D1472692

*A Critical Bibliography of
French Literature*

A Critical Bibliography of French Literature

VOLUME IV

Supplement

THE EIGHTEENTH CENTURY

Edited by

RICHARD A. BROOKS

Richmond College of the City University of New York

SYRACUSE UNIVERSITY PRESS

1968

Library of Congress Catalog Card: 47-3282
First edition 1968, Syracuse University Press
Syracuse, New York
ALL RIGHTS RESERVED

Printed in Belgium

For OTIS E. FELLOWS *and* NORMAN L. TORREY

INTRODUCTION

THE SERIES of critical bibliographies of French literature undertaken by the Syracuse University Press under the general editorship of the late David C. Cabeen is widely recognized as the standard reference work of its type in the field. The guiding principle of the work is that of critical selectivity: the series provides for the specialist and advanced student of French literature bibliographical information about those books and articles of which he should be aware in the pursuit of further study. Insofar as possible, the bibliographies attempt to present an objective survey of various specialized fields by scholars known in the United States for their particular interest or competence with regard to a given subject or author. Moreover, every collaborator has worked in close consultation with the volume editor. Nevertheless, in a work of this scope and complexity, errors or omissions are bound to occur. The editor urges all users of this work to call them to his attention, as it is our hope that the material presented in this volume may be brought up to date periodically.

The period since 1950 has been marked by a great flourishing of studies of eighteenth-century French literature both in Europe and in the United States. The purpose of the present work is to survey that body of scholarship in the spirit of Volume IV, *The Eighteenth Century,* edited by George R. Havens and Donald F. Bond (1951). No attempt has been made to reassess the material covered by that work. Our intention here is rather to continue and update the pioneering work of our predecessors. Only occasionally have we introduced items before 1950 omitted from the 1951 volume. Although the present bibliography is an independent work, the scholar or student will use it to maximum advantage in conjunction with its predecessor.

It is my privilege to record here my thanks to Otis E. Fellows, of Columbia University, who first encouraged me to undertake this project. I am also indebted to Robert J. Clements, Henry A. Grubbs, Georges May, Paul M. Spurlin, George R. Havens, and Geo. Winchester Stone, Jr., for providing me counsel at different stages of this work. Without the devoted secretarial assistance of Françoise Mottier and Ada M. Squiers, this volume could not have gone to press. I am most grateful to the reference departments of the Columbia University Library, the New York Public Library, and the New York University Library for their knowledgeable cooperation. This work was greatly helped by a grant from the Arts and Science Research Fund of New York University.

RICHARD A. BROOKS

January, 1967
New York, New York

EDITOR'S NOTE

THE BIBLIOGRAPHICAL forms adopted for this volume have been selected to provide the greatest amount of information consistent with clearness and brevity. To this end, the forms of the H. W. Wilson Company, with some modifications, were chosen for periodicals, and those of the Library of Congress for books. The strongest argument for the use of the Library of Congress forms is that its catalog is likely to be the one source available to most potential users of this work. Whenever Library of Congress practice—particularly in the spelling of proper names—was found to differ from established scholarly usage, the more familiar forms were adopted with appropriate cross-references.

No effort has been made to eliminate duplicate titles. Indeed, some items are repeated in different sections. Usually, the main entry will be found in the section most directly related to the general subject matter of the work. E.g., Georges May's *Le dilemme du roman au XVIII⁰ siècle* has its main entry under "General Studies and Aspects of the 18th-Century Novel" and a secondary entry under "English and American Influences and Relations." Occasionally, where the contents of a study do not allow such classification, the first appearance of the item constitutes its main entry. Subsequent appearances of an item usually offer material of further interest, but carry only the title and a cross-reference to the main entry.

Last names of eighteenth-century writers are abbreviated to an initial (e.g., V. for Voltaire) in sections devoted principally to them. No place of publication is given for books published in Paris.

Reference numbers in this volume begin at 3320. All cross-references bearing numbers below 3320 are to Volume IV, *The Eighteenth Century*, edited by George R. Havens and Donald F. Bond.

LIST OF ABBREVIATIONS

With some slight modifications, titles of serials conform to their listing in the *Union List of Serials in Libraries of the United States and Canada. Third Edition* (New York, H. W. Wilson Co., 1965), *New Serial Titles, 1950–1960* (Washington, The Library of Congress, 1961), and *New Serial Titles. 1964 Cumulation* (Washington, The Library of Congress, 1965). Variant titles are sometimes indicated in brackets to facilitate reference.

AAA   American academy of political and social science. Annals
AASP   American antiquarian society. Proceedings
ABo   Annales de Bourgogne
ABr   Annales de Bretagne
AC   Antiquité classique
ADI   Hague. Academy of international law. Recueil des cours
AdMidi Annales du Midi; revue archéologique, historique et philologique
AESC   Annales; économies, sociétés, civilisations
AFLC   Cagliari. Università. Facoltà di lettere e filosofia. Annali
AFLT   Toulouse. Université. Faculté des lettres. Annales : littératures
AGBB   Association Guillaume Budé. Bulletin
AGSK   Akademie der Wissenschaften und der Literatur, Mainz. Geistes- und sozialwissen-
         schaftliche Klasse. Abhandlungen
AHR   American historical review
AHRF   Annales historiques de la Révolution française
AHSJ   Archivum historicum societatis Jesu
AIHS   Archives internationales d'histoire des sciences
AJJR   Société Jean-Jacques Rousseau. Annales
AJS   American journal of sociology
AK   Archiv für Kulturgeschichte
AL   American literature; a journal of literary history, criticism and bibliography
ALB   Besançon. Université. Annales littéraires
ALM   Archives des lettres modernes; études de critique et d'histoire littéraire
AMPR   Académie des sciences morales et politiques. Revue des travaux et comptes-rendus
AMT   Australian mathematics teacher
An   Annales [Annales conferencia]
AnAix   Aix-Marseille. Université. Faculté des lettres. Annales
AnB   Année balzacienne
AnC   *See* An

AnProp	Année propédeutique
AnSc	Annals of science; a quarterly review of the history of science since the Renaissance
AntA	Antike und Abendland; Beiträge zum Verständnis der Griechen und Römer und ihres Nachlebens
APP	Annales de philosophie politique
APSP	American philosophical society. Proceedings
APSR	American political science review
APST	American philosophical society. Transactions
AQ	American quarterly
Archiv	Archiv für das Studium der neueren Sprachen
ArL	Archivum linguisticum; a review of comparative philology and general linguistics
ARSP	Archiv für Rechts- und Sozialphilosophie
ASR	American sociological review
ASSM	Société historique et archéologique de l'arrondissement de Saint-Malo. Annales
ATSL	Accademia toscana di scienze e lettere "La Colombaria". Atti e memorie
AUL	Lyons. Université. Annales
AUMLA	A.U.M.L.A. [Australasian universities modern language association. *Issuing body varies*.]
AUP	Paris. Université. Annales
AUS	Saarbrücken. Universität des Saarlandes. Annales universitatis saraviensis. Philosophie-lettres
AV	Ateneo veneto; rivista
AvS	Avant-scène
B	Bibliotheck; a journal of bibliographical notes and queries mainly of Scottish interest
BA	Books abroad
BAB	Association des bibliothécaires français. Bulletin
BABN	Banco di Napoli. Bollettino dell'archivio storico
BBB	Bulletin du bibliophile et du bibliothécaire
BBF	Bulletin des bibliothèques de France
Bbib	Bulletin of bibliography
Bcol	Book collector
BDB	Paris. Bibliothèque nationale. Bulletin de documentation bibliographique
BEC	Bibliothèque de l'École des chartes
Bel	Belfagor; rassegna di varia umanità
BH	Annales de la Faculté des lettres de Bordeaux et des universités du Midi. Bulletin hispanique
BHR	Bibliothèque d'humanisme et renaissance; travaux et documents
BLS	Strasbourg. Université. Faculté des lettres. Bulletin
BO	Botteghe oscure
BR	Bucknell review
BRP	Beiträge zur romanischen Philologie
BSAHA	Vieux papier
BSHL	Société historique et archéologique de Langres. Bulletin
BSHP	Société de l'histoire du protestantisme français. Bulletin
BSLP	Société de linguistique de Paris. Bulletin
BuHM	Bulletin of the history of medicine
BuR	*See* BR
C	Criticism; a quarterly for literature and the arts
CahB	Cahiers de Bruges

CahH	Cahiers d'histoire (Universités de Clermont-Ferrand, Grenoble et Lyon)
CahHM	*See* CaHM
CaHM	Cahiers haut-marnais
CahN	Cahiers naturalistes
CAIEF	Association internationale des études françaises. Cahiers
CamJ	Cambridge journal
CAT	Cahiers d'analyse textuelle
CathHR	Catholic historical review
CBFL	Critical bibliography of French literature
CCRB	Compagnie Madeleine Renaud-Jean-Louis Barrault. Cahiers
CDS	Cahiers du sud
Cfr	Classe de français; revue pour l'enseignement du français
CHM	Cahiers d'histoire mondiale; Journal of world history; Cuadernos de historia mundial
CHR	Canadian historical review
CL	Comparative literature
Clex	Cahiers de lexicologie
CLS	Comparative literature studies (College Park, Maryland)
CMF	Časopis pro moderní filologii
Conv	Convivium; rivista di lettere, filosofia e storia
CPl	Cahiers de la Pléiade
CPMP	California. University. Publications in modern philology
Cr	Critique; revue générale des publications françaises et étrangères
Crev	Contemporary review
CSE	Cairo studies in English
CSoc	Contrat social; revue historique et critique des faits et des idées
CSt	Critica storica
CUAS	Catholic university of America. Studies in Romance languages and literatures
CUSH	Colorado. University. Studies. Series in history
CulF	Culture française (Bari)
CulM	Cultura moderna; rassegna delle edizioni Laterza
Daed	Daedalus
DF	Deutschland-Frankreich [Ludwigsburg. Deutsch-französisches Institut. Veröffentlichungen]
Dia	Dialogues; revue des problèmes culturels et de l'enseignement dans le monde
DLit	Deutsche Literaturzeitung für Kritik der internationalen Wissenschaft
DS	Diderot studies
DU	Deutsche Universitätszeitung (Göttingen)
DV	Deutsche Vierteljahrsschrift für Literaturwissenschaft und Geistesgeschichte
EA	Études anglaises
ECr	Essays in criticism
EDH	Royal society of literature of the United Kingdom. Essays by divers hands
EG	Études germaniques : Allemagne, Autriche, Suisse, pays scandinaves et néerlandais
EHR	English historical review
EJ	Economic journal
EL	Études de lettres
ELEC	Études de littérature étrangère et comparée
EMisc	English miscellany; a symposium of history, literature and the arts
Enat	Éducation nationale
EnC	Enseignement chrétien; revue de l'enseignement secondaire

Enc	Encounter; literature, arts, politics
EP	Études de presse
EPar	Écrits de Paris; revue des questions actuelles
Esp	Esprit; revue internationale
EspCr	Esprit créateur
Est	English studies (Amsterdam)
Et	Études
Eur	Europe
EurL	Europa letteraria
F	Filosofia (Turin)
FAZ	Frankfurter allgemeine Zeitung
FDLM	Français dans le monde
FE	Frantsuzskii ezhegodnik
FHS	French historical review
FILLM	International congress of modern languages and literatures. Actes, proceedings, etc.
FL	Figaro littéraire
Flam	Flambeau; revue belge des questions politiques et littéraires
Fmod	Français moderne; revue de synthèse et de vulgarisation linguistiques
FR	French review
FrAR	French-American review
FS	French studies
GBA	Gazette des beaux-arts
GCFI	Giornale critico della filosofia italiana
Germ	Germanistik; internationales Referatenorgan mit bibliographischen Hinweisen
Gids	Gids
Grev	Germanic review
GRM	Germanisch-romanische Monatsschrift
GSLI	Giornale storico della letteratura italiana
H	Historia
HAHR	Hispanic-American historical review
HelC	Hellénisme contemporain
Herm	Hermathena; a series of papers on literature, science and philosophy by members of Trinity college, Dublin
Hist	Historian
HJ	Hibbert journal; a quarterly review of religion, theology and philosophy
HLB	Harvard university. Harvard library bulletin
HR	Hispanic review; a quarterly journal devoted to research in the Hispanic languages and literatures
HT	History today
Hum	Humanitas (Brescia)
HZ	Historische Zeitschrift
IDC	Paris. Université. Institut de droit comparé. Travaux et recherches
IFWB	Institut français de Washington. Bulletin
IHist	Information historique
IHRB	London. University. Institute of historical research. Bulletin
IL	Information littéraire
IMGS	International musical society; Internationale Musik-Gesellschaft; Société internationale de musique. Sammelbände
IS	Italian studies; a quarterly review

IT	Illustre théâtre; la vie et l'histoire de la Comédie Française
Ital	Italica
IUHS	Indiana. University. Humanities series
JA	Jardin des arts
JAAC	Journal of aesthetics and art criticism
JAMS	American musicological society. Journal
JEGP	Journal of English and Germanic philology
JHI	Journal of the history of ideas
JHMS	Journal of the history of medicine and allied sciences
JMH	Journal of modern history
JPE	Journal of political economy
Jph	Journal of philosophy
JPNP	Journal de psychologie normale et pathologique
JRLB	John Rylands library. Bulletin
JS	Journal des savants
JSH	Journal of southern history
JWCI	London. University. Warburg institute. Journal of the Warburg and Courtauld institutes
KFLQ	Kentucky foreign language quarterly
KNeo	Kwartalnik neofilologiczny
LB	Leuvensche bijdragen; tijdschrift voor moderne philologie
Le	Livre et l'estampe
LetF	Lettres françaises (Paris)
LetN	Lettres nouvelles
LH	Association Guillaume Budé. Lettres d'humanité
LHB	Lock Haven bulletin
LHM	American society legion of honor magazine
LI	Lettere italiane, con une sezione di studi danteschi (Arona)
Libr	Library
Littératures	*See* AFLT
Lmod	Langues modernes
LN	*See* LetN
Lnéo	Langues néo-latines
LR	Lettres romanes
LSUSH	Louisiana state university studies. Humanities series
MA	Modern age; a conservative review
ManG	Manchester guardian weekly
MASALP	Michigan academy of science, arts and letters. Papers
MédF	Médecine de France
MélCB	Mélanges de linguistique française offerts à M. Charles Bruneau, professeur à la Sorbonne. Geneva, Droz, 1954.
MemCo	Commission des antiquités du département de la Côte d'Or. Mémoires
MerF	Mercure de France
MF	Musik-Forschung
ML	Modern languages; a review of foreign letters, science and the arts
MLAN	Music library association. Notes
Mlet	Music and letters
MLF	Modern language forum
MLJ	Modern language journal

MLN	Modern language notes
MLQ	Modern language quarterly
MLR	Modern language review; a quarterly journal devoted to the study of medieval and modern literature and philology
MN	Monde nouveau
MP	Modern philology
MQ	Musical quarterly
MR	Music review
MRA	Mainzer romanistische Arbeiten
MRo	Marche romane
MS	Moderna språk
MuK	Maske und Kothurn; Vierteljahrsschrift für Theaterwissenschaft
MVHR	Mississippi Valley historical review
NA	Nuova antologia; rivista di lettere, scienze ed arti
NCr	Nouvelle critique; revue du marxisme militant
NCSL	North Carolina. University. Studies in comparative literature
Neo	Neophilologus; a modern language quarterly
NFJG	Goethe-Gesellschaft. Goethe [Neue Folge des Jahrbuchs der Goethe Gesellschaft]
NFS	Nottingham French studies
NL	Nouvelles littéraires, artistiques et scientifiques
NNRF	Nouvelle revue française [Nouvelle nouvelle revue française]
NQ	Notes and queries for readers and writers, collectors and librarians
NR	Neue Rundschau
NRRSL	Royal society of London. Notes and records
NS	Neueren Sprachen; Zeitschrift für den neusprachlichen Unterricht
n.s.	new series
NSN	New statesman [New statesman and nation]
OLib	Œuvres libres; romans, nouvelles, récits, histoire, théâtre
Or	Orpheus; rivista di umanità classica e cristiana (Catania)
OrL	Orbis litterarum; revue internationale d'études littéraires
Os	Osiris; studies on the history and philosophy of science, and on the history of learning and culture
PBA	British academy for the promotion of historical, philosophical and philological studies. Proceedings
PBSA	Bibliographical society of America. Papers
Per	Personalist
pér.	période
Phist	Pennsylvania history
PhR	Philosophical review
PIFF	Grenoble. Université. Institut français de Florence. Publications
PIMUP	Paris. Université. Institut de musicologie. Publications
PMHB	Pennsylvania magazine of history and biography
PMLA	Modern language association of America. Publications
PoS	Political studies
PP	Philologica pragensia
PPR	Philosophy and phenomenological research
PQ	Philological quarterly; a journal devoted to scholarly investigation in the classical and modern languages
ProvH	Provence historique

PRRM	Pensée; revue du rationalisme moderne
PSP	*See* APSP
PSQ	Political science quarterly
PUGL	Grenoble. Université. Faculté des lettres et des sciences humaines. Publications
PULC	Princeton university library chronicle
QJE	Quarterly journal of economics
RassF	Rassegna di filosofia
RassM	Rassegna musicale
RBP	Revue belge de philologie et d'histoire
RCSF	Rivista critica di storia della filosofia
RDM	Revue des deux mondes
RE	Revue d'esthétique
REAn	Annales de la Faculté des lettres de Bordeaux et des universités du Midi. Revue des études anciennes
REc	Revue économique (Paris)
RecT	*See* ThR
REG	Utrecht. Rijksuniversiteit. Instituut voor vergelijkend literatuuronderzoek. Registen van de aanwinsten
REP	Revue d'économie politique
REtI	Revue des études italiennes
RevHM	Hommes et mondes
RF	Rivista di filosofia
RFor	Romanische Forschungen; Organ für romanische Sprachen, Volks- und Mittellatein
RFRG	Revista de filologie romanică si germanică
RGB	Revue générale belge
RGS	Revue générale des sciences pures et appliquées
RHAF	Revue d'histoire de l'Amérique française
RHB	Revue historique de Bordeaux et du département de la Gironde
RHD	Revue d'histoire diplomatique
RHES	Revue d'histoire économique et sociale
Rhist	Revue historique
RHL	Revue d'histoire littéraire de la France
RHS	Revue d'histoire des sciences et de leurs applications
RHT	Revue d'histoire du théâtre
RHV	Revue historique vaudoise
RIF	*See* RF
RInsP	Rice institute of liberal and technical learning. Rice institute pamphlets
RIP	Revue internationale de philosophie
RIPC	Politique; revue internationale des doctrines et des institutions [Revue internationale d'histoire politique et constitutionnelle]
RJa	Romanistisches Jahrbuch
RLC	Revue de littérature comparée
RLI	Rassegna della letteratura italiana
Rlir	Revue de linguistique romane
RLM	Rivista di letterature moderne e comparate
RLR	Revue des langues romanes
RM	Revue de musicologie
RMéd	Revue de la Méditerranée
Rmet	Review of metaphysics

RMM	Revue de métaphysique et de morale
RMR	Rocky Mountain review (Billings, Montana)
RomN	Romance notes
RoP	Romance philology
RPar	Revue de Paris
RPF	Revista portuguesa de filologia
Rpol	Review of politics
RPP	Revue politique et parlementaire
RPr	Romanistica pragensia
RR	Romanic review
RScH	Revue des sciences humaines
RSCI	Rivista di storia della chiesa in Italia
RSHist	Schweizerische Zeitschrift für Geschichte; Revue suisse d'histoire; Rivista storica svizzera
RSI	Rivista storica italiana
RSSHN	Revue des sociétés savantes de Haute Normandie
Rsu	Présence et revue de Suisse [Revue de Suisse]
Rsyn	Revue de synthèse
RUB	Brussels. Université libre. Revue
RUL	Quebec. Université Laval. Revue de l'université Laval
s.	series
SA	Studi americani; rivista annuale dedicata alle lettere e alle arti negli Stati Uniti d'America
SAQ	South Atlantic quarterly
sér. gén.	série générale
SF	Studi francesi
Sfil	Studia filozoficzne
SG	Studium generale; Zeitschrift für die Einheit der Wissenschaften im Zusammenhang ihrer Begriffsbildungen und Forschungsmethoden
ShJ	Shakespeare Jahrbuch
ShQ	Shakespeare quarterly
ShS	Shakespeare survey; an annual survey of Shakespearian study and production
SiGy	Siculorum gymnasium
SN	Studia neophilologica
SP	North Carolina. University. Studies in philology
SRF	*See* SRLF
SRL	Saturday review [Saturday review of literature]
SRLF	Saggi e ricerche di letteratura francese
StCl	Stendhal club; revue trimestrielle (Lausanne)
StGR	The French mind; studies in honour of Gustave Rudler. Ed. by Will Moore, Rhoda Sutherland and Enid Starkie. Oxford, Clarendon press, 1952
StS	Studi storici; rivista trimestrale
SuF	Sinn und Form
suppl.	supplement
SVEC	Geneva. Institut et musée Voltaire. Studies on Voltaire and the eighteenth century
Sym	Symposium; a journal devoted to modern foreign languages and literatures
TAS	Technique, art, science; revue de l'enseignement technique
TBR	New York Times book review
TC	Twentieth century

TDR	Tulane drama review
ThR	Theatre research; Recherches théâtrales
TLS	Times literary supplement (London)
TMAix	Aix-Marseille. Université. Faculté des lettres. Travaux et mémoires
Tmod	Temps modernes
TN	Theatre notes
Tpop	Théâtre populaire; revue trimestrielle d'information sur le théâtre
Tro	Table ronde; revue mensuelle
TSJC	Cahiers de la tour Saint-Jacques
TVUB	Brussels. Université libre. Tijdschrift
TWA	Wisconsin academy of sciences, arts and letters. Transactions
UNCR	North Carolina. University. Studies in the Romance languages and literatures
UTQ	University of Toronto quarterly
Vel	Veltro
VFH	Vlaamse filologencongres. Handelingen
Vfil	Voprosy filosofii
VIst	Voprosy istorii
VL	Vie et langage
VMHB	Virginia magazine of history and biography
VW	Vie wallonne; revue mensuelle illustrée
WB	Weimarer Beiträge
WMQ	William and Mary quarterly
WPHM	Western Pennsylvania historical magazine
WSCL	Wisconsin studies in contemporary literature
WWa	Wort und Wahrheit
WZUB	Berlin. Universität. Wissenschaftliche Zeitschrift. Gesellschafts- und sprachwissenschaftliche Reihe
WZUL	Leipzig. Universität. Wissenschaftliche Zeitschrift. Gesellschafts- und sprachwissenschaftliche Reihe
WZUR	Rostock. Universität. Wissenschaftliche Zeitschrift. Gesellschafts- und Sprachwissenschaften [Gesellschafts- und sprachwissenschaftliche Reihe]
YCGL	Yearbook of comparative and general literature
YFS	Yale French studies
YWML	Year's work in modern language studies
ZFSL	Zeitschrift für französische Sprache und Literatur
ZLGS	Zeitschrift für Literatur und Geschichte der Staatswissenschaften
ZPF	Zeitschrift für philosophische Forschung
ZRG	Zeitschrift für Religions- und Geistesgeschichte
ZRP	Zeitschrift für romanische Philologie

LIST OF CONTRIBUTORS

ALFRED OWEN ALDRIDGE
University of Illinois

BARRY S. BROOK
Queens College of the City University of New York

RICHARD A. BROOKS
Richmond College of the City University of New York

JOHN W. CHAPMAN
University of Pittsburgh

CLIFTON C. CHERPACK
Wesleyan University

LESTER G. CROCKER
Western Reserve University

HUGH M. DAVIDSON
Ohio State University

OTIS E. FELLOWS
Columbia University

DIANA GUIRAGOSSIAN
Indiana University

BASIL J. GUY
University of California, Berkeley

ADRIENNE HYTIER
Vassar College

J. ROBERT LOY
Brooklyn College of the City University of New York

JEANNE MONTY
Tulane University

MADELEINE FIELDS MORRIS
Queens College of the City University of New York

ROBERT NIKLAUS
University of Exeter

JOHN N. PAPPAS
Fordham University

JEAN A. PERKINS
Swarthmore College

MERLE L. PERKINS
University of Wisconsin, Madison

SPIRE PITOU
University of Delaware

OLGA RAGUSA
Columbia University

HENRY H. H. REMAK
Indiana University

JEAN SAREIL
Columbia University

KENNETH R. SCHOLBERG
Michigan State University

EDWARD D. SEEBER
Indiana University

EVA MARIA STADLER
*Borough of Manhattan Community
College of the City University of
New York*

ROBERT E. TAYLOR
University of Massachusetts, Amherst

VIRGIL W. TOPAZIO
Rice University

ARAM VARTANIAN
New York University

FERNAND VIAL
State University of New York at Albany

ARTHUR M. WILSON
Dartmouth College

MARY T. WILSON
Norwich, Vermont

MELVIN ZIMMERMAN
University of Maryland

TABLE OF CONTENTS

Supplement to
VOLUME IV

CHAPTER I. BACKGROUND MATERIALS

(Nos. 3320–3541)

BARRY S. BROOK, HUGH M. DAVIDSON, ADRIENNE D. HYTIER, SPIRE PITOU, JEAN SAREIL, EVA MARIA STADLER, *and* ROBERT E. TAYLOR

Bibliographies
(Nos. 3320–3376)

ROBERT E. TAYLOR

See individual authors. *See also* such general studies as *Nature and culture* by Lester G. Crocker (4123), *L'idée de nature en France dans la première moitié du XVIII*e *siècle* by Jean Ehrard (4126), *L'idée du bonheur dans la littérature et la pensée françaises du XVIII*e *siècle* by Robert Mauzi (4136), etc. *See also* such current bibliographies as the " Bibliographie analytique internationale des publications relatives à l'archivistique et aux archives " appearing in *Archivum* since 1952, the "Annual Bibliography " appearing in PMLA, *The year's work in modern languages*, etc.

Baldensperger, Fernand, and **Werner P. Friederich.** Bibliography of comparative literature. Chapel Hill, Univ. of North Carolina, Studies in comparative literature, 1950. xxiv, 701 p. **3320**

Monumental bibliography, together with its supplements. Seventh part (p. 482–550) concerned with French contributions. Supplements to this work appear in YCGL.

Reviews: B. Munteano in RLC 26: 273–86, 1952; S. Skard in JEGP 52: 229–42, 1953.

Barbier, Antoine Alexandre. Dictionnaire des ouvrages anonymes. 3e éd. revue et augmentée par Olivier Barbier, René et Paul Billard. Hildesheim, Georg Olms, 1963. 4 v. **3221**

A most important work once again available.

Battisti, Carlo. Note bibliografiche alle traduzioni italiane di vocabolari enciclopedici e tecnici fancesi nella seconda metà del Settecento. Florence, Institut français de Florence, 1955. 72 p. **3322**

Introduction of real interest to student of ideas, p. 7–48. Bibliography, p. 49–70,

lists all Italian translations of dictionaries, encyclopedias and scientific works (in alphabetical order by original author, editor, or title.) Author notes that Diderot in Italy " più che come enciclopedista, fu conosciuto come autore di drammi lacrimosi e come romanziere " (p. 57). Indeed, a 3-volume translation of the *belle lettere* of Diderot, d'Alembert, and Marmontel appeared, but not the *Encyclopédie* itself. Except for Chambers (in 21 v.), one translation from German, and one 18th-century Italian study of new technical words, all items are translations from the French, including the Robert James medical dictionary where the Diderot translation was used. List of authors in the introduction, p. 71–72.

Billioud, Jacques. Le livre en Provence du XVIe au XVIII siècle. Marseilles, Saint-Victor, 1962. 300 p. **3323**

Excellent study of books and bibliography. Ch. 1 of Part II (p. 85-106) lists all books of science, erudition, and entertainment printed in Provence for period covered. Ch. 2 of Part II (p. 107–27) does the same for gazettes, almanachs, guide books, etc. Elsewhere book collectors and libraries are listed (p. 131-209). Ch. 2 of Part IV (p. 235–38) deals with the illicit commerce of books by unlicensed merchants, but not with prohibited books; it is suggested (p. 241) that because of the severity of the laws and rigorous enforcement only books with a *privilège* were printed in Provence.

Brenner, Clarence D. A bibliographical list of plays in the French language, 1700–1789. Berkeley, California, 1947. iv, 229 p. **3324**

Fine tool. Anonymous plays are listed first, then authors are arranged by alphabetical order. Includes an index of titles. Work is not paginated. Completeness is not claimed (nor achieved), but 11,662 titles are listed.

1

— The Théâtre Italien : its repertory, 1716–1793. Berkeley and Los Angeles, Univ. of California press, 1961. *See* 3607.   **3325**

A compilation of real value. All daily performances are listed by date together with figures for receipts and attendance, except in few cases where such figures are not known (particularly between April 10, 1725, and March 1, 1728). Plays given entirely or partly in Italian are so indicated; authors are not given. Index of titles.

Cassell's encyclopaedia of literature. Ed. by Sigfrid Henry Steinberg. London, Cassell, 1953. 2 v.   **3326**

Well written, soundly compiled with a respectable bibliography for and about each author.

Castaing, Roger. Almanachs galants et chantants français de format in-64 (1785–1829). BBB 57–69, 1962.   **3327**

Complement of the article on almanachs in-128 appearing in same journal in 1959. Almanachs are listed by publishers.

— Almanachs minuscules français. BBB 1–15, 1959.   **3328**

A more complete listing than that of Grand-Carteret (*Les almanachs français: bibliographie, iconographie.* [Alisié, 1896].) *See also* articles by Jules Duhem, *Glanes pour Grand-Carteret, almanachs français et livres congénères* in same review, 1952 and following.

Chancerel, L. Pour un inventaire des affiches des XVIIe et XVIIIe siècles. RHT 3 : 255–60, 1951.   **3329**

Arranged chronologically for the various Archives, bibliography tries to list what few theater posters remain for the period. Descriptive method.

Coleman, Charles. Bibliographie descriptive de la critique des auteurs principaux du XVIIe siècle publiée dans le Journal de Verdun, 1710–1750. RUL 11 : 217–35, 1956–57.   **3330**

Very important bibliography, with a most interesting introduction on the thinking of the period. Descartes was most cited scientist (often in rejection of Newton); Boileau, most cited man of letters, was used as a guide even for the novel. Corneille was apparently more popular than Racine, and Molière was much preferred to the new *comédie larmoyante.* La Fontaine was most cited creative writer.

Cordié, Carlo. Avviamento allo studio della lingua e della letteratura francese. Milan, Marzorati, 1955. 1, 1222 p.   **3331**

A selected but general bibliography of French literature, culture, and language. The 18th-century section (p. 335–414) is perhaps too short, but the presentation is fine.

Review : P. Jourda in RLR 72 : 223–26, 1955–58.

Dacier, Emile. Des livres précieux sans en avoir l'air : les anciens catalogues de ventes. BBB 117–42, 1952.   **3332**

Most interesting article on bibliographical catalogs and on interesting annotations sometimes found in them.

Defourneaux, Marcelin. L'Inquisition espagnole et les livres français au XVIIIe siècle. Presses univ. de France, 1963. 214 p.   **3333**

Except for *Sources et bibliographie* (p. 5–12) and *Catalogue des livres français condamnés (1747–1807)* (p. 167–205), this important study of censorship, of inquisitorial procedure, of the fate of French books in 18th-century Spain, and of the diffusion of condemned volumes is more a book about books than a strict bibliography. Books of high moral content not based on the Church (e. g., *La chaumière indienne* of Bernardin de Saint-Pierre) were quite as violently attacked as so-called pornography (e. g., *Justine ou les malheurs de la vertu* by Sade). Index, p. 207–12. Well-documented volume.

Dictionary of French literature. Ed. by Sidney D. Braun. Philosophical Library, 1958. xiii, 362 p.   **3334**

Not overly satisfactory as bibliographical tool.

Dictionnaire biographique des auteurs de tous les temps et de tous les pays. Ed. by Robert Laffont and Valentino S. Bompiani. S.E.D.E., 1957–58. 2 v.   **3335**

The bibliographical material following each entry, when appropriate, is brief but adequate and up to date. An excellent tool for the nonspecialist. In charge of the bibliographical material : Alexandre Labzine, Michel Mourre, Bernard Noël, Maud Sissung. Editor-in-chief : Jacques Brosse.

Dictionnaire des lettres françaises. Le dix-huitième siècle. Publié sous la direction du Cardinal Georges Grente. (Assistant directors : Albert Pauphilet, Louis Pichard, Robert Barroux). *See* 3381.   **3336**

Excellent tool, bibliographical and otherwise, for study of 18th-century French literature. Subjects and authors are arranged in one alphabetical listing.

Dictionnaire des œuvres de tous les temps et de tous les pays : littérature, philosophie, musique, sciences. Ed. by Robert Laffont and Valentino S. Bompiani. S.E.D.E., 1952–55. 5 v. **3337**

The works are listed, described, and discussed in alphabetical order by titles. Last volume contains an index of authors, a chronological table, and the list of collaborators. Although frequently a useful bibliography in itself, it does not often supply additional bibliographical material for each work. Moreover, rarer works, of interest to the specialist, are not listed at all. Editor-in-chief : Jacques Brosse.

Dictionnaire des personnages littéraires et dramatiques de tous les temps et de tous les pays. Ed. by Robert Laffont and Valentino S. Bompiani. S.E.D.E., 1963. 669 p. **3338**

Quite useful and beautifully illustrated. Editor-in-chief : Jacques Brosse.

Dubled, Henri. Le catalogue-matières de la Bibliothèque Inguimbertine de Carpentras et son intérêt pour l'histoire de la bibliothéconomie et des sciences au XVIII᷎e siècle. ProvH 13:91–97, 1963. **3339**

Of more interest to the student of library science than to the student of literature and ideas.

Durand-Vaugaron, L. Inventaire d'un fonds de librairie à Rennes en 1725. ABr 64:329–46, 1957. **3340**

Details of a 34-leaf ms listing what books were destroyed by fire in the total destruction of a bookshop in Rennes. A list with obvious interests and limitations.

Ferrand, Louis. Les livres de colportage. BSAHA 23:317–23, 1961–63. **3341**

Article on the so-called *Bibliothèque bleue*, followed by a bibliography of the more important studies of the subject.

Fromm, Hans. Bibliographie deutscher Übersetzungen aus dem Französischen, 1700–1948. Baden-Baden, Kunst und Wissenschaft, 1950–53. 6 v. *See* 5825. **3342**

Monumental compilation, much of which necessarily beyond the scope of 18th-century France, though that area is perhaps most voluminously represented. Voltaire alone has 25 p. Last volume

contains list of translators, p. 431–538, and a list of German authors whose original French works have been translated into German, p. 335–427. Friedrich II alone has 21 p. in this last list.

Gallet-Guerne, Danielle. Les sources de l'histoire littéraire aux Archives nationales. Imprimerie nationale, 1961. v, 161 p. **3343**

A most important bibliographical source book in an area that is widely dispersed and difficult to control. An index (p. 155–59) lists all authors mentioned.

Gandilhon, René. Bibliographie générale des travaux historiques et archéologiques publiés par les sociétés savantes de la France. Période 1910–1940. Imprimerie nationale, 1944–61. 5 v. **3344**

A most important compilation listing the studies made between 1910 and 1940 by all the learned societies of France. Purely literary as well as more biographical items are included.

Gilbert, P. Le dictionnaire et les dictionnaires : les dictionnaires en France au XVIII᷎e siècle. Cfr 9:209–23, 1959. **3345**

Interesting critical bibliographical article. It follows two earlier articles in the same journal on 17th-century dictionaries, 6:212–22, 1957, and the *Dictionnaire de l'Académie française*, 7:339–47, 1958.

Giraud, Jeanne. Manuel de bibliographie littéraire pour les XVI᷎e, XVII᷎e et XVIII᷎e siècles français, 1921–1935. 2᷎e éd. Vrin, 1958. 304 p. **3346**

This volume is a reprint of the 1st ed. and adds nothing to it.

— Manuel de bibliographie littéraire pour les XVI᷎e, XVII᷎e et XVIII᷎e siècles français, 1936–1945. Nizet, 1956. xiii, 270 p. **3347**

Splendid continuation of a monumental bibliography.

Golden, Herbert H., and Seymour O. Simches. Modern French literature and language; a bibliography of homage studies. Cambridge, Harvard univ. press, 1953. 158 p. *See* 3485. **3348**

Fine bibliography of items that are often missed. Work is divided by centuries, literary and intellectual relations, and the language itself. Index of authors makes it particularly useful.

Reviews : A. Ewert in FS 8:88, 1954; H. Keller in ZRP 73:169, 1957; H. Lancaster in MLN 69:302–03, 1954; Y. Malkiel in RoP 8:169, 1954–55; J. Orr in MLR 49:272, 1954.

Gordon, L. S. Quelques résultats de l'étude du livre prohibé en France (seconde moitié du 18ᵉ siècle). FE 89–120, 1959.   **3349**

The résumé in French (p. 119–20) is far from just to a very well-documented article written in Russian. Perhaps too much is made of notion that much of the Enlightenment material was read by the " people " and was written by penniless plebeian intellectuals.

Gove, Philip Babcock. The imaginary voyage in prose fiction; a history of its criticism and a guide for its study, with an annotated check list of 215 imaginary voyages from 1700 to 1800. London, Holland press, 1961. 445 p.   **3350**

Excellent reprint of the 1941 ed.

Hampton, John. Les traductions françaises de Locke au xviiiᵉ siècle. *See* 5600.   **3351**

Excellent bibliographical article on the diffusion of Locke's ideas.

Howard, Alison K. Montesquieu, Voltaire and Rousseau in eighteenth century Scotland; a check list of editions and translations of their works published in Scotland before 1801. B 2²:40–63, 1959.   **3352**

Interesting, informative list of 80 items. 3 eds. of the *Lettres persanes*, 5 (including one in French) of the *Considérations ... des Romains*, 10 (including one in French) of *De l'esprit des lois*, 4 of the *English letters*, 4 of *Mahomet*, 3 (including one in French) of the *Siècle de Louis XIV*, 3 of *Candidus*, 4 of *An essay on crimes and punishments*, 4 of *Emilius*, with fewer eds. of other works. In addition the *Works* of Rousseau came out in 10 v., but no trace has been found of the *Collected works* of Voltaire which were to come out in 20 v.

Jaffe, Adrian H. Bibliography of French literature in American magazines in the 18th century. East Lansing, Michigan State college press, 1951. vii, 27 p.   **3353**

Short introduction on use of magazines as a source of information. Items are arranged by year of publication, from 1758 to 1799, and alphabetically by titles within each year. Rightly so, items of political, historical, religious, or social interest are not excluded. List of periodicals consulted, p. 21–26. Index, p. 27.

Jallut, Marguerite. Les bibliothèques de Marie-Antoinette. *In* : Mélanges d'histoire du livre et des bibliothèques offerts à Monsieur Frantz Calot. Librairie d'Argences, 1960. p. 325–32.   **3354**

Interesting article about books and bibliography, although not a bibliography in itself.

Josserand, Pierre. Table générale de la Revue d'histoire littéraire de la France. Années 1909–1939. Geneva, Droz, 1953. 182 p.   **3355**

The continuation of an invaluable index.

Kaminer, Liubov' Veniaminovna. Bibliografiia i kritiko-bibliograficheskie zhurnaly vo Frantsii perioda prosveshcheniia, 1750–1789. (Bibliographies et revues littéraires en France au siècle des lumières, 1750–1789.) Moscow, Editions de la Chambre du livre de l'U.R.S.S., 1959. 246 p.   **3356**

In addition to subject suggested by title, author gives a sketch of the history of the periodic press in France in the 17th and 18th centuries. Except for a second title page, entire work, including index, is in Russian.

Klapp, Otto. Bibliographie der französischen Literaturwissenschaft. Frankfurt am Main, Vittorio Klostermann, 1960– . *See* 5878.   **3357**

Monumental series with presentation in both German and French. Designed to cover all studies, critical editions, complete works, theses, and significant book reviews. Schoolbooks and reprints are not included. An invaluable tool in all areas of French studies.

Langlois, Pierre, and **André Mareuil.** Guide bibliographique des études littéraires. Edition revue et augmentée d'un appendice : Contribution de la critique étrangère. Hachette, 1960. xxxii, 254 p.   **3358**

Despite errors and omissions, this relatively elementary guide can be useful. The appendix does not greatly improve the 1st ed. of 1958 since its 32 p. include very little foreign scholarship, and then almost exclusively German.

Review : P. Riberette in BBF 6:497–99, 1961.

Lebel, Gustave, *et al.* Bibliographie des revues et périodiques d'art parus en France de 1746 à 1914. GBA 38:5–64, 1951. (Publ. separately by Editions de la Gazette des beaux-arts, Paris, 1960.)   **3359**

Of real interest since many art magazines were (and are) also devoted to literature. Titles are listed in alphabetical order. A table lists all titles in chronological order. Only a fraction concerned with 18th century.

Lelièvre, Pierre. La bibliothèque de Richard Mique, architecte de la reine Marie-Antoinette. *In* : Mélanges d'histoire du livre et des bibliothèques offerts à Monsieur Frantz Calot. Librairie d'Argence, 1960. p. 333–36. **3360**
Interesting bibliographical article of a wider interest than the title might suggest.

Lenardon, Dante A. An annotated list of articles dealing with Italian literature appearing in the Journal encyclopédique from 1756–1793. Ital 40:52–61, 1963. **3361**
Interesting comments and bibliography, particularly for the last 20 years of the journal which are too aften neglected.

Malclès, Louise-Noëlle. La bibliographie. Paris, 1960. 114 p. (Issued as a supplement to Bibliographie de la France, pt. 2 [Chronique], Jan. 29–March 4, 1960.) **3362**
Excellent general study with chapters 4 and 5 (p. 42–55) devoted to the 18th century.

— Les sources du travail bibliograhique. Geneva, Droz, 1950–58. 3 v. in 4. **3363**
Finest universal guide to bibliography published in French. V. 1 lists general and national bibliographies. The two parts of v. 2 deal with bibliographies in the humanities. Last volume deals with the sciences. French literature is treated in first part of v. 2, p. 230–302.

Méras, Mathieu. La bibliothèque de l'abbaye de Grandselve au début du XVIIIe siècle. AdMidi 73:81–94, 1961. **3364**
A description of the inventory of works once held in the library of the Abbaye de Grandselve in Languedoc. Classified by subject matter. Holdings were vast, but in philosophy only one commentary on Descartes and nothing by him; in literature nothing at all by Corneille, Racine, or Molière; almost no 16th-century humanists aside from Erasmus and Montaigne. An important list for those who would understand the limitations of the early Englightenment.

The Oxford companion to French literature. Ed. by Sir Paul Harvey and J.-E. Heseltine. Oxford, Clarendon press, 1959. x, 776 p. **3365**
A handy reference guide, but of no great bibliographical worth.

Proust, Jacques. Diderot et le XVIIIe siècle français en U.R.S.S. *See* 4994. **3366**
Limited but precious bibliography of Russian studies on the French 18th century and on Franco-Russian relations. Lists also Russian eds of the *philosophes* and Russian studies on them. Diderot himself figures no more in this study than d'Holbach, Rousseau, Voltaire, etc.

— Travaux soviétiques récents sur le XVIIIe siècle français. RHL 61:589–92, 1961. *See* 4144. **3367**
Brief but very important critical bibliography covering the years 1958–61. Not a supplement to author's *Diderot et le XVIIIe siècle français en U.R.S.S.* (3366) which appeared in same review in July–Sept. 1954

Quérard, Joseph-Marie. La France littéraire ou dictionnaire bibliographique des savants, historiens et gens de lettres de la France. Maisonneuve & Larose, 1964. 12 v. **3368**
An excellent reprint making this work available again for purchase.

— Les supercheries littéraires dévoilées. Maisonneuve & Larose, 1964. 3v. **3369**
Excellent reprint making this work available again for purchase.

Rancœur, René. Revue d'histoire littéraire de la France : bibliographie littéraire. Colin, 1955- . **3370**
This yearly publication is more than a gathering together of the quarterly bibliographies of the RHL. It contains many unusual items from *numéros spéciaux*, as well as items on living authors not covered before.

Reynaud, Henry-Jean. Notes supplémentaires sur les livres à gravures du XVIIIe siècle. Geneva, Bibliothèque des érudits, 1955. 580 p. **3371**
A bibliography in alphabetical order by authors and anonymous titles of the precious and the beautiful in 18th-century illustrated books. This book is itself a work of art. The descriptions, however, are brief; the artist is identified wherever possible but in general the engravings are not described. Many beautiful illustrations.

Ronsin, Albert. La librairie et l'imprimerie en Bourgogne d'après une enquête de 1764. ABo 32:126–37, 1960. **3372**
A bibliography of publishers, sellers, and printers of books listed alphabetically by towns.

Saffroy, Gaston. Bibliographie des almanachs et annuaires administratifs, ecclésiastiques et militaires français de l'Ancien Régime et des almanachs et annuaires généalogiques et nobiliaires du xvie siècle à nos jours. Gaston Saffroy, 1959. xvi, 109 p.   **3373**

Excellent compilation, most of which is devoted to the 18th century.

Speziali, Pierre. Manuscrits inédits du xviiie siècle (fonds genevois). RHS 9:165–68, 1956.   **3374**

Interesting bibliographical article on largely unstudied manuscripts at Geneva, many of which, however, fall outside the realm of belles-lettres.

Ventre, Madeleine. L'imprimerie et la librairie en Languedoc au dernier siècle de l'Ancien Régime, 1700–1789. Mouton, 1958. xi, 288 p.   **3375**

Excellent study of all aspects of book production and sale, including censorship, repressive police measures, inspections, etc. Most secretly sold books were religious in nature (Jansenist or Protestant): very few were *galant*, libertine, or philosophic (such as the *Pucelle d'Orléans*, the *Bijoux indiscrets*, the works of Fontenelle, essays by Rousseau, etc.). Work concludes with an index of all prohibited books mentioned (p. 284–88).

Review : F. Orlando in SF 4:160–61, 1960.

Zambon, Maria Rosa. Bibliographie du roman français en Italie au xviiie siècle; traductions. Florence, Sansoni antiquariate and Paris, Didier, 1962. xxxii, 120 p. (PIFF) *See 3747.*   **3376**

A publication of prime importance for the study of the dissemination of French thought in the 18th century. A few examples of numbers of separate editions of one or more novels: Fénelon, 54; Baculard d'Arnaud, 38; the abbé Prévost, 35; Mme de Riccoboni, 20; Lesage, 18; Marmontel, 15; Rousseau, 13; Florian, 10; Marivaux, 9; Voltaire, 8; Diderot, 3 (of which two were of *La religieuse*).

Histories of Literature
(Nos. 3377–3387)

Hugh M. Davidson

Billy, André. La littérature française du xviiie siècle. *In* : Neuf siècles de littérature française. Ed. by Emile Henriot. Delagrave, 1958. p. 273–366.   **3377**

Individual chapters on Voltaire, Montesquieu, Buffon, Diderot, Rousseau; other chapters group authors and works by topics or genres. Eclectic work : combines cultural history, biography, résumés, appreciation of form. Useful but not particularly unified or penetrating survey. Short winded on great figures; almost nothing on international aspects of Enlightenment. Good basic bibliography now needs supplementing, e.g., for recent work on Montesquieu, Diderot, Rousseau.

Reviews : P. Moreau in RHL 59:249–53, 1959; F. Soumande in RUL 13:156–59, 1958–59; A. Viatte in RUL 13:609–12, 1959.

Bornecque, Pierre, and Jacques-Henry. La France et sa littérature. Lyons, IAC, 1957. V. 2 : De 1715 à nos jours. p. 265–404.   **3378**

A combination of cram-book and small encyclopedia. Thousands of facts, judgments, analyses, and quotes arranged in tabular form. Includes historical, political, social, economic, literary, artistic, and biographical information and events; historical and literary maps, etc. Exasperating at times as 18th-century literature is cut and dried under a system of three *parties,* four *époques,* and eleven *mouvements.* Still, provocative general views result and the extraordinary mine of factual data lends itself to various uses. Has *lexiques,* indexes of several kinds, and select bibliography of French titles.

Brereton, Geoffrey. A short history of French literature. Baltimore, Penguin books, 1954. 368 p.   **3379**

Part II, a series of chapters entitled *From the Renaissance to the Revolution,* treats " general " prose, novel and short story, tragedy, comedy, and poetry in such a way that 18th-century writers are seen in unusual light—as working within broadly defined genres that go in relatively unbroken lines back to the 16th century. A rapid survey, done with taste, that suggests lines of thought for further investigation. Basic bibliography; index.

Review : G. Watts in FR 28:543–44, 1954–55.

Cazamian, Louis François. A history of French literature. Oxford, Clarendon press, 1955. p. 206–87.   **3380**

Traditional historical framework (transition from Classical Age to Enlightenment, then on to pre-Romanticism) and critical vocabulary, but notable from time to time for independent and discriminating judgments; e. g., the chapter on Voltaire or the remarks on Louis Racine and other minor figures. Interesting *rapprochements* and allusions based on author's knowledge of English literature and thought. Well written; no need for him to apologize for writing in a language other than his own! Short biographical sketches in footnotes; index of names, titles, topics; no bibliography.

Reviews : P. Jones in FS 10:256–57, 1956; W. Moore in MLR 51:429–31, 1956; H. Ryland in FR 29:512–13, 1955–56.

Dictionnaire des lettres françaises. Le dix-huitième siècle. Publié sous la direction du Cardinal Georges Grente. (Assistant directors : Albert Pauphilet, Louis Pichard, Robert Barroux). Fayard, 1960. 2 v. *See* 3336. **3381**

Contains articles on general topics (*c.* 150 of these), on major and minor writers, on personages both well known and obscure. Long list of distinguished contributors. Excellent reference work in spite of inevitable variation in quality of entries. Funck-Brentano's introductory essay, based on generic rather than chronological principles, has enlightening remarks; serves, however, as review rather than as synthesis. Main articles give clear sense of complex movements in ideas, literature, and other arts and some grasp of the many levels of thought and action involved in the Enlightenment and Revolution. Good for browsing (e.g., articles on *Apologistes, Musique, Nature*) as well as for reference. Bibliographical indications at end of most articles always useful, but must be checked for adequacy up to date of publication; *see also* p. 19–32 for general survey of research tools, documentary sources, and *Discographie.* Index of general articles on genres, institutions, influences, etc., at end of v. 2.

Hatzfeld, Helmut A. Literature through art; a new approach to French literature. New York, Oxford univ. press, 1952. p. 102–19. **3382**

In *The rococo of the 18th century, 1715–1789,* the fourth of 6 chapters dealing with epochs of French literature and art, author undertakes comparative analysis and appreciation of texts and pictures in terms of themes such as eroticism, mask and disguise, *esprit.* Brief treatment of big subject; valuable because it makes explicit the problems of historians and critics of literature who wish to study works and details of works on basis of *Geistesgeschichte*

and comparative esthetics. (For statement of "Consequences for Literary Criticism," *see also* ch. 7.) Two bibliographies : one for chapters, the other for the approach in general; index of artists and authors.

Reviews : C. Gilbert in RR 43:309–12, 1952; M. Wandruszka in NS n. s. 1: 226–27, 1952.

Havens, George R. The age of ideas; from reaction to revolution in eighteenth-century France. New York, Collier books, 1962. 480 p. First published in 1955 in illustrated ed. (New York, Holt). *See* 4131. **3383**

Since " ideas live only in people, " history of literature and of the period are approched via biography. Striking *tableaux* and narrative sections; author has eye for telling detail and anecdote : an imaginative but not imagined account, with documentation given in notes at end. Covers span from revocation of Edict of Nantes to coming of Napoleon. Single chapters on Bayle, Fénelon, Fontenelle, Beaumarchais; 4 each on Montesquieu, Voltaire, Rousseau, and Diderot. Important works analyzed, quoted, discussed in each case. Interesting excursions; *see,* e. g., chapter on Montesquieu in America. For general reader as well as specialist. Detailed index of names, titles, topics.

Reviews : F. Green in RHL 57:254–55, 1957; N. Torrey in RR 46:299–301, 1955; F. Vial in FR 29:268–70, 1955–56.

Histoire des littératures. Ed. by Raymond Queneau. V. 3 : Littératures françaises, connexes et marginales. Gallimard, 1958. p. 525–883. (Encyclopédie de la Pléiade) **3384**

Contains 12 chapters on the period, each with bibliography at end : A. Adam, *Ouvertures sur le XVIIIᵉ siècle*; Y. Belaval, *Au siècle des lumières*; J. Fabre, *Marivaux*; Etiemble, *Montesquieu*; J. van den Heuvel, *Voltaire*; J. Thomas, *Diderot*; J. Fabre, *J.-J. Rousseau, Beaumarchais,* and *Le théâtre au XVIIIᵉ siècle*; Etiemble *La poésie au XVIIIᵉ siècle, Prosateurs du XVIIIᵉ siècle* and *Les écrivains français et la Révolution.* Not a unified history of 18th-century literature; rather, 12 elegant and valuable essays representing some of best French scholarship. Coverage and point of view varies with author's temperament and preferences in each case. Suggestive revisions of details, no big surprises. *Table analytique,* indexes of names and works help, but hardly a reference tool.

Mornet, Daniel. The development of literature and culture in the XVIIIth century. *In* : The European inheritance. Ed. by Sir Ernest Barker, Sir George Clark, and P. Vaucher. Oxford, Clarendon press, 1954. 2:283–352. *See* 4952.   **3385**

Remarkable survey compresses great erudition into fewer than 70 p. Three periods are distinguished : *c.* 1700–1750, 1750–1789, 1789–1815. The earlier two correspond to the predominance of France, then of England, the " North, " and Germany in European culture and literature; the last takes in the diverse movements that accompanied and followed the Revolution. Truly European in scope; so much so that authors and works are inevitably submerged in international trends. Valuable, nonetheless, as rich and readable background study. 8 p. of documents at end of section; index of names and subjects at end of volume.

Saulnier, Verdun L. La littérature française du siècle philosophique. 5th ed. rev. Presses univ. de France, 1958. 134 p. (Que sais-je ?, 128)   **3386**

For period 1715–1802, treats four literary " generations " against background of facts from various domains. Groupings sometimes questionable, but work generally gives lively sense of differences in authors and their productions. Many suggestive views and *formules*; author has talent for finding apt quotations to illustrate his points. Short, fact-filled section at end entitled *L'Europe française.* Bibliography of basic works in French (a *liste d'initiation*) good to date of publication. Index of names.

Vier, Jacques. Histoire de la littérature française : XVIIIᵉ siècle. Colin, 1965. V. 1 : L'armature intellectuelle et morale. 352 p.   **3387**

Short chapters on Saint-Simon, Fontenelle, Bayle; longer treatments of Montesquieu, Voltaire, Rousseau, Diderot, Buffon as the " grands maîtres du chœur philosophique." Substantial, vigorous essays based on wide reading of the authors and of recent scholarship. Vivid portraits in each case, followed by some analysis of works but mostly synoptic discussion of themes and positions. Chapters on Rousseau and Buffon especially notable. Chronologies at head of each chapter; up-to-date bibliography (mainly works in French) at end; no index. Author announces in preface a second volume covering evolution of genres in the period.

Historical and Political
Background*
(Nos. 3388–3402)

ADRIENNE D. HYTIER

Augé-Laribé, Michel. La révolution agricole. A. Michel, 1955. 435 p.   **3388**

Posthumous work by a long-time specialist of agricultural problems and history. Well documented and readable; avoids excessive use of technical vocabulary.

Barber, Elinor G. The bourgeoisie in 18th century France. Princeton, Princeton univ. press, 1955. xi, 165 p.   **3389**

Sociological study of the *bourgeoisie* during the Enlightenment.

Reviews : J. Egret in Rhist 217:160, 1957; L. Gershoy in AHR 61:699, 1955–56; J. McManners in EHR 71:672–73, 1956.

Corvisier, André. L'armée française de la fin du XVIIᵉ siècle au ministère de Choiseul; le soldat. Presses univ. de France, 1964. 2 v.   **3390**

A very thorough and interesting study of the French army between 1700 and 1763, based both on published and unpublished material (especially the *Contrôles de troupes*); includes an excellent bibliography and index, numerous tables, graphs and appendixes. Indispensable for an understanding of the society of the 18th century.

Fabre, Jean. Stanislas-Auguste Poniatowski et l'Europe des lumières. Institut d'études slaves, 1952. iii, 746 p.   **3391**

Most interesting and valuable; reveals many hitherto little-known aspects of 18th-century political and literary life. Extremely well documented; many almost inaccessible Polish sources have been used.

* It must be stressed once again that this section is extremely selective; many interesting works have had to be omitted. The reader will find additional titles in the *Bibliographie de la France*, in the *American historical association's guide to historical literature*, in the *Bibliographie annuelle de l'histoire de France du Vᵉ siècle à 1939*, and in the bibliographies of the *Revue historique*, of the *Journal of modern history*, and of the books indicated here.

Faÿ, Bernard. La grande Révolution, 1715–1815. Le livre contemporain, 1959. 476 p. **3392**

" Je me suis peu servi de documents officiels, car ils mentent d'ordinaire... les papiers intimes de ceux qui ont fait ou subi la Révolution m'ont semblé les documents les plus sûrs " (p. 467–68). Alas, there are no references and no bibliography. The author's interpretations are usually interesting, sometimes original and even brilliant, but not always thoroughly convincing. Particularly in Book IV, *La Révolution orléaniste*, the reader would like more substantiation for the arguments presented.

Ford, Franklin L. Robe and sword; the regrouping of the French aristocracy after Louis XIV. Cambridge, Harvard univ. press, 1953. xii, 280 p. **3393**

Deals with " the situation of the nobility and especially the *noblesse de robe* in 1715, the elements which underlay the magistracy's rise to power and prestige in the ensuing period, and... the overt indications of aristocratic regrouping in the politics, social relationships, and intellectual trends of the years between 1715 and 1748." Based partly on archival material.

Reviews : H. Hill in JMH 27:77–78, 1955; R. Palmer in AHR 59:614–16, 1953–54; M. Thomson in EHR 70:335, 1955.

Godechot, Jacques Léon. La contre-révolution, doctrine et action, 1789–1804. Presses univ. de France, 1961. 426 p. **3394**

Interesting and original work. Deals not only with what the author calls the " action " of the *contre-révolution* (revolts, espionage, plots) but also with doctrines which explain it.

Gooch, George Peabody. Louis XV; the monarchy in decline. New York, Longmans, Green, 1956. xiv, 285 p. **3395**

Agreeable review of well-known facts. Review : J. McManners in EHR 72: 753, 1957.

Jacomet, Pierre. Vicissitudes et chutes du Parlement de Paris. Hachette, 1954. 251 p. **3396**

A popular treatment of an important aspect of 18th-century political life in France. Readable but not scholarly. No bibliography, no references.

Kunstler, Charles. La vie quotidienne sous Louis XV. Hachette, 1953. 348 p. **3397**

Amusing tidbits and anecdotes on 18th-century society in France, with special special emphasis on the immorality of the times. Neither a complete nor a systematic study. As in the other volumes of the series of the *Vie quotidienne*, brief bibliographies, and no indexes. See also by the same author, *La vie quotidienne sous la Régence*, Hachette, 1960.

Mauro, Frédéric. L'expansion européenne (1600–1870). Presses univ. de France, 1964. 417 p. (" Nouvelle Clio," l'histoire et ses problèmes, 27) **3398**

" La nouvelle collection répond à l'orientation imprimée de nos jours aux études historiques en matière de recherche et d'enseignement. Il s'agit de donner aux lecteurs le sentiment du dynamisme de l'histoire, une idée de ses conquêtes, de sa complexité, de ses doutes." Precisely for that reason, although there is, and, intentionally so, some overlapping with the volumes of the " old " Clio series, one may doubt whether this new collection will completely supersede it, at least for some time to come.

This volume, among the first of the series to be published, certainly augurs well for the others. It contains much new and critically assessed material, and will certainly prove very useful to students and scholars. In the same series, v. 36 by Jacques Godechot, *Les révolutions, 1770–1799* (1963, 410 p.), is also of interest to students of this period.

Mousnier, Roland, Ernest Labrousse, and Marc Bouloiseau. Le XVIIIe siècle : révolution intellectuelle, technique et politique (1715–1815). Presses univ. de France, 1953. 567 p. **3399**

Very general history of the world from the death of Louis XIV to the fall of Napoleon. The most interesting and most useful sections are those dealing with non-Western countries and with the development of the sciences (mathematics, medicine, astronomy, physics, chemistry, the natural sciences) and of modern techniques (particularly in the army, in the navy, in industry, and in agriculture). The political and diplomatic history of Western Europe is inadequately treated.

Reviews : L. Gershoy in AHR 59: 81–83, 1953–54; A. Goodwin in EHR 69:338, 1954.

Préclin, Edmond. Le XVIIIe siècle. Presses univ. de France, 1952. 2 v. (" Clio," introduction aux études historiques, 7) **3400**

Worthy of its predecessors in the "Clio" series. Probably the most useful single work on the historical and political background of the 18th century. Contains excellent, terse summaries of events and trends, judiciously selective bibliographies and penetrating *état actuel des questions*.
Reviews : A. Goodwin in EHR 69:341, 1954; A. Guérard in AHR 59:80–81, 1953–54.

Vaillé, Eugène. Histoire générale des postes françaises. Presses univ. de France, 1947–55. 6 v. **3401**
Scholarly study of a complex subject. Indirectly throws much light on 18th-century life; also very interesting analysis of the postal relations between France and other countries.

Zeller, Gaston. Les temps modernes. Hachette, 1953–55. 2 v. (Histoire des relations internationales, 2–3) **3402**
V. 2, *De Louis XIV à 1789*, 375 p. Like the other volumes of this excellent series, this one, by the late Gaston Zeller, attempts to give as broad and comprehensive a picture as possible of relations between states and to show the most important factors and trends in international politics. Clear, informative, interesting, and useful; perhaps a little rapid.
Reviews : A. Goodwin in EHR 71: 490–91, 1956; J. Mitchell in AHR 61:680, 1955–56.

The Salons
(Nos. 3403–3426)

Eva Maria Stadler

General Studies
(Nos. 3403–3404)

Herold, J. Christopher. Love in five temperaments. New York, Atheneum, 1961. 337 p. *See* 3626. **3403**
Well-written biographical essays on Mme de Tencin, Mlle Aïssé, Mme de Staal, and Mlle de Lespinasse. Delightful reading, but not a contribution to scholarship.

Nicolson, *Sir* Harold George. The salons (1660–1789). *In his* : The age of reason. London, Constable, 1960 and Garden City, Doubleday, 1961. p. 214–33. **3404**
General survey. Readable and informative for nonspecialist. Treats the intellectual and cultural influence of the

salons from the Hôtel de Rambouillet to the Revolution. Mme du Maine, Mme de Lambert, Mme de Tencin, Mme Geoffrin, Mme du Deffand, Mme de Choiseul, Mme Necker, and Mlle de Lespinasse. Bibliography, but no notes or scholarly apparatus.

Salonnières
(Nos. 3405–3426)

Condorcet, Marie Louise, etc., *marquise* **de.** 1764–1822.
Salon : 1787–92.

Valentino, Henri. Mme de Condorcet; ses amis et ses amours (1764–1822). Perrin, 1950. 282 p. **3405**
Biography of Mme de Condorcet with chapter devoted to *Le salon des Condorcet*. Provides information on *habitués* including Beaumarchais, Cabanis, Destutt de Tracy, Lafayette, and Turgot. Written for popular audience, but interesting.

Du Deffand, Marie Anne, etc., *marquise.* 1696–1780.
Salon : 1730–80.

Du Deffand, Marie Anne, etc., *marquise, et al.* Lettres inédites de Madame du Deffand, du président Hénault et du comte de Bulkeley au baron Carl Fredrik Scheffer (1751–1756). Ed. by Gunnar von Proschwitz. SVEC 10:267–412, 1959. *See* 3428. **3406**
Only 13 letters of Mme du Deffand had been published for the years 1751–54 prior to this ed. This collection adds 10 more of her letters. Bibliography, index, and scholarly introduction.

Duisit, Lionel. Madame du Deffand épistolière. Geneva, Droz, 1963. 128 p. *See* 3429. **3407**
The literary, esthetic, intellectual, and biographical import of Mme du Deffand's letters. Interesting book ans sound method, but rather brief. Bibliography.
Reviews : M. Launay in RHL 64:484–85, 1964; J. Sareil in RR 56:66–67, 1965.

— Mme du Deffand et Voltaire : le mythe du progrès et la décadence du goût. FR 36: 284–92, 1962–63. **3408**
Interesting analysis of Mme du Deffand's character. Her essentially aristocratic, political conservatism and sureness of taste contrasted with her moral and religious skepticism. Based on extracts of her correspondence with Voltaire.

Gooch, G. P. Four French salons. II. Mme du Deffand. Crev 180:26–33, 1951. **3409**
Anecdotal account of Mme du Deffand and her relations with *le président* Hénault and Mlle de Lespinasse. Not a contribution to scholarship.

— Four French salons. IV. Mme du Deffand and Horace Walpole. Crev 180:148–57, 1951. **3410**
Description of quasi-maternal friendship of Mme du Deffand and Walpole.

Klerks, Wilhelm. Mme du Deffand; essai sur l'ennui. Assen, Van Gorcum, 1961. 110 p. *See* 3431. **3411**
A study of boredom in the character of Mme du Deffand and how this trait was influenced by cultural and sociological factors. A rather far-fetched psychological exercise.

Michel, François. La marquise et le philosophe (Voltaire et Mme du Deffand). NCr 7:71–87, June 1955. **3412**
A Marxist interpretation of the relationship.

Tenenbaum, Louis. Mme du Deffand's correspondence with Voltaire. FR 27: 193–200, 1953–54. **3413**
Author sees the du Deffand-Voltaire correspondence as defining " the tug of war between the *philosophes* and the respectful skeptics . . . who opposed their excesses."

Epinay, Louise Tardieu des Clavelles, *dame* de la Live d'. 1726–83.
Salon : 1750–73.

Epinay, Louise, etc., d'. Histoire de Madame de Montbrillant; les pseudo-mémoires de Madame d'Epinay. Ed. by Georges Roth. Gallimard, 1951. 3 v. **3414**
The *Histoire de Montbrillant* is a long *roman à clef* with an autobiographical basis. Grimm and perhaps Diderot were involved in its composition and also assume rôles in the work under fictitious names. First critical ed. of the complete text preceded by a scholarly introduction with information on the genesis of the work, on its mss, and history of its publication.

Hoffmann, Paul. L'histoire de Madame de Montbrillant ou l'école de la femme. RScH n. s. 110:161–72, 1963. **3415**
Author considers these pseudo-memoirs an important document on the condition of women in the 18th century. At the same time, he considers Mme d'Epinay's analysis of passion and sensibility in this work superior to that in any contemporary novel.

Truc, Gonzague. Mme d'Epinay et Grimm. RevHM 7:114–19, Sept. 1952. **3416**
Analysis of the Grimm-d'Epinay liaison in the light of the *Histoire de Mme de Montbrillant*.

Valentino, Henri. Mme d'Epinay, 1726–1783; une femme d'esprit sous Louis XV. Perrin, 1952. 345 p. **3417**
A biography of Mme d'Epinay based on her correspondence (particularly with Galiani) and on the *Histoire de Mme de Montbrillant*.

Genlis, Stéphanie Félicité, etc., *comtesse* de. 1746–1830.
Salon : 1772–89.
Also see section on Minor Novelists.

Genlis, Stéphanie Félicité, etc., *comtesse* de. Dernières lettres d'amour; correspondance inédite de la comtesse de Genlis avec le comte Anatole de Montesquiou. Ed. by André Castelot. Grasset, 1954. 302 p. **3418**
Correspondence of Mme de Genlis with Ambroise Anatole Augustin, *comte* de Montesquiou-Fezensac. Preface by the *duc* de La Force.

Geoffrin, Marie Thérèse. 1699–1777.
Salon : 1730–76.

Fabre, Jean. Les caprices de Mme Geoffrin. *In his* : Stanislas-Auguste Poniatowski et l'Europe des lumières. *See* 3391. p.292–312. **3419**
Well-documented account of relationship between Mme Geoffrin and the Polish king, Stanislaus II. Seems to destoy legend that this was " le plus bel amour du XVIIIe siècle " and shows political interest Poniatowski had in this friendship.

Gooch, G. P. Four French salons. I. Mme Geoffrin. Crev 179:345–53, 1951. **3420**
Pleasant, informative portrait of Mme Geoffrin, but nothing new here for scholar.

Lambert, Anne Thérèse, etc., *marquise* de. 1647–1733.
Salon : 1698–1733.

Delorme, Suzanne. Le salon de la marquise de Lambert, berceau de l'Encyclopédie. RHS 4:223–27, 1951.   **3421**

Sees Mme de Lambert's salon, frequented by Fontenelle, La Motte, Marivaux, and Montesquieu, as receptive to " new ideas." Goes so far as to assert that it was here that " l'*Encyclopédie* naquit en esprit "!

Lespinasse, Julie Jeanne, etc., de. 1732–76.

Salon : 1764–74.
Also see section on d'Alembert.

Lespinasse, Julie Jeanne, etc., de. Les plus belles lettres de Mademoiselle de Lespinasse. Ed. by Claude Roy. Calmann-Lévy, 1962. 160 p.   **3422**

Unannotated ed. of some 60 letters or fragments addressed to Guibert. Chatty introduction on love and literature for general public.

Bouissounouse, Janine. Julie de Lespinasse : ses amitiés, sa passion. Hachette, 1958. 320 p. *In English as* : Julie, the life of Mademoiselle de Lespinasse : her salon, her friends, her loves. Trans. by Pierre de Fontnouvelle. New York, Appleton-Century-Crofts, 1962. 309 p. *See* 3432.   **3423**

Interesting *ouvrage de vulgarisation*, well documented, but not addressed to scholars. Reliable and sympathetic, but not much new material here.

Garcin, Philippe. L'amour et l'absence dans les lettres de Mlle de Lespinasse. CDS 302:109–22, 1951. *See* 3433.   **3424**

Interesting and original essay. Interpretation of the effects of absence, imagination, lucidity, and emotion in Julie's love letters.

Gooch, G. P. Four French salons. III. Julie de Lespinasse. Crev 180:93–100, 1951.   **3425**

An account of Julie's life after leaving Mme du Deffand which concentrates on describing her " romantic and tormented soul."

Necker, Suzanne Curchod. 1739–94.

Salon : 1765–88.

Gooch, G. P. Four French salons. V. Mme Necker. Crev 180 : 223–33, 1951.   **3426**

Entertaining and anecdotal.

Letter Writers and Authors of Memoirs
(Nos. 3427–3434)

JEAN SAREIL

Because of the nature of the subject, much of the material in this section is also treated under Salons to which the reader is referred.

Charles Pinot Duclos

Meister, Paul. Charles Duclos, 1704–1772. *See* 4088.   **3427**

A very serious and intelligent study of one of the most important secondary figures in the 18th century. This book supersedes all previous works on the same subject.

Madame du Deffand

Du Deffand, Marie Anne, etc., *marquise, et al.* Letters inédites de Madame du Deffand, du président Hénault et du comte de Bulkeley au baron Carl Fredrik Scheffer (1751-1756). Ed. by Gunnar von Proschwitz. *See* 3406.   **3428**

An important mass of unpublished documents which may not add much to what we know of the historical events or of the people involved in this correspondence. They are, however, good examples of their talent as letter writers. A book to read for those interested in these specific years.

Duisit, Lionel. Madame du Deffand épistolière. *See* 3407.   **342**

The author considers Madame du Deffand only as a writer and his viewpoint is very objective. The book is short and readable although it adds little to our knowledge of the subject.

Judrin, Roger. D'une effrayante nudité. NNRF 19:87–93, Jan. 1962.   **3430**

Brief article providing a good analysis of Mme du Deffand's character.

Klerks, Wilhelm. Madame du Deffand; essai sur l'ennui. *See* 3411.   **3431**

A technical investigation on boredom which is at times rather . . . boring. The book will be more useful for a specialist in psychology than for the literary scholar.

Julie de Lespinasse

Bouissounouse, Janine. Julie de Lespinasse : ses amitiés, sa passion. *See* 3423.   **3432**

Good biography which does not bring new material to the subject but tries to give a much more sympathetic presentation of the Encyclopedists than Ségur (123) in his authoritative study of the same heroine.

Garcin, Philippe. L'amour et l'absence dans les lettres de Mademoiselle de Lespinasse. *See* 3424. **3433**

Good psychological study of the effect of absence and *dénuement* on her tragic disposition towards love.

Mitchiner, Margaret. A muse in love : Julie de Lespinasse. London, Bodley head, 1962. 222 p. **3434**

Vivid biography which does not pretend to be a scholarly contribution to the subject.

Music
(Nos. 3435–3459)

BARRY S. BROOK

In addition to studies recently published, the present supplement contains a few essential early items omitted by Wolf Franck in his superb contribution to the 1951 edition either because he was unable to examine them personally at the time or for lack of space. It includes several specialized research tools, e. g., early and current encyclopedias that the student of literature will find helpful. It does not include entries describing the many important 18th-century periodicals dealing with music, e. g., *Journal de musique théorique et pratique* and *Almanach musical*. These may be found listed in La Laurencie (3451, 3: 261–62), Brook (3436, 1:643–44) and, in some cases, in the Chronological List of Periodicals in CBFL, IV, 2804–66.

[Bobillier, Marie] *pseud.*, **Michel Brenet.** Les concerts en France sous l'ancien régime. Fischbacher, 1900. 407 p. **3435**

Invaluable historical panorama of concert life in France based on an indefatigable search of archival, periodical, and memoir sources. In two parts : *Avant le XVIIIᵉ siècle*, which begins with Middle Ages, and *Pendant le XVIIIᵉ siècle*, which takes up about three-fourths of the book. Available facts about composers, directors, performers and repertoire—including the very obscure—are carefully chronicled for a wide variety of concerts, public and private, aristocratic and bougeois, provincial and Parisian. Valuable narrative summary of the develop-

ment of the greatest of Parisian concert institutions, *Le Concert Spirituel*, from its founding by Philidor in 1725. Important for those interested in performance practice, esthetics, and sociology. Excellent footnotes equal almost one third of the text. Well indexed.

N. B. A similar volume by Constant Pierre entitled *Le Concert Spirituel, 1725–90, précédé d'une historique des concerts publiques à Paris* was announced for publication also in 1900 and is often listed in bibliographies, but it never appeared in print. It is one of the most persistent bibliographical ghosts in music history. Probably withdrawn to avoid unfavorable comparison with Bobillier, the ms has recently been rediscovered in Paris.

Brook, Barry S. La symphonie française dans la seconde moitié du XVIIIᵉ siècle. 1962. 3 v. (PIMUP, 3) **3436**

First full-length portrait of a long-neglected area in music history, redressing balance between our knowledge of orchestral and operatic music in France. Contents include : 1. *Etude historique*; 2. *Catalogue thématique et bibliographique*; 3. *8 partitions inédites*. Based on a study of 1200 French symphonic works by 150 composers and detailed scrutiny of periodicals, memoirs, and archival sources. Includes discussion of concert life, publication activities, esthetic and sociological questions. Extensive scholarly apparatus, thematic catalog, appendixes, etc. Some material drawn from this study has been published in two articles : *The symphonie concertante : an interim report* in MQ 47: 493–516, 1961, and *Simon Le Duc l'aîné, a French symphonist at the time of Mozart* in MQ 48:498–513, 1962.

Reviews : B. Churgin in JAMS 17: 224–27, 1964; J. LaRue in MQ 49:384–88, 1963; M. Pincherle in RM 49:131–33, 1963; H. Robbins Landon in MF 17: 435–39, 1964; F. Sternfeld in Mlet 44: 388–90, 1963; R. Stevenson in MLAN 20:466–69, 1963.

Burney, Charles. An eighteenth-century musical tour in France and Italy. Ed. by Percy A. Scholes. London, Oxford univ. press, 1959. xxxv, 328 p. **3437**

V. I of *Dr. Burney's musical tours in Europe.* Dr. Johnson called Burney " one of the first writers of his age for travels." Burney made two tours of Europe in 1770 and 1772, " undertaken to collect materials for a general history of music." The result was 2 v. of oft-quoted, much-translated reportage : *The present state of music in France and Italy* (1771) and *The present state of music in Germany, The Netherlands, and United Provinces* (1773). For these publications, Burney had been persuaded to leave out all passages in his journal referring to nonmusical matters. Scholes' edition rectifies this omission, for the French-Italian tour at least, from surviving mss in Burney's hand. " The two complementary accounts, the manuscript and printed book, have now been woven together into one connected narrative in the form in which Burney originally intended the book to be published." Special brackets carefully encase the extensive new material and the whole is conscientiously annotated. Makes for superb reading and invaluable history notwithstanding Burney's view of French music as " notoriously hateful to all the people of Europe but themselves." Includes lively descriptions of musical life in Paris and of his meetings with " many literary and musical notabilities," e. g., Grétry, Balbastre, Diderot, Voltaire, and Rousseau.

Burton, Humphrey. Les académies de musique en France au xviiie siècle. RM 37: 122–47, 1955. **3438**

Well-documented account of the activities of amateur concert societies (*académies*) in provincial France.

Champigneulle, Bernard. L'âge classique de la musique française. Aubier, 1946. 351, [1] p. **3439**

Honest *ouvrage de vulgarisation* surveying both 17th and 18th centuries. Although it lays the usual stress on operatic activities, it does not ignore religious or instrumental music. Well-annotated, good bibliography, *index biographique*, printed on very poor paper.

Choron, Alexandre-Etienne, and **François Fayolle.** Dictionnaire historique des musiciens. Valade, 1810–11. 2 v. **3440**

Contemporary biographical dictionary still very useful for French 18th-century figures. Includes those " qui se sont illustrés en une partie quelconque de la musique et des arts qui y sont relatifs tels que Compositeurs, Ecrivains, didacticues, Théoriciens, Poëtes, Acteurs lyriques ...." Corections and additions by J. B. B. Roquefort published in *Magasin encyclopédique* (June 1911, p. 448 ff. and Jan. 1912, p. 217 ff.) and as a separate pamphlet of 40 p.

Cucuel, Georges. Quelques documents sur la librairie musicale au xviiie siècle. IMGS 13:385–92, 1911–12. **3441**

Important supplement to 304 listing numerous publishing *privilèges* from 1726–83.

Daval, Pierre. La musique en France au xviiie siècle. Payot, 1961. 292 p. **3442**

Despite its promising title, this work, written for popular consumption, ignores the last third of the century completely and provides only a sketchy portait of the first two thirds. The " tableau d'ensemble, en situant le phénomène musical dans son cadre " that the author sets out to achieve is unfulfilled. Based largely on secondary sources. Bibliography ignores numerous essential French monographs and lists not a single non-French reference. Although some chapters may provide usable introductions to their subjects, this book is of minimal value.

Ecrits de musiciens (XVe–XVIIIe siècles). Ed. by Jacques-Gabriel Prod'homme. 3rd ed. Mercure de France, 1912. 455 p. **3443**

General anthology of letters, prefaces, dedications, autobiographies, etc. Half of volume devoted to 18th century. Mainly original French sources : Couperin, Campra, Rameau, Leclair, Gluck, etc. Some translations from German writings. Helpful notes. No index. Complements Pincherle (3456) and Tiersot (3453).

Encyclopédie de la musique. Publié sous la direction de François Michel en collaboration avec François Lesure et Vladimir Fédorov. Fasquelle, 1958–61. 3 v. **3444**

Best recent music lexicon in French language. Biographical and terminological. Uneven. Valuable for many extended entries on obscure figures and subjects. Lavishly illustrated.

Encyclopédique méthodique. Musique, publiée par MM. [Nicolas-Etienne] Framery et [Pierre-Louis] Guinguené. Tome premier. A-G. Panckoucke, 1791. 760 p. Tome second. H-Z. [Above authors with] [Jérôme-Joseph] de Momigny. Agasse, 1818. 560 p., 114 p. music supplement. **3445**

Maligned by Fétis, the leading 19th-century music lexicographer, as a work that " ne peut être d'aucune utilité," it is valuable precisely because it is a conglomeration of conflicting and heterogeneous articles on the same subject by different authors. A typical multiple entry, e.g., *concerto*, gives Rousseau's *Dictionnaire* definition in its entirety; this is followed by an article by Framery and another by Guinguené amplifying and criticizing Rousseau's and each other's views. Additional authorities may also appear as authors of articles or be quoted *in extenso*. The time span from Rousseau (1768) to v. 1 (1791) and v. 2 (1818) provides insight into changing taste and meanings. V. 2 marred somewhat by Momigny's reiteration of his very curious views of music theory.

Fétis, François-Ioseph. Biographie universelle des musiciens et bibliographie générale de la musique. Deuxième édition entièrement refondue et augmentée de plus de moitié. Firmin Didot, 1860–65. 8 v. Supplément et complément. Ed by Arthur Pougin. Firmin Didot, 1878–80. 2 v. **3446**

Major 19th-century biographical dictionary of music. Especially valuable for obscure figures but must be used with considerable discretion. Fétis was a man of extraordinary energy and productivity : teacher, theorist, composer, librarian, author, lexicographer, and journal editor; his dictionary is his most important legacy. Often pungently opinionated, replete with inaccuracies and even whole-cloth invention, this work remains an indispensable, if exasperating, source of information for 18th-century musicians and their works. Poungin's supplement is more dependable and less readable.

Girdlestone, Cuthbert M. Jean-Philippe Rameau, his life and work. London, Cassel, 1957. vii, 627 p. **3447**

The first large-scale study of the life and works of Rameau. Thorough, scholarly job; valuable appendix and bibliography. Joins Masson's study of Rameau's operas (334) in re-establishing the stature of Rameau as a major composer, thus rectifying the usual overemphasis on his reputation as a theorist. Particularly valuable to the student of literature for its astute discussions of librettos and librettists.

Reviews : A. Bon. in RassM 29:77–79, 1959; E. Lebeau in RM 41:128–29, 1958; W. M. in Mlet 39:73–76, 1958.

Gougelot, Henri. La romance française sous la révolution et l'empire; étude historique et critique. Melun, Legrand, 1938. 371 p. **3448**

Standard study of this peculiarly French genre. In 3 parts : *L'aspect littéraire*, *Les compositeurs*, and *La musique des romances*, preceded by a valuable introduction, *La romance française avant la révolution*. *L'aspect littéraire* deals with subjects, mode of presentation and poetic form. Beautifully produced volume amply endowed with accoutrements of scholarship.

Grout, Donald J. A short history of opera. 2nd ed. New York, Columbia univ. press, 1965. xviii, 852 p. **3449**

Excellent, up-to-date survey. Although French opera appears to receive less space than its partisans may think it deserves, the student of French literature will be rewarded by concise in-context discussion of major trends, composers, and librettists. Famous for its 184 p. bibliography, 52 p. on the 18th century alone !

La Borde, Jean-Benjamin de. Essai sur la musique ancienne et moderne. Pierres, 1780. 4. **3450**

The *financier dilettant*, La Borde, was *premier valet de chambre* to Louis XV, Governor of the Louvre, and *fermier-général*. He studied music with Dauvergne and Rameau and composed a number of *opéras comiques* and parodies which, although violently attacked by Grimm, contained many tunes that found favor with the public. He is known for having set the text of the *privilège du roi* to music and for his *Choix de chansons* (1773, 4 v.), one of the most beautifully illustrated works of the century. His *Essai*, a French counterpart to the more famous English compendia of the same period by Hawkins and Burney, contains over 2500 p. and is lavishly provided with engraved illustrations, charts, tables, musical exemples, complete texts of poems, and, as a supplement to each volume, *67 chansons à quatre parties*, one part per volume to facilitate singing. Avowed purpose is given in the *Avant-propos* : " Nous n'avons eu d'autre projet que celui de rassembler dans un seul ouvrage presque tout ce qui nous a paru écrit de bon sur la Musique, dans plusieurs milliers de volumes." The work, " composé sans prétention," took 30 years to complete. Uneven conglomeration though it may be, it remains a useful source of documentation and opinion for early music, especially for 18th-century music and poetry; v. 3 and 4 are actually an enormous and insufficiently known biographical dictionary of composers, performers, poets, librettists, etc. Despite certain prejudices, e. g., against Rousseau, and lack of intellectual probing, La Borde provides much valuable comment and levelheaded insight into the taste and esthetics of his time. Indexed.

La Laurencie, Lionel de. L'école française de violon de Lully à Viotti; études d'histoire et d'esthétique. Delagrave, 1922–24. 3 v.
3451

Monumental study devoted almost entirely to the 18th century and crammed with the fruit of many years of painstaking primary research. Detailed study of the lives and music of some 60 musicians, many deservedly recalled from total obscurity. However, as suggested by its subtitle, *Etudes d'histoire et d'esthétique*, it ranges far beyond a purely technical monograph to embrace the entire panorama of musical and artistic life of its time. As such this work, indispensable to the music historian, can be of substantial value to the literary scholar as well. Voluminous notes, bibliographies, catalogs, and index.

— Le goût musical en France. Joanin, 1905. 359 p.
3452

Chapters 5 and 6, *Les querelles esthétiques* and *La critique et les genres* (p. 153–227), deal with the 18th century. Viewpoint philosophical rather than historical. Not one of the author's most important or mature works, it is still useful for its documentation and its discussion of the development of musical criticism. Not indexed.

Lettres de musiciens écrites en français du XVe au XXe siècles. Ed. by Julien Tiersot. Turin, Bocca, 1924–37. 2v. **3453**

Originally published serially in *Rivista musicale italiana*, this abundant anthology of autographs, letters, and documents was chosen from the superb collections of the Bibliothèque du Conservatoire. Tiersot, an able scholar, has added extensive commentaries, annotations, reproductions of signatures, complete letters, and portraits. About 300 p. of v.1 are devoted to the 18th century, with chapters on the *opéra, opéra comique, contemporains de la Révolution, fondateurs du Conservatoire*. Would benefit greatly from index. Supplemented by Pincherle (3456) and Prod'homme (3443).

Lowinsky, Edward E. Taste, style and ideology in eighteenth-century music. *In* : Aspects of the eighteenth century. Ed. by Earl R. Wasserman. Baltimore, Johns Hopkins press, 1965. p. 163–205. **3454**

Superb summation of profound change from the baroque to the rococo in music by one of this country's leading musicologists. Since it was originally prepared for a humanistic rather than musicological conference, the student of literature will find it doubly rewarding. Deftly places the *querelle des bouffons* in proper perspective; provides a lucid evaluation of Rousseau's role as both philosophical architect and musical embodiment of changing taste and style; challenges conventional characterization of Couperin as a rococo rather than a basically baroque composer. Very extensive literary (and musical) quotations in the original and in translation.

Mellers, Wilfred H. François Couperin and the French classical tradition. London, Dobson, 1950. 412 p. **3455**

The only comprehensive study of Couperin *le Grand* (1668–1733) in any language. Parts II and III are concerned with his music and theoretical writings. Part I deals with his life and—especially important for the cultural historian—with standards, manners, and philosophy as related to literature, painting, architecture, and music. Extensive scholarly apparatus: appendixes, biographical notes, *catalogue raisonné*, and indexes.
Review: Anon. in MR 12:232–34, 1951; R. Donington in Mlet 32:157–60, 1952; P. Lang in MQ 38:167–71, 1952.

Musiciens peints par eux-mêmes; lettres de compositeurs écrites en français (1771–1910). Ed. by Marc Pincherle. Cornuau, 1939. 251 p. **3456**

Compiler's personal collection of autographs is the basis for this anthology. Reproduces two dozen unique 18th-century letters by Mondonville, Piccini, Philidor, Le Sueur, Monsigny, Grétry, etc. Excellently annotated and indexed. Supplements Tiersot (3453) and Prod'homme (3443).

Die Musik in Geschichte und Gegenwart; allgemeine Enzyklopädie der Musik. Ed. by Friedrich Blume. Kassel, Bärenreiter, 1949- . v **3457**

12 v. to date (A-Sym). Largest, most authoritative music encyclopedia ever produced. Each volume contains about 1000 tightly crammed double-column pages. Plan was to have each entry of considerable length, based on fresh research and written by the outstanding scholar on the subject. Provides an

enormous amount of unique material on
18th-century French music, musicians,
librettists, publishers, and related topics.
Contributors include most of the leading
specialists in the field, French and foreign.
In most cases, therfore, MGG offers the
latest scholarly word, the most voluminous bibliographies, and lists of works,
etc. Well illustrated. Indispensable
reference tool.

Striffling, Louis. Esquisse d'une histoire
du goût musical en France au xviii^e
siècle. Delagrave, 1912. 286 p.   **3458**
" L'abrégé d'un cours libre fait à la
Faculté des Lettres de l'Université de
Dijon." Although lacking a point of
view of its own and relying sometimes too
heavily on secondary sources for its
judgments, it provides a unified portrait
of 18th-century musical taste without, as
is often the case, neglecting instrumental
music. Liberal quotations from contemporary authors. Good notes but no
index.

Vallas, Léon. Un siècle de musique et
de théâtre à Lyon, 1688–1789. Lyons,
Masson, 1932. vii, 559 p.   **3459**
Detailed scholarly compendium of a
vast amount of source data woven into
an impressive portrait of a century of
musical and theatrical life. Includes
major contributions to the biographies
of Rameau, Leclair, and many others.
Table des noms cités, biographical and
bibliographical suplements.

History of the Language
(Nos. 3460–3542)

SPIRE PITOU

Baldinger, Kurt. Autour du Französisches
etymologisches Wörterbuch. RPF 4:342–73,
1951.   **3460**
Draws heavily from 18th-century
French dictionaries to illustrate the pit-
falls into which trusting lexicographers
and their readers may fall. Cites widely
from Pomey (1700 ed.), Furetière-Trévoux
(1743, 1771 eds.), and Richelet (1759 ed.).
Urges greater use of specialized works
instead of general dictionaries to avoid
perpetuating errors.

Barrell, R. A. Three philosophical terms
which France owes to Germany : esthétique,
psychologie, statistique. ArL 11:48–61,
1959.   **3461**

Describes the entrance of *esthétique*
and *statistique* into French by locating the
first appearances of these two words in
their modern meanings. Also studies
pre-1700 connotations of *psychologie* in
addition to examining the more recent
semantic changes that this word has
undergone.

Benveniste, E. Quelques latinismes en français moderne. Fmod 23:1–12, 1955.   **3462**
Indicates influence of Linnaeus on
18th-century entomological vocabulary
(p. 6–11), but this aspect of his topic is
not pursued far enough. *See* Fmod 24:
51–56, 1956.

**Bibliographie des thèses littéraires
d'intérêt lexicologique** (1940–1960).
Clex 2:152–74, 1960.   **3463**
A topically arranged bibliography easily
scanned for items pertaining to 1700–1800
period. Headings arranged by author
and topic. For the 1959–62 continuation,
see B. Quémada and P. Wexler, *Bibliographie des études lexicologiques* in Clex
4:73–124, 1964.

Bibliographie linguistique. Utrecht and
Anvers, 1953–63. 11 v.   **3464**
A most comprehensive report for each
year published by the Comité international permanent de linguistes. Includes
books, articles, reviews, and homage
volumes. Attempts to cover every aspect
of linguistic scholarship. Well organized
by subject and easily consulted for titles
dealing with 1700-1800 French. A basic
guide.

Bruneau, Charles. Petite histoire de la
langue française. Colin, 1955–58. 2 v. **3465**
First volume, subtitled *Des origines à
la Révolution*, contains chapter on *Le
siècle des lumières: 1688–1789.* Describes
the fixing of the language, grammars,
dictionaries, neologisms, and the styles
of La Bruyère, Marivaux, and the *philosophes*. Concluding pages devoted to
nonliterary language. An excellent introduction.
Reviews : A. Gill in MLR 51:461,
1956; G. Gougenheim in BSLP 54^2:
120–22, 1959; J. Pignon in Fmod 27:
75–77, 1959; T. Reid in FS 10:373–74,
1956; M. Riffaterre in RR 51:216–19,
1960; S. Ullmann in RoP 14:58–61,
1960–61.

Brunot, Ferdinand, and **Charles Bruneau.**
Précis de grammaire historique de la langue

française. 4th ed. Masson, 1956. xxxvii, 641 p.   **3466**

Contains a pertinent *sommaire chronologique* of often ignored but no less important events in the history of the evolution of the language from 1716 to 1798 (p. xxiv–xxvi). Excellent account; still useful.

Cahiers de l'Association internationale des études françaises. 9:219–300, 1956.
                                    3467

The second half of this volume is announcedly committed to *Le langage populaire dans les œuvres littéraires françaises jusqu'à la Révolution*, but this title is too ambitious. The 5 essays comprising the publication are devoted exclusively to pre-1715 topics.

Cohen, Marcel. L'Encyclopédie et l'orthographe académique. Eur 72:22–26, Dec. 1951.   **3468**

Describes the arguments for a renovation in spelling set forth in the *Encyclopédie*. Brief and too reliant upon the previous work of Charles Beaulieux. *See* 71.

— Grammaire et style, 1450–1950. Editions sociales, 1954. 237 p.   **3469**

A collection of articles originally published in *Europe* and *Lettres françaises*. Contains essays on Fénelon and the French sentence, spoken French in 1700 and the concern of the *Encyclopédie* over the confusion in contemporary spelling. Reviews: C. Barbier in ArL 8:79–81, 1956; A. Dauzat in Fmod 23:229–30, 1955; M. Lejeune in REAn 57:136, 1955.

— Nouveaux regards sur la langue française. Editions sociales, 1963. 315 p.   **3470**

A work of rather general nature containing a score of interesting observations on 18th-century French. These remarks are indexed separately and easily consulted (p. 311), but this volume is not a continuous or detailed presentation of the history or the nature of the language in the 18th century.

Collison, Robert L. Dictionaries of foreign languages. New York, Hafner, 1955. xviii, 210 p.   **3471**

Contains a brief history of French lexicography with listings of specialized French dictionaries, glossaries, and vocabularies concerned with the professions, trades, and sciences. Contains a brief but basic bibliography.

Condillac, Etienne Bonnot de. Œuvres philosophiques. V. 3. Ed. by Georges Le Roy. Presses univ. de France, 1951. 604 p.   **3472**

This third volume contains the text of Condillac's hitherto unpublished *Dictionnaire des synonymes*. In his preface, Mario Roques describes and traces the history of the ms of this work. A bibliography and an index of names and ideas or concepts are appended. Most of Condillac's entries are more suited to a dictionary than to a simple list of undefined synonyms.
Review : O. Jodogne in LR 8:191–92, 1954.

Dainville, François de. Une querelle de régent autour de l'enseignement français des mathématiques (1737). Fmod 19:193–96, 1951.   **3473**

Furnishes interesting insights into the history of the introduction of French as the language of instruction in French schools during the 18th century. Of more than local interest although the essay was prompted by the accidental retrieval of a ms from the municipal archives of Bordeaux.

David, Madeleine. L'emploi du terme hiéroglyphe au 18ᵉ siècle. Comptes rendus du groupe linguistique d'études chamito-sémitiques 7:98–101, 1954–57.   **3474**

Describes the 18th-century fascination with " the marvelous invention of writing " and the reasons for the confused notions then prevalent. A brief but interesting document on 18th-century linguists' interest in the origin of written language.

Deloffre, Frédéric. Une préciosité nouvelle, Marivaux et le marivaudage. *See* 3699. **3475**

Studies the first manifestations of *marivaudage* and Marivaux' linguistic theories. Detailed consideration of his style, vocabulary, syntax, and word order. Thorough indexes and exhaustive bibliography. An important and impressive work.

Deneckere, Marcel. Histoire de la langue française dans les Flandres, 1770-1823. Tongeren, Broeders, 1954. 384 p.   **3476**

Describes the role of the French language in the schools, press, theater, government, Masonic lodges, Catholic Church, literature. Demonstrates that *la francisation* of the nobility and rising middle class dates back to 1770. Extensive bibliography.

Reviews : A. Cosemans in RBP 34: 462–64, 1956; G. Gougenheim in RoP 11:67–71, 1957–58; W. Hempel in RFor 69:220–25, 1957; H. Weinrich in Archiv 193:225, 1956–57.

Dubois, Jean, and **R. Lagane.** Dictionnaire de la langue française classique. Belin, 1960. xii, 507 p. **3477**

The authors describe the scope of their work as extending from the last generation of the 16th century through the first generation of the 18th century, a feature that endows their dictionary with a wider range and greater depth than achieved by Cayrou, *Le français classique* (1948). A grammatical index is appended. Indispensable for the period of transition.

Reviews : G. Gougenheim in BSLP 57²:74–76, 1962; J. Pignon in Fmod 30:73–74, 1962.

Ducháček, Otto. Le champ conceptuel de la beauté en français moderne. Prague, Stáliní pedagogické nakladatelství, 1960. 215 p. **3478**

Discusses such words as *beau, beauté, bellement, enjoliver, joliesse* as the core of the beauty concept before establishing and analyzing the connotations of such words as *attrayant, ravissant, impeccable.* Bibliography and lengthy conclusions with illustrative charts. Scattered examples drawn from, or in some instances, traced to the 18th century.

Review : K. Baldinger in ZRP 78: 613–14, 1962.

El Nouty, Hassan. Le panthéisme dans les lettres françaises au xviiie siècle. RScH n. s. 100:435–57, 1960. *See* 4372. **3479**

Discusses the origin of word *panthéisme* and traces its history from Toland through D'Holbach. Also defines meanings that this word came to have and assesses influence upon the age.

Escoffier, S. La littérature dialectale à Lyon entre le xvie et le xixe siècle. Rlir 27: 192–210, 1963. **3480**

Adopts ingenious procedure of drawing from local songs for his examples. P. 202–08 devoted to 18th century. Bibliography.

Flutre, L.-F. De quelques termes de la langue commerciale utilisée sur les côtes de l'Afrique occidentale au xviie et xviiie siècles d'après les récits de voyages du temps. Rlir 25:274–89, 1961. **3481**

Lists about 40 commercial and slaving terms commonly understood only by navigators, missionaries, and agents of East and West India companies. Refers to other works pertinent to subject.

— De quelques termes usités aux xviie et xviiie siècles sur les côtes de l'Afrique occidentale et qui ont passé dans les récits des voyageurs français du temps. *In :* Etymologica. Walther von Wartburg zum siebzigsten Geburtstag, 18. Mai 1958. Tübingen, Niemeyer, 1958. p. 209–38. **3482**

Comments on about 70 vocables with Portuguese, Arabic, Spanish, English, Brazilian, and African etymons. Names of animals and plants are excluded. Ten of his 23 source books date from 18th century. Words are divided into 3 categories : those pertaining to local dignitaries, to various activities and social conditions, to certain indigenous objects and customs.

François, Alexis. Histoire de la langue française cultivée des origines à nos jours. Geneva, Jullien, 1959. 2 v. **3483**

The 4th chapter of v. 2 (p. 3–158) is devoted exclusively to the 18th century and is evolved from the author's distinction between *la langue cultivée* and *la langue écrite.* Discusses the universality of French, its adaptability in an age of ideas, the spectrum of its vocabulary and styles, its various literary performances. Each of the 16 sections in the chapter on the 18th century is accompanied by a bibliography of the subject treated.

Reviews : H. Christmann in Erasmus 13:523–26, 1960; P. Rickard in FS 16: 86–87, 1962; M. Riffaterre in RR 50: 276–78, 1959; A. Rosellini in SF 4:394–95, 1960; P. Zumthor in Museum 64:221–23, 1959.

Garapon, Robert. La fantaisie verbale et le comique dans le théâtre français du moyen âge à la fin du xviie siècle. Colin, 1957. 368 p. **3484**

The last section of the study concerns the 1660-1715 period (p. 277-335). Conclusion : "... le jeu verbal est moribond à l'aube du xviiie siècle " with the changes in theatrical fare and public taste. Bases his concluding pages largely upon Boursault, Brueys, Dancourt, Regnard.

Review : J. Pignon in Fmod 25:311–12, 1957.

Golden, Herbert H., and **Seymour O. Simches.** Modern French literature and language; a bibliography of homage studies. *See* 3348. **3485**

An extremely handy bibliography of more than 1500 essays included in over 300 homage volumes devoted to post-1500 French literature and language. Besides the sections on the history of the language in the 18th century, there are sections on the *philosophes* and the genres in the 1700's that are linguistic as well as literary in nature. A most welcome and time-saving tool.

Gonon, M. Mots de français local à Pouilly-lès-Feurs de 1395 à 1916. Rlir 26:90–100, 1962. **3486**

Discusses 4 categories of words : *La maison, Les travaux des femmes, Travaux des hommes-outillages.* Most of his examples are drawn from 18th-century sources.

Goosse, André. Les emplois modernes de " l'on." ZRP 75:269–305, 1959. **3487**

Reports 18th-century judgments on the propriety of the *l'on* construction. Also traces its history. Bibliography contains useful list of 1706-*an* VII grammars.

Gossen, Carl Theodor. Neufranz. gamin. *In:* Etymologica. Walther von Wartburg zum siebzigsten Geburtstag, 18. Mai 1958. Tübingen, Niemeyer, 1958. p. 297–311. **3488**

Summarizes previous misinformation about etymology of *gamin* and finds it defined and used for the first time in the *Encyclopédie* after the entry *verrerie.* Also discusses its semantics.

Gossman, Lionel. Old French scholarship in the eighteenth century : the glossary of LaCurne de Sainte-Palaye. FS 12:346–61, 1958. **3489**

Investigates the contributions to Romance language studies by 18th-century scholars and points to their concern with the written rather than the spoken language in spite of their having been " fascinated by the relations between the spoken and written language in classical and imperial times."

Gougenheim, G. La valeur psychologique des temps dans le monologue de Figaro. JPNP 44:472–77, 1951. **3490**

Analyzes the 5 longer passages in the monologue that employ past tenses, usually the imperfect. Argues that these strong and sometimes sudden changes in tense are not the result of chance but

fall into a psychological pattern. Links Figaro's use of the imperfect to its use in modern French. Reproduces the variants of the first text from the ms in the Bibliothèque Nationale.

Guilbert, L., and J. Dubois. Formation du système préfixal intensif en français moderne et contemporain. Fmod 29:87–111, 1961. **3491**

Studies such prefixes as *archi-, extra-, sur-,* and *ultra-* from time of the Renaissance and notes a regression in their use during the pre-Revolutionary period.

Henry, Albert. Etudes de syntaxe expressive, ancien français et français moderne. Presses univ. de France, 1960. 174 p. **3492**

Has interesting material in essay on the fortunes of *ça* in the 18th century (p. 75–100) although other 9 chapters contain little or nothing of importance to the French language in this period.

Review : S. Escoffier in Rlir 25:458–59, 1961.

Hepp, Noémi. Esquisse du vocabulaire de la critique littéraire de la Querelle du Cid à la Querelle d'Homère. RFor 69:332–408, 1957. **3493**

Deals almost exclusively with the 17th century but contains for this reason a certain amount of information about the sources of 18th-century critical terminology. Must be considered marginal although it will be of use in any future consideration of the vocabulary of literary criticism in the following age.

Hull, Alexander. Note on the development of the modern French vowel system. Word 13:60–64, 1957. **3494**

Discusses the validity of F. Brunot's statement that, by the 18th century, there is no longer " at the base a spoken language, that writing reproduces . . . a written language, fixed." Approaches the problem from the point of view of the phonetic evolution of French and challenges notion that the phonemic structure of modern French could have been molded by orthography.

Imbs, Paul. L'emploi des temps verbaux en français moderne. Klincksieck, 1960. viii, 269 p. **3495**

Has a brief discussion of the use of the past definite in the 18th century with examples drawn from Diderot and Voltaire (p. 87–89). Most of the other discussion and examples, however, are concerned with modern French.

International federation of modern languages and literatures. 8th congress, Paris, 1961. Langue et littérature. Actes du VIIIe congrès de la Fédération internationale des langues et littératures modernes. Les Belles Lettres, 1961. 448 p. (FILLM,8) **3496**

Contains a short note by Ronald Grimsley, *Un aspect du vocabulaire personnel de J.-J. Rousseau* (p. 367–69), discussing Rousseau's expression *se suffire à soi-même*. Cites and interprets a dozen instances of Rousseau's use of this phrase. This same volume also contains Robert Shackleton's *Quelques néologismes de Montesquieu* (p. 356–57), a self-explanatory title.

Krauss, Werner. Zur Lexikologie der Aufklärung. RFor 66:384–96, 1955. **3497**

Takes issue with Georges Matoré, *La méthode en lexicologie* (1953), in matter of latter's discussion of word categories. Specifically, he treats *boutique-Laden und magasin-Warenlager* as applied to the book business. Also discusses *charlatanisme* and relates his argument to the commercial and philosophic attitudes of the 18th century.

Kukenheim, Louis. Esquisse historique de la linguistique française et de ses rapports avec la linguistique générale. Leiden, Universitaire Pers, 1962. 205 p. **3498**

The 12th chapter of his first section, entitled *Des origines à 1800 : préhistoire de la linguistique générale*, considers the contributions of 18th-century grammarians especially although other aspects of the history of pre-Romantic linguistic studies are not forgotten. Brief bibliography.

Laplatte, C. Langues parlées à Strasbourg en 1789. Fmod 21:140, 1953. **3499**

Supports his thesis of the *perméabilité* of spoken " Alsatian " and refers to previous publications dealing with the language of Alsace. Especially valuable, therefore, on account of bibliographical references despite its brevity.

LeGuin, Charles A. Roland de la Platière and the universal language. MLR 55: 244–49, 1960. **3500**

A report of contemporary reasons why French was deemed worthy and unworthy of being adjudged a universal language before 1789. The nature, progressiveness, and literary usage of a language as well as the customs, prestige, religion, laws and situation of the country speaking the language are taken as the criteria for determining universality.

LeHir, Yves. Esthétique et structure du vers français. *See* 3556. **3501**

Principal concern is with versification, but its bond to language is stressed constantly. Indicates the stultifying effect of grammarians upon poetry in the 18th century. Discusses the tendency to deprecate the ordinary manner of pronunciation in conversation as well as certain other features of the oral language (p. 77–107).

Lévy, Paul. La langue allemande en France : pénétration et diffusion des origines à nos jours. Lyons-Paris, IAC, 1950–52. 2 v. *See* 5830. **3502**

The 4th and 5th chapters of v. 1 offer a detailed study of the waxing and waning of the prestige of the German language in France during 1650–1789. Describes the impact of the presence of royalty and nobility in France, of the influence of soldiers, students, scholars, merchants. French attitudes toward the German language are described as is the latter's effect upon the philosophic movement.

Reviews : W. Chambers in MLR 47: 258–59, 1952; J. van Dam in LB 41:107, 1951; A. Dauzat in Fmod 21:62–63, 1953; W. Leopold in JEGP 52:105–08, 1953; V. Pisani in Paideia 9:62–65, 1954; J. Sofer in Sprache 3:48–50, 1954; W. von Wartburg in ZRP 67:408, 1951; P. Zumthor in Museum 58:247–48, 1953.

Lexicologie et lexicographie françaises et romanes; orientations et exigences actuelles, Strasbourg, 12–16 novembre 1957. Editions du Centre national de la recherche scientifique, 1961. 293 p. **3503**

Contains a detailed and up-to-date bibliography devoted to *le français régional* (p. 164–74). The text of a discussion on this topic follows (p. 174–76). The bibliography and comment often concern and are nearly always applicable to aspects of 18th-century French.

Marivaux, Pierre Carlet de Chamblain de. Le paysan parvenu. Ed. by Frédéric Deloffre. Garnier, 1959. lxxvi, 468 p. **3504**

Offers a glossary filled with 18th-century terms that demand explanation, if they are to be understood fully today.

Review : G. Gougenheim in Fmod 28:307–08, 1960.

— Le petit-maître corrigé. Ed. by Frédéric Deloffre. *See* 3693. **3505**

Contains a history and discussion of the word *petit-maître* in the 17th and 18th centuries with an account of the roles this personage played in the theatre and the language he used in his various stations (p. 11–107).

Matoré, G., and A. Greimas. La naissance du génie au XVIIIe siècle. Fmod 25:256–72, 1957. **3506**

Noting that innovators were suspect in the 17th century but encouraged in the 18th century, authors examine this change in attitude by considering neologisms and the successive meanings of *génie*, *esprit*, and *talent*.

MLA international bibliography of books and articles on the modern languages and literatures. PMLA 1951- . V. 66- . **3507**

Each volume contains sections on language and the 18th century. A valuable tool.

Modern language journal. Published by the National federation of modern language teachers associations. 1951- . V. 35- . **3508**

Contains sections listing American doctoral theses written in the field of modern languages with separate sections devoted to linguistics and to Romance languages. Gives name of institution conferring degree, title of thesis and author, but no indication as to whether or not dissertation has appeared in printed form.

Mourot, Jean. Sur la ponctuation de Diderot. Fmod 20:287–94, 1952. *See* 5213. **3509**

Diderot's habits of punctuating adjudged typical of 18th-century practices in this area. Relates his orthography with the article on punctuation in the *Encyclopédie* and the pronouncements of such codifiers as Grimarest.

Munteano, B. Survivances antiques : l'abbé Du Bos, esthéticien de la persuasion passionnelle. RLC 30:318–50, 1956. **3510**

Analyzes Du Bos' concept of rhetoric and his use of such words as *instruire*, *plaire*, *impression*. Largely esthetic, but is of linguistic interest in showing how rhetoric, or the art of persuasion, came to a new definition.

Mylne, Vivienne. Notes on eighteenth-century interjections. MLR 52:28–34, 1957. *See* 3582. **3511**

Studies interjections in fifty 1715–1789

French plays. Demonstrates that this part of speech was governed by its own conventions and reflected social status and personality of characters using it.

Nardin, Pierre. La recette stylistique des Lettres persanes. Fmod 20:277–86, 1952; 21:13–28, 101–09, 1953. **3512**

Besides describing the literary ingredients and devices that endow Montesquieu's style with its charm, essayist discusses his Latinisms and archaisms.

Pitou, Spire. Vocables of fashion in Meunier's Les modes (1704). RomN 5:49–52, 1963. **3513**

Calls attention to older and newer terms of fashion in dress and coiffure. Complements B. Quémada's *Les termes de mode dans la "Comédie des mots à la mode" de Boursault* in Fmod 21:283–91; 22:29–37, 1953–54.

Politzer, Robert L. A detail in Rousseau's thought : language and perfectibility. MLN 72:42–47, 1957. **3514**

Discusses Rousseau's theories of the origin of language and depicts him as wavering between making language dependent upon or fostering perfectibility. Insists upon Rousseau's peculiar dilemma : his inability to deal conclusively with the problem of the origin of language despite its pertinence to his other theses.

— Rousseau on language education. MLF 41:23–34, June 1956. **3515**

Reviews Rousseau's recommendations for language teaching and study, his ideas on semantics and grammar. Describes his point of view as "sensationalistic, pragmatic, romantic."

Pop, Sever. Bibliographie des questionnaires linguistiques. Louvain, Commission d'enquête linguistique, 1955. 168 p. **3516**

An extensive listing of questionnaires circulated by linguists, but only the items for 1759, 1779, and 1790 merit mention here. There is interesting material in these three entries, however, especially in the areas of botany, pharmacy, medicine, dialectology. The 1790 section contains invaluable data for any investigation of the universality of French during the Revolution.

Review : M. Paiva Poléo in RPF 7: 473–74, 1956.

Prévost, Antoine François, *called* **Prévost d'Exiles.** Histoire du chevalier des Grieux et de Manon Lescaut. Ed. by Georges Matoré. *See* 3773. **3517**

Most of the nearly 3000 glosses are devoted to linguistic questions since the purpose of this ed. is to bind the text itself to the economic, political, and social environments in which it was created. Discusses the post-1700 theorists of style and the vocabulary employed in the novel. Also contains a valuable bibliography of *Ouvrages sur la langue du XVIIIᵉ siècle* (p. 227).

Proschwitz, Gunnar von. Gustave III de Suède et la langue française; recherches sur la correspondance du roi. Göteborg, Akademiförlaget, 1962. 220 p. **3518**

Studies Gustavus III's use of the French language. The first half of the book contains separate chapters on the conversational and literary aspects of his style, his efforts to bring the French tongue to Sweden, his vocabulary. The remainder of the study is devoted to a *lexique* of his letters (p. 85-178). Bibliography and index of names and words included. A fascinating account of the spread of French to Scandinavia in the 18th century.

— Introduction à l'étude du vocabulaire de Beaumarchais. *See* 3680. **3519**

Studies Beaumarchais' vocabulary as an illustration of the transfomation of the French language around the middle of the 18th century. Examines his vocabulary in the areas of literature, politics, and fashion. Draws upon the 1765-85 period for examples. Extensive and useful bibliography and lexicons.

— Notes sur le vocabulaire français du XVIIIᵉ siècle. SN 27:226-36, 1955. **3520**

Finds earlier datings for more than 50 words. A continuation of Hasselrot's list in SN 26:168-69, 1953-54.

Quémada, Bernard. Introduction à l'étude du vocabulaire médical (1600-1710). Les Belles Lettres, 1955. 199 p. (ALB, 2ᵉ s., II, fascicule 5) **3521**

Includes many examples from 18th century and covers first decade of this age when experimental medicine was making its start and when other innovations were being made in surgery by Dionis and in pharmacy by Chomel and Alexandre. Includes a detailed bibliography for 1700-10 (p. 184-88). *See* especially notes 9, p. 12; 87, p. 35; 100, p. 85.

Review : J. Bourguignon in Rlir 22: 372-73, 1958.

Rocher, Ludo. Les philologues classiques et les débuts de la grammaire comparée. RUB 10:251-86, 1957-58. **3522**

Not too pertinent. Points only fleetingly to the initial dismay or puzzlement among philologists at introduction of Sanskrit studies.

Rommel, Alfred. Die Entstehung des klassischen französischen Gartens im Spiegel der Sprache. Berlin, Akademie-Verlag, 1954. 212p. **3523**

An exhaustive lexicon of hortological nomenclature in the classical period. Although Rommel states in his preface that his study is limited to 1500-1710 period, many of his examples and definitions are drawn from 18th-century works. He offers an appendix containing a list of 25 dictionaries published between 1700-1801 (p. 196).

Reviews : W. Mettmann in RFor 67: 123-24, 1955-56; J. Sofer in Archiv 198:124-25, 1961-62; P. Wexler in ZRP 74:322-27, 1958.

Rothwell, W. Winds and cardinal points in French. ArL 7:29-56, 1955. **3524**

Most of the discussion is in the maritime realm, but the terms involved are seen as finally becoming part of the landsman's vocabulary when the industrial revolution and the steam engine make him feel the need for " a valid system of orientation." Curiously enough, the word *orientation* is not included in the exposition. Nor are the etymologies of the points of the compass considered on a comparative level.

Saisselin, Rémy G. Une grammaire de poche au siècle des lumières. FR 31:534-37, 1957-58. **3525**

Describes the organization, wordgroups, and some of the model conversations in Antoine Perger's *Volkommene französische Grammatig* [sic], published in 1713 at Brussels. A brief but lively piece.

Salvucci, Pasquale. Linguaggio e mondo umano in Condillac. *See* 4264. **3526**

Discusses Condillac's ideas on language, communication, society, and action. Philosophical rather than philological approach.

Struble, George G. The French in Pennsylvania prior to 1800. FR 27:50-58, 1953-54. **3527**

Traces the original French spellings of

Pennsylvania Dutch family names and describes the extent to which French was spoken by Washington's army at Yorktown. The émigrés are followed as far west as Ohio. *Also see* Alexander Gibson, *The story of Azilum* in FR 27:92–98, 1953–54.

Switten, Marlou. Diderot's theory of language as the medium of literature. *See* 5250. **3528**

Considers the 18th-century debate over the adaptability of French to poetic expression. Views of the *grammairiens-philosophes* are examined.

Tinsley, Lucy, *Sister.* The French expressions for spirituality and devotion : a semantic study. Washington D. C., Catholic univ. of America press, 1953. xxvli, 302 p. **3529**

Contains a chapter on the later 17th and entire 18th centuries. Sees the reaction against organized religion and the aggravation arising from politico-religious strife as clarifying forces aiding in the defining of the vocabulary of spirituality and devotion. Special attention paid to the history of the words *dévotion* and *piété.* Extensive bibliography.

Reviews : H. Godin in FS 8:378–80, 1954; W. Rothwell in ArL 6:153–55, 1954; K. Sneyders der Vogel in Neo 39:68, 1955; S. Ullmann in RoP 9:46–48, 1955–56; J. Williams in MLR 50:338–39, 1955.

Vidos, B. E. Mots créés, mots empruntés et curiosités lexicologiques. RPF 4:269–309, 1951. **3530**

Chooses words used in the textile industry during the 17th and 18th centuries to describe the economico-linguistic process whereby the recipients of goods (France and Spain) and not the producing countries (Flanders, Germany, Holland) influence the formation of words. Bases his discussion on J. Savary des Bruslons' *Dictionnaire universel de commerce* (1759–65).

Vossler, Karl. Langue et culture de France; histoire du français littéraire des origines à nos jours. Preface and trans. by Alphonse Juilland. Payot, 1953. 341 p. **3531**

Translation of the author's *Frankreichs Kultur im Spiegel seiner Sprachentwicklung* (1913). Reproduces chapter on 1710–89 French which equates the language with contemporary historical events and cultural trends. Notes the influence of abstract thinking on French and

describes its acceptance of foreign terms to assimilate new concepts. Old, but still a standard perennial.

Wagner, Robert-Léon. Introduction à la linguistique française. Lille, Giard, 1947. 142 p. **3532**

Has sections on bibliographies, periodicals, grammars, dictionaries, as well as on stylistic topics, phonetics, vocabulary, semantics.

— Supplément bibliographique à l'introduction à la linguistique française, 1947–53. Geneva, Droz, 1955. 71 p. **3533**

Designed as a sequel to the *Introduction à la linguistique française*, this compilation deals principally with grammatical topics but also offers valuable sections on general bibliographies and bibliographies dealing with philology and linguistics.

Reviews : A. Ewert in FS 10:188, 1956; K. Sneyders der Vogel in Neo 40:77, 1956.

—, and J. Pinchon. Grammaire du français classique et moderne. Hachette, 1962. 640 p. **3534**

Destined for students, this book presents the elementary notions about the development of French in order to furnish them with the history as well as the facts of grammatical rules. Hence the examples are drawn from all sources as well as the 18th century.

Waisbord, Bernard. La conversation de Diderot. Eur 405–06: 163–72, 1963. **3535**

Describes Diderot's manner of conversing and the topics he discussed rather than attempting to examine the structure of his speech. A few extant transcripts of his conversations are reproduced.

Wartburg, Walther von. Evolution et structure de la langue française. 5th ed. Berne, A. Francke, 1958. 294 p. **3536**

This fifth edition has been revised and " slightly augmented " without modifying seriously " the general disposition of the book." Still quite useful as an orientation.

Reviews : K. Baldinger in ZRP 74: 158–61, 1958; L. Harmer in ArL 12: 67–71, 1960.

Weinrich, Harald. Die clarté der französischen Sprache und die Klarheit der Franzosen. ZRP 77:528–44, 1961. **3537**

Considers the reasons why and the degree to which French was considered a universal language in the 18th century.

Wexler, Peter J. La formation du vocabulaire des chemins de fer en France (1778–1842). Geneva, Droz, 1955. 159 p. **3538**

Describes the earliest texts dealing with railways and explains some of the curious difficulties that his topic offers in the field of semantics. What his pre-1800 section lacks in quantity is compensated for in interest (p. 13–27). Index and detailed bibliography.

Reviews : A. Dauzat in Fmod 21:151–52, 1953; T. Hope in ArL 8:85–86, 1956; R.-L. Wagner in BSLP 51: 97–101, 1955.

The year's work in modern language studies. Cambridge, Cambridge univ. press, 1951- . V. 13- . **3539**

A basic bibliographical tool. Describes and evaluates many articles and books instead of merely listing them. An excellent orientation. The sections on language and the 18th century are easily consulted.

Yvon, H. Convient-il de distinguer dans le verbe français des temps relatifs et des temps absolus ? Fmod 19:265–76, 1951. **3540**

Examines the notions of tense possessed by grammarians of the 18th century, the terms they employed to designate these notions, and the different ways in which they understood these terms.

— La notion d'article chez nos grammairiens. Fmod 23:161–72, 241–55, 1955. **3541**

A complete and well-documented account of 18th-century grammarians' concepts of and ideas about the definite article. Discussed are Régnier-Desmarais, Restaut, N. Fr. de Wailly, the *Encyclopédie*, Duclos, and Beauzée. For the very end of the pre-Romantic phase of this topic, *see* Fmod 24:1–3, 1956.

Zumthor, Paul. Fr. étymologie : essai d'histoire sémantique. In : Etymologica. Walther von Wartburg zum siebzigsten Geburtstag, 18. Mai 1958. Tübingen, Niemeyer, 1958. p. 873–93. **3542**

Zumthor appraises the importance of Turgot's article on *étymologie* in the *Encyclopédie* and points to other 18th-century definitions and uses of this word. Sees 1750–1800 period as time when *étymologie* became part of the vocabulary of the educated public and simultaneously entered the expanding vocabulary of the new science of linguistics.

CHAPTER II. POETRY

(Nos. 3543–3569)

CLIFTON C. CHERPACK

L'art poétique. Ed. by Jacques Charpier and Pierre Seghers. Seghers, 1956. 715 p.
3543

The editors' choice of the most interesting statements about the art of poetry from the ancients to mid-20th century. Section on 18th century includes citations from Marmontel, Diderot, Chénier, Du Bos, Voltaire, and Delille. Useful to all students of poetic tradition.

Barquissau, Raphaël. Les poètes créoles du XVIIIᵉ siècle (Parny, Bertin, Léonard). J. Vigneau, 1949. 249 p.
3544

Seeks to determine influence of the *tempérament créole* on the works of these poets. Mostly biographical. For critical views, Henri Potez' *L'élégie en France* (410) still most useful.

Chénier, André. Poems. Ed. by Francis Scarfe. Oxford, Blackwell, 1961. xxvi, 144 p.
3545

Seventy-eight poems and fragments with a scholarly and sensitive introduction and helpful notes. Biographical section especially interesting on end of poet's life. Critical section emphasizes his relation to "the European tradition."
Reviews : J. Falvey in MLR 58:434–35, 1963; R. Fargher in FS 18:64–65, 1964.

Cherpack, Clifton. The structure of Chénier's L'invention. PMLA 72: 74–83, 1957.
3546

Argues that close reading of text and review of external evidence suggest that, in spite of apparently consistent forensic structure, the poem may be " composed of fragments juxtaposed or linked by a clever editor " (p. 83).

Etiemble, René. La poésie au XVIIIᵉ siècle. *In :* Histoire des littératures. *See* 3384. 3:815–30.
3547

A sarcastic, scornful glance at poetic theory and practice of time to reveal

that nothing in these domains, except for an occasional premonitory note, is worth serious attention. Remarkable as modern statement of " Romantic prejudice." *Also see* p. 555–59 and 603–09 of this volume for differing views.

Fabre, Jean. André Chénier, l'homme et l'œuvre. Hatier-Bovin, 1955. 240 p. **3548**

The most important study of Chénier's life and works since Dimoff; handier and, since it emphasizes last poems, more inclusive. Little new in biographical section, but critical pages stimulating. Fails, however, to situate Chénier in relation to great poets of France.
Reviews : P. Dimoff in RHL 58:80–84, 1958; C. Girdlestone in MLR 51:439, 1956; H. Grubbs in RR 47:68–69, 1956; A. Pizzorusso in RLM 10:293–95, 1957.

— Un thème préromantique : le nouveau monde des poètes d'André Chénier à Mickiewicz. *In :* Comparative literature. Proceedings of the second congress of the international comparative literature association. Chapel Hill, Univ. of North Carolina press, 1959. 2:382–400. *See* 5747. **3549**

Discusses reasons for interest of poets in this subject and reasons, largely nonliterary, for their failure to transform it into great poetry, or even into " myth ".

Finch, Robert. The sixth sense; individualism in French poetry, 1686–1760. Toronto, Univ. of Toronto press, 1966. x, 411 p. **3550**

Well-documented contribution to a revaluation of 18th-century poetry by centering on the " individualist " poets, so classified because of their concern for feeling, qualities, pleasure, individualism, and lyricism, as well as their involvement with other arts, especially music. Poets studied are Saint-Evremond, Perrault, Fénelon, Fontenelle, La Motte, Chaulieu, La Fare, J.-B. Rousseau, Gresset, Lefranc de Pompignan, Bernis, Louis

Racine, and Lebrun. Also sections on Du Tillet, Du Bos, André, and Batteux. More concerned with the " idea " and description of poetry than with analysis and interpretation of texts, but many poetic samples given. A major contribution, to be read as corrective to traditional views. Cf. Gilman *infra*.

Gilman, Margaret. The idea of poetry in France; from Houdar de La Motte to Baudelaire. Cambridge, Harvard univ. press, 1958. xi, 324 p. **3551**

Important study of attitudes of poets and critics toward poetry (mainly lyric) : its essence, composition, constituent elements, and relation to reality. Indispensable for period covered and future research, but flawed by oversimplification of connections between theory and practice and by acceptance of traditional view of poetic sterility in 18th century. Main emphasis on ideas of Diderot and Baudelaire.

Reviews : B. Bart in Sym 14:65–69, 1960; H. Dieckmann in MLN 76:75–81, 1961; M. Riffaterre in RR 51:115–22, 1960; A. Rodway in CL 15:86–87, 1963; J. Seznec in FS 13:353–55, 1959; A. Steele in MLR 55: 447–48, 1960.

Gros, Léon-Gabriel. Houdar de La Motte, accusateur et défenseur de la poésie. CDS 38:189–94, 1951. **3552**

A somewhat enigmatic introduction to La Motte's *Discours sur la poésie en général*, arguing that we can learn much from this bad poet : " son argumentation fausse repose sur des observations justes, parfois illuminantes ...."

— Poésie bien-disante, poètes maudits. CDS 48:3–9, 1959. **3553**

Disagrees slightly with Roudaut's theses on " les exercices poétiques " (3566) but agrees that 18th-century poetry unjustly scorned.

Klemperer, Victor. Delilles Gärten : ein Mosaikbild des 18. Jahrhunderts. Berlin, Akademie-Verlag, 1954. 65 p. **3554**

After brief review of critical reaction to Delille, relates aspects of *Les jardins* to ideas and interests of the age. Finds little originality in poem, except in smoothness of synthesis, but is unwilling to regard it as superficial. Compare with Mornet's studies of " preromanticism."

— Die französische Lyrik der Rousseauzeit. *In:* Forschen und Wirken; Festschrift zur 150-Jahr-Feier der Humboldt-Universität zu Berlin, 1810–1960. Ed. by Willi Göber and Friedrich Herneck. Berlin, VEB Deutscher Verlag der Wissenschaften, 1960. 3:243–73. **3555**

Taken from unpublished second volume of author's *Geschichte der französischen Literatur im 18. Jahrhundert.* Treats new poetic spirit at end of century and, especially, the works of Colardeau, Dorat, and Lebrun. Nothing particularly new in treatment but good synthetic view.

Le Hir, Yves. Esthétique et structure du vers français d'après les théoriciens, du XVIe siècle à nos jours. Presses univ. de France, 1956. 275 p. *See* 3501. **3556**

Ch. 3 is a rapid, often indignant sampling of 17 works on French prosody written in 18th century. Traditional conclusion : poets and theoreticians had " forgotten " the incommunicability of inspiration.

Reviews : M. Descotes in Erasmus 10:153–55, 1957; M. Hougardy in RBP 35:813–15, 1957; P. Jourda in RHL 59: 253–54, 1959; R. Pouillart in LR 12: 200–01, 1958; A. Steele in MLR 52: 602–03, 1957; W. Suchier in ZFSL 68: 112–13, 1958.

— L'expression du sentiment amoureux dans l'œuvre d'André Chénier. LR 9:177–204 1955. **3557**

A study thick with citations to show how rarely Chénier, in his portrayal of love, was able to overcome the obstacles of the over-intellectualized poetic language of his age and a certain lack of personal inspiration. Standard of comparison not clear.

— Rhétorique et stylistique de la Pléiade au Parnasse. Presses univ. de France, 1960. 207 p. **3558**

Ch. 3 of second part presents another view, this time from standpoint of formal rhetoric, of obstacles set up by theoreticians between 18th-century poets and a more supple and evocative kind of poetry. Actual influence of theory on practice remains a moot point.

Review : S. Ullmann in FS 16:58–59, 1962.

Munteano, Basil. Le problème de la peinture en poésie dans la critique française du XVIIIe siècle. *In:*Actes du cinquième congrès international des langues et littératures modernes : les langues et littératures modernes et leurs relations avec les beaux-arts.

Florence, Valmartina, 1955. p. 325–38. (FILLM, 5) **3559**
Compact review of *ut pictura poesis* doctrine from ancients through 18th century followed by discussion of *poésie descriptive* as largely unsuccessful attempt to realize it due to inadequacies of language. Interesting but debatable definition of pre-Romanticism.

Murdoch, Ruth T. Newton and the French muse. *See* 5608. **3560**
A " French footnote " to M. Nicolson's *Newton demands the muse.* Reviews Newtonian influence, mostly of the *Optics*, on Voltaire, Chénier, Saint-Lambert, Bernis, and Delille, concluding that they failed to reconcile new subject matter with old poetic language and forms.

Nardis, Luigi de. Saint-Lambert, scienza e paesaggio nella poesia del Settecento. Rome, Ateneo, 1961. 142, lxxxiv p. **3561**
Biographical study, based necessarily on much indirect evidence, takes up two thirds of work. Comments on poetry emphasize desire to innovate, especially by incorporation of new scientific knowledge. Appends 1796 text of *Les saisons* without critical apparatus.
Reviews : J. Deshayes in RHL 63: 320–21, 1963; L. Rebay in RR 55:133–35, 1964.

Natoli, Glauco. La crisi della poesia e i minori dell'età voltairiana. *In his:* Figure e problemi della cultura francese. Messina, G. D'Anna, 1956. p. 249–94. **3562**
Reacts against traditional contempt for 18th-century French poetry. Emphasizes its serious aspects, and stresses work of Colardeau, Malfilâtre, and Gilbert as attempts to break restraints of traditional form and language.

Parny, Evariste Désiré de Forges, *vicomte* de. Le chevalier de Parny et ses poésies érotiques. Ed. by Léon de Forges de Parny. Editions de la Cité vivante, 1949. 182 p. **3563**
A relative of the poet reproduces the 1778 edition of the *Poésies érotiques* and a few unedited texts without critical apparatus, and adds a long biographical introduction designed to correct errors in earlier works.

Payne, Richard J. Nicolas Gilbert, jeune poète et critique. RUL 7:413–31, 1952–53. **3564**

Résumé of a dissertation (Laval) tracing the evolution of poet's ideas. Necessarily superficial, but useful synthesis. Short on literary criticism.

Pizzorusso, Arnaldo. La poetica arbitraria di Rémond de Saint-Mard. RLM 5:5–25, 1954. **3565**
Useful summary of ideas of this little-read but imaginative and forward-looking critic. Little attempt to set him in critical tradition of age. For that see Gilman's *Idea of poetry* (3551), p. 275–76 especially.

Roudaut, Jean. Les exercices poétiques au xviiiᵉ siècle. Cr 18:533–47, June 1962. **3566**
Attacks deprecation of 18th-century poetry on grounds that it is not like 19th-century poetry. Sees it as " un exercice spirituel du langage." Author's articles most interesting of recent work on poetry of 18th century, but point of view sometimes blurred, and without elaboration not likely to overthrow traditional view.

— Les logiques poétiques au xviiiᵉ siècle. CDS 48:10–32, 1959. **3567**
An attempt to rehabilitate 18th-century " poésie logique," but also an affirmation that analogical thinking found not in poets at this time, but in erudites like Father Castel and Court de Gébelin. Some curious poetic texts appended.

— Les machines et les objets dans la poésie du xviiiᵉ siècle. NNRF 16:180–92, July 1960. **3568**
Discusses and exemplifies interest of poets in mechanical devices and their frequent inability (through linguistic inadequacies) and unwillingness (through hostility) to describe them precisely or to extract from them *un état d'âme.* Suggests further investigations.

Venzac, Gérard. Jeux d'ombre et de lumière sur la jeunesse d'André Chénier. Gallimard, 1957. 332 p. **3569**
An ingenious reconstruction of Chénier's early life with the aid of documents of varying obscurity and considerable religious zeal, but adds little solid material to earlier biographies. An appended *essai d'iconographie* by G. Sarraute represents original research.

CHAPTER III. DRAMA

(Except Voltaire and Diderot)

(Nos. 3570–3717)

ROBERT NIKLAUS

General Studies and Dramatic Theory
(Nos. 3570–3587)

Attinger, Gustave. L'esprit de la commedia dell'arte dans le théâtre français. *See* 5931.
3570

An important study which traces the influence of the *commedia dell'arte* on the French theater from the 16th century to our time and, stressing the contribution of individual players, shows how theatrical convention and realism were fused. The chapters on Regnard and Marivaux are particularly significant. His enthusiasm for the "spirit" of *commedia dell'arte* leads the author to distrust the literary approach to the theater.

Bergman, Gösta M. La grande mode des pantomimes à Paris vers 1740 et les spectacles d'optique de Servandoni. RecT 2:71–81, 1960.
3571

Of historical interest.

Breitholtz, Lennart. Le théâtre historique en France jusqu'à la Révolution. Uppsala, Lundequistska Bokhandeln, 1952. 394 p.
3572

Historical plays by Voltaire, De Belloy, Baculard d'Arnaud, Sedaine, and Mercier are considered primarily for their significance in the evolution of a genre. Considerable background information on the development of costume, décor, etc., the reception of plays by spectators, journalists, and other critics. The approach is broader than that of C. D. Brenner's *L'histoire nationale dans la tragédie française au XVIIIᵉ siècle* (Berkeley, 1929) and extended to non-French subjects and genres other than tragedy. Index and bibliography inadequate.

Reviews : W. Howarth in FS 8:70–71, 1954; R. Lebègue in RLC 27:469–72, 1953; J. Lough in MLR 49:375–76, 1954; R. Mortier in RBP 32:567–69, 1954; J. Scherer in RHL 55:518, 1955.

Fabre, Jean. Le théâtre au XVIIIᵉ siècle. *In :* Histoire des littératures. *See* 3384. 3:791–813.
3573

A thoughtful general survey for scholars and students.

Green, F. C. Charles-Nicolas Cochin and le chevalier de Chaumont : two eighteenth-century reformers in playhouse design. FS 17:148–54, 1963.
3574

Deals with Cochin's *Projet d'une salle de spectacle pour un théâtre de comédie* (1765) and Chaumont's *Exposition des principes qu'on doit suivre dans l'ordonnance des théâtres modernes* (1769), both of which challenge the rectangular shape of French playhouses. Supplements information presented by historians of the theatre and T. E. Lawrenson's study, *The French stage in the seventeenth-century*.

Havens, George R. The age of ideas : from reaction to revolution in eighteenth-century France. *See* 3383.
3575

Discusses Beaumarchais and other playwrights *passim*.

Howarth, W. D. The theme of Tartuffe in eighteenth-century comedy. FS 4:113–27, 1950.
3576

References to J.-B. Rousseau, Dufresny, Dancourt, Destouches, Gresset, Bret, Palissot de Montenoy, Mercier, Voltaire, Dorat, Cailhava d'Estandoux, Lantier, Bièvre, Chéron, Beaumarchais (*L'autre Tartuffe, ou la mère coupable*), *Le Tartuffe révolutionnaire, ou le terroriste*, La Montagne, Gosse, Laroche, etc.

— The theme of the droit du seigneur in the eighteenth-century theatre. FS 15:228–40, 1961.
3577

Useful background information for the study of Beaumarchais and others.

Leclerc, Hélène. Le théâtre et la danse en France, 17ᵉ, 18ᵉ siècles; exposition au

Cabinet des Dessins. RHT 11:327–31, 1959. **3578**

Provides interesting information on 18th-century costumes and décor based on drawings and engravings by D. Rabel, C. Deruet, J. Callot, Bérain, C. N. Cochin *fils*, G. J. de Saint-Aubin, F. Bibiena (for Opéra de Nancy), J. L. David, Radel, Watteau, Greuze, P. N. Guérin, etc. Illustrated.

Lough, John. Paris theatre audiences in the seventeenth and eighteenth centuries. London, Oxford univ. press, 1957. vii, 293 p. **3579**

Contains important documentary information, available only in the original sources, about size, composition, taste, and behavior of theater audiences. Comprehensive and scrupulously fair. Reviews : W. Howarth in FS 12:369–70, 1958; R. Lebègue in JS 141–43, 1957; R. Nelson in RR 48:304–06, 1957; R. Picard in RScH n. s. 87:335–39, 1957; G. Védier in MLN 73:137–39, 1958.

Messner, Charles. The French theatre : a bibliography. YFS 5:113-17, 1950. **3580**

Includes references to the 18th-century French theater.

Myers, Robert L. The dramatic theories of Elie-Catherine Fréron. Geneva, Droz, 1962. 207 p. *See* 5498. **3581**

A sound doctoral thesis consisting of 4 chapters devoted to Fréron's life and his views on tragedy, the *drame*, and comedy as expressed in *L'année littéraire* (1754–75). Adds little of great significance to works by F. C. Green, Cornou, H. C. Lancaster. Reviews : C. Cherpack in MLN 78:220–21, 1963; J. Lough in FS 18:53–54, 1964; L. Sozzi in SF 7:361-62, 1963; R. Waldinger in RR 55:214–15, 1964.

Mylne, Vivienne. Notes on eighteenth-century interjections. *See* 3511. **3582**

An analysis of linguistic interjections and the conventions that governed their use, based on a study of 50 French plays, written and performed 1715–89. Useful references to Marivaux and Beaumarchais.

Niklaus, Robert. Diderot et Rousseau : pour et contre le théatre. DS 4:153–89, 1963. **3583**

A study of common attitudes and of fundamental divergences on the subject of the theater and its function.

— La propagande philosophique au théâtre au siècle des lumières. SVEC 26:1223–61, 1963. **3584**

The study surveys philosophical propaganda in tragedy, comedy, and *drames*, challenging the concept of genre in the French 18th-century theater. *Also see* Ridgway (4684).

Sauvy, Alfred. Théâtre et société au XVIIIe siècle. AESC 16:535–44, 1961. **3585**

Includes Table of Contents of *Théâtre français ou recueil de toutes les pièces françaises restées au théâtre* (Geneva, 1767–69), and analytical table of plays reproduced in *Théâtre français*.

Védier, Georges. Origine et évolution de la dramaturgie néo-classique. L'influence des arts plastiques en Italie et en France : le rideau, la mise en scène et les trois unités. Presses univ. de France, 1955. 215 p. **3586**

Deals only incidentally with the 18th century, and chiefly concerned with the theater curtain. Review : J. Scherer in RHL 58:77–78, 1958.

Voisine, Jacques. Amphitryon, sujet de parodie. CAIEF 12:91–101, 1960. **3587**

Discusses dramatic parody and comedy with particular reference to parodies of Molière's play including *Parodie d'Amphitrion* (1713) attributed to Raguenet and *Amphitromanie* (1786, rev. 1788).

Tragedy
(Nos. 3588–3591)

Cherpack, Clifton. The call of blood in French classical tragedy. Baltimore, Johns Hopkins press, 1958. 136 p. **3588**

The theme of *le cri du sang* is studied from Alexandre Hardy to the end of the 18th century, excluding melodrama. Voltaire's use of the theme in *Mahomet* is well analyzed. Review : R. Knight in FS 13:164–65, 1959; F. Orlando in RLM 12:170–72, 1959; P. Ronge in Archiv 196:97,1959–60; J. Scherer in RHL 59:549-52, 1959.

Lancaster, Henry Carrington. French tragedy in the reign of Louis XVI and the early years of the French Revolution, 1774–1792. Baltimore, Johns Hopkins press, 1953. x, 181 p. **3589**

A compendium of significant facts about performances, content, and reputation of the 62 tragedies. Follows method of preceding volume in Lancaster's series.

DRAMA 31

Plays discussed include those by Ducis, La Harpe, Marie-Joseph Chénier, Baculard d'Arnaud, Legouvé, Paul-Ulric Dubuisson.
Reviews : J. Scherer in RHL 55:80–81, 1955; R. Shackleton in FS 8:272–74, 1954.

— French tragedy in the time of Louis XV and Voltaire, 1715–1774. *See* 535A. **3590**
This inventory deals with some 150 tragedies performed at the Comédie Française. Its scope extends beyond tragedy to such works as Fontenelle's *Ericie* (1768), which was published as a *drame* in 1769. The notion of genre was losing its force in the eyes of the public and Lancaster has shown the influence of theatergoers on playwrights other than Voltaire and Beaumarchais.
Reviews : C. Brenner in RR 41:302–04, 1950; R. Shackleton in FS 6:161–62, 1952.

Lockert, Lacy. Neo-classical tragedy in the eighteenth century. *In his :* Studies in French classical tragedy. Nashville, Vanderbilt univ. press, 1958. p. 476–508. **3591**
A useful survey of a neglected subject.

Drama of the Revolution
(Nos. 3592–3594)

Ault, H. C. Charles IX ou l'école des rois : tragédie nationale. MLR 48:398–406, 1953. **3592**
An account of M.-J. Chénier's *tragédie nationale* which was performed in Nov., 1789, and provided the most successful first night of the century.

Congrès des sociétés savantes de Paris et des départements. Actes du 77ᵉ congrès (Grenoble, 1952). Imprimerie nationale, 1952. 603 p. **3593**
Includes : B. F. Hyslop, *Le théâtre parisien pendant la Terreur*, p. 401–10 and Yves Le Hir, *Servan, avocat général au parlement de Grenoble, auteur dramatique*, p. 35–52.

Rivoire, Jean-Alexis. Le patriotisme dans le théâtre sérieux de la Révolution, 1789–1799. Gilbert, 1950. 245 p. **3594**
" The book is readable and usable, splendidly annotated, with a good bibliography and index.... analyses of plays are brief and the quotations are held to a minimum. Within the limits set for himself, M. Rivoire has done a highly commendable

job." (Kenneth McKee in review *infra*.)
Review :K. McKee in RR 42:295–97, 1951.

Theater of the Fairs
(No. 3595)

Spaziani, Marcello. Per una storia della commedia foraine; il periodo 1713–36. *In :* Studi in onore di Carlo Pellegrini. Società editrice internazionale, 1963. p. 255–77. **3595**
An important study by the author of *Il teatro minore di Lesage* (Rome, Studi e ricerche, 1957), *Corneille e Racine alla foire* in his *Francesi in Italia e Italiani in Francia* (Rome, 1961), p. 51–80, and *Le origini italiane della commedia foraine* in SF 6:225–44, 1962. Contains an invaluable appendix on the repertory of the *théâtre de la foire* for the years 1713–36.

Opera
(Nos. 3596–3602)

Chailley, Jacques. Le récitatif d'opéra, sténographie de la déclamation théâtrale des XVIIᵉ et XVIIIᵉ siècles. RHT 15:247-48, 1963. **3596**
A useful note.

Doolittle, James. A would-be philosophe : Jean-Philippe Rameau. PMLA 74:233-48, 1959. **3597**
A clear and informative account of Rameau's philosophical aspirations presented in their historical context.

Langlois, Rose-Marie. L'opéra de Versailles. Horay, 1958. 153 p. **3598**
A well-documented study.
Review : F. Orlando in SF 3:328, 1959.

Leclerc, Hélène. Les Indes galantes (1735-1952). RHT 5:259–85, 1953. **3599**
Mme Leclec has supplemented Charles Malherbe's introduction to the Durand ed. of this *Opéra-ballet héroïque* by Rameau which Paul Dukas revised in 1902. She reviews the question of sources and provides information on exoticism, décor, and staging, as well as an account of performances of the work since 1735. Mme France Vernillat has added a note on costume. Illustrated.

Les monuments historiques de la France n. s. 3:1–63, 1957. **3600**
Special number devoted to the Opéra de Versailles. Contents include following articles pertinent to 18th-century theater :

Jean Feray, *Les théâtres successifs du château de Versailles*, p. 3–18; *L'inauguration de l'Opéra en 1770 (textes et documents)*, p. 19–27; Pierre Verlet, *Décors et costumes de l'Opéra de Versailles pour les spectacles de 1770*, p. 28–34.

Nagler, Alois W. Maschinen und Maschinisten der Rameau-Ära. MuK 3:128–40, 1957. **3601**

Useful background information.

Verlet, Pierre. Gabriel et la construction de l'Opéra de Versailles. JA 33:555–61, 1957. **3602**

Very brief.

Comédie Française
(Nos. 3603–3605)

Bergman, Gösta M. Le décorateur Brunetti et les décors de la Comédie-Française au XVIIIᵉ siècle. ThR 4:6–28, 1962. **3603**

Useful information on staging.

Lancaster, Henry Carrington. The Comédie Française, 1701–1774 : plays, actors, spectators, finances. APST n. s. 41⁴:593–849, 1951. **3604**

A continuation to the year of the death of Louis XV of Lancaster's earlier work on the period 1680–1701. Based on the registers and provides factual information about performances, finance, and management, enabling the reader to follow up the success of individual plays and giving data on which to approach wider questions.

Reviews : J. Hytier in RR 43:293–95, 1952; J. Lough in MLR 48:346–47, 1953; J. Scherer in RHL 54:103–04, 1954; R. Shackleton in FS 6:369–70, 1952.

Lough, John. A Paris theatre in the eighteenth century. UTQ 27:289–304, 1957–58. **3605**

An informed and concise article on the Comédie Française in the 18th century, on playgoers who belonged chiefly to the upper and middle ranks of society until the last two decades of the *ancien régime*, on the nature of disturbances in the *parterre*, on the *jeux d'entr'acte* in Beaumarchais' *Eugénie*, and on the stage settings and costumes up to the time of Talma.

Théâtre Italien
(Nos. 3606–3612)

Boyer, Ferdinand. La construction de la Comédie Italienne à Paris (1780–1783). SF 7:287–91, 1963. **3606**

A useful note on plans for the new 1780 building.

Brenner, Clarence D. The Théâtre Italien : its repertory, 1716–1793, with a historical introduction. Berkeley, Univ. of Calif. press, 1961. xii, 531 p. *See* 3325 and 5933. **3607**

Analogous to H. C. Lancaster's 2 v. on Comédie Française for 1680–1774. List of daily perfomances, titles of plays, receipts, attendance. Description of registers. Historical introduction of 35 p. Index of titles of plays. A work of outstanding value although the registers are less complete than those of the Comédie Française for the same period. Performances given at court have been listed. No index of persons nor of playwrights. An essential handbook to be supplemented by reference to the *Mercure de France* in cases where there are deficiencies in the registers.

Reviews : H. Kurz in MLJ 47:37–38, 1963; H. Lagrave in RHT 14:250–53, 1962; J. Lough in FS 16:182–83, 1962; J. Loy in RR 54:61–62, 1963.

Courville, Xavier de. Jeu italien contre jeu français. CAIEF 15:189–99, 1963. **3608**

Supplements X. de Courville's major study (3609) and criticizes severely but justly Gazagne's biased views on Marivaux' alleged sensuality and Planchon's realistic presentation of *La seconde surprise de l'amour*.

— Lélio, premier historien de la comédie italienne et premier animateur du théâtre de Marivaux. Librairie théâtrale, 1958. 304 p. *See* 5898. **3609**

A continuation of and conclusion to X. de Courville's earlier work on Riccoboni published in 1943 and 1945. Important for the understanding of Italian comedy, of Riccoboni's dramatic theories, and of Riccoboni and Marivaux (last ch.). *See* 528.

Reviews : L. Chancerel in RHT 12:47–50, 1960; A. Pizzorusso in SF 4:551–52, 1960.

Dieckmann, Herbert. Claude Gillot, interprète de la commedia dell'arte. CAIEF 15:201–24, 1963. *See* 5937. **3610**

Gillot, by his accurate presentation of the *jeu* of the Italian players, has enabled us to fill lacunæ pointed out by Gherardi. Dieckmann's standpoint is that of the literary rather than the art historian. An original and important contribution usefully illustrated.

Nicoll, Allardyce. The world of Harlequin; a critical study of the commedia dell'arte. Cambridge, Cambridge univ. press, 1963. xiv, 243 p.   **3611**
An indispensable work of reference on the *commedia dell'arte*. Superficial, however, on its career in France.

Niklaus, Thelma. Harlequin phoenix; or the rise and fall of a Bergamask rogue. London, Bodley Head and New York, Braziller, 1956. 259 p.   **3612**
This work deals *passim* with history of Italian comedy in the French 18th-century theater and devotes a chapter to Marivaux.

Provincial Stage
(Nos. 3613–3618)

Ambard, Robert. La comédie en Provence au xviiie siècle. Aix-en-Provence, La Pensée universitaire, 1956. 269, 3 p. (TMAix, 4)   **3613**
Informative.

Bossuat, André. Le théâtre à Clermont-Ferrand aux xviie et xviiie siècles. RHT 13:103–71, 1961.   **3614**
An historical survey with useful appendixes on the plays performed. The data on actors, singers, and musicians at Clermont-Ferrand have been drawn from local archives.

Dollot, René. Il teatro S. Pietro di Trieste et son répertoire français (1690–1801). RLC 24:437–46, 1950.   **3615**
The period dealt with is 1776–1801 when the plays for the most part are *drames*, in some cases translated from English.

Lowe, Robert W. Les représentations en musique dans les collèges de Paris et de Province (1632–1757). RHT 15:119–26, 1963.   **3616**
Some useful data.

Mesuret, Robert. La scène bordelaise au xviiie siècle de Servandoni à Gonzalès. RHT 5:175–78, 1953.   **3617**
Useful data on provincial theater.

Richard, Jean. Les projets de Cellerier pour la construction d'une salle de spectacle à Dijon (1787-1788). MemCo 24:257–67, 1954–58.   **3618**
Provides further evidence of interest in the building of theaters.

Actors
(Nos. 3619–3628)
See also Courville (3609).

Ambrière, Francis. Le théâtre et la vie : auteurs et comédiens pendant la Révolution Française. AESC 114:41–52, Apr. 1960.   **3619**
Intersting but very short.

Chancerel, Léon. Giovanna Rosa Balotti, dite Silvia. CCRB 28:52–57, Jan. 1960.   **3620**
A brief but useful note on the great actress who played the lead in most of Marivaux' best plays.

Chevalley, Sylvie. Talma, comédien français. RHT 14:337–57, 1962.   **3621**
A general survey of his career with dates of perfomances in which he took part. A list of plays performed at the Théâtre Français and a table of the number of performances in each part for each year as provided for the period 1787–1826.

Coèle, René-Thomas. Farceurs français et italiens : trois toiles peintes du Musée des Arts décoratifs et une gravure conservée en Autriche. RHT 12:127–30, 1960.   **3622**
The paintings, most probably of the early 18th century (1700), are reproduced, and the Italian players portrayed are tentatively identified.

Conlon, P. M. Voltaire's literary career from 1728 to 1750. See 4573.   **3623**
A sudy of Voltaire's relationship with censors, printers, actors, contemporary literary and scientific figures, academies and court of Louis XV. Some useful light on the Comédie Française and actors who played leading roles in Voltaire's own plays.

Cramer, Lucien. Les Cramer, une famille genevoise; leurs relations avec Voltaire, Rousseau et Benjamin Franklin-Bache. Geneva, Droz, 1952. viii, 101 p. *See* 5784.   **3624**
On Gabriel Cramer, a distinguished amateur actor and on theatrical performances at Ferney.

Dabcovich, Elena. Die Selbstdarstellung einer Schauspielerin. *In :* Formen der Selbstdarstellung; Festgabe für Fritz Neubert. Berlin, Duncker und Humblot, 1956. p. 53–60.   **3625**
Concerned with Mlle Clairon.

Herold, J. Christopher. Love in five temperaments. *See* 3403.   **3626**
A popular but interesting study of Mlle Clairon and other women.

Lorenz, Paul. Adrienne LeCouvreur (1692–1730). RDM 287–309, Sept.–Oct. 1956.   **3627**
Informative.

Pollitzer, Marcel. Grandes actrices : leur vie, leurs amours. La Colombe, 1958. 171 p.   **3628**
A popular biography of the lives of the three actresses Lecouvreur, Dumesnil, and Clairon, among others.

Dramatists
(Nos. 3629–3656)

For Beaumarchais and Marivaux see the special sections on those authors. For Voltaire, Rousseau and Diderot see chapters VII, VIII, and IX.

Arnaud, François Thomas Marie de Baculard d'. Une lettre inédite d'Arnaud à Duclos sur l'affaire de Berlin présentée par René Duthil et Paul Dimoff. SVEC 6: 141–46, 1958.   **3629**
Of interest in that it brings out Baculard d'Arnaud's plight on being peremptorily ordered to quit by Frederick the Great.

Derla, Luigi. Di alcuni esempi di poesia sombre in un dramma di Baculard d'Arnaud: Les amants malheureux. Aevum 32: 191–97, 1958.   **3630**
Deals competently with a minor work.

— Il teatro di Baculard d'Arnaud. SF 4: 434–55, 1960.   **3631**
A detailed study with a useful bibliographical appendix.

Pitou, Spire. Une tragédie retrouvée de Belin : Vononez, 1701. RScH n. s. 117: 119–25, 1965.   **3632**
This play by Belin figures in the repertory of the Comédie Française. The text follows closely Tacitus, *Annals, II.* Of marginal interest.

Vercruysse, Jérôme. Pages peu connues de Voltaire : Le factum de Rapterre contre Giolot Ticalani. Minard, 1961. 20 p. (ALM, 37)   **3633**
A critique of Catilina by Crébillon *père.*

Desvignes, Lucette. Dancourt, Marivaux et l'éducation des filles. RHL 63:394–414, 1963. *See* 3701.   **3634**
Indicates convincingly a number of Marivaux' debts to Dancourt.

Müller, Franz W. Dancourt's Prologue des trois cousines; Probleme der Molière-Imitatio in der Komödie der Frühaufklärung. Archiv 196:113–44, 1959-60.   **3635**
Brings out Dancourt's debt to Molière and provides background information on early 18th-century comedy.

Eerde, John van. A note on Fontenelle's Histoire du théâtre français jusqu'à Corneille. *See* 4206.   **3636**

— Le théâtre de Fontenelle. *See* 4207.   **3637**
Important, but a full-length study of Fontenelle's theater has still to be undertaken.

Kail, Andrée. Note sur le théâtre de Fontenelle. *See* 4213.   **3638**
Useful in that it shows Fontenelle as foreshadowing the *drame.*

Dieckmann, Herbert. Diderot und Goldoni. *See* 5137.   **3639**
Important.

Jonard, Nicolas. La fortune de Goldoni en France au xviiie siècle. RLC 36:210–34, 1962. *See* 5940.   **3640**
Goldini was invited to go to Paris in 1762 in order to revive the *commedia dell'arte*; instead he attempted a sweeping reform of the theater. His success in Paris is here ascribed to his scenarios. Differences between French and Italian tastes are well brought out.

Mamczarz, Irena. Les intermèdes de Carlo Goldoni dans le théâtre français au xviiie siècle. CAIEF 15:225–35, 1963. *See* 5941.   **3641**
Interesting.

Presles, Claude des. Goldini et l'Opéra-Comique. RHT 15:136–44, 1963.   **3642**
Information on Goldoni as a libretto writer, music lover, and ardent Picciniste and on the Italian composers who set his work to music from the 18th century to the present day.

La Force, Auguste, *duc* de. Un élève de Racine : La Grange-Chancel. RDM 505–11, Apr. 1, 1953.   **3643**
A brief note on this mediocre playwright.

Landois, Paul, *supposed author.* The first French tragédie bourgeoise : Silvie, attributed to Paul Landois. Ed. by Henry Carrington Lancaster. Baltimore, Johns Hopkins press, 1954. xx, 61 p. **3644**

The text of this one-act play of 1741 and its prologue is reproduced together with the *Prologue des trois spectacles* (from *Théâtre français,* Paris, 1737, 12: 461–72), *Histoire de Monsieur des Frans et de Silvie* (from *Les illustres Françoises,* 2:199–220), and *Histoire de Monsieur du Puis et de Madame de Londé* (from *Les illustres Françoises,* 3:113–19). The short introduction, p. xi–xx, is most useful for the understanding of this overlooked play, which has an important place in the history of the *drame.*

Review : W. Howarth in FS 9:269–71, 1955.

Yarrow, P. J. The plays of La Tournelle : the Oedipus theme in the early eighteenth century. FS 6:101–13, 1952. **3645**

An analysis of the 4 Oedipus plays published in 1730 and 1731 by La Tournelle which have been neglected by writers on the Oedipus theme in French classical tragedy : *Oedipe ou les trois fils de Jocaste, Oedipe et Polibe, Oedipe ou l'ombre de Laïus, Oedipe et toute sa famille.* These plays are to be found in the B. N. and in the Arsenal.

Lesage, Alain René. Crispin, rival de son maître, comédie. Ed. by T. E. Lawrenson. Univ. of London press, 1961. 109 p. **3646**

The introduction, in addition to dealing with the plot and its sources, considers the play and its staging, and indentifies the actors in the play's première. An important section deals with Crispin from 1654 to 1853.

Sauro, Antoine. Turcaret. Bari, Adriatica, 1957. 117 p. **3647**

Provides an account in French of the history of Lesage's play and its influence. Assesses its dramatic and documentary value.

Spaziani, Marcello. Lesage e il teatro comico al principio del '700. Rome, De Santis, 1959. 141 p. **3648**

Useful for background information on the French theater of second rank.

— Il teatro minore di Lesage; studi e ricerche. Rome, Signorelli, 1957. 194 p. **3649**

A reliable guide for Lesage's *Théâtre espagnol* and his *Théâtre de la foire.*

Describes and analyzes 95 extant plays and 5 that have been lost. Invaluable as a work of reference.

Reviews : F. Deloffre in RScH n. s. 91:422–23, 1958; P. Groult in LR 13: 418–20, 1959; H. Kurz in MLN 75: 375–76, 1960.

Temple Patterson, H. Poetic genesis : Sébastien Mercier into Victor Hugo. Geneva, Institut et musée Voltaire, 1960. 315 p. (SVEC, 11) **3650**

Deals incidentally with Mercier as dramatist.

Reviews : A. Freer in SF 4:353–54, 1960; S. Ullmann in FS 15:169–71, 1961.

Pitou, Spire. Pellegrin's tragedy Polydore (1705). MLR 54:299–31, 1959. **3651**

A brief analysis of Pellegrin's first and much-criticized tragedy.

— Le petit-maître de campagne again. MLN 74:123–27, 1959. **3652**

The play, listed as rare by Lancaster, is available in the Arsenal library and is here subjected for the first time to a close analysis.

Staaks, Walter. The theatre of Louis-Benoît Picard. CPMP 28:359–462, 1944–52. **3653**

An abridgment of a sound doctoral thesis on a secondary author, of importance in his day, who wrote 83 works for the theater, including propaganda plays from 1789 to 1795, comic operas or vaudeville, and "high comedy" without resorting to melodrama.

Reviews : W. Howarth in FS 7:271–72, 1953; H. Hunt in MLR 48:348–49, 1953.

Brockett, O. G. The function of dance in the melodramas of Guilbert de Pixérécourt. MP 56:154–61, 1959. **3654**

Shows how Pixérécourt skillfully exploited dance to serve his dramatic purposes. Of some historical significance.

Engel, Claire-Eliane. L'abbé Prévost à la scène. *See* 3802. **3655**

Manon Lescaut has given birth to 10 plays and 3 films from *Manon ou la courtisane vertueuse* (London, 1774) in the manner of Diderot to a modern adaptation *Manon 49* by Clouzot (1949) with Cécile Aubry and Michel Auclair. Engel also examines *Cleveland oder der irrende Philosoph* (Zelle, 1765).

Calame, Alexandre. Regnard, sa vie et son œuvre. Presses univ. de France, 1960. 504 p.   **3656**

A full and definitive study. Reviews : W. Ince in FS 16:273–74, 1962; P. Mélèse in RHT 14:378–79, 1962.

Beaumarchais
(Nos. 3657–3688)

Beaumarchais, Pierre-Augustin Caron de. Théâtre de Beaumarchais. Le barbier de Séville, Le mariage de Figaro, La mère coupable. Ed. by Maurice Rat. Garnier, 1956. 469 p.   **3657**

The introduction is lively and well informed but needs to be supplemented by reference to Arnould's eds. of the *Barbier* (3668) and the *Mariage* (3663).

— Théâtre. Lettres relatives à son théâtre. Gallimard, 1957. 855 p. (Bibliothèque de la Pléiade)   **3658**

Useful but contains inaccuracies. *See also* 3675.

— Le barbier de Séville; comédie en quatre actes présentée par Léon Lejealle, accompagnée d'une étude de G. Matoré sur la langue de Beaumarchais. Didier, 1960. 111 p.   **3659**

A popular ed.

— Le barbier de Séville. Ed. by E. J. Arnould. Oxford, Blackwell, 1963. xli, 132 p.   **3660**

The introduction provides a useful discussion of the genesis of the play, its originality, the mss and previous eds. The text is the best critical ed. to date, although all variants are not given. *See also* 3666 and 3668.
Review : J. Hampton in FS 18:63–64, 1964.

— Beaumarchais par lui-même. Ed. by Philippe Van Tieghem. Editions du Seuil, 1960. 188 p.   **3661**

Reveals a B. fluctuating between self-interest and sensibility and caught up in an ambiguous philosophical position. Discusses influences on his ideas. An excellent choice of texts to support the author's argument. Good on *Tarare*. Useful chronology.
Reviews : P. Blanchart in RHT 13: 375–78, 1961; C. Borgal in Cr 17:950–58, Nov. 1961.

— La folle journée, ou le mariage de Figaro. Ed. by Annie Ubersfeld. Editions sociales, 1957. 206 p.   **3662**

Important defense of *Le mariage de Figaro* as a play of ideological and political significance. One-sided. Fails to take into account factors listed by R. Pomeau in his review *infra*, especially B.'s concern for liberty. Lacking in subtlety but very useful.
Review : R. Pomeau in RHL 59: 554–55, 1959.

— Le mariage de Figaro. Ed. by E. J. Arnould. Oxford, Blackwell, 1952. xlv, 172 p.   **3663**

The text of the 1st ed. of the play justifiably modified by two slight emendations, with a selection of variants. The notes on the preface are particularly useful.
Review : W. Howarth in FS 7:168–69, 1953.

— Le mariage de Figaro; ou, la folle journée. Mise en scène et commentaires de Jean Meyer. Editions du Seuil, 1953. 301 p. **3664**

A detailed and illuminating commentary on the production of the play.

— Notes et réflexions. Introduction by Gérard Bauër. Hachette, 1961. 187 p. **3665**

Contains some interesting *inédits*.

Arnould, Emile Jules François. Le barbier de Séville et la critique. FS 16:334–47, 1962.   **3666**

This important article deals with the various mss, their chronology and relationship to the 1st ed. Criticizes Loménie and Lintilhac and challenges the view first expressed by Lintilhac that the *Barbier* was originally a *parade*.

— Beaumarchais and the opera. Herm 79: 75–88, 1952.   **3667**

An excellent note referred to in Arnould's ed. of the *Barbier de Séville*.

— La genèse du Barbier de Séville. Dublin, Dublin univ. press, 1965. 506 p.   **3668**

The first scholarly critical ed. of the *Barbier*. It reproduces the text of the 5-act play in its entirety and all the variant readings of the 3 other known mss, as well as that of the first impression and 1st ed. In addition we have the *Compliment de clôture* and the *Lettre modérée*. Some new data drawn from the family archives. Refutes Lintilhac's statement that the *Barbier* was first a *parade*. A fundamental work of great importance.
Review : R. Niklaus in MLR 61: 323–25, 1966.

Bémol, Maurice. Un petit problème franco-espagnol : d'où vient Figaro ? *In:* Actes du 4e congrès national de la Société française de littérature comparée. Didier, 1961. p. 39–53. *Also in:* Littératures 9:34–53, 1961. **3669**

Inconclusive and unconvincing.

Brenner, C. D. The eighteenth-century vogue of Malbrough and Marlborough. MLR 45:177–80, 1950. **3670**

A note on the origin and popularity of Malbrough with special reference to *Malbrough s'en va-t-en guerre* and Chérubin's *romance* in *Le mariage de Figaro,* Act 1, scene 7.

Cox, Cynthia. The real Figaro; the extraordinary career of Caron de Beaumarchais. London, Longmans, 1962; New York, Coward McCann, 1963. 212 p. **3671**

A popular biography which utilizes unpublished material to be found in England.

Denkinger, Marc. Le quatrième mariage de Beaumarchais. MASALP 39:429–38, 1954. **3672**

Contains some hitherto unpublished data.

Fabre, Jean. Beaumarchais. *In:* Histoire des littératures. *See* 3384. 3:773–89. **3673**

An excellent general survey.

Hampton, John. Research on Le mariage de Figaro. FS 16:24–32, 1962. **3674**

Excellent *mise au point* and judicious handling of speculative theories.

Morton, Brian N. Beaumarchais' first play, Eugénie. RR 57:81–87, 1966. **3675**

A copy of *Eugénie*, dated 1762, in the Falconner Madan collection, but originally in the Archives de la Comédie Française, was presented to the British Museum in 1961. It predates previously known eds. by 5 years. Morton has examined the 7 known mss of *Eugénie* and the eds. of 1767 and of 1762. He lends support to B.'s own statement about the composition of the play, one endorsed by R. Pomeau but challenged by P. Pia, M. Allem and P. Courant in their eds. of B.'s plays. Important.

Nardis, Luigi de. L'affaire Goëzman. *In his:* Il sorriso di Reims. Rocca son Casciano, Capelli, 1960. p. 157–72. **3676**

Some background information.

Nicolini, Fausto. Una probabile fonte del Barbier de Séville del Beaumarchais. NA 470:159–66, June 1957. **3677**

On *La précaution inutile* (1692) published in Gherardi's *Théâtre italien.*

Place, Edwin B. Beaumarchais and bibliography. FR 29:57–58, 1955–56. **3678**

A useful note.

Pomeau, René. Beaumarchais, l'homme et l'œuvre. Hatier-Boivin, 1956. 206 p. **3679**

Deals succinctly with all the aspects of B.'s life and work, stressing the playwright's personality as the great unifying factor and its expression as the key to his genius. Excellent account of the *Mémoires.* Good analysis of plots and characters in the plays. Essential *mise au point.*

Reviews : C. Brenner in RR 49:68–69, 1958; M. Dunan in RHD 71:280–81, 1957; L. Guichard in RHL 58:389–91, 1958.

Proschwitz, Gunnar von. Introduction à l'étude du vocabulaire de Beaumarchais. Stockholm, Almqrist and Wiksell; Paris, Nizet, 1956. xii, 386 p. (Romanica Gothoburgensia, 5) *See* 3519. **3680**

Studies B.'s use of new words, linking them with contemporary events.

Reviews : E. Arnould in FS 16:379–80, 1962; B. Guy in RoP 12:307–09, 1958–59; 13:167, 1959–60; F. Mackenzie in MLR 52:598–99, 1957; A. Pizzorusso in SF 2:324–25 1958; B. Quémada in Fmod 26:237–40, 1958; R. Pomeau in RHL 58:236–37, 1958; M. Riffaterre in RR 49:214–15, 1958.

Proust, Jacques. Précisions nouvelles sur les débuts de Pierre Augustin Caron de Beaumarchais. SF 7:85–88, 1963. **3681**

Throws new light on B. as an inventor.

Ratermanis, J. B., and **W. R. Irwin.** The comic style of Beaumarchais. Seattle, Univ. of Washington press, 1961. 140 p. **3682**

A substantial but not wholly satisfactory study which deals mainly with texts but discusses also theories of comedy. The analysis of B.'s comic style is insufficiently rigorous. Concentrates on minutiae of the comic.

Reviews : J. Hampton in FS 17:266–67, 1963; W. Howarth in MLR 58:267–68, 1963; K. McKee in RR 59:300–02, 1963.

Scherer, Jacques. La dramaturgie de Beaumarchais. Nizet, 1954. 258 p. **3683**

An exhaustive study of B.'s literary

and dramatic technique, successfully following the method of Scherer's *La dramaturgie classique en France*. B.'s work is seen as deriving from the *parade* and the *drame*. Links between *parades* and comedies are stressed.

Reviews : F. Green in MLR 51:275–77, 1956; W. Howarth in FS 9:67–69, 1955.

— Les parades de Beaumarchais.   IL 3: 43–50, 1951.   **3684**

Although Arnould has questioned their importance as a source of the *Barbier de Séville*, the *parades* deserve attention since they form a significant part of B.'s general dramatic background.

Sedwick, B. Frank. Cervantes' El celoso extremeño and Beaumarchais' Le barbier de Séville.   FR 28:300–08, 1954–55. *See* 5960.   **3685**

Contains an account of B.'s 11 months in Spain.

Seebacher, Jacques. Autour de Figaro : Beaumarchais, la famille de Choiseul et le financier Clavière.   RHL 62:198–228, 1962.   **3686**

This article brings out B.'s lack of revolutionary purpose and at the same time the revolutionary situation implicit in his *Folle journée*. The author is no doubt right in examining closely B.'s relations with the milieu of Choiseul and in concluding that it has no bearing on *Le barbier de Séville*, although it does help to explain aspects of *Le mariage de Figaro* and *La mère coupable*.

Spink, J. S. A propos des drames de Beaumarchais.   RLC 37:216–26, 1963.   **3687**

Deals with English sources of the *drame* (Lillo and Moore), with B. as a writer of *drames* and his influence in England, particularly that of *Les deux amis* on Colman the elder's *Man of business* (1774).

Vier, Jacques. Le mariage de Figaro; miroir d'un siècle, portrait d'un homme.   1957. 48 p. (ALM, 6, Nov. 1957)   **3688**

A lively appreciation followed up in ALM, 39, 1961.

Marivaux
(Nos. 3689–3717)

Marivaux, Pierre Carlet de Chamblain de. Théâtre. Ed. by Bernard Dort. Le Club fançais du livre, 1961–62. 4 v. **3689**

Useful annotations. The *postface* has

appeared separately in Tmod 17:1058–87, 1961–62. Dort has also republished M.'s *Théâtre complet* for Editions du Seuil, 1964.

— Arlequin poli par l'amour.   Ed. by Robert Niklaus and Thelma Niklaus.   London, Univ. of London press, 1959. 103 p. **3690**

Production notes and a transcription of the music by Mouret have been appended to the text. The introduction situates the text and M.'s major contribution to theater in the context of Italian comedy.

Reviews : A. Freer in SF 5:158, 1961; W. Ince in FS 14:253–54, 1950; N. Leov in AUMLA 14:82, 1960.

— Les fausses confidences.   Ed. by H. T. Mason.   London, Oxford univ. press, 1964. 120 p.   **3691**

The introduction is based on a careful reading of some of M.'s lesser known plays as well as on his masterpieces. The author has detected sadistic overtones in the work.

— Marivaux par lui-même; images et textes présentés par Paul Gazagne.   Editions du Seuil, 1954. 190 p.   **3692**

A well-documented and lively work the late director of the Comédie Française which links the plays to the novels and overstresses sensuality as underlying M.'s genius at the expense of his sensibility and *marivaudage*.

— Le petit-maître corrigé.   Ed. by Frédéric Deloffre.   Geneva, Droz, 1955.   292 p. *See* 3505.   **3693**

Important. Supplements author's *Une préciosité nouvelle, Marivaux et le marivaudage* by dwelling on dramatic tradition left out of main study. The introduction provides a full study of the *petit-maître*, the history of the term, and a literary background to the play, listing 60 plays with notes on the dramatic treatment of the character common to them all. The *petit-maître* is seen as a type rather than as a character or as belonging to a " condition."

Cahiers de la compagnie Madeleine Renaud–Jean-Louis Barrault 28: Jan. 1960.   **3694**

Issue devoted to M. with articles by Jean-Louis Barrault, Jacques Scherer, Jean-Louis Bory, André Frank, Pierre Bertin, Léon Chancerel, Touchard Lafosse, and Claude des Presles.

Cismaru, Alfred G. Agnès and Angélique : an attempt to settle the relationship. FR 35:472–77, 1962–63. **3695**

Contrary to the view held by most critics, the author considers Agnès as the more modern of the two heroines.

Courville, Xavier de. Le merveilleux dans le théâtre de Marivaux. RHT 15:29–35, 1963. **3696**

Comments on Lesage and the *théâtre de la foire, Arlequin poli par l'amour, La surprise de l'amour, Le prince travesti, La double inconstance,* and *Les îles.*

Daniels, May. Marivaux, precursor of the théâtre de l'inexprimé. MLR 45:465–72, 1950. **3697**

Raises some interesting points but, as the author has to agree, M. does not go as far as Jean-Jacques Bernard in his exploration of the dramatic value of pure silence.

Deloffre, Frédéric. Aspects inconnus de l'œuvre de Marivaux. RScH n. s. 73:5–24, 1954; 74:97–115, 1954. **3698**

Réflexions sur l'esprit humain à l'occasion de Corneille et de Racine, a treatise first published in the *Mercure de France* in 1755 and 1757, is attributed to M. M.'s dramatic art shown to rest on a theoretical basis.

— Une préciosité nouvelle, Marivaux et le marivaudage; étude de langue et de style. Les Belles Lettres, 1955. 603 p. (AUL 3ᵉ série. Lettres, 27) *See* 3475. **3699**

An indispensable study of M.'s language and style.

Reviews : J. Lacant in Archiv 196: 232–34, 1959–60; R. Lathuillère in RHL 56:579–82, 1956; R. Mortier in RBP 34: 755–57, 1956.

— Sources romanesques et création dramatique chez Marivaux. AUS 3:59–66, 1954. **3700**

Deals with *Arlequin poli par l'amour, Le legs,* and *Le triomphe de l'amour.*

Desvignes, Lucette. Dancourt, Marivaux et l'éducation des filles. *See* 3634. **3701**

Comments on education of young girls as presented on the stage and, in particular, influence of Dancourt's *La Parisienne* (1691) on *L'école des mères* and *La mère confidente.*

Dort, Bernard. A la recherche de l'amour et de la vérité: esquisse d'un système marivaudien. Tmod 17:1058–87, 1961–62. **3702**

A subtle analysis of M.'s theater, stressing the *épreuve* as opposed to *conflit* characteristic of the classical theater. *See also* 3689.

L'esprit créateur 1:165–202, 1961. **3703**

Special number on M. with articles by F. Deloffre, E. J. H. Greene, O. A. Haac, W. S. Rogers and H. Walker.

Fabre, Jean. Les grands écrivains du XVIIIᵉ siècle : Marivaux. *In:* Histoire des littératures. *See* 3384. **3704**

An excellent general survey.

Greene, Edward Joseph Hollingsworth. Marivaux. Toronto, Univ. of Toronto press, 1965. x, 368 p. **3705**

Contains an excellent *état présent* of M. scholarship. Some reservations need to be made about the benign figure of the playwright which is presented.

Review: H. Mason in FS 20:410–11, 1966.

Koch, Philip. On Marivaux's expression 'se donner la comédie'. RR 56:22–29, 1965. **3706**

A study of M.'s use of this expression brings out convincingly his profession of faith in a moderate, earth-centered optimism.

McKee, Kenneth N. The theatre of Marivaux. With an appreciation by Jean-Louis Barrault. New York, New York univ. press, 1958. 277 p. **3707**

Contains a chronological survey of all M.'s plays, full synopses, contemporary and later criticism with useful cross-references, and an account of performances to the present day. Handy work of reference. Some revision required of sections dealing with theatrical background, especially *commedia dell'arte.*

Reviews : X. de Courville in RHT 12: 42, 1960; O. Haac in MLQ 21:92–93, 1960; W. Howarth in FS 14:361–62, 1960; R. Marshall in MLN 75:72–74, 1960; R. Mauzi in RHL 60:233–34, 1960; P. Meyer in RR 50:290–92, 1959; R. Niklaus in MLR 54:431–32, 1959.

Marshall, Robert G. Some recent studies on Marivaux. Sym 9:147–51, 1955. **3708**

A useful critical survey.

Matucci, Mario. Marivaux e l'Arlecchino selvaggio del Nouveau Théâtre Italien. *In:* Studi in onore di Carlo Pellegrini. Turin, Società editrice internazionale, 1963. p. 289–99. **3709**

An informed and interesting article on a neglected subject.

Meister, Anna. Zur Entwicklung Marivaux'. Berne, Francke, 1955. 93 p. (Studiorum romanicorum collectio turicensis, 8)   **3710**

Inspired by Georges Poulet's essay on M. in *La distance intérieure*, but heavy in style and ponderous in interpretation. Some interesting light on M. the man, but the contrast established between M. who wrote *Le paysan parvenu* and the later comedies and the earlier M. of the *Vie de Marianne* may be due to differences in the characters portrayed and not to internal evolution.

Reviews : M. Daniels in MLR 51: 436–37, 1956; L. Guichard in RHL 57:244–45, 1957.

Meyer, Marlyse M. La convention dans le théâtre d'amour de Marivaux. Sâo Paulo, 1961. 195 p.   **3711**

A thesis written in 1955 which attempts to reconcile the Italian and classical conventions, and is largely founded on an analysis of *Le jeu de l'amour et du hasard*.

Review : P. Blanchart in RHT 14: 254–55, 1962.

Morel Jacques. Le triomphe de l'amour au T. N. P. Et 289:260–68, 1956.   **3712**

An interesting notice of the performance of this little studied play.

Niklaus, Robert. Marivaux et la comédie italienne. *In:* Studi in onore di Carlo Pellegrini. Turin, Società editrice internazionale, 1963. p. 279–87. *See* 5918   **3713**

Studies the genesis of M.'s art, establishing the determining role of Italian comedy. A comparative study.

Nurse, Peter H. Molière, précurseur de Marivaux. RScH n.s. 100:379–84, 1960.   **3714**

Both dramatists, having depicted the beginnings of love, are shown to belong to the same tradition. Interesting but fails to bring out common debt to *commedia dell'arte*. *See also* the same author's *Marivaux and Molière* in ML 41:102–05, 1960.

Rousset, Jean. Marivaux et la structure du double registre. SF 1:58–68, 1957. *Also in his:* Forme et signification. Corti, 1962. p. 45–64.   **3715**

A highly intelligent and sound study of one of the mainsprings of M.'s dramatic technique.

Ruggiero, Ortensia. Marivaux e il suo teatro, saggio critico. Milan, Fratelli Bocca, 1953. xix, 237 p.   **3716**

A detailed examination of M.'s plays, characters, and dramatic technique, the latter closely related to his *marivaudage*. Useful, if rather general.

Scherer, Jacques. Analyse et mécanisme des Fausses confidences. CCRB 28:11–19, Jan. 1960.   **3717**

Thorough.

Addenda

Niklaus, Robert. Beaumarchais : Le barbier de Séville. London, Edward Arnold, 1968. 58 p.   **3717A**

A detailed study and analysis of the play.

Ratermanis, J. B. Etude sur le comique dans le théâtre de Marivaux. Geneva, Droz, 1961. 268 p.   **3717B**

Some shrewd observations, but little justification for the categories used.

CHAPTER IV. PROSE FICTION

(Except MONTESQUIEU, VOLTAIRE, ROUSSEAU, and DIDEROT)

(Nos. 3718–4115)

RICHARD A. BROOKS, DIANA GUIRAGOSSIAN, BASIL GUY, *and* J. ROBERT LOY

General Studies and Aspects
of the 18th-Century Novel
(Nos. 3718–3740)

DIANA GUIRAGOSSIAN

Atkinson, Geoffroy. Le sentiment de la nature et le retour à la vie simple (1690–1740). Geneva, Droz, 1960. 89 p. **3718**
Frequently utilizes the minor novels of the period.
Reviews : J. Clemens in REG 5:3–4, 1960; Gita May in RR 52:138–40, 1961.

Barchilon, Jacques. Uses of the fairy tale in the eighteenth century. SVEC 24:111–38, 1963. **3719**
A general survey of the vogue of the fairy tale in its various manifestations during the Enlightenment.

Crocker, Lester G. Human nature in the novel. *In his:* An age of crisis; man and world in eighteenth-century French thought. *See* 4122. p. 404–46. **3720**
In this study of French 18th-century morality, the author uses 9 novelists as partial proof that the age moves inexorably toward Sade's extreme espousal of evil.

Deloffre, Frédéric. Le problème de l'illusion romanesque et le renouvellement des techniques narratives de 1700 à 1715. *In:* La littérature narrative d'imagination; des genres littéraires aux techniques d'expression. Colloque de Strasbourg, 23–25 avril 1959. Presses univ. de France, 1961. p. 115–33. **3721**
Author sees novel rejecting illusion through history and groping for new fictional devices which inevitably lead toward the formulation of the *roman de l'individu.* Short, pointed analysis of the structure of Challes' *Les illustres françaises* concludes this study.

Etiemble, René. Prosateurs du XVIIIe siècle. *In:* Histoire des littératures. *See* 3384. 3:833–68. **3722**
Contains incisive comments on the major and minor novelists of the period.

Green, Frederick Charles. Some observations on technique and form in the French seventeenth- and eighteenth-century novel. *In:* Stil- und Formprobleme in der Literatur; Vorträge des 7. Kongresses der Internationalen Vereinigung für moderne Sprachen und Literaturen in Heidelberg. Ed. by Paul Böckmann. Heidelberg, Winter, 1959. p. 208–15. **3723**
Before the invention of printing, there existed a close and dramatic relationship between the storyteller and his audience. The novelist of the 17th and 18th century, we are told, had to elaborate new techniques which would preserve the essential *échange* and dialogue between himself and his readers. Short and precise survey of the various techniques mentioned.

Kibédi Varga, A. La désagrégation de l'idéal classique dans le roman français de la première moitié du XVIIIe siècle. SVEC 26:965–98, 1963. **3724**
Traces the change in the classical novel brought about by such writers as Madame de Fontaines, Madame de Tencin, and Madame Riccoboni on the one hand and Crébillon *fils* and Duclos on the other. " La complexité croissante de l'intrigue, la transformation des attitudes morales, l'individualisation et l'amoindrissement du personnage " (p. 998) are, according to the author, the main lines of the disintegration of the classical ideal in the French novel. Good article.

Laufer, Roger. Style rococo, style des lumières. *See* 4134. **3725**
The author tells us that by rococo style he means the mixture of realism and reverie or fantasy, a detached view to-

ward life, the smile of a La Tour portrait, all of which admirably suit the new philosophy of the Enlightenment. To him, this represents a fundamental unity in the age. Of greater significance, perhaps, are those chapters that analyze with ingenuity and subtlety the structure and meaning of 5 of the greatest novels of the day : *Les lettres persanes, Manon Lescaut, L'ingénu, Le neveu de Rameau,* and *Les liaisons dangereuses.*

Loos, Erich. Die Gattung des Conte und das Publikum im 18. Jahrhundert. RFor 71:113–37, 1959.   3726

After defining the *conte* as opposed to the *nouvelle,* the author gives a detailed survey of the evolution of the genre from La Fontaine to Diderot.

Loy, J. Robert. Love/vengeance in the late eighteenth-century French novel. EspCr 3:157–66, 1963. *See* 3948.   3727

This rapid view of a vast theme has nevertheless good, original insights and offers interesting reading.

McGhee, Dorothy M. The cult of the conte moral; the moral tale in France, its emergence and progress. Menasha, Banta, 1960. 126 p.   3728

Brief development of the genre down through the 18th century. Notes in profusion.

Review : Gita May in RR 53:233–34, 1962.

— Fortunes of a tale : the philosophical tale in France, bridging the eighteenth and nineteenth centuries. Menasha, Banta, 1954. 74 p.   3729

Offered as a companion volume to *Voltairian narrative devices* (1782), amplifies already published article (724). Agreeably written. A list of the *contes* discussed would have been welcome.

Mauzi, Robert. L'idée du bonheur dans la littérature et la pensée françaises au XVIIIᵉ siècle. *See* 4136.   3730

In his monumental study concerning the problem of pleasure and happiness in 18th-century France, Mauzi draws on a large number of novels for source material

May, Georges Claude. Le dilemme du roman au XVIIIᵉ siècle; étude sur les rapports du roman et de la critique, 1715–1761. New Haven, Yale univ. press, 1963. 294 p. *See* 5548.   3731

This important book makes no pretense at being a comprehensive study of the

18th-century French novel. Its main purpose is to restate certain perplexing problems in the field and to provide a clearer idea of the development of 18th-century fiction. It fulfills this function admirably and shows the writer's impressive erudition and ability to think creatively. A significant milestone in criticism of the French novel. Invaluable bibliography.

Reviews : H. Amer in NNRF 21:1097–99, 1963; T. Combe in MLR 60:624–25, 1965; R. Ellrich in RR 54:299–300, 1963; D. Guiragossian in DS 6:263–74, 1964; J. van den Heuvel in IL 16:214, 1964; J. Loy in EspCr 5:185–89, 1965; K. Maurer in Archiv 200:394–97, 1963; J. Sgard in RHL 65:121–22, 1965; A. Vartanian in FR 39:644–47, 1965–66.

— L'histoire a-t-elle engendré le roman?; aspects français de la question au seuil du siècle des lumières. RHL 55:155–76, 1955.   3732

Important study throwing new light on one aspect of the development of French fiction. The subject receives further attention in 3731.

Milner, Max. Le diable dans la littérature française de Cazotte à Baudelaire, 1772–1861. Corti, 1960. 2 v.   3733

Part one—covering the years 1772–1815 —of this vast and penetrating study should be useful to those interested in the 18th century in general and the novel of the period in particular.

Reviews : H. Amer in NNRF 16:511–12, 1960; L. Cellier in RHL 64:114–17, 1964; R. Jouanny in SF 9:506–10, 1965; R. Kampmann in Archiv 200:313–20, 1964; J. Morel in RScH n.s. 101:122–25, 1961; P. Sipriot in Tro 157:143–45, Jan. 1961; A. Viatte in RLC 35:506–09, 1961.

Mylne, Vivienne. The eighteenth-century French novel : techniques of illusion. New York, Barnes and Noble, 1965. viii, 280 p.   3734

A work of real distinction, this clearly written, intelligently conceived book goes far toward filling the need of an up-to-date, comprehensive evaluation of the 18th-century French novel. The over-all aim of the volume is to study the literary devices that create the illusion of reality. The evolution of various fictional techniques—false memoirs, the epistolary novel, and the picaresque narrative being a few—are traced with a sure touch in this impressive contribution to our

understanding of fiction under the Ancien
Régime.
Review : Georges May in FS 20:62–65,
1966.

Quatre romans dans le goût français.
Ed. by Claude Roy. Le Club français du
livre, 1959. 311 p.   **3735**
Four psychological novels (Madame de
Genlis, *Mademoiselle de Clermont;* Madame de Tencin, *Mémoires du comte de
Comminges;* Duclos, *Madame de Selves;*
Vivant Denon, *Point de lendemain*)
presented attractively and with helpful
general introduction as well as short
prefaces for each. According to the editor,
all four bear witness to the persistence of
the tradition of *La princesse de Clèves.*

Romanciers du XVIII° siècle. Ed. by
Etiemble (with the collaboration of Marguerite du Cheyron for v. 2). Gallimard,
1960–65. 2 v. (Bibliothèque de la Pléiade).
                                           3736
Useful prefaces, notes, and bibliographies accompany wholly reliable texts of
sixteen 18th-century works of fiction.
Novels of such major writers as Lesage,
Prévost, Sade, and Bernardin de Saint-
Pierre, not appearing elsewhere in the
Pléiade series, are included as well as
works of the following : Hamilton,
Crébillon *fils,* Duclos, Cazotte, Vivant
Denon, Louvet de Couvrai, and Sénac de
Meilhan.

Rousset, Jean. Une forme littéraire : le
roman par lettres. *In his:* Forme et signification; essais sur les structures littéraires
de Corneille à Claudel. Corti, 1962. p. 65–
108.   **3737**
Perhaps the most fascinating chapter in
this rich, seminal study of structures. A
careful analysis of the genre and the various possibilities it offers is followed by an
exacting study of such epistolary novels as
La nouvelle Héloïse and *Les liaisons dangereuses.* Useful bibliography of French
epistolary novels. *Also see* chapter on
Marivaux ou la structure du double registre.
Reviews : R. Judrin in NNRF 21:531–
32, 1963; W. Moore in MLR 60:620–21,
1965; J. Robichez in IL 16:124, 1964.

Turnell, Martin. The art of French fiction :
Prévost, Stendhal, Zola, Maupassant, Gide,
Mauriac, Proust. New York, New Directions, 1959. 394 p.   **3738**
This controversial but highly readable
book often strains for the paradox; this is
particularly true in the author's treatment

of the abbé Prévost, who is the only 18th-
century novelist given serious attention.

— The novel in France : Madame de La
Fayette, Laclos, Constant, Stendhal, Balzac,
Flaubert, Proust. New York, New Directions, 1951. xv, 432 p.   **3739**
The 18th century is represented by
Laclos and his famous epistolary novel.

Versini, L. De quelques noms de personnages dans le roman du XVIII° siècle. RHL
61:177–87, 1961.   **3740**
With the evolution of the novel, the
author tells us, names of exotic or *galant*
origin are replaced by others seemingly
more plausible and realistic which, in
turn, assume a symbolic significance.
Instead of Clitandre or Tanzaï, for
instance, Valmont or Valville. Persuasive
and interesting.

Foreign Influences
(Nos. 3741–3747)
(*See also* Chapter XI)

DIANA GUIRAGOSSIAN

Bundy, Jean D. Fréron and the English
novel. RLC 36:258–66, 1962.   **3741**
Conscientious study based on numerous
reviews in Fréron's 2 major periodicals :
Lettres sur quelques écrits de ce temps and
the *Année littéraire.*

Defourneaux, Marcelin. Les lettres péruviennes en Espagne. *See* 4097.   **3742**

Fluchère, Henri. Laurence Sterne, de
l'homme à l'œuvre; biographie critique et
essai d'interprétation de Tristram Shandy.
Gallimard, 1961. 734 p.   **3743**
This prize-winning study should henceforth be consulted by anyone interested in
Sterne. The impressive bibliography includes a section devoted to the French
translations of Sterne's works.

Fredman, Alice Green. Diderot and Sterne.
See 5152.   **3744**
Well-presented study in which the
author arrives at the conclusion that
Diderot's debt to Sterne, particularly for
Jacques le fataliste, has received undue
emphasis.

May, Georges. The influence of English
fiction on the French mid-eighteenth-century novel. *In:* Aspects of the eighteenth
century. Ed. by Earl R. Wasserman. Baltimore, Johns Hopkins press, 1965. p. 265–
80.   **3745**

The author comes to the conclusion that perhaps the most important aspect of this influence is the prestige it lent the genre. Argument convincingly presented.

Roddier, Henri. Robert Challes inspirateur de Richardson et de l'abbé Prévost. *See* 4076.   **3746**

Zambon, Maria Rosa. Bibliographie du roman français en Italie au XVIIIe siècle; traductions. *See* 3376.   **3747**
    Important work, the author's first step toward a comprehensive study of the vogue of the French novel in 18th-century Italy. Stresses the clandestine infiltration of French philosophic writing. The three main sections are : a catalog of novels by authors, a catalog by titles, and a list of libraries and special collections.

Alain-René Lesage
(Nos. 3748–3771)

BASIL GUY

Editions

Lesage, Alain-René. Le diable boiteux [and] Gil Blas. *In:* Romanciers du XVIIIe siècle. *See* 3736. 1:265–1197.   **3748**
    First attempt in recent years to provide an authentic text which conforms to the best eds. published under the author's supervision.

— Histoire de Gil Blas de Santillane. Ed. by Maurice Bardon. Garnier, 1955. 2 v. **3749**
    Standard reprint; first published in this format in 1942. *Apparatus criticus* superficial and insufficient, although acceptable as far as it goes.

— Histoire de Gil Blas de Santillane. Ed. by Raymond Dumay. Club français du livre, 1959. xxvi, 684 p.   **3750**
    Standard reprint. Introduction emphasizes the biographical element (*see* 3759), but annotation insufficient.

Criticism

Alter, Robert. The incorruptibility of the picaresque hero. *In his:* Rogue's progress : studies in the picaresque novel. Cambridge, Harvard univ. press, 1964. p. 11–34. **3751**
    The most recent and one of the more honest attempts to understand Gil Blas through his morality.

Bardon, Maurice. Mendoza, Lesage, Beaumarchais. TDR 6⁴:125–29, 1962. **3752**

Attempts to replace L. in a tradition running from 17th-century Spain to late 18th-century France and to evaluate his role as intermediary. Although primarily concerned with the theater, some attention is paid to L.'s work in general.

Cordié, Carlo. Avventure postume di Gil Blas di Santillana. *In his:* La guerra di Gand. Florence, Le Monnier, 1958. p. 55–72. **3753**
    Examination and listing of imitations by Féval, da Ponte, and Borsieri (Gil Perez), adding a note on Napoleon, reader of *Gil Blas*. Written originally in 1946.

— Intorno al Lesage. Or 4:105–10, 1957. *See* 5897.   **3754**
    Two notes. One concerns a likely derivation from Folengo's burlesques; the other, an imitation of *Gil Blas* in the 19th-century Milanese periodical *Il conciliatore.*

— Introduzione al Gil Blas de Santillane. *In his:* Saggi e studi di letteratura francese. Padua, Cedam, 1957. p. 86–99.   **3755**
    General appreciation of the novel in relation to its influence and universal appeal.

Crocker, Lester G. Human nature in the novel. *In his:* An age of crisis. *See* 4122. p. 404–10.   **3756**
    Probes the depths of L.'s pessimism in relation to conflicting ideas of his times, but not very original in its conclusions.

Dédéyan, Charles. A.-R. Lesage : Gil Blas. Centre de documentation universitaire, 1956. 115 p. (Les cours de Sorbonne)   **3757**
    Originally presented as a course at the Sorbonne. Systematically reviews all the literature thus far available with some suggestive developments from the point of view of literary history, but disappointing where ideas or questions of style and technique are concerned.

— Lesage et Gil Blas. S.E.D.E.S., 1965. 2 v. **3758**
    A reworking of 3757 for a wider reading public.

Dumay, Raymond. Lesage, écrivain par amitié. LN 6:676–90, May 1958.   **3759**
    Reworking of Dumay's preface to an ed. of *Gil Blas*. General appreciation, with emphasis on biographical detail.

Etiemble, René. Préface [au Diable boiteux et à Gil Blas]. *In:* Romanciers du xviiie siècle. *See* 3736. 1:249–64.   **3760**

Interesting and worthwhile considerations of these novels as literature, with an excellent *mise au point* of the textual problems they present, especially *Gil Blas*.

Galotti, Jean. Une journée de Lesage. NL 1–2, Feb. 12, 1959.   **3761**

A brief biographical sketch.

Giudici, Enzo. Brevi appunti per un'edizione critica del Diable boiteux. *In:* Studi in onore di Vittorio Lugli e Diego Valeri. Venice, Pozza, 1961. 2:473–506.   **3762**

Excellent review of textual and interpretive problems, with some suggestions for their solution and several illuminating insights.

Iknayan, Marguerite. The fortunes of Gil Blas during the Romantic period. FR 31:370–77, 1957–58.   **3763**

An historical review, showing the decline of L.'s prestige.

Judrin, Roger. Sur les pas de Gil Blas. NNRF 26:513–15, 1965.   **3764**

" Que furent Lesage et son illustre laquais ? ... Lesage ... fut Gil Blas " (p. 513). Brief excursus into the importance of the theater, the moral, and the style for the modern reader.

Lacoste, Edmond. Sur Gil Blas. *In his:* Essais et réflexions d'humanisme. Lille, Giard, 1961. p. 14–24.   **3765**

General and suggestive appreciation emphasizing the universality and value of the picaresque hero.

Lebois, André. Le breton Lesage et le filibustier. *In his:* Littérature sous Louis XV. Denoël, 1962. p. 105–27.   **3766**

Chapter of a generally illuminating book relating to L.'s *Beauchêne*.

Mylne, Vivienne. Lesage and conventions. *In her:* The eighteenth-century French novel. *See* 3734. p. 49–72.   **3767**

Part of author's general concern with the development of the techniques of reality and illusion. Accurate and satisfying as far as it goes, but lacking any real perspective for renewing our appreciation of the novel's ultimate structure and meaning.

— Structure and symbolism in Gil Blas. FS 15:134–45, 1961.   **3768**

Reviews present estimate of novel without, however, adding to our understanding or appreciation, despite the title.

Sablé, J. Gil Blas entre Panurge et Figaro. FDLM 15:40–43, Mar. 1963.   **3769**

Gil Blas is here seen as a " neuter " character, but with a conscience tested by circumstance, the eternal *primum vivere*.

Stackelberg, Jürgen von. Die Moral des Gil Blas. RFor 74:345–60, 1962.   **3770**

Attempts to appraise the morality of the novel in relation to its novelistic background. Superseded by Alter (3751).

Wagner, N. Quelques cadres d'étude pour Gil Blas. IL 8:29–38, 1956.   **3771**

Pedagogical study consisting of brief notes, some very suggestive, susceptible of further development.

Antoine François Prévost, *called*
Prévost d'Exiles
(Nos. 3772–3852)

Basil Guy

Works

Le Gazetin

Weil, Françoise. L'abbé Prévost et le Gazetin de 1740. SF 6:474–86, 1962. *See* 5511.   **3772**

Brief presentation and critical ed.

Manon

Prévost, Antoine François, *called* Prévost d'Exiles. Histoire du chevalier des Grieux et de Manon Lescaut. Ed. by Georges Matoré. Geneva, Droz, 1953. xli, 234 p. *See* 3517.   **3773**

A critical ed. based on 1731 text that pays particular attention to style and vocabulary in its introduction. Bibliography, p. 221–27.

— Histoire du chevalier des Grieux et de Manon Lescaut. Ed. by Robert Sabatier. Bordeaux, Delmas, 1955. 213 p.   **3774**

Standard reprint of 1753 ed., with a slight but charming commentary on the " lesson " of the novel by way of introduction.

— Histoire du chevalier des Grieux et de Manon Lescaut. Ed. by Paul Vernière. Colin, 1957. 231 p.   **3775**

Standard reprint of 1753 ed., preceded by illuminating appreciation of the work as literary creation.

— Histoire du chevalier des Grieux et de Manon Lescaut. Texte de l'édition de 1759. Ed. by C.-E. Engel and Max Brun. Club des libraires de France, 1960. 388 p.   **3776**

One of the most controversial eds. in recent times because of the choice of text upon which the ed. is based. See the long review-article of Jean Sgard *infra*. Bibliography, p. 329–88.

— Histoire du Chevalier des Grieux et de Manon Lescaut. Ed. by Louis Bovey. Lausanne, Editions Rencontre, 1961. 220 p.   **3777**

The introduction points out problems raised by this novel for the modern reader and is accompanied by notes which are satisfactory, even though on occasion they are insufficient or incomplete.

— Histoire du chevalier des Grieux et de Manon Lescaut. Ed. by Clifford King. London, Harrap, 1963. lxxvi, 226 p.   **3778**

Primarily a classroom presentation of 1753 ed., with generally satisfactory editing and annotation, considering the level to which it is directed.
Review : M.-R. de Labriolle-Rutherford in FS 18:64, 1964 (unfavorable).

— Histoire du chevalier des Grieux et de Manon Lescaut. Ed. by Frédéric Deloffre and Raymond Picard. Garnier, 1965. clxxvii, 340 p.   **3779**

An excellent ed. of text and variants. Should replace all others currently available. The introduction, which seems especially valuable, deals with historical, social, textual, linguistic, and moral problems raised by the novel in definitive fashion. Bibliography and index.
Reviews : M.-R. de Labriolle-Rutherford in FS 20:187–88, 1966; J. Piatier in Le Monde p. 10, April 7, 1965.

— Manon Lescaut. Ed. by Jean-Louis Bory. Club du meilleur livre, 1958. xlviii, 203 p.   **3780**

Text of 1731 with introduction emphasizing the moral problem of the novel. Introduction also published separately (3791).

— Manon Lescaut. *In:* Romanciers du XVIIIe siècle. Ed. by Etiemble. 1:1217–1371. *See* 3736.   **3781**

Text of 1753 with good presentation, commentary and notes, including an excellent *mise au point* of recent studies.

— Mémoires d'un homme de qualité [and] Manon Lescaut. Ed. by J. Ducarre. Hachette, 1958. 346 p.   **3782**

Careful presentation of 1753 text by P. specialist, but introduction, despite or perhaps because of author's meticulousness, is disappointing.

Translations

— Geschichte des Chevaliers des Grieux und der Manon Lescaut. Trans. by W. Widmer. Hamburg, Fischer, 1962. 182 p.   **3783**

Brief appreciation at end (p. 176–82) by F.-W. Müller deals with historical importance of the novel and the appearance of Manon as a literary type.

— Manon Lescaut. Trans. by L.W. Tancock. Harmondsworth, Penguin, 1949. 190 p.   **3784**

The translation is satisfying, in keeping with the standard set by the rest of the series, but the introduction is disappointing.

— Manon Lescaut. Trans. by Donald M. Frame. New York, New American Library, 1961. 191 p.   **3785**

Follows the text of 1753 with variants of the 1731 ed. The brief introduction helps to situate the novel for the modern American reader. Some notes, generally satisfactory.

Criticism

L'abbé Prévost : actes du colloque d'Aix-en-Provence, 20 et 21 décembre, 1963. Aix-en-Provence, Ophrys, 1965. xxvii, 270 p. (AnAix n.s., 50)   **3786**

Transactions of a congress held to commemorate the 200th anniversary of P.'s death. Twenty-five communications treat of (1) his life, (2) *Manon*, (3) other works, (4) themes common to most of his novels, (5) his relations and influence abroad.
Review : R. Mortier in RLC 38:334–35, 1964.

Auerbach, Erich. The interrupted supper. *In his:* Mimesis. Princeton, Princeton univ. press, 1953. p. 395–401.   **3787**

Excellent stylistic analysis of the type for which Auerbach was best known, relating specifically to the realism of *Manon* and the historic change it represents in the development of Western literature.

Aury, Dominique. La fille perdue. *In her:* Lecture pour tous. Gallimard, 1958. p. 199–217. **3788**

Interesting, if slight appreciation of the morality of *Manon*, prepared originally as the introduction to a new ed.

Bonnerot, Jean. Une préface à Manon Lescaut. BBB 182–83, 1959. **3789**

Brief appreciation, centering largely in the choice of text for an edition : 1731 or 1733 ? *See*, in this section, titles by C.-E. Engel and M. Brun, J. Ducarre, H. Roddier, and J. Sgard.

Bory, Jean-Louis. Manon, l'amour et l'argent. RPar 65:83–90, April 1958. **3790**

Appraises two familiar themes of *Manon*, but without surpassing Auerbach (3787).

— Manon, ou les désordres du monde. *In his:* Pour Balzac et quelques autres. Julliard, 1960. p. 113–50. **3791**

A reworking of his introduction to an ed. of *Manon.*

Brun, Max. Contribution à l'étude des premières éditions des Mémoires et aventures d'un homme de qualité et de Manon Lescaut publiées de 1728 à 1763. BBB 1–21, 1954; 155–78, 1955; 1–18, 1956. **3792**

Important work of eminent bibliophile, opting for the ed. of 1733 as the original ed. (and not that of 1731) because of typographical and other evidence. For contrary views, *see* Ducarre (3801) and article of Roddier in RHL 59:207–13, 1959.

Busson, Henri. La théologie de l'abbé Prévost. *In his:* Littérature et théologie. Presses univ. de France, 1962. p. 195–242. **3793**

Intelligent and convincing re-examination of P.'s religion from orthodox point of view, using the *Véritable abbé Prévost* of C.-E. Engel (3808) as point of departure for refuting the " Jansenist " interpretation.

Cellier, Léon. Manon et le mythe de la femme. IL 5:35–38, 1953. **3794**

Manon cannot be said to represent uniquely *la petite femme* since she is a composite of at least 3 other characters : Regency, classical, and mythical.

Cooper, Berenice. The abbé Prévost and the Jesuits. TWA 43:125–32, 1954. **3795**

Brief examination of the facts in P.'s life and their interpretation by him, especially in *Cleveland.*

— The Protestantism of the abbé Prévost. TWA 50:295–305, 1961. **3796**

Succinct statement of P.'s religious attitudes which does not, however, add to the presentation of C.-E. Engel's *Véritable abbé Prévost* (3808).

Coulet, Henri. L'abbé Prévost et Racine. *In:* Actes du premier congrès international racinien. Uzès, Peladan, 1962. p. 95–107. **3797**

A reworking of the now familiar commonplaces regarding P.'s stylistic debt to Racine. The closer analysis of Karl Maurer (3832) is to be preferred.

Crocker, Lester G. Human nature in the novel. *In his:* An age of crisis. *See* 4122. p. 410–14. **3798**

Centers attention on des Grieux but oversimplifies presentation of his character so that a few promising insights are left undeveloped and several questions relating to the moral of the novel unanswered.

Crowley, Francis J. Voltaire, Prévost and Cardinal Alberoni. RR 55:256–59, 1964. **3799**

Brief biographical note, dealing with a minor aspect of P.'s supposed political activity.

Deloffre, Frédéric. Un morceau de critique en quête d'auteur : le jugement du Pour et contre sur Manon Lescaut. RScH n.s. 106:203–12, 1962. *See* 5502. **3800**

Draws attention to anomalies in the review of *Manon* in P.'s own journal. An important article.

Ducarre, Joseph. Sur la date de Manon Lescaut. RHL 59:205–07, 1959. **3801**

Prefers 1731 as the original 1st ed. to be used for textual study. Against the presentation of C.-E. Engel and M. Brun. *See* article by Roddier in RHL 59:207–13, 1959, upholding Ducarre.

Engel, Claire-Eliane. L'abbé Prévost à la scène. RScH n.s. 104:467–75, 1961. *See* 3655. **3802**

Historical review of various scenic adaptations of *Manon*, including the film of 1949.

— L'abbé Prévost archéologue. RScH n.s. 86:123–32, 1957. **3803**

Title misleading in that this article deals mainly with the sources of Italian descriptions in some of P.'s novels.

— L'abbé Prévost collaborateur d'une revue neuchâteloise.   SVEC 2:225–32, 1956. *See* 5503.   **3804**

P.'s collaboration in the *Mercure suisse* with a sometimes helpful collation of texts.

— L'abbé Prévost romancier baroque.   RScH n.s. 100:385–97, 1960.   **3805**

Rather forced attempt to see in P. many of the devices now considered characteristic of the Baroque.

— L'état des travaux sur l'abbé Prévost. IL 9:146–49, 1957.   **3806**

Excellent *mise au point*, especially in describing the 1759 ed. of *Manon* which contains more revisions than previously noted.

— L'Ordre de Malte et la vie intellectuelle. *In her:* L'Ordre de Malte en Méditerranée. Monaco, Editions du Rocher, 1957. p. 277– 313, *passim*.   **3807**

Interesting review of P.'s relations with the Order and its importance in supplying him with material, especially in the creation of des Grieux. For supplementary material on the same topic, *also see* Engel's *L'abbé Prévost et l'Ordre de Malte* in MédF 91:113–21, 1958.

— Le véritable abbé Prévost. Monaco, Editions du Rocher, 1957. 302 p. *See* 5689. **3808**

One of the most controversial publications on P. to appear in recent years. The two most debated points are : the date of the original 1st ed. of *Manon*, and Prévost's conversion to Anglicanism while in England, a development which, claims the author, permeated his attitude thereafter.   Important, but marred by many significant misprints.

Review : J. Candaux in RScH n.s. 95:207–09, 1959; Ph. de F. in BSHP 104: 255–57, 1958; M.-R. de Labriolle-Rutherford in FS 13:166–67, 1959; A. Pizzorusso in SF 3:319, 1959; H. Rod-dier in RHL 59:207–13, 1959 (unnecessarily severe).

— La vie secrète de l'abbé Prévost. RScH n.s. 67:199–214, 1952.   **3809**

Biographical sketch based on new documents revealing further proof of P.'s *crise de protestantisme* and adding to the delineation of his paradoxial character.

Etiemble, René. Histoire du chevalier des Grieux et de Manon Lescaut. MN 11:20– 33, Dec. 1956.   **3810**

A general appreciation.

— Préface [à Manon Lescaut]. *In:* Romanciers du xviiie siècle. *See* 3736.   1:1199–1216. **3811**

Valuable reappraisal of the novel and its problems, especially in relation to the modern reader.

Fiedler, Leslie. The beginnings of the anti-bourgeois sentimental novel in America. *In his:* Love and death in the American novel. New York, Criterion, 1960.   p. 81–105, *passim*.   **3812**

P., Richardson, and the growth of bourgeois sentimentality in America.

Frautschi, Richard L. Manon Lescaut : the exemplary attitude. FR 37:288–95, 1963–64. **3813**

Attempts to relate the *Avis de l'auteur* to the tale itself and to use it in explaining the moral.   The ambiguity of des Grieux makes identification easier, so that his gradual, if paradoxical, enlightenment provides the main claim to our attention.

Guyon, Bernard. Notes sur l'art du roman dans Manon Lescaut.   *In:* Hommage au doyen Etienne Gros.   Gap, Louis-Jean, 1959. p. 185–92.   **3814**

Excellent review of the form, style, and ultimate meaning of the novel, with insights into the problems it raises *as a novel* and offering some solutions.

Hammer, Charles, Jr. Goethe, Prévost and Louisiana. MLQ 16:332–38, 1955.   **3815**

Studies the influence of P. on Goethe, especially during the period of *Dichtung und Wahrheit.*

Henriot, Emile. La vie agitée de Prévost, père de Manon Lescaut. H 34:676–83, 1963. **3816**

Elegant résumé of P.'s life in light of recent studies.

Kaminker, Jean-Pierre. L'abbé Prévost. Eur 415–16:5–55, Nov.–Dec. 1963.   **3817**

Excellent general appreciation of life, work, and importance.

— Chronologie de Prévost. Eur 415–16:59–64, Nov.–Dec. 1963.   **3818**

Tabulation of important dates in P.'s life, with minor commentaries.

Labriolle-Rutherford, Marie-Rose de. Un inédit sur l'abbé Prévost.   FS 9:227–37, 1955.   **3819**

Examines a brochure of 28 pages at the B.N. which brings to light evidence on why P. left England for Holland in 1730. Publishes most important and interesting letters of this brochure.

— Le Pour et contre et les romans de l'abbé Prévost (1733–1740). RHL 62:28–40, 1962. **3820**
A close examination of P.'s critical and creative work and their interrelations.

— Le Pour et contre et son temps. Geneva, Institut et musée Voltaire, 1965. 2 v. (SVEC, 34–35) *See* 5506. **3821**
Excellent survey of P.'s periodical, arranged topically, including : *La scène dramatique, Le roman, Les lettres étrangères*, etc. Lacks appendix with complete listing of references and general index for checking any author or topic rapidly. Review : E. Briggs in FS 20:188–90, 1966.

— Les procédés d'imitation de l'abbé Prévost dans le Pour et contre (1733–1740). RLC 29:258–70, 1955. *See* 5559. **3822**
Minute examination of several telling passages in P.'s journal which reveal the truth of the author's opening statement : " il n'y a pas de création absolue. "

— La scène tragique dans le Pour et contre de l'abbé Prévost (1733–1740). RHT 14:211–26, 1962. *See* 5508. **3823**
Various reviews and comments in P.'s journal are an excellent source for showing the evolution of stage presentation and dramatic criticism. A good introduction to the same sort of material in Grimm.

— Les sources du Pour et contre (1733–1734). RLC 33:239–57, 1959. *See* 5509. **3824**
English sources for some of the early articles in P.'s journal. An exact list for v. 1 to 4 is supplied.

Lafarge, Catherine. The emergence of the bourgeoisie [Furetière, Robert Challes, Prévost]. YFS 32:40–49, 1964. **3825**
Brief mention of P.'s treatment of the middle class with the importance of their ethic for the development of the " realistic " novel.

La Force, Auguste, *duc* de. En relisant Manon Lescaut. RDM 650–60, Dec. 15, 1954. **3826**
Of 3 sections, the first and third (*Roman vécu* and *Echo racinien*) are least important since they treat in general terms of the topics announced in the subheadings. The second (*Réminiscences*) is both more interesting and more important for P.'s

biography. Gives some details of the relations of the author's family with the creator of *Manon*.

— Le vrai des Grieux. NL 5, Jan. 8, 1953. **3827**
Slight article attempting to identify the hero of *Manon*.

Laufer, Roger. L'histoire du chevalier des Grieux et de Manon Lescaut. *In his:* Style rococo, style des lumières. *See* 4134. p.73–96. **3828**
Brilliant approach to the novel and what it can tell us about a developing 18th-century style, in line with the author's thesis in this controversial volume.

Légier-Desgranges, Henry. La légende de Manon Lescaut à la Salpêtrière. MédF 96:37–46, 1958. **3829**
After examining hospital records and anecdotal history, author finds no reason to believe the model for Manon was ever detained there. Takes up some points of the 1922 study by M. Henry, *La Salpêtrière sous l'Ancien Régime*.

Lernet-Holenia, Alexander. Die wahre Manon. NR 69:699–717, 1958. **3830**
The author claims to have discovered the originals for Manon and des Grieux in a certain Toinon Levieux and a chevalier de Viantaix, whose stories he sketches.

Martins, Antonio C. L'histoire du marquis de Rosambert par l'abbé Prévost : mémoires ou roman ? AnAix n.s. 34:53–86, 1961. **3831**
Formulates an important question concerning all of P.'s creative work, but in relation to a relatively unfamiliar text. The point of view originally stated in the author's *O padre Prévost* (Lisbon, 1956). Review : D.-H. Parageaux in RLC 36:314–16, 1962.

Maurer, Karl. Der Récit des Chevalier des Grieux. *In:* Wort und Text : Festschrift für Fritz Schalk. Frankfurt am Main, Klostermann, 1963. p. 315–29. **3832**
Interesting, intelligent, and convincing discussion of the style of *Manon*, especially in its relation to Racinian devices.

Minář, Jaroslav. Společenská skutečnost v románě abbého Prévosta. (La réalité sociale dans le roman de l'abbé Prévost.) CMF 44:161–71, 1962. **3833**
Social realism in *Manon*. While interesting, this article is not comparable with Lukač's use of the same method in other

contexts. Accompanied by a résumé in French.

Mylne, Vivienne. Prévost : The new realism. *In her:* The eighteenth-century French novel. *See* 3734. p. 73–103. **3834**
Perhaps the best chapter in this book treating of the techniques of reality and illusion, complementing nicely the work of Laufer (3828).

Paris. Bibliothèque nationale. Manon Lescaut à travers deux siècles. 1963. vii, 48 p. **3835**
Documents relating to the novel and its influence. Catalog by Edmond Pognon and Gérard Willemetz.

Picard, Raymond. L'univers de Manon Lescaut. MerF 341:606–22, 1961; 342:87–105, 1961. **3836**
Good general appreciation of *Manon* as a great novel by virtue of its complete representation of reality, both concrete and psychological.

Plazolles, L.-R. Manon Lescaut. AnProp 10:185–91, 1957–58. **3837**
Brief presentation which mentions a few of the problems that hinder modern appreciation of the novel, but neither so well developed nor so far reaching as Guyon's *Notes* (3814).

Poulet, Georges. L'abbé Prévost. *In his:* Etudes sur le temps humain. Plon, 1950. p. 146–57. **3838**
Remarkable essay in line with author's thesis of the importance of " human time " in understanding literature.

Remak, Henry H. H. Goethes Gretchenabenteuer und Manon Lescaut : Dichtung oder Wahrheit? *In:* Formen der Selbstdarstellung : Festgabe für Fritz Neubert. Berlin, Duncker und Humblot, 1956. p. 379–95. **3839**
More important for *Faust* than for *Manon*, but casts very illuminating asides on the fundamental problem common to both regarding a biographical interpretation of literature.

Roddier, Henri. L'abbé Prévost et le problème de la traduction au xviiie siècle. CAIEF 8:173–81, 1956. *See* 5692. **3840**
Good appreciation of P.'s rôle as intermediary, especially concerning his translations of Richardson.

— L'abbé Prévost, homme de lettres et journaliste. RLC 29:161–72, 1955. *See* 5510 and 5693. **3841**

Interesting article tracing P.'s career as journalist from 1728 to 1740. Sees in it a drain on P.'s energies and genius as a creative writer, even though inspired, of necessity, by his search for personal freedom.

— L'abbé Prévost, l'homme et l'œuvre. Hatier-Boivin, 1955. 200 p. *See* 5694. **3842**
Like most volumes in the *Connaissance des lettres* collection, a valuable *mise au point* up to date of publication.
Reviews : G. Havens in RR 47:60–62, 1956; M.-R. de Labriolle-Rutherford in MLR 51:437–38, 1956; S. Pitou in BA 30:181, 1956.

Sauro, Antoine. Manon Lescaut. Bari, Adriatica, 1955. 138 p. **3843**
Manual-type presentation of the novel, its background, form and meaning, prepared for an Italian public.

Seylaz, Jean-Luc. Structure et signification dans Manon Lescaut. EL 2nd series 4:97–108, 1961. **3844**
Good, detailed, and subtle analysis of the form of *Manon*. Conclusions regarding interpretation are somewhat subject to caution, but article remains a model of its type.

Sgard, Jean. A propos du texte de Manon Lescaut : éditions de 1756 et de 1759. SF 5:89–93, 1961. **3845**
Prefers text of 1753 to that of 1759, touted by C.-E. Engel (3806), and makes certain suggestions which, if developed more fully, might lead to a re-evaluation of P.'s methods of composition.

— Prévost : de l'ombre aux lumières (1736–1746). SVEC 27:1479–87, 1963. **3846**
Despite his general disapproval of the *philosophes*, P.'s attachment to their cause can best be seen in the *Pour et contre* where his feelings also find adequate expression, whence his importance for our understanding of 18th-century ambivalence. Important.

— Prévost et Voltaire. RHL 64:545–64, 1964. **3847**
Personal relations and affinities of two men. Particularly interesting are P.'s remarks in the *Pour et contre* on Voltaire's *Lettres anglaises*. Examines P.'s form of literary expression and underlines its differences from that of Voltaire.

Shaw, Edward P. Malesherbes, the abbé Prévost and the first French translation of

Sir Charles Grandison. MLN 69:105–09, 1954. *See* 5682. **3848**

P.'s translation both encouraged and licensed by Malesherbes, some of whose unpublished papers were consulted.

Smith, Albert B., Jr. The abbé Prévost's Cleveland : fatality vs. religion. RomN 4:33–35, 1962–63. **3849**

Brief mention of an important problem in P. but not particularly well developed nor convincing.

Trompeo, Pietro Paolo. Manon Lescaut, romanzo rigorista. *In his:* Vecchie e nuove rilegature gianseniste. Naples, Ed. scientifiche italiane, 1958. p. 151–56. **3850**

Excellent review of the " Jansenist " thesis from an Italian point of view, but must be used with caution and supplemented by the *Véritable abbé Prévost* of C.-E. Engel (3808) and Busson's article (3793).

Turnell, Martin. The abbé Prévost. *In his:* The art of French fiction. Norfolk, New Directions, 1959. p. 31–60. **3851**

Consists of three parts : A priest-novelist; *Manon;* forgotten novels. Attempts to present P. in light of recent criticism to an Anglo-Saxon public. The third part is perhaps the best. Select bibliography, p. 380–81.

Verbiest, F. Lily. Le chevalier des Grieux commandeur de la Braque à Vieux-Tournhout ? RGB 99:59–80, Sept. 1963. **3852**

Until p. 65, nothing new. Thereafter, records of the Knights of Malta reveal that details in the life of Charles-Alexandre de Grieu correspond almost exactly with those given by P. in his novel.

Bernardin de Saint-Pierre
(Nos. 3853–3861)

RICHARD A. BROOKS

Saint-Pierre, Jacques Henri Bernardin de. Paul et Virginie. Ed. by Pierre Trahard. Garnier, 1958. clxxiii, 319 p. **3853**

Provides text of 1806 ed. with variants from other eds. published during Bernardin's lifetime. Lengthy description of an intermediary ms on which *Paul et Virginie* based and reproduction of most interesting parts provide picture of author at work. Introduction gives historical and background information on novel and its future, but few esthetic insights for appreciation of work itself.

Reviews : A. C. in RBP 38:216, 1960; L. Crocker in MLN 75:163–64, 1960; A. Pizzorusso in SF 3:498, 1959.

Fabre, Jean. Une question de terminologie littéraire : Paul et Virginie, pastorale. AFLT 2:167–200, 1953. *Also in his:* Lumières et romantisme. Klincksieck, 1963. p. 176–99. **3854**

Reviews criticism of *Paul et Virginie* and of Bernardin with conclusion that both author and work have been neglected by scholars. Defines place and originality of *Paul et Virginie* as a pastoral with appeal for further original research and studied attention to " une œuvre trop populaire et un écrivain trop délaissé " (p. 191).

Henriot, Emile. L'auteur de Paul et Virginie était-il un homme suave ? H 35:114–20, 1964. **3855**

"... avec une âme médiocre, Bernardin de Saint-Pierre a été un remarquable artiste et un très gracieux moment de l'histoire de la prose française " (p. 120). Briefly reviews biography of Bernardin to his detriment.

Kasterska, Marya. Le vrai roman d'amour de Paul et Virginie. H 25:207–15, 1959. **3856**

Bernardin and Marie Lubomirska-Radziwill.

Sauro, Antoine. Etudes sur la littérature française du 18e siècle. 3 : Paul et Virginie. Bari, Adriatica, 1956. 115 p. **3857**

An unsympathetic and somewhat superficial account of Bernardin's biography and of *Paul et Virginie*.

Review : R. Virolle in RHL 59:230–31, 1959.

Snow, Sinclair. The similarity of Poe's Eleonora to Bernardin de Saint-Pierre's Paul et Virginie. RomN 5:40–44, 1963–64. **3858**

Textual comparisons between the two works. " . . . it is clear that Poe was familiar with at least a portion of the writings of St. Pierre, and it is likely that he read *Paul and Virginia* in the Hunter translation, London, 1796 " (p. 44).

Toinet, Paul. Au sujet de Paul et Virginie. BBB 93–95, 1962. **3859**

Additions to Toinet's bibliography of *Paul et Virginie* published in BBB, 1961 (3861).

— Paul et Virginie : répertoire bibliographique et iconographique. Maisonneuve et Larose, 1963. 204 p.   **3860**
> Lists nearly 700 French eds., translations, and adaptations of *Paul et Virginie*. Detailed commentary on entries, with particular attention to 18th- and early 19th-century eds. Iconographic section lists paintings, drawings, posters, tapestries, etc., inspired by *Paul et Virginie*. Meticulous work by eminent collector. Iconography appeared previously in BSAHA 22:141–71, 1959.
> Review : M.-T. Laureilhe in BBF, BDB 9:275–77, 1964.

— Répertoire bibliographique et iconographique de Paul et Virginie de Bernardin de Saint-Pierre. BBB 147–252, 1961.   **3861**
> Bibliography and iconography of *Paul et Virginie*.

Nicolas Edme Restif de La Bretonne
(Nos. 3862–3915)

BASIL GUY

Restif de La Bretonne, Nicolas Edme. Les contemporaines. Club français du livre, 1952. xxiv, 328 p.   **3862**
> *Restif et Les contemporaines* by H. Fabureau, p. v–xxiv. Excellent selection, probably the best since that of Grand-Carteret in 1910. Introduction by Fabureau is informative and valuable.

— Les contemporaines. Les Yeux ouverts, 1962. 3 v.   **3863**
> A facsimile reprint containing *Les contemporaines, ou aventures des plus jolies femmes du temps présent*, *Les contemporaines du commun*, and *Les contemporaines graduées*. Interesting and valuable, especially from a bibliophile's point of view.

— L'enfance de monsieur Nicolas. Ed. by Gilbert Rouger. Club des libraires de France, 1955. 355 p.   **3864**
> Good choice of texts from *Monsieur Nicolas*, with a sane and valid appreciation of R. for today.

— Ingénue Saxancour. Ed. by Gilbert Lély. Pauvert, 1960. xxxvii, 213 p.   **3865**
> First reprint of this work generally available in long while. " Présentation " rather facile and arch. Reissued in somewhat different format in 1961.

— Louise et Thérèse. OLib n.s. 143:249–70, 1958.   **3866**
> Little-known text reprinted because of its interest for the modern reader and for the light it sheds on R.'s understanding of feminine psychology.

— Monsieur Nicolas, ou le cœur humain dévoilé. Edition nouvelle revue sur les textes originaux. Pauvert, 1959. 6 v.   **3867**
> Although not critical, this is an excellent ed. of an important work long unavailable in complete form.

— Les nuits de Paris. Ed. by Henri Bachelin. Firmin-Didot, 1960. viii, 319 p.   **3868**
> A facsimile reprint of the 1788 ed. Introduction, notes, and bibliography (p. 305–15).

— Les nuits de Paris. Ed. by Marc Chadourne and Marcel Thiébaut. Hachette, 1960. 296 p.   **3869**
> *Introduction historique* by Chadourne, p. 7–22; *Restif et son œuvre* by Thiébaut, p. 23–30; *Notes* by H. André-Bernard, p. 267–91. Characteristic work presented with taste and insight, but without the pretentiousness of Bachelin (3868). The introduction by Chadourne is somewhat frenzied, but valuable, while other contributions make this small volume important and agreeable.

— Les nuits de Paris. Textes choisis, présentés et annotés par Patrice Boussel. Union générale, 1963. 379 p.   **3870**
> Standard reprint, generally available. " Présentation " of little value.

— Œuvres érotiques : Le pornographe, L'anti-Justine, Dom Bougre (morceaux choisis). Arcanes, 1953. 302 p.   **3871**
> Important reprint of several of R.'s most scabrous works. Almost impossible to obtain.

— La paysanne pervertie, ou les dangers de la ville, histoire d'Ursule R...., mise-au-jour d'après les véritables lettres des personnages. Preface by André Maurois. Cercle du livre précieux, 1959. xxviii, 495 p.   **3872**
> Elegant and necessary reprint of another important work by R. The introduction by Maurois later adapted for inclusion in his *De La Bruyère à Proust* (3905).

— Les plus belles pages de Restif de la Bretonne. Preface by Félicien Marceau. Mercure de France, 1964. 272 p.   **3873**
> This is an anthology of bits and pieces that is most unsatisfying. The value of the book is in the preface by Marceau.

— Le 14 juillet 1789. OLib n.s. 182:267–72, 1961. **3874**
Brief political text important for understanding R. during the Revolution.

— Sara. Introduction by Marcel Béalu. Nouvelle Office d'édition, 1963. 187 p. **3875**
Agreeable reprint of one of the more decently amorous incidents in *La vie de mon père*.

— La vie de mon père. Ed. by G. Rouger. Cercle des amateurs de livres et d'art typographique, 1960. 2 v. in 1. **3876**
Issued in portfolio and slide-case without pagination, this ed. is an admirable typographic exercise almost impossible to obtain.

— La vie de mon père. Introduction by Jean Desmeuzes. Club des amis du livre progressiste, 1962. xxxii, 250 p. **3877**
The best available ed. of this important work by R. The introduction by Desmeuzes is a model of its kind.

— La vie de mon père. Introduction by Emile Mireaux and note by H. André-Bernard. Hachette, 1963. 232 p. **3878**
Also contains *La femme du laboureur* from *Les contemporaines*, v. 13 (1783). A somewhat truncated ed. for the general public, but valuable for André-Bernard's notes.

Translation

— Les nuits de Paris, or the nocturnal spectator; a selection. Trans. by Linda Asher and Ellen Fertig. Introduction by Jacques Barzun. New York, Random House, 1964. xxii, 375 p. **3879**
This text follows closely the choice of André-Bernard *supra*, but Barzun's presentation, while a good introduction to R. for the Anglo-Saxon reader, is rather superficial and unconvincing. Bibliography included in Notes, p. 357–75.

Criticism

Aury, Dominique. On dévore du Restif. NNRF 14:690–96, 1959. **3880**
Penetrating analysis of R.'s importance for today as seen in new eds. of his works and in Chadourne's study.

Chadourne, Marc. Eros and Restif. YFS 11:12–17, 1953. **3881**
A brief appreciation of R., attempting to vindicate him against charges of " im-morality " made by Victorian prudery (and our own).

— Jean-Jacques et Nicolas, Restif et Rousseau. Eur 391–92:189–98, Nov.–Dec. 1961. **3882**
Comparison of the two authors stressing biographical, literary, and psychological factors with an appreciation of their respective influence and its value.

— Restif de la Bretonne, ou le siècle prophétique. Hachette, 1958. 363 p. **3883**
A moving and spirited reappraisal of Restif and his works, frequently accompanied by analyses in detail since until time of publication few texts were readily available. Not, however, without exaggeration, showing traces of the author's excessive enthusiasm. Important.
Reviews : J.-A. Bédé in RR 51:53–59, 1960; J. Bloch-Michel in Preuves 111:77–80, 1960; G. Brée in FR 33:301–02, 1959–60; F. Green in FS 13:358–60, 1959; R. Lalou in An 100:35–36, 1959; R. Niklaus in MLR 55:451, 1960; G. Spagnoletti in EurL 4:145–50, 1960; M. Thiébaut in RPar 66:140–53; Feb. 1959.

— Restif de la Bretonne : prophet and precursor. LHM 27:345–59, 1956. **3884**
The first fruits of Chadourne's labors on R., culminating in his study and in his ed. of *Les nuits*.

— Restif de la Bretonne revisité. RPar 64:20–31, July 1957. **3885**
General appreciation arranged for a wide public in Chadourne's attempt to revitalize interest in R.

Childs, James Rives. Restif de la Bretonne : témoignages et jugements, bibliographie. Briffaut, 1949. 367 p. **3886**
Indispensable work of reference.
Review : J. Robert in FR 25:231–33, 1951–52.

Chinard, Gilbert. An eighteenth-century interpretation of the struggle for existence : Rétif de la Bretonne's École des pères. APSP 102:547–54, 1958. **3887**
Enlightening excursion into one of R.'s less familiar works.

Citron, Pierre. *In his:* La poésie de Paris dans la littérature française de Rousseau à Baudelaire. Editions de Minuit, 1961. 1:112–16. **3888**
R. and freedom in Paris. His use of the neologism *l'inconussion;* what he under-

stands by " freedom " without idealizing his reaction.

Courbin, J.-C.   Encore un mot sur Restif. BBB 96–106, 1962.   **3889**
> R. and Nougaret. The illustrations of *Monsieur Nicolas.*

— Le plus fort des pamphlets, un ouvrage peu connu de Rétif. BBB 69–75, 1960.   **3890**
> Examines a work of R. : *L'ordre des paysans aux Etats Généraux,* Noillac, 26 février 1789.

Courbin-Demolins, J.-C.   A propos d'un texte inconnu sur Restif de la Bretonne. BBB 93–101, 1959.   **3891**
> Mention of R. in a piece by Nougaret from 1787.

— Les femmes féïques de Binet. L'Oeil 81: 22–31, 1961.   **3892**
> Invented the neologism *féïque* to describe the elongated creatures of the engraver Binet who illustrated his works.

Crocker, Lester G.   Human nature in the novel. *In his:* An age of crisis. *See* 4122. p. 437–41.   **3893**
> A brief examination of R.'s work showing how it portrays " the ultimate consequences of the eighteenth-century moral impasse which resulted from the destruction of objective ethical universals by the new materialism."

Eaubonne, Françoise d' [*pseud.* of Martine Okapi]. Restif, ou le Loth du ruisseau. *In her:* Eros noir. Le Terrain vague, 1962. p. 75–144.   **3894**
> An effort to do more than draw attention to R. Attempts to vindicate him and his point of view along the lines of Mme de Beauvoir's *Faut-il brûler Sade?*

Grubbs, Henry A.   Further light on the Dernière aventure of Rétif de la Bretonne. MLN 66:151–55, 1951.   **3895**
> Note on hitherto missing part of *Mes inscriptions* in B.N. on affair with Sara Debée.

Guillot, Gérard.   Restif de la Bretonne par et pour les femmes. Eur 427–28:56–65, Nov.–Dec. 1964.   **3896**
> Close and profitable examination of women in works by R. with some interesting conclusions about him and his deformation of reality.

Guilly, Paul.   Au pays de Restif. *In:* Demeures inspirées et sites romanesques. Ed.

by Raymond Lecuyer.   S.N.E.P.-Illustration, 1949–58. 3:109–16.   **3897**
> A visit to R.'s Burgundy.

Ioanisian, A. R.   Restif et le communisme utopique. PRRM n.s. 78:91–103, 1958. **3898**
> Brief article nicely complementing Chadourne's views on this same subject in his book.

Lély, Gilbert.   Le marquis de Sade et Rétif de la Bretonne. MerF 331:364–66, 1957.
                                                      3899
> *See* under Sade (4028).

Losito, Luigi.   Restif de la Bretonne. *In his:* Panorama. Bari, Collana di Culture française, 1963. p. 5–11.   **3900**
> A general appreciation, which originally appeared in *Culture française* (1958), shortly before Chadourne's book but lacking the enthusiasm of the latter.

Marceau, Félicien.   Un prolétaire de la littérature : Restif de la Bretonne. NL 1, 10, Nov. 12, 1964.   **3901**
> R. viewed as a writer forced to earn a living by his pen, whence his proletarian outlook and his prophetic utterances. Originally prepared as a preface to the edition of R. in the collection *Les plus belles pages ....*

Mars, François L.   Julien Sorel et Restif de la Bretonne. StCl 1:306–07, 1958–59. **3902**
> A brief note comparing the two personalities and mentioning possible influences.

Martin, Angus.   Restif de la Bretonne devant la critique : 1950–1963. SF 9:278–83, 1965.
                                                      3903
> *Etat présent.* Essential. Last 2 p. a model of common sense, exactness, and sensitivity.

Matthews, J.H.   Une source possible de Nana ? Le ménage parisien de Restif de la Bretonne. CahN 1:504–06, 1955–60.   **3904**
> Compares 2 texts and mentions possible influences, but inconclusive.

Maurois, André.   Restif de la Bretonne et la paysanne pervertie. *In his:* De La Bruyère à Proust. Fayard, 1964. p. 66–81.   **3905**
> Eminently readable stylistic considerations of R. and his work, both in particular and in general.

Mylne, Vivienne.   Restif de la Bretonne and Laclos : the culmination of the letter-novel.

In her: The eighteenth-century French novel. *See* 3734. p. 221–44. **3906**

General stylistic considerations of R. attempting to explain his success as a purveyor of " realism," but not very convincing.

Peyrefitte, Roger. Le spectateur nocturne. Flammarion, 1960. 160 p. **3907**

A dramatic presentation in 4 parts, giving author's conception of R.'s life.

Pinset, Jacques. Les origines instinctives de la Révolution française, I. RHES 39:198–228, 1961. **3908**

Stimulating interpretation of R.'s reporting on popular feeling in Paris during the 18th century. Point of view different from that of Porter (3910).

Plessis, Jean. Restif de la Bretonne et l'inscriptiomanie. VL 95:115–22, 1960. **3909**

Examination of well-known aspect of R.'s biography underlining its importance.

Porter, Charles A. Imperiled pedestrian. YFS 32:55–67, 1964. **3910**

Informative and entertaining appreciation of R.'s view of the Parisian street-scene as " the Destroyer."

— Restif, Rousseau and M. Nicolas. RR 54:262–73, 1963. **3911**

Points out specific ways in which R. emulated Rousseau, especially in the composition of his own " autobiography."

Rouger, Gilbert. Une journée au pays de Restif. NL 4, Aug. 6, 1959. **3912**

General reflections on R. inspired by a visit to Burgundy.

Spagnoletti, Giacinto. Il ritorno di Restif de la Bretonne. EurL 4:145–50, 1960. **3913**

General review, for Italian public, of recent renewed interest in R.

Thérive, André. Restif de la Bretonne. EPar 120–27, April 1961. **3914**

A brief general appreciation. The man more important than his works to modern reader?

Tuzet, Hélène. Deux types de cosmogonies vitalistes, I. Restif de la Bretonne, ou le cœur humain dévoilé. RScH n.s. 100:495–506, 1960. **3915**

Illuminating interpretation of R. in terms of one of his *idées maîtresses*.

Pierre-Ambroise-François Choderlos de Laclos
(Nos. 3916–3970)

J. Robert Loy

Editions

Laclos, Pierre-Ambroise-François Choderlos de. Laclos par lui-même. Images et textes présentés par Roger Vailland. Editions du Seuil, 1958. 191 p. **3916**

Excellent running analysis and commentary with choice of texts. Good use of L.'s poetry to establish his bourgeois timidity and ambition, his resentment of established class, and profeminist sentiments. Good analysis of libertinage supported by pertinent texts. Its four " figures " are according to Vailland : choice, seduction, fall, and rupture. One of best cases yet made for L. as a serious reformer and great novelist far from tradition of Sade.

— Les liaisons dangereuses; ou, lettres recueillies dans une société et publiées pour l'instruction de quelques autres. Preface by Armand Hoog. Editions du Bateau ivre, 1946. 2 v. **3917**

— Les liaisons dangereuses. Etablissement du texte, introduction et notes par Jean Mistler. Monaco, Editions du Rocher, 1948. xxxvii, 113 p. **3918**

— Les liaisons dangereuses. Introduction by Dominique Aury. Lausanne, Guilde du livre, 1950. 483 p. **3919**

— Les liaisons dangereuses. Ed. by Yves Le Hir. Garnier, 1952. 464 p. **3920**

— Les liaisons dangereuses. Ed. by Roger Vailland. Club français du livre, 1957. xxviii, 540 p. **3921**

— Les liaisons dangereuses. Preface by André Malraux. Gallimard, 1958. 443 p. (Le Livre de poche, 354–55) **3922**

— Les liaisons dangereuses. Avec préface de Roger Vailland suivi de Les liaisons dangereuses et les écrivains d'aujourd'hui. Textes de Jean Cocteau, Paul Guth, Jean Dutourd, Pierre-Henri Simon. Les Amis du club du livre du mois, 1960. 2 v. **3923**

All are serious eds. with introductions of value to serious readers. Listed here to record recent eds. with names of their editors.

Criticism

Aldridge, A. Owen. Lolita and Les liaisons dangereuses. WSCL 2³:20–26, 1961. **3924**

Cécile-Lolita a pornographic creation were it not for style. Both owe special character to author's innuendo/euphemism and humorous detachment (cf. *Fanny Hill*). Other valid parallels and contrasts drawn. Interesting article.

Aury, Dominique. La révolte de Mme de Merteuil. CPl 12:89–101, 1951.   **3925**

Witty essay situating Merteuil's conduct against accepted " game " of her period. She revolts against woman/slave whose only arms are tears. A personal, temperamental, nonreasoning revolt to preserve her greatest passion—her freedom.

Bertin, Alfeo. Il creatore di un mito : Choderlos de Laclos. Il Ponte 17:372–80, 1961.   **3926**

Studies problem of *Liaisons dangereuses* in terms of life of L. Valmont and Merteuil two projections of same entity : he an intuitive incarnation, she more interiorized. They are without spiritual quality that rises to sphere where art of love is predicate of spiritual self. L. creates naively *not* a new *ideal* but *myth* of his time.

Brun, Max. Contribution bibliographique à l'étude des éditions des Liaisons dangereuses portant le millésime 1782. BBB 49–173, 1958; 44–56, 1961.   **3927**

Essential article for problems related to all eds. of *Liaisons dangereuses;* facsimiles.

Castel-Çagarriga, G. Les clefs des Liaisons dangereuses. RDM 682–99, April 15, 1961.   **3928**

Attempt to trace down persons behind fictional characters of *Liaisons dangereuses* in Grenoble society. Castel-Çagarriga provides key for all main characters : Mme de Montmaur for Merteuil, Antoine d'Agoult for Valmont, thus providing L. with revenge for their betrayal. Somewhat romanced presentation but important article drawing on wide documentation.

Cherpack, Clifton. A new look at Les liaisons dangereuses. MLN 74:513–21, 1959.   **3929**

Actually long review article of Seylaz (3961). Interesting article full of insights, particularly the *confiance-confidence* pattern and importance of time in the novel, playing down role of intelligence somewhat.

Choderlos de Laclos, Etienne Fargeau. Le fils de Laclos; carnets de marche du commandant Choderlos de Laclos (An XIV–1814). Ed. by Louis de Chauvigny. Lausanne, Payot, 1912. 254 p.   **3930**

Peripheral document important for tone, milieu, and certain details surrounding life of L.'s legitimized son and for suggestions concerning another vital side of the father. Followed by letters to Mme Laclos from Mme Pourrat, *Tout-Paris* matron and friend of many well known, including Chénier.

Croce, Sara. La première édition ignorée des Liaisons dangereuses dans une traduction inachevée. Bel 13:704–14, 1958.   **3931**

Slight article on first translation of *Liaisons dangereuses* into Italian in 1909 with comments on relative value of several subsequent translations.

Cucuel, Georges. La vie de société dans le Dauphinois au XVIIIe siècle. RHL 35:344–74, 1935.   **3932**

Research and souvenirs of backdrop of J.-J. Rousseau, Stendhal and L. Key to L.'s literary creations—in part superseded by later work—tied, in part, to souvenirs of Stendhal. Such research leads " moins à des certitudes qu'à la réunion d'un faisceau de probabilités. "

Delmas, André Albert and Yvette. A la recherche des Liaisons dangereuses. Mercure de France, 1964. 485 p.   **3933**

Certainly most ambitious work on fortunes and literary progeny of *Liaisons dangereuses* yet published. Reasonably comprehensive, well balanced, and objective. From immediate reactions (1782–1815) through romantic hell (1815–1850) and travesty (1850–1914), the authors point up valid point of L.'s final critical triumph and sympathetic understanding of *Liaisons dangereuses* only in past 50 years. Although ranked high, recent Italian criticism somewhat slighted in short appendix on *Liaisons dangereuses* abroad. Serious, thorough, essential. Index helpful if incomplete.

Review : W. de Spens in Tro 203:132, 1964.

Derla, Luigi. Questioni di critica laclosiana. SF 4:278–89, 1960.   **3934**

Intelligent, essential article on problems of interpretation of *Liaisons dangereuses* particularly in light of recent critical estimates of Malraux, Pizzorusso, Natoli, Ruff, Seylaz, and Cherpack. Valmont, a complete character, seen in evolution from *libertin* to *homme sensible*. Adds to Seylaz that *Liaisons dangereuses* is a " myth " of fatal passion and Jansenist sin.

Dutourd, Jean. Choderlos de Laclos. *In his:* Le fond et la forme. Gallimard, 1958. p. 133–38. **3935**
Short but concentrated remarks on role of L. in French literature. *Liaisons dangereuses* most French of all novels; Valmont and Merteuil cruel, but gay *à la française*, continually living in the flesh but least fleshly of all novel heroes. Their cruelty all the more unpardonable and French for being *raisonnable* and of the 18th century.

Esmonin, Edmond. La société grenobloise au temps de Louis XV, d'après les Miscellanea de Letourneau. *In his:* Etudes sur la France des XVIIᵉ et XVIIIᵉ siècles. Presses univ. de France, 1964. p. 471–94. (PUGL, 32) **3936**
Slim but interesting background material on genesis of *Liaisons dangereuses*. " Force nous est donc de conclure que Letourneau ... n'apporte aucune confirmation indiscutable de la thèse traditionnelle sur la clef des *Liaisons dangereuses*."

Faurie, Jacques. Essai sur la séduction. Table ronde, 1948. 225 p. **3937**
Important long essay, admirably organized. Author, wishing to fill lacunae in psychological studies (i.e., no proper essay on seduction), finds the *séducteur parfait* in Valmont and, incidentally, gives his interpretation of novel.

Gay, Peter. Three stages on love's way. Enc 47:8–20, 1957. **3938**
L.'s use of epigraph from *Nouvelle Héloïse* not an accident for *Liaisons dangereuses* a mirror image of Rousseau's novel. As latter's cult of sincerity hides insincerity, so cult of insincerity in *Liaisons dangereuses* hides sincerity. These 2 works placed in direct opposition to Diderot.

Greshoff, C. J. Laclos' Les liaisons dangereuses. *In his:* Seven studies in the French novel. Capetown, A. A. Balkema, 1964. p. 26–38. **3939**
Stimulating short essay concentrating on unique quality of *Liaisons dangereuses* as the novel of courtly love that reintroduces cruelty and barbarity. In an analysis of characters as victims, executioners,

and neutral representatives of society, Greshoff makes a convincing case for the Luciferian evil exemplified by Merteuil's artificial and sick intellect.

Grimsley, Ronald. Don Juanism in Les liaisons dangereuses. FS 14:1–15, 1960. **3940**
Good study of elements of Don Juanism in Valmont although " his activity is not absolutely lucid since it is permeated by a sort of self-conscious reflection. " Mme de Tourvel provokes the dilemma; Merteuil triumphs from it.

Guy, Basil. The prince de Ligne, Laclos and the Liaisons dangereuses : two notes. RR 55:260–67, 1964. **3941**
An excellent, compact article important for details on historical background of *Liaisons dangereuses*. Also random critical remarks of prince de Ligne on novel valuable as reflection of contemporary opinion. Guy carefully concludes : "... the testimony of the prince de Ligne ... should henceforth be considered along with [Tilly and Stendhal] as the starting point for any appreciation of the *Liaisons dangereuses* and its historical background."

Hoffmann, Paul. Aspects de la condition féminine dans Les liaisons dangereuses. IL 15:47–53, 1963. **3942**
Readable, well-organized discussion of *Liaisons dangereuses* as document in continuing interest of L. for social status of women in 18th century. Merteuil as pioneer in this direction but also a victim of her own liberation. *Liaisons dangereuses* a meditation on powers given to women by nature.

Hudon, E. Sculley. Love and myth in Les liaisons dangereuses. YFS 11:25–38, 1953. **3943**
Analyzes kinds of love in novel (classic, pre-Romantic, tragic, etc.), then attempts to define L.'s realism in an artistic creation of myth. Finds the sense of the *Liaisons dangereuses* to be in its reassertion of human fallibility " in protean world of art." Some provocative ideas.

Koppen, Erwin. Laclos' Liaisons dangereuses in der Kritik (1782–1850). Wiesbaden, Steiner, 1961. viii, 109 p. (MRA, 4) **3944**
Divided into two parts : until 1789, and up to Napoleonic *coup d'état*. Well-done collection of critical material with comment, always enriching. In general,

CRITICAL BIBLIOGRAPHY OF FRENCH LITERATURE

" die Geschichte der Interpretation der *Liaisons dangereuses* ist . . . die Geschichte einer Fehlinterpretation." The idea of a cynical, Sadean production flourished to end of period despite efforts of L.'s friends at rehabilitation. Author suggests same erroneous " legend " remains today.
Review : R. Grimsley in FS 17:180–82, 1963.

Laufer, Roger. La structure dialectique des Liaisons dangereuses. PRRM n.s. 93:82–90,
3945

Subtle study of the aspects of libertinage in *Liaisons dangereuses*. " L'idée géniale de Laclos ... consiste à avoir fait des complices un homme et une femme." Valmont playing sentimental seduction becomes feminine; Merteuil, bent on pure physical possession, becomes male. The *présidente*'s role above all that of the *bourgeoise*. " Les *Liaisons dangereuses* nous montrent la défaite des libertins comme conséquence de leur embourgeoisement." The work is for Laufer a triumph of bourgeois sentiment and rationalization. He thus limits usual critical appraisal of Valmont and Merteuil as perverse monsters and of the novel as the waging of a libertine war. Important article.

Loiseau, Yvan. Rivarol, Laclos et la monarchie française. RDM 291–302, July–Aug. 1958.
3946

Excellent, short confrontation of two key 18th-century personalities and their theories of monarchy : L. for whom the office, close to people, is important, and Rivarol for whom the person of king is sacred.

— Le vrai Laclos. *In his:* Rivarol, suivi de le vrai Laclos. La Palatine, 1961. p. 199–236.
3947

Short monograph providing details of L.'s biography. Genealogical table on p. 237.

Loy, J. Robert. Love/vengeance in the late eighteenth-century French novel. *See* 3727.
3948

Study, centering on *Liaisons dangereuses*, suggests that a confusion of heart for head and love for vengeance, rather than nihilistic immoralism, explains novel of period.

Macchia, Giovanni. Il sistema di Laclos. *In his:* Il paradiso della ragione. Bari, Laterza, 1960. p. 216–29.
3949

Good analytical article on rereading L., with particular attention to problem of

genre of the work. L. omits much of earlier divertissement, " da un compromesso tra il memorialismo, la confessione e il racconto induce il romanzo epistolare ad una forma autonoma."

Marat, Janine. Les liaisons dangereuses : roman de l'intelligence pure. RSu 1:138–41, 1951.
3950

Slight but perceptive pages on the novel's action : attempt of pure intellect (Merteuil and Valmont) to play rather than live. " Peut-être, à tout prendre, l'intelligence est-elle le seul personnage des *Liaisons dangereuses*."

Maurois, André. Laclos. *In his:* De La Bruyère à Proust. Fayard, 1964. p. 82–97.
3951

Good, inclusive general article on the novel, the milieu and role of L. in history of French literature.

May, Georges. Racine et Les liaisons dangereuses. FR 23:452–61, 1949–50.
3952

May makes provocative article out of L.'s preference for Racine over Corneille. L.'s quotation from *Britannicus* points up degree to which L. and Racine have written classical tragedies of *duperie*. May compares their structures to architecture of Versailles. " C'est la fidélité aux mêmes principes esthétiques qui conduit Racine et Laclos à s'exposer aux mêmes critiques."

— The witticisms of monsieur de Valmont. EspCr 3:181–87, 1963.
3953

Interesting study of Valmont as master of the *double-entendre* and of L.'s art in thus involving reader in accepting him as deceiver and cheat.

Mead, William. Les liaisons dangereuses and moral usefulness. PMLA 75:563–70, 1960.
3954

Provocative article, with some subjective judgments, but nicely documented, showing L. both as moralizer and moralist. In the more important role of moralist, he seems to be writing at once the antidote to extreme rationalism and to extreme *sensibilité*, this latter in direct reply to both Rousseau and Richardson. Far from their disciple, L. is revealed as a novelist of the intelligence, balancing reason and sensibility.

Natoli, Glauco. Dalle Liaisons dangereuses alla Femme vertueuse. *In his:* Figure e problemi della cultura francese. Messina, G. D'Anna, 1956. p. 209–48.
3955

Excellent, sensitive article, tracing male-female modes in fiction, rational-sentimental motivation from 17th century to L., and previewing changes in literary ideals thereafter. Valid comparisons with *Comte de Valmont* and especially with *Le femme vertueuse* (1787) in which appears the penultimate *roué* in person of Mermeuil.

Pichois, Claude. Un roman inconnu et inachevé de Choderlos de Laclos. SRLF 1:87–148, 1960. **3956**

Somewhat misleading title. Pichois has made happy discovery of the fact that L. projected a novel based on P.-L. Lacretelle's 1802 play, *Le fils naturel.* He writes an historical account of L.'s project and prints his *Observations sur Le fils naturel* as they appeared, unfinished, in v. 4 of Lacretelle's *Œuvres* (1824).

Pizzorusso, Arnaldo. La struttura delle Liaisons dangereuses. AFLC 19²:50–88, 1952. **3957**

The opposition nature-society is of constant validity for L. *Liaisons dangereuses* represents anti-nature. Novel, by definition for L., demands integration of social morality with genre. Sentimental side of novel is but ornament to psychological architecture. Society a grand theater and characters in novel must embrace role as actors. Pizzorusso, adding to May (3952), shows theatricality of structure of *Liaisons*, i.e., order and art of novel when compared to usually suggested sentimental precursors (*Nouvelle Héloïse, Clarissa*, etc.).

Pomeau, René. Le mariage de Laclos. RHL 64:60–72, 1964. **3958**

Pomeau reviews sincerity of L.'s intentions and concern of critics to know real L. behind *bon père, excellent époux.* Situated in his military career, the liaison and marriage with Marie Duperré (details of her family background) clarify L.'s relatively non-*galant* personal life after *Liaisons dangereuses* and during writing of *Education des femmes.*

Rousset, Jean. Le roman par lettres—Les liaisons dangereuses. *In his:* Forme et signification. Corti, 1962. p. 65–103. **3959**

Interesting pages on *Liaisons dangereuses* as representative of epistolary form considered along with *Nouvelle Héloïse* and *Mémoires de deux jeunes mariées.* L., by letter form, has filled his novel with " ce désordre qui peut seul peindre le sentiment."

Salomon, Jean-Jacques. Liberté et libertinage : Les liaisons dangereuses. Tmod 5:55–70, 1949. **3960**

Intelligent, important study of interpretive tradition of the *Liaisons dangereuses* as strategy, intellect, *gloire.* The true *libertin* not a *sensuel* but a mystifier whose real object is the soul of his equal, the seduced or betrayed one. " Le libertin s'est choisi libre : ... ce choix n'est compréhensible qu'en référence à Dieu."

Seylaz, Jean-Luc. Les liaisons dangereuses et la création romanesque chez Laclos. Geneva, Droz, 1958. 156 p. **3961**

Epistolary form becomes with Laclos " un moyen de création—l'accord de la matière romanesque et du genre." Detailed study of ways in which letters give tone, meaning, and reality to the various characters. A second part studies what Seylaz calls " une mythologie de l'intelligence." Serious study filled with advised admiration for L. as great novelist.
Reviews : C. Cherpack in MLN 74:513–21, 1959; L. Gossman in RR 49:302–04, 1958; F. Green in FS 13:62–65, 1959; R. Marclay in EL 1:113–19, 1958; F. Orlando in SF 3:103–05, 1959; A. Pizzorusso in RHL 60:73–76, 1960.

Simon, Pierre-Henri. Laclos fut-il marxiste ? RPar 61:125–30, Dec. 1954. *Also in his:* Le jardin et la ville. Editions du Seuil, 1962. p. 191–96. **3962**

Actually, review of Vailland (3916). Simon agrees with L.'s moral sincerity in *Liaisons dangereuses;* of L.'s involvement and preaching less sure. Slight but of interest.

Solaroli, Libero. Laclos. Preface by Pietro Paolo Trompeo. Rome, Ateneo, 1952. 195 p. **3963**

A solid life and works (rapid estimate of fortune in conclusion) that tries to avoid all previous easy explanations of the L. problem by judicious use of recent material insisting on his various " careers " : " Aveva mancato tutto : la carriere militare, quella litteraria e quella politica." Giraudoux' estimate (922) of L., he says, is brilliant but not true. Important study.

— Laclos e Nelson. *In:* Studi sulla letteratura dell'Ottocento in onore di Pietro Paolo Trompeo. Ed. by Giovanni Macchia and Glauco Natoli. Naples, Edizioni scientifiche italiane, 1959. p. 87–95. **3964**

Slight but interesting article on circumstances bringing L. in contact with Nelson in 1803. Correction of details concerning fort on S. Paolo.

— Nuovi elementi per la biografia di Laclos. RLM 9:36–38, 1956.   **3965**

Details and suggestions, linked to discovery in Brindisi of L.'s tombstone, on L.'s Italian travels, his son, other probable *inédits*.

Thelander, Dorothy R. Laclos and the epistolary novel. Geneva, Droz, 1963. 167 p. *See* 5680.   **3966**

Central plot is " variation of classic recognition theme " to which epistolary technique is well suited. Play between appearance and reality closer to 20th-century literature. Interesting study of genre.
Reviews : W. Krauss in DLit 85:306–07, 1964; J. Monty in MLJ 48:118–19, 1964.

Vartanian, Aram. The marquise de Merteuil : a case of mistaken identity. EspCr 3:172–80, 1963.   **3967**

Closely reasoned portrait of Merteuil as " a woman who has decided, on her own initiative, to free herself altogether from the position of passivity and inferiority of her sex " and of her catalytic influence on all characters of the novel.

Willemetz, Gérard. La véritable deuxième édition originale des Liaisons dangereuses. BBB 45–52, 1957.   **3968**

Notes on what Willemetz calls sole true second ed. of *Liaisons dangereuses* with facsimiles.

Wolpe, Hans M. J. Le double jeu des Liaisons dangereuses. RFor 72:30–50, 1960.   **3969**

Criticism begins by holding J.-J. Rousseau in higher esteem than L. but ends by reversing values. Wolpe studies separation of sentiment expressed in and effect produced by letters. L., like Thomas Mann, understood irony and ambiguity of passion, thus *double jeu*. Excellent article.

Wurmser, André. Encore à propos des Liaisons dangereuses; de l'amour sottement considéré comme une hallucination. LetF 3, Sept. 2, 1954.   **3970**

Slight but interesting article on occasion of publication of Vailland (3916). Parallels L.-Stendhal : " Stendhal semblable à Laclos et dressé contre lui, Stendhal qui se moquera violemment des libertins,

incapables de goûter la joie de vivre et la joie d'aimer ...."

Donatien Alphonse François, *comte, called marquis* de Sade
(Nos. 3971–4061)

BASIL GUY

Editions

Sade, Donatien Alphonse François, *comte, called marquis* de. Œuvres complètes. Pauvert, 1958 [i.e., 1960] –1963. 13 v.   **3971**

1.   Les infortunes de la vertu. Edition nouvelle, précédée de La douteuse Justine, ou Les revanches de la pudeur, par Jean Paulhan et un plan du roman par Maurice Heine. 1959 [i.e., 1962]. xlvi, 199 p.

2.   Justine, ou les malheurs de la vertu. Préface de Georges Bataille, 1958 [i.e., 1960]. xxxvi, 417 p.

3–5.   Les crimes de l'amour. Introduction de Gilbert Lély. 1961. 3 v.

6.   Historiettes, contes et fabliaux. Dorci. 1962. 300 p.

7.   Dialogue entre un prêtre et un moribond, et autres opuscules. Préface de Maurice Heine. 1961. 139 p.

8–11.   Aline et Valcour, ou le roman philosophique. Préface de Pierre Klossowski. 1963. 4 v.

12.   Ecrits politiques. Oxtiern. 1963. 172 p.

13.   La marquise de Gange. Introduction de Gilbert Lély. 1963. vi, 323 p.

The foregoing titles now alone comprise the Pauvert ed., since the famous trial of the publisher by the French government (*see* 4045) caused 4 other titles (*Les 120 journées de Sodome, La nouvelle Justine, Histoire de Juliette, La philosophie dans le boudoir*) to be removed from circulation and to be declared " épuisés, [ne pouvant] faire l'objet que de ré-éditions hors commerce."

— Œuvres complètes. Edition définitive. Cercle du livre précieux, 1962–64. 15 v.   **3972**

1–2.   Vie du marquis de Sade, avec un examen de ses ouvrages, par Gilbert Lély. Nouvelle édition revue et corrigée et en maints endroits refondue. Postface d'Yves Bonnefoy. 1962. 2 v.

3.   Justine, ou les malheurs de la vertu. Préface de A. Hesnard et de Maurice Heine. La philosophie dans le boudoir. Préface de Pierre Klossowski. 1963. 563 p.

4–5. Aline et Valcour, ou le roman philosophique. Préface de Jean Fabre.
1962. 2 v.

6–9. La nouvelle Justine, ou les malheurs
de la vertu, suivie de l'Histoire de
Juliette, sa sœur, ou les prospérités du
vice. Préfaces de Maurice Blanchot,
Georges Bataille, Pierre Klossowski,
et Maurice Heine. 1963. 4 v.

10. Les crimes de l'amour, nouvelles
héroïques et tragiques, suivies de
L'auteur des Crimes de l'amour à
Villeterque, Folliculaire. Préfaces de
Jean Fabre et de Pierre Klossowski.
1964. 522 p.

11. La marquise de Gange, précédée des
Opuscules politiques et d'Oxtiern, ou
les malheurs du libertinage. Préfaces
de Pierre Naville, Camille Schuwer et
Gaëtan Picon. 1964. 430 p.

12. Correspondance, 1759–1814. Préface
et postface de Gilbert Lély. 1964.
650 p.

13. Les 120 journées de Sodome ou
l'école du libertinage. Préfaces de
Maurice Heine, A. Hesnard, Henri
Pastoureau et Pierre Klossowski.
1964. 438 p.

14. Opuscules. Historiettes, contes et
fabliaux. Les infortunes de la vertu.
Préfaces de Maurice Heine et d'Antoine Adam. 1963. 472 p.

15 et dernier. Histoire secrète d'Isabelle de
Bavière, reine de France. Précédée
des Notes littéraires, des Notes pour
les Journées de Florbelle et d'Adé-
laïde de Brunswick, princesse de
Saxe. Postface de Jean-Jacques Bro-
chier. 1964. 534 p.
Elegant, select ed. (despite the title)
for the general public, prepared in competition with Pauvert ed. *supra* and
attempting to profit by the interest it
aroused. The texts chosen conform to the
best eds. available. The introductions,
etc., utilize the best work of recent years
where apposite, and publish rare or out-
of-print studies by such famous critics as
Maurice Heine and Pierre Klossowski.
Review: J. Lacan in Cr 19:291–313,
Apr. 1963.

Separate Titles

— Cahiers personnels (1803–1804). Ed. by
Gilbert Lély. Corrêa, 1953. 128 p. **3973**
An important collection of documents,
interesting for the light they shed on S.'s
later career.

— Le carillon de Vincennes : lettres inédites.

Ed. by Gilbert Lély. Arcanes, 1953. 103 p.
3974
Unpublished letters from Vincennes,
some important, others not, forming a
nice complement to ed. of letters by
Daumas *infra*.

— Cent onze notes pour la Nouvelle Justine.
Ed. by Maurice Heine. Paris, 1956. 159 p.
(Le Terrain vague, 4) **3975**
Notes for a reworking of the novel,
discovered by Maurice Heine and edited
by him. Interesting for the light they
throw on S.'s ulterior considerations when
dealing with a work of " imagination."

— Dorci, ou la bizarrerie du sort. Suivi de
Dialogue entre un prêtre et un moribond.
Avec une notice sur l'auteur. Pernette, 1957.
94 p. **3976**
First recent ed., limited to 500 copies, of
Dorci (but *see* 3971, v. 6) followed by a
standard reprint of the *Dialogue*. The
" Notice " is of small value.

— Histoire de Sainville et de Léonore. Introduction by Gilbert Lély. Union générale,
1962. 371 p. **3977**
Reprint of one of the *Crimes de l'amour*
for the general public with a good introduction.

— Histoire secrète d'Isabelle de Bavière, reine
de France. Ed. by Gilbert Lély. Gallimard,
1953. 332 p. **3978**
The 1st ed. of a new famous *supercherie*.
Basically an historical novel in the *genre
troubadour*, the documents on which it is
supposedly founded have been proved
false by Lély. *See also* 4034 and Lély's ed.
for the Club français du livre (1964),
translated into Italian the same year.

— Histoire secrète d'Isabelle de Bavière, reine
de France. Foreword by Gilbert Lély. Club
français du livre, 1964. xl, 285 p. **3979**
Text of Lély's 1953 ed., but the introduction and commentary have been
reworked in light of his later discoveries
and conclusions. Translated into Italian
in 1964 and published in Milan by Suger,
316 p.

— Les infortunes de la vertu. Edition nou-
velle précédée de La douteuse Justine ou
Les revanches de la pudeur. Ed. by Jean
Paulhan. Pauvert, 1959. lxiv, 203 p. **3980**
Standard reprint famous for the lengthy
but convincing introduction by Paulhan.
The ed. of the *Œuvres complètes*, with this
as v. I, never appeared.

— Les infortunes de la vertu. Suivies des Historiettes, contes et fabliaux. Introduction by Gilbert Lély. Union générale, 1965. 512 p.   **3981**

> Textual reprint of v. 1 and 6 of Pauvert ed. (3971) with the addition of a brief commentary for the general reader.

— Lettre à Marie-Dorothée de Rousset. Ed. by Gilbert Lély. CPl 12:148–55, 1951. **3982**

> Unpublished letter from S. to one of the women with whom he became involved in a celebrated court case with overtones both comic and tragic, as mentioned by Lély in his presentation.

— Lettres aux femmes. Cercle du livre précieux, 1965. 188 p.   **3983**

> An interesting and ingenious choice of documents spanning S.'s life whose value is lessened by the absence of commentary and notes.

— Lettres choisies. Preface by Gilbert Lély. Pauvert, 1963. 269 p.   **3984**

> Letters, mostly unedited, from the years 1777–94, which show different attitudes of S. toward the Revolution.

— La marquise de Gange, roman. Texte conforme à l'édition unique de 1813. Preface by Gilbert Lély. Amiot, 1957. 225 p.   **3985**

> The first modern ed. of an atypical novel by S. with an informative introduction.

— Mon arrestation du 26 août [1778]. Lettre inédite, suivie des Etrennes philosophiques. Ed. by Gilbert Lély. Hughes, 1959, 43 p.   **3986**

> Interesting account of an early incarceration by S. himself, accompanied by an important opuscule and excellent notes by a leading S. scholar.

— Monsieur le 6; lettres inédites (1778–1784). Ed. by Georges Daumas. Julliard, 1954. 286 p.   **3987**

> Introduction by Gilbert Lély and notes are good. Contains 47 letters, all but one unpublished heretofore, written from Vincennes.

— Nouvelles exemplaires. Selected and ed. by Gilbert Lély. Club français du livre, 1958. 401 p.   **3988**

> A selection of novellas from the *Crimes de l'amour* and other works presented in an elegant format for the general public in meticulous but too insistent fashion by Lély, prompting in part the strictures of Wilson (4060).

— Séïde, conte moral et philosophique. Introduction by Gilbert Lély. MerF 316:210–15, Oct. 1952.   **3989**

> Unpublished project from Arsenal ms. A *Zadig*-like tale on the relativity of virtue and vice.

— La vanille et la manille. Ed. by Yvon Belaval. CPl 12:156–59, 1951.   **3990**

> An important letter from S. to his wife underlining the nature of their relationship and her importance to him.

Translations

— Adelaide of Brunswick. Trans. by Hobart Ryland from an unpublished manuscript recently discovered among the papers left by the marquis de Sade. Washington, Scarecrow, 1954. 168 p.   **3991**

> One of S.'s last pieces taking up theme of *Justine:* the reward of virtue here below is misery. So far as this reviewer is aware, the original text is not yet generally available, but *see* v. 15 of *Livre précieux* ed. (3972). For a brief appreciation, *see* Pick (4047).

— The bedroom philosophers. Paris, Olympia press, 1957. 226 p.   **3992**

> *La philosophie dans le boudoir*, translated by Pieralessandro Casavini. An amusing version of this important work in a style best characterized as " breezy."

— The complete Justine, Philosophy in the bedroom, and other writings. Compiled and trans. by Richard Seaver and Austryn Wainhouse. With introductions by Jean Paulhan and Maurice Blanchot. New York, Grove press, 1965. xxii, 753 p.   **3993**

> The essay by Paulhan (p. 3–36) is a translation of *Le marquis de Sade et sa complice*, originally published in 1946; that by Blanchot (p. 37–72) forms part of his *Lautréamont et Sade*, published in 1949. The chronology (p. 73–119) and notes derive from Lély's *Vie du marquis de Sade*. A good bibliography (p. 744–52) completes this excellent work.

— De Sade quartet. Trans. by Margaret Crosland. London, Owen, 1963. 158 p.   **3994**

> Four stories from *Contes et fabliaux.*

— Justine, or good conduct well chastised. Trans. by Pieralessandro Casavini. Paris, Olympia press, 1959. 330 p.   **3995**

— The marquis de Sade : an essay by Simone de Beauvoir [trans. by Annette Michelson] with selections from his writings chosen [and trans.] by Paul Dinnage. New York, Grove press, 1953. 236 p.   **3996**

The essay by Mme de Beauvoir is an American reprint of the English translation of her *Faut-il brûler Sade?*

— The 120 days of Sodom; or, the romance of the school for libertinage. Paris, Olympia press, 1957. 3 v.   **3997**

Trans., together with a prefatory essay by Georges Bataille, by Pierallesandro Casavini.

— Selected writings. Selected and trans. by Leonard de Saint-Yves. New York, British Book center, 1954. 306 p.   **3998**

Brief introduction for each piece, but not critical. Originally published in 1953 by Owen in London.
Review : R. Pick in SRL 19, July 24, 1954.

— Opere scelte. Ed. by Gian Piero Brega and trans. by Pino Bava. Milan, Feltrinelli, 1962. cxxxiv, 524 p.   **3999**

A selection of texts—imaginative, critical, and biographical—in a smooth Italian version, with an excellent appreciation of S., his life and works.

Criticism

Bataille, Georges. Sade. *In his:* La littérature et le mal. Gallimard, 1957. p. 111–38.
4000

Important collection of papers written over the years by one of the most influential critics in the renewed approach to S. Includes : *Sade et la prise de la Bastille, La volonté de destruction de soi, La pensée de Sade, La frénésie sadique, Du déchaînement à la conscience claire, La poésie du destin de Sade.*

Beauvoir, Simone de. Faut-il brûler Sade ? Tmod 74:1002–33, Dec. 1951; 75:1197–1230, Jan. 1952.   **4001**

Probably the most stimulating discussion of S. since the war, giving by the sharpness of its views a new depth to our understanding of S.

Blanchot, Maurice. Français, encore un effort. NNRF 26:600–18, 1965.   **4002**

Prepared as an introduction to a volume in the collection *Libertés*. Penetrating analysis of limits between madness and reason in light of S., his time—and our own.

Camus, Albert. La négation absolue. *In his:* L'homme révolté. Gallimard, 1951. p. 54–67.   **4003**

Thirteen pages of luminous and rigorous demonstration of the precept that " God is dead." One of the more positive—and overlooked—contributions to the literature on S. in recent years.

Cleugh, James. The marquis and the chevalier. New York, Duell Sloan and Pearce, 1952. 295 p.   **4004**

No new material on S.; somewhat better on Sacher-Masoch, but generally disappointing.

Crocker, Lester G. Sade and the Fleurs du mal. *In his:* Nature and culture. *See* 4123. p. 398–429.   **4005**

An illuminating analysis of S. and his point of view in the " nihilist dissolution " of 18th-century ethical thought.

Drummond, Walter. Philosopher of evil. Evanston, Regency books, 1962. 158 p. **4006**

A general appreciation which, without being original, succeeds in doing justice to the subject for a general public.

Dupé, Georges. Le marquis de Sade. OLib n.s. 136:27–76, 1957.   **4007**

Valuable reappraisal not only of S., but of recent work on him in France.

Eaubonne, Françoise d' [*pseud.* of Martine Okapi]. Sade ou l'éros-vengeance. *In her:* Eros noir. Le Terrain vague, 1962. p. 145–233.   **4008**

Plausible, if outspoken attempt to vindicate S. and his work along lines earlier laid down by Madame de Beauvoir. No new material.

Endore, S. Guy. Satan's saint. New York, Crown, 1965. 312 p.   **4009**

Recreation in manner for which author is well known of S., his life, times and ideas. Attempts mainly to profit by renewed interest in subject inspired by some of the entries in this bibliography. Nothing new. " Notes " (including bibliographical references), p. 307–12.

Etiemble, René. Prosateurs du XVIIIe siècle. *In:* Histoire des littératures. *See* 3384. 3:862–65.   **4010**

Brief, but stimulating. Etiemble asks why S. never mentions Laclos and points out that the *Cahiers* of 1803–04 indicate that S. would have liked to emulate Laclos.

Faye, Jean-Pierre. Au secours de Sade. Esp 29:623–26, Nov. 1961.   **4011**

Brief, topical article showing the parallels which may be drawn between S. and certain modern authors like Céline, all to the honor of S.

Fiedler, Leslie. Prototypes and early adaptations. *In his:* Love and death in the American novel. New York, Criterion, 1960. p. 106–24, *passim.*   **4012**

The origins of " American Gothic " in S. and in the tale of terror.

Fleischmann, Wolfgang B. The divine marquis under the shadow of Lucretius. RomN 4:121–26, 1963.   **4013**

Examination of a didactic poem by S., *La vérité*, published by Lély in 1961, that finds clear borrowings from and resemblances with Lucretius as well as less convincing suggestions about the 19th and 20th centuries' cult of violence.

Fowler, Albert. The marquis de Sade in America. BA 31:353–56, 1957.   **4014**

A general review which continues and develops the article by Ryland (4052).

Gaudon, Jean. Lamartine lecteur de Sade. MerF 343:420–38, 1961.   **4015**

A comparison of certain passages of the *Chute d'un ange* with *Juliette*, whence it appears that Lamartine did more than adapt his predecessor.

Gear, Norman. The divine demon; a portrait of the marquis de Sade. London, F. Muller, 1963. 223 p.   **4016**

General biography and appreciation, tendentious in overstating the case for S. Review : Anonymous in TLS 32, Jan. 10, 1964.

Gorer, Geoffrey. The life and ideas of the marquis de Sade. New York, Norton, 1963. 250 p.   **4017**

Still considered by some to be the best presentation in English. Brought up to date and revised in this ed. First published in 1934 under title : *The revolutionary ideas of the marquis de Sade.* See Pick (4047).

— The marquis de Sade. Enc 18:72–78, April 1962.   **4018**

Brief general remarks for an English-speaking public.

Habert, Gabriel. Le marquis de Sade, auteur politique. RIPC n.s. 7:147–213, 1957.   **4019**

Excellent treatment. Approaches S. from historico-sociological point of view. Questions like S. and Malthus, S. and Machiavelli nicely analyzed, with now and then interesting suggestions susceptible of further development. Review : E. Benedetti in SF 4:160, 1960.

Heine, Maurice. Le marquis de Sade. Ed. by Gilbert Lély. Gallimard, 1950. 382 p.   **4020**

Posthumous papers of one of the first serious students of S., presented by his equally serious successor, Gilbert Lély.

The house of Sade. YFS 35: 1965. 122 p.   **4021**

Eleven articles by students of S., some well-known and established French authors (Pastoureau and Klossowski) and others, mostly professors in America (Georges May, Mark Temmer, Raymond Giraud, Jacques Guicharnaud). The issue is divided into 3 unequal parts : Novelist, Philosopher, Fomenter. The first includes a translation into English of a large segment of the *Idée sur le roman*, based on the 1946 Palimugre ed. The second contains articles originally published as prefaces to volumes of the *Œuvres complètes* as edited by the Cercle du livre précieux. The third deals with Sade's " influence " and includes stimulating discussions by Jeremy Mitchell (of Swinburne), J. H. Matthews (of surrealism), Joseph McMahon (of Durrell), and Michel Beaujour (of Peter Weiss and *Marat/Sade*).

Lacan, Jacques. Kant avec Sade. Cr 19:291–313, Apr. 1963.   **4022**

Basically a review of the *Œuvres complètes* (3972), but going far beyond usual limits. Notes the similarities between the two authors, especially if the former were better known and the latter were treated seriously, for each, at about the same time and in his own way attempted to reason about the human condition. Dense and difficult, but searching.

Lacretelle, Jacques de. Une épouse modèle : la marquise de Sade. FL 1, 4, Feb. 10, 1962.   **4023**

Curious historico-biographical inquiry with some very questionable generalities which aroused the rather indignant rebuttal of Lucien Feuillade in LN 29:147–60, Oct. 1962.

Lély, Gilbert. L'évasion du marquis de Sade à Valence d'après des documents inédits. Tro 101:108–16, May 1956.   **4024**

Presents results of sound historical research, typical of author's efforts on behalf of S.

— Introduction aux 120 journées de Sodome. MerF 331:497–504, 1957. **4025**
Excellent historical and bibliographical appreciation.

— La jalousie conjugale du marquis de Sade. LN 4:674–82, May 1956. **4026**
Appraisal of Sade's attitude in relation to his creativity.

— Une maîtresse du marquis de Sade : Mademoiselle Colet, de la Comédie italienne. CPl 12:137–47, 1951. **4027**
Two unpublished letters reveal the friendship of S. for this actress whom he almost married.

— Le marquis de Sade et Rétif de la Bretonne. MerF 331:364–66, 1957. **4028**
Brief excursus into the bitter hostility of the two authors. More important for S. than for Restif.

— La mort du marquis de Sade d'après des documents inédits. BO 18:20–26, 1956. **4029**
Important biographical details revealed in unpublished correspondence.

— Répertoire des œuvres du marquis de Sade suivi d'un tableau synoptique. RScH n.s. 70:133–47, 1953. **4030**
Analysis of printed works available to date, as also of papers in collections of Xavier, comte de Sade.

— Sade a-t-il été jaloux de Laclos ? NNRF 1: 1124–29, 1953. **4031**
Sade's jealousy indicated by various references in his works and letters motivated by a desire not only to emulate but to improve upon Laclos. *See also* Etiemble (4010).

— Sade et la berline de Varennes (24 juin 1791). MN 104:137–44, Oct. 1956. **4032**
An attempt to assess Sade's political views and reactions in the first part of the Revolution.

— Sade n'est pas l'auteur du pamphlet de Zoloé. MerF 328:182–84, 1956. **4033**
Brief analysis, invoking reasons why this work cannot be by S.

— Une supercherie littéraire de Sade : Isabelle de Bavière. MerF 340:476–88, 1960. **4034**
" Le présent texte ... annule et remplace [l']Avant-Propos à *Isabelle de Bavière* et le

chapitre correspondant de [la] *Vie du marquis de Sade.*" Detailed and circumstantial investigation of the inspiration, motives, and calligraphy of the text to prove that the novel is not based on archives, but solely on Sade's imagination. The resultant contradiction with Sade's other works is carefully noted and analyzed.

— Vie du marquis de Sade. Gallimard, 1952–57. 2 v. **4035**
Most important study to date. Based on several unpublished sources. Thorough and enlightened, although sometimes a bit turgid in style and, so, difficult. New appraisals and insights. Seemingly unsurpassed in its exactness. Translated into English by Alec Brooks as *The marquis de Sade, a biography* (London, Elek, 1961).
Reviews : H. Amer in NNRF 11:724–26, 1958; Y. Bonnefoy in Cr 14:387–95, May 1958; A. Rousseaux in FL 2, Feb. 8, 1958; H. Vallat in SF 2:451–53, 1958.

Leyser, Hans. Sade, oder der andere Florestan; eine Skizze zur Tragikomödie der Intelligenz. Antaios 2:515–26, 1960–1961. **4036**
Stimulating discussion of a general psychological problem for which S. provides the point of departure.

Lobet, Marcel. Du mal de Sade à l'ennui de Benjamin Constant. RGB 100:21–33, Sept. 1964. **4037**
Interesting article which begins with remarks about Klossowski and then examines in detail the romantic illness characterized by the vogue of *journaux intimes*, especially in Constant, while making frequent asides on the condition of modern man.

Luckow, Marion. Sade. *In her:* Die Homosexualität in der literarischen Tradition; Studien zu den Romanen von Jean Genet. Stuttgart, Enke, 1962. p. 6–11. **4038**
Brief, superficial treatment. Does not renew subject nor bring to it the additional materials of contemporary reappraisal.

Lund, Mary G. The century of de Sade. MA 8:38–44, 1963. **4039**
Establishes a neat parallel of S. with Durrell and Henry Miller, including some very apposite remarks on S. himself, such as " S. was the founder of a new science, that concerned with sexual abnormalities, and he was its principal victim " (p. 38).

Marchand, Max. Du marquis de Sade à André Gide; essai de critique psychopathologique et psychosexuelle. Oran, Fouque, 1956. 145 p. **4040**

Interesting examination of the topic, but not exhaustive.

Mead, William. The marquis de Sade : politics on a human scale. EspCr 3:188–98, 1963. **4041**

Clear, intelligent, and suggestive article, exploring the lesson of freedom as taught by S. and as it may be applied today.

Milner, Max. *In his:* Le diable dans la littérature française de Cazotte à Baudelaire. *See* 3733. 1:185–91. **4042**

Continues the examination of this topic in relation to S. begun by Klossowski in *Recherches philosophiques IV* (1934–35).

Oliver, A. Richard. Charles Nodier and the marquis de Sade. MLN 75:497–502, 1960. **4043**

Intriguing speculations on the meeting of Nodier and S., especially as reported by the former.

Paulhan, Jean. Le marquis de Sade et sa complice; ou, les revanches de la pudeur. Lilac, 1951. 130 p. **4044**

Sade's heroines, especially Justine, are S. himself. Reprinted in revised and shortened form as a preface to the Pauvert ed. of *Les infortunes de la vertu* (1959).

Pauvert, Jean-Jacques, *defendant.* L'affaire Sade; compte-rendu exact du procès intenté par le Ministère public aux Editions Jean-Jacques Pauvert. Pauvert, 1957. 137 p. **4045**

Depositions before the bar of G. Bataille, A. Breton, J. Cocteau, J. Paulhan and others, with the complete text of the defense by M. Garçon. Essential document for understanding S. in our day. Reviews : W. Babilas in Archiv 194: 356–57, 1957–58; Werner Weber *in his:* Zeit ohne Zeit (Zürich, Manesse, 1959), p. 126–32.

Paz, Octavio. Corriente alterna. Sur 274: 35–46, Jan.–Feb. 1962. **4046**

Excellent article on the powerful attraction exerted by S. on the modern reader. Examines carefully and intelligently Sade's reason for writing and his success in explaining the inexplicable and, so, in coming close to the real nature of man.

Pick, Robert. The madman of Charenton. SRL 19, 32, July 24, 1954. **4047**

Basically a review of recent work on S. in English, but goes beyond a mere résumé to give several suggestive details.

Picon, Gaëtan. Sade et l'indifférence. *In his:* L'usage de la lecture. Mercure de France, 1960. 1:55–64. **4048**

Renewed attempt at a reinterpretation of S. following a more philosophical line than many articles examined here, and more successfully.

Rahenalt, A. M. Theatricum sadicum : der Marquis de Sade und das Theater. Emsdetten, Johannson, 1965. 341 p. **4049**

A learned and fascinating investigation of the attraction which the theater had for S. If, in our own day, merely a few scenes from *La philosophie dans le boudoir* have been adapted for the stage, in his own time S. was by turns author, actor, and producer for private theaters and ended his life as director of a theater in the madhouse at Charenton.

Rougemont, Denis de. Don Juan et Sade. *In his:* L'amour et l'occident. Rev. ed. Plon, 1956. p. 194–98. **4050**

Brief note with illuminating insights into the amorous coefficients of sadism.

Ryland, Hobart. Anatole France, le marquis de Sade et Courtilz de Sandras. KFLQ 4:200–04, 1957. **4051**

Brief note showing influence and development of sadism.

— Recent developments in research on the marquis de Sade. FR 25:10–15, 1951–52. **4052**

Gives in brief compass an interesting and valuable *état présent*.

Schmidt, Albert-Marie. Duclos, Sade et la littérature féroce. RScH n.s. 62–63:146–55, 1951. **4053**

More important for Duclos than for S., but author's particular emphasis gives the key to still another worthwhile interpretation of S.

Serra, Dante. L'avventurosa vita del marchese de Sade. Milan, Ceschina, 1950. 304 p. **4054**

A popular and unimportant interpretation of Sade's life for an Italian public. Also published under title : *Il marchese di Sade; la sua vita e suoi tempi.*

Taylor, Robert E. The marquis de Sade and the first psycopathia sexualis. *In:* An analysis of the Kinsey reports on sexual behavior

in the human male and female. Ed. by
Donald P. Geddes. New York, Dutton,
1954. p. 193–210 **4055**

> Brief sketch of Sade's importance for
> modern sexology with indications of topics
> for further investigation.

— The SEXpressive S in Sade and Sartre.
YFS 11:18–24, 1953. **4056**

> The common denominators in appre-
> ciating two seemingly disparate authors
> are sexual satisfaction and personal
> liberty.

Thody, Philip. The case of the marquis de
Sade. TC 162:41–52, 1957. **4057**

> Restatement of Sade's meaning and
> value for today prepared primarily for an
> Anglo-Saxon public.

Weiss, Peter. The persecution and assas-
sination of Jean-Paul Marat as performed by
the immates of the asylum of Charenton
under the direction of the marquis de Sade;
a play, English version by Geoffrey Skelton.
Verse adaptation by Adrian Mitchell. Introduction by Peter Brook. New York, Atheneum, 1966. x, 117 p. **4058**

> Originally published in German by
> Suhrkamp at Frankfurt/Main. Intro-
> duction, p. v–vii; characters, p. viii–x;
> music composed for the first British pro-
> duction of the play by R. C. Peaslee,
> p. 110–17. Although not properly a
> learned work of scholarship, this play is so
> exact in its recreation of the last years of
> the life of S. and so important for our
> understanding of him today by reason of
> the controversy which it has aroused,
> that it is impossible not to mention it here.

Willard, Nedd. Le génie et la folie à travers les
œuvres du marquis de Sade. *In his:* Le génie
et la folie au XVIIIe siècle. Presses univ. de
France, 1963. p. 131–64. **4059**

> General survey of the themes an-
> nounced in the title, but neither far-
> reaching nor effective.

Wilson, Edmund. The documents on the
marquis de Sade. *In his:* The bit between
my teeth. New York, Farrar, Straus and
Giroux, 1965. p. 174–227. **4060**

> A supplement to and a correction of an
> earlier essay, *The vogue of the marquis de
> Sade.* Rather critical of the work of Lély.
> Brief sketch of life, some notes on his
> correspondence, with an appreciation of
> recent eds. of his work. Was S. psycho-
> logically impotent (p. 179)?

— The vogue of the marquis de Sade. *In his:*
Eight essays. New York, Doubleday, An-
chor, 1954. p. 167–80. **4061**

> Essay, published originally in *The New
> Yorker*, attempts to appreciate recent
> renewal of interest in S. A good antidote
> to the excesses of Heine, Gorer, and Lély.

Minor Novelists
(Nos. 4062–4115)

DIANA GUIRAGOSSIAN

Letessier, Fernand. Une source de Chateaubriand : Le voyage du jeune Anacharsis en
Grèce. *See* 5641. **4062**

> This careful confrontation of the 18th-
> century novel with the *Essai sur les
> révolutions* concludes that the abbé Bar-
> thélemy's influence has been exaggerated.

Parreaux, André. William Beckford, auteur
de Vathek (1760–1844); étude de la création
littéraire. Nizet, 1960. 577 p. *See* 5565. **4063**

> Definitive work on the English writer
> who presented his one famous gothic tale
> in French. Ch. 5, *Vathek et le roman
> gothique terrifiant*, and ch. 6, *Vathek et le
> conte oriental au XVIIIe siècle*, are of
> particular interest. Valuable selective
> bibliography. Index.
> Reviews : M. Milner in RHL 62:427–
> 49, 1962; F. Moussa-Mahmoud in EA
> 15:138–47, 1962; C. Pichois in MerF 343:
> 307–11, 1961.

Keys, Allwyn Charles. Antoine Bret (1717–
1792), the career of an unsuccessful man of
letters. Auckland, Univ. of Auckland, 1959.
86 p. **4064**

> Careful, objective study of a minor
> writer who is nonetheless representative
> of his time.
> Reviews : W. Barber in FS 15:67–69,
> 1961; R. Shackleton in AUMLA 13:90–
> 92, 1960; S. Weil in SF 5:165, 1961.

Lebois, André. Un roman noir en 1702 : Le
comte de Vordac. *In his:* Littérature sous
Louis XV, portraits et documents. Denoël,
1962. p. 69–103. **4065**

> Stresses the abbé Cavard's deft handling
> of gothic elements. The author calls
> for a critical ed. of this early 18th-century
> novel : " Vordac, ou le premier bréviaire
> de l'égotisme; le premier traité de la
> chasse au bonheur; le premier art de
> ' vivre dangereusement, ' dangereusement
> pour les autres " (p. 103). This excellent
> study is both lively and scholarly.

Cazotte, Jacques. Le diable amoureux. *See* 3736. **4066**

Aury, Dominique. L'aventure de Jacques Cazotte. NNRF 9:781–89, 1957. *Also in her:* Lecture pour tous. Gallimard, 1958. p. 185–98. **4067**
In this elegant presentation of *Le diable amoureux*, the emphasis is on the handling of the fantastic. While reflecting past occult superstitions and traditions, the novel also reveals specific secrets of the 18th-century illuminati.

Castex, Pierre. Le précurseur français. *In his:* Le conte fantastique en France de Nodier à Maupassant. Corti, 1951. p. 25–41. **4068**
Considers Cazotte as the true creator of the fantastic tale in France.
Reviews : H. Godin in FS 6:262–63, 1952; J. Pommier in RHL 52:241–45, 1952.

Décotes, Georges. Logique et fantastique dans Le diable amoureux. RScH n.s. 119: 305–17, 1965. **4069**
This short novel, we are told, presents two essentially contradictory aspects to the reader : (1) a psychological study; (2) an irrational adventure leading to an esthetics of the fantastic. In view of these two elements, certain events in the novel may be given diametrically opposed interpretations. Convincing *exposé*.

Dresden, S. Madame de Charrière et le goût du témoin. Neo 45:261–78, 1961. **4070**
A general, somewhat superficial treatment of Madame de C.'s life and works.

Guyot, Charly. Madame de Charrière, la Hollande au xviiie siècle et la culture française. MN 103:129–43, 1956. **4071**
Finds that the originality of Madame de C.'s novels resides " dans la vérité du sentiment et dans la parfaite adéquation de l'expression à l'idée " (p. 134).

Challes, Robert. Les illustres françoises [par Robert Chasles]. Edition critique publiée avec des documents inédits par Frédéric Deloffre. Les Belles Lettres, 1959. 2 v. **4072**
Invaluable ed. of the novel which is now generally considered of the greatest importance in the history and evolution of French fiction. By his subtle use of realism and especially psychology, Challes adumbrates Diderot, Stendhal, and Balzac among others. An introduction which is a model of erudition and precision, notes,

a bibliography, and an index complete this impeccable piece of scholarship.
Reviews : H. Coulet in RHL 61:351–52, 1961; J. Hubert in RR 51:226–29, 1960; P. Jourda in SF 4:351–52, 1960; J. Morel in IL 12:119–20, 1960; D. Potts in FS 15:66–67, 1961; R. Pouilliart in LR 16: 302–05, 1962.

Deloffre, Frédéric. A la recherche de Robert Chasles, auteur des Illustres françaises; documents inédits. RScH n.s. 95:233–54, 1959. **4073**
The author has painstakingly unearthed an important series of documents which enable him to throw considerable new light on the life and times of C.

— Un mode préstendhalien d'expression de la sensibilité à la fin du xviie siècle. CAIEF 11:9–32, 1959. **4074**
Title of article misleading for Challes's novel was published in 1713. The choice of the title was motivated by the framework of the Congress at the Collège de France where it was presented. Perceptive observations on C.'s narrative art. *See also* 3721.

Mirandola, Giorgio. Robert Chasles e le Lettres portugaises. SF 9:271–75, 1965. **4075**
Short, precise parallel showing that C. was well acquainted with the famous letters.

Roddier, Henri. Robert Challes inspirateur de Richardson et de l'abbé Prévost. RLC 21:5–38, 1947. **4076**
Conscientious study of sources and influences. Prévost and Richardson became acquainted with C.'s novel through the translation of Mrs. Penelope Aubin, an obscure English novelist. Points out the debt incurred by three of the most famous novels of the 18th century : *Manon Lescaut, Pamela*, and *Clarissa*.

Castel-Çagarriga, G. Le roman de Sophie Cottin; documents inédits. RDM 120–37, May–June 1960. **4077**
Adds a few details to our knowledge of the life of this minor novelist through a number of unpublished documents. Complements in some measure the study by Sykes (4078).

Sykes, Leslie Clifford. Madame Cottin. Oxford, Blackwell, 1949. ix, 432 p. **4078**
Definitive study in French on Madame Cottin. Part of her life drawn in large

measure from some 200 unpublished
letters. Book also ties writer's novels in
with the tradition of the 18th-century
sentimental novel. Appendix : *choix de
lettres, inédits.* Good bibliography.
Reviews : R. Fargher in FS 4:269–70,
1950; O. Fellows in BA 25:36, 1951.

Crébillon [*fils*], Claude. Les égarements du
cœur et de l'esprit. Ed. by Etiemble. Colin,
1961. xxxi, 219 p. **4079**
Excellent introduction, studded with
the usual paradoxes of C.'s self-appointed
champion. *See also* 3736.
Reviews : E. Caramaschi in SF 6:155–
56, 1962; P. Delbouille in RBP 42:274–
76, 1964; M.-J. Durry in NNRF 19:527–
29, 1962; M. Foucault in Cr 18:597–611,
July 1962.

Cherpack, Clifton. An essay on Crébillon
fils. Durham, Duke univ. press, 1962.
xv, 190 p. **4080**
The definitive work on this unjustly
neglected novelist who is gradually coming into his own has yet to be written.
The present study, however, offers a
generally well-informed introduction to
C.'s fiction. Dominant themes are outlined and straightforward summaries of
plots are given.
Reviews : D. Day in MLR 44:145–46,
1964; J. Sgard in RHL 63:474–75, 1963;
L. Sozzi in SF 7:160–61, 1963; A. Vartanian in EspCr 3:87–89, 1963.

Day, Douglas A. Crébillon fils, ses exils et
ses rapports avec l'Angleterre; avec deux
lettres inédites. RLC 33:180–91, 1959.
See 5646. **4081**
Shows how little and how poorly C.'s
life is known. Corrects errors repeated by
biographers, especially relating to C.'s
presumed three exiles. There is, according to Day, no proof that C. ever went to
England. His popularity was great among
such illustrious Englishmen as Walpole,
Gray, Sterne, Hume, etc., however, and
he established personal relationships with
them during their visits to France.

— On the dating of three novels by Crébillon
fils. MLR 56:391–92, 1961. **4082**
Establishes with the support of documents the dates of the original eds. of
Tanzaï et Néadarné (1734), *Ah! quel conte*
(1754), and *Le sopha* (Feb. 1742).

Macchia, Giovanni. Il sorriso di Crébillon
fils. *In his:* Il paradiso della ragione; studi
letterari sulla Francia. Bari, Laterza, 1960.
p. 208–15. **4083**

Shrewd insights on the importance of
C. in the development of the psychological novel in France.

Haac, Oscar A. L'amour dans les collèges
jésuites : une satire anonyme du dix-
huitième siècle. SVEC 18:95–111, 1961.
4084
The title of the article is somewhat
misleading. It is, in fact, a detailed and
meticulously documented account of the
burlesque novel *L'amour apostat* by
Augustin Delmas, a Jesuit father. Effectively combining realism and satire, this
" intelligent, lively " novel gives us
valuable, firsthand details about life in the
Jesuit colleges of the day. Biographical
sketch of Delmas appears as appendix.

Denon, Dominique-Vivant. Point de lendemain. *See* 3735. **4085**

Duclos, Charles Pinot. Les confessions du
comte de ***. *See* 3735. **4086**

— Madame de Selves. (Episode from Les
confessions du comte de ***.) *See* 3735.
4087
Meister, Paul. Charles Duclos, 1704–1772.
Geneva, Droz, 1956. 278 p. *See* 3427. **4088**
Indispensable for the study of D. Adds
much to our knowledge of the man whom
Meister considers superior to his work.
Last third of the book is devoted to an
analysis of D.'s fictional and moralisitic
productions. Unpublished letters, a good
bibliography, and an index complete this
conscientious monograph.
Reviews : F. Green in MLR 52:439–42,
1957; A. Pizzorusso in SF 1:499–500,
1957; J. Spink in FS 22:71–72, 1958.

Schmidt, Albert-Marie. Duclos, Sade et la
littérature féroce. *See* 4053. **4089**
Illuminating parallel between *Histoire
de Madame de Luz* and *Justine.* In the
confrontation of the two unfortunate
heroines of these novels, the author
establishes a disquieting similitude of
doctrine and tone between Duclos and
the inmate of Charenton.

Humphrey, George. Victor ou l'enfant de la
forêt et le roman terrifiant. FR 33:137–46,
1959–60. **4090**
In viewing the influence of Thomson,
Young, Gray, and especially Mrs. Rad-
cliffe on Ducray-Duminil, the author
establishes the lack of originality of the
French writer.

Genlis, Stéphanie-Félicité Ducrest de Saint-Aubain. Mademoiselle de Clermont. *See* 3735. **4091**

Berthoud, Dorette. Le duc de Chartres et Madame de Genlis en Suisse. RPar 69:108–18, Feb. 1962. **4092**

Throws new light on the sojourn of Madame de Genlis and her former pupil in Switzerland during the Terror. Unpublished documents utilized.

Wahba, Magdi. Madame de Genlis in England. CL 13:221–38, 1961. **4093**

At the end of the 18th century, the reputation of Madame de Genlis in England was more widespread than that of Voltaire and Rousseau. Well documented but somewhat verbose.

Walker, T. C. Madame de Genlis and Rousseau. RR 43:95–108, 1952. **4094**

Detailed account of Madame de Genlis' relationship with and changing attitudes toward Jean-Jacques.

Wyndham, Violet. Madame de Genlis, a biography. New York, Roy publishers, 1960. 304 p. **4095**

Pleasantly written biography, particularly appropriate for the general, cultivated reading public. Reliable sources and anecdotes in abundance.

Review: F. Orlando in SF 4:359, 1960.

Mish, Charles C. Madame de Gomez and La belle assemblée. RLC 34:212–25, 1960. **4096**

Having recalled the considerable esteem and popularity enjoyed both in France and in England by Madame de Gomez, author of innumerable romances in the heroic tradition, the critic analyzes her most popular work, *Les journées amusantes*, translated into English as *La belle assemblée*, and considers it as the " representative " piece of fiction of the 1720's. Highly worthwhile article.

Defourneaux, Marcelin. Les lettres péruviennes en Espagne. *In:* Mélanges offerts à Marcel Bataillon par les hispanistes français et publiés par les soins de Maxime Chevalier, Robert Ricard et Noël Salomon. Bordeaux, Féret et fils, 1962. p. 412–23. (BH, 64 *bis*) **4097**

Madame de Graffigny's best-seller enjoyed a tremendous success in Spain through unreliable translations, when it was already forgotten in France. Highly commendable scholarship.

Schmidt, Albert-Marie. Grainville et le récit d'anticipation. LetN 41–43, Nov. 11, 1959. **4098**

Excellent brief account of the pitiful existence of the author of an early specimen of science fiction.

Hamilton, Anthony. Mémoires du Chevalier de Gramont. Texte établi, annoté et présenté par Claire-Eliane Engel, avec une notice bibliophilique de Max Brun. Monaco, Editions du Rocher, 1958. 353 p. **4099**

Good critical ed. of these lively and remarkably well-written pseudo-memoirs. *See also* 3736.

Review : F. Orlando in SF 4:153, 1960.

Duhamel, Georges. Vues sur Hamilton. MerF 307:5–20; 238–55, 1949. **4100**

Composed in 1944, this lively article contains delightful portraits of Hamilton and his brother-in-law, Gramont, and a subtle analysis of Hamilton's art.

Engel, Claire-Eliane. Le véritable chevalier de Gramont. RDM 298–315, May 15, 1960. **4101**

Well-documented article which follows the life of Philibert de Gramont, Hamilton's brother-in-law and model, from the conclusion of the *Mémoires* in 1664 to his death in 1707.

Barchilon, Jacques. A note on the original text of Beauty and the beast. MLR 56:81–82, 1961. **4102**

In a 1756 ed. of *Le magasin des enfants* by Madame Le Prince de Beaumont, acquired by the Houghton Library of Harvard, the author has found the original text of the famous tale. Stresses her mastery of style and remarkable handling of material.

Louvet de Couvrai. Les aventures du chevalier de Faublas. *See* 3736. **4103**

Dutourd, Jean. Faublas. *In his:* Le fond et la forme : essai alphabétique sur la morale et le style. Gallimard, 1958. 1:79–91. **4104**

Lively, sympathetic presentation of the novel and its charming hero.

Rustin, J. Amour, magie et vertu : Les veillées de Thessalie (1731–1741) de Mademoiselle de Lussan. BLS 41:287–302, 1962–63. **4105**

Generally known as an author of historical romances, Mlle de Lussan adroitly combines the pastoral genre, the novel of witchcraft, and the fairy tale under the same cover. The narrative technique of the novelist is greatly admired in this scholarly article.

Maubert de Gouvest, Jean-Henri. Les lettres iroquoises [présentées par] Enea Balmas. Nizet, 1962. 250 p. **4106**

Les lettres iroquoises, one of the numerous books inspired by the success of the Lettres persanes, occupies a more important place in the history of ideas than in the evolution of the novel. Substantial introduction precedes the text of 43 letters. Bibliographical footnotes.

Reviews : D. d'Angeli in CulF 10:201–04, 1963; R. Mercier in RLC 38:159–60, 1964.

Vianu, Hélène. De la mouche au Neveu de Rameau. RScH n.s. 112:503–15, 1963. **4107**

Hints that Diderot might have used a passage in Mouhy's novel as a source. Good article, presented in a lively style.

Juin, Hubert. Un portrait d'Andréa de Nerciat. In his: Chroniques sentimentales. Mercure de France, 1962. p. 61–91. **4108**

Short, provocative essay on N.'s life and works. This minor novelist's clandestine fiction is, the author declares, far better written and much closer to depicting 18th-century immorality than has been generally supposed.

Laufer, Roger. Un roman oublié du début du xviiie siècle : L'infortuné napolitain ou les aventures et mémoires du signor Rosselly. RScH n.s. 110:153–59, 1963. **4109**

According to Laufer, this novel deserves to be remembered for both its historical and its literary value. Sound reconstruction of the biography of the author, Lucio Roselli, a Neapolitan refugee living in Holland. Contemporary writers—widely quoted—testify to the success of the work.

Sénac de Meilhan, Gabriel. L'émigré. See 3736. **4110**

Stavan, Henry A. Un roman de 1793 : L'émigré de Sénac de Meilhan. RScH n.s. 119:319–27, 1965. **4111**

This sketchy analysis concentrates on two characters who presumably represent the dual personality of the author.

Tencin, Claudine Alexandrine Guérin de. Mémoires du comte de Comminges. See 3735. **4112**

Derla, Luigi. Saggio sui Mémoires du comte de Comminges di Claudine de Tencin. Contributi del Seminario di filologia moderna dell'Università Cattolica del Sacro Cuore di Milano, serie francese 1:75–104, 1959. **4113**

Examines the novel in the framework of 18th-century French fiction. The structure of Madame de T.'s story suggests a close affinity with La princesse de Clèves, but the Cornelian ideal implicit in the 17th-century novel is replaced by that of romantic sensibility. The Comte de Comminges also foreshadows the roman noir. Thoroughgoing analysis.

Herold, J. Christopher. Madame de Tencin. In his: Love in five temperaments. See 3403. **4114**

Based on secondhand information but highly readable, sprightly presentation of Madame de Tencin.

Tiphaigne de la Roche, Charles-François. Giphantie : textes présentés par Elie-Charles Flamand. NNRF 19:964–75, 1962. **4115**

Excerpts from this little-known example of science fiction are preceded by a brief review of the strange life and works of its author, a Norman physician.

CHAPTER V. LE MOUVEMENT PHILOSOPHIQUE

(Nos. 4116–4396)

Lester G. Crocker, John N. Pappas, Jean Perkins, Virgil W. Topazio, *and* Aram Vartanian

General Studies
(Nos. 4116–4165)

Lester G. Crocker

Albaum, Martin. The moral defenses of the physiocrats' laissez-faire. JHI 16:179–97, 1955. **4116**

Useful analysis of basic assumptions underlying physiocratic theories and their implementation in theory.

Amann, Peter. Taine, Tocqueville, and the paradox of the Ancien Régime. RR 52: 183–95, 1961. **4117**

Analyzes relation between the two writers, leading to explanation of inconsistency in Taine's work.

Aspects de l'illuminisme au XVIIIᵉ siècle. Ed. by H. Roudil. *In:* TSJC 2–4:1960. 223 p. **4118**

Collection of essays of unequal quality and interest on 19 aspects of Illuminism.

Besse, Guy. Marx, Engels et le XVIIIᵉ siècle français. SVEC 24: 155–70, 1963. **4119**

Excellent précis from Marxist viewpoint. Less inclusive than Rihs (4145), but more pointed. Emphasis on Rousseau. Like all Marxist articles on subject, limited to what Marx, Engels, or orthodox doctrine says relationship is, and omits many of deeper, more significant elements.

Bredvold, Louis I. The brave new world of the Enlightenment. Ann Arbor, Univ. of Michigan press, 1961. 164 p. **4120**

A thoroughly distorted view of the Enlightenment, in the tradition of its Christian enemies, with Burke held up as the savior.

Review : L. Crocker in JMH 34:331–32, 1962.

Cobban, Alfred. In search of humanity. New York, Braziller, 1960. 254 p. *See* 4938. **4121**

Attempt to re-examine character of Enlightenment and its role in history. Really an apology : some excellent analyses and useful, if sketchy, summaries. Arbitrarily excludes from Enlightenment whatever does not fit into predetermined scheme and judgments. Distorted or oversimplified as general picture, though accurate in many particulars. Continues older tradition of seeing Enlightenment as all " light " and as simple unilinear development.

Reviews : Anon. in TLS 484, July 29, 1960; C. Brinton in AHR 66:694–95, 1960–61; L. Coser in AJS 66:411, 1960–61; O. Fellows in SRL 20–21, Aug. 20, 1960; A. Goodwin in EHR 77: 167–68, 1962.

Crocker, Lester G. An age of crisis; man and world in eighteenth-century French thought. Baltimore, Johns Hopkins press, 1959. xx, 496 p. *See* 4545. **4122**

First volume of a synthetical reinterpretation of Enlightenment, with axis on moral problems. Broad study of period. Finds its organic wholeness in dynamic tension of polarities. Postulates relation among metaphysics, psychology, ethics, and politics. This volume studies first two as ground for ethical decisions. Emphasis on challenge of moral skepticism. Three sections : Man in the Universe, Freedom and Determinism, Human Nature and Motivation.

Reviews : A. Bingham in MLR 56: 273–74, 1961; C. Brinton in AHR 65: 893–94, 1959–60; H. Brown in JHI 22: 121–30, 1961; C. Hendel in Ethics 72: 202–13, 1961–62; J. Loy in RR 51:132–35, 1960; P. Meyer in MLQ 21:182–84, 1960; L. Rosenfield in FR 35:333–34, 1961–62; A. Scaglione in SF 4:504–06, 1960; R. Shackleton in FS 16:180–82, 1962; L. Thielemann in CL 12:267–70, 1960.

— Nature and culture; ethical thought in the French Enlightenment. Baltimore, Johns Hopkins press, 1963. xx, 540 p. **4123**

Concluding volume deals with ethical theory. " Nature and Genesis of Moral Experience" includes study of natural law theories, moral sense, experiential theories, conscience, justice and law, reason and feeling. " Moral Values " analyzes " Utilitarian Synthesis," most characteristic of period, opposition to it, and " Nihilistic Dissolution," culminating in Sade. Import of ethical theories for politics (liberal and regimented or collectivist societies). In both, historical role of Enlightenment a dual one, born of its own inner tensions. Polarity of nature and culture seen as most defining dynamic tension of Enlightenment.

Reviews : A. Bingham in MLR 60:119–20, 1965; P. Meyer in MLQ 25:110–15, 1964; R. Oake in FR 38:574–76, 1964; J. Roger in RHL 64:490–92, 1964; D. Schier in MP 67:167–69, 1964; R. Shackleton in FS 20:65–67, 1966; P. Vernière in DS 6:353–62, 1964.

— Recent interpretations of the French Enlightenment. CHM 8:426–56, 1964. **4124**

Critical examination of general interpretations of the Enlightenment from 1920 to present. Sees marked shift in attitudes and radical re-examination of period with cataclysm of World War II as watershed. Newer views uncover greater complexity and closer relation to trends and crises of later times.

Desautels, Alfred R. Les Mémoires de Trévoux et le mouvement des idées au xviiie siècle (1701–1734). Rome, Institutum historicum S. I., 1956. xxvii, 256 p. *See* 5529. **4125**

Careful study of evolution of ideas in *Journal de Trévoux* with regard to developments in metaphysics, physics, ethics, education, Jansenist and other theological disputations, and the fight against religious skepticism.

Reviews : R. Mercier in RHL 59:224–25, 1959: J. Pappas in FR 31:81–83, 1957–58; A. Pizzorusso in SF 1:497, 1957; R. Shackleton in FS 13:65–67, 1959.

Ehrard, Jean. L'idée de nature en France dans la première moitié du xviiie siècle. S.E.V.P.E.N., 1963. 2 v. **4126**

Vast erudition and penetrating analyses. Includes science, theology and religion, metaphysics, esthetics, ethics, politics. Less effort at interpretation and synthesis.

" Nature " considered dominant idea of period (*see* Mauzi [4136], " happiness "). Reservations possible about " isolationist " crosscutting as valid general interpretation (perspective, numerous meanings of thematic idea). Nevertheless, important and suggestive study.

Fabre, Jean. Lumières et romantisme. Klincksieck, 1963. xii, 302 p. **4127**

Studies, written with virtuosity and brilliance, on the themes of energy and nostalgia from Rousseau to Mickiewicz. Introduction a valuable commentary on attitudes to Enlightenment. Chapters on Voltaire, Diderot and Rousseau of particular interest.

Fleischmann, Wolfgang B. The debt of the Enlightenment to Lucretius. SVEC 25:631–43, 1963. **4128**

Lucretius' influence largely literary and conventional; its forms and limits are examined. Claims he was too antireligious for the *philosophes*. For contrary view, *see* Roger (4146).

Frankel, Charles. The faith of reason. New York, King's crown press, 1948. x, 165 p. **4129**

Penetrating study of idea of progress in relation to present impasse of that idea. Search for what was right and wrong in 18th-century concepts. Emphasis on two approaches to scientific method, their influence on view of history. Some serious reservations must be made to author's method and conclusions.

Reviews : C. Brinton in Nation 724, June 26, 1948; H. Parker in JMH 21:142–43, 1949; G. Sabine in AHR 54:126–27, 1948–49.

Gawlick, Günter. Cicero and the Enlightenment. SVEC 25:657–79, 1963. **4130**

Cicero's influence on several English and French writers of the early 18th century.

Havens, George R. The age of ideas. *See* 3383. **4131**

Excellent introduction to major 18th-century authors. Scholarly but most readable.

Healey, F. G. The Enlightenment view of homo faber. SVEC 25:837–59, 1963. **4132**

Useful account of development of interest in crafts and craftsmen from Bacon and Colbert to apogee of *manufactures;* writings on subject, especially

Encyclopédie and *Descriptions des arts et métiers;* place of movement in Enlightenment.

Labriolle-Rutherford, Marie-Rose de. L'évolution de la notion du luxe depuis Mandeville jusqu'à la Révolution. SVEC 26:1025–36, 1963.   **4133**
Raises important questions but treatment is inadequate, even inaccurate (art. *Luxe* attributed to Diderot). Good on defense of inequality.

Laufer, Roger. Style rococo, style des lumières. Corti, 1963. 154 p. *See* 3725.
                                              4134
A brilliant if not always convincing attempt to reduce the 18th century to the rococo, defined as a tension between reason and sensibility, classicism and baroque, bourgeois and aristocratic.
Reviews: P. Brady in SF 7:511–14, 1963; J. Cocking in FS 19:91–92, 1965; A. Pizzorusso in Bel 19:738–42, 1964.

Lough, John. An introduction to eighteenth-century France. London, Longmans, 1960. 349 p.   **4135**
Solid and interesting study of background of social, political, and economic life in 18th-century France. Invaluable for students.
Reviews: Anon. in TLS 430, July 8, 1960; E. Acomb in AHR 66:796–97, 1960–61; C. Brinton in CHR 41:235–37, 1960; A. Freer in SF 5:564, 1961; D. Potts in MLR 56:426–27, 1961; R. Shackleton in FS 15:368–70, 1961.

Mauzi, Robert. L'idée du bonheur dans la littérature et la pensée françaises au XVIIIᵉ siècle. Colin, 1960. 725 p. *See* 3730.   **4136**
Vast study containing many valuable ideas, but too long and insufficiently synthesized. Subtle analyses of feelings and ideas, including literary works and personal documents. Fine realization of complexity of period. Courageous exploration of false compromises and failures in Enlightenment's quest for happiness and attempt to reconcile it with moral values. Emphasizes pessimism. Overlooks or underestimates several important factors in climate of the age.
Reviews: L. Crocker in MLQ 24:79–87, 1963; C. Guyot in RHL 62:429–32, 1962; J. Loy in MLN 78:216–20, 1963; Gita May in RR 52:140–44, 1961; J. Spink in FS 17:172–73, 1963.

Meyer, Paul H. The attitude of the Enlight-

enment towards the Jew. SVEC 26:1161–1205, 1963. *See* 4163.   **4137**
Illuminating and well-written contribution to little-known area. Traces evolving attitudes in western Europe from 1648 to 1789. Emphasizes *philosophes'* combination of liberalism (tolerance, rights, equality) and contrary anti-Jewish prejudice. Shows that many factors led to emancipation of Jews.

— The French Revolution and the legacy of the philosophes. FR 30:429–34, 1956–57.
                                              4138
Brief but interesting summary of attitudes toward French Revolution among those *philosophes* who experienced it.

Mortier, Roland. Unité ou scission du siècle des lumières? SVEC 26:1207–21, 1963.   **4139**
Insists convincingly on complexity of Enlightenment within over-all unity: a *concert discordant.* Emphasizes importance of nonrational (passions, uneasiness); separation between Rousseau and Romanticism, and his affinity to *philosophes.* Criticizes P. Hazard. Contrary to Romanticism, Enlightenment wishes to harmonize reason and feeling. Calls attention to current revisions in interpretation of Enlightenment.

Neill, Thomas P. The physiocrats' concept of economics. QJE 63:532–53, 1949.   **4140**
Good analysis of basic presuppositions, theories, and methods of physiocratic school. Somewhat more philosophical than following article.

— Quesnay and physiocracy. JHI 9:153–73, 1948. *See* 5431.   **4141**
Good analysis of methods and tenets of physiocratic school with emphasis on Quesnay.

Pappas, John N. Berthier's Journal de Trévoux and the philosophes. Geneva, Institut et musée Voltaire, 1957. 238 p. (SVEC, 3) *See* 4662 and 5532.   **4142**
After brief history of *Journal de Trévoux,* studies period under Berthier's editorship (1745–62), particularly its relationships with Montesquieu, Voltaire, Rousseau, Diderot, the *Encyclopédie,* and the Enlightenment in general.
Reviews: R. Taylor in MLN 74:465–66, 1959; F. Vial in RR 49:129–32, 1958.

Popkin, Richard H. Scepticism in the Enlightenment. SVEC 26:1321–45, 1963.
                                              4143

Important and original contribution situating Enlightenment in relation to mainstream of epistemological thought. Traces evolution of attitudes to skepticism and refusal of Enlightenment, wrapped up in utilitarian optimism, to recognize significance of its challenge, fundamental to modern thought. Enlightenment, however, did not avoid this challenge in moral speculation, thus splitting the dual problem posed by Sextus Empiricus.

Proust, Jacques. Travaux soviétiques récents sur le XVIIIᵉ siècle français. *See* 3367.
4144
A useful list with brief commentary.

Rihs, Charles. L'influence du siècle des lumières sur la formation du matérialisme historique. SVEC 26:1389–1416, 1963. **4145**
A Marxist view of the relation of the *philosophes* to Marxist theory. Considered as fathers of Communism, but differences also stressed. Prolix yet incomplete (e.g., on Rousseau); goes over much already well known. Worth reading despite undisguised prejudice and propaganda.

Roger, Jacques. Les sciences de la vie dans la pensée française du XVIIIᵉ siècle. Colin, 1963. 842 p. **4146**
Most complete and illuminating study of ideas and systems concerning living nature in 18th century.
Reviews : L. Crocker in RR 56:142–45, 1965; Jean-Jacques in RUL 18:780–81, 1963–64; Y. Laissus in RHS 17:182–91, 1964; M. Roelens in RScH n.s. 116:595–600, 1964; A. Vartanian in DS 6:339–52, 1964.

Rosso, Corrado. Moralisti del bonheur. Turin, Edizioni di Filosofia, 1954. 99 p.
4147
Scholarly work, still valid for the figures discussed (Gassendi, Levesque de Pouilly, Robinet) despite broader study of Mauzi (4136).

Sagnac, Philippe. La formation de la société française moderne. Presses univ. de France, 1945–46. 2 v. **4148**
Important study of social and political structure and evolution with attention to intellectual forces.
Reviews : L. Gottschalk in JMH 20:137–48, 1948; G. L. in Rhist 202:288–89, 1949.

Saisselin, Rémy. Le passé, le goût et l'histoire. SVEC 27:1445–55, 1963. **4149**

Defends thesis that 18th century was not entirely or essentially relativist. Interesting for observations on Voltaire's historiography and affinity between history and *bon goût*.

Sampson, Ronald Victor. Progress in the age of reason. Cambridge, Harvard univ. press, 1956. 259 p. **4150**
Reinterpretation of meaning of idea of progress in terms of concepts of scientific method and philosophies of history which superseded natural law theories. Goes over some of same ground as Frankel (4129), but new emphasis on utopianism and preparation for control of behavior. Exaggerates optimism of period. Too narrow in breadth. Arbitrary selection does not adequately represent Enlightenment. Relation between decline of natural law and philosophies of history not convincing. Includes French and German writers. Emphasizes weaknesses of Enlightenment.
Reviews : S. Idzerda in AHR 63:658–59, 1957–58; R. Jones in Hist 21:215–16, 1958–59; R. Milliband in PSQ 28:298–300, 1957; J. Plamenatz in PoS 5:330–32, 1957; A. Taylor in NSN 53:518, 1957.

Stelling-Michaud, Sven. Lumières et politique. SVEC 27:1519–43, 1963. **4151**
Main currents of 18th-century political thought as seen from the Marxist viewpoint of class struggle and economic interests, and in relation to Marxist doctrine into which some aspects of it flowed. Often disputable, but thought-provoking and not to be overlooked.

Stromberg, R. N. History in the eighteenth century. JHI 12:295–304, 1951. **4152**
Distinguishes interest in history and " historical-mindedness." 18th-century historians founded modern historical methods. But historicism prevented by preconceptions used in approaching past experience by abstract, analytical, and universalist idea of man and by didactic use of history to discover and teach laws and truths. Also, emphasis on accidental and capricious, rather than theory of causation or understanding of organic continuity of culture. Du Bos and Vico exceptions.

Talmon, Jacob Leib. The rise of totalitarian democracy. Boston, Beacon press, 1952. xi, 366 p. **4153**
Revolutionary study of the Enlightenment as seedbed of modern totalitarianism of the left. Marks a clear break with earlier

interpretations which view Enlightenment as fountainhead of liberalism only. Some dubious assertions resulting from limited knowledge of the period. Greater part of book devoted to French Revolution and Babouvist conspiracy.

Reviews : Anon. in TLS 350, May 30, 1952; R. Crossman in NSN 44:578, 1952; G. Lefèbvre in Rhist 211:144–46, 1954; S. Possony in AAA 282:177–78, 1952; G. Sabine in PhR 62:147–51, 1953; A. Taylor in ManG 4, Feb. 6, 1952.

Tonelli, Giorgio. The law of continuity in the eighteenth century. SVEC 27:1619–38, 1963.   **4154**

Sketchy view, not without interest, of debate over principle of continuity and its implications, which was characterized by ineptitude and intrusion of personal prejudices and polemics.

Topazio, Virgil W. Art criticism in the Enlightenment. SVEC 27:1639–56, 1963. *See* 5491.   **4155**

Useful account of development of art criticism. Re-evaluates some forgotten figures and downgrades role and value of Diderot.

Trevor-Roper, Hugh. The historical philosophy of the Enlightenment. SVEC 27: 1667–87, 1963.   **4156**

Masterly analysis of development of historical writing in the 18th century. Favorable to Enlightenment historiography, as compared with 19th century. Contrasts with Stromberg (4152).

Vernière, Paul. L'idée d'humanité au XVIIIᵉ siècle. SG 15:171–79, 1962.   **4157**

Important article tracing rise and development of the idea of " humanity " in 18th century.

— Spinoza et la pensée française avant la Révolution. Presses univ. de France, 1954. 2 v.   **4158**

Brilliant study of Spinozism—its influence, its diffusion, its deformations, the quarrels around it—from 1663 to end of period. Combines philosophical and historical approach. Emphasis on relation to Leibnizianism, empiricism, and materialism.

Reviews : R. Mercier in RHL 57:252–54, 1957; J. Spink in FS 9:271–73, 1955.

Voitle, Robert. The reason of the English Enlightenment. SVEC 27:1735–74, 1963.   **4159**

Incisive analysis of forms and limits of reason in 17th– and early 18th-century England; relations between reason and sentiment.

Vyverberg, Henry. Historical pessimism in the French Enlightenment. Harvard univ. press, 1958. viii, 253 p.   **4160**

Sound investigation of questions which neither Frankel (4129) nor Sampson (4150) had asked : how widespread was doctrine of progress, what shadings did it have, what currents opposed or denied it. Traces roots and progress of pessimism. Fully understands relation of Sade to Enlightenment and his significance. Broken and sketchy development.

Reviews : I. Berlin in FS 14:167–70, 1960; L. Gershoy in AHR 64:945–46, 1958–59; J. Schapiro in JMH 32:61–62, 1960.

Weightman, John G. Critical judgment and eighteenth-century literature. AUMLA 18: 153–66, 1962.   **4161**

Challenges overevaluation of 18th-century literature. Trenchant, provocative, controversial.

Weil, F. La franc-maçonnerie en France jusqu'en 1755. SVEC 27:1787–1815, 1963.   **4162**

Erudite, somewhat discursive inquiry into early years (1735–55) of Freemasonry in the provinces.

Weinryb, Bernard D. Enlightenment and German-Jewish Haskalah. SVEC 27:1817–47, 1963.   **4163**

Differs from P. Meyer's article (4137) in emphasis on internal evolution of Jewish thought and feeling. Brilliant scholarship and insights, but some simplified ideas about Enlightenment (e.g., the " natural order " was an ancient order to which we should return).

White, Howard B. The influence of Bacon on the philosophes. SVEC 27:1849–69, 1963.   **4164**

Bacon's influence on d'Alembert, Montesquieu, and Rousseau. Some interesting points, but turgid and diffuse.

Willey, Basil. The eighteenth-century background; studies on the idea of nature in the thought of the period. London, Chatto and Windus, 1940. viii, 302 p. **4165**

First-rate study of connection between " nature " and " reason " (including providentialism, optimism, natural morality) in England, followed by Humean revolution and new association of nature and feeling. Includes chapter on d'Holbach.

Pierre Bayle
(Nos. 4166–4186)

JEAN A. PERKINS

Bayle, Pierre. Historical and critical dictionary; selections. Translated with an introduction and notes by Richard H. Popkin, with the assistance of Craig Brush. Indianapolis, Bobbs-Merrill, 1965. xliv, 456 p. **4166**

Contains selections from 40 articles and an excellent brief introduction which outlines the main problems in the study of B. Includes a useful critical bibliography.

Adam, Antoine. Pierre Bayle. *In his:* Histoire de la littérature française au dix-septième siècle. Domat, 1956. 5:229–50. **4167**

An excellent introduction to B.'s life and works. Defends point of view that B. remained a Christian thinker. Suggests a number of interesting topics for further research.

Barber, William Henry. Leibniz in France, from Arnauld to Voltaire; a study in French reactions to Leibnizianism, 1670–1760. *See* 5815. **4168**

Chapters 4 and 5 give a scholarly and interesting account of the intellectual interplay between B. and Leibniz, showing the difference in their views on reason and liberty.

— Pierre Bayle : faith and reason. *In:* StGR, p. 109–25. **4169**

A pioneer study replacing B. in Calvinist intellectual milieu in which reason is denigrated and faith offered as only answer to ultimate questions. Review : A. Barbier in FS 7:59–61, 1953.

Garin, Eugenio. Per una storia dei rapporti fra Bayle e l'Italia. ATSL n.s. 9:209–21, 1958–59. **4170**

B.'s ideas about Italy and his influence there, primarily on Vico. Complements article by Thijssen-Schoute in Dibon (4173) and supersedes Courines (1122).

Haase, Erich. Einführung in die Literatur des Refuge; der Beitrag der französischen Protestanten zur Entwicklung analytischer Denkformen am Ende des 17. Jahrhunderts.

Berlin, Duncker und Humbolt, 1959. 587 p. **4171**

Monumental study of the main currents of thought among French Protestants in exile, primarily B., Jurieu, and Le Clerc. B. is seen against background of refugee problems and quarrels, and his contribution to modern historiography is stressed. Rex calls this the " most substantial contribution to French literature of the later Seventeenth Century since Hazard's *La crise de la conscience européenne* " (BHR 23:206, 1961).
Reviews : E. Labrousse in BSHP 105:194–97, 1959; J. Orcibal in RHL 61:254–57, 1961; R. Popkin in MLN 76:273–76, 1961; W. Rex in BHR 23:206–12, 1961.

— Quelques pages inédites de la correspondance de Bayle. BSHP 103:267–88, 1957. **4172**

Nine unpublished letters with careful documentation and good instructions. Shows what needs to be done on B.'s correspondence.

Historisch genootschap Roterodamum. Pierre Bayle, le philosophe de Rotterdam. Ed. by Paul Dibon and R. H. Popkin. Amsterdam, Elsevier and Paris, Vrin, 1959. 255 p. **4173**

Contents: P. Dibon, *Redécouverte de Bayle;* R. H. Popkin, *Pierre Bayle's place in 17th-century scepticism;* N. C. Hazewinkel, *Pierre Bayle à Rotterdam;* A. Robinet, *La philosophie de Pierre Bayle devant les philosophies de Malebranche et de Leibniz;* L. Kolakowsky, *Pierre Bayle, critique de la métaphysique spinoziste de la substance;* P. J. S. Whitmore, *Bayle's criticism of Locke;* E. R. Labrousse, *Les coulisses du Journal de Bayle;* R. Shackleton, *Bayle and Montesquieu;* C. L. Thijssen-Schoute, *La diffusion européenne des idées de Bayle;* E. Haase, *Un épilogue à la controverse Jurieu-Bayle;* R. H. Popkin, *An unpublished letter of Pierre Bayle to Pierre Jurieu;* E. R. Labrousse, *Documents relatifs à l'offre d'une chaire de philosophie à l'Université de Franeker au printemps de 1684;* E. R. Labrousse, *Documentation iconographique; Index des noms de personnes.*
Essential work. First 2 essays are most controversial with attempt to replace B. in 17th-century stream of ideas. Labrousse's article on B.'s *Journal* draws on unpublished correspondence to show background of *Nouvelles de la république des lettres.*
Reviews : A. Crisafulli in RR 52:62–64, 1961; A. Deregibus in SF 4:299–303,

1960; H. Dieckmann in JHI 22:131–36, 1961; J. Lameere in RIP 13:361–63, 1959; D. Potts in YWML 21:66–67, 1959; H. Robinson in AHR 65:378–79, 1959–60; K. Sandberg in MP 58:128–30, 1960–61; J. Spink in FS 15:64–65, 1961; R. Vancourt on Cr 16:879–92, Oct. 1960; R. Zuber in RHL 61:257–58, 1961.

Labrousse, Elisabeth. Inventaire critique de la correspondance de Pierre Bayle. Vrin, 1961 [i.e., 1960]. 413 p.   **4174**

Indispensable guide to B.'s correspondence, showing desperate need for a scholarly ed., which is now in preparation by Labrousse in the series AIHS. Introduction gives critical history of ms collections and eds. Followed by 2 lists, a chronological one and an annotated alphabetical one of 260 correspondents.
Reviews : W. Barber in FS 16:179–80, 1962; D. Potts in YWML 23:64, 1961.

— La méthode critique chez Pierre Bayle et l'histoire. RIP 11:450–66, 1957.   **4175**

An important study of B.'s critical method showing how he cast doubt on all aspects of historical fact, including the witness himself. This was an extension of the Cartesian method to a new area which caused his readers to undergo " une prise de conscience critique " (p. 466).

— Obscurantisme et lumière chez Pierre Bayle. SVEC 26:1037–48, 1963.   **4176**

Shows major differences between B. and *philosophes* and how the latter misunderstood his anticlericalism as being anti-Christian.

— Pierre Bayle. The Hague, Nijhoff, 1963–64. 2 v.   **4177**

Definitive biography supplementing Desmaizeaux with new research. Stresses Calvinist upbringing and continuing Protestant influence throughout B.'s life. In basic agreement with Bastide (1115) on problem of authorship of *Avis aux réfugiés*. V. 2 organized around 3 major themes : factual truth, rational truth, and revealed truth. Out of these B. evolved his own doctrine of tolerance based on liberty of conscience.
Reviews : C. Butterworth in Rmet 17: 306, 1963–64; H. Robinson in AHR 69: 829–30, 1963.

Mason, Haydn T. Pierre Bayle and Voltaire. London, Oxford univ. press, 1963. x, 159 p. *See* 4657.   **4178**

Rather a disappointing book. Skirts most of major issues about B.'s thought but does show how B. is intertwined in most of major concerns of 18th century and how B. was farther ahead in some areas than Voltaire and later thinkers.
Review : W. Barber in FS 18:378–79, 1964; J. Pappas in MP 62:260–63, 1965.

Nedergaard, Leif. La genèse du Dictionnaire historique et critique de Pierre Bayle. OrL 13:210–27, 1958.   **4179**

Analysis of a ms notebook of B. begun in 1674 which demonstrates clearly his original idea of *Dictionnaire* as merely a corrected edition of Moréri.

Popkin, Richard H. The sceptical precursors of David Hume. PPR 16:61–71, 1955–56.   **4180**

The skeptical tradition up to Hume, especially B. and Huet. Sees *Dictionnaire* as a *Summa pyrrhonica* and attempts to prove skepticism led B. to " blind, inexplicable faith " (p. 67).

Rex, Walter. Essays on Pierre Bayle and religious controversy. The Hague, Nijhoff, 1965. xv, 271 p.   **4181**

A major study of B. in context of 17th-century French Protestantism. Analyzes theological traditions and sources in the *Pensées diverses sur la comète*, the *Commentaire philosophique*, and the article on David.

— Pierre Bayle, Louis Tronchin et la querelle des Donatistes. BSHP 105:97–121, 1959.   **4182**

Shows influence of Tronchin, a Cartesian philosopher, during B.'s rediscovery of Calvinism and particularly on 3rd part of the *Commentaire philosophique*.

— Pierre Bayle : the theology and politics of the article on David. BHR 24:168–89, 1962; 25:366–403, 1963.   **4183**

An important new interpretation of one of the most controversial articles in the *Dictionnaire*. Shows B. was upholding conservative Calvinist interpretation of justification, sanctification, and political power. *Also in* 4181.

Sandberg, K. C. Pierre Bayle's sincerity in his views on faith and reason. SP 61:74–84, 1964.   **4184**

Argues in favor of B.'s sincerity on basis of freedom of press in Holland and also of B.'s own personality, which did not lend itself to irony. The first part is more convincing than the second, although it ignores the unfortunate outcome of B.'s quarrel with Jurieu.

Talluri, Bruna. La polemica fra Bayle e Jurieu dal 1690 al 1692. ATSL n.s. 9:225–54, 1958–59.   **4185**

Good analysis of B.'s opposition to Jurieu's theories of popular sovereignty. Claims B. wrote *Avis aux réfugiés*, but Labrousse proves B. merely edited it. *See* 4177.

Vernière, Paul. Bayle devant le spinozisme. *In his:* Spinoza et la pensée française avant la Révolution. *See* 4158. 1:288–306.   **4186**

B.'s violent attack on Spinoza in 2nd ed. of *Dictionnaire* covers up their mutual aim of separating philosophy from Christianity. B. disliked the *Ethics*, and he confused *natura naturans* with *natura naturata*, a mistake which was to continue through the 18th century. *See also* Kolakowsky in Dibon (4173).

Bernard Le Bovier de Fontenelle
(Nos. 4187–4233)

ARAM VARTANIAN

Editions

Fontenelle, Bernard Le Bovier de. Entretiens sur la pluralité des mondes. Digression sur les anciens et les modernes. Ed. by Robert Shackleton. Oxford, Clarendon press, 1955. 218 p.   **4187**

Gives text of 1742 ed. of *Entretiens* on acceptable grounds that it represents purest and final form, and original text (1688) of *Digression* because of insignificance of later variants. Shackleton has added an introduction (p. 1–50), devoted almost wholly to a balanced discussion of *Entretiens* from a merely historical standpoint. It concerns, among other topics, historical moment of appearance of *Entretiens;* sources probably utilized by F.; relationship of Fontenellean cosmology to Copernicus, Descartes, and Newton; F.'s role in Enlightenment as seen through *Entretiens*, etc. In his concisely informative notes, editor has adduced all important variants of texts; an all but exhaustive bibliography lists 17th- and 18th-century eds. of *Entretiens* (but no translations). Altogether, a very reliable and elegant presentation of 2 basic but not easily obtainable works by F.

Reviews : S. Delorme in RHS 10:375–77, 1957; O. Fellows in RR 47:63–65, 1956; C. Gillispie in Isis 47:452–53, 1956; G. Havens in FS 10:71–73, 1956.

— Lettres galantes. Ed. by Daniel Delafarge. Les Belles Lettres, 1961. 229 p. (AUL 3ᵉ série : Lettres, 35)   **4188**

In this critical ed., which is also a modest attempt to rehabilitate F.'s little-read and generally deprecated *Lettres de M. le chevalier d'Her*** (better known as *Lettres galantes*), Delafarge has followed the text of the 1742 ed., on the plausible grounds that it contains the final version of the work. The editor has added an informative introduction (p. 9–39), which discusses such questions as the composition and publication of the *Lettres galantes*, its probable literary sources, its reputation from the 17th to the 20th century, etc.

— Testament de Fontenelle. Rsyn 82:32–35, 1961.   **4189**

Gives, without comment, the text of F.'s will.

Criticism

Adam, Antoine. Fontenelle écrivain. AUP 27:402–05, 1957.   **4190**

An eloquent *éloge*, but little else.

— Fontenelle, homme de lettres. Rsyn 82:37–42, 1961.   **4191**

Provocative article. Seeks to defend F., the *homme de lettres*, against a lack of sympathy and occasional denigration by both his contemporaries and posterity. Contends that F., contrary to the ordinary view, was really a partisan of " pure poetry." Finds in his *préciosité*, so often reproached against him, evidence of a special humanism—of a conception of man as the product, above all, of social and esthetic factors.

Atkinson, Geoffroy. Précurseurs de Bayle et de Fontenelle (La comète de 1664–1665 et l'Incrédulité sçauante). RLC 25:12–42, 1951.   **4192**

Solid, erudite contribution to study of 17th-century free thought. Without raising question of direct influences on F. or Bayle, shows that in period 1664–70 there were prevalent critical and skeptical attitudes toward supernatural, le *merveilleux*, etc., that anticipated fuller critiques of F. and Bayle concerning religious and popular superstition. Atkinson describes and documents these tendencies in reference to reflections provoked, in England, France (and even North America), by comet of 1664–65.

Bertrand, Joseph. Fontenelle ou M. Teste au XVIIᵉ siècle. RGB 93:74–86, 1957.   **4193**

Does not quite live up to promise of title. In attempt to define " spirit " of F., author emphasizes familiar traits of *ironie souriante, sagesse paradoxale,* skepticism, disillusionment with human nature—in short, all those qualities which, in F.'s case, skirt the edge of despair, only to be retrieved by his wit, sense of balance, and buoyancy of style and thought.

Birembaut, Arthur. Fontenelle et la géologie. RHS 10:360–74, 1957.   **4194**

Informative article, based essentially on comments of F. as editor of yearly *Histoire de l'Académie des sciences,* concerning various memoirs on geological subjects. Author shows that F. followed, intelligently and appreciatively, work being done in geology, and that, to his mind, these researches already served to separate biblical doctrines of Creation, Deluge, etc., from method of a rational and empirical explanation of geological phenomena.

Callot, Emile. Fontenelle. *In his:* La philosophie de la vie au XVIIIᵉ siècle. Rivière, 1965. p. 29–63.   **4195**

The only study devoted specifically to F.'s " biological philosophy ". Even so, most of it is a restatement of F.'s general position in science, for there is not in fact much to say about his opinions in biology—a field with which he concerned himself only incidentally. Nevertheless, Callot sees in this minor aspect of Fontenellean thought a historically faithful expression of the development of biology in the first half of the 18th century. F. is described as representing a transitional stage, by means of which the Cartesian mechanical approach was rendred more experimental and empirical, in order to yield the mechanistic and naturalistic hypotheses typical of the biological science of the *philosophes.*

— Un maître à penser : Fontenelle. *In his:* Six philosophes français du XVIIIᵉ siècle. Annecy, Gardet, 1963. p. 39–75.   **4196**

An informed, succinct survey of F.'s life, personality, and contributions to belles-lettres, philosophy, and science. Author's purpose is to show that, while F.'s was not a creative mind in science or philosophy, he had special talent of interpreting and adapting thought of 17th century (particularly Cartesianism) to effect transition between it and following century.

Canguilhem, Georges. Fontenelle, philosophe et historien des sciences. AUP 27:384–90, 1957.   **4197**

Mise au point of how F. managed to transform the inheritance of Cartesianism in logic and science into a conception of the historical evolution of scientific knowledge. Article remains somewhat on surface because of its brevity, but is not lacking in worthwhile *aperçus.*

Cosentini, John W. Fontenelle's art of dialogue. New York, King's crown press, 1952. xi, 240 p.   **4198**

Detailed—even fastidious—examination of literary form and various techniques present in *Dialogues des morts.* Author considers, among other aspects of F.'s art, dialectical method of exposition of ideas, relationship to Platonic dialogues and to " Socratic irony," satirical characterization of interlocutors, history of genre before and during F.'s time, etc. Work has merit of conscientious and thorough treatment, and is valuable as only full-length study available of *Dialogues.* But it lapses at times into critical naïveté, repetitiousness, and a taste for the trivial, which make reader conscious how distant this analysis of F.'s art is from that art itself.

Review : A. Crisafulli in RR 45:63–64, 1954.

Counillon, J.-F. Fontenelle, écrivain, savant, philosophe. Fécamp, Imprimeries réunies L. Durand, 1959. 186 p.   **4199**

Work that won *grand prix* of Académie de Rouen during commemoration of F. in 1957. Balanced, interestingly and often eloquently composed essay on various aspects of F.'s life, personality, literary and scientific writings and ideas, which seeks to place him in mainstream of cultural evolution from 17th to 18th century. But offers nothing original in materials or interpretations; quotes over-liberally views of other critics, sometimes undiscriminatingly as to source or value; and generally sets its subject in a glowing, eulogistic light, while side-stepping problematic themes.

Delorme, Suzanne. Des Eloges de Fontenelle et de la psychologie des savants. *In:* Mélanges Georges Jamati. Ed. du Centre national de la recherche scientifique, 1956. p. 95-100.   **4200**

Suggestive article, proposing that the

éloges be investigated with a view to determining the psychological portrait of the scientist in the age of F. and as seen by him. In outlining a " psychological questionnaire " to be applied to each *éloge*, Delorme seems interested, more exactly, in a characterological study of the possible historical-cultural variations in the type of the *savant*. A fascinating project which, however, is not pursued further.

— Fontenelle, l'homme et son temps. Rsyn 82:3–31, 1961.   **4201**

An introduction to the *Journées Fontenelle* represented by the series of articles in *Rsyn* for 1961. As such, it merely situates F. biographically and literarily in his time, without attempting to go beyond a secondhand, though admittedly graceful, presentation.

— Tableau chronologique de la vie et des œuvres de Fontenelle, avec les principaux synchronismes littéraires, philosophiques et scientifiques. RHS 10:289–309, 1957. **4202**

First part of article is convenient table of literary, scientific, and philosophical dates and events in their chronological relationship to career of F. Second part is a " contribution à la bibliographie de F.," which, without pretending to be exhaustive, makes additions to Shackleton's bibliography of *Pluralité des mondes* (*see* 4187) and furnishes one for *Eloges*.

— La vie scientifique à l'époque de Fontenelle, d'après les Eloges des savants. Archeion 19:217–35, 1937.   **4203**

Based almost wholly on information in *Eloges*, article reconstitutes certain important aspects of scientific life in late 17th and early 18th centuries, as observed by F. Although it has the merit of including a great many elements in its composite picture, article suffers from rapidity and superficiality of treatment, resembling an index.

Dupont-Sommer, André. Fontenelle, historien des religions. AUP 27:390–96, 1957.
4204

Gives résumé with lengthy quotations —as if no one had read the book—of *Origine des fables*. Almost no critical evaluation; worthless from scholarly standpoint.

Eerde, John van. Fontenelle's reflections on language. MLJ 41:75–77, 1957. **4205**

From random remarks by F. concerning language, author would like to show that

" Fontenelle's thoughts on language reflect . . . the man whose ideas are familiar through such works as the *Dialogues des morts*, *Les entretiens*, and *La digression sur les anciens et les modernes*." But material cited is too meager to indicate that F. extended his philosophical attitudes in any deliberate or meaningful fashion to subject of language.

— A note on Fontenelle's Histoire du théâtre français jusqu'à Corneille. MLQ 17:301–03, 1956.   **4206**

Modestly informative article which points out that F.'s account of French theater, owing to its anticlerical and antireligious elements, may be considered early example of *histoire philosophique*.

— Le théâtre de Fontenelle. SF 6:279–83, 1962. *See* 3637.   **4207**

Useful article. Seeks to define general character of F.'s theater by situating it between ideal of Cornelian tragedy (of which he was admirer and would-be imitator) and 18th-century trend toward sentimental moralizing and genre-mixing. Concludes that, because of an ambiguous position between two inconsistent conceptions of drama, F. was unable to realize a new and viable form of theater. *See* Kail (4213).

Fayol, Amédée. Fontenelle. Debresse, 1961. 126 p.   **4208**

A chatty vulgarization, superficial, unmethodical, and full of stereotyped notions concerning F.

Folkierski, Wladyslaw. Voltaire contre Fontenelle, ou la présence de Copernic. *In:* Literature and Science. Oxford, Blackwell, 1955. p. 174–84. (FILLM, 6)   **4209**

Author's main point is that Voltaire's discovery of literary form of *conte philosophique* in case of *Micromégas* was provoked by his antagonism to F.'s method of popularizing science in *Entretiens*. But article lacks critical balance in failing to see that, in *Micromégas*, Voltaire was as much a continuator as an opponent of F. with respect to philosophical and human implications of hypothesis of a plurality of worlds.

Garcin, Philippe. Fontenelle, ou la métaphysique du bavardage. Cr 12:1011–23, Dec. 1956.   **4210**

Ingenious analysis of basis of F.'s style. Starting out from general interpretation of Grégoire (4212), author contends that F.'s overelaborate use of language has function of compensating for impossibility, owing to his radical skepticism, of making any substantial affirmation of truth : " F. se retranche par l'art d'écrire du désespoir de penser juste .... Par l'exercice assidu de la parole, [il] ne veut cependant échapper qu'à l'angoisse de former sur le monde et sur lui-même une opinion désastreuse " (p. 1019–20). Article suffers, however, from Garcin's own (Fontenellean ?) talent for preciosity and for mimicking while analyzing *la métaphysique du bavardage*.

Grégoire, François. Le dernier défenseur des tourbillons : Fontenelle. RHS 7:220–46, 1954.   **4211**

Excellent article. Based on careful analysis of arguments by means of which F. defended *tourbillons* against attractionism, it shows that his stubborn and, finally, futile loyalty to Cartesian hypothesis was owing to motives of a broad philosophical kind, and only secondarily to relative merits in technical sense of vortex or attraction theory. Concludes, convincingly, that F. preferred Cartesian explanation because it conformed to a scientific method that sought to comprehend nature, basically, in terms of *intuitions sensibles immédiates*.

— Fontenelle, une philosophie désabusée. Nancy, Georges Thomas, 1947.   xxxix, 474 p.   **4212**

Essential study; the only major reinterpretation of F. since Carré (1175). Renouncing a methodical or general treatment of the subject, Grégoire seeks to penetrate the " enigma " of F. and thereby to define fundamental spirit or attitude from which his thought springs. He concentrates on those aspects of F.'s activity that seem to be the most promising and which turn out to be, primarily, the preoccupation with science. *Chemin faisant*, Grégoire gives the most probing and informed discussion available of F.'s scientific views. His general thesis is that F.'s skepticism and pessimism concerned not merely social institutions, religious beliefs, and moral conduct, but went far deeper and involved a negative evaluation of even reason and science, making of him ultimately " un savant apôtre d'une science en laquelle il ne croit pas " (xix). Challenging the familiar image of a rationalistic F., precursor of the *philosophes*, the book insists on a basic contradiction between his overt, official position and his " true," usually (but not always) masked nihilism; and attempts, moreover, to trace this " existential "

antinomy and resultant *désabusement* to their more purely personal and human motives. Grégoire's interpretation is surely controversial and exaggerates (however brilliantly) the total significance of the many paradoxical elements in Fontenellean thought. But it is cogently argued and supported by an impressive grasp of the history of science and philosophy and of F.'s part in both. It has therefore deserved the considerable impact it has made in recent years on F. criticism.

Kail, Andrée. Note sur le théâtre de Fontenelle. FR 36:133–37, 1962–63. *See* 3638.   **4213**

Compact, well-documented article which amplifies on Gaiffe's classing of F. among precursors of *drame*. By examining F.'s " preface " to collected ed. of his plays, as well as plays themselves, author assesses how close he came to Diderot's theory of an intermediate *genre* between tragedy and comedy.

Krauss, Werner. Fontenelle und die Republik der Philosophen. RFor 75:11–21, 1963.   **4214**

Argues for F.'s authorship of *La république des philosophes* (first published in 1768) on the basis of parallels between certain of its leading themes and ideas present elsewhere in F.'s works, particularly in his utopian *Ma république*. Krauss makes a fair case for his attribution; but since no decisive evidence is presented, the question must still be regarded as not settled definitively.

La Harpe, Jacqueline de. Des inédits de Fontenelle : sa correspondance avec J.-P. de Crousaz. RHV 62:90–108, 1954.   **4215**

Reproduces, with explanatory comment, 6 letters from F. to the Lausanne philosopher, Crousaz, and 3 from Crousaz to F. The letters show, besides the versatility of F.'s interests, a certain diplomatic *souplesse* and *bonhomie* that were no doubt required in his official position.

Marsak, Leonard M. Bernard de Fontenelle: in defense of science. JHI 20:111–22, 1959.   **4216**

Solid article. Argues that F. sought to bring to science a new and positive value, and to increase public esteem for it, by showing how the practice of science imposed on the investigator a morality of its own, typified by such ideal qualities as dedication to truth, selflessness, humility, cooperativeness, and tranquillity of spirit.

While the idea of this study is not altogether original, Marsak has explored and documented it more fully than others.

— Bernard de Fontenelle : the idea of science in the French Enlightenment. Philadelphia, American philosophical society, 1959. 64 p. (TAPS n.s., 49⁷)   **4217**

Author's thesis is to take F.'s " critical empiricism " as key to explication of his thought, and to apply it successively to his positions in metaphysics, scientific method, epistemology, morals, anthropology, and sociology. Ch. 5, *The methodology of science*, is essentially the same as 4218 and ch. 6, *The meaning of science*, duplicates 4216. Although F.'s empiricist and experimentalist tendencies were generally recognized, Marsak has made an important contribution in exploring more fully this aspect of subject. However, he tends to attribute more consistency and deliberateness to F.'s " critical empiricism " than is justified in case of an obvious eclectic with penchant for paradox and contradiction; as a result, he has oversimplified an excessively subtle and elusive phenomenon—the mind of F.
Reviews : S. Lytle in Isis 52:111–12, 1961; R. Mortier in RBP 41:546–49, 1963.

— Cartesianism in Fontenelle and French science, 1686–1752. Isis 50:51–60, 1959.
                                   4218
Challenges generally accepted view that F. was, albeit with qualifications, an heir of Cartesianism and seeks to establish instead a sharp contrast between Fontenellean and Cartesian attitudes to science. Marsak's thesis rests on a particularly narrow and dogmatic definition of Cartesianism which does not do justice to either its ambiguities or its potential of growth and adaptation. His argument tends toward paradox in its inability to explain historical facts of F.'s life-long and tenacious advocacy of Cartesian *tourbillon* physics.

Martin, Geneviève. Retouches au portrait de Fontenelle : pièces inédites. RHS 10: 310–33, 1957.   **4219**
Article based on correspondence of *Académie des sciences, belles-lettres et arts de Rouen*, insofar as it concerned F. Although most of this material was already known, author examines documents more thoroughly and publishes several *inédits*. Even so, texts cited, while revealing a less " egotistical " F., do not alter greatly familiar character-portrait of him.

Retouches in question are mostly corroborative.

Maurois, André. Le double centenaire de Fontenelle. AUP 27:406–15, 1957. *Also in:* RPar 64:13–22, May 1957.   **4220**
A pleasantly written, warm appreciation that adds nothing to knowledge about F.

McKie, Douglas. Fontenelle et la Société Royale de Londres. RHS 10:334–38, 1957.
                                   4221
Reproduces several letters from F. to Newton, Hans Sloan, and Royal Society. McKie seems unaware that letters to Newton were already published. Material illustrates spirit of cooperation and mutual admiration that helped growth of internationalism in science during 18th century.

Munot, Philippe. Un texte d'idées : De l'origine des fables (extrait) de Fontenelle. CAT 3:67–85, 1961.   **4222**
Stylistic analysis of key passage from *Origine* describing credulity of prehistoric peoples for *faux merveilleux* and consequent rise of myths. Without examining ideas themselves, Munot's aim is to clarify " mise en forme littéraire " of ideas... " et d'apprécier dans quelle mesure l'écrivain a su servir le penseur." Useful analysis, even if, occasionally, it " clarifies " the obvious.

Paris. Bibliothèque Nationale. Fontenelle, 1657–1757; exposition organisée pour le troisième centenaire de sa naissance et le deuxième centenaire de sa mort. 1957. vii, 42 p.   **4223**
Catalog of the exhibition, describing 164 displayed items. Many of these are individual works by F., usually in the original editions. Others include documents concerning his life, a few letters by him, scientific, philosophical, or literary works having a significant link with his career, portraits of contemporaries, etc. Particularly useful for the detailed bibliographic descriptions it gives.

Pintard, René. Fontenelle et la société de son temps. AUP 27:396–401, 1957.   **4224**
An evocation of the social circles frequented by F., his friends and acquaintances, a few *bons mots*, his manner in company—in short, nothing new.

Pizzorusso, Arnaldo. Considerazioni sul metodo e sulla filosofia di Fontenelle. SRLF 2:81–131, 1961.   **4225**
Valuable study, interested in defining

certain constants in methodology and philosophical outlook of F., with which to approach particularly his poetics. Author finds that these are best revealed in what Cartesianism came to mean to F., i.e., a geometrically lucid explanation of nature, hostile to all mystification. F.'s humanistic use of such criteria was limited, however, by deterministic features of his psychology, which saw human condition in historically static, mechanically repetitive light. It was example of *savant* (as observed in *Eloges*), disinterestedly searching for objective truth, that eventually expressed for F. highest form of human virtue.

— Fontenelle e l'idea di progresso. Bel 18: 150–80, 1963.   **4226**

Meticulous, judicious re-examination of F.'s conception of history and his opinions on the question of progress and on the relationship of " ancients " to " moderns." Author strives to bring out all the subtleties—and ambiguities—of F.'s general position, which, as it turns out, cannot be stated categorically. Pizzorusso's interpretation of Fontenellean doctrine of progress differs from others, in particular, by concluding that F. tended to see history of art and poetry as influenced positively by advancement of reason and objective knowledge, rather than as constant in manner of morals.

Poulet, Georges. Fontenelle. *In his:* Etudes sur le temps humain. Plon, 1950. p. 133–45.   **4227**

According to the author's analysis, time was conceived by F. in such a way as to save the ephemerality and insubstantiality of man's world—to *economize*, as much as possible, its being. The Fontenellean sense of time accomplished this by projecting into the future, in the form of continual postponements, the pleasures, ideas, or passions comprising human experience; it prevented these from destroying themselves by weighing too heavily, as it were, upon the present moment, and created instead, through change in time, a life-prolonging *légèreté*. Like Poulet's book in general, this chapter is marked by a subtle suggestiveness of style and content, rather than by explicitness or rigor.

Robinet, André. Considérations sur un centenaire (Notes soumises aux historiens de Fontenelle). RMM 63:283–98, 1958.   **4228**

Important study. Robinet attempts to show that, contrary to general opinion,

basic principles of F.'s thought evolved historically. *Schéma d'évolution* here offered includes following phases : (1) pastoral idealism, prompting F. first to realize his " dream " in poetry and opera; (2) revolt against real, historical order of things in name of *rêve*, expressing itself in antireligious, subversive *Relation de Bornéo* and *Histoire des oracles*; (3) transformation of this revolt, under threat of censorship, into general progressivist thesis concerning *devenir de la raison*, as seen in *Entretiens, Dialogues, Digression,* and *Origine;* (4) final stage, when F., seeking to fit concept of infinity into world-picture of rationalist-empiricist reality, raised physics (in *L'existence de Dieu*, etc.) to level of natural theology. Though overschematized, article corrects what has been blind spot in F. criticism.

— Malebranche dans la pensée de Fontenelle. Rsyn 82:79–86, 1961.   **4229**

Suggestive article, though a bit elusive. Robinet's main idea is that, after his *Doutes sur le système des causes occasionnelles*, F.'s antagonism toward Malebranche changed, on the whole, to sympathy. The author attributes this to F.'s eventual realization that the notion of infinity had, in Malebranchean philosophy, a positive role to play in the analysis of natural phenomena. It remains somewhat unclear, however, from a historical standpoint, to what extent Malebranche might merely have benefited indirectly, in F.'s estimation, from the discovery and application to physics of infinitesimal calculus.

Sacy, Samuel S. de. Fontenelle avec nous. LN 6:38–48, 1958.   **4230**

Relates F. primarily to *fin de siècle* represented by decline of classicism and of reign of Louis XIV. F. is seen, amid this decadence, as transitional figure, leading way gracefully and constructively to a new cultural era. While neither original nor scholarly in aim, article manages to talk about its subject in a Fontenellean tone and idiom.

Saisselin, Rémy G. Fontenelle : le parfait honnête homme. Le Bayou 72:521–26, Winter 1958.   **4231**

Informal but curious article. Its first part maintains that F. was perfect personification of *honnêteté;* but author relies too much on *lieux communs* and anecdotes to make his point. Second part, subtitled *Maximes sur l'honnête homme*, is an *abrégé*, in form of aphorisms (some of which are excellent), of decline, during 18th century and afterwards, of ideal represented by F.

Vendryès, Joseph. Hommage à la mémoire de Fontenelle (1657–1757). AUP 27:379–83, 1957. **4232**

An introduction, polite and innocuous, to the papers which followed in the *hommage solennel* organized at the Sorbonne on the occasion of F.'s tercentenary.

Wais, Kurt. Selbstanalyse Fontenelles und Fénelons in ihren Totengesprächen. *In his:* Französische Marksteine von Racine bis Saint-John Perse. Berlin, De Gruyter, 1958. p. 33–54. **4233**

Perceptive and scholarly article, analyzing various ways in which dialogue form allowed F. and Fénelon to give expression to contrary impulses of their nature. Concerning F. in particular, author concludes that *Dialogues des morts* mirrored " der Widerstreit zwischen seiner Entdeckung, wie selig das Unbewusste sei, und seinem Bewusstsein, selber zu den traurigen Opfern des glücklos skeptischen Intellekts zu zählen " (p. 53).

Julien Offray de La Mettrie
(Nos. 4234–4254)

ARAM VARTANIAN

La Mettrie, Julien Offray de. L'homme machine; a study in the origins of an idea. Critical ed., with an introductory monograph and notes by Aram Vartanian. Princeton, Princeton univ. press, 1960. 264 p. **4234**

First critical ed., based on 1751 text revised by L., together with variants of preceding eds. Accompanying monograph (p. 1–138) is an attempt to assess thought and historical role of L., with *Homme machine* serving as a general focus. It offers, among other things, interpretation of *Homme machine*, study of its sources, its place in development of L.'s thought, reaction of 18th century to its materialist and atheist theses, and relevance of man-machine idea since Enlightenment, particularly at present time. Extensive notes on text occupy p. 199–249. Reviews : M. Baym in EspCr 1:158–60, 1961; H. Brown in MP 58:217–18, 1961; O. Fellows in MLN 77:212–13, 1962; L. Rosenfield in RR 52:233–35, 1961; P. Rossi in RIF 54:103–06, 1963; D. Thomas in Mind 71:275–76, 1962.

— La Mettrie : textes choisis. Ed. by Marcelle Tisserand. Editions sociales, 1954. 199 p. **4235**

Contains discerning selections from (principally) *Traité de l'âme, L'homme machine, Système d'Epicure, L'homme plante.* Inasmuch as L.'s philosophical works have not been reprinted in collected form since 18th century, present texts, though not extensive, fill real need. Preface is competently written, though strives too hard to fit L.'s ideas and his historical role into Marxist framework. Notes on text are of minimal sort.

— Réponse à l'auteur de La machine terrassée. Réimpression avec notes par P. Lemée. Lyon, Dodeman, 1944. 16 p. **4236**

Makes available text of this extremely rare opuscule.

— L'uomo macchina ed altri scritti. Ed. by Giulio Preti. Milan, Feltrinelli, 1955. xxx, 189 p. **4237**

Contains the texts, in Italian translation by G. Preti, of *L'homme machine, L'homme plante*, and *Discours sur le bonheur;* also a preface summarizing L.'s place in 18th-century thought and his interest for the present-day reader. No attempt at a critical presentation has been made; essentially a popular ed.

Callot, Emile. La Mettrie. *In his:* La philosophie de la vie au xviiie siècle. Rivière. 1965. p. 195–244. **4238**

On the whole, a thoughtful, balanced, circumstanced analysis of L.'s biological philosophy, that brings out its specific features and originality, as well as its long-run theoretical value, in the development of biological doctrines in the 18th century, primarily in France. Despite the author's general competence with the subject, this chapter would have profited from a wider acquaintance with recent work on L. and on 18th-century science.

Desné, Roland. L'humanisme de La Mettrie. PRRM n.s. 109:93–110, 1963. **4239**

Consists for most part of commentary on Vartanian's critical edition of *Homme machine* (4234). In the process, Desné develops evidence for L.'s characteristic attitude of " medical humanitarianism " in regard to perfectibility of man and pursuit of happiness. This side of L.'s intentions as materialist and doctor, insufficiently noted in past, deserves further treatment.

Falvey, J. F. The individualism of La Mettrie. NFS 4:15–27, 66–78, 1965. **4240**

Probing and important study. Tracing the individualistic emphasis of L.'s thought, Falvey finds its culmination in the "amoralism" of the *Discours sur le bonheur*, in the light of which he tends to appreciate its author's materialism generally. His thesis is that an atomistic theory of matter corresponded logically and scientifically, in L.'s thinking, with his radical individualism in psychology and ethics; and this atomism is thereupon used to deny that L. was a true mechanist, despite appearances to the contrary. Falvey has built his case on two questionable assumptions : first, that atomistic features in L.'s highly eclectic definition of matter are necessarily antimechanistic in implication; secondly, that the "man-machine" theory, as L. understood it, was less favorable than atomism to an individualistic, amoralistic view of man.

— La Mettrie, L'homme plus que machine, and La machine terrassée : a question of authorship. MLN 75:670–81, 1960.   **4241**

Questions, with good reason but inconclusively, L.'s authorship of satirical pamphlet, *La machine terrassée*, hitherto attributed to him without exception. By placing work in appropriate context among his writings, argues that internal evidence fails to support supposition that he could have written it for purposes of ironic autocriticism. But these objections, given L.'s talent for mystifying *non sequiturs*, seem on the whole oversubtle.

Gunderson, Keith. Descartes, La Mettrie, languages, and machines. Philosophy 39: 193–222, 1964.   **4242**

Tightly reasoned article which examines how Cartesian *bête machine* was related to L.'s extension of it into *homme machine* and how status of problem in 17th and 18th centuries prefigured similiar discussions today about "thinking machines." Taking test of "language ability" as key to issue, author contends, on one hand, that Descartes was right, in special sense, to deny intelligence to animals in contrast to man; and, on other hand, that L.'s transformation of *bête machine* into *homme machine* reflected basic misunderstanding of original doctrine. Author's method neglects historical aspects of linkage in favor of logical analysis.

Guthke, Karl S. Haller, La Mettrie und die anonyme Schrift L'homme plus que machine. EG 17:137–43, 1962.   **4243**

Prints newly discovered letter, dated June 12, 1748, from Elie Luzac to Haller, in which former protests false attribution of *Homme plus que machine* (made in

Haller's *Göttingische Zeitungen*) to L. and declares that he is author. Article leaves no further room for doubt that Luzac— and neither L. nor Haller—was in fact author. *See* 1216A; 4250.

Lemée, Pierre. Julien Offray de La Mettrie, St.-Malo (1709) – Berlin (1751), médecin, philosophe, polémiste; sa vie, son œuvre. Mortain, Imprimerie du Mortainais, 1954. 272 p.   **4244**

Brings together in final form fruits of lifetime of research on L., of which earlier, less finished version was published in series of articles between 1923 and 1936 (*see* 1212). Offers most detailed and reliable account of specially confused subject of L.'s published works, though some bibliographic problems still remain unsolved. Enriches L.'s none-too-complete biography by number of important findings. But in discussions of various aspects of his activity as philosopher and writer, Lemée, primarily a *bibliophile* and *amateur*, tends to be somewhat superficial, with uncritical exposition often taking place of analysis of L.'s ideas and their relationship to 18th-century and more recent thought. Book is unfortunately full of typographical errors.

— La Mettrie : Réflexions philosophiques sur l'origine des animaux. ASSM 1954–55, p. 32–34.   **4245**

Describes briefly only known copy of this pamphlet.

Metz, W. Julien Offray de La Mettrie. Janus 49:235–72, 1960.   **4246**

Surely the most extraordinary interpretation of L. to appear yet. The author, convinced that everyone has been mistaken in thinking L. a materialist and atheist, argues that his affirmations of the "man-machine" and related doctrines were merely an ironic disguise meant to ridicule materialism and atheism and to suggest quite the opposite opinions to his readers, who, however, were unable to get the point of the *persiflage*. The sort of textual evidence and logic with which Metz tries to overturn the unanimous view that L. was a sincere materialist and atheist is, to put it mildly, inadequate to the task. The translation into English of the Dutch original is rather poor and the proofreading very faulty—which does not make things better.

Perkins, Jean A. Diderot and La Mettrie. SVEC 10:49–100, 1959. *See* 5221.   **4247**

Useful study. Seeks to show that,

despite general similarities, there are significant differences between L. and Diderot which reflect developments that took place in materialist science in latter part of 18th century. Main weakness of discussion, however, is its reliance on rigid, oversimplified formulas (i.e., " mechanical materialism," " dynamical materialism," etc.) to characterize positions of L. and Diderot, when actually problems of interpretation are often, in both cases, too complex to permit categorical comparison.

— Voltaire and La Mettrie. SVEC 10:101–11, 1959. *See* 4667. **4248**

Valuable article. Discusses Voltaire's relationship, both positive and negative, to L. in light of his comments written on margins of latter's works. Nothing startlingly new is revealed by this method, but what was generally known or supposed is more fully documented.

Pflug, Günther. Julien Offray de Lamettrie und die biologischen Theorien des 18. Jahrhunderts. DV 27:509–27, 1953. **4249**

Substantial article; proposes to discount purely philosophical sources of L.'s ideas (Cartesianism, Lockeanism, etc.) in favor of influence of biological and medical doctrines prevalent in period. Though such a shift in emphasis was needed, author goes too far in that direction, with result that his study lacks sense of proportion. Also, specific interpretations of relationship between 18th-century science and thought of L. remain, at more than one point, open to question.

Saussure, Raymond de. Haller and La Mettrie. JHMS 4:431–49, 1949. **4250**

Unscholarly article, full of factual errors; author is dilettante in field. Presents hypothesis, now quite untenable (*see* 4243), that Haller, who invented canard that L. was author of *Homme plus que machine*, might himself have been its author. Only worthwhile point in article is suggestion, quite plausible on face of it, that Haller might have attributed *Homme plus que machine* to L. in retaliation to Frenchman's perfidious dedication of *Homme machine* to him.

Starke, Manfred. Die politische Position La Mettries. *In:* Neue Beiträge zur Literatur der Aufklärung. Berlin, Rütten und Loening, 1964. p. 129–53, 360–73. (Neue Beiträge zur Literaturwissenschaft, 21) **4251**

Uneven article. Points up L.'s hostility to authoritarianism, sympathy for sufferings of poor and other victims of oppression, advocacy of an independent-minded, individualistic role for human beings in society, etc. From this, however, Starke argues that L.'s " political position " was one of popular social revolution against ruling classes. Since L. himself never affirmed as much, and even stressed nonpolitical nature of his atheism and materialism, Starke's thesis must rely on Marxist presuppositions, on forcing of texts, and on conjectures about what L. " really meant " when he said something quite different. Author's doctrinaire approach has spoiled what might have been a valuable study of a neglected aspect of L.'s thought.

Steinkraus, Warren E. Is La Mettrie out of date? Per 43:180–88, 1962. **4252**

Thought-provoking article which takes the current unpopularity of L. in philosophical circles as a test-case for examining the facile tendency to judge philosophers of the past according to prevailing " fashions." Decides that, by any serious attempt to clarify the meaning of " up to date," L. and those holding similar views could not be considered out of date; hence that the contemporary tendency to ignore him represents usually an act of intellectual sloth or blind *parti-pris*.

Vartanian, Aram. Trembley's polyp, La Mettrie, and eighteenth-century French materialism. JHI 11:259–86, 1950. *Reprinted, abridged, in:* Roots of scientific thought : a cultural perspective. Ed. by Philip P. Wiener and Aaron Noland. New York, Basic Books, 1957. p. 497–516. **4253**

Shows that L. was first to exploit significantly implications of Trembley's dramatic discovery of regenerative powers of fresh-water hydra, in direction of a materialist philosophy based on concept of self-determining, autonomously creative Nature.

Willard, Nedd. Le génie et la folie à travers l'œuvre de La Mettrie. *In his:* Le génie et la folie au dix-huitième siècle. Presses univ. de France, 1963. p. 106–30. **4254**

L. is studied, along with other representative French writers of the 18th century, regarding the relationship believed to exist between genius and madness. Actually, L. turns out not to be a significant exponent of the problem. Most of the present chapter is an unoriginal account of his views on human nature, with frequent paraphrasing of his texts. The part dealing specifically with the relationship of genius and madness is meager and negative in its import, for L., seeing the problem differently from the book's main premises, simply conceived of *génie* and *folie* as two altogether antithetical states of mind.

Etienne Bonnot de Condillac
(Nos. 4255–4265)

VIRGIL W. TOPAZIO

Condillac, Etienne Bonnot de. Lettres inédites à Gabriel Cramer. Ed. by Georges Le Roy. Presses univ. de France, 1953. 116 p. **4255**

Contains 9 autograph letters and an autograph *mémoire*. Correspondence instigated by Cramer's disagreement with some ideas in *Essai sur l'origine des connoissances humaines*. Discussion and elucidation of the theses within the *Essai* make these letters a good complement to the *Essai* and announce the *Traité des sensations*. Preceded by an excellent short introduction by Le Roy.

— La logica; o, los primeros elementos del arte de pensar. Estudio preliminar por Guillermo Morón. Trans. by Bernardo María de la Calzada. Caracas, Academia de la historia, 1959. 189 p. **4256**

Important introduction (p. 11–46) for the influence of C. on generations of university students in Venezuela during the 19th century. In this regard, notes the particular importance of C.'s *Logique*, first translated in 1812, the original Caracas text of which is given here. Morón asserts that C.'s sensationalistic doctrine " forma la generación de los intelectuales de la independencia."

Cherpack, Clifton. Warburton and some aspects of the search for the primitive in eighteenth-century France. *See* 5629. **4257**

Article includes a discussion of the influence of Warburton on the linguistic theories of C. Direct evidence of latter's indebtedness can be traced only in the *Essai sur l'origine des connoissances* of 1746. The works of Warburton seen as particularly influential are the *Divine legation* and the *Essai sur les hiéroglyphes*.

Herzog, Wilhelm. Condillac. *In his:* Grosse Gestalten der Geschichte. Munich and Bern, Francke, 1960. 2:148–51. **4258**

A summary of C.'s philosophy, his position and importance in the eighteenth century, and his influence on future thinkers. Includes a discussion of influence of Locke.

Jimack, Peter D. Les philosophes sensualistes : Condillac, Buffon, Helvétius. *In his:* La genèse et la rédaction de l'Emile de Jean-Jacques Rousseau. *See* 4846. p. 318–44. **4259**

Jimack studies important resemblances and influences of the *sensualistes* discernible in Rousseau's *Emile*. Author finds that influence of Helvétius was largely negative; Rousseau cited him only in refutation. By contrast, influence of Buffon and C. was positive and important although Rousseau would not allow Emile to read Buffon. Interesting and significant.

Lefèvre, Roger. Hommage à Condillac. CahH 1:349–64, 1956. **4260**

An excellent summary of C.'s role as the 18th-century continuator of Locke's metaphysics reinforced by Newton's physics. It reviews the importance of C.'s works and the breadth of their undertaking. A commendable study for a capsule knowledge of C.

Parenti, Roberto. Il pensiero storico di Condillac. RCSF 17:167–79, 309–20, 1962; 18:32–43, 1963. **4261**

Valuable discussion of C.'s historical thought seen as an outgrowth of his *storicità del linguaggio*. Notes influence of Montesquieu and affinity for Rousseau. Sees historical development implicit in pages of *Storia generale degli uomini e degli imperi*, written for Ferdinando di Borbone, future Duke of Parma, of whom C. was preceptor from 1758 to 1765.

Ryding, Erik. La notion du moi chez Condillac. Theoria 21:123–30, 1955. **4262**

A philosophical inquiry into C.'s admittedly limited reduction of the *moi* to impressions received through the senses. The sovereignty of sense perception not seen as absolute in the *Essai* and *Traité des sensations*.

Salvucci, Pasquale. Condillac filosofo della communità umana. Milan, Nuova Accademia, 1961. 133 p. **4263**

Worthwhile monograph on biographical and philosophical aspects of C. Emphasizes his preoccupation with epistemology, his typically 18th-century refutation of Cartesianism and reliance on empiricism and observation. Following a Lockean line of thought, C. contends that man developed into the sentient superior animal through the development of language which in turn made him master of his destiny. A sound and well-written work which unfortunately has neither an index nor a bibliography. Review : L. Sozzi in SF 7:561, 1963.

— Linguaggio e mondo umano in Condillac. Urbino, S.T.E.U., 1957. 132 p. *See* 3526. **4264**

A succinct but useful and interesting discussion of C.'s sensationalism. Comparison with ideas of Locke, Berkeley, Diderot, and others. Salvucci contends that C. was consistently a phenomenalist, but one primarily concerned with man and the human world. Contains index but no bibliography. Review : V. Stella in Gmet 15:668–70, 1960.

Thomas, M. Condillac et " L'instinct n'est rien." Scientia 91:271–79, 1956. **4265**

A learned and convincing refutation of C.'s concept of instinct as an inferior degree of intelligence which in effect minimized the distinction between man and animal.

Jean Lerond d'Alembert
(Nos. 4266–4298)

JOHN N. PAPPAS

Alembert, Jean Lerond d'. Discours préliminaire de l'Encyclopédie (1751). Einleitung zur Enzyklopädie von 1751. Ed. by Erich Köhler. Hamburg, Felix Meiner, 1955. xxix, 270 p. **4266**

Bilingual ed. Introduction presents Encyclopedists as symbols of *bourgeoisie.* Shows limitations of d'Al.'s ideas on progress and history of language. Underlines d'Al.'s consciousness of link between the *Encyclopédie* and the Renaissance. Reviews : F. Venturi in FS 10:266–67, 1956.

— Testament de Jean le Rond d'Alembert, [and] Inventaire après décès de M. Le Rond d'Alembert. CahHM 24:8–9, 1951. **4267**

Useless for serious work. *Inventaire* only a small extract of original ms in the Minutier central.

Belaval, Yvon. Les protagonistes du Rêve de d'Alembert. *See* 5276. **4268**

Discusses reasons for Diderot's choice of d'Al. and Mlle de Lespinasse. Their personal relations studied. Distinguishes between these elements and their artistic transformation in *Le rêve.* A valuable contribution to the subject.

Bouissounouse, Janine. Jean Le Rond d'Alembert. *In her:* Julie de Lespinasse : ses amitiés, sa passion. *See* 3423. p. 57–78. **4269**

Standard version of d'Al.-Lespinasse affair utilizing usual sources plus some unpublished letters (not given *in extenso*). Intended for popular readership (sources of quotations often not indicated) but a reliable summary of past scholarship. Author disagrees with some by suggesting that Julie really loved d'Al.

Briggs, J. Morton, Jr. D'Alembert : philosophy and mechanics in the eighteenth century. CUSH 3:38–56, 1964. **4270**

Studies d'Al.'s position in the *vis viva* controversy. D'Al.'s principle ignores motive causes; concentrates on objective description of mechanical phenomena. His dynamics is not a philosophical system and allows him little freedom for conjecture. Despite his sensationalistic epistemology, d'Al. remains faithful to Cartesian search for ultimate truth. He helped work an accommodation of Newtonian and Cartesian thought; was a founder of analytical mechanics.

Broglie, Louis de. Un mathématicien, homme de lettres : d'Alembert. AUP 22 (spec. no. 1): 27–37, Oct. 1952. **4271**

Stresses d'Al.'s mathematical accomplishments. D'Al. opens way for Lagrange. His one weakness in mathematics : his " paradoxes " on statistics of probability. Weak in discussing d'Al. as *homme de lettres.* Mayer's article (4286) is more fruitful.

—, and Robert Barroux. D'Alembert. *In:* Dictionnaire des lettres françaises : XVIIIe siècle. *See* 3381. 3¹:58–63. **4272**

Section by Broglie a brief, standard résumé of d'Al.'s biography. Barroux deals with d'Al.'s *Histoire des membres de l'Académie française.* Stresses its importance in the history of literary criticism and suggests that Sainte-Beuve may have been influenced by it. Bibliography includes mss.

Butts, Robert E. Rationalism in modern science : d'Alembert and the esprit simpliste. BR 8:27–39, 1958–59. **4273**

Excellent presentation of Cartesian side of d'Al. Contrast made between his professed empiricism end his *esprit simpliste* or scientific credo grounded in Cartesian rationalism, utilizing mathematical modes of thought. By " putting a question to nature " in a mathematical vocabulary, d'Al. orders nature according to the question in the tradition of Galileo, Descartes, and Leibniz, rather than Hume, and is a precursor of modern science which operates on the same scientific credo.

Casini, Paolo. D'Alembert epistemologo. RCSF 19:28–53, 1964.   **4274**

Author sees a shift in d'Al.'s position from Cartesian stress on logical consistency and desire to establish a " chain " of knowledge in the *Discours préliminaire* to an empirical skepticism in the *Eléments de philosophie* which questions validity even of mathematical truths and stresses accumulation of facts. Disputes Cassirer's contention that d'Al. elaborates a *métaphysique des sciences* (*see* 4273 for another view).

Costabel, Pierre. La mécanique dans l'Encyclopédie. RHS 4:267–93, 1951.   **4275**

Considers abbé Bossut's guide for reading d'Al.'s *Encyclopédie* articles. Shows many of them to be based on his *Traité de dynamique.* Underlines d'Al.'s failure to build satisfactory scientific method by limiting himself too exclusively to " effects " and to mathematics. Points to d'Al.'s recourse to metaphysical arguments in later years, contradicting his own method, and his honesty in admitting its limitations. A penetrating analysis.

Durry, Marie-Jeanne. Autographes de Mariemont. Nizet, 1955. 1²:486–98. **4276**

Contains 3 letters of d'Al. to Rameau, Morellet and Formey, plus verses, some already published. Errors in Ch. Henry corrected.

Folman, Michel. Les impuissants de génie. Debresse, 1957. 139 p.   **4277**

Unscholarly, superficial treatment of question. Loose conception of *impuissant* permits author to include Voltaire, Rousseau, and many others in this category. Approximately one page summarizes usual allegation on d'Al.'s supposed impotence.

Grimsley, Ronald. D'Alembert and Hume. RLC 35:583–95, 1961. *See* 5586.   **4278**

Studies relations between d'Al. and Hume through their correspondence, utilizing several unpublished letters. Concludes that d'Al. was interested in Hume mainly as a useful ally on the *philosophe* cause. D'Al. tried to elicit anticlerical publications from him and asked support or aid for individual *philosophes.*

— D'Alembert and J.D. Michaelis : unpublished correspondence. RLC 35:258–61, 1959.   **4279**

Letters between d'Al. and the orientalist and Biblical scholar whom d'Al. had recommended to Frederick II. Michaelis asks d'Al. to intercede with Franklin for his son in America.

— D'Alembert at Potsdam (1763) : an English comment. RLC 35:114–15, 1961. *See* 5862.
                                              4280

Presents unpublished reports of English envoy to Berlin concerning d'Al.'s visit to Frederick II. Envoy dismisses rumors that visit is political, suggesting mutual *amour propre* as motive. Gives interesting information concerning fears of members of Berlin Academy that d'Al. might be named their president.

— Jean d'Alembert, 1717–83. Oxford, Clarendon press, 1963. 316 p.   **4281**

A much-needed study utilizing materials unavailable to or ignored by previous writers. Excellent, scholarly coverage in topical form. Emphasis is often synthetical rather than biographical. Chapters on d'Al. and the *Encyclopédie*, Voltaire, Rousseau, some monarchs, the religious question, the Parlements, and 3 rewarding chapters on d'Al.'s philosophy. Much new documentation, good bibliography, indexed.

Reviews : E. Briggs in FS 18:54–56, 1964; M. Rezler in DS 6:323–37, 1964; A. Wilson in JMH 36:335–36, 1964.

— Quelques lettres inédites de Jean d'Alembert. RHL 62:74–78, 1962.   **4282**

Unpublished letters of d'Al. gleaned from various Paris libraries presented with little critical comment.

— Une lettre inédite de Jean d'Alembert. RHL 59:376, 1959.   **4283**

Letter to Swedish ambassador concerning Gustavus III's discourse. Exaggeratedly eulogistic tone interesting as indication of d'Al.'s manner of courting foreign monarchs.

Laissus, Yves. Une lettre inédite de d'Alembert. RHS 7:1–5, 1954.   **4284**

Letter to Durival dated Jan. 1, 1758. Important in dating d'Al.'s defection from *Encyclopédie.*

Ley, Hermann. Zur Bedeutung D'Alemberts : eine philosophiegeschichtliche Untersuchung. WZUL 3:48–60, 1951–52. *Also in French as:* Sur l'importance de d'Alembert. PRRM n.s. 44:49–57, 1952; 46:39–50, 1953. **4285**

Polemical but interesting as example of attempts to fit *philosophes* into a pre-Marxian mould. *Encyclopédie* viewed as an instrument of materialist philosophy against feudal ideology. Attacks critics linking the " Lockean materialist " d'Al. to the " idealistic " positivists, the descendants of Berkeley and Hume. Cartesian elements in his thought are dismissed. Cassirer's view that d'Al. ceases to be Lockean in mathematics attacked as a " reactionary falsification." Schinz, Schalk, and others refuted as representing views of declining imperialism. A long digression on the development of the *arts mécaniques* gives interesting information. D'Al.'s concern here viewed as participation in the class struggle. The scholar will continue to rely on Maurice Muller (1285) for a more objective view.

Mayer, Jean. D'Alembert et l'Académie des Sciences. *In:* Literature and science. Proceedings of the sixth triennial congress, Oxford 1954 (International federation for modern languages and literatures). Oxford, Blackwell, 1955. p. 202–05. (FILLM, 6) **4286**

A short but rewarding view of some of d'Al.'s mistakes and shortcomings as well as his strong points. Good critical evaluation of his scientific works, with details on his polemics on probability, inoculation, etc. Touches on relations with Diderot.

McCormick, C. A. Leopardi and d'Alembert : a possible source for the Canto notturno. IS 14:75–83, 1959. **4287**

Author notes in Leopardi's *Zibaldone* various quotations from d'Al. concerning emptiness of life and misery of man. D'Al.'s theme of the relative capacities of man and animals for happiness is noted in the penultimate stanza of the *Canto;* his melancholy letter to Frederick II over the death of Mlle de Lespinasse is pointed to as a possible source of the *Vecchierel bianco* stanza.

Pappas, John N. D'Alembert et la querelle des bouffons, d'après des documents inédits. RHL 65:479–84, 1965. **4288**

Presents unpublished documents showing that despite his public espousal of cause of Italian opera, d'Al. favored French opera. His loyalty to Encyclopedists suggested as reason for keeping his personal opinion secret.

— D'Alembert et Mme Corneille, d'après des documents inédits. RScH n.s. 105:39–47, 1962. **4289**

D'Al.'s polemic with Linguet over d'Al.'s alleged refusal to aid Mme Corneille. Utilizes unpublished documents from Académie française.

— Diderot, d'Alembert et l'Encyclopédie. DS 4:191–208, 1963. *See* 4325 and 5086. **4290**

Studies fluctuations in Diderot-d'Al. friendship. Suggests that d'Al.'s defection from *Encyclopédie* less from fear than from differences with Diderot on policies and rivalry for leadership of *philosophes.* Hypothesis offered as an attempt to explicate letters of Diderot on the subject.

— Rousseau and d'Alembert. PMLA 75:46–60, 1960. **4291**

Disputes assertions by Fuchs, Boiteux, and others that d'Al. was Rousseau's consistent enemy. Shows that d'Al. appreciated Rousseau's works and tried to dissuade Voltaire from attacking him. Rousseau's public accusation against d'Al. in the Hume affair turns d'Al. against him. *See* Grimsley (4281) for similar findings.

— Voltaire and d'Alembert. *See* 4664. **4292**

Studies Voltaire-d'Al. friendship. Questions traditional view of a faint-hearted d'Al. refusing to follow his " master's " urgings to fight for *philosophe* cause. Presents their differences as based on disparate views of their individual role in the struggle and of tactics to be followed. D'Al. does not so much implement Voltaire,'s policies as he attempts to utilize them for his own purposes.

Rezler, Marta. The d'Alembert question : a study in problematics. DS 6:323–37, 1964. **4293**

Review article of Grimley's *Jean d'Alembert* (4281). Considers other studies as well and presents points concerning d'Al. needing further exploration. A generally balanced evaluation of Grimsley's work.

— The Voltaire-d'Alembert correspondence : an historical and bibliographical re-appraisal. SVEC 20:9–139, 1962. *See* 4683.   **4294**

A very useful and important contribution for future studies on d'Al. Rectifies errors in past eds. of his correspondence, notably in the Belin ed. where the *Supplément* to the correspondence in v. 5 is proved spurious. Disputes conclusions of recent scholars (Pomeau, Wilson, etc.) and points out problems to be resolved. A sometimes provocative but worthwhile study. Reviews: J. Brumfitt in FS 18:173–74, 1964; J. Pappas in RR 55:128–29, 1964; R. Pomeau in RHL 64:304–05, 1964.

Rice, Howard C., Jr. A d'Alembert letter re-examined. PULC 18:189–93, 1956–57.   **4295**

Reprints and translates entire letter of d'Al. to Servan, including passages previously omitted or changed by Servan's biographer, De Portets, in 1825.

Stackelberg, Jürgen von. D'Alemberts Apologie der gelehrten Bildung (Apologie de l'étude). DU 13:40–49, 1958.   **4296**

Praises D'Al. as a critic. Takes issue with Lanson's depreciation of his " arid " style and translates the *Apologie de l'étude* as proof of his thesis.

— Rousseau, d'Alembert et Diderot traducteurs de Tacite. SF 2:395–407, 1958. *See* 5248.   **4297**

Compares translations by each author. Diderot dramatizes Tacitus, Rousseau makes him grandiloquent, d'Al. makes him speak the refined language of the salon. Concludes that Diderot is best interpreter.

Varloot, Jean. Genèse et signification du Rêve de d'Alembert; naissance d'un chef d'œuvre. *In:* Diderot, Denis. Le rêve de d'Alembert. Ed. by Jean Varloot. Editions sociales, 1962. p. vii–lv.   **4298**

Studies relations between Diderot and d'Al. Has valuable insights and new interpretations.

The *Encyclopédie*
(Nos. 4299–4347)

JEAN A. PERKINS

Le bicentenaire de l'Encyclopédie. Enat 16: May 8, 1952.   **4299**

D. Mornet, *L'Encyclopédie et son influence en France au XVIIIe siècle*, p. 3–5;

M. Roques, *Les collaborateurs artistiques de l'Encyclopédie*, p. 6–8; P. Couderc, *D'Alembert et la science du ciel*, p. 9–10; P. Clarac, *L'Encyclopédie et les problèmes d'éducation*, p. 11–12.

The most interesting of these items are analyzed in the appropriate alphabetic category. The articles by Clarac, Couderc, and Roques also appear in AUP 22: special no., Oct. 1952 (4302).

Casini, Paolo. Diderot philosophe. *See* 5123.   **4300**

Ch. 3 appraises Diderot's contribution to the *Encyclopédie* through his articles on religion and the history of philosophy. Overlaps Proust (4327) to some extent but is particularly good on Baconian influence and on Diderot's concept of *Encyclopédie* as an educational force : " il programma di una recostruzione della società su basi razionale " (p. 315).

Cherpack, Clifton. Warburton and the Encyclopédie. CL 7:226–39, 1955. *See* 5630.   **4301**

Describes modification of Warburton in such articles as *Ame* and *Athées* by Yvon, *Ecritures, Hiéroglyphe, Obélisque,* and *Onéirocrite* by Jaucourt. Notes parallels with Vico.

2e centenaire de l'Encyclopédie française. AUP (special no.) 22: Oct. 1952. 267 p. **4302**

J. Sarrailh, *Allocution*, p. 4–5; J. Thomas, *Le rôle de Diderot dans l'Encyclopédie*, p. 7–25; L. de Broglie, *Un mathématicien, homme de lettres: d'Alembert*, p. 27–37; R. Pintard, *Voltaire et l'Encyclopédie*, p. 39–56; P. Grosclaude, *Malesherbes et l'Encyclopédie*, p. 57–79; G. Lefebvre, *L'Encyclopédie et la Révolution française*, p. 81–90; M. Roques, *L'art et l'Encyclopédie*, p. 91–109; J.-J. Mayoux, *Les doctrines littéraires de Diderot et l'Encyclopédie*, p. 111–22; G. Friedmann, *L'Encyclopédie et le travail humain*, p. 123–35; J. Fourastié, *L'Encyclopédie et la notion de progrès économique*, p. 137–49; M.-M. Janot, *Quelques aspects de la chimie dans l'Encyclopédie*, p. 151–68; L. Plantefol, *Les sciences naturelles dans l'Encyclopédie*, p. 169–84; L. Binet, *Biologie et médecine dans l'Encyclopédie*, p. 185–93; P. Couderc, *L'Encyclopédie et l'astronomie*, p. 195–211; P. Clarac, *L'Encyclopédie et les problèmes d'éducation*, p. 213–40; H. Bédarida, *L'Encyclopédie et l'Italie*, p. 241–64; J. Sarrailh, *Conclusion*, p. 265–67.

A series of lectures delivered at the Sorbonne in 1952. The most interesting of these items are analyzed in the appropriate alphabetic category. The articles by Clarac, Couderc, and Roques also appear in Enat 16: May 8, 1952 (4299).

Diderot et l'Encyclopédie. RHL 51:306–72, 1951. **4303**

N.L. Torrey, *L'Encyclopédie de Diderot: une grande aventure dans le domaine de l'édition*, p. 306–17; H. Dieckmann, *L'Encyclopédie et le fonds Vandeul*, p. 318–32; L.J. Thielemann, *Thomas Hobbes dans l'Encyclopédie*, p. 333–46; P. Vernière, *Le spinozisme et l'Encyclopédie*, p. 347–58; N.S. Hoyt, *Méthode et interprétation de l'histoire dans l'Encyclopédie*, p. 359–72.

The most interesting of these items are analyzed in the appropriate alphabetic category.

Dieckmann, Herbert. The concept of knowledge in the Encyclopédie. *In:* Dieckmann, Herbert, Harry Levin, and Helmut Motekat. Essays in comparative literature. St. Louis, Washington univ., 1961. p. 73–107. **4304**

The Encyclopedists saw their work not only as a vast storehouse but as a coherent system of knowledge. In this they were influenced by Bacon but went far beyond him in their structural concept of knowledge. *See* Pappas (4325).

— L'Encyclopédie et le fonds Vandeul. RHL 51:318–32 1951. **4305**

Describes a number of items of interest, especially a document which gives a list of articles by d'Holbach which appear in Assézat-Tournaux as Diderot's and a ms description of the plates for *Bas* in which the text differs from that published in the *Encyclopédie*.

— The sixth volume of Saint-Lambert's works. RR 42:109–21, 1951. **4306**

The discovery of this extremely rare volume permits certain attribution of 13 articles to Saint-Lambert, including *Génie*, which had been attributed to Diderot.

L'Encyclopédie et la pensée du XVIIIe siècle. Rsyn n.s. 28:10–77, 1951. **4307**

M. Le Roy, *1751–1951. L'Encyclopédie et les encyclopédistes*, p. 10–45; J. Thomas, *Diderot, les encyclopédistes et le grand Rameau*, p. 46–67; P. Vernière, *La critique biblique dans l'Encyclopédie et les sources spinozistes*, p. 68–77.

The most interesting of these articles are analyzed in the appropriate alphabetic category.

L'Encyclopédie et le progrès des sciences et des techniques. Ed. by Suzanne Delorme and René Taton. Presses univ. de France, 1952. viii, 233 p. **4308**

A series of articles, originally appearing in v. 4 and 5 of RHS, about scientific knowledge in the *Encyclopédie*. General consensus is that it is representative of the 1750's but is by no means revolutionary in this field. The articles of most interest to literary students are analyzed separately in the appropriate alphabetic categories.

L'Encyclopédie et son rayonnement à l'étranger. CAIEF 2:1952. **4309**

Gilbert Chinard, *L'Encyclopédie et le rayonnement de l'esprit encyclopédique en Amérique (also in:* Dia 2:34–46, 1951), p. 3–22; S. Dresden, *L'Encyclopédie aux Pays-Bas*, p. 23–30; Jean Fabre, *L'Encyclopédie en Pologne*, p. 31–45; Charly Guyot, *Le rayonnement de l'Encyclopédie en Suisse*, p. 47–60; D. M. Lang, *L'Encyclopédie en Russie et au Caucase*, p. 61–65; John Lough, *Le rayonnement de l'Encyclopédie en Grande-Bretagne (longer version in:* FS 6:289–307, 1952), p. 67–75; J. Sarrailh, *Note sur l'Encyclopédie en Espagne* p. 77–83; F. Schalk, *Le rayonnement de l'Encyclopédie en Allemagne*, p. 85–91 (*also in German in* GRM n.s. 3:50–57, 1953).

A series of lectures given at the Collège de France on Aug. 27, 1951, which show that *Encyclopédie* had very little influence in America or Holland, primarily technical influence in Great Britain, Germany, Poland, and Spain. Should be supplemented by Venturi (4338) on influence in Italy and by Mortier (4323) on reception in Germany.

Review: R. Sayce in FS 8:183–84, 1954.

Fage, Anita. Les doctrines de population des Encyclopédistes. Population 6:609–24, 1951. **4310**

Analysis of 34 articles about theories of population and its relationship to wealth, agriculture, and luxury. Shows Diderot, Jaucourt, and d'Amilaville united in favor of increasing population and St. Lambert alone favoring luxury and recognizing importance of industry.

Grimsley, Ronald. Turgot's article Existence in the Encyclopédie. StGR, p. 120–51. **4311**

A close analysis of Turgot's article showing main philosophical problem encountered by French sensationalism and solution offered in principle of causality by both Turgot and d'Alembert.

Grosclaude, Pierre. Malesherbes, témoin et interprète de son temps. Fischbacher, 1961. xiv, 806 p. **4312**

Chapter on *Malesherbes et l'Encyclopédie* (p. 101–38) enlarges on material published in RScH n.s. 91:351–80, 1958. Particular attention is paid to Malesherbes' conduct in the crises of 1752 and 1759. Interesting discussion of individual censors and their problems. Rather vague on certain details. Suggests Malesherbes may have decided to suppress *Encyclopédie* in order to assure its continued publication but presents no real proof for this statement.
Reviews : J.-D. Candaux in RSHist 12:561–63, 1962; A. Delorme in Rsyn n.s. 83:376–79, 1962; J. Egret in Rhist 229: 228–30, 1963; Ph. de F. in BSHP 108: 92–98, 1962; W. Krauss in DLit 84:997–1000, 1963; G. Mongrédien in MerF 345: 350–54, 1962; R. Rigodon in IHist 25: 90–91, 1963; L. Sozzi in SF 8:166–67, 1964.

Guyot, Charly. Le rayonnement de l'Encyclopédie en Suisse française. Neuchâtel, 1955. 148 p. **4313**

Expanding his article in CAIEF (4309), Guyot notes that most readers used *Encyclopédie* for scientific information. Gives the reactions of Bonnet and Haller based on unpublished correspondence and notebooks. Makes a close comparison of Paris and Yverdun eds.
Reviews: P. Kohler in RHL 57:249–52, 1957; A. Pizzorusso in SF 1:148, 1957.

Hoyt, Nelly Schargo. Méthode et interprétation de l'histoire dans l'Encyclopédie. RHL 51:359–72, 1951. **4314**

Proves that almost one-tenth of *Encyclopédie* articles deal with historical subjects. Jaucourt took over from Mallet after first four volumes and saw history as a critical science in early research stages but an art later on.

Huard, Georges. Les planches de l'Encyclopédie et celles de la Description des arts et métiers de l'Académie des Sciences. RHS 4:238–49, 1951. **4315**

A detailed comparison of the plates published in these two rival publications shows that Patte's charge of plagiarism has some basis. The text of the *Encyclopédie* articles corresponds to the unpublished plates of Réaumur.

Kafker, Frank A. A list of contributors to Diderot's Encyclopedia. FHS 3:106–22, 1963. **4316**

An alphabetical list giving names in 18th-century form, dates of birth and death, some of their contributions to *Encyclopédie*, and sources of biographical information. Should be used only in conjunction with a list furnished by Proust (4327) and Lough (4319).

Lough, John. The contemporary influence of the Encyclopédie. SVEC 26:1071–83, 1963. **4317**

Supplements Mornet (4322), showing that reactions were rare in contemporary correspondence, memoirs, and periodicals. Only real source for this type of information is in attacks on *Encyclopédie*. Main controversy lasted from 1750 to 1760. Price of *Encyclopédie* made it less influential than it might otherwise have been.

— Louis, chevalier de Jaucourt (1704–1780), a biographical sketch. *In:* Essays presented to C. M. Girdlestone. Univ. of Durham, Newcastle upon Tyne, 1960. p. 193–217. **4318**

Supplements Schwab (4332) giving information based on ms material and documents in notarial archives.

— The problem of the unsigned articles in the Encyclopédie. SVEC 32:327–90, 1965. *See* 5317. **4319**

A compendium of all known information about the authorship of these articles.

Marcu, Eva. Un encyclopédiste oublié : Formey. RHL 53:296–305, 1953. **4320**

Gives list of 81 articles which this Huguenot *savant* living in Berlin ceded to the *Encyclopédie* and discusses most important ones.

Mayer, Jean. Diderot, homme de science. *See* 5201. **4321**

Makes rather prudent use of *Encyclopédie*. Some excellent pages on Diderot's concept of *Encyclopédie* and its central position in his faith in progress and in his eventual discouragement in this area (p. 412–32). Index is to names only.

Mornet, Daniel. L'Encyclopédie et son influence en France au XVIIIe siècle. *See* 4299. p. 3–5. **4322**

Sees *Encyclopédie* as a *summa* of French thought in 1750's, especially of idea of progress. Gives 2 interesting lists of subscribers. *See* 4317.

Mortier, Roland. Diderot en Allemagne, 1750–1850. *See* 5207. **4323**

P. 139–81 reinforce findings of Schalk

(4331) that influence of *Encyclopédie* was confined almost entirely to its technical worth. Useful review of reactions in contemporary journals.

Pappas, John N. Berthier's Journal de Trévoux and the philosophes. *See* 4142. p. 163–96. **4324**

By quoting from reviews in the *Journal de Trévoux*, Pappas shows clearly that Berthier favored idea of the *Encyclopédie* until Diderot became the editor. Suggests that Diderot may have had one of Berthier's articles suppressed by the censors in view of certain remarks in the Berthier-Diderot correspondence. Berthier's reviews of the 1st v. were detached and impartial, but after Nov., 1753, he never mentioned either Diderot or the *Encyclopédie* by name.

— Diderot, d'Alembert et l'Encyclopédie. *See* 4290. **4325**

Proves Diderot and d'Alembert were already friends in 1746. Draws on unpublished material to document quarrel between them in 1759 and points out that grounds for d'Alembert's break with *Encyclopédie* existed in rivalry between them and in different concepts of what an encyclopedia should be. Seems to have ignored discussion of this point in Vernière (4341).

Paris. Bibliothèque nationale. Diderot et l'Encyclopédie; exposition commémorative du deuxième centenaire de l'Encyclopédie. *See* 5088. **4326**

An extremely useful catalog of the exhibit held in Paris in 1951, giving bibliographical information about precursors, editors, collaborators, and critics of *Encyclopédie*.

Proust, Jacques. Diderot et l'Encyclopédie. Colin, 1962. 621 p. *See* 5335. **4327**

Essential work incorporating most recent research. Excellent bibliography. Somewhat confused format since it wavers between study of *Encyclopédie* itself and the evolution of Diderot's thought in period 1760 to 1765. Interesting attempt to situate *Encyclopédie* in society of times by studying bourgeois background of almost all of collaborators and most of the subscribers. Rather too strictly limits Diderot's articles to those which have an asterisk and those which were reproduced by Naigeon in his 1780 ed. Strengthens Diderot's position as editor. A résumé is given in AUP 33:655–

57, 1963; IHist 25:161–67, 1963; IL 15:192–97, 1963.

Reviews : L. Crocker in MLQ 24:274–80, 1963; J. Decobert in RSch n.s. 112:551–54, 1963; R. Desné in DS 6:251–62, 1964; M. Duchet in AESC 19:953–65, 1964; W. Krauss in DLit 85:410–11, 1964; M. Launay in Esp 32:8–9, Aug.–Sept. 1964; C. Le Guin in AHR 69:749–50, 1963–64; J. Lough in FS 18:164–65, 1964; R. Mortier in SF 8:110–15, 1964; R. Sauzet in RHist 230:554–58, 1963; F. Schalk in Archiv 201:316–19, 1964–65; J. Varloot in PRRM n.s. 111:87–97, 1963; A. Wilson in JMH 35:406–07, 1963.

— La documentation technique de Diderot dans l'Encyclopédie. RHL 57:335–52, 1957. **4328**

Supplements Huard (4315) on plates and clarifies Diderot's method of working on technical subjects.

Roger, Jacques. Les sciences de la vie dans la pensée française du XVIIIe siècle. *See* 4146. **4329**

Ch. 3 on *Diderot et l'Encyclopédie* shows the influence of Buffon on Diderot's article *Animal* and documents preponderant influence of Bordeu's theories of *sensibilité* in most of biological articles, especially those by Fouquet and Menuret.

Roques, Mario. L'art et l'Encyclopédie. *See* 4302. p. 91–109. **4330**

Discusses the 3 main contributors in this field; Cahusac, Watelet, and Jaucourt. Also analyzes the psychological approach to artistic creation as seen in the articles *Génie*, erroneously assumed to be by Diderot; *Enthousiasme* by Cahusac; and *Verve* by Jaucourt.

Schalk, Fritz. Zur Vorgeschichte der Diderot'schen Enzyklopädie. RFor 70:30–53, 1958. *See* 5672. **4331**

Chiefly on background of thought in Bacon. *See also* Casini (4300), who is more perceptive about the differences to be found.

Schwab, Richard N. The chevalier de Jaucourt and Diderot's Encyclopédie. MLF 42:44–51, 1957. **4332**

Gives history of Jaucourt's collaboration with *Encyclopédie* showing how he bankrupted himself in the process. *See* 4318.

— The extent of the chevalier de Jaucourt's contribution to Diderot's Encyclopédie. MLN 72:507–08, 1957. **4333**

Estimates Jaucourt contributed 28% of all articles or 24% of total text, but 44% of text in last 4 v. alone.

Strangué, M. M. L'Encyclopédie de Diderot et ses traducteurs russes [in Russian with brief French résumé]. FE 76–88, 1959 [1961].   **4334**

Shows there were 2 periods of interest : the first about 1767 resulted in 3 collections of articles translated into Russian, but these were not the more philosophic ones; the second between 1769 and 1775 resulted in the translation of such important articles as *Monarchie absolue, Droit naturel, Economie politique, Morale, Luxe,* and *Goût.* Supplements the article by Lang in CAIEF 2:61–65, 1952. *See* 4309.
Review : J. Proust in RHL 61:592, 1961.

Taton, René. Les mathématiques selon l'Encyclopédie. RHS 4:255–66, 1951. *Also in* 4308. p. 52–63.   **4335**

Points out that d'Alembert wrote most of his articles before 1754 so they do not reflect the discoveries of Lagrange. A great deal was copied from Chambers. Supplements Pappas (4325).

Thomas, Jean. Le rôle de Diderot dans l'Encyclopédie. *See* 4302. p. 7–25. *Also in:* Dia 3:96–109, 1952.   **4336**

Weighs Diderot's faults as editor against his virtues. Cursory but interesting.

Torrey, Norman L. L'Encyclopédie de Diderot: une grande aventure dans le domaine de l'édition. RHL 51:306–17, 1951.   **4337**

Stresses economic importance of the enterprise to the French publishing business as a whole and shows how this fact contributed to saving *Encyclopédie* in its 3 crisis periods of 1749, 1752, and 1759.

Venturi, Franco. L'Encyclopédie et son rayonnement en Italie. CAIEF 3:11–17, 1953.   **4338**

True role of *Encyclopédie* in Italy was not as a *machine de guerre* but as *une somme de savoir.* Discusses Lucques and Livourne eds. at some length. Supersedes Lévi-Malvano (1314).

— Le origini dell'Enciclopedia in Inghilterra. Itinerari 2:200–20, 1954.   **4339**

Based on letters written by John Mills in 1745 clarifying his part in the inception of the *Encyclopédie.* D'Alembert is mentioned as a collaborator in a letter of June 21, 1745.

Vernière, Paul. La critique biblique dans l'Encyclopédie et ses sources spinozistes. Rsyn n.s. 28:68–77, 1951.   **4340**

Behind the orthodox sources which are named, such as Chambers, the *Dictionnaire de Trévoux,* and Brucker, are other unacknowledged ones, including Spinoza. Main influence of Spinoza is in scientific approach to study of Jewish antiquity.

— L'Encyclopédie de Diderot et d'Alembert. Rsyn n.s. 26:134–54, 1950.   **4341**

Outlines the aims of Diderot and d'Alembert and shows how they differed in their ideal of what *Encyclopédie* should be. *See* Pappas (4325).

— Le spinozisme et l'Encyclopédie. RHL 51:347–58, 1951.   **4342**

Spinoza was attacked as the symbol of *l'esprit de système,* and Yvon completely misread him. Vernière's arguments about Diderot's contradictions are vitiated by discovery that Diderot did not write article *Spinoza. See* 4327.

Watts, George B. The Geneva folio reprinting of the Encyclopédie. APSP 105:361–67, 1961.   **4343**

Supplements his earlier article (4344), giving further information about agreements between Panckoucke and Cramer. Illustrated to show differences between Paris ed. and Geneva reprint.

— The Swiss editions of the Encyclopédie. HLB 9:213–35, 1955.   **4344**

Detailed descriptions of 4 distinct versions of *Encyclopédie* published in Switzerland, one of which was a reprint by Cramer of Paris ed., often confused with original today.

Weis, Eberhard. Geschichtsschreibung und Staatsauffassung in der französischen Enzyklopädie. Wiesbaden, F. Steiner, 1956. viii, 285 p.   **4345**

An important book on historical and political theory in the *Encyclopédie* and the *Suppléments.* Weis examines their concept of the Middle Ages in some detail, showing that Henri IV was their ideal king. He also discusses their ideas about state of nature, social contract, equality, liberty, property, etc., and shows how Rousseau in *Economie politique* differed from most of the other Encyclopedists.

Reviews : J. Egret in Rhist 218:161–62, 1957; A. Goodwin in EHR 73:163–64, 1958; K. von Raumer in HZ 188:311–26, 1959; C. Rosso in SF 2:503, 1958; A. Wilson in AHR 62:973–74, 1956–57.

Wilson, Arthur M. Diderot : the testing years, 1713–1759. *See* 5103. **4346**

The best presentation of Diderot's day-to-day participation in and contribution to *Encyclopédie* up to 1759. Especially useful in analysis of many little-known articles. Also gives an excellent history of the publication of the *Encyclopédie* to this date.

— Why did the political theory of the Encyclopedists not prevail? A suggestion. FHS 1:283–94, 1960. *See* 5673. **4347**

A thought-provoking article showing differences between political theory of the Encyclopedists and those of Rousseau and the physiocrats. Suggests Rousseau prevailed during Revolution in part because of necessity for strong government and of appeal to nationalism.

Claude Adrien Helvétius
(Nos. 4348–4367)

ARAM VARTANIAN

Helvétius, Claude-Adrien. De l'esprit; introduction et notes par Guy Besse. Editions sociales, 1959. 190 p. **4348**

Useful selection of texts. Introduction is rather long (p. 8–64), but unoriginal and oriented toward Marxist interpretation. Volume addressed to " popular " rather than scholarly audience.

Review : R. Pomeau in RHL 61:264–65, 1961.

— Notes de la main d'Helvétius, publiées d'après un manuscrit inédit avec une introduction et des commentaires par Albert Keim. Alcan, 1907. viii, 116 p. **4349**

Ms of private jottings, reflections, etc., by H., apparently prior to publication of *De l'esprit*, is given in its integral state, without editing of order, spelling, or punctuation. Though these " notes " (never meant by H. for posterity) are of very unequal value and interest and make a somewhat chaotic impression, many of them are excellent maxims or revealing remarks, and, taken all together, offer basis for studying growth of H.'s ideas, personality, and characteristics of his style.

Alciatore, Jules C. Stendhal et Helvétius; les sources de la philosophie de Stendhal. Geneva, Droz, 1952. vi, 300 p. **4350**

Painstaking study, in which all points of contact between Stendhal and thought of H. (in period 1802–30) are fastidiously described, compared, evaluated, with aim of proving that " le sensualisme d'Helvétius, modifié, approfondi et élargi par les œuvres des idéologues, constitue le fond d'où sont sorties presque toutes les théories psychologiques, sociales, et esthétiques de Stendhal " (p. 284). Although author succeeds in showing that influence of H. on Stendhal was in fact greater than previously supposed, he greatly exaggerates this influence as result of ignoring other possible sources and of making excessive appraisals of Stendhal's affinities with H. on particular points. What is most typically *beylien* tends to escape this type of *rapprochement*. Exposition suffers, also, from undigested clutter of trivia and tiresome repetition.

Reviews : J. Deschamps in FS 7:171–72, 1953; O. Fellows in RR 44:299–302, 1953; F. Green in MLR 48:349–50, 1953; M. Le Yaouanc in RHL 54:230–33, 1954.

Andlau, Béatrice d'. Helvétius, seigneur de Voré (avec des documents inédits). Fernand Sorlot, 1939. 168 p. **4351**

Purpose of book, by a descendant of H., is to describe his life as *châtelain* of his country estate of Voré in Le Perche. Utilizing abundant family archives and other documents, author deals with physical character of property, its domestic régime, role of H. as wise and generous administrator, and even history of Voré before and after his ownership. Reconstructs an aspect of [H.'s experience that was obviously very important to him but which had been largely neglected by biographers in favor of his more dramatic social and intellectual activities among Parisian *philosophes*. Book is written with quaint combination of chatty informality and fastidious documentation.

Baumgarten, Arthur. Helvetius. *In:* Grundpositionen der französischen Aufklärung. Berlin, Rütten und Loening, 1955. p. 3–25. (Neue Beiträge zur Literaturwissenschaft, 1) **4352**

General essay on H., not particularly informative or illuminating on any special problem. Maintains, within framework of Marxist view of history, that utilitarian social ideals of H. could not have been realized under capitalist system, a fact that he never grasped because his period had no inkling of economic laws of development which make structure of society dependent on means of production.

Creighton, Douglas G. Man and mind in Diderot and Helvétius. PMLA 71:705–24, 1956. *See* 5126.   **4353**

Substantial article, which takes issue with those critics who have classed H. and Diderot indiscriminately together as " sensationalists." Emphasizes basic contrasts between H.'s reductivist, dogmatizing environmentalism and more supple physiological psychology of Diderot, which recognized complexity and individuality of human nature. Author remains, however, within limits of a confrontation, without investigating broader philosophical or psychological implications of Diderot-Helvétius " debate " for history of thought.

Cumming, Ian. Helvetius : his life and place in the history of educational thought. London, Routledge and Kegan Paul, 1955. xi, 260 p.   **4354**

Excellent work; balanced presentation, interestingly written. Author has, in particular, merit of elucidating H.'s ideas on education in relation, not merely to doctrines and practice of pedagogy in period, but to its philosophical currents and social reality, as well as to H.'s own personality and experience. Rather than dry, specialized discussion, work is thus evocation of large segment of French Enlightenment itself, seen and described from focal point of H.'s life and mind. Gives special attention to fruition of his pragmatism in education among British utilitarians, Bentham, James Mill, Godwin, etc. There is, however, tendency to " glorify " H. who, despite estimable qualities, had moral and intellectual failings on which author chooses not to dwell critically. Useful bibliography.

— Helvétius in England. EA 16:113–23, 1963. *See* 5676.   **4355**

Informative but somewhat dry and congested account of H.'s visit to England in 1764. Describes his frequentations, movements, and impressions. Shows that, in general, he failed to see what was basically wrong with British life in 18th century, tending to exaggerate those qualities in which country was superior to France and to minimize the rest. H. did, however, criticize England's " commercialism " and haphazard " constitution."

Horowitz, Irving L. Claude Helvetius : philosopher of democracy and enlightenment. New York, Paine-Whitman, 1954. 204 p.   **4356**

Marxist interpretation of H. within context of similiar explanation of economic, social, and ideological history of 18th-century France. Somewhat rambling in structure; polemical and partisan in spirit, causing author to present what supports dialectical materialist thesis and to suppress what does not. Within these limits, much of what he says is plausible, provided reader brings his own corrective sense of balance. Horowitz contends that, historically, 2 contradictory schools of thought were indebted to H. : bourgeois utilitarianism, represented by Bentham and his followers; and socialism and communism, culminating in Marx and Engels. On closer examination, he claims that only latter school has remained, to this day, true heir of ideals of humanitarian enlightenment and social democracy advocated by H.

Jimack, Peter. Les influences de Condillac, Buffon et Helvétius dans l'Emile. AJJR 34:107–36, 1956–58. *Also in his:* La genèse et la rédaction de l'Emile de Jean-Jacques Rousseau. *See* 4846. Ch. 13.   **4357**

Scholarly treatment, utilizing for comparative purposes various ms versions of *Emile.* As regards H., author contends that, although Rousseau subscribed generally to sensualist thesis in *Emile,* he did not do so in sense of *De l'esprit* (i.e., *sentir, c'est juger*), which represented passive and simplistic conception of mind. Reacting against such an extreme position, Rousseau instead followed closely sensualist psychology of Condillac and to lesser degree that of Buffon.

Koebner, Richard. The authenticity of the letters on the Esprit des lois attributed to Helvétius. IHRB 24:19–43, 1951. *See* 4446.   **4358**

Important article, impugning for first time authenticity of much-quoted letters in question. Argues that they are inconsistent in content and terminology with what author of *De l'esprit* could logically be expected to have expressed 10 years earlier on occasion of *Esprit des lois.* Koebner suggests that " letters " were forged during period of French Revolution by abbé Lefebvre-La Roche, H.'s literary executor and editor, in order to combat conservative influence of Montesquieu's ideas. Plausible, though inconclusive, discussion.

Ladd, Everett C., Jr. Helvétius and d'Holbach : la moralisation de la politique. JHI 23:221–38, 1962. *See* 4374. **4359**

Judicious comparison of political thought of H. and d'Holbach, stressing general continuity in application of utilitarian ethics to problems of political reorganization in *ancien régime*. Seeks also—not always successfully—to clarify specific differences in their respective programs of governmental and social reform. Concludes that neither H. nor d'Holbach, despite philosophic breadth of their principles, was able to see beyond practical limits of either a constitutional, or enlightened, monarchy.

Maublanc, René. Un poète inconnu : Helvétius. Eur 72:26–39, Dec. 1951. **4360**

Somewhat amateurish and superficial, but principal study available of H.'s poetry, which is discussed in terms of several of its dominant philosophical themes. Describes Voltaire's role as mentor to the aspiring poet. Arrives at unobjectionable conclusion that, if H. was far from being great poet, his poems are nonetheless still readable for ideas they express—at times with epigrammatic eloquence.

McConnell, Allen. Helvétius' Russian pupils. JHI 24:373–86, 1963. **4361**

Measures extent of H.'s influence on Alexander Radishchev (1749–1802), forerunner of Russian radical intelligentsias. Discussion based primarily on latter's *Journey from St. Petersburg to Moscow* (1790), which reflected H.'s ideas faithfully in denunciation of despotism, but somewhat less so with respect to anticlericalism, utilitarian principle, power of education to reform society, and " calculus of pleasure."

Momdzhian, Khachik N. La philosophie d'Helvétius. Traduit du russe par M. Katsovitch. Moscow, Editions en Langues étrangères, 1959. 445 p. [Originally published as : Filosofiĭa Gel'vetsiĭa, Moscow, 1955.] **4362**

Most systematic among recent attempts to assimilate H. to Marxist interpretation of intellectual history. Author adheres to stock formulas and dogmatic stereotypes of Communist world view, evaluating materialism and atheism of 18th century exclusively through opinions of Marx, Engels and Lenin, who are frequently and slavishly cited as final authorities on French Enlightenment. Conclusion that emerges is twofold. It is claimed, on one hand, that H. as materialist failed to reach truly dialectical and proletarian standpoint because he remained on level of "mechanical " and " metaphysical " materialism and an " idealistic " conception of history in keeping with limited " progressivism " of " revolutionary *bourgeoisie* " of his period. On other hand, H. is praised as " progressive " insofar as his utilitarian atheism and materialism represented fundamental attack against feudal structure, religion, and class exploitation of *ancien régime*, and helped thereby to prepare French Revolution and rise of utopian socialism and communism in 19th century.

Ozanam, Didier. La disgrâce d'un premier commis : Tercier et l'affaire de l'Esprit (1758–1759). BEC 113:140–70, 1955. **4363**

Excellent article. Based on new documents, explains *affaire de l'Esprit* from vantage point of unfortunate role played in it by royal censor, Jean-Pierre Tercier, *premier commis* at *Ministère des Affaires Etrangères*. Reveals that culmination of *affaire* in Tercier's dismissal was only incidentally related to subject itself of *De l'esprit*, but resulted from Mme de Pompadour's opposition to secret Polish policy of Louis XV in which Tercier was active. The latter, a loyal and able, but unwary, civil servant, emerges as principal dupe and scapegoat of whole business. *See* 4365.

Rostand, Jean. La conception de l'homme selon Helvétius et selon Diderot. RHS 4: 213–22, 1951. *See* 5232. **4364**

Mediocre article, notwithstanding author's reputation. Summarizes opposing positions of Diderot and H.-organicist vs. environmentalist, genetic vs. educative—as if no one knew anything about subject. Affirms that modern psychology has, on the whole, vindicated more nuanced opinions of Diderot. Perceptively accredits H., however, with having glimpsed the profound role played in formation of total personality by seemingly trivial factors in environment of infancy and childhood.

Smith, David W. Helvétius; a study in persecution. Oxford, Clarendon press, 1965. viii, 248 p. **4365**

Well-written, seemingly definitive study, based on examination of all available materials, that clarifies obscure and often paradoxical motives and forces behind *cause célèbre* of suppression of *De l'esprit*.

Building on researches of Ozanam (4363), author demonstrates that objective content of *De l'esprit* had relatively little to do with magnitude and history of *affaire*. Various controlling factors woven skillfully into reconstruction of *affaire* in its entirety are : struggles between Church and Encyclopedists; contest between Jansenists and Jesuits; rivalry between *Parlement de Paris* and Royal Chancellor regarding censorship rights; secret foreign policy of Louis XV; court intrigues among Mme de Pompadour, Choiseul, and Queen; and impact of *De l'esprit* on ideological conflicts of age, furthering a cleavage among the *philosophes* themselves. Invaluable bibliography.

— The publication of Helvétius's De l'esprit (1758–59). FS 18:332–44, 1964.   **4366**

Factually rich article, which distinguishes among 3 known versions of " 1st ed." of *De l'esprit* and gives history of each. In particular, reveals subterfuges by which publisher Durand succeeded, despite ban on the book and confiscation of typeset by censor's office, in flooding the market with copies of *De l'esprit*. Lists variants among 3 versions.

Topazio, Virgil W.   Diderot's supposed contribution to Helvétius' works. PQ 33:313–29, 1954. *See* 5257.   **4367**

Effectively refutes Meister's vague, uncorroborated statement (echoed by subsequent critics) that Diderot wrote some pages of *De l'esprit*, by examination of his limited personal relations with H. at time, no less than by internal evidence of his *Réflexions sur l'esprit*. Author rightly points out, moreover, that there are in fact no pages in *De l'esprit* which, by their style or content, suggest Diderot's intervention.

Paul Henri Thiry, *baron* d'Holbach
(Nos. 4368–4385)

Virgil W. Topazio

Holbach, Paul Henri Thiry, *baron* **d'.** Textes choisis. Ed. by Paulette Charbonnel. Editions sociales, 1957. 198 p.   **4368**

Selections from works of 1st and 2nd periods, the scientific and antireligious, are preceded by a 74 p. introduction that is informative and enlightening. *See* especially the section on *Science et conscience*.

— Ausgewählte Texte. Ed. by Manfred Naumann. Berlin, Akademie Verlag, 1959. vii, 320 p.   **4369**

Selections from major works to establish H.'s contribution to a systematized explanation of universe on materialistic grounds in spite of limited state of natural sciences of that time. Contains excellent bibliography; also opinions of contemporaries.

Besthorn, Rudolf.   Zeitgenössische Zeugnisse für das Werk Holbachs. *In:* Neue Beiträge zur Literatur der Aufklärung. Berlin, Rütten und Loening, 1964. p.185–94, 391–96.   **4370**

In this contemporary look at the works of H., Besthorn pays particular attention to the question of authorship and the claims and disclaimers regarding the degree of contributions and collaboration by H.'s *philosophe* friends like Diderot, Naigeon, and Suard. Besthorn concludes with most present-day specialists that H. undoubtedly wrote the *Système social, Système de la nature,* and *Morale universelle.*

Booy, J. Th. de.   L'abbé Coger, dit Coge Pecus, lecteur de Voltaire et de d'Holbach. SVEC 18:183–96, 1961. *See* 4616   **4371**

Defines Coger's interest in works of Voltaire and H.; summarily treats the dissemination of antireligious literature in 18th century and discusses role of publisher Marc-Michel Rey. Projects a special study on date and circumstances of publication of the *Christianisme dévoilé.*

El Nouty, Hassan.   Le panthéisme dans les lettres françaises au XVIIIe siècle : aperçus sur la fortune du mot et de la notion. *See* 3479.   **4372**

An excellent article on the changing patterns of pantheism since Toland's first use of the word in 1709. A major part of article treats H.'s revival of a pantheism made to conform to his rigorous materialism, thus differing from Spinoza's identification of God and Nature. Voltaire, as El Nouty points out, used Spinozist principles to combat atheism of H.   As sentiment supplanted Reason (particularly with Rousseau), the position of H. and his disciples lost ground and a rehabilitation of pantheism resulted.

Gross, Georg.   Holbach oder Voltaire? WZUR 4:335–44, 1954–55.   **4373**

Continues investigation of authorship of works attributed to H. Position taken is that he cannot be considered sole author of all works attributed to him. Exceptions like *Le système de la nature, La contagion sacrée,* and *La théologie portative* are made. Concludes that *L'histoire critique de Jésus Christ, ou analyse raisonnée des Evangiles* was the work of Voltaire.

Ladd, Everett C., Jr. Helvétius and d'Holbach, la moralisation de la politique. *See* 4359. **4374**

A useful and interesting study of political ideas of Helvétius and H. Shows that despite their differences (Helvétius, the psychologist with a light and anecdotal style; H., the moralist with an often tedious and repetitive manner), they both pursued the same goal, *la moralisation de la politique,* and applied a utilitarian standard to all actions which were seen as motivated by self-interest. Also attempts to define what in the minds of the *philosophes* constituted a good society.

Lough, John. Le baron d'Holbach : quelques documents inédits ou peu connus. RHL 57:524–43, 1957. **4375**

A much-needed addition for biographical data on H. Fruit of years of research and great scholarship. Also introduces some new documents to cast additional light on some old controversies. An indispensable article for any H. scholar.

Manuel, Frank E. The eighteenth century confronts the gods. Cambridge, Harvard univ. press, 1959. 336 p. **4376**

Contains a short chapter on H., *Baron d'Holbach's contagion sacrée* (p. 228–41). Summarizes his explanations for existence and creation of gods. H. supplemented the ancient fear theory by two psychological postulates, a doctrine of projection and a principle of analogy.

Maublanc, René. L'athéisme de d'Holbach. PRRM n.s. 77:121–26, 1958. **4377**

Essentially a *compte-rendu* of Paulette Charbonnel's *Textes choisis du baron d'Holbach* (4368). Explores, by liberal use of quotes from H.'s works, the antireligious position of H. based on political and social preoccupations.

Naumann, Manfred. D'Holbach und das Materialismusproblem in der französischen Aufklärung. *In:* Holbach, Paul Henri Thiry, *baron* d'. System der Natur : oder von den Gesetzen der physischen und der moralischen Welt. Trans. by Fritz-Georg Voigt. Berlin, Aufbau, 1960. p. v–lvii. **4378**

Excellent introduction. Scholarly study of H.'s position in French Enlightenment and his importance in the development of materialism. Contains index of names to be found in *Système de la nature.*

— Zur Publiakationsgeschichte des Christianisme dévoilé. *In:* Neue Beiträge zur Literatur der Aufklärung. Berlin, Rütten und Loening, 1964. p. 155–83, 373–90. **4379**

Extensive treatment of the background and importance of H.'s *Christianisme dévoilé.* Concludes that author's aims were neither historiographic nor particularly original, with the exception of the political views of chapters 14 and 16. H. summarized sources and currents which had preceded him in an effort to reach as wide a reading public as possible.

Pappas, John. Voltaire et la guerre civile philosophique. *See* 4666. **4380**

Scholarly study of the rift between the Voltaire and Diderot-H. factions. Emphasizes role of d'Alembert in influencing Voltaire to adopt moderate position as a defender of religion and the monarch against extreme attacks of the H. materialistic and atheistic faction.

Topazio, Virgil W. Diderot's supposed contribution to d'Holbach's works. PMLA 69:173–88, 1954. *See* 5256. **4381**

Conclusion of the author is that Diderot's contribution to H.'s works was negligible if not nonexistent. Problem obviously not settled to the satisfaction of many Diderot scholars.

— D'Holbach, apostle of atheism. MLQ 17: 252–60, 1956. **4382**

A useful study of H.'s antireligious position which is seen as consistent, logical, and unwavering. His complete willingness to forsake fame or publicity obviated any need to compromise his philosophic position; the result was an unremitting atheism unparalleled in the 18th century.

— D'Holbach's conception of nature. MLN 69:412–16, 1954. **4383**

The point made is that H.'s Nature was either *le grand tout* which comprised the whole of the universe, or a human nature which served as the foundation of his secular morality. Principally it was the latter.

— D'Holbach's moral philosophy; its background and development. Geneva, Institut

et musée Voltaire, 1956. 180 p. *See* 5678.
4384

A succinct study of the " complexity of ancestral traits " which manifested themselves in the formulation of H.'s moral philosophy. Careful attention is paid to both English and French contributions to the baron's thought. H. presented as the culmination of the currents of atheism, determinism, and materialism. Contains useful index and bibliography.

Review : L. Thielemann in RR 48: 215–19, 1957.

Venturi, Franco. Postille inedite di Voltaire ad alcune opere di Nicolas-Antoine Boulanger e del barone d'Holbach. SF 2:231–40, 1958.
4385

A scholarly use of Voltaire's marginalia on his copies of Boulanger's *Recherches sur l'origine du despotisme oriental* and H.'s *Christianisme dévoilé*. The *Recherches* unfortunately, in Voltaire's eyes, undermine kings as well as priests; he found even less palatable the more atheistic and materialistic *Christianisme* which, according to Voltaire, was too vague and filled with errors.

Marie Jean Antoine Nicolas Caritat,
marquis de Condorcet
(Nos. 4386–4396)

JOHN N. PAPPAS

Condorcet, Marie, etc. Sketch for a historical picture of the progress of the human mind. Introduction by Stuart Hampshire. Trans. by June Barraclough. New York, Noonday, 1955. xvi, 202 p.
4386

Brief introduction on C.'s life and work that contributes nothing new. Makes available in English translation an essential text of the Enlightenment.

Reviews : H. Grange in RLC 32:138, 1958; R. Shackleton in FS 10:176, 1956.

Aldridge, Alfred Owen. Condorcet et Paine; leurs rapports intellectuels. *See* 5791.
4387

Disproves claims of C.'s biographers that Paine's *Réponse à quatre questions* was written to refute C. Both *Réponse* and *Lettre à l'abbé Sieyès* first published in C.'s *Le républicain* in collusion with Paine and Sieyès to prepare the public for republicanism. Studies personal relations between C. and Paine. Concludes that Paine helped accelerate C.'s philosophy while C. gave him hope, if not faith, in perfectibility of man. No profound cross-influence found. A valuable contribution to the subject.

Bouissounouse, Janine. Condorcet : le philosophe dans la Révolution. Hachette, 1962. 320 p.
4388

Presents C. as heir to Voltaire's struggle for reform and liberty. His role in writing and fostering the republican constitution recounted; his struggle against intolerance including that of Robespierre, leading to his denunciation and death under the Terror also related. Intended for popular readership (lacks scholarly trappings—footnotes, references, etc.), but well documented, reliable. Has bibliography and index. Unpublished documents and revolutionary newspapers utilized, throwing some new light on the subject (e.g., Suard's role during C.'s last days).

Reviews : J. Godechot in AHRF 35: 239–41, 1963; L. Sozzi in SF 7:365, 1963.

— De la calomnie à l'histoire. Preuves 151: 55–60, 1963.
4389

Defends C. against accusations, perpetuated by Sainte-Beuve, of opportunism by both monarchists and Girondists during the Revolution.

Cento, Alberto. Condorcet e l'idea di progresso. Florence, Parenti, 1956. 147 p.
4390

Part I considers development of C. as a *philosophe* under influence of Turgot and d'Alembert, seeking reforms in bourgeois terms with distrust for the masses. Revolution presented in Marxian terms. C. accused of vacillation and opportunism during Revolution (*see* 4387 and 4389 for a different view). Part II considers C.'s idea of progress in relation to freedom vs. determinism and history vs. anti-history. Anti-historic mode of thought of Enlightenment contrasted with historicism and positivistic determinism. C.'s concept is a revolt against history with faith in biological laws of progress and in self; it represents the will of the bourgeoisie to reshape the world to its liking.

Review : F. Orlando in SF 1:325–36, 1957.

— Un riassunto ignorato dell'Esquisse di Condorcet : il proemio dell'Antologia. RLM n.s. 11:160–66, 1958.
4391

By comparing texts, Cento shows that Giuseppi Giusti's preface to the *Antologia* is based on ideas of C.'s *Esquisse*.

Gentile, Francesco. La trasformazione dell'idea di progresso da Condorcet à Saint-Simon. RIP 14:417–44, 1960. **4392**

Based on Saint-Simon's marginal comments to C.'s *Esquisse*. Saint-Simon attracted by anticlerical passages. Modifies C.'s concept of continuous progress to one of alternating rhythm between critical and organizational stages. Author points to Turgot's influence on C.

Gooch, G. P. Condorcet and human perfectibility. *In his:* French profiles. London, Longmans, 1961. p. 145–54. **4393**

Emphasizes approvingly C.'s faith in the perfectibility of man. Largely a résumé of C.'s *Esquisse*.

Granger, Gilles-Gaston. La mathématique sociale du marquis de Condorcet. Presses univ. de France, 1956. viii, 178 p. **4394**

Stresses C. as basically a mathematician. His originality lies in his attempt to apply the methodology of this science to social questions, thus creating a *mathématique sociale.* Decisive influence of d'Alembert and Turgot shown.

Reviews : H. Grange in RLC 32:135–38, 1958; M. Israël in SF 1:503–04, 1957.

Manuel, Frank E. Marquis de Condorcet : the taming of the future. *In his:* The prophets of Paris. Cambridge, Harvard univ. press, 1962. p. 53–102. **4395**

Utilizing unpublished ms material, author underlines C.'s dilemma in reconciling individual rights with requirements of organized scientific society dedicated to accelerating human progress. Progress of human species finally takes precedence over the individual in C.'s later years. A penetrating and illuminating analysis.

Reviews : D. Thomson in FS 17:194–95, 1963.

Taton, René. Condorcet et Sylvestre-François Lacroix. RHS 12:127–58, 243–62, 1959. **4396**

Two-part article showing C.'s influence on Lacroix' career in mathematics. C. obtained teaching posts for him in Paris and led him to study the theory of probabilities. Part I has interesting history of the *Musée* founded by Pilatre de Rozier and later called the *Lycée.* Author underlines its importance in influencing the educational reforms of the Revolution. Part II deals with C.'s influence in Lacroix' *Mémoire* on probabilities in maritime insurance and his maneuvers in the Académie des Sciences to have Lacroix obtain the prize. A worthwhile study utilizing many unpublished letters and documents.

CHAPTER VI. CHARLES-LOUIS DE SECONDAT,
baron de LA BRÈDE ET DE MONTESQUIEU

(Nos. 4397–4478)

J. ROBERT LOY

Editions

Montesquieu, Charles-Louis de Secondat, *baron* **de La Brède et de.** Œuvres complètes. Ed. by Roger Caillois. Gallimard, 1949–51. 2 v. (Bibliothèque de la Pléiade) **4397**

Practical, compact, well-annotated text. No correspondence and not as complete as Nagel (4398). Valuable preface.

— Œuvres complètes. Ed. by André Masson. Nagel, 1950–55. 3 v. **4398**

Far excels all previous eds. Valuable introductory material for each section by known scholars. Excellent notes and apparatus. The essential ed. for scholars. Reviews : Anon. in TLS 266, April 23, 1954; R. Kemp in NL 3, Sept. 16, 1954.

— Œuvres complètes. Préface de Georges Vedel. Présentation et notes de Daniel Oster. Editions du Seuil, 1964. 1117 p. **4399**

" Il a écrit un véritable *Discours de la méthode* de la sociologie et de la science politique; il ne possède point véritablement une méthodologie " (Préface). "Pour parler le langage moderne, il réconcilie le monde normatif et le monde de la nature." Attractive one-volume ed. of principal works, essays, travel journal, *spicilège*, *pensées*, and poetry with short collection of aphorisms. Review : J. Bertrand in RGB 100: 134–35, Aug. 1964.

— De l'esprit des loix. Ed. by Jean Brèthe de La Gressaye. Les Belles Lettres, 1950–58. 3 v. **4400**

Robert Shackleton calls this ed., with reason, " une édition magistrale." Henceforward *the* text of the *Lois*.

— Histoire véritable. Edition critique par Roger Caillois. Lille, Giard, 1948. xxvi, 82 p. **4401**

Important ed.; text difficult to find heretofore. Caillois publishes a corrected text that reflects suggestions to M. from his friend J.-J. Bel. Appendix includes a " préambule ajouté ... pour transformer en dialogue la version remaniée " and a *Critique de l'Histoire véritable* by Bel. Review : M.-L. Dufrenoy in FR 24: 262, 1950–51.

— Les lettres persanes. Ed. by Antoine Adam. Geneva, Droz, 1954. xxviii, 434 p. **4402**

This critical ed. provides a serious scholarly presentation of text with valuable notes.

— Les lettres persanes. Ed. by Paul Vernière. Garnier, 1960. xlv, 399 p. **4403**

The best text available with introduction, rich notes, bibliographical material, and variants. Review : P. Berselli Ambri in RLM 15: 446–49, 1962.

— Montesquieu par lui-même. Images et textes présentés par Jean Starobinski. Editions du Seuil, 1957. 190 p. **4404**

Long introduction and well-chosen representative texts. Starobinski presents, in his usual brilliant style, excellent portrait of M. and continues with ever-provocative, brief, penetrating analysis of works. He seizes the person well; " le monde n'a pas pour lui [M.] de face nocturne .... Montesquieu ne s'avance vers aucun lieu qui soit sans retour." He illuminates the apparent contradiction in his thought between absolute *nature humaine* and relative *machine*, between M.'s *mécanisme* and the century's vitalism, between M.'s *liberté* and Rousseau's, although here some conclusions are open to question and subject to caution. Important contribution to M. studies.

— Politique de Montesquieu. Ed. by Jean Ehrard. Colin, 1965. 331 p. **4405**

Intelligent and interesting selection of texts with useful and cogent 40-page introduction by editor. Texts given under three headings : politics and nature of things, liberty and forms of government, elements of social happiness.

Translation

The Persian letters. Ed., trans., and introd. by J. Robert Loy. New York, Meridian, 1961. 352 p. **4406**

Contains short appendix with variants. Reviews : L. Gossman in MLN 77:322–25, 1962; G. Laidlaw in RR 52:302–04, 1964.

Criticism

Althusser, Louis. Montesquieu; la politique et l'histoire. Presses univ. de France, 1959. 119 p. **4407**

Useful, well-organized handbook; perhaps superior to most. Judgments solid and documented if, at times, overgeneralized : e.g., " c'est parce qu'il plaidait la cause d'un ordre dépassé qu'il se fit l'adversaire de l'ordre présent que d'autres devaient dépasser."
Review : J. E. in Rhist 222:477–78, 1959.

Ayrault, R. Schiller et Montesquieu : sur la genèse du Don Carlos. EG 3:233–40, 1948. **4408**

Studies Schiller play through portrait of Phillip II as example of monarchy in disintegration, eventually into despotism. Interesting, somewhat conjectural essay.

Barrière, Pierre. Les éléments personnels et les éléments bordelais dans les Lettres persanes. RHL 51:17–36, 1951. **4409**

Sees in Lettres persanes correspondence and contradiction between M.'s ideas and his real existence in Bordeaux. Rica and Usbek are two sides of M.; the Persians, Bordelais; the women, M.'s friends and wife; etc. Barrière presents imposing list of personal and intellectual parallels. " Son œuvre, si nettement influencée par celle de Montaigne, apparaît comme un véritable examen de conscience intellectuel et moral." Important contribution.

— L'expérience italienne de Montesquieu. RLM n.s. 3:15–28, 1952. See 5884. **4410**

Good estimate of importance of Italian travels in M.'s intellectual formation. This influence was perhaps as vital as his English experience according to Barrière.

Baskin, Mark Petrovich. Charles Louis Montesquieu, vwidayushiisya fransuskii mwislitel XVIII veka. (Charles Louis Montesquieu, outstanding French thinker of the eighteenth century.) Moscow, Znanie, 1955. 23 p. **4411**

Slight but interesting pamphlet. Some good ideas, but M.'s " struggle " against feudal absolutes and religion as well as his part in consciously prepared bourgeois revolution exaggerated.

Berlin, Isaiah. Montesquieu. London, Oxford univ. press, 1956. 30 p. Also in: PBA 41:267–96, 1955. **4412**

Important. One of best jugements d'ensemble on writer, thinker, and man.

Berselli Ambri, Paola. L'opera di Montesquieu nel Settecento italiano. Florence, Olschki, 1959. viii, 236 p. See 5889. **4413**

After routine review of M.'s Italian voyage, author studies reputation of M. at Vatican from 1748 to Revolution; also his reputation and influence in Tuscany, Piedmont, Venice, Naples, and in Austrian Italy. Lois more important than Lettres persanes and Romains. " Ma ciò che majormente piacque agli Italiani del tempo fu il relativismo...."

Beyer, Charles-Jacques. Montesquieu et la censure religieuse de l'Esprit des lois. RScH n.s. 70:105–31, 1953. **4414**

Orderly and important review of M.'s encounters with religious authority using and filling out documents already published (e.g., L. Bérard's ed. of Bottari's report, etc.). Using texts of the Lois, Beyer explains the kind of modifications in 1757 ed. of Lois made by M. who " ne pensait être un moins bon chrétien pour croire en une morale, une science politique et même une politique libre de toute intervention directe de l'autorité religieuse."

— Montesquieu et le relativisme esthétique. SVEC 24:171–82, 1963. **4415**

Using documents made available since 1947, Beyer reappraises M.'s esthetics (cf. Dargan, 1546). He sees in various stages of Essai sur le goût same intellectual development as in the Lois between classical esthetic of absolute along with relative esthetic measured in terms of period, place, and civilization.

Bordeaux. Bibliothèque municipale. Montesquieu, 1689–1755. Exposition organisée à la Bibliothèque municipale pour commémorer le deuxième centenaire de la mort de Montesquieu. Bordeaux, 1955. 148 p.   **4416**

Interesting catalog of M. material, including facsimiles, portraits, material on life, property, family, works, etc., and bibliography.

Bresky, Dushan. Schiller's debt to Montesquieu and Adam Ferguson. CL 13:239–53, 1961.   **4417**

Precisions on the influence, direct or otherwise, of M. on Schiller, including the intermediary of Ferguson. Interesting and serious article, although hypothetical at times as all such studies must be. Schiller in both *Don Carlos* and *Fiesko von Genua* very probably reflects the complex ideal of M.: a democratic monarchy.

Cabeen, David C. A supplementary Montesquieu bibliography. RIP 9:409–34, 1955.   **4418**

Additions and precisions to 1458, done with Cabeen's usual efficiency.

Caillois, Roger. Montesquieu ou la révolution sociologique. CPl 8:179–94, 1949. **4419**

Stimulating essay on basic unity of M.'s thought and literary life. Caillois sees *Lettres persanes* as necessary prerequisite in M.'s sociological revolution, as " la démarche de l'esprit qui consiste à se feindre étranger à la société où l'on vit, à la regarder du dehors et comme si on la voyait pour la première fois." Presents convincing case for seeing in M. a divorce of *moraliste* and *sociologue*.

Carayol, Elisabeth. Des lettres persanes oubliées. RHL 65:15–26, 1965.   **4420**

Le fantasque (a weekly appearing from May 24 to Oct. 4, 1745) by author of *Chef d'œuvre d'un inconnu,* friend of M., published 8 presumed fragments of new *Lettres persanes.* Carayol studies relations between M. and St.-Hyacinthe and comments on new letters.

Chevallier, Jean-Jacques. Montesquieu ou le libéralisme aristocratique. RIP 9:330–45, 1955.   **4421**

Solid study of M. and *la résistance aristocratique* historically, sociologically, and from point of view of M.'s intellectual development. *La résistance* becomes *libéralisme* but remains alert to dangers of sick monarchies.

Congrès Montesquieu. Actes du Congrès Montesquieu, Bordeaux, 23–26 mai 1955. Bordeaux, Delmas, 1956. 366 p.   **4422**

Collection of papers read at bicentenary

congress of M.'s death, held at La Brède. Papers fall into 4 categories : The Man, Sources and Ideas, Law and Political Science, and Religion. A partial and selective list of papers follows : Paul Bastid, *Montesquieu et les Jésuites,* p. 305–26; A. Bertière, *Montesquieu, lecteur de Machiavel,* p. 141–58; Charles-Jacques Beyer, *Montesquieu et l'esprit cartésien,* p. 159–73; Roger Caillois, *Montesquieu et l'athéisme contemporain,* p. 327–36; Sergio Cotta, *L'idée de parti dans la philosophie politique de Montesquieu,* p. 257–63; M. Eisenmann, *Le système constitutionnel de Montesquieu et le temps présent,* p. 241–48; F. T. H. Fletcher, *Montesquieu et la politique religieuse en Angleterre au XVIII* *siècle,* p. 295–304; W. Folkierski, *Montesquieu et Vico,* p. 127–40; François Gébelin, *La clef du Temple de Gnide d'après la Correspondance de Montesquieu,* p. 83–97; André Masson, *Les dernières ratures des Lettres persanes,* p. 71–82; Robert Shackleton, *La religion de Montesquieu,* p. 287–94; Paul M. Spurlin, *L'influence de Montesquieu sur la constitution américaine,* p. 265–72; Paul Vernière, *Montesquieu et le monde musulman, d'après l'Esprit des lois,* p. 175–90.

Cotta, Sergio. L'illuminisme et la science politique : Montesquieu, Diderot et Catherine II. RIPC n.s. 16:273–87, 1954. *See* 5125.   **4423**

Serious and interesting contribution to 18th-century studies. Cotta proposes to show that whereas M. " se propose d'élaborer une science *empirique* de la société," by studying *what it is,* Voltaire *et al.* see things in the light of what ought to be. M. represents a crucial point in 18th-century political philosophy. Diderot's reaction to M. the most interesting and meaningful for comprehension of *philosophes.* " Pour Diderot l'unique gouvernement possible est la démocratie ... le problème politique ... rapporté à son noyau central : qui *doit* être souverain, *vrai* souverain ? " Cotta concludes : " La profonde conviction de Montesquieu [Laws are expressions of historical social situations] ... n'est même pas comprise par Diderot," who is still in the Platonic world of nature-reason.

— Montesquieu e la scienza della società. Turin, Ramella, 1953. 420 p.   **4424**

Essential study. Cotta examines M.'s religious-metaphysical convictions and finds them in harmony with his scientific theories. He then studies M.'s early political ideas chronologically by work, and finds the gradual introduction of ethical thought into the political as the obvious effect of his travels. He finally traces M.'s thought from the political to the sociological in the *Lois*.

— Montesquieu et Filangieri; notes sur la fortune de Montesquieu au xviiᵉ siècle. RIP 9:387-400, 1955.   **4425**

Cotta regrets absence of study in form of M. in Italy. Sober study of influences on Filangieri as representative of basic M.-*philosophe* split between " what is " and " what ought to be " and basic incomprehension of M.'s position and ideas among Italian enlighteners.

— Montesquieu, la séparation des pouvoirs et la constitution fédérale des Etats Unis. RIPC n.s. 4:225-47, 1951.   **4426**

Re-examines classic academic problem by logical steps : (1) evidence shows influence; (2) influence not exclusive; (3) terrain of opinion prepared to receive influence. Assays originality of M. (compared to Locke and English constitution) in his theory of separation. M.'s theory already in Book II before famous chapter on England. The founding fathers " adoptèrent la formule [de Montesquieu] à la réalité sociale américaine." An important article that serves as a corrective to long-accepted ideas of Parrington and Beard.

Courtney, C. P. Montesquieu and Burke. Oxford, Blackwell, 1963. xv, 204 p. *See* 5685.   **4427**

A short, reasonably well-documented survey of the career of Edmund Burke with comment on probable influence by M. on Burke's thinking during periods of debate on British constitution, American independence, India, French Revolution and Ireland. Shows that with physical decline of George III and beginning of parliamentary reform, the whole British constitution as comprehended by M. ceases to exist. Concludes that with the French Revolution, M.'s particular determinism becomes unpalatable to Burke although, in contrast to general liberal opinion of times, he continues to admire M.'s intellectual orientation.

Reviews : I. Berlin in MLR 60:449-52, 1965; J. Ehrard in RHL 65:128, 1965; M. Fuchs in EA 17:192-94, 1964.

Crisafulli, Alessandro S. Montesquieu's Histoire véritable : sources and originality of its satirical device. SP 50:59-67, 1953. **4428**

Shows Lucian as source for satirical device of M.'s fiction. Also, however, *Les aventures merveilleuses du mandarin Fum-Hoam, conte chinois* by Thomas Gueulette (1723). M.'s originality not only in different use of Gueulette's transmigration device but in all the common points between the two fictions. Incidentally, date of work now certainly subsequent to *Lettres persanes*. Forthright, sober study of important aspect of M. as a novelist.

— A neglected English imitation of Montesquieu's Lettres persanes. MLQ 14:209-16, 1953.   **4429**

Details of influence of *Lettres persanes* and of Lyttleton's *Letters from a Persian in England to his friend in Ispahan* on *Letters from an Armenian in Ireland to his friends in Trebisond* (1756). England obviously chose satiric element of M. rather than erotic and romanesque aspects. Article preparatory to a longer study of history of pseudo-oriental epistolary literature.

Derathé, Robert. Montesquieu et Jean-Jacques Rousseau. RIP 9:366-86, 1955. **4430**

Well-organized presentation of similarities and differences of two seminal political philosophers : M., the describer of what is and Rousseau, the writer of what ought to be. The *volonté générale* and the balance of powers are " la croisée des chemins où [M. and Rousseau] se séparent pour devenir les chefs de deux écoles politiques radicalement opposées."

— La philosophie des Lumières en France : raison et modération selon Montesquieu. RIP 6:275-93, 1952.   **4431**

After a valid survey of the beginning of philosophic spirit in France, Derathé studies M. as characteristic *philosophe* in his avowed aim of introducing the spirit of moderation into lawmaking—*modération*, along with *douceur*, being M.'s notion of *raison*.

Desgraves, Louis. Le IIᵉ centenaire de la mort de Montesquieu (Bordeaux, mai–juin 1955). RHB n.s. 4:363-71, 1955. **4432**

Chronique régionale useful for succinct description of ceremonies, exposition, and congress held on occasion of centenary of M.'s death.

Deuxième centenaire de l'Esprit des lois de Montesquieu, 1748-1948; conférences organisées par la ville de Bordeaux. Bordeaux, Delmas, 1949. 309 p.   **4433**

As Cabeen says (4418), somewhat hastily edited. A list of communications, some of them important, follows : Pierre Barrière, *L'humanisme de L'esprit des lois*, p. 31–64; Léon Bérard, *L'esprit des lois devant la Congrégation de l'Index*, p. 241–309; Jean Brèthe de La Gressaye, *L'esprit des lois vu de La Brède*, p. 65–78; Maurice Creyx, *Biologie et médecine dans l'œuvre de Montesquieu*, p. 79–125; Georges Davy, *Montesquieu et la science politique*, p. 127–71; Maurice Duverger, *Montesquieu et notre temps*, p. 227–40; André Masson, *Naissance et fortune de L'esprit des lois*, p. 11–29; William Stewart, *Montesquieu et l'Angleterre*, p.173–225.

Dimoff, Paul. Cicéron, Hobbes et Montesquieu. AUS 1:19–47, 1952. *See* 5686. **4434**

Completing lacunae of Dedieu, studies documentable influence of Hobbes on M. Shows contradiction between Cicero's and Hobbes' notion of source of law, both of which were known to M. *Lettres persanes* seen as a reply to Hobbes; also *Traité des devoirs*. After 1729, Hobbes less present in M.'s thinking in *Lois* and M. seems content with having already refuted the important part of Hobbes' thought. For whatever reasons, M. never thought to destroy Hobbes.

Dubroca, Joseph. La pensée de Montesquieu n'est-elle pas méconnue ? PRRM n.s. 99:87–97, 1961. **4435**

Diffuse but stimulating article on the true guidelines of M.'s thought which for Dubroca is not " déiste et réactionnaire."

Durkheim, Emile. Quid Secundatus politicae scientiæ instituendæ contulerit. Trans. into French by Armand Cuvillier. *In his:* Montesquieu et Rousseau, précurseurs de la sociologie. Rivière, 1953. p. 25–113. *Also in English in his:* Montesquieu and Rousseau : forerunners of sociology. Trans. by Ralph Manheim. Foreword by Henry Peyre. Ann Arbor, Univ. of Michigan press, 1960. p. 1–64. **4436**

Same as 1552. The study has not lost any of its essential force. The new translation by director of *Petite bibliothèque sociologique internationale* would appear closer to Durkheim's thought than the former one.

Ehrard, Jean. Les études sur Montesquieu et l'Esprit des lois. IL 11:55–66, 1959. **4437**

Valuable article reviewing and judging recent eds. of texts and critical studies. Also sketch and suggestions for study of genesis of the *Lois* with good bibliography.

One conclusion : the unity of the *Lois* less in perfect coherence of its composition than in personality of its author. Underlines importance of vocabulary study for comprehension of M. : e.g., *cause* and *raison* of institutions.

Eylaud, J.-M. Montesquieu chez ses notaires de La Brède. Bordeaux, Delmas, 1956. 194 p. **4438**

Statistics on M.'s dealings with his lawyers (agents), Latapie and Giraudeau, conscientiously collected by Dr. Eylaud. Also inventory lists of M.'s furnishings at La Brède, Martillac, Baron, and rue Porte-Dijeaux.
Review : C. Dartigue–Peyrou in AdMidi 69:171–74, 1957.

Fleckniakoska, J.-N. Essai sur les sources du panorama de l'Espagne et de son empire dans l'œuvre de Montesquieu. RHB n.s. 5: 167–92, 1956. *See* 5953. **4439**

Interesting article on M.'s long ambivalent interest in Spain and examination of his ideas on Hispania and of the Spanish sources he very probably used (although without knowledge of Spanish). Article goes in right direction to fill important lacunae.

Göhring, Martin. Montesquieu : Historismus und moderner Verfassungsstaat. Wiesbaden, Franz Steiner, 1956. 51 p. **4440**

Slight but interesting essay including biographical data. Compares two " systems " open to M., that of abbé Du Bos following divine rights and that of Boulainvilliers going back to Franks. Also compares M. to Machiavelli with advantage given to former. Underlines M.'s contribution to one-world, family-of-nations idea.

Grimsley, Ronald. The idea of nature in the Lettres persanes. FS 5:293–306, 1951. **4441**

Serious article proposing to study norms of *reason* and *nature* as used by M. in *Lettres persanes*. M. clearly did not intend *relativity* as his final word but rather aims at new norm of reason derived from serious consideration of the relativity of sentimental or emotional reaction to nature. A good introduction to a vast and vastly interesting problem.

Groethuysen, Bernard. Le libéralisme de Montesquieu et la liberté telle que l'entendent les républicains. Eur 37:2–16, Jan. 1949. **4442**

Important article concerning M.'s ideas on liberty. M. essentially humanist : " tout son système repose sur la reconnaissance de la nature humaine et ses droits."

— Philosophie de la Révolution française, précédée de Montesquieu. Gallimard, 1956. 306 p. **4443**

Unfinished ms on M. Dense, somewhat disorganized collection of quotations. Insists on limits of reason so well seen by M.; discusses intelligently role of social morality vs. church morality, despotism of monarch vs. national destiny and providence. Alix Guillain, who prepared publication, says that Groethuysen shows how the revolutionaries, while recognizing their debt to M.'s constructive reasoning, " ne pouvaient s'en tenir au relativisme de *L'esprit des lois*." Review : H. Jauss in Archiv 195:355–57, 1958–59.

Henry-Bordeaux, Paule. L'élection mouvementée de Montesquieu à l'Académie française. RDM 498–510, Mar.–Apr. 1959. **4444**

Succinct review of circumstances surrounding M.'s election during years 1721–28 that clarifies academician/barrister struggle of honor.

Kassem, Badreddine. Décadence et absolutisme dans l'œuvre de Montesquieu. Geneva, Droz, 1960. 286 p. **4445**

Problem of decadence fundamental in M. Author studies absolutism and intolerance, e.g., Jesuits in France, M.'s theory of despotism, his views of corruption in Europe, and his conclusions on decadence. Especially good on M. as judge of Islamic culture and Orient. Concludes that M.'s politics is really morality. Solid study if somewhat diffuse; useful bibliography.

Koebner, Richard. The authenticity of the letters on the Esprit des lois attributed to Helvétius. *See* 4358. **4446**

Cabeen comments (4418) : " Careful research for the purpose of establishing the fact that the letters were forgeries, written by abbé Martin Lefebvre La Roche."

Laufer, Roger. La réussite romanesque et la signification des Lettres persanes de Montesquieu. RHL 61:188–203, 1961. **4447**

Re-examining M.'s remarks in the *Réflexions*, Laufer purports to show how internal study of *Lettres persanes* can support critical notion that M.'s originality in work lies in synthetic unity of philosophic criticism and harem plot. Author sees *Lettres persanes* and *Diable boiteux* as examples of rococo style, contrary to lingering postclassicism of most other contemporary literature. Some interesting ideas.

Laurain-Portemer, Madeleine. Le dossier des Lettres persanes : notes sur les cahiers de corrections. RHB n.s. 12:41–81, 1963. **4448**

Important article for textual scholarship giving details of M.'s corrections, facsimile pages from *grand* and *petit cahiers de corrections*, and several pages tracing corrections through 3 stages : *grand, petit*, and final *grand*. Appended, an interesting unpublished caricature of M. during Italian travels.

Ludwig, Mario. Montesquieu und die Engländer. AK 46:97–107, 1964. *See* 5687. **4449**

M. perhaps shows more " Kenntnisse, Objektivität, kritischen Scharfblicke und Wohlwollen " than any other Frenchman viewing England. By analysis of life and works, Ludwig makes interesting and convincing study about why this should be so. Nothing new, but succinct.

Marchand, Jean. Bibliographie générale raisonnée des œuvres de Montesquieu. BBB 49–62, 1960. **4450**

Slight article giving, only for *Lettres persanes*, a résumé of bibliographical problems and suggestion for a new *essai de classement* for 1st eds.

Mauriac, Pierre. Une source méconnue de L'esprit des lois. RDM 192–202, Mar.–Apr. 1962. **4451**

Details of probable Spanish source : *Examen des esprits propres et naiz aux sciences* (French transl., 1613) by Jean Huarte. M. had it in his library at La Brède.

Mercier, Roger. Le roman dans les Lettres persanes : structure et signification. RScH n.s. 108:345–56, 1962. **4452**

Important article showing that the literary and philosophic center of the *Lettres persanes* (with change of insistence according to social backdrop of various fictional episodes : e.g., Ibrahim, Aphéridon, and Astarté, Roxane, Troglodytes, etc.) is the problem : happiness or virtue ? The consistent conclusion : virtue without liberty is not possible. Thus, another proof of the unity of fiction-idea in the *Lettres persanes*. Article written before that of Laufer (4447).

— La théorie des climats des Réflexions critiques à L'esprit des lois. RHL 53:17–37, 159–74, 1953. **4453**

First part of article traces development of idea that climate influences human mind and action from Du Bos through Rémond de St. Mard, de la Villate, the abbé d'Espiard, Feijoo, Hume (*et al.*) to M. In the second, Mercier studies the close connection between such theory and a general skepticism. Mercier concludes with examination of development of these ideas from *Essai sur les causes* ... to final form in the *Lois*. There, climate is but one of the determinants of the *esprit général*. Importance of M.'s contribution not in originality, therefore, but in care with which he subjected several theories to *experience* to extract one limited theory.

Merquiol, André. Montesquieu et la géographie politique. RIPC n.s. 7:127–46, 1957. **4454**

Political geography a modern science but end product of long tradition owing much to M. Merquiol provides workmanlike résumé of influences on M., analyzes implications of M.'s thinking on climate and terrain, and studies destiny of theory of climate after the *Lois*. Distinguishes between M.'s determinism in human realm and in realm of objects.

Oake, Roger B. Montesquieu's analysis of Roman history. JHI 16:44–59, 1955. **4455**

Rome's success neither " proof of a divine plan " nor " ideal model for politicians." Oake takes reasoned exception to some of Laboulaye's commentary. Rome for M. a timocratic republic, and results follow from that fact. " Roman appetite for *gloire* inevitably destroyed liberty." M. revolutionary not only in absence of Providence from history but in assuming existence of discoverable laws of human behavior. The relative and absolute once more combined.

— Montesquieu's religious ideas. JHI 14: 548–60, 1953. **4456**

Man's religious activity seen by M. as essentially social activity; religion considered within historical framework. Free will an observed fact with which political and religious systems must be consonant. Perceptive article distinguishing between M.'s traditional Catholicism and his intellectual inquiry.

La pensée politique et constitutionnelle de Montesquieu; bicentenaire de L'esprit des lois, 1748–1948. Ed. by Boris Mirkine-

Guetzévitch and Henri Puget. Recueil Sirey, 1952. 328 p. (IDC : Travaux et recherches, 8) **4457**

Pierre Barrière, *L'humanisme de L'esprit des lois*, p. 97–115; Paul Bastid, *Montesquieu et les États-Unis*, p. 313–21; Jean Brèthe de La Gressaye, *L'histoire de L'esprit des lois*, p. 69–96; René Cassin, *Montesquieu et les droits de l'homme*, p. 183–90; Charles Eisenmann, *La pensée constitutionnelle de Montesquieu*, p. 133–160; André Gardot, *De Bodin à Montesquieu*, p. 41–68; Jean Graven, *Montesquieu et le droit pénal*, p. 209–54; André Marie, *Conclusion*, p. 323–28; Boris Mirkine-Guetzévitch, *De L'esprit des lois à la démocratie moderne*, p. 11–24; Boris Mirkine-Guetzévitch, *De la séparation des pouvoirs*, p. 161–81; J.-P. Niboyet, *Montesquieu et le droit comparé*, p. 255–71; Marcel Prélot, *Montesquieu et les formes de gouvernement*, p. 119–32; Henri Puget, *L'apport de L'esprit des lois à la science politique et au droit publique*, p. 25–38; Henri Puget, *Montesquieu et l'Angleterre*, p. 275–311; Pierre Rain, *Montesquieu et l'histoire*, p. 191–207.

Polska Akademia nauk. Komitet nauk prawnych. Monteskiusz i jego dzieło; sesja naukowa w dwusetną rocznicę śmierci; Warszawa, 27–28 X 1955. Ed. by Juliusz Bardach and Konstanty Grzybowski. Wrocław, Zakład im Ossolińskich, 1956. 364 p. **4458**

A series of Polish communications read at anniversary celebration with a brief résumé of proceedings and papers in French. Papers read include : Juliusz Bardach, *Conclusion;* Andrzej Burda, *La doctrine constitutionnelle de Montesquieu;* Karol Koranyi, *Le fond historique de l'œuvre de Montesquieu;* Kazimierz Opałek, *Montesquieu en Pologne;* Stanisław Pławski, *Les problèmes du droit pénal dans les œuvres de Montesquieu;* Jerzy Wróblewski, *La théorie du droit de Montesquieu.* Each communication followed by a discussion.

Rantzau, Johann Albrecht von. Politische Wirkungen antiker Verstellungen bei Montesquieu. AntA 5:107–20, 1956. **4459**

Solid, important discussion of M.'s complex ideas on political liberty which author sees as a mixture of Ancient ideals and Middle-Ages tradition. Good discussion of importance of Frankish idea in M.'s synthesis and a skillful contrast of Rousseau's more discussed *Gleichheit* (opposed to M.'s liberty) in light of Benjamin Constant's 1819 essay.

Rat, Maurice. Grammairiens et amateurs de beau langage : Montesquieu. VL 72:129–32, 1958. **4460**

Short note showing examples (starting with the *Romains*) of shift in M.'s style from artifice and elegance to a classic style grounded in Latin.

Robinet, André. Ouvrages ayant appartenu à Malebranche recueillis par Montesquieu. RHB n.s. 8:266–67, 1959. **4461**

Check list of titles once belonging to Malebranche in M.'s library at La Brède.

Roddier, Henri. De la composition de L'esprit des lois : Montesquieu et les oratoriens de l'Académie de Juilly. RHL 52:439–50, 1952. **4462**

Excellent article showing influence upon M.'s sense of composition, in the *Lettres persanes* and the *Lois*, of the particular brand of Cartesianism disseminated by the Oratorians. Good case made for importance of *Entretiens sur les sciences* of *père* Lamy. Author shows more clearly than most the eclectic nature of M.'s method : logic, experiment, historic, or genetic method. Excellent illumination on several problem passages of the *Lettres persanes* and the *Lois*.

Roger, G. L'audience de Montesquieu. Eur 119–20:203–11, Nov.–Dec. 1955. **4463**

Slight but useful article on the size and nature of M.'s public and probable influence on his century.

Rombout, Machiel Willem. La conception stoïcienne du bonheur chez Montesquieu et chez quelques-uns de ses contemporains. Leiden, Universitaire Pers Leiden, 1958. 118 p. **4464**

Important, short, concise study of problem vital to century. Conclusion : " Montesquieu est vraiment réaliste. Tout en bâtissant son état pour le bonheur de ses prochains, il dit qu'on peut être heureux et qu'on ne peut pas le devenir."

Rosa, Mario. Sulla condanna dell'Esprit des lois e sulla fortuna di Montesquieu in Italia. RSCI 14:411–28, 1960. **4465**

Article motivated by Berselli Ambri's book (4413). Attempts to detail M.'s conflict with Rome and concludes with précis of M.'s literary fortunes in various sections of Italy. Interesting, well-documented article.

Rostand, Jean. Montesquieu (1689–1755) et la biologie. RHS 8:129–36, 1955. **4466**

Interesting by reason of author. Discussion of M.'s early papers on science concerning biology. M. seems naïve to us, says Rostand, for he kept much of Cartesian mechanism. But occasionally in *Observations sur l'histoire naturelle* and elsewhere, " avec un peu de bon vouloir on pourrait ranger Montesquieu parmi les quelques-uns qui, avant Lamarck et Geoffroy Saint-Hilaire, ont pressenti la grande idée de l'évolution."

Rowbotham, Arnold H. China in the Esprit des lois : Montesquieu and Mgr. Foucquet. CL 2:354–59, 1950. **4467**

A slight article assaying sources of M.'s knowledge of China. Rowbotham concludes that any confusion in M.'s mind reflects conflict of evidence between official Jesuit information (Du Halde) and information resulting from conversations with Foucquet.

Scaglione, Aldo. Montesquieu e Algarotti : nota sulla storiografia settecentesca. SF 2:249–53, 1958. **4468**

Precisions and suggestions on comparative study of two writers. M.'s influence not as enduring as Machiavelli's.

Schalk, Fritz. Montesquieu und die europäischen Traditionen. *In:* Forschungsprobleme der vergleichenden Literaturgeschichte. Ed. by Kurt Wais. Tübingen, Max Niemeyer, 1951. p. 101–18. *Also in his:* Studien zur französischen Aufklärung. Munich, Hueber, 1964. p. 107–26. **4469**

M. seen as part of trilogy of French political thought with Bodin and J.-J. Rousseau. M. situated in development from old (monarchy, unity, absolute, etc.) to new in reference to Bodin, Rousseau, English thinkers, physiocrats, and after. Interesting, well-limited, important article.

Shackleton, Robert. The evolution of Montesquieu's theory of climate. RIP 9:317–29, 1955. **4470**

Shackleton proposes to study development of M.'s ideas on climate chronologically. First interest in polluted air of Rome. Tight study of important detail through 4 stages : Rome, *esprit général*, Arbuthnot's essay, Espiard. Shackleton maintains importance of *Essai sur les causes* which he dates 1736–1743.

— La genèse de L'esprit des lois. RHL 52:425–38, 1952. **4471**

By close study of ms of *Lois* and the handwriting of M.'s secretaries, Shackleton proposes, in sober, scholarly fashion, a chronology of sections of the *Lois*, e.g., date of composition of chapter on England. Essential article.

— Montesquieu : a critical biography. London, Oxford univ. press, 1961. xiv, 432 p.   **4472**

A major work by outstanding M. scholar. Richly documented and soberly written, the biography traces M.'s life and provides short, expert analyses of his works in chronological order. Studies M. under important headings : conception of law, theory of governments, liberty, climate, history of laws, and religion. Excellent on moral aspects of M.'s conception of law and on clarification of *esprit général*. A treasure-trove of facts. Valuable bibliography of M.'s works.

Reviews : S. Cotta in RIF 54:481–83, 1963; S. Cotta in SF 8:310–11, 1964; P. Gay in JMH 35:78–79, 1963; L. Gossman in MLN 79:89–94; J. Lough in FS 16:62–64; 1962; A. Masson in Cr 18:87–91, Jan. 1962; R. Mercier in RLC 38:156–59, 1964; M. Oakeshott in MLR 57:442–44, 1962.

— Montesquieu and Machiavelli : a reappraisal. CLS 1:1–13, 1964. *See* 5921.   **4473**

Excellent, sober study clarifying and correcting what has already been written on subject by chronological study of M.'s mss. Striking passages of Machiavelli, in contemporary French translation, set beside passages of M. " Reading Machiavelli stimulated Montesquieu to reflect on the extent and ... limits of personal policies in the history of states, on historical causation, and above all on the relation between history and politics."

— Montesquieu : two unpublished documents. FS 4:313–21, 1950.   **4474**

Important article. Details on Shackleton's discovery of volume II of *Geographica* and catalog of M.'s library.

Trevor-Roper, Hugh. L'esprit de Montesquieu. NSN 745–46, Nov. 17, 1961.   **4475**

Occasioned by Shackleton's biography of M., this is best thumbnail sketch of M. Succinct estimate of M., condemned both by authorities and *philosophes*, especially Voltaire.

Vidal, Enrico. Saggio sul Montesquieu; con particolare riguardo alla sua concezione dell'uomo, del diritto e della politica. Milan, Giuffrè, 1950. 223 p.   **4476**

Cabeen reports (4418) : " Best in Italian up to its date of publication ... a most useful publication."

Weil, Françoise. Les lectures de Montesquieu. RHL 57:494–514, 1957.   **4477**

Careful article of which large part a list of books read by M., especially in connection with the *Lois* and the *Romains*. Perhaps susceptible to some argument, the list established by author is always seriously justified and clearly explained. General conclusion arising therefrom : M. spent much more time in Paris (including scholarly pursuits) than heretofore supposed. Helpful chronological list of readings with suggested notations of place read (La Brède or Paris).

— Le manuscrit des Geographica et L'esprit des lois. RHL 52:451–61, 1952.   **4478**

Description of ms and contents of *Geographica* by editor of this section of Nagel ed. of *Œuvres complètes* (4398). Complements Dodds (1484) on sources of the *Lois*. Role of *Geographica* as first step in M.'s research and importance of his remarks on readings. The *Geographica* not used for the *Lois* before 1741. M. quotes exclusively from this personal source book and not the original work in question; he incorporates his first reactions of *Geographica* almost *verbatim* into the *Lois*. Valuable chronology of M.'s research and thinking on China.

CHAPTER VII. FRANÇOIS-MARIE AROUET DE VOLTAIRE

(Nos. 4479–4769)

RICHARD A. BROOKS

Bibliography

Alatri, Paolo. Le renouveau voltairien en Italie. Tro 122:176–81, Feb. 1958. **4479**
An account of Italian scholarship on V. between 1950 and 1957.

— Studi volterriani. Bel 12:133–58, 1957. **4480**
An appraisal of post-World War II scholarship on V. until about 1956.

Besterman, Theodore. The Institut et musée Voltaire and its collections. *In his:* Voltaire essays, and another. *See* 4542. p. 114–23. **4481**
A description of the publishing activities, printed and ms collections, and museum pieces at the Institut et musée Voltaire. Taken from the guide to the Institut.

— The manuscripts of the Institut et musée Voltaire. SVEC 6:293–95, 1958. **4482**
A brief account of ms material in the possession of the Institut and of which a detailed inventory had not yet been prepared.

— A provisional bibliography of Italian editions and translations of Voltaire. SVEC 18: 263–310, 1961. **4483**
Bibliography restricted to separately published works and excludes publications in contemporary periodicals, drama collections, anthologies, etc. No claim for completeness even within its limits because of imperfect state of present knowledge of 18th-century Italian literature and lack of comprehensive national Italian libraries. Author urges Italian scholars to carry on from this preliminary study. Includes indexes of titles, translators, editors, etc.

— Some eighteenth-century Voltaire editions unknown to Bengesco. SVEC 8:123–242, 1959. **4484**
Description of a number of 18th-century Voltaire eds. unlisted in Bengesco (1618), but excluding translations. Author makes no claim of setting up a formal bibliography; only a catalog of his important collection. Nevertheless, a valuable supplement to Bengesco. Indexed.

— Voltaire's correspondence. Crev 181:357–61, 1952. *French version in:* RSu 2⁵:106–11, 1952. **4485**
Briefly summarizes publication of V.'s correspondence by Beaumarchais and Moland and justifies publication of his new critical ed.

Delattre, André. Répertoire chronologique des lettres de Voltaire non recueillies dans les éditions de sa correspondance générale. Chapel Hill, 1952. xii, 201 p. (UNCR,17) **4486**
Author claims to list nearly 4,000 letters newly found since Moland ed. At least half of his entries, however, are in Moland ed. and many are not strictly letters. Superseded by Besterman ed. of V.'s correspondence (4509).
Reviews : T. Besterman in SVEC 1: 220–24, 1955; H. Lancaster in MLN 67:488–89, 1952.

Evans, Hywel Berwyn. A provisional bibliography of English editions and translations of Voltaire. SVEC 8:9–121, 1959. **4487**
Author makes no claim of completeness and hopes " that it may provoke corrections and additions " for preparation of definitive bibliography. Contains 578 entries includhing sets and doubtful works. Includes index of titles, translators, and editors. Valuable contribution.
Review : J. Brumfitt in FS 14:69, 1960.

Flower, Desmond, and **J. S. G. Simmons.** Voltairiana in the U.S.S.R. TLS 276, May 16, 1958. **4488**
Authors list and summarize major contributions of V.S. Lîublinskiĭ, Soviet V. scholar who had extended access to V. library. These include : (1) a 200-page contribution on V. in *Literaturnoe nasled-*

stvo, 29/30 (*Russkaya kul'tura i Frantsiya*, 1, Moscow, 1937; (2) a paper on V.'s marginalia in *Vol'ter: stat'i i materialy*, ed. by M. P. Alekseev, Leningrad, 1947; (3) a contribution in *Vol'ter: stat'i i materialy*, ed. by V. P. Volgin, Moscow-Leningrad, 1948; (4) the *Pis'ma Vol'tera* of 1956 (4526) described in detail in this article; (5) and an essay on sources for history of religion in V.'s library in *Ezhegodnik Muzeya istorii religii i ateizma*, 1, Moscow, Akademiia nauk, 1957.

Leningrad. Publichnaia biblioteka. Biblioteka Vol'tera; katalog knig. (Bibliothèque de Voltaire; catalogue des livres.) Ed. by M. P. Aperceev and T. N. Kopreeva. Moscow, Akademiia nauk SSSR, 1961. 1166 p. **4489**

Definitive work on V.'s Ferney library now preserved in Soviet Union. Important bibliographical study containing 3,867 titles, introductions, and appendixes. Titles and bibliographical information in French followed by abbreviations in Russian (with translations at beginning of works) to indicate notes in V.'s hand or Wagnière's, corrections, reading markers, and volumes whose pages were completely or partially uncut. Brief French summaries of Russian introductions. Mine of information about V.'s intellectual preoccupations. Supersedes Havens and Torrey (4499).
Reviews : D. Flower in Bcol 10⁴:501-09, 1961; A. Miller in RR 55:56-58, 1964; J. Minář in CMF 44:252-53, 1962; L. Onu in RFRG 7:181-84, 1963; R. Pomeau in RHL 62:609-10, 1962.

Liublinskii, Vladimir Sergeevich. La bibliothèque de Voltaire. RHL 58:467-88, 1958. **4490**

States that V. marginalia published to date represent only small fraction of those in V. library preserved in Leningrad. Gives résumé of studies made on V. library and brief summary of results obtained from study of V. materials in Soviet Union by Soviet and non-Soviet scholars. Provides history of catalog of V. library published in Soviet Union and suggests several research projects. Interesting introduction to recent Soviet scholarship on V. *See also* by same author *Voltaire and his library* in Bcol 7:139-51, 1958.

Malcolm, Jean. Table de la bibliographie de Voltaire par Bengesco. Geneva, Institut et musée Voltaire, 1953. 127 p. **4491**

An index of Bengasco's *Voltaire:*

bibliographie de ses œuvres (1618). An important reference work facilitating use of Bengesco's vital but unmethodical bibliography. Includes index of first lines of V. poems cited by Bengesco and Bengesco's *errata* and additions.

Maslen, Keith I. Some early editions of Voltaire printed in London. Libr 14:287-93, 1959. **4492**

A bibliographical note on eds. of the *Histoire de Charles XII* and *Alzire* printed in London wholly or partly by William Bowyer and not recorded by Bengesco or other authorities. An appendix provides a list and description of other works of V. wholly or partly printed by Bowyer.

Montagu, Jennifer. Inventaire des tableaux, sculptures, estampes, etc. de l'Institut et musée Voltaire. SVEC 20:223-47, 1962. **4493**

Enumeration and description of iconography of V. and contemporaries in V. museum in Geneva. Does not include holdings of V. library connected with same institution.

Pomeau, René. Etat présent des études voltairiennes. SVEC 1:183-200, 1955. **4494**

Discusses status of V. scholarship with respect to eds., notebooks, correspondence, works of erudition, literary studies, and philosophy. Maintains that V. still remains one of most poorly known of great French writers. Suggests areas for further investigation : additional critical eds. of specific works, particularly *Essai sur les mœurs* (*see* 4512) and the *Siècle de Louis XIV*; a new biography of V. based on information revealed by Besterman's new ed. of the correspondence; V.'s relations with Frederick II; Voltaire as an historian (*see* 4623); the art of V.'s *contes* and dialogues; and V.'s scientific ideas after 1750. Useful bibliographical references but not as critical as CBFL, v. 4.

Séguin, J. A. R. Voltaire and the Gentleman's magazine, 1731-1868; an index compiled and ed. with an introd. by J. A. R. Séguin. New York, Paxton, 1962. x, 134 p. *See* 5560. **4495**

A chronological listing and index of items referring to V. in the *Gentleman's magazine* of London from 1731 to 1868. Annotated.

Studies on Voltaire and the eighteenth century. Ed. by Theodore Besterman. Geneva, Institut et musée Voltaire, 1955–. v. **4496**

An important series of scholarly articles and monographs, in English or French, on all aspects of V. and French literature of the 18th century. V. 1 entitled : *Travaux sur Voltaire et le dix-huitième siècle.* An essential source of information edited by one of the great authorities on V.

Varbanetz, N. V., and T. N. Kopreeva. La bibliothèque de Voltaire à Léningrad. Horizons 109:121–29, June 1960. **4497**
A general account of the history of V.'s library and its importance to scholarship. Authors note intention of Soviet scholars to publish in years to come " toutes les notes et remarques de Voltaire sur ses livres " (p. 129). *See Biblioteka Vol'tera* (4489).

Vercruysse, J. Notes sur les imprimés et les manuscrits de la collection Launoit. SVEC 20:249–59, 1962. **4498**
Notes on the V. collection donated by count de Launoit to the Royal Library of Belgium in 1954. Notes fall into 3 categories : (1) V. works not listed in Bengesco's bibliography; (2) V. works insufficiently described by Bengesco; (3) Voltaire works in the collection containing ms notes. Useful bibliographical contribution.

Voltaire, François-Marie Arouet de. Voltaire's catalogue of his library at Ferney. Ed. by George R. Havens and Norman L. Torrey. Geneva, Institut et musée Voltaire, 1959. 285 p. (SVEC, 9) **4499**
Tentative ed. of catalog of V. library at Ferney. Supersedes 400 titles published in authors' article in MP 27:1–22, 1929. Introduction describes catalog of Ferney library and its history, and analyzes character of V.'s books. Contains 2 lists : (A) copy of Ferney catalog and (B) attempt to identify titles owned by V., whether in Ferney catalog or not. Important source for various aspects of V.'s career. V.'s marginalia indicated, but only for limited number of volumes examined personally by authors. Editors limited by their restricted access to V.'s books in Leningrad. Invaluable as a bibliographical contribution, but better firsthand ed. of this catalog provided in Russian in *Biblioteka Vol'tera* (4489).
Reviews : W. Bottiglia in RR 50:292–94, 1959 with editors' rejoinder in RR 51:156–58, 1960; J. Brumfitt in FS 14:70, 1960; J. Loy in MLN 75:453–55, 1960.

Watts, George B. Voltaire and Charles

Joseph Panckoucke. KFLQ 1:179–97, 1954. *See* 5492. **4500**
Summarizes V.'s relations with C. J. Panckoucke, one of his publishers and successor to Michel Lambert of Paris. Interesting information on publication of V.'s works from 1760 to Kehl ed.

Editions

Châtelet-Lomont, Gabrielle Emilie (Le Tonnelier de Breteuil) *marquise* du. Les lettres de la marquise Du Châtelet. Ed. by Theodore Besterman. Geneva, Institut et musée Voltaire, 1958. 2 v. **4501**
This ed. of correspondence of Mme du Châtelet is based largely on mss, except for her letters to Saint-Lambert. It replaces Asse ed. of 1878 which contained 246 letters, errors in dating, and suppressions of numerous passages. Present ed., invaluable for V. scholarship, contains 486 letters. Includes introductory notes useful for a biography of Mme du Châtelet and letters proving her liaisons with Maupertuis, the duc de Richelieu, as well as V. and Saint-Lambert. Editor suggests greater influence of Mme du Châtelet on V.'s ideas than hitherto supposed. An essential contribution.
Review : O. Fellows in RR 50:216–18, 1959; A. Freer in SF 3:322, 1959; N. Torrey in MLN 74:466–68, 1959.

Friedrich II, *der grosse, king of Prussia.* L'anti-Machiavel. Ed. by Charles Fleischauer. Geneva, Institut et musée Voltaire, 1958. 382 p. (SVEC, 5) *See* 5907. **4502**
Critical ed. of Frederick's *Anti-Machiavel* showing V.'s contributions. Introduction provides historical material on V.'s part in its publication and significance of his corrections and contributions. Appendix contains bibliography of eds. of the *Anti-Machiavel* published during Frederick's lifetime. Index. Basic to a study of V.-Frederick relationship.
Reviews : O. Haac in MLQ 20:299–300, 1959; E. Marcu in RR 51:135–36, 1960.

Vercruysse, J. Articles inédits de Voltaire pour le Dictionnaire de l'Académie française. SVEC 37:7–51, 1965. **4503**
Presents text of 115 articles by V. intended for the *Dictionnaire de l'Académie* and included by Beuchot in his ed. of the *Dictionnaire philosophique.* Corrects bibliographical data of Bengesco (1618) and Naves (1316). Brief introduction.

Voltaire, François-Marie Arouet de.
L'Akakia de Voltaire. Ed. by Charles
Fleischauer. SVEC 30:7–145, 1964.   **4504**

Critical ed. of V.'s satire of Maupertuis
with detailed historical background (p. 7–
93), a bibliography of eds. of the *Akakia*
before its inclusion in the *Œuvres complètes*, the texts of the Luzac ed. of the
Diatribe and of the Breitkopf ed. for the
rest of the *Histoire*, and significant
variants. An important contribution.

— Candide. Trans. and ed. by Peter Gay;
a bilingual edition. New York, St. Martin's
press, 1963. xxxvi, 299 p.   **4505**

Intended for school use. Contains both
the French original and an English translation by Gay. Introduction does not
contain all background information important to study of *Candide*, and some
facts subject to caution. Translation not
always accurate.
Review: R. Brooks in FR 37:239–40,
1963–64.

— Candide ou l'optimisme. Ed. by René
Pomeau. Nizet, 1959. 297 p.   **4506**

A critical ed. Pomeau's introduction
concentrates on biographical and esthetic
material, whereas Morize (1631) emphasized sources and historical background.
Uses text of 1771 Cramer ed. and includes corrections and additions of 1761
text in critical material. Concludes that
V. sketched *Candide* in Jan., 1758, edited
it in July, finished it in Oct., and went
over it again in Dec. Includes interesting
esthetic observations on composition of
the tale, movement, style, and psychology
of characters. Does not replace Morize's
monumental work, but is based on later
scholarship and useful alongside Morize.
Review: H. Coulet in RHL 61:84–85,
1961.

— Correspondance. Ed. by Theodore Besterman. Gallimard, 1964 [c. 1963]–. v. (Bibliothèque de la Pléiade)   **4507**

Besterman reproduces most of V.'s
letters from his comprehensive Geneva
ed. (4509) and includes a number of
additional letters, published as supplements in SVEC, as well as V.'s love letters to Mme Denis. Documentation and
biographical, bibliographical and historical appendixes, as well as indications of
ms sources and material on *établissement
de textes* found in Geneva ed. eliminated
here. Completely in French with Besterman's notes translated by Mireille Zarb.
Fine for general reader, but scholar will
prefer Besterman's Geneva ed.

— Correspondance avec les Tronchin. Ed.
by André Delattre. Mercure de France,
1950. xliii, [1], 796 p.   **4508**

See 1635B.
Reviews: H. Lancaster in MLN 66:
345–46, 1951; R. Pomeau in RHL 53:550–
53, 1953; J. Smiley in RR 43:62–64, 1952.

— Correspondence. Ed. by Theodore Besterman. Geneva, Institut et musée Voltaire, 1953–65. 107 v.   **4509**

A monument of scholarship and now
the standard ed. for V.'s correspondence
with number and accuracy of texts of
letters to and from V. vastly increased
over Moland (1628). Text of each letter
in French followed by 4 sets of notes in
English on mss, eds., textual notes, and
commentary. Each volume contains con-
cordance between Moland and Besterman
eds.; chronological list of letters; list of
letters arranged by correspondents; keys
to bibliographical abbreviations, pseu-
donyms, and nicknames used in correspondence. These are cumulated in v. 99–
102 which also contain an inventory of
mss, bibliography of printed correspondence, list of works cited, list of uniden-
tifiable letters, index of V.'s quotations,
and index of annotated words. Concluding volumes will contain a general index.
Choice of type, paper, and illustrations
add to general excellence of this ed. Supplements are published in SVEC.
Reviews: H. Coulet in SF 2:434–41,
1958; P. Guillaud-Brandon in LH 16:
131–54, 1957; H. Lancaster in MLN 69:
145–47, 1954; R. Leigh in MLR 49:236–
44, 1954; MLR 51:269–73, 338–43, 1956;
MLR 52:279–82, 393–97, 1957; MLR 53:
434–36, 550–52, 1958; MLR 54:565–70,
604–08, 1959; MLR 57:565–71, 606–12,
1962; Tro 122:164–75, Feb. 1958; F.
Orlando in SF 4:552–55, 1960; SF 5:559–
61, 1961; R. Pomeau in RHL 53:548–50,
1953; RHL 56:262–67, 1956; RHL 61:
82–84, 1961; F. Taylor in FS 8:163–65,
1954; N. Torrey in RR 45:147–50, 1954;
RR 46:63–64, 1955.

— Dictionnaire philosophique. Chronologie
et préface par René Pomeau. Garnier-
Flammarion, 1964. 380 p.   **4510**

Very brief preface by René Pomeau
(p. 9–13). Text used is that of Naves ed.
(1639), but without notes, variants, or
other critical apparatus.

— Essai sur les mœurs et l'esprit des nations.
Ed. by Jacqueline Marchand. Editions
sociales, 1962. 304 p.   **4511**

Annotated extracts with a general introduction (p. 7–60) on the background, sources, content, and fortune of the *Essai*.

— Essai sur les mœurs et l'esprit des nations et sur les principaux faits de l'histoire depuis Charlemagne jusqu'à Louis XIII. Ed. by René Pomeau. Garnier, 1963. 2 v. **4512**

First complete and separate ed. of the *Essai sur les mœurs* since 1835. Essentially a reproduction of text of Kehl ed. with marginal notes indicating evolution of work from 1st complete ed. of 1756. Selection of variants from earlier versions and the 1765 ed. of the *Philosophie de l'histoire*. Footnotes indicate V.'s sources and method of working as indicated by notes and markers in his library. Lengthy introduction treats history of composition of the *Essai*, V.'s philosophy of history, and influence of the work in 18th and 19th centuries. Bibliography and index. Valuable contribution.
Reviews : P. Alatri in CulF 11:153–54, 1964; J. Brumfitt in FS 19:188–89, 1965.

— Le Henriade. Ed. by Owen R. Taylor. Geneva, Institut et musée Voltaire, 1965. 3 v. (SVEC, 38, 39, 40) **4513**

First critical ed. and study in depth of *La Henriade*. Editor reproduces text of 1775 *édition encadrée* but eliminates changes and additions made by Kehl editors which he feels V. did not authorize. First volume is a copious introduction that discusses at length the work's composition and publication, V.'s conception of the epic, sources of the *Henriade*, its fortune after 1730, its influence and the text (mss and printed eds.). V. 2 provides *pièces relatives* including pertinent material long omitted from eds. of V. and the text of the poem itself. V. 3 treats literary and historical sources of poem and gives critical text of the *Essai sur les guerres civiles* in both its French and English versions. Work concluded by lengthy bibliography. A painstaking and exhaustive work of scholarship.

— L'ingénu; histoire véritable. Ed. by William R. Jones. Geneva, Droz, 1957. 192 p. **4514**

An updating of the editor's 1936 critical ed. (1641).

— L'ingénu, and Histoire de Jenni. Ed. by J. H. Brumfitt and M. I. Gerard Davis. Oxford, Blackwell, 1960. lxiii, 147 p. **4515**

Meaty introduction on background and significance of the two *contes*, the art of V.'s *contes*, and a selective bibliography. Annotated. Recent scholarship taken into account.
Reviews : J. Lough in FS 15:69–70, 1961; J. Sareil in RR 52:65–66, 1952.

— Les lettres d'Amabed. Ed. by Alexandre Jovicevich. Editions universitaires, 1961. lxxviii, 87 p. **4516**

In this critical ed. of V.'s last *conte*, editor concludes that character portraits are very weak and that work is unsuccessful because of V.'s haste and lack of restraint. Jovicevich collated 10 eds. of *conte* appearing between 1769 and 1775, but critical material confined to variations in spelling. Editor's investigation of sources for the *conte* leads to nothing essentially new.
Reviews : R. Pomeau in RHL 63:477, 1963; J. Sareil in RR 53:229–30, 1962.

— Lettres d'amour de Voltaire à sa nièce. Ed. by Theodore Besterman. Plon, 1957. 207 p. *English edition:* The love letters of Voltaire to his niece. Ed. and trans. by Theodore Besterman. London, Kimber, 1958. 158 p. **4517**

A collection of letters of V. to Mme Denis from 1740 to 1750, most of which had been previously unpublished. Shows that V.'s *liaison* with his niece began around autumn of 1744 and necessitates rewriting of V.'s biography for 1744 to 1749. Introduction provides biographical material on Mme Denis and her relationship with V. from 1737 on and indicates history of mss of these letters now preserved in Pierpont Morgan Library in New York.
Reviews : R. Leigh in MLR 53:434–36, 1958; R. Pomeau in RHL 61:82–84, 1961.

— Lettres inédites à Constant d'Hermenches. Ed. by Alfred Roulin. Corrêa, 1956. 215 p. **4518**

These letters now included in Besterman ed. of V.'s correspondence (4509).
Review : C. Govaert in Le Thyrse 58: 362–63, 1956.

— Lettres inédites à son imprimeur Gabriel Cramer. Ed. by Bernard Gagnebin. Geneva, Droz, 1952. xliii, 316 p. **4519**

Contains previously unpublished letters of V. to Gabriel Cramer, his principal publisher during years of this correspondence (1755–77), but not an integral ed. of the V.-Cramer correspondence. Editor's introduction provides biographical information about Philibert and Gabriel Cramer, their relations with V.,

the publishing activities of the Cramers, and the clandestine diffusion of some of V.'s works. More complete version of this correspondence now available in Besterman (4509).
Reviews : G. Havens in RR 45:207–11, 1954; R. Pomeau in RHL 53:550–53, 1953; F. Taylor in FS 8:165–66, 1954.

— Lettres inédites aux Tronchin. Ed. by Bernard Gagnebin. Geneva, Droz, 1950. 3 v.   **4520**
   See 1635A.
   Reviews : H. Lancaster in MLN 66: 345–46, 1951; R. Pomeau in RHL 53:550–53, 1953; J. Smiley in RR 43:62–64, 1952.

— Mélanges. Ed. by Jacques van den Heuvel. Preface by Emmanuel Berl. Gallimard, 1961. xxxii, 1553 p. (Bibliothèque de la Pléiade)
                                                 4521
   Some 70 works of V. presented in chronological order and in their entirety, except for the *Akakia*. Selection provides reader with good idea of development and variety of V.'s thought. Period after 1770 skimpy. Abundant, reliable notes, although American scholarship not sufficiently taken into account. Quite useful.
   Reviews : W. Bottiglia in FR 36:102–03, 1962–63; C. Cordié in RLM 15:152–54, 1962.

— La mort de César. Edition accompagnée de textes complémentaires. Ed. by A.-M. Rousseau. S.E.D.E.S., 1964. 197 p.   **4522**
   Unannotated text of the play along with V.'s preface to 1736 ed., the *Lettre de M. Algarotti ... sur la tragédie de Jules César par M. de Voltaire*, V.'s preface to *Brutus* (*Discours sur la tragédie à Mylord Bolingbroke*), V.'s translation of the first 3 acts of Shakespeare's *Julius Caesar* and his brief introduction to and commentary on it. In introductory pages (p. 5–37), editor studies genesis and history of play and the accompanying texts. Brief bibliography.

— Œuvres historiques. Ed. by René Pomeau. Gallimard, 1957. 1813 p. (Bibliothèque de la Pléiade)   **4523**
   Contents include : *Remarques sur l'histoire, Nouvelles considérations sur l'histoire, Histoire de Charles XII, roi de Suède, Textes relatifs à l'Histoire de Charles XII, Anecdotes sur le csar Pierre le Grand, Le siècle de Louis XIV, Supplément au Siècle de Louis XIV, Du protestantisme et de la guerre des Cévennes, Défense de Louis XIV contre l'auteur des Ephémérides, Précis du siècle de Louis XV, Histoire de la guerre de 1741* (*extraits*). Editor reproduces texts

from Kehl ed. with correction of obvious errors and typographical mistakes and omissions. Not a critical ed., but does provide textual variants. Preface by Pomeau (p. 7–24) offers appreciation of V.'s role as historian. Bibliography, notes, and index of principal names of persons. A very useful collection of V.'s historical texts made available in a handy and handsome ed.

— Philosophical dictionary. Trans. with an introduction and glossary by Peter Gay. Preface by André Maurois. New York, Basic Books, 1962. 2 v.   **4524**
   Translation, with few exceptions, follows text of Naves ed. (1639). Unannotated, but a lengthy introduction (p. 4–52) and a glossary of unfamiliar names (p. 607–52) provide comment on background of the *Dictionnaire* and on text itself.

— La philosophie de l'histoire. Ed. by J. H. Brumfitt. Geneva, Institut et musée Voltaire, 1963. 327 p. (SVEC, 28)   **4525**
   A critical ed. of V.'s most complete work on ancient history, the *Philosophie de l'histoire*, which later became Introduction to *Essai sur les mœurs*. Includes a critical introduction (p. 11–79), critical apparatus (p. 261–78), and commentary (p. 279–323). An important ed. for study of modern historiography.
   Review : M. Laurent-Hubert in RHL 65:5112–15, 1965.

— Pis'ma Vol'tera. (Textes nouveaux de la correspondance de Voltaire.) Ed. by Vladimir Sergeevich Liublinskiĭ. Moscow, Akademiĭa nauk SSSR, 1956. 430 p.   **4526**
   Amends some volumes of Besterman ed. of correspondence (4509) because of Besterman's lack of access to Leningrad library. First of 2 v. on mss of V.'s correspondence in Soviet Union. Questions authenticity of Besterman's copies of V. letters in Leningrad and regrets Western ignorance of Soviet V. scholarship. First part contains 20 letters of V. to comte d'Argental, his wife, and his brother. Story of *Voltairomanie* and the *Préservatif* now subject to revision on basis of this correspondence. Information on *mise en scène* of *Sémiramis*. Introduction and notes in Russian with a brief summary in French. Contains Russian translations of letters.
   Reviews : R. Leigh in MLR 52:607–09, 1957; J. Loy in RR 50:62–67, 1959; R. Pomeau in RHL 58:234, 1958; F. Taylor in FS 11:278–80, 1957.

— Les plus belles lettres de Voltaire. Ed. by Marcel Jouhandeau. Calmann-Lévy, 1961. 155 p. **4527**

A selection of V. letters from 1722 to 1755 with an introduction by Marcel Jouhandeau. Very sparsely annotated; ed. of no use for scholarly purposes.

— Politique de Voltaire. Ed. by René Pomeau. Colin, 1963. 254 p. **4528**

Authoritative 50-page *Présentation* by Pomeau of V.'s political theory and practice followed by selection of texts setting forth his political and economic thought.

Reviews : P. Alatri in CulF 10:231–35, 1963; M. Launay in RHL 65:123–25, 1965; J. Sareil in DS 6:373–74, 1964; L. Sozzi in SF 7:558–59, 1963.

— Select letters. Trans. and ed. by Theodore Besterman. London, Nelson, 1963. xii, 180 p. **4529**

A representative selection of 141 letters of V. in English translation that attempts to provide reader with view of important aspects of V.'s life and activities. All texts given in full prefatory notes that add to reader's understanding. Introduction (p. 1–11) provides appreciation of V. as letter writer.

— Le taureau blanc. Ed. by René Pomeau. Nizet, 1956. lxxii, 99 p. **4530**

A critical ed. Gives a history of the ms and indicates various eds. of the *conte*. Dates composition of *Le taureau blanc* as 1771–72. Editor includes an essay on *Le taureau blanc* and biblical criticism, discusses V.'s relations with the *Correspondance littéraire*, and includes a chapter on the style and art of V.'s *contes*. Completely annotated. Index of references. Replaces Moland ed. of this work.

Review : H. Coulet in RHL 58:234–35, 1958.

— Traité de métaphysique. Ed. by H. Temple Patterson. 2nd ed. Manchester, Manchester univ. press, 1957. xv, 76 p. **4531**

Reprinting of Patterson's 1st ed. of this text (1652) originally published in 1937 with minor updating in light of more recent scholarship, particularly Wade's study of the *Traité de métaphysique* in his *Studies on Voltaire* (1812).

— Voltaire par lui-même. Ed. by René Pomeau. Éditions du Seuil, 1955. 190 p. **4532**

An attempt to interpret essence of V.

by an outstanding authority with a sure knowledge of his subject and the critical literature but in framework that requires him to be very selective and brief. Includes selections from V.'s works and illustrations.

Review : F. Taylor in FS 10:263–65, 1956.

— Voltaire's England. Ed. by Desmond Flower. London, Folio society, 1950. xvi, 190 p. *See* 5714. **4533**

Translated extracts from a number of V.'s works and his correspondence, revealing his attitudes toward England and the English. Illustrated with 18th-century engravings of England by Hogarth.

— Voltaire's notebooks. Ed. by Theodore Besterman. Geneva, Institut et musée Voltaire, 1952. 2 v. **4534**

Introduction details history of the notebooks, which provide much information on V.'s reading, and their connection with his own publications. The *sottisier* previously published contained only about half of ms faultily transcribed. Besterman's ed. not based on original ms but on microfilm enlargement. Important to a study of V.'s ideas and their development. For reservations, *see* N. L. Torrey's review *infra*.

Reviews : H. Lancaster in MLN 68: 435–36, 1953; F. Taylor in FS 7:69–71, 1953; N. Torrey in RR 44:219–22, 1953.

— Zadig ou la destinée. Ed. by Verdun L. Saulnier. Droz, 1946. xxxvii, 102 p. **4535**

Does not replace critical ed. of Ascoli (1653). Text not annotated and based on that of last ed. of 1756 for which V. made significant corrections. Introduction summarizes information on contemporary and literary sources. Editors offers questionable hypotheses about origin of *Zadig* and of V.'s pessimism.

Review : M. Davis in FS 5:172–73, 1951.

— Zadig ou la destinée; histoire orientale. Edition critique avec une introduction et un commentaire par Georges Ascoli. 2e tirage revu et complété par Jean Fabre. Didier, 1962. 2 v. **4536**

Reproduces Ascoli's critical ed. of *Zadig* (1653) originally published in 1929 with correction of very small number of errors and additional commentary in *Notes complémentaires* based on recent scholarship (including consideration of the ms of the several chapters of the future *Zadig* extant in V.'s library in

Leningrad). In his *Note sur le deuxième tirage*, Fabre indicates strengths and limitations of Ascoli's work in light of present-day scholarship. An important scholarly ed. once again made available.

— Zadig ou la destinée. Ed. by M. Colesanti. Florence, Sansoni, 1963. xliv, 154 p.   **4537**

Annotated ed. with ample introduction that summarizes major phases in V.'s career and defines V.'s narrative art while showing close relationship between his fictional works and philosophical output. Editor sees *Zadig* as a *roman d'essai* containing V.'s *morale provisoire*. Also included are texts of *Jeannot et Colin*, the *Petite digression*, and the *Aventure indienne*. Review : L. Sozzi in SF 8:558, 1964.

General Biography or Criticism

Adam, Antoine. Voltaire et les lumières. Eur 361-62:8-19, May–June 1959.   **4538**

A very good, concise introduction to V. as a philosopher of the Enlightenment by one who believes in the modernity and importance of V. today.

Addamiano, Natale. Voltaire. Rome, Azione letteraria italiana, 1956. 769 p.   **4539**

A review of V.'s life and works for an Italian public by an admirer who sometimes loses objectivity in defending his hero. Lively.
Review : R. Pomeau in RHL 58:382–83, 1958.

Barthes, Roland. Le dernier des écrivains heureux. *In his:* Essais critiques. Editions du Seuil, 1964. p. 94–100.   **4540**

A stimulating essay that poses the paradox of a happy V. (" pessimisme du fond et allégresse de la forme ") whose antinomy of intelligence and intellectuality leads to anti-intellectualism. Worthwhile reading.

Belaval, Yvon. L'esprit de Voltaire. SVEC 24:139–54, 1963.   **4541**

" ... l'esprit voltairien se définirait : une irritabilité morale. Sa vitesse de réaction est la rapidité d'un style. Voltaire enrage. La bêtise n'est pas son fort. Et que de bêtises partout " (p. 149). Interesting general appreciation.

Besterman, Theodore. Voltaire essays, and another. London, Oxford univ. press, 1962. 181 p.   **4542**

A collection of 11 essays by an outstanding authority on V. Contents include : (1) *Voltaire: discours inaugural* (on the opening of the Institut et musée Voltaire); (2) *Voltaire judged by Flaubert;* (3) *Voltaire and the Lisbon earthquake: or, the death of optimism;* (4) *Voltaire's commentary on Frederick's "L'art de la guerre";* (5) *Voltaire's love-letters;* (6) *Emilie Du Châtelet: portrait of an unknown woman;* (7) *Le vrai Voltaire par ses lettres;* (8) *The Institut et musée Voltaire and its collections;* (9) *The terra-cotta statue of Voltaire made by Houdon for Beaumarchais;* (10) *Voltaire: with a glance at Johnson and Franklin;* (11) *The love of manuscripts.* Review : N. Torrey in RR 54:134–46, 1963.

— Le vrai Voltaire par ses lettres. SVEC 10:9–48, 1959. *Also in his:* Voltaire essays, and another. See 4542. p. 74–113.   **4543**

Well-written and important article for understanding V.'s unique role in epistolary genre.

Ceitac, Jane. Doctrine humanitaire et esprit voltairien. Flam 43:211–24, 1960; 386–415, 1961.   **4544**

An enthusiastic if disorganized and haphazard presentation of V. as a believer in humanity.

Crocker, Lester G. An age of crisis : man and world in eighteenth-century French thought. See 4122.   **4545**

According to preface of work, it is " a synthetical study of French ethical thought during the Age of Enlightenment." No claim of being exhaustive with regard to separate authors involved, but an attempt at a perspective of " the complex, interacting currents of 18th-century intellectual history." Refers to V.'s ethical and religious ideas throughout book, emphasizing his pessimism.

— Voltaire's struggle for humanism. SVEC 4:137–69, 1957.   **4546**

Author perceives dichotomy in desire of 18th-century thinkers to look upon both reason and nature as normative concepts and in their inability to resolve ensuing contradictions. Sees conflict exemplified throughout V.'s writings, and explains contradictions in V.'s thought as a result of " practical propagandist consequences." Thought-provoking abstract essay.

Delattre, André. Voltaire, l'impétueux. Mercure de France, 1957. 105 p.   **4547**

An attempt to explain character of V. by use of categories of modern psychology. Emphasizes emotional shock of V.'s youth to account for his repression of feeling and disparagement of human nature; sees his struggle against Christianity aroused by his reaction to piety of his father and Jansenist brother. Psychological interpretation emphasized to neglect of historical and intellectual currents.

Reviews : R. Mercier in RHL 58:541, 1958; H. Perret in EnC 73:253–54, 1959–60; N. Torrey in RR 49:67–68, 1958.

Endore, S. Guy. The heart and the mind : the story of Rousseau and Voltaire. London, Allen, 1962. 360 p.   **4548**
See 4549.

— Voltaire ! Voltaire ! New York, Simon and Schuster, 1961. 507 p.   **4549**
A biographical novel for which the author is claimed to have done research " including days and nights in the Voltaire library in Ferney (*sic*) " ! A shorter version published in England as *The heart and the mind; the story of Rousseau and Voltaire* (London, Allen, 1962, 360 p.).

French thought in the eighteenth century; Rousseau, Voltaire, Diderot. Presented by Romain Rolland, André Maurois, and Edouard Herriot, with an introduction by Geoffrey Brereton. New York, David McKay, 1953. p. 131–245.   **4550**
General essay on V. by Maurois followed by selections in English translation which include : *Candide, Babouc's vision, Micromegas, Lord Chesterfield's ears,* and passages from the *Philosophical dictionary.* This section originally published as *The living thoughts of Voltaire, presented by André Maurois* (New York, Longmans, Green, 1939). Original French version : *Les pages immortelles de Voltaire choisies et expliquées par André Maurois* (Corrêa, 1938).

Gilles, B. Voltaire : son temps, sa vie, son œuvre. Centre de documentation universitaire, 1952. 145 + 4 + 10 p.   **4551**
An adequate general introduction to V. with emphasis on the biographical.

Girnus, Wilhelm. Voltaire. Berlin, Aufbau, 1958. 99 p.   **4552**
A brief general introduction to V. for a Marxist-oriented public. " Marx *und* Voltaire, das klingt gut, das klingt harmonisch; das gibt einen freudigen hellen Ton : den Ton der Zukunft " (p. 99). No notes, no references, no bibliography.

Gross, Rebecca H. Voltaire, nonconformist. New York, Philosophical Library, 1965. 162 p.   **4553**

By reviewing some generally known information about V.'s life and work as well as 18th-century background and through liberal quotation of host of critics, author's purpose is to demonstrate V.'s nonconformism. Neither an adequate synthesis nor a contribution to scholarship.

Havens, George R. Voltaire. *In his:* The age of ideas. *See* 3383. p. 157–220.   **4554**
A general introduction to great figures of the French Enlightenment by prominent scholar. While written for general public, author makes no recourse to novelized biography nor to diluting material. Contains valuable bibliographical guide. Recommended to all students of period.

Heuvel, J. van den. Voltaire. *In:* Histoire des littératures. *See* 3384. 3:711–28.   **4555**
A rapid review of the man and his works with an attempt to establish an " essential " V. Selective bibliography.
" Un badinage aussi tenace que les erreurs qu'il faut tuer et retuer encore, immédiat comme un réflexe, opiniâtre comme une machination, tel est l'esprit de Voltaire.... Cet accord intime entre l'ironie et la pitié agissante, cela, c'est le secret de Voltaire " (p. 726–27).

Lanson, Gustave. Voltaire. Edition revue et mise à jour par René Pomeau. Hachette, 1960. 247 p.   **4556**
Reprint of Lanson's classic study of V. (1672) with an appendix (p. 224–42) by René Pomeau in which aspects of Lanson's work are updated or discussed in light of more recent scholarship. Bibliography includes recent eds. and critical studies of V. A valuable work made available once again.

Leithäuser, Joachim G. Er nannte sich Voltaire; Bericht eines grossen Lebens. Stuttgart, Cotta, 1961. 375 p.   **4557**
A full-length biography of V. for a German public. Author familiar with recent scholarship, but no notes, no references, no index. Brief critical bibliography.
Review : R. Krämer-Badoni in FAZ Aug. 12, 1961.

Meyer, Adolph Erich. Voltaire : man of justice. London, Quality press, 1952. 250 p.   **4558**
General biography of V. aimed at popular audience. Emphasis on events and personalities rather than on intellectual trends or literary analysis. No

indication of source of quotations and no credit to other scholars. Bibliography includes no work on V. published after 1925. Little new in this work.

Nicolson, *Sir* **Harold George.** Skepticism. *In his:* The age of reason. Garden City, Doubleday, 1961. p. 89–107.   **4559**

For the general reader having no knowledge of V. Contains good number of clichés.

Topazio, Virgil W. Voltaire, philosopher of human progress. PMLA 74:356–64, 1959.   **4560**

Article examines constructive side of V.'s philosophy which author sees as restoration of dignity of individual and improvement of social conditions interfering with human rights. Attempts to upgrade V.'s reputation as a philosopher, to show that V.'s philosophical knowledge was not superficial but encyclopedic, and that, while he sought to destroy fanaticism, he also had specific, practical ideas of a constructive nature.

Vial, Fernand. Voltaire, sa vie et son œuvre (avec textes complets annotés). Didier, 1953. 678 p.   **4561**

Very useful introduction to life and work of V. Includes account of his career and 536 p. of extracts of V.'s works with notes and solid introductions. Summarizes V.'s metaphysical, ethical, and general philosophic ideas and describes his propagandistic techniques. As often as possible, reproduces complete V. texts.

Reviews : C. Cherpack in MLN 71: 156–58, 1956; A. Viatte in FR 28:199–200, 1954–55.

Voltaire, François-Marie Arouet de. Candide and the critics. Ed. by Milton P. Foster. Belmont, Calif., Wadsworth, 1962. x, 182 p.   **4562**

A useful guide to study of *Candide*. Donald M. Frame's annotated translation of *Candide* is followed by a series of 22 critical essays or excerpts on the book, all of which have previously appeared elsewhere, by critics dating from the 18th century to the present. Among these are Torrey, Wade, Bottiglia, Havens, *et al.*

Wade, Ira O. The search for a new Voltaire; studies in Voltaire based upon material deposited at the American philosophical society. Philadelphia, American philosophical society, 1958. 206 p. (APST n.s., 48⁴)   **4563**

A group of miscellaneous studies on V. of differing importance. Additional information provided about V., but no radically " new Voltaire " presented here. Interesting account of V.'s working with his notebooks and his methods of composition from documentary reading related in *Voltaire's method of working* (p. 58–82). Second part of monograph (p. 115–99) contains an inventory of 2 collections of mss by or about V., one gathered by André Delattre and the other, the Ricci collection of the B.N.

Reviews : J.-D. Candaux in SVEC 8: 243–51, 1959; W. Crittenden in Per 40: 425, 1959; G. Havens in RR 50:133–37, 1959; F. Orlando in SF 4:155, 1960; F. Taylor in FS 13:355–56, 1959.

Specialized Biographical Studies

Alatri, Paolo. Voltaire e Ginevra. *In:* Ginevra e l'Italia; raccolta di studi promossa dalla Facoltà valdese di teologia di Roma. Ed. by Delio Cantimori *et al.* Florence, Sansoni, 1959. p. 613–49.   **4564**

V.'s relations with the city of Geneva. *See also* the author's *Note sul periodo ginevrino di Voltaire e sulle sue corrispondenze coi Tronchin e coi Cramer* (Milan, Dante Alighieri, 1957 [?], 127 p.).

Beer, Gavin de. Voltaire's British visitors. SVEC 4:7–136, 1957. *See* 5718.   **4565**

An attempt to identify numerous British visitors of V. during his residence in Switzerland. Transcription of written accounts of visits reprinted in chronological order. Index and notes on sources. Good basis for future study of V.'s British relations. Supplements providing additions, amplifications, and corrections in SVEC 10:425–38, 1959 and 18:237–62, 1961.

Review : R. Leigh in MLR 53:437–39, 1958.

Bellugou, Henri. Voltaire et Frédéric II au temps de la marquise du Châtelet, un trio singulier. Marcel Rivière, 1962. 219 p.   **4566**

First volume of a projected 2-volume study of the relations of V. and Frederick. Period covered is from 1735 to 1749. No startling revelations, but additional information based on Besterman ed. of V.'s correspondence. Book marred by disregard for chronology, sloppy citation of texts, and excessively familiar style.

Review : A. Bertière in RHL 64:678–79, 1964.

Bingham, Alfred J. Voltaire and the abbé Bergier : a polite controversy. MLR 59:31–39, 1964. **4567**

A gentle religious controversy between V. and the abbé Nicolas-Sylvain Bergier, royal confessor, canon of the cathedral of Notre-Dame, and scholar on origin of languages and pagan religions.

Boiteux, L. A. Voltaire et le ménage Suard. SVEC 1:19–113, 1955. **4568**

Aspects of V.'s relations with the family of Suard, editor of the *Gazette littéraire de l'Europe*, and with Panckoucke by virtue of marriage of his daughter to Suard. Contains previously unpublished texts. Rather disorganized presentation.

Brumfitt, J. H. Voltaire and Warburton. SVEC 18:35–56, 1961. *See* 5720. **4569**

An account of the affinities and hostility between the two men.

Candaux, Jean-Daniel. Des documents nouveaux sur la mort de Voltaire ? SVEC 20:261–63, 1962. **4570**

Refutes small monograph of André Lebois, *La mort chrétienne de monsieur de Voltaire* (4585). Shows that notebook of Duvivier, husband of Mme Denis, containing information on V.'s death was merely transcription of a printed account which had already appeared in the *Supplément au journal politique des Deux-Ponts* (1778).

Ceitac, Jane. Voltaire et l'affaire des natifs. Geneva, Droz, 1956. 222 p. **4571**

Natifs were Genevan-born children of French Huguenot refugees who were economically and politically handicapped but who were principal skilled artisans of Geneva's industry. V. sought to apply principles of toleration outlined in *Traité sur la tolérance* to them. Book is thoroughly documented and contains new material from State Archives and Public Library of Geneva. Corrects Desnoiresterres and gives favorable picture of V. in his efforts to obtain civil and political equality for *natifs*. Work poorly organized and edited; documentary material not well integrated.

Reviews : N. Torrey in RR 48:307–08, 1957.

Chapuisat, Edouard. Voltaire et Mallet Du Pan. AMPR 105¹:152–64, 1952. **4572**

V.'s relations with Jacques Mallet Du Pan, pioneer of modern political journalism. New material based on mss in libraries of Geneva and Neuchâtel.

Conlon, P. M. Voltaire's literary career from 1728 to 1750. Geneva, Institut et musée Voltaire, 1961. 350 p. (SVEC, 14) *See* 3623. **4573**

Not actually an analysis of V. as a writer but contains number of historical chapters on V.'s relations with censors, publishers, theatrical world, other contemporary writers, the Académie française and other learned societies, and the French court. Uneven and somewhat repetitive because of its organization. Does not analyze any of V.'s writings but does give some interesting information on this somewhat lesser known period of V.'s life.

Reviews : J. Broome in MLR 57:444–45, 1962; J. Brumfitt in FS 16:64–66, 1962.

Donvez, Jacques. De quoi vivait Voltaire ? Deux Rives, 1949. 178 p. **4574**

Clear presentation of V.'s financial activities. Study published before Besterman ed. of the correspondence and could therefore be supplemented with further information.

Review : R. Pomeau in RHL 55:367–68, 1955.

Engel, Claire-Eliane. Voltaire est-il l'auteur des lettres de Mlle Aïssé ? RDM 530–39, Aug. 1953. **4575**

Suggests that letters of Charlotte Elisabeth Aïssé published in Paris in 1787 were written by V. Purely conjectural.

Fabre, Jean. Stanislas-Auguste Poniatowski et l'Europe des lumières. *See* 3391. p. 126–27, 312–30, 632–37. **4576**

A monumental study of cultural, philosophic, political, and religious affairs of 18th-century Europe as seen by the unstable and errant king of Poland. Chapters on salon of Mme Geoffrin, Grimm's correspondence, and relations with V. Based on thorough, firsthand documentation and wide knowledge of field.

Fields, Madeleine. Voltaire and Rameau. JAAC 21:457–65, 1962–63. **4577**

An account and analysis of their collaboration and subsequent hostility based on the Besterman ed. of V.'s correspondence.

Gagnebin, Bernard. Le médiateur d'une petite querelle genevoise. SVEC 1:115–223, 1955. **4578**

Describes V.'s involvement in Genevan

politics through his writing of a *compliment* for the *parti des natifs*, a group of descendants of Huguenot refugees born in Geneva but deprived of political rights. V.'s relationship with the *natifs* treated at much greater length by Ceitac (4571).

Garçon, Maurice. Voltaire et la tolérance. Tro 122:122–32, Feb. 1958.   **4579**
Voltaire and toleration with another résumé of the Calas affair. Nothing new here.

Gooch, G. P. Catherine the Great and Voltaire. *In his:* Catherine the Great and other studies. London, Longmans, Green, 1954. 292 p. *Also in:* Crev 182:214–20, 288–93, 1952.   **4580**
A summary of V.'s relations with Catherine II of Russia, based largely on their correspondence. No attempt at interpreting significance of their relationship. Bibliographical note on studies of Catherine II appears on p. 107–08. For a more critical approach, see ch. 3 of Peter Gay's *Voltaire's politics* (4640) and p. 384–85 of that work for further bibliography.

— Madame du Châtelet and her lovers. II: Voltaire. Crev 201:44–48, 1961.   **4581**
Readable summary of V.'s relationship with Mme du Châtelet. Nothing new here for scholar.

— Voltaire in England. *In his:* French profiles: prophets and pioneers. London, Longmans, Green, 1961. p. 44–61. *Also in:* Crev 195:349–53, 1959; 196:31–36, 90–98, 1959. *See* 5726.   **4582**
Account of V.'s early stay in England and a summary of the ideas of the *Lettres anglaises*. Well written, but largely derivative.

Guillemin, Henri. François-Marie Arouet, dit Zozo, dit Voltaire. Tro 122:81–108, Feb. 1958. *Also in his:* Eclaircissements. Gallimard, 1961. p. 25–60.   **4583**
A Catholic who sees no reason to reject V. because of his beliefs. Contains a critique of Pomeau's thesis (4677) that V. was a sincere, passionate deist and believes with Mornet in V.'s atheism. Distinguishes between private and public V. with some fine psychological insights. Speculates over V.'s childhood and his parental relationship to explain " contradictions " of his character. A very suggestive, sensitive, and challenging essay.

Henriot, Emile. Voltaire inédit. *In his:* Courrier littéraire, xviiie siècle. Nouvelle

édition augmentée. Michel, 1961. 1:261–67.   **4584**
On the correspondence with the Tronchins.

Lebois, André. La mort chrétienne de monsieur de Voltaire; documents inédits. Minard, 1960. 31 p. (ALM, 32) *Substantially same material reprinted as:* Le trépas chrétien de m. de Voltaire. *In his:* Littérature sous Louis XV. Denoël, 1962. p.297–323.   **4585**
Supposedly new information on V.'s death, but *see* Candaux (4570).

Lecercle, J.-L. Querelles de philosophes : Voltaire et Jean-Jacques Rousseau. Eur 361–62:105–17, May–June 1959.   **4586**
A résumé of the hostile relations between V. and Rousseau on both the personal and ideological level.

Mitford, Nancy. Voltaire in love. New York, Harper, 1957. 320 p.   **4587**
A witty, polished account of V. and Mme du Châtelet served up with delight but not for the scholar. No documentation.

Monier, M.-E. Jean-Baptiste du Tertre, notaire de Voltaire et premier commis du Département des finances. RSSHN 31:17–31, 1963.   **4588**
Biographical information about Jean-Baptiste du Tertre, a notary of V., extracted from his memoirs.

Myers, Robert L. A literary controversy in 18th-century France : Voltaire vs. Desfontaines. RInsP 44²:94–116, 1957. *See* 5495.   **4589**
A review of V.'s relations with the abbé Desfontaines in the light of the newly published Besterman ed. of the correspondence (4509). Article tends to increase V.'s guilt in their controversies.

Nivat, Jean. Quelques énigmes de la correspondance de Voltaire. RHL 53:439–63, 1953. *See* 5734.   **4590**
Author attempts to identify personages and decipher secret language of V.'s correspondence with Mme Denis from Alsace in 1753 and 1754 and to reconstruct the story of V.'s life during that year. A fascinating account that illuminates V.'s relations with Mme Denis, the French court, and Frederick the Great. For some reservations on Nivat's conclusions, *see* V.'s *Correspondence*, ed. by Theodore Besterman, letter no. 4890,

n. 2 and editor's introduction to v. 23, p. xxi.

— Voltaire et les ministres. Tro 122:43–59, Feb. 1958.   **4591**
An analysis of a significant aspect of V.'s character : his courting favor with and adulation of public officials. Article important in understanding V.'s personal aspirations and the nature and extent of his critique of the *ancien régime*.

Nixon, Edna. Voltaire and the Calas case. New York, Vanguard press, 1961. 224 p.
                                                4592
Another account of the Calas case. Clear, readable, and lively, but does not explain fundamental question of Catholic reaction in Toulouse to Protestantism. Bibliography; no index. *See* Bien (4613).

Orieux, Jean. Les enchantements de l'exil : Voltaire à Cirey. RPar 72:68–79, Jan. 1965.
                                                4593
Tidbits of Mme de Graffigny's visit to Cirey in Dec., 1738, served to a popular audience.

— François-Marie Arouet, l'enfant du siècle. RDM 550–63, July–Aug. 1964; 100–12, Sept.–Oct. 1964.   **4594**
An account of V.'s early years until his affair with Olympe Dunoyer. No documentation or scholarly apparatus.

Pomeau, René. La confession et la mort de Voltaire d'après des documents inédits. RHL 55:299–317, 1955.   **4595**
A detailed re-examination of circumstances surrounding confession, death and burial of V. with new documentation. To the question : " Did V. die a good Catholic ? " Pomeau replies, " Qualis vita, talis mors." A fascinating account.

— Nouveau regard sur le dossier Calas. Eur 398:57–72, June 1962.   **4596**
In contrast to Bien (4613), author sees Calas case as result of religious emotion preventing opinion in Toulouse from judging Calas with objectivity. " L'affaire Calas rappelle le danger des égarements, et démontre comment les préventions d'une foule peuvent être attisées par l'action d'un appareil, église, ligue, parti ..." (p. 71–72).

— Voltaire au collège. RHL 52:1–10, 1952.
                                                4597
Updates and corrects 19th-century studies on this subject by Beaune, Pierron, and Desnoiresterres.

— Voltaire en Angleterre : les enseignements d'une liste de souscription. AFLT 3:67–76, 1955.   **4598**
Uses subscription list for 1728 London ed. of *La Henriade* to derive information about V.'s English journey and contacts. Concludes that V. was acquainted with principal representatives of English thought. Suggests that V.'s stay in London ended by a disagreement since thereafter he turned away from interest in British politics and diplomacy. However, author still admits that V.'s last months in England shrouded in obscurity.

Price, J. Roy. Voltaire's name again. FR 31: 53–54, 1957–58.   **4599**
Suggests that V. drew his name from Voltaire, an antireligious character in Jobert's play *Balde, reine des Sarmantes* (1651).

Stern, Jean. Voltaire et sa nièce, Mme Denis. La Palatine, 1957. 332 p.   **4600**
A biographical summary of the relationship of V. and Mme Denis over the years. Account of their incestuous relationship based on the *Lettres d'Alsace* (1635) published in 1938, but not on the *Lettres d'amour de Voltaire à sa nièce* published by Besterman in 1957. Consequently, chronology and reason offered for their affair would have to be revised. Documentation and sources indicated in footnotes, but no bibliography or index. Useful background material.
Review : M. Dunan in RHD 71:261–63, 1957.

Vallotton, Henry. Catherine II et ses correspondants : Voltaire, Diderot, Grimm et J.-J. Rousseau. RDM 659–74, Aug. 15, 1954.   **4601**
Section on V. summarizes and quotes part of the Voltaire-Catherine correspondence. Nothing new here for scholar.

Studies of Style, Ideas, Sources, or Influence

Alciatore, Jules C. Stendhal et les romans de Voltaire. StCl 3^{10}:15–23, 1961.   **4602**
In spite of Stendhal's low regard for V., author shows Stendhal read and admired his novels greatly. Suggests possible similarities between *L'ingénu*, *Zadig*, and *La princesse de Babylone* on the one hand, and *Le rouge et le noir* and *La chartreuse de Parme* on the other. *See also* Ferdinand Boyer, *Les lectures de Stendhal* (Champion, 1925).

— Stendhal lecteur de La pucelle. StCl 2:325–34, 1959–60.   **4603**

References to *La pucelle* in the works of Stendhal over the years and suggestions about his ambivalent attitude to V.

Allain, Mathé. Voltaire et la fin de la tragédie classique française. FR 39:384–93, 1965–66.
4604

V.'s failure to revivify French classical tragedy seen as an ineluctable part of the changing scheme of philosophical values in the Enlightenment from those of the closed society of the 17th century.

Aubery, Pierre. Voltaire et les Juifs : ironie et démystification. SVEC 24:67–79, 1963.
4605

Article attempts to clear V. of charges of anti-Semitism traditionally attributed to him. Maintains that V. always judged Jews equitably and urges distinction between V.'s criticism of Biblical Jews and his attitude toward contemporary Jews. Nevertheless, in midst of article, author admits " tendencies " toward anti-Semitism in V. Article too brief to establish clear premises and review of critical literature on this complex subject.

Bach, Max. Sainte-Beuve and Voltaire. FR 31:109–15, 1957–58.   **4606**

Sainte-Beuve's varying reactions to V. with a stress on political factors.

Barber, William Henry. Leibniz in France, from Arnauld to Voltaire. *See* 5815.   **4607**

In an important study on a field that had previously been treated inadequately, author discusses effect of Leibniz' thought in France from 1670 to 1760. Recounts Leibniz' relations with Arnauld and his effort to bring about a reunion of the Protestant and Catholic churches, but emphasis is on Leibniz' connection with Bayle and V. Treatment of V. and Leibniz limited by failure to show relationship of Leibniz to persistence and continuity of V.'s ideas.

— Voltaire and Quakerism : Enlightenment and the inner light. SVEC 24:81–109, 1963. *See* 5716.   **4608**

Author suggests that V.'s interest in the Quakers not due simply to their eccentricity or to their usefulness in his campaign of religious propaganda. Sees fundamental affinities between Enlightenment and Protestantism, relationship of Voltairian deism to radical Protestantism, and parallels between Enlightenment and

Quaker doctrine of " inner light." Suggestive and thought provoking.

Baym, Max I. John Fiske and Voltaire. SVEC 4:171–84, 1957.   **4609**

Studies influence of V. on John Fiske (1842–1901), American historian and man of letters, who admired V. for contributions to science of history, his efforts in spreading Newtonianism in France, breadth of his interests, his criticism of theology, his poetic genius and wit, and as a founder of philosophy of history. Good basis for more complete study. Good bibliography.

Besterman, Theodore. Voltaire, absolute monarchy, and the enlightened monarch. SVEC 32:7–21, 1965.   **4610**

Law, derived from justice and reason, is the foundation of civilized society and of V.'s political ideas. V. rejected more formal doctrines of physiocratic thinkers but their major political ideas are seen as having their basis in V.'s teachings and as being shared by him.

— Voltaire jugé par Flaubert. SVEC 1:133–58, 1955. *English version in his:* Voltaire essays. *See* 4542. p. 13–23.   **4611**

Author demonstrates important influence of V. on Flaubert, Flaubert's thorough knowledge of V.'s work, and his sympathy with V.'s ideals. Includes Flaubert's unpublished notes on the *Essai sur les mœurs*. Article takes exception, convincingly, to comparatively minor importance accorded V. in Flaubert's thought by René Dumesnil in his *Gustave Flaubert*. Illuminating study.

— Voltaire's commentary on Frederick's L'art de la guerre. SVEC 2:61–206, 1956. *Also in his:* Voltaire essays. *See* 4542. p. 42–54 (without text of poem).   **4612**

Includes the previously unpublished text of V.'s comments on Frederick II's poem *L'art de la guerre*. No study had ever been made of *L'art de la guerre*, which Besterman judges as " confused in structure, feeble in execution, commonplace in poetic style." Poem of interest for information about Frederick's personality and ideas, and particularly as a sustained illustration of V.'s poetic principles. Commentary clearly shows that V.'s criticism of Frederick could be direct and caustic.

Bien, David D. The Calas affair; persecution, toleration, and heresy in eighteenth-century

Toulouse. Princeton, Princeton univ. press, 1960. 199 p. **4613**

A critical review of testimony at Calas trial as well as a study of Catholic attitudes toward Protestantism around Toulouse from 1750's to beginning of Revolution. Book provides a " revision of the conventional explanation and interpretation of both the intellectual and emotional setting and the Calas case itself which, in the polemical writing of Voltaire . . . is represented as a signal illustration of religious superstition and intolerance. With these explanations, the author is not in full accord " (Leo Gershoy in review *infra*).

Reviews : E. Barber in AJS 67:222–23, 1961–62; P. Gay in PSQ 76:309–11, 1961; L. Gershoy in AHR 67:119–20, 1961–62; A. Lee in ASR 26:489–90, 1961; H. Short in HJ 59:280, 1961; H. Trevor-Roper in NSN 62:121, 124, July 28, 1961.

Bingham, Alfred J. Voltaire and the New Testament. SVEC 24:183–218, 1963. **4614**

Outline of V.'s criticism of New Testament, Christian dogmas and institutions between early and later Christianity. Important source of information on V.'s attitudes toward New Testament scattered over many of his works and fundamental to assessment of his religious views.

Bongie, Laurence L. Crisis and the birth of the Voltairian conte. MLQ 23:53–64, 1962. **4615**

Conjectures that V. turned to the conte as a genre starting in 1747–48 because of a personal crisis over the problem of evil. Sensible, but little new here.

Booy, J. Th. de. L'abbé Coger, dit Coge Pecus, lecteur de Voltaire et de d'Holbach. *See* 4371. **4616**

Information from archives of the 18th-century Amsterdam printer and bookseller, Marc-Michel Rey, regarding abbé François Marie Coger, professor of rhetoric at the Collège Mazarin and enemy of V., and his purchases of books of V. and d'Holbach. Includes a *Catalogue des ouvrages commandés par Coger* [from Rey].

Boulier, Abbé Jean. Voltaire et Dieu. Eur 361–62:48–68, May-June 1959. **4617**

A sympathetic essay which concludes that because of his sense of justice and pity for the unfortunate, V. made a contribution to the " religious progress " of humanity. Written for a popular audience.

Brombert, Victor. Voltaire dans le Journal de Delacroix. FR 30:335–41, 1956–57. **4618**

Describes Delacroix' admiration in his *Journal* for V.'s artistry as a prose writer, his personality, his taste. Suggests that many Romantics' ideas firmly entrenched in the 18th century. Nevertheless, recalls Delacroix' criticism of V.'s *excès d'esprit* and narrowness of his esthetic ideas. Interesting brief article which could be elaborated into broader study.

Brooks, Richard A. Voltaire and Garcilaso de la Vega. SVEC 30:189–204, 1964. *See* 5949. **4619**

V.'s debt to the Spanish historian of Inca civilization and its importance in the *Essai sur les mœurs* and *Candide*.

— Voltaire and Leibniz. Geneva, Droz, 1964. 150 p. **4620**

The relationship of Leibniz to continuity of V.'s ideas and in context of his career. A study of two temperamentally different approaches to enigma of theodicy.

Reviews : W. Barber in FS 20:191–92, 1966; O. Haac in MLN 80:532–35, 1965.

Brown, Harcourt. Science and the human comedy : Voltaire. Daed 87:25–34, 1958. **4621**

The interaction of the sciences and humanities in the case of V. with suggestion that his *contes philosophiques* can be understood not only in terms of sensibility or literary form but in relation to his interest in natural sciences as well. Stimulating, thought-provoking essay.

Brumfitt, J. H. History and propaganda in Voltaire. SVEC 24:271–87, 1963. **4622**

An inquiry into V.'s objectivity as an historian with conclusion that his goal was enlightenment rather than pure information. V.'s historical writing contains moral and political judgments, but his propaganda restrained by his need for prudence in face of censorship and by a sincere regard for impartiality and truth as standards for historical writing. Interesting, informative, well-organized article.

— Voltaire, historian. London, Oxford univ. press, 1958. 178 p. **4623**

Devotes attention to historians who were predecessors of V. and analyzes V.'s historical works in chronological order. Weighs strengths and weaknesses of V.'s historiography and demonstrates growth of a critical attitude in it as he matures. Good bibliography. Careful, thorough work.

Reviews : P. Meyer in FR 32:593–94, 1958–59; F. Taylor in FS 12:370–72, 1958.

Caramaschi, Enzo. Du Bos et Voltaire. SVEC 10:113–236, 1959. **4624**

A rehabilitation of the abbé Du Bos in framework of a stimulating contribution to study of 18th-century historiography, esthetics, and criticism.

Cherpack, Clifton. Voltaire's criticism of Petrarch. RR 46:101–07, 1955. **4625**

Ambivalent attitude of V. toward Petrarch in *Essai sur les mœurs* and in his article in the *Gazette littéraire de l'Europe* in 1754 with conclusion that V.'s qualified admiration of Petrach was due to latter's " historical importance and the musical charm of his verse, rather than . . . the ' profundità dell'anima del poeta ' " (p. 107).

Cornu, Marcel. Le second Voltaire. Eur 361–62: 136–51, May–June 1959. **4626**

Title of article derives from description of Mérimée by Turgeniev. Mérimée's style, cosmopolitanism, and ideology as they were influenced by V. Rather general and insufficiently documented for scholarly purposes.

Dagens, Jean. La marche de l'histoire selon Voltaire. RFor 70:241–66, 1958. **4627**

Presentation of V.'s " static and cyclical " conception of course of history as opposed to evolution of history consistent with idea of progress, followed by a discussion of V.'s analysis of age of Louis XIV, the Middle Ages and the Renaissance, and concluding with a description of V.'s philosophy of history. A knowledgeable survey.

Day, Douglas A. Voltaire and Cicero. RLC 39:31–43, 1965. **4628**

V.'s admiration of Cicero as a man, statesman, orator, and philosopher. Cicero " was more than just a philosophical ally; he became Voltaire's *alter ego* " (p. 93).

Dédéyan, Charles. Voltaire et la pensée anglaise. Centre de documentation universitaire, 1956. 232 p. (Les cours de Sorbonne) **4629**

A manual-type summary of V.'s relation to English literary, scientific, political, social, philosophic, and religious thought.

Deneckere, Marcel. La conscience européenne chez Voltaire. CahB 2:43–54, 1952. **4630**

Author shows V.'s recognition of the limitations of nationalism, his dilemma in seeing no way to escape its evils, and his vision of unity of Europe on cultural rather than political level. While V. did not believe in the inherent superiority of the white man, he saw European civilization in the forefront of Enlightenment. Suggestive basis for a broader study of V.'s European consciousness.

Desné, Roland. Voltaire et les beaux-arts. Eur 361–62:117–27, May-June 1959. **4631**

V. as an art lover, collector, speculator, and critic. Despite his limited knowledge of art, his reflections on taste and history in *Siècle de Louis XIV* and *Essai sur les mœurs* gave fine arts a new importance. Suggestive, if brief treatment of the subject.

Diaz, Furio. Voltaire storico. Turin, Einaudi, 1958. 323 p. **4632**

An account of V.'s merits as an historian by an admirer who fails to see his limitations in light of modern historiography.

Reviews : J. Brumfitt in RSI 71:500–05, 1959; A. Dufour RSHist 10:589–92, 1960; G. Gargallo di Castel Lentini in SiGy n.s. 14:204–11, 1961; F. Orlando in SF 4:354, 1960.

Dimaras, C. Th. La fortune de Voltaire en Grèce. *In:* Mélanges offerts à Octave et Melpo Merlier à l'occasion du 25ᵉ anniversaire de leur arrivée en Grèce. Athens, 1956. 1:199–222. **4633**

V.'s influence and fortune in Greece from 1765 to 1820. " Au début l'œuvre du philosophe est agréée par les lettrés, qui, en l'occurrence, sont en même temps les représentants de la pensée religieuse; au second tour l'Eglise et les clercs réagissent violemment, et enfin les idées nouvelles symbolisées par le nom de Voltaire prévalent de façon définitive. Cinquante ans de la vie intellectuelle grecque sont enfermés dans ce schéma " (p. 201).

Duchet, Michèle. Voltaire et les sauvages. Eur 361–62:88–97, May–June 1959. **4634**

V.'s humanism derives nothing from

observation of primitive societies. " Tout retour en arrière lui semble une dangereuse régression, et le ' primitivisme ' une hérésie intellectuelle, dans un monde où scintillent déjà les lumières des villes futures, métropoles du capitalisme industriel " (p. 94). A useful delineation of V.'s thinking on this important 18th-century theme.

Duckworth, Colin. Flaubert and Voltaire's Dictionnaire philosophique. SVEC 18: 141–67, 1961. **4635**
Flaubert's interest in and debt to V. based on an unpublished Flaubert ms containing quotations from and his comments on *Dictionnaire philosophique*. Flaubert's reactions to V. on a wide range of subjects. Important article based on primary research.

Fabre, Jean. Deux définitions du philosophe: Voltaire et Diderot. Tro 122:135–52, Feb. 1958. *Also in his:* Lumières et romantisme. *See* 4127. p. 3–18. **4636**
Author reviews relations of V. and Diderot, taking into account critical literature on subject, and, seeing an essential antagonism between the two, suggests numerous reasons for it ranging from differences of age and social situation to psychological analysis. Fundamentally sees Diderot and V. at odds over the conception of the *philosophe*. Interesting insights and well written.

Fields, Madeleine. Voltaire et le Mercure de France. SVEC 20:175–215, 1962. *See* 5536. **4637**
Studies the image of V. in the *Mercure de France*, a periodical which represented opinion of governing conservative class. Well written and based on painstaking research. A valuable contribution to our knowledge of 18th-century opinion of V.

Flowers, Ruth Cave. Voltaire's stylistic transformation of Rabelaisian satirical devices. Washington, Catholic univ. of America press, 1951. v, 138 p. (CUAS, 41) **4638**
A close textual study in comparative stylistics in which the author analyzes satirical techniques of Rabelais and V. and their relationship. Bibliography and a useful index that includes satirical subjects and devices employed by both authors.

Folena, Gianfranco. Divagazioni sull'italiano di Voltaire. *In:* Studi in onore di Vittorio Lugli e Diego Valeri. Venice, Pozza, 1961. 1:391–424. *See* 5905. **4639**

On V.'s " lungo e amoroso ' commercio ' ... con la lingua italiana." A detailed study.

Gay, Peter. Voltaire's politics : the poet as realist. Princeton, Princeton univ. press, 1959. 417 p. **4640**
Emphasizes V.'s realism and relativism as a political thinker, tries to destroy notion of V. as zealous, idealistic believer in abstract reason and shows his constant involvement in practical politics. Central thesis is V.'s defense of *thèse royale* (absolute monarchy) against *thèse nobiliaire* (intermediary feudal powers). Although largely based on secondary works, contains new material on V. and Genevan politics and his relation to the *natifs*. Explains V.'s contradictory political attitudes as result of empirical approach. Contains bibliographical essay. Valuable study.
Reviews : D. Brogan in Enc 78:88–90, March 1960; J. Brumfitt in FS 14:365–66, 1960; E. Cahm in SVEC 12:111–16, 1960; L. Crocker in RR 50:294–97, 1959; W. Moore in MLR 55:449–51, 1960; R. Pomeau in RHL 61:87–88, 1961; E. Weis in HZ 193:146–49, 1961.

Girard, René. Classicism and Voltaire's historiography. LHM 29:151–60, 1958. **4641**
Purports to discuss V.'s conception of historiography and its relationship to classicism but actually concentrates on contrast between 17th-century ideal of *honnête homme* and modern tendency toward specialization. Interesting article, but little to do with V. *per se.*

Gooch, G. P. Voltaire as historian. *In his:* Catherine the Great and other studies. London, Longmans, Green, 1954. p. 199–274. *Also in his:* French profiles : prophets and pioneers. London, Longmans, Green, 1961. p. 62–136. **4642**
General indication of V.'s importance as an historian with a summary of his major historical works. No attempt at a critique of V. as historian or a study of his role in historiography. Convenient for layman, but little new here for scholar.

Gordon, L. S. Voltaire, lecteur de Bayle et de Necker. FE 469–80, 1961. **4643**
A study of V.'s marginal notes on works of Bayle and on Necker's *Sur la législation et le commerce des grains* found in V.'s library in Leningrad. V.'s approbation of and debating with the former and his

hostility to the latter. Article in Russian with brief French résumé.

Grappin, Pierre. Goethe und Voltaire. DF 3:201–12, 1963.   **4644**

On V.'s influence on Goethe concluding with undocumented hypothesis that V. was model of the aging Faust.

Guerlac, Henry. Three eighteenth-century social philosophers : scientific influences on their thought. Daed 87:8–24, 1958.   **4645**

Relationship of V.'s belief in Newton's theory of scientific probability to his critique of French judicial system. Concludes that V., despite his technical and mathematical deficiencies, understood implications of Newton's thought and method better than any other French literary figure in 18th century.

Guicharnaud, Jacques. Voltaire and Shakespeare. LHM 27:159–69, 1956. *See* 5727.   **4646**

V.'s antagonism to Shakespeare because of his commitment to French classicism. Little new in this article.

Guiragossian, Diana S. Voltaire's facéties. Geneva, Droz, 1963. 140 p.   **4647**

A study of V.'s *facéties* (short anonymous works written on the spur of the moment), their role in his war on the *infâme*, and the techniques he used to create satire and wit.

Reviews : P. Aubery in MLN 81:251–53, 1966; A. Pizzorusso in RLM 16:304, 1963; R. Waldinger in RR 55:215–16, 1964.

Guiral, Pierre. Quelques notes sur le retour de faveur de Voltaire sous le Second Empire. *In:* Hommage au doyen Etienne Gros. Gap, Imprimerie Louis-Jean, 1959. p. 193–204.   **4648**

V. admired by Lamartine, Hugo, Michelet, Sainte-Beuve, a number of minor Second Empire authors, and the periodical press. The campaign for and against the subscription to the 1867 ed. of V.'s *Œuvres complètes* (Bengesco #2178) published by the newspaper *Le siècle.* A number of interesting details about V.'s fortune under the Second Empire.

Guy, Basil. The French image of China before and after Voltaire. Geneva, Institut et musée Voltaire, 1963. 468 p. (SVEC, 21)   **4649**

The Chinese image from Montaigne to French Revolution, importance of V. and first two chapters of the *Essai sur les mœurs*

in making China philosophically fashionable, and decline of Chinese vogue after 1760. Appendixes include list of significant works in which V. mentions China. Documentation, bibliography, but no index.

Reviews : W. Appleton in RR 55:216–17, 1964; R. Pomeau in RHL 64:308–09, 1964; R. Shackleton in FS 18:272–73, 1964.

Haac, Oscar A. Voltaire and Leibniz : two aspects of rationalism. SVEC 25:795–809, 1963.   **4650**

Article summarizes results of previous studies on subject by Barber, Wade, and Bottiglia; briefly reviews V.'s comments on Leibniz; discusses significance of garden theme in *Candide;* raises the dubious question of whether Leibniz was an ally or foe of V.; and, not unexpectedly, concludes that the two men " never speak the same language." Little significantly new.

Krös, Börje. Voltaire et la Grèce. HelC 9:6–31, 1955.   **4651**

V. as an admirer of Ancient Greece because of its literary and artistic contributions and its political liberty. Finds V.'s chapters on history of Byzantium inaccurate and superficial and maintains V. had little knowledge of contemporary Greece, his attitude toward it coinciding with political viewpoint of Catherine II of Russia. Nevertheless, he had important influence on contemporary opinion toward Greece.

Leigh, R. A. An anonymous eighteenth-century character-sketch of Voltaire. SVEC 2:241–72, 1956.   **4652**

Fascinating account of the history of a malicious character sketch of V., appearing at least as early as 1735, which reveals contemporary opinion of V. and established a critical image of him throughout the rest of the 18th century and later. Portrait of V., inspired by image of a *bel esprit* of early Paris salons, was perpetuated without great change throughout rest of his career. Well documented.

Liublinskiǐ, Vladimir Sergeevich. Du nouveau sur Voltaire et la Russie. Eur 361–62:97–105, May–June 1959.   **4653**

On Russian studies concerning V. and their importance, especially as they relate to Russian history.

— Voltaire et la guerre des farines. AHRF 31:127–45, 1959. *Also in:* Pages d'histoire

des mouvements sociaux et des relations
internationales publiées à la mémoire
d'Eugène Tarlé. Moscow, Editions de l'Académie des sciences de l'U.R.S.S., 1957. **4654**
V.'s *Diatribe à l'auteur des Ephémérides*
as a literary echo of the *guerre des farines*
(1775), the riots against Turgot's decree
for the circulation of grain.

— Voltaire-Studien. Trans. by Wolfgang
Techtmeier. Berlin, Akademie-Verlag,
1961. 190 p. **4655**
German translation of 4 Russian essays:
(1) *Religionsgeschichtliche Quellen in der
Bibliothek Voltaires;* (2) *Randbemerkungen
Voltaires;* (3) *Voltaire und der "Mehlkrieg"*
(French trans., *see* 4654); (4) *Ein unbe-
kanntes Voltaire-Autograph in Puschkins
Papieren.* Issued prior to publication of
Russian catalog of V.'s library, first two
essays deal with sources of information
concerning religious questions in V.'s
library; third essay is on V. and the *guerre
des farines;* the last essay, originally
published in 1935, deals with a previously
unknown autograph ms of V. found in
1934 among Pushkin's papers; a sheet
containing 13 verses making up beginning
of famous letter of Feb., 1737 to Frederick on one side and 23 verses of Juvenal
and Persius.
Reviews : H. Dieckmann in Archiv
200:311–13, 1963–64; M. Naumann in
DLit 84:579–81, 1963; J. Vercruysse in
RBP 61:971–72, 1963.

Marchou, Gaston. Le chevalier de La
Barre et la raison d'état. RPar 72:112–25,
July–Aug. 1965. **4656**
The La Barre affair seen as part of
struggle of *parlements* and the Jesuits.

Mason, Haydn T. Pierre Bayle and Voltaire.
See 4178. **4657**
A scholarly and careful treatment of
Bayle's influence on V. A chronological
presentation of V.'s familiarity with and
reaction to Bayle's work followed by a
comparison of attitudes between the two
in chapters entitled : *The critical outlook,
The problem of evil, Atheism and morality,
Spinoza and agnosticism,* and *Methods and
aims.* Presentation of problem of evil and
of V.'s attitude toward Spinoza weak, and
book lacks historical perspective. Nevertheless, fills important need in history of
ideas.

— Voltaire and Manichean dualism. SVEC
26:1143–60, 1963. **4658**
Traces V.'s long-term interest in the
subject from time of *Remarques sur Pascal*

with conclusion that V. rejects Manicheism because of an " impulse towards an
optimistic view of human nature " and
his association of Manicheism with
Christian doctrine of original sin. Author
suggests that V. created character of
Martin in *Candide* with Pierre Bayle in
mind and shows relationship of Martin's
arguments to Bayle's writings. Well-
documented article that enlightens complex subject of V.'s varying reactions to
optimism and pessimism.

Maurois, André. Voltaire : romans et
contes. *In his:* De La Bruyère à Proust.
Fayard, 1964. p. 43-53. **4659**
A polished essay serving as an introduction to V.'s *contes* that does not
propose to say anything fundamentally
new on the subject.

Meikle, Henry W. Voltaire and Scotland.
EA 11:193–201, 1958. *See* 5731. **4660**
Publication of V.'s works in 18th-cen-
tury Scotland, his treatment of the
Forty-five, his relationship to the historians Hume and Robertson, and to
the economist Adam Smith, and his very
limited influence on Scottish thought.
Interesting article that could be further
developed. *See also* Paul Meyer, *Voltaire
and Hume as historians* (4743).

Nichols, Elizabeth. Dom Calmet, " qui n'a
raisonné jamais . . . ." FR 31:296–99, 1957–
58. **4661**
V.'s contradictory attitude toward Dom
Augustin Calmet. His apparent respect
for the Benedictine theologian and
historian in his correspondence and his
ironic and harsh attacks on him in *Dictionnaire philosophique.*

Pappas, John N. Berthier's Journal de
Trévoux and the philosophes. *See* 4142.
4662
P. 85–137 are concerned with V. and
Journal de Trévoux. Author describes
V.'s early admiration for the Jesuits, their
attempts to encourage him to stay within
fold of Catholic religion, and their subsequent hostility. Interesting, systematic,
well-documented account.

— La rupture entre Voltaire et les jésuites.
LR 12:351–70, 1959. **4663**
Reviews V.'s relations with Jesuits and
suggests reasons for his open break with
them coming only as late as 1759. Interesting article, but question of chronology
in V.'s attack on Jesuits not entirely
settled. English version in author's

Berthier's Journal de Trévoux and the philosophes (4142).

— Voltaire and d'Alembert. Bloomington, Indiana univ. press, 1962. vi, 183 p. (IUHS, 50) *See* 4292.   **4664**

A study of the intellectual relationship of V. and d'Alembert centering on the *Encyclopédie* venture and the struggle on behalf of *philosophie*. The personal or biographical is underplayed. Ch. 5, *Civil war*, originally appeared in French as *Voltaire et la guerre civile philosophique* (4666). An excellent, scholarly monograph.

Reviews : J. Brumfitt in FS 18:56–57, 1964; L. Gossman in MLN 79:94–97, 1964; J. Proust in RHL 64:105, 1964; F. Spear in BA 73–74, Winter 1964; R. Waldinger in RR 55:130–31, 1964.

— Voltaire and the problem of evil. EspCr 3: 199–206, 1963.   **4665**

Article maintains that V., under attack by the atheist coterie of d'Holbach, accepted, in later life, very optimism he ridiculed in *Candide*. A complex question which had better probably be resolved in a longer study.

— Voltaire et la guerre civile philosophique. RHL 61:525–49, 1961. *English version in his:* Voltaire and d'Alembert. *See* 4664. p. 81–128.   **4666**

The differing attitudes—metaphysical and political—of V. and d'Alembert, on the one hand, and the Diderot-d'Holbach group, on the other, in their war on *l'infâme*. A well-written, authoritative, and important article.

Perkins, Jean A. Voltaire and La Mettrie. *See* 4248.   **4667**

Personal relations of La Mettrie and V.; latter's reaction to *Anti-Sénèque* and to La Mettrie's atheism and materialism. Article partly based on V.'s marginal notes and markers in La Mettrie's works.

— Voltaire and the natural sciences. SVEC 37: 61–76, 1965.   **4668**

Author rejects commonly accepted opinion that V. did not keep up with scientific progress in his later years. Concludes that V. valued experimental method and did not abandon science, but was not sanguine about its ability to reveal mysteries of universe.

Perkins, Merle L. Voltaire and the abbé de Saint-Pierre. *See* 5413.   **4669**

V. was interested in Saint-Pierre's

ideas on religious and governmental reform. At the same time, criticized the abbé's demeaning appraisal of the value of arts and sciences and the accomplishments of the Sun King. He also found the abbé's utopianism unacceptable.

— Voltaire and the abbé de Saint-Pierre on world peace. *See* 5414.   **4670**

V.'s position on principal issues raised by Saint-Pierre, particularly in the *Paix perpétuelle*, major object of V.'s attack. Interesting conclusion that V. was more of an idealist than Saint-Pierre.

— Voltaire on the source of national power. SVEC 20:141–73, 1962.   **4671**

Purpose of study is to ascertain V.'s conclusions on the reasons for national weakness and his positive ideas on the source of national power. Good résumé of topic, but somewhat uncritical with regard to enlightened despotism and progressiveness of Peter the Great and Catherine.

— Voltaire's concept of international order. Geneva, Institut et musée Voltaire, 1965. 342 p. (SVEC, 36)   **4672**

Study presents V.'s thinking on international order with reference to following categories : V.'s knowledge of nations of earth, his experience with European politics, his attitudes toward international law, projects for peace, enlightened despotism, his views on sources of war, sovereignty, national power, and foreign policy. These topics are organized "into a structure designed to coordinate Voltaire's beliefs about the affairs of nations, beliefs which Voltaire never bothered to build into a system " (p. 14–15). Appendixes include illustrative V. texts and lists of books in V.'s library arranged by categories and pertinent to topic of monograph. Fully documented and based on firsthand research.

— Voltaire's principles of political thought. MLQ 17:289–300, 1956.   **4673**

Purpose of article is to show a consistent theoretical basis underlying V.'s political thinking and to uncover " the postulates on which Voltaire's ' system ' rests." " For the sake of conciseness and significant juxtaposition in the treatment of Voltaire's argument, an arrangement which is not his own and which joins materials taken from many of his works has been followed " (p. 289). Paper has a number of fine insights, although perhaps an oversystematic V. emerges because of method followed.

Pichois, Claude. Préromantiques, rousseau-istes et shakespeariens (1770–1778). RLC 33:348–55, 1959. *See* 5735.   **4674**

Pierre Le Tourneur, monumental translator of Shakespeare in 18th-century France, as an enemy of V. and admirer of Rousseau. Interesting aspect in changing history of 18th-century esthetics.

— Voltaire et Shakespeare : un plaidoyer. ShJ 98:178–88, 1962. *See* 5736.   **4675**

Author believes that to understand V.'s attitude toward Shakespeare it is necessary to understand opposition between *génie* and *goût* in 18th-century esthetics. Thus, although V. found Shakespeare barbarous because of his violation of *les règles*, he admired his genius which brought life to stage and gave flight to his imagination. Also suggests that as a precise translator of Shakespeare (after 1734), V. was Shakespeare's most faithful servant in 18th-century France, superior to the pre-Romantic translation of Le Tourneur. Contains useful bibliography.

Pintard, René. Voltaire et l'Encyclopédie. AUP 22:39–56, Oct. 1952.   **4676**

Complements Raymond Naves' *Voltaire et l'Encyclopédie* (1316). Describes intentions and fears of Diderot and d'Alembert in their collaboration with V. and latter's attempt to use article *Genève* to win over Genevan ministers to deism. Discusses *Encyclopédie*'s role in transforming V. from the *impatient manœuvrier des Délices* to the *diabolique patriarche de Ferney* and its relationship to the *Dictionnaire philosophique*. Well-written and urbane presentation.

Pomeau, René. La religion de Voltaire. Nizet, 1956. 516 p.   **4677**

A capital work on 18th-century French literature that shows thorough knowledge of V. scholarship. Impartial presentation of controversial subject. Conclusion of work not unexpected: V. was a deist and his religion was one of passionate faith and sincere conviction, consisting of a love of God, of reason, and justice. Includes controversial characterological study of V. as an aid in interpreting his religion. Important background material. Excellent bibliography.

Reviews : A. Adam in RScH n.s. 84: 491–93, 1956; T. Besterman in SVEC 4: 295–301, 1957; F. Orlando in RLM 12:

83–86, 1959; H. Perret in EnC 73:251–53, 1959–60.

— Voltaire conteur : masques et visages. IL 13:1–5 1961.   **4678**

The omnipresence of V. in the *contes* through characters that diversify his being while preserving his identity. An intriguing article that demonstrates the very personal role V. played in his *contes*.

— Voltaire européen. Tro 122:28–42, Feb. 1958.   **4679**

The many ways in which V. was a European and not simply a Frenchman. *See also* Deneckere (4630).

Proschwitz, Gunnar von. Gustave III et les Lumières : l'affaire de Bélisaire. SVEC 26: 1347–63, 1963.   **4680**

Gustavus III, king of Sweden, as an admirer of V., p. 1350–52.

Ramsey, Warren. Voltaire and l'art de peindre. SVEC 26:1365–77, 1963.   **4681**

Article considers implications of V.'s belief that poetic imitation largely involves particulars whereas painting has a more universal quality. Sees characteristics of V.'s verse as great movement, images in motion, lack of vision in depth, lack of guiding metaphors, and highly flexible use of caesura. Analyzes briefly three V. poems from around 1756. Fine, suggestive article on a neglected aspect of V. studies.

Rezler, Marta. Voltaire and the Encyclopédie : a re-examination. SVEC 30:147–87, 1964.   **4682**

The first part of a projected longer study in which Rezler amends or adds to Naves' conclusions (1316) on following questions : V.'s absence from *Encyclopédie* at outset, initial circumstances of his collaboration, his attitude toward *Encyclopédie* and its editors, etc. Initial conclusion is that no personal feelings kept V. from participating in *Encyclopédie* at outset; rather events connected with V.'s private life and beyond control of all concerned delayed his collaboration until 1754.

— The Voltaire-d'Alembert correspondence : an historical and bibliographical re-appraisal *See* 4294.   **4683**

Aim of study is to show need of comprehensive work on Voltaire-d'Alembert friendship. Surveys critical literature on the subject and concludes treatment has been generally superficial and arbitrary.

Contains a bibliographical history of the correspondence and a list of letters belonging to the Voltaire-d'Alembert correspondence added since Kehl ed. Concludes that there are important missing gaps in the correspondence but that essential relationship indicated by letters extant. Meticulous piece of scholarship, although sometimes quite technical.

Ridgway, Ronald S. La propagande philosophique dans les tragédies de Voltaire. Geneva, Institut et musée Voltaire, 1961. 260 p. (SVEC, 15)   **4684**

Treats basic philosophical ideas of V. as they appear in his tragedies, including deism, anti-Christian propaganda, and theme of despotism. Establishes following categories for V.'s theatre : political, Christian, philosophical, moral, historical, and pamphlet tragedy. Conclusions : V.'s propaganda destroyed his plays and he was unable to be great dramatist because of hasty writing, poor characterization, and his effort to embody ideas of Enlightenment in forms of classicism. Judicious and well written.
Reviews : J. Brumfitt in FS 16:185–87, 1962; H. Hastings in RR 52:304–06, 1961.

Rihs, Charles. Voltaire; recherches sur les origines du matérialisme historique. Geneva, Droz, 1962. 228 p.   **4685**

A study of V.'s historiography in relation to the providential and materialist conceptions of history. Number of facts and conclusions subject to caution.
Reviews : R. Desné in Eur 405–06:324–34, Jan.-Feb. 1963; W. Krauss in DLit 85:633–36, 1964; R. Mortier in RBP 42: 731–35, 1964.

Robinove, Phyllis S. Voltaire's theatre on the Parisian stage, 1789–1799. FR 32:534–38, 1958–59.   **4686**

Includes statistics of performances of 19 V. plays from 1789 to 1799 and concludes that V.'s popularity as a dramatist in Revolutionary period due to his expressing in the theater aspirations of the time. Useful information based on contemporary periodicals.

Rosenthal, Jerome. Voltaire's philosophy of history. JHI 16 : 151–78, 1955.   **4687**

An examination of V.'s philosophy of history and a critique of its principles. The author treats notions of selectivity, teleology, oral and written history, moral standards in historical judgment, time and timelessness in history, the meaning

of superstition, the shortcomings and influence of V.'s historical method. Important article.

Rowe, Constance. Voltaire and the state. New York, Columbia univ. press, 1955. xi, 254 p.   **4688**

First part of work contains standard, brief biography of V.; second half, an inquiry into V.'s political views. Information on V.'s opinions on government, international affairs, economics and education, but little that is new. Author's main points already made by Lanson and Brailsford and work marred by failure to study V.'s ideas in chronological sequence and by misprints.
Reviews : J. Brumfitt in FS 11:355–56, 1957; G. Havens in RR 47:218–20, 1956.

Saisselin, Rémy G. Goût et civilisation. RE 15:30–42, 1962.   **4689**

Taste as a criterion of judgment in analysis of history by V., who explains its course, according to Saisselin, not in terms of a philosophy of progress but as a series of oscillations striving for classical perfection but achieving it only in its great moments. A suggestive and useful notion within limits.

Sareil, Jean. Anatole France et Voltaire. Geneva, Droz, 1961. 502 p.   **4690**

Thorough study with good bibliography. Large part of work consists of comparison of views of both authors on wide-ranging subjects. Painstaking work with large number of quoted passages. Valuable contribution.
Reviews : J. Brumfitt in FS 16:80–81, 1962; G. Havens in RR 53:236–38, 1962; W.-G. Klostermann in Archiv 200: 77-80, 1963-64; W. Krauss in DLit 83:637–39, 1962; H. Peyre in FR 35:334–35, 1961–62; M. Spaziani in SF 6:514–15, 1962; A. Vandegans in RHL 63:136–37, 1963; R. Wiarda in Neo 46:77–80, 1962.

—— La répétition dans les contes de Voltaire. FR 35:137–46, 1961–62.   **4691**

Content and form coalesce in the Voltairian *conte* through the device of repetition which serves as both a plot-unifier and as a basic source of the author's humor. Interesting stylistic study.

Saunders, Richard M. Voltaire's view of the meaning of history. UTQ 22:44–54, 1952–53.   **4692**

V.'s philosophy of history seen as struggling between two conceptions : (1) history as the revelation or progress in the unfolding of human reason and (2) history as a proof of the constancy and imperfection of human nature leading V. to pessimism and to a belief in the meaninglessness of history.

Seznec, Jean. Falconet, Voltaire et Diderot. SVEC 2:43–59, 1956. *See* 5095. **4693**

Falconet's low esteem of V.'s art appreciation in the *Essai sur l'histoire générale*, *Temple du goût*, and *Dictionnaire philosophique*. Diderot's defense of V.'s judgment.

Sgard, Jean. Prévost et Voltaire. RHL 64: 545–64, 1964. **4694**

A study of their esthetic and intellectual affinities, their collaboration, and the break in their relations.

Sivolape, I. I. Voltaire sur les mouvements révolutionnaires des xviie et xviiie siècles. FE 370–87, 1960. **4695**

Article examines V.'s views on English " bourgeois revolution " of 17th century, the Fronde and other revolutionary movements of 17th and 18th centuries. Concludes, not surprisingly, that although he was personally opposed to revolutionary transformation of society, V.'s works unconsciously contributed to upheaval of 1789. Article in Russian with brief French summary.

La table ronde. 122: Feb. 1958. **4696**

An entire issue devoted to V. Articles include : (1) André Maurois, *Voltaire au présent*, p. 9–14; (2) Emmanuel Berl, *Situation de Voltaire*, p. 15–26; (3) Jean Cocteau, *Voltaire académicien*, p. 27; (4) René Pomeau, *Voltaire européen*, p. 28–42; (5) Jean Nivat, *Voltaire et les ministres*, p. 43–59; (6) Theodore Besterman, *Le désastre de Lisbonne et l'optimisme de Voltaire*, p. 60–74; (7) André Thérive, *Dieu et Voltaire*, p. 75–80; (8) Henri Guillemin, *François-Marie Arouet, dit Zozo, dit Voltaire*, p. 81–108; (9) Hugo Friedrich, *Candide (1759)*, p. 109–15; (10) Jacques van den Heuvel, *Le conte voltairien ou la confidence déguisée*, p. 116–21; (11) Maurice Garçon, *Voltaire et la tolérance*, p. 122–32; (12) Alain, *Tortures*, p. 133–34; (13) Jean Fabre, *Deux définitions du philosophe: Voltaire et Diderot*, p. 135–52; (14) Pierre Sipriot, *Au temps des lumières*, p. 153–58; (15) Bertrand Russell, *Sous l'influence de Voltaire*, p. 159–63; (16) R. A. Leigh, *La correspondance de Voltaire par Besterman*, p. 164–75; (17) Paolo Alatri, *Le renouveau voltairien en Italie*, p. 176–81.

Taylor, Samuel. La collaboration de Voltaire au Théâtre français (1767–69). SVEC 18:57–75, 1961. **4697**

V.'s participation with Henri Rieu in the 14-volume series of the *Théâtre français ou recueil de toutes les pièces françaises restées au théâtre* (Geneva, 1767–69) whose aim was to follow evolution of French drama. Collection interesting to critic as a reflection of dramatic taste of the period and to bibliographer since many plays included in the series represent *éditions inconnues*. Article followed by bibliographical analysis of the *Théâtre français*.

Thérive, André. Dieu et Voltaire. Tro 122:75–80, Feb. 1958. **4698**

An *ad hominem* dismissal of V.'s anti-Christian rationalism. Rejects values of Enlightenment and sees Voltaire as a tragic figure unable to reconcile himself with God. Interesting as a contemporary Catholic viewpoint on Voltaire. *See also* Guillemin (4583).

Thielemann, Leland. Voltaire and Hobbism. SVEC 10:237–58, 1959. *See* 5738. **4699**

V.'s reserved admiration for Hobbes' anticlericalism and his views on Church and State. V.'s attack on ideas of legendary Hobbism : natural wickedness of man, right of the stronger, natural state of war, and justice of convention. Judicious and important article, although it does not sufficiently take into account V.'s contradictory attitudes toward nature and society.

Tumins, Valerie A. Voltaire and the rise of Russian drama. SVEC 27:1689–1701, 1963. **4700**

Popularity of V. in Russia in 19th and 20th centuries, although V. did not have great influence on Russian stage because he was too classical for a theater stressing national modes. Interesting, although rather generalized study of the subject. V. and Russia is an important subject largely unknown to Western scholars.

Varloot, Jean. Voltaire et le matérialisme. Eur 361–62:68–75, May-June 1959. **4701**

Examination of V.'s difficult religious position in which he is represented as struggling between indifference and faith and opposing both Christians and atheists. A useful summary.

Vercruysse, J. La fortune de Bernard Nieuwentydt en France au xviiie siècle et les notes marginales de Voltaire. SVEC 30:223–46, 1964.   **4702**

Rapid account of the French reputation of the Dutch physician and author of the *Existence de Dieu démontrée par les merveilles de la nature;* reactions of Rousseau, Diderot, La Mettrie, and V. with reproduction of latter's marginal notes on a copy of Nieuwentydt's work.

— Les Provinces-Unies vues par Voltaire. SVEC 27:1715–21, 1963.   **4703**

V.'s attitude to the Netherlands as gleaned from observations spread throughout his works and correspondence. His interest in Dutch commerce and science, but his displeasure with Dutch publishing business and its piracy of author's rights and privileges. Interesting sidelights.

Vignery, J. Robert. Voltaire's economic ideas as revealed in the romans and contes. FR 33:257–63, 1959–60.   **4704**

Suggestions from the *contes* on V.'s ideas concerning luxury, foreign commerce, colonialism, agriculture, and taxation. Author believes *L'homme aux quarante écus* has been overemphasized as a source for V.'s economic ideas.

Wade, Ira O. Voltaire's quarrel with science. BuR 8:287–98, 1958–59.   **4705**

Author sees science and metaphysics as inseparable disciplines for V. and suggests that, starting in 1758, V. became dissatisfied with science because of its inability to answer fundamental questions about nature of universe. According to Wade, this critical attitude toward science coincided with Lisbon earthquake, Seven Years' War, and author's personal experiences at Potsdam. However, he sees V. as not rejecting science but looking upon it more cautiously.

Waldinger, Renée. Voltaire and reform in the light of the French Revolution. Geneva, Droz, 1959. 118 p.   **4706**

Clear account of general way in which V.'s ideas on social reform developed. Shows relationship of V.'s demands for reform with the *cahiers de doléances* and revolutionary legislation of 1789 to 1791. Too vast a subject for this small book. Good description of V.'s social ideas, but not strong on interpretation.

Reviews : W. Barber in MLR 55:448–49, 1960; J. Brumfitt in FS 14:367–68, 1960; P. Burgelin in RLC 35:675–77, 1961; A. Freer in SF 4:155, 1960; H. Jauss in Archiv 197:91–92, 1960–61;

W. Krauss in DLit 83:890–91, 1962; P. Meyer in MLN 75:624–27, 1960; R. Mortier in RBP 39:94–96, 1961; J. Pappas in LR 15:181–84, 1961; R. Pomeau in RHL 61:87–88, 1961; L. Thielemann in RR 51:296–98, 1960.

Wilson, Arthur M.   Leningrad, 1957 : Diderot and Voltaire gleanings. FR 31:351–63, 1957–58.   **4707**

Interesting information on V.'s comments on Diderot's works and on articles in *Encyclopédie* based on brief examination of V.'s library at Leningrad.

Wilson-Jones, Kenneth R. Voltaire's letters and notebooks in English (1726–29). *In:* Studies in comparative literature. Ed. by Waldo F. McNeir. Baton Rouge, Louisiana State univ. press, 1962. p. 120–29. (LSUSH, 11)   **4708**

What V.'s early letters and English notebooks reveal about his knowledge and practice of English language and his impressions of England and the English.

Studies of Individual Works

Barber, William Henry. L'Angleterre dans Candide. RLC 37:202–15, 1963. *See* 5715.   **4709**

Melancholy, inhumanity, *esprit de parti,* and poor taste are English characteristics found in *Candide.* Penn's American colony as a possible source for V.'s Eldorado. Incidental article.

— The genesis of Voltaire's Micromégas. FS 11:1–15, 1957.   **4710**

Concludes that *Micromégas* is a reworking of the earlier *Baron de Gangan* with expression of V.'s ideas and attitudes of the early 1750's. Although, as author admits, subject cannot now be settled with finality, article is closely reasoned. *Also see* Nedergaard-Hansen (4746).

— Voltaire : Candide. London, Arnold, 1960. 62 p.   **4711**

A concise critical evaluation of *Candide* of use to both the general reader and the specialist.

Reviews : J. Brumfitt in FS 15:70–71, 1961; J. Sareil in RR 52:64–65, 1961.

Besterman, Theodore. Note on the authorship of the Connaissance des beautés. SVEC 4:291–94, 1957.   **4712**

Concludes that the *Connaissance des beautés* (1749) was not written by V., but by David Durand, French Protestant minister who lived in London.

— Voltaire et le désastre de Lisbonne : ou, la mort de l'optimisme. SVEC 2:7–24, 1956. *Also in :* Tro 122:60–74, Feb. 1958. *English version in his:* Voltaire essays, and another. *See* 4542. p. 24–41. **4713**

Description of the earthquake of 1755 and its relationship with the demise of optimism in Europe which author attributes largely to influence of V.'s *Poème sur le désastre de Lisbonne*. Well-written synthesis of subject with valuable bibliographical references. More extensive treatment of subject in Thomas D. Kendrick, *The Lisbon Earthquake* (Philadelphia, Lippincott, 1957).

— Voltaire's love letters. TLS 524, Aug. 30, 1957. *Also in his* : Voltaire essays, and another. *See* 4542. p. 55-60. **4714**

The story of V.'s love letters to his niece Mme Denis. *Also see* 4517.

Bingham, Alfred J. Voltaire and the Encyclopédie méthodique. SVEC 6:9–35, 1958. **4715**

Analysis of use made of V.'s works in composition of Panckoucke's *Encyclopédie méthodique:* 880 passages from V.'s works, including 320 taken from the *Encyclopédie*, and 450 references to V. and his works, including 115 from the *Encyclopédie*.

Bjurström, Per. Mises en scène de Sémiramis de Voltaire en 1748 et 1759. RHT 8: 299–320, 1956. **4716**

A close study of the different *mises en scène* used for *Sémiramis* between 1748 and 1759 with new information based on ms sources and accompanied by interesting contemporary engravings to illustrate article.

Booy, Jean Th. de. Diderot, Voltaire et les Souvenirs de Madame de Caylus. RScH n.s. 109:23–38, 1963. *See* 5053. **4717**

Diderot did not publish the *Souvenirs de Mme de Caylus* and the work enjoyed V.'s " patronage " but not his authorship.

Bottiglia, William F. Voltaire's Candide; analysis of a classic. Geneva, Institut et musée Voltaire, 1959. 280 p. (SVEC, 7). *Also* 2nd ed., rev., 1964. 325 p. (SVEC, 7A) **4718**

" Never before in the two hundred years of its existence, has *Candide* been subjected to such a searching analysis " (N. L. Torrey in review *infra*). Successful combination of historical and literary approach with a discussion of philosophic tale as a genre, *Candide* in its social setting,

and themes and structure of *Candide*. Good analysis of V.'s style and strong on literary analysis and interpretation, but unconvincing discussion of " Il faut cultiver notre jardin." Underplays importance of Pope and Leibniz, of problem of evil, and of pessimistic strain in *Candide*. Reviews : J. Brumfitt in FS 14:68–69, 1960; L. Crocker in FR 33:425–27, 1959–60; O. Fellows in MLN 74:754–55, 1959; A. Freer in SF 3:494, 1959; R. Pomeau in RHL 61:85–87, 1961; N. Torrey in RR 50:218–20, 1959.

Brun, Max. Contribution à l'étude d'une édition in-4° du Siècle de Louis XIV publiée en Angleterre un an après l'originale. Le 26:134–45, 1961. **4719**

Data about a 1752 London ed. of the *Siècle de Louis XIV* published in French by R. Dodsley and evidently not in Bengesco, B.N., British Museum, or Institut et musée Voltaire. Reproduction of title page.

Candaux, Jean-Daniel. Les débuts de François Grasset. SVEC 18:197–235, 1961. **4720**

The affair of the ms of *La pucelle*, p. 223–28.

— La publication de Candide à Paris. SVEC 18:173–78, 1961. **4721**

Disputes Wade's contention in *Voltaire and Candide* (4766) that work appeared in Paris by Jan. 15, 1759.

Carney, Edward. Voltaire's Candide and the English reader. MS 52:234–51, 1958. **4722**

On early English eds. of *Candide* and some 18th-century sources of and reactions to *Candide*.

Castex, Pierre-Georges. Voltaire : Micromégas, Candide, L'ingénu. Centre de documentation universitaire, 1960. 110 p. (Les cours de Sorbonne) **4723**

A manual-type study of the 3 *contes* with information on their genesis, background, art, and meaning. Presentation takes recent scholarship into account, but character of monograph reduces complexity of the *contes* and provides too " pat " answers to number of problems surrounding them. Nevertheless, quite good for student use.

Cazeneuve, Jean. La philosophie de Voltaire d'après le Dictionnaire philosophique. Synthèses 181–82:14–21, June–July 1961. **4724**

An analysis of V.'s philosophical ideas in the *Dictionnaire philosophique* with an appreciation of their contradictions, weaknesses, and lasting value. The limitations of V. as an original thinker, but the lasting effects of his activist philosophy : " Il n'a pas grande place dans la philosophie; mais dans l'histoire des idées, il est un grand philosophe " (p. 31). Useful *mise au point*.

Černý, Václav. Voltaire et Lomonosov, historiens rivaux de Pierre le Grand. RScH n.s. 110:173–206, 1963.   **4725**

An account of the relations of V. and M. V. Lomonosov and the *Histoire de Pierre le Grand* based on new documentation. Supplements E. Šmurlo, *Voltaire et son œuvre; histoire de l'empire de Russie sous Pierre le Grand* (Prague, 1929) and Lortholary (4742).

Chenais, Margaret. New light on the publication of the Pucelle. SVEC 12:9–20, 1960.   **4726**

Hypothesizes on the publication of *La pucelle* by interpreting a code used in two V. letters.

Coulet, Henri. La candeur de Candide. AFLA 34:87–99, 1960.   **4727**

An analysis of the character of Candide that leads author to conclusion that Candide has learned nothing from his experiences. Consequently, he views the work as essentially pessimistic without a humanistic conclusion. Not very convincing.

Derche, Roland. Oedipe de Voltaire. *In his:* Quatre mythes poétiques. S.E.D.E.S., 1962. p. 42–51.   **4728**

A close study of V.'s *Oedipe* with an indication of the author's criticism of and debt to Corneille, reasons for the great popularity of *Oedipe* in the 18th century, and V.'s *Oedipe* in relation to Sophocles'. Succinct and useful.

Falke, Rita. Eldorado : le meilleur des mondes possibles. SVEC 2:25–41, 1956.   **4729**

Discusses general characteristics of utopian writings, particularly Fénelon's *Télémaque*. Sees Eldorado as illustration of V.'s thesis that religious toleration is the *sine qua non* for world peace, and concludes that his thesis was too optimistic in light of subsequent history. Interesting, but essentially only one aspect of a complex subject.

Fields, Madeleine. La première edition

française de la Princesse de Babylone. SVEC 18:179–82, 1961. *See* 5535.   **4730**

Discusses 1st French ed. of the *Princesse de Babylone* in its shortened version in the *Mercure de France* for July 1, 1768. This ed. unmentioned by Moland or Bengesco. Sole example of a Voltaire *conte* published in official journal without government intervention.

Florenne, Yves. Voltaire ou de la raison et de la déraison par alphabet. Eur 398:40–53, June 1962.   **4731**

A general appreciation of the *Dictionnaire philosophique* with particular attention to V.'s anti-Semitism.

Gagnebin, Bernard. L'édition originale de Candide. BBB 169–81, 1952.   **4732**

Reopens question of original ed. of *Candide* by disagreeing with Tannery (1842) that Paris ed. published by Michel Lambert was the first. Concludes that " l'édition genevoise de *Candide* doit être considérée comme l'originale, parce qu'elle a été faite sous les yeux de l'auteur et sur son manuscrit et qu'elle est sortie de presse le 15 janvier 1759 " (p. 181). For rebuttal of Gagnebin, *see* Wade (4764).

Gay, Peter. Voltaire's Idées républicaines; a study in bibliography and interpretation. SVEC 6:67–105, 1958.   **4733**

An interesting background study of politics in Geneva with conclusion that the *Idées républicaines* was published in Nov. or Dec., 1765. Corrects date of 1762 given by Beuchot and Bengesco.

Gengoux, Jacques. Zadig et les trois puissances de Voltaire. LR 16:115–47, 266–74, 340–62, 1962.   **4734**

The nature and relationship of *corps*, *esprit*, and *cœur*—*les trois puissances*—in *Zadig* and the significance of this triad in V.'s thought. Lengthy and somewhat obscure article with few real conclusions.

Gobert, David L. Comic in Micromégas as expressive of theme. SVEC 37:53–60, 1965.   **4735**

Study would demonstrate " how ' large equals small ' constitutes the comic theme on the levels of action and language " (p. 53). Theme of *Micromégas* is found to be the coexistence of man's insignificance and his grandeur.

Gossman, Lionel. Voltaire's Charles XII : history into art. SVEC 25:691–720, 1963.   **4736**

Author sees *Charles XII* as a transformation of history into esthetic form, typical of 18th century itself, which sought to transform life of society into esthetic form. Sees 18th-century historical writing as an art rather than a science. Premise of article is V.'s " profound affinity with the culture of the baroque."

Guinard, Paul J. Une adaptation espagnole du Zadig au 18ᵉ siècle. RLC 32:481–95, 1958.   **4737**

A study of the *Instrucción para un joven que desea conducirse bien* (1759), a didactic Spanish adaptation of *Zadig* in which V.'s genius is dissipated through a literal translation burdened by interpolation, paraphrase, and commentary that destroy the original.

Hartley, K. H. The sources of Voltaire's Mariamne. AUMLA 21:5–14, 1964. *See* 5728.   **4738**

Josephus, Lodovico Dolce, Tristan L'Hermite, and Elijah Fenton as possible sources of *Mariamne*.

Jovicevich, Alexander. Sur la date de composition de L'homme aux quarante écus. Sym 18:251–57, 1964.   **4739**

"... il ne faut pas exclure la possibilité d'une ébauche de cette œuvre à la fin de 1763 ou au commencement de 1764 " (p. 257).

Leigh, R. A. Rousseau's letter to Voltaire on optimism (18 August 1756). SVEC 30:247–309, 1964.   **4740**

A meticulous textual study based on collation of 7 mss and the early printings of Rousseau's letter. An important contribution.

Lichtenstein, Julius. The title of Voltaire's Zadig. FR 33:65–67, 1959–60.   **4741**

Contests Ascoli's contention that V. derived name Zadig from *L'histoire de la sultane de Perse* by Chec Sadé. Suggests that the name actually derives from the Hebrew word *zadik*, denoting a completely righteous man. Speculative, but interesting.

Lortholary, Albert. Le mirage russe en France au xviiiᵉ siècle. Boivin, 1951. 409 p. *See* 5078.   **4742**

Account of French attitude toward Russia in 17th and 18th centuries. Author maintains that myth of the cultural and political enlightenment of Peter the Great spread in France largely because of

V.'s writings and that in *Histoire de l'empire de Russie sous Pierre le Grand,* V. was more of a legend-maker than historian. Work discusses Catherine II's relations with V., Diderot, d'Alembert, etc. Well-documented and important work with fine treatment of notion of enlightened despotism.

Reviews : F. Hemmings in FS 6:78–80, 1952; H. Lancaster in MLN 68:208–09, 1953.

Meyer, Paul H. Voltaire and Hume as historians : a comparative study of the Essai sur les mœurs and the History of England. PMLA 73:51–68, 1958. *See* 5732.   **4743**

Compares the *Essai sur les mœurs* and the *History of England* to show parallel strengths and weaknesses of V. and Hume as historians and as philosophers of history. Sees greatest contribution of both in stimulating interest in writing of history and in freeing historical writing from antiquarianism and eulogizing. Well-documented essay.

Monty, J. R. Le travail de composition d'Alzire. FR 35:383–89, 1961–62.   **4744**

A study of the composition of *Alzire* based on Besterman correspondence. Concludes that general outline and tone of play never significantly changed from V.'s original conception of them and that his main criterion was to follow esthetics of Boileau and Racine. Amends Lion's view (1779) of V.'s dramatic working methods.

Nedergaard-Hansen, Leif. Sur la date de composition de L'histoire des voyages de Scarmentado. SVEC 2:273–77, 1956. **4745**

Dates this *conte* in 1753 and suggests some autobiographical allusions : Scarmentado would be V. after his quarrel with Frederick, and the ending of the tale—" Je fus cocu, et je vis que c'était l'état le plus doux de la vie "—would refer to V.'s situation at Lunéville with Mme du Châtelet seen from later perspective. Ingenious presentation.

— Sur l'identité de Baron de Gangan avec Micromégas, et d'autres contributions à la compréhension des contes de Voltaire. OrL 9:222–32, 1954; 10:429–42, 1955. **4746**

Presents arguments to show that *Micromégas* probably a reworking of *Baron de Gangan* and therefore first of V.'s *contes*. Shows similarity of subject of *Micromégas* to V.'s interests in late 1730's.

Nivat, Jean. L'ingénu de Voltaire, les jésuites et l'affaire La Chalotais. RScH n.s. 66:97–108, 1952.		**4747**

Amends W. R. Jones ed. of *L'ingénu* by showing tale's close relationship to contemporary events, particularly the La Chalotais affair (1765–67). Author's thesis : because of his desire to retain his influence at Versailles and his refusal to be associated with Jansenist defenders of La Chalotais, V. did not wish to be involved directly, but his public answer to the La Chalotais affair was given indirectly in form of *L'ingénu*.

Perkins, Merle L. Concepts of necessity in Voltaire's Poème sur le désastre de Lisbonne. KFLQ 3:21–28, 1955.		**4748**

Sees primary purpose of the *Lisbonne* as the attempt to reconcile man to the human condition.

— Dryden's The Indian emperour and Voltaire's Alzire. CL 9:229–37, 1957. *See* 5575.		**4749**

Author finds substantial influence of the *Indian emperour* on *Alzire*. Structure of Dryden's play is seen as enabling V. to adapt heroic genre to serious philosophic purpose.

Pomeau, René. En marge des Lettres philosophiques : un essai de Voltaire sur le suicide. RScH n.s. 75:285–94, 1954.		**4750**

Reproduces 1739 text of V.'s essay on suicide which the *Œuvres complètes* contain only in fragmentary form. Suggests that the essay may date back to 1726 when V. was going through crisis occasioned by the Rohan incident and by death of his sister. While the essay was not very original, considers it a useful indication of V.'s then still undeveloped talent as a prose writer. Interesting article on V.'s early career.

— Une esquisse inédite de L'ingénu. RHL 61:58–60, 1961.		**4751**

Author analyzes what he believes to be first sketch of *L'ingénu*, a note found among V. mss in Leningrad. Unable to date it or to determine whether V. developed this outline. Main modification between it and final version is inclusion of a love motif in latter. Shows that V.'s *contes* were not mere improvisations.

— Histoire d'une œuvre de Voltaire : le Dictionnaire philosophique portatif. IL 7:43–50, 1955.		**4752**

The relationship of the *Portatif* to Bayle's dictionary and to the *Encyclopédie*, the origin and development of the *Portatif*, its relationship to V.'s propagandistic campaigns, and some 18th-century reactions to the work.

Pruner, Francis. Recherches sur la création romanesque dans L'ingénu de Voltaire. Minard, 1960. 47 p. (ALM 30, Mar.–Apr. 1960)		**4753**

On supposed keys to characters and events in *L'ingénu*. Rather conjectural.

Quignard, Jacques. Un établissement de texte : le Siècle de Louis XIV de Voltaire. LR 5:305–38, 1951.		**4754**

The genesis of the *Siècle de Louis XIV*, the various eds. of the work in V.'s lifetime, his major modifications of the work and their significance.

Rigal, Juliette. L'iconographie de La Henriade au xviiie siècle ou la naissance du style du troubadour. SVEC 32:23–71, 1965.		**4755**

A study of the evolution of style in illustrations of the *Henriade* from the 1728 London ed. to the 1805 Paris ed. with engravings by Moreau *le jeune*.

Rousseau, André-Michel. En marge de Candide : Voltaire et l'affaire Byng. RLC 34:261–73, 1960.		**4756**

V.'s reaction to the Byng case, based on the Besterman ed. of V.'s correspondence and ms material. Supplements Morize (1631).

Sareil, Jean. De Zadig à Candide, ou permanence de la pensée de Voltaire. RR 52:271–78, 1961.		**4757**

Author questions opposition of *Zadig* and *Candide* on basis of antithesis of optimism and pessimism and finds more similarities than differences between the two *contes*.

Siegel, June Sigler. Voltaire, Zadig, and the problem of evil. RR 50:25–34, 1959.		**4758**

Author sees *Zadig* as an apology for *engagement* and a call to arms against evil, particularly in the political sphere. Sees importance of *Zadig* in separating physical universe from man's moral realm. Interesting elucidation of V.'s moral position, but argumentation based on *Zadig* is thin.

Tobin, Ronald W. The sources of Voltaire's Mahomet. FR 34:372–78, 1960–61.		**4759**

Boulainvilliers' *Vie de Mahomed* and Jean Gagnier's *Vie de Mahomed* are shown to be sources of V.'s *Mahomet* by textual comparisons. Author rejects Humphrey Prideaux' *Life of Mahomet* as a source.

Topazio, Virgil W. Voltaire's Pucelle : a study in burlesque. SVEC 2:207–23, 1956. *See* 5923. **4760**

Relates the *Pucelle* to Ariosto's *Orlando furioso* and judges the latter superior to V.'s burlesque. Sees *La pucelle*, in spite of its levity, as focusing on serious issues of religious fanaticism and social abuse and considers it a distinguished masterpiece.

Torrey, Norman L. Candide's garden and the Lord's vineyard. SVEC 27:1657–66, 1963. **4761**

Discusses two important metaphors of Voltaire : the cultivation of Candide's garden, which the author interprets as " minding one's own business and being of no use to the world"; and working in the Lord's vineyard, which Voltaire used as the equivalent of *écrasez l'infâme*. Author sees double implication in *Candide:* we should mind our own business and cultivate our gardens and " behind it, but only by implication, lay the tremendous task of uprooting the noxious weeds" (p. 1666).

Vidal, Gaston. Une publication de Voltaire demeurée inconnue : Le médiateur d'une grande querelle. BBB 283–92, 1953; 49–70, 1956. **4762**

Attributes the anonymous 75 p. pamphlet on Jesuits dated 1762 and entitled *Le médiateur d'une grande querelle* to V. Evidence problematical.

Wade, Ira O. Dulard and Voltaire. FR 35: 546–52, 1961–62. **4763**

Similarities between *Candide* and Dulard's *Œuvres diverses* which had preceded it, but no conclusion regarding influence.

— The first edition of Candide; a problem of identification. PULC 20:63–88, 1959. **4764**

A review and examination of information regarding first printed ed. of *Candide* with the conclusion that V. had a trial ed. of the work set up at end of Dec., 1758, and dated 1759 and that this was in all likelihood published in Amsterdam by Marc-Michel Rey. Bengesco 1434 (Morize 59ᵃ) became subsequently the authoritative ed. Article, thus, disagrees with Bengesco, Morize, and Gagnebin (4732) that Cramer edition published in Geneva was 1st ed. of *Candide. Also see* Desmond Flower, *Candide: a perennial problem* in Bcol 8:284–88, 1959.

— A manuscript of Voltaire's Candide. APSP 101:93–105, 1957. **4765**

A description of the La Vallière ms of *Candide* found by the author in the Arsenal Library and an indication of variants between it and the Morize ed.

— Voltaire and Candide; a study in the fusion of history, art and philosophy. With the text of the La Vallière manuscript of Candide. Princeton, Princeton univ. press, 1959. xvi, 369 + 82 p. **4766**

A controversial study, based on the La Vallière ms of *Candide,* which also contains much useful background information.

Reviews : J.-D. Candaux in SVEC 18: 173–78, 1961; H. Coulet in RHL 62:103, 1962; B. Gagnebin (sharply critical) in BBB 22–31, 1960; C. Rouillard in MP 60: 145–49, 1962–63.

Watts, George B, Voltaire and Le catéchumène. KFLQ 4:212–16, 1957. **4767**

From Panckoucke's account of V.'s mss for the Kehl ed. in the *Encyclopédie méthodique,* author provides evidence that Charles Bordes and not Voltaire was the author of the heterodox *Le catéchumène* of 1768.

Weightman, J. G. The quality of Candide. *In:* Essays presented to C. M. Girdlestone. Newcastle upon Tyne, Univ. of Durham, 1960. p. 333–47. **4768**

An important essay on *Candide* with a number of fresh insights. Author finds lesson of *Candide* to be that there is " no verbal or intellectual solution to the problem of evil, but that we go on living even so, and even when we think we have no faith " (p. 338). Convinced that *Candide* is a masterpiece on the order of *Don Quixote* and *Faust,* Weightman finds that its quality is indicated by its being " a work in which an unappealable sense of the mystery and the horror or life is accompanied, at every step, by an instinctive animal resilience " (p. 340).

Weitz, Morris. Candide, the burden of philosophy. *In his:* Philosophy in literature. Detroit, Wayne State univ. press, 1963. p. 5–21. **4769**

A brief analysis of themes of *Candide* with the conclusion that man cannot achieve utopian happiness, in V.'s view, because he is " a bipolar creature, oscillating between his restlessness of anxiety and his lethargy of boredom " (p. 21).

CHAPTER VIII. JEAN-JACQUES ROUSSEAU

(Nos. 4770–4985)

JOHN W. CHAPMAN

Bibliography

Annales de la Société Jean-Jacques Rousseau. Geneva, Jullien, 1905– . **4770**

Continuation of 1858. Each volume includes bibliography containing analyses of R. publications from major centers of scholarship. An important source of bibliographical information for all concerned with R. Indispensable.

Sénelier, Jean. Bibliographie générale des œuvres de J.-J. Rousseau. Presses univ. de France, 1950. 282 p. **4771**

Not based on firsthand research. Numerous errors, including eds. that do not exist and omitting large number that do. Unmethodical.

Review : B. Gagnebin in AJJR 32:231–55, 1950–52.

Voisine, Jacques. Etat des travaux sur Jean-Jacques Rousseau au lendemain de son 250e anniversaire de naissance (1712–1962). IL 16:93–107, 1964. **4772**

A review of the present state of R. studies including a survey of recent commemorative volumes, eds. of R.'s works, principal contributions of 20th-century scholarship and recent general studies. Includes suggestions for further investigation in sections on unresolved problems of R. scholarship and the future of R. studies. Very useful.

Editions

Plan, Pierre-Paul. Table de la correspondance générale de J.-J. Rousseau, avec une introduction et des lettres inédites publiées par Bernard Gagnebin. Geneva, Droz, 1953. xi, 266 p. **4773**

Bernard Gagnebin in his introduction : [Cette table] " n'est pas un simple index des noms cités, mais une vraie table analytique et descriptive. Les principaux personnages sont identifiés et leurs relations avec Rousseau étudiées de manière critique. ... cette table constitue l'histoire des relations de Rousseau avec ses correspondants."

Review : D. N. in AJJR 33:344–45, 1953–55.

Rousseau, Jean-Jacques. Œuvres complètes. Edition publiée sous la direction de Bernard Gagnebin et Marcel Raymond. Gallimard, 1959– . v. (Bibliothèque de la Pléiade) **4774**

Splendidly produced ed. of R.'s works. The commentaries are biographical in orientation and uniformly excellent. Indispensable for further research.

Contents : I. *Les confessions, Dialogues, Les rêveries du promeneur solitaire, Fragments autobiographiques*. Ed. by Bernard Gagnebin, Robert Osmont, and Marcel Raymond. 1959. cxviii, 1970 p. II. *La nouvelle Héloïse, Théâtre, Poésies, Essais littéraires*. Ed. by Henri Coulet, Bernard Guyon, Charly Guyot, and Jacques Scherer. Bibliographical notices by Bernard Gagnebin. 1961. ciii, 2052 p. III. *Du contrat social, Ecrits politiques*. Ed. by François Bouchardy, Jean-Daniel Candaux, Robert Derathé, Jean Fabre, Sven Stelling-Michaud, and Jean Starobinski. Bibliographical notices by Bernard Gagnebin. 1964. cclv, 1964 p.

Reviews : I. T. Besterman in SVEC 10: 519–21, 1959; F. Bouchardy in AJJR 35: 379–84, 1959–62; L. Crocker in MLN 75:529–32, 1960; F. Green in FS 14:171–72, 1960; R. Grimsley in RLC 35:681–82, 1961; P. Jourda in RLR 74:82–83, 1960; R. Leigh in MLR 57:104–07, 1962; F. Orlando in SF 4:354–55, 1960; H. Roddier in RHL 62:111–15, 1962; J. Voisine in RHL 62:104–11, 1962. II. J.-L. Bellenot in AJJR 35:84–91, 1959–62; O. Fellows in RR 54:136–37, 1963; F. Healey in MLR 58:265–67, 1963; Georges May in MLN 77:519–28, 1962; J. Voisine in RHL 64:309–12, 1964. III. J. Broome in MLR 61:317–19, 1966.

— A la rencontre de Jean-Jacques Rousseau; textes et documents réunis par Bernard Gagnebin. Geneva, Georg, 1962. 74 p. **4775**

Selections, excerpts from mss, and illustrations beautifully and skillfully arranged.

— Les confessions. Ed. by J.-L. Lecercle. Club des amis du livre progressiste, 1962. xliv, 633 p. **4776**

Review : M. Françon in RR 55:131–32, 1964.

— Correspondance complète. Ed. by R. A. Leigh. Geneva, Institut et musée Voltaire, 1965– . v. **4777**

A new and critical ed. of R.'s correspondence. Leigh analyzes the defects of the Dufour-Plan ed. (1883) of R.'s correspondence and the principles of his enlarged ed. in AESC 35:263–86, 1963.

— Discours sur l'origine et les fondements de l'inégalité parmi les hommes. Introduction, commentaires et notes explicatives par J.-L. Lecercle. Editions sociales, 1954. 191 p. **4778**

Sympathetic and historical introduction.

Review : M. Françon in AJJR 33:345–48, 1953–55

— Julie ou la nouvelle Héloïse. Ed. by René Pomeau. Garnier, 1960. lvii, 829 p. **4779**

Based on Mornet ed. (1898). Deals with problem of variants through selection from the mss and references to Rey's 1763 ed. Tries to balance viewpoints of Mornet and Osmont (4806) in historical and critical introduction.

Review : J. Broome in MLR 57:260–61, 1962.

— Political writings. Trans. and ed. by Frederick Watkins. Edinburgh and New York, Nelson, 1953. xliii, 330 p. **4780**

Contains *The social contract, Considerations on the government of Poland*, and Part I of the *Constitutional project for Corsica*. Analytic and judicious introduction by the editor. R.'s political thought judged a failure owing to the incompatible liberal and totalitarian assumptions upon which it is based.

— Les rêveries du promeneur solitaire. Ed. by Henri Roddier. Garnier, 1960. xcvii, 234 p. **4781**

J. Lough in review *infra:* " this excellent volume is a valuable addition to the ... Classiques Garnier."

Reviews : J. Lough in MLR 56:617–18, 1961; R. Mortier in RLC 35:677–80, 1961; F. Orlando in SF 6:360–61, 1962; R. Osmont in RHL 63:477–80, 1963.

— Rousseau juge de Jean-Jacques : dialogues. Texte présenté par Michel Foucault. Colin, 1962. xxiv, 333 p. **4782**

Reprints text of Pléiade ed. (4774). Editor sees the *Dialogues* as anti-*Confessions*.

Review : M. Launay in RHL 63:680–81, 1963.

— Rousseau par lui-même; images et textes présentés par Georges May. Editions du Seuil, 1961. 191 p. **4783**

Comprehensive and biographical interpretation of R.'s thought, making judicious use of quotations from his writings, and supported throughout with evocative illustrations.

Reviews : L. Crocker in Sym 17:304–07, 1963; B. Gagnebin in AJJR 35:340–42, 1959–62; R. Trousson in RBP 40:1058–60, 1962; I. Wade in RR 53:295–97, 1962.

Commemorative Volumes and Journals

Annales de la Société Jean-Jacques Rousseau 35: 1959–62. 457 p. **4784**

Contains : *Entretiens sur Jean-Jacques Rousseau organisés par la Société J.-J. Rousseau à l'institut universitaire des Hautes Etudes à Genève les 16 et 17 juillet 1962*. Penetrating presentations by Bronislaw Baczko, Pierre Burgelin, Robert Derathé, Jean Fabre, Henri Gouhier, Bernard Guyon, R. A. Leigh, Robert Mauzi, Robert Osmont, Arnaldo Pizzorusso, Robert Ricatte, John S. Spink, and Kurt Wais. Participants in the discussion on the papers include Bouchardy, Buenzod, Candaux, Dehaussy, Eigeldinger, Gagnebin, Grosclaude, Jost, Meyer, Munteano, Pire, Poulet, Rang, Raymond, Rousset, Starobinski, Stelling-Michaud, and Trahard. Indispensable.

Annales de philosophie politique. Rousseau et la philosophie politique. 5:1965. 256 p. **4785**

Interpretative articles by Hans Barth, Pierre Burgelin, Sergio Cotta, Lester G. Crocker, Robert Derathé, Iring Fetscher, Carl J. Friedrich, Stanley Hoffmann, Bertrand de Jouvenel, and John Plamenatz.

Annales historiques de la Révolution Française. V. 34, no. 170, Oct.-Dec. 1962. **4786**

Collection of illuminating articles on R.'s historical influence. See especially those by B. Leśnodorski on Poland, R. R. Palmer on the United States, and Albert Soboul on the French Revolution.

Baud-Bovy, Samuel, *et al.* Jean-Jacques Rousseau. Neuchâtel, La Baconnière, 1962. 262 p.   **4787**

A commemorative volume of excellent articles on diverse topics by Baud-Bovy, Derathé, Dottrens, Gagnebin, Guéhenno, Guyot, Lévi-Strauss, Raymond, Rousset, Schaerer, Starobinski, and Stelling-Michaud. Sponsored by Université ouvrière de Genève.

Le contrat social. V. 6, no. 3, May-June, 1962; v. 6, no. 6, Nov.-Dec. 1962.   **4788**

See especially articles by Robert Derathé on R. and monarchy, Zygmunt Jedryka on R. and freedom, and Yves Lévy's comparison of R. and Machiavelli.

Europe. Numéro spécial consacré à Jean-Jacques Rousseau.   391–92: Nov.–Dec. 1961. 320 p.   **4789**

Biographical and interpretative articles by Fabre, Grosclaude, Havens, Nemo, Pomeau, Starobinski, della Volpe, and others.

Review : C. Guyot in AJJR 35:336–37, 1959–62.

Jean-Jacques Rousseau et son oeuvre; problèmes et recherches. Commémoration et colloque de Paris (16–20 octobre 1962) organisés par le Comité national pour la commémoration de Rousseau. Klincksieck, 1964. xxxi, 374 p.   **4790**

Commemorative volume of short, incisive articles penetrating the frontiers of research. Contributions by : Pierre Burgelin, Bernard Gagnebin, Ronald Grimsley, Charly Guyot, Michel Launay, R. A. Leigh, Robert Osmont, Raymond Polin, Marcel Raymond, Henri Roddier, Jean Starobinski, and Jacques Voisine.

Review : M. Duchet in AESC 18:149–55, 1963.

Journées d'étude sur le Contrat social, Dijon, 1962. Etudes sur le Contrat social de Jean-Jacques Rousseau.   Les Belles Lettres, 1964. 539 p. (PUD, 30)   **4791**

Noteworthy studies of sources, aspects, and historical influence of R.'s political thought, including essays by Burgelin, Chevallier, Cotta, Davy, Derathé, Godechot, Gouhier, Lacharrière, Polin, Soboul, Starobinski, Stelling-Michaud, and della Volpe.

Yale French studies. Jean-Jacques Rousseau. 28:1961–62.   **4792**

Commemorative volume of short articles dealing with various aspects of his

thought. *See* especially those by Lester G. Crocker, *The priority of justice or law,* and Bertrand de Jouvenel, *Rousseau, the pessimistic evolutionist.*

Biographical

Baud-Bovy, Samuel. Rousseau musicien. *In:* Jean-Jacques Rousseau. *See* 4787. p. 51–66.   **4793**

An appraisal of R.'s musical compositions in which his preference for simplicity is revealed.   " Les plus belles mélodies de Rousseau ne sont d'ailleurs pas ses mélodies en musique, mais ses mélodies en prose " (p. 64).

Cranston, Maurice. Rousseau in England. HT 11:599–606, 1961. *See* 5698.   **4794**

Sympathetic and judicious account of R.'s relations with David Hume.

Gagnebin, Bernard. Verité et véracité dans Les confessions. *In:* Jean-Jacques Rousseau et son œuvre : problèmes et recherches. *See* 4790. p. 7–20.   **4795**

" Ce refus d'assumer le poids de ses fautes est un des aspects les plus troublants de la psychologie de Jean-Jacques " (p. 20).

An analysis of R.'s moral deficiencies, challenged in the discussion following by Jean Guéhenno.

— Une vie tourmentée.   *In:* Jean-Jacques Rousseau. *See* 4787. p. 11–32.   **4796**

Brief and sympathetic exposition of the main periods of R.'s life.

Gay, Peter. Introduction. *In:* Cassirer, Ernst. The question of Jean-Jacques Rousseau. New York, Columbia univ. press, 1954. p. 1–30.   **4797**

An appreciation of Cassirer's interpretation of R. placed in the context of both previous and more recent efforts. Gay asserts the desirability of interpreting R.'s political ideas in the light of his total outlook and distinguishes sharply between political speculation and prescription.

Green, Frederick Charles. Jean-Jacques Rousseau; a critical study of his life and writings.   Cambridge, Cambridge univ. press, 1955. 376 p.   **4798**

Impressive intellectual biography, distinguished for its sensitivity to the spirit of R.'s writings and life. Less successful in its treatment of his political thought which is held to be somewhat mysterious.

Reviews : J.-D. Candaux in AJJR 34: 180–83, 1956–58; J. Chapman in APSR

50:599–600, 1956; J. Spink in MLR 51: 601, 1956.

Grimsley, Ronald. Jean-Jacques Rousseau; a study in self-awareness. Cardiff, Univ, of Wales press, 1961. 338 p. **4799**
Illuminating analysis of R.'s personality and morality which is distinctive for the use made of concepts drawn from modern psychology and existentialist philosophy. Reviews : P. Burgelin in RLC 36:618– 20, 1962; Georges May in RR 53:269–79, 1962; T. Morris in MLR 60:118–19, 1965; J. Spink in FS 17:68–69, 1963; J. Starobinski in AJJR 35:352–53, 1959– 62; J. Voisine in RHL 64:485–90, 1964.

Guéhenno, Jean. Jean-Jacques. Grasset and Gallimard, 1948–52. 3 v. **4800**
Monumental investigation of R.'s life and thought based upon detailed examination of his correspondance. Sympathetic and unsurpassed for its psychological and moral acumen. Reviews : C. Berkowe in RR 54:62–64, 1963; P. Kohler in RHL 54:224–26, 1954; M. Raymond in AJJR 33:325–35, 1953– 55; N. Torrey in RR 44:297–99, 1953.

Jimack, P. D. Rousseau and the primacy of self. SVEC 32:73–90, 1965. **4801**
An attempt to trace R.'s belief in personal independence to its roots in his personality and experience. " The ideal of self-sufficiency contained in the *Nouvelle Héloïse* and *Emile* derives from the same source, Rousseau's own experience of unhappiness " (p. 85).

Jost, François. Jean-Jacques Rousseau Suisse; étude sur sa personnalité et sa pensée. Fribourg, Editions universitaires, 1961. 2 v. *See* 5865. **4802**
Fascinating and not entirely successful attempt to account for R.'s personality and attitudes in terms of his Swiss origins. Reviews : F. Green in FS 17:70–71, 1963; C. Guyot in AJJR 35:368–75, 1959–62; G. Heuberger in Sym 18:371–73 1964; M. Launay in RHL 64:108–10, 1964; Georges May in RR 53:269–79, 1962; A. Viatte in RLC 36:620–22, 1962.

Lapassade, Georges. L'œuvre de J.-J. Rousseau : structure et unité. RMM 61: 386–402, 1956. **4803**
An attempt to explain the structure and unity of R.'s writings in the light of his personal experience.

Mornet, Daniel. Rousseau, l'homme et l'œuvre. Boivin, 1950. 187 p. **4804**

Classic study distinguished for its objectivity, now superseded by the work of Starobinski and others. Reviews : O. Fellows in RR 42:293–95, 1951; M. Françon in MLQ 12:250–52, 1951; P. Kohler in RHL 54:223-24, 1954; J. Spink in MLR 46:521–22, 1951.

Nemo, Maxime. L'homme nouveau : Jean-Jacques Rousseau. La Colombe, 1957. 178 p. **4805**
Suggestive and speculative interpretation of R.'s significance based on the novelty of his attitudes toward life and nature. Not scholarly. Review : M. Raymond in AJJR 34: 195–96, 1956–58.

Osmont, Robert. Remarques sur la genèse et la composition de La nouvelle Héloïse. AJJR 33:93–148, 1953-55. **4806**
The source and unity of the novel are not to be found in the personal experiences immediately preceding its composition; rather it is the fruit of R.'s moral insight and reflection.

Poulet, Georges. Expansion et concentration chez Rousseau. Tmod 16:949–73, 1960–61. **4807**
" Bien loin de conduire au bonheur, l'expansion par les sensations et par l'imagination anticipatrice a pour fin inévitable le malheur. Telle est la leçon que Rousseau tire de sa propre expérience " (p. 958).
Brilliantly suggestive analysis of R.'s psychological experience and the moral conclusions which he drew from it.

Raymond, Marcel. Rousseau et Genève. *In:* Jean-Jacques Rousseau. *See* 4787. p. 225–37. **4808**
R.'s thought owes much both to his Genevan experience and to the works of his predecessors, neither of which should be given priority over the other.

Starobinski, Jean. Jean-Jacques Rousseau : la transparence et l'obstacle. Plon, 1957. 340 p. **4809**
Spectacular and provocative attempt to account for the unity of R.'s thought in terms of his search for spiritual union, ultimately thwarted by ineradicable pride. This fundamentally psychological explanation of the nature of the coherence possessed by R.'s work deserves comparison with more philosophical and theoretical efforts. Reviews : M. Blanchot in NNRF 11: 1057–66, 1958; R. Jean in CDS 48:474,

1959; F. Orlando in RLM 13:116–20, 1960; R. Osmont in RHL 60:71–73, 1960; A. Rowbotham in BA 32:392–93, 1958; F. Schalk in RFor 73:213–17, 1961; P.-H. Simon in AJJR 34:228–40, 1956–58; J. Voisine in IL 11:79–80, 1959.

Philosophical and Religious

Baczko, Bronislaw. Rousseau i problemy alienacji. Sfil 24:25–71, 1961.   **4810**
Analysis and appreciation of R.'s sociological theory of alienation.

Barth, Karl. Protestant thought : from Rousseau to Ritschl. Trans. by Brian Cozens. New York, Harper, 1959. p. 58–118.   **4811**
" It is from Rousseau onwards and originating from Rousseau that the thing called theological rationalism, in the full sense of the term, exists : a theology for which the Christian spirit is identical with the truly humane spirit . . ." (p. 117).
Presentation of R.'s religious outlook as rationalist and humanist.

Burgelin, Pierre. L'idée de place dans l'Émile. RLC 35:529–37, 1961.   **4812**
Study supportive of the author's thesis that R.'s philosophical outlook is fundamentally rationalist.

— Jean-Jacques Rousseau et la religion de Genève. Geneva, Labor et fides, 1962. 60 p.   **4813**
Comparative and comprehensive analysis of R.'s religious ideas, which are held to be Christian and are seen as directed to the adaptation of Christianity to modern needs.
Review : G. Manzini in Hum 18:192–95, 1963.

— Kant lecteur de Rousseau. *In:* Jean-Jacques Rousseau et son œuvre : problèmes et recherches. *See* 4790. p. 303–15.   **4814**
Superb comparative analysis of the thought of R. and Kant, with emphasis on religious, moral, and political aspects. R. is seen as the moralist of politics, whereas Kant gives priority to the ethical. Contrast posed between R.'s *contrat social* and Kant's *contrat éthique*. For Burgelin, "Kant est inintelligible sans Rousseau qui le précède " (p. 315).

— La philosophie de l'existence de J.-J. Rousseau. Presses univ. de France, 1952. 597 p.   **4815**
Magisterial presentation and inter-

pretation of R.'s philosophy of life in which he is portrayed as essentially a rationalist; consistent with the appraisals of Cassirer and Derathé. Résumé in AUP 21:422–24, 1951. Jean Fabre in his review *infra:* "... jamais interprétation aussi complète ni mieux équilibrée n'avait été proposée de la pensée de Rousseau."
Reviews : J. Fabre in AJJR 33:304–23, 1953–55; A. Ouy in MerF 314:751–52, 1952.

Cassirer, Ernst. The question of Jean-Jacques Rousseau. Trans. and ed. by Peter Gay. New York, Columbia univ. press, 1954. 129 p.   **4816**
Brilliant interpretation of the unity of R.'s thought and writings in terms of his concern for moral freedom, derived from his rationalism and Protestantism.

Chapman, John W. Rousseau—totalitarian or liberal ? New York, Columbia univ. press, 1956. viii, 154 p.   **4817**
" There is an unresolved tension in Rousseau's thought between radical Christian emphasis on moral creativity and Platonic willingness to impose order and value on human life at the expense of moral liberty and dignity " (p. 73).
Reviews : L. Hamori in AJJR 34:193–94, 1956–58; F. Watkins in APSR 51:1104–07, 1957.

Cobban, Alfred. New light on the political thought of Rousseau. PSQ 66:272–84, 1951.   **4818**
An appreciation of Robert Derathé's monumental contributions to the understanding of R.'s philosophy and politics.

Cotta, Sergio. Philosophie et politique dans l'œuvre de Rousseau. ARSP 49:171–89, 1963.   **4819**
"... la primauté rousseauiste de la politique signifie que la vie et la loi politiques sont la source et la règle de la vie morale " (p. 187).
R.'s philosophy leads him to give priority to politics over ethics.

— La position du problème de la politique chez Rousseau. *In:* Etudes sur le Contrat social de Jean-Jacques Rousseau. *See* 4791. p. 177–90.   **4820**
His conception of the natural goodness of man leads R. to replace divine grace with political democracy. Human will displaces natural law as the ultimate ethical standard, and this implies a totalitarian form of political activity.

— Théorie religieuse et théorie politique chez Rousseau. APP 5:171–94, 1965. **4821**

" Le transfert, plus ou moins conscient, de ce concept spirituel de liberté propre au christianisme sur le plan politique, en fausse inévitablement l'essence et implique une évidente contradiction : comment peut-on se soustraire au mal et à l'erreur en suivant un précepte purement humain, et donc sujet lui aussi au mal et à l'erreur ?" (p. 187).

Provocative and stimulating analysis of the connections between R.'s religious views and political principles.

Dautry, Jean. Saint-Simon et Jean-Jacques Rousseau. AHRF 34:465–81, 1962. **4822**

Comparative analysis of R.'s religious thinking in which he is held to adhere to fundamentally Christian conceptions.

" Le futur auteur du *Nouveau christianisme*, qui traita toute sa vie religieuse comme de pures institutions humaines, était insensible au Dieu d'essence chrétienne de Rousseau et de Robespierre " (p. 479).

Derathé, Robert. La religion civile selon Rousseau. AJJR 35:161–70, 1959–62. **4823**

" Ce qui domine dans cette conception de la religion civile, c'est le souci de ne pas séparer la communauté religieuse et la communauté politique, et de faire en sorte que les citoyens relèvent d'une seule autorité. Cela correspond chez Rousseau à un besoin profond de son âme ainsi qu'à une exigence systématique d'unité " (p. 169).

The civil religion is a threat to tolerance and liberty of conscience.

— L'unité de la pensée de Jean-Jacques Rousseau. *In:* Jean-Jacques Rousseau. *See* 4787. p. 203–18. **4824**

R. offers two alternative ideals, those of natural and social man, both of which promise freedom and happiness, his ultimate values.

Eméry, Léon. Rousseau l'annonciateur. Lyon, Audin, 1954. 170 p. **4825**

Comprehensive examination of R.'s thought with emphasis upon its unity and contemporary relevance.

Review : M. Raymond in AJJR 35: 318, 1959–62.

Glum, Friedrich. Jean-Jacques Rousseau, Religion und Staat; Grundlegung einer demokratischen Staatslehre. Stuttgart, Kohlhammer, 1956. 418 p. **4826**

R. is presented as a theorist of democracy, inspired by the Christian conception of natural law. Robert Derathé in his review *infra*: " Le caractère religieux de la pensée politique de Rousseau se manifeste surtout dans la notion d'ordre. L'ordre tel que le conçoit Rousseau est un ordre divin, ou, s'il s'agit d'un ordre institué par les hommes, comme celui qui est issu du contrat social, cet ordre n'en doit pas moins s'insérer dans le cadre de l'ordre cosmique ou moral de nature divine."

Review : R. Derathé in AJJR 34:185–87, 1956–58; W. Ritzel in ZPF 11:626–31, 1957.

Gouhier, Henri. Ce que le Vicaire doit à Descartes. AJJR 35:139–54, 1959–62. **4827**

" La règle cartésienne prescrit un comportement tel que l'évidence paraît quand le sujet historique disparaît. Au contraire, la règle du Vicaire vise moins l'évidence que la certitude, parce qu'il s'agit, cette fois, de la certitude du sujet historique, engagé dans le drame de son existence " (p. 144).

R. is concerned more with subjective certainty than with objective validity.

— Nature et histoire dans la pensée de Jean-Jacques Rousseau. AJJR 33:7–48, 1953–55. **4828**

The originality and unity of R.'s philosophy of life are to be grasped in the light of his belief that nature offers standards and principles that may be used to appraise the contingencies of historical development. The concept of nature displaces the concept of grace and in so doing becomes a sort of grace, having reference not to the deficiencies of nature, but rather to the deformities of history.

Grimsley, Ronald. Rousseau and Kierkegaard. CamJ 7:615–26, 1954. **4829**

Their contrasting outlooks reveal " a distinction which has persisted in various forms throughout the whole history of European culture—a distinction which may perhaps be best summed up as that usually made between nature and grace " (p. 626).

Comparative analysis reveals that for R. the concept of nature is paramount, whereas for Kierkegaard grace is vital.

Guéhenno, Jean. Hommage à Jean-Jacques. *In:* Jean-Jacques Rousseau. *See* 4787. 249–58. **4830**

" Il a réveillé dans tout l'Occident,

puis dans le monde, les forces de l'âme, augmenté l'inquiétude qui seule peut nous maintenir sur le chemin de la justice et de la liberté, sur notre chemin d'hommes " (p. 258).
A magnificent appreciation of R.'s moral significance.

Guyot, Charly. La pensée religieuse de Rousseau. *In:* Jean-Jacques Rousseau. *See* 4787. p. 127–51.   **4831**
A comprehensive examination of his religious thinking shows him best described as a liberal Protestant.

Haymann, Franz. La loi naturelle dans la philosophie politique de J.-J. Rousseau. AJJR 30:65–109, 1943–45.   **4832**
Path-breaking article pointing toward later rationalist interpretations of R.'s thought.

Mauzi, Robert. Le problème religieux dans La nouvelle Héloïse. *In:* Jean-Jacques Rousseau et son œuvre : problèmes et recherches. *See* 4790. p. 159–69.   **4833**
" Dans la religion de Julie comme dans celle de Saint-Preux, la Révélation disparaît en somme à peu près complètement au profit de la raison et de la conscience " (p. 166).
Argues that R.'s religious orientation gives priority to rational and moral considerations.

Munteano, Basil. Les contradictions de J.-J. Rousseau : leur sens expérimental. *In:* Jean-Jacques Rousseau et son œuvre : problèmes et recherches. *See* 4790. p. 95–111.   **4834**
" Ennemi par nature de tout rationalisme idéalisant, ainsi que des généralités abstraites qu'il engendre, Rousseau restera jusqu'au bout un pragmatiste, disons, pour mieux préciser, un *pragmatiste du mouvement ...*" (p. 109).
Emphasizes the exploratory and empirical character of R.'s thought, which is traced to the dualistic nature of his personality oscillating between the sociable and the solitary. Compare with Derathé's emphasis on his rationalism and with other efforts to reveal the unity of his work.

Plamenatz, John. Pascal and Rousseau. PolS 10:248–63, 1962.   **4835**
" Rousseau was perhaps the first to translate certain ideas familiar to the theologian into political terms. Just as the Spirit which is in each of the faithful is yet more than he is, so the General

Will is in every citizen and yet is more than his will " (p. 262).
Plamenatz's interpretation of the relations between R.'s religious and political ideas tends to support the view of R. as fundamentally liberal in outlook. Compare Cotta's authoritarian or totalitarian appraisal (4820).

Raymond, Marcel. La rêverie selon Rousseau et son conditionnement historique. *In:* Jean-Jacques Rousseau et son œuvre : problèmes et recherches. *See* 4790. p. 77–92.   **4836**
Comparative analysis of the significance of R.'s reveries as a form of communication with nature.

Röhrs, Hermann. Jean-Jacques Rousseau; Vision und Wirklichkeit. Heidelberg, Quelle und Meyer, 1956. 246 p.   **4837**
Comprehensive examination of R.'s life and thought, in which he is portrayed as a fundamentally religious thinker, intensely sensitive to transcendent ideals, in the light of which reality may be appraised and reconstructed. Jean Starobinski in his review *infra:* " Aux yeux de l'auteur, les deux pôles entre lesquels Rousseau oscille sont l'affrontement de la *réalité* et la *vision* d'un monde possible qui constituerait soit la forme achevée, soit la source primitive de notre monde dégénéré."
Review : J. Starobinski in AJJR 34: 188–90, 1956–58.

Schaerer, René. Jean-Jacques et la grande famille. *In:* Jean-Jacques Rousseau. *See* 4787. p. 187–201.   **4838**
Brilliant historical study of the philosophical sources and consequences of R.'s thought. In this perspective R. is held to have seen that happiness and virtue are morally united.

Thomas, Jacques-François. Le pélagianisme de J.-J. Rousseau. Nizet, 1956. 153 p.   **4839**
R. is seen as psychologically disposed to assert the doctrine of natural goodness in opposition to that of original sin.
Review : F. Bouchardy in AJJR 35: 321–22, 1959–62.

Wahl, Jean. La bipolarité de Rousseau. AJJR 33:49–55, 1953–55.   **4840**
In agreement with Cassirer and Groethuysen and inspired by Poulet, Wahl argues that R.'s thought is exploratory, informed by a sensitivity to alternative

possibilities, and hence its unity must be conceived as dialectical.

Psychological and Educational

Baczko, Bronislaw. Rousseau et l'aliénation sociale. AJJR 35:223-33, 1959-62. **4841**
R. offers a phenomenology of alienation, the causes of which are injustice and inequality and the consequence of which is moral crisis. Only through moral freedom and justice can authenticity be achieved.

Burgelin, Pierre. L'éducation de Sophie. AJJR 35:113-30, 1959-62. **4842**
Critical appraisal of R.'s views on feminine education, the point of which is not so much development of self as preparation for dealing with the male, an education which R. considers in accord with the natural order.

Château, Jean. Jean-Jacques Rousseau; sa philosophie de l'éducation. Vrin, 1962. 254 p. **4843**
Thorough and comprehensive exposition of R.'s educational ideas, placed in the context of his life and writings, with attention to sources and relevance.

Dottrens, Robert. Jean-Jacques Rousseau éducateur. *In:* Jean-Jacques Rousseau. *See* 4787. p. 101-26. **4844**
" La conception fonctionnelle de l'enfance ... résulte de la prise en considération des phénomènes psychiques, du point de vue de leur structure, de leur fonction, de leur évolution " (p. 124).
An analysis of the dependence of R.'s educational theory upon his psychology, and an appraisal of his contributions in the light of modern thought.

Grosclaude, Pierre. La politique dans l'œuvre de Jean-Jacques Rousseau. RPP 65: 43-50, Feb. 1963. **4845**
Illuminating treatment of R.'s political philosophy with special reference to the role of education in the formation of appropriate political sentiment.

Jimack, Peter D. La genèse et la rédaction de l'Emile de J.-J. Rousseau : étude sur l'histoire de l'ouvrage jusqu'à sa parution. Geneva, Institut et musée Voltaire, 1960. 425 p. (SVEC, 13) **4846**
An account of existing mss, of the work's composition, and of its publication. An important contribution to the study of *Emile.*
Reviews : P. Burgelin in AJJR 35:363-

68, 1959-62; R. Grimsley in MLR 57: 103-04, 1962; F. Jost in RLC 36:622-25, 1962; P. Meyer in RR 54:64-66, 1963; G. Pire in RHL 62:611-13, 1962.

Lévi-Strauss, Claude. Jean-Jacques Rousseau, fondateur des sciences de l'homme. *In:* Jean-Jacques Rousseau. *See* 4787. p. 239-48. **4847**
" La révolution rousseauiste, préformant et amorçant la révolution ethnologique, consiste à refuser des identifications obligées, que ce soit celle d'une culture à cette culture, ou celle d'un individu, membre d'une culture, à un personnage ou à une fonction sociale, que cette même culture cherche à lui imposer " (p. 245).
R.'s humanity and universalism both appreciate the individual in and disengage him from his social environment.

Osmont, Robert. Jean-Jacques Rousseau et la jalousie. AJJR 35:73-86, 1959-62. **4848**
" Pour pouvoir condamner plus sûrement la jalousie, Rousseau en a fait une passion d'amour-propre issue de la rivalité sociale; dès lors elle n'a plus rien d'une passion primitive; elle appartient à une nature dégradée " (p. 83-84).
Jealousy, according to R., is unnatural, the product of pride and competition, and a threat to authenticity and happiness.

Pire, Georges. De l'influence de Sénèque sur les théories pédagogiques de J.-J. Rousseau. AJJR 33:57-92, 1953-55. **4849**
"... l'influence de Sénèque, tout importante qu'elle soit, ne se manifeste presque jamais d'une manière évidente dans les œuvres de Rousseau " (p. 85).
R.'s educational theory owes much to Seneca, but much also to others and to his own experience.

— Jean-Jacques Rousseau; lecteur de Pierre Charron. RLC 36:481-94, 1962. **4850**
"... il a exercé une influence originale et directe sur la pédagogie de Rousseau, lequel peut être considéré comme le père de la pédagogie moderne " (p. 494).
Illuminating analysis of Charron's influence on R.

Pizzorusso, Arnaldo. La comédie de Narcisse. AJJR 35:8-20, 1959-62. **4851**
R.'s proclivity for introspection and his need for recognition are foreshadowed in this work. Starobinski's comment in the discussion following : " On pourrait enfin observer, si l'on recourt aux notions de la psychiatrie contemporaine, que le délire de persécution doit être mis en

relation avec les tendances narcissiques " (p. 27).

Poulet, Georges. Rousseau. *In his:* Etudes sur le temps humain. Edinburgh, Edinburgh univ. press, 1950. p. 186–217. **4852**
Penetrating analysis of relationships between R.'s psychological theory and his personality and experience.

Rang, Martin. Le dualisme anthropologique dans l'Emile. *In:* Jean-Jacques Rousseau et son œuvre : problèmes et recherches. *See* 4790. p. 195–203. **4853**
" S'il y a synthèse dans *l'Emile*, elle est constituée plutôt par la coexistence de ces deux manières de vivre et de penser, par l'intime relation de leurs principes : l'indépendance d'une part, la sensibilité d'autre part, principes qui sont conçus comme restrictions mutuelles et dont cependant aucun ne dément l'autre " (p. 201–02).
Moral sensibility arises from the interplay of reason and feeling according to the principles of human dynamics. R.'s psychology is neither behaviorist nor determinist.

— Rousseaus Lehre vom Menschen. Göttingen, Vandenhoeck und Ruprecht, 1959. 617 p. **4854**
Erudite presentation of R.'s psychological and educational theories in historical perspective.
Reviews : P. Burgelin in RMM 65:199–209, 1960; J. Knoll in ZRG 13:263–66, 1961; F. Orlando in SF 4:355, 1960; J. Starobinski in AJJR 35:331–33, 1959–62.

Roddier, Henri. Education et politique chez J.-J. Rousseau. *In:* Jean-Jacques Rousseau et son œuvre : problèmes et recherches. *See* 4790. p. 183–93. **4855**
R.'s educational and political theories have in common the aim of freedom and are based on an identical psychology.

Spink, John S. Les premières expériences pédagogiques de Rousseau. AJJR 35:93–103, 1959–62. **4856**
" Pour Rousseau, la loi ne se maintient que par les bonnes mœurs et les bonnes mœurs par l'éducation, mais l'éducation n'est pas possible quand les mœurs ne sont pas bonnes et les bonnes mœurs supposent le souci du bien général, qui est la patrie " (p. 100).
Biographical data are used to elucidate the development of R.'s thought on education and its relation to his political theory.

Starobinski, Jean. Discours sur l'origine et les fondements de l'inégalité. *In:* Rousseau, Jean-Jacques. Œuvres completes. *See* 4774. 3:xlii–lxxi. **4857**
A sensitive and subtle exposition of the *Discours* which produces a novel interpretation. Inequality has its origins in man's divorce from and antagonism to nature. Loss of immediacy of contact with nature leads to reflection, comparison, and competition, the consequence of which is alienation. Men, alienated from nature and themselves, seek inequality, and by doing so create unhappiness through mutual frustration of their moral potentialities.

— Jean-Jacques Rousseau et le péril de la réflexion. *In his:* L'œil vivant. Gallimard, 1961. p. 91–190. **4858**
" Le schématisme assez pauvre de l'anthropologie sensualiste est fécondé chez Rousseau par tout ce qui reste vivant de la pensée judéo-chrétienne. Il en résulte non un système, mais un tumulte d'idées qui contribuera pour beaucoup à l'extraordinaire élan politique et philosophique de la fin du xviiie siècle " (p. 161).
According to Starobinski, R.'s quest for personal unity and identity unleashed a new conception of the self, fatal to simplistic psychologies and productive of moral and political energy. A masterful analysis which makes use of a remarkable range of knowledge and concepts.
Reviews : M. Eigeldinger in AJJR 35: 348–51, 1959–62; M. Launay in RHL 63: 504–06, 1963; R. Niklaus in MLR 57: 450–51, 1962.

— J.-J. Rousseau et les pouvoirs de l'imaginaire. RIP 14:43–67, 1960. **4859**
" Dans l'état de nature, l'imagination est corruptrice; dans l'état de nos sociétés imparfaites, elle est la seule ressource des âmes vertueuses et tendres " (p. 64).
Brilliant analysis of the role of imagination in R.'s life and writings.

— Rousseau et Buffon. *In:* Jean-Jacques Rousseau et son œuvre : problèmes et recherches. *See* 4790. p. 135–46. **4860**
Penetrating analysis of the extent to which R. relied upon Buffon's work, revealing R.'s originality, especially in the *Discours sur l'origine de l'inégalité.*

Ethical and Social

Allers, Ulrich S. Rousseau's Second discourse. Review of Politics 20:91–120, 1958. **4861**

Study of the *Second discourse* concerned especially with R.'s conception of freedom and its relation to equality.

" ... Rousseau believes that there is but one form of freedom, which is obtained through the internal equilibrium of inclinations and which is predicated upon the equality of all " (p. 119).

Baczko, Bronislaw. Hegel a Rousseau. Sfil 9:87–120, 1958; 10:136–69, 1959. **4862**

" The problems of alienation and negation in social life, which are of fundamental importance for Hegelian dialectic and historicism, can be found also in Rousseau, even though entangled in a style of thinking which is in many ways opposed to that of Hegel and linked with a different social ideal " (p. 169, English summary).

Distinguished comparative analysis of R.'s and Hegel's theories of alienation.

Balaval, Yvon. La théorie du jugement dans l'Emile. *In:* Jean-Jacques Rousseau et son œuvre : problèmes et recherches. *See* 4790. p. 149–57. **4863**

" ... unissant Descartes à Locke, Rousseau professe un innéisme génétique. Cette genèse nous élève de la vie à l'esprit —du sensitif à l'intellectuel, du psychologique au moral, du nécessaire au libre. Elle est l'œuvre du jugement " (p. 150).

Examination of the nature and sources of R.'s theory of moral judgment in which rational and emotional processes are seen as interdependent. This is one of few analyses of R.'s metaethics.

Bloom, Allan. Jean-Jacques Rousseau. *In:* History of political philosophy. Ed. by Leo Strauss and Joseph Cropsey. Chicago, Rand McNally, 1963. p. 514–35. **4864**

Comprehensive and cogent analysis of R.'s political theory with emphasis upon its moral component, combined with an attempt to place his work in a historical perspective. Freedom is seen as the source rather than the actualizer of morality, and hence R. emerges as a romantic, not a rationalist thinker.

Bouchardy, François. Discours sur les sciences et les arts. *In:* Rousseau, Jean-Jacques. Œuvres complètes. *See* 4774. 3:xxvii–xli. **4865**

Primarily biographical account of the occasion of and influences on the composition of the *Discours*.

Bretonneau, Gisèle. Valeurs humaines de J.-J. Rousseau. La Colombe, 1961. 307 p. **4866**

Comprehensive, thorough, and remarkably sensitive analysis and exposition of R.'s psychological and ethical theories, dynamic in its emphasis on their developmental nature, which makes them relevant especially for educational theory and practice.

Reviews : Anon. in AUP 32:111–12, 1962; J.-D. Candaux in AJJR 35:335–36, 1959–62.

Burgelin, Pierre. Le social et le politique chez Rousseau. *In:* Etudes sur le Contrat social de Jean-Jacques Rousseau. *See* 4791. p. 165–76. **4867**

Society is the creation of reason, not feeling, and social order, the purposes of which are freedom, virtue, wisdom, and happiness, is a political achievement.

Collinet, Michel. L'homme de la nature ou la nature de l'homme. CSoc 6:147–54, 1962. **4868**

" L'homme naturel de Rousseau appartient aux créations mythiques sur l'origine de l'espèce; mais ce mythe lui parut nécessaire pour doter l'homme réel d'une existence antérieure aux vicissitudes de l'histoire, sans rapport avec une justice sociale trop soumise aux circonstances politiques pour obtenir l'adhésion de la conscience " (p. 154).

R.'s conception of the natural embodies a vision of harmony which offers psychological security to men exposed to historical and social injustice.

Crocker, Lester G. The priority of justice or law. YFS 28:34–42, 1961–62. **4869**

R.'s conventionalism is revealed in the priority which he gives to law over justice; for him human salvation is to be obtained by the establishment of appropriate and unchanging conventions.

— The relation of Rousseau's Second discours and the Contrat social. RR 51:33–44, 1960. **4870**

" At bottom, what Rousseau desired most urgently to avoid was a thoroughly competitive society, and to create in its stead a cooperative (or collective) society " (p. 40).

R. is presented as an illiberal thinker anxious to obtain social stability and psychological security at the expense of change and opportunity.

— Rousseau et la voie du totalitarisme. APP 5:99–136, 1965. **4871**

" Le paradoxe de Rousseau est que son point de départ est humaniste : l'homme n'est pas asservi à la nature, et appelé à se créer; mais son aboutissement est un système antihumaniste par la dissolution du moi distinctif dans le moi commun " (p. 135–36).

To be compared with Derathé's introduction to the *Discours sur l'économie politique* (4774).

Dehaussy, Jacques. La dialectique de la souveraine liberté dans le Contrat social. *In:* Etudes sur le Contrat social de Jean-Jacques Rousseau. *See* 4791. p. 119–41. **4872**

Social equality not only makes for freedom but is also implied by R.'s prescriptions that there be no factions and that the law apply equally to all in his ideal society. Social equality would promote agreement and prevent oppression.

Derathé, Robert. Discours sur l'économie politique. *In:* Rousseau, Jean-Jacques. Œuvres complètes. *See* 4774. 3:lxii–lxxxi. **4873**

Biographical, analytical, and historical account of the *Discours*, showing its relation to R.'s other writings, and of special interest for its presentation of R.'s conception of society.

— L'homme selon Rousseau. *In:* Etudes sur le Contrat social de Jean-Jacques Rousseau. *See* 4791. p. 203–17. **4874**

The unity of R.'s thought derives from his concern with human nature and the human condition. His conceptions of the natural man and the citizen both aim at the ideals of liberty and equality.

Fetscher, Iring. Rousseaus politische Philosophie; zur Geschichte des demokratischen Freiheitsbegriffs. Neuwied, Luchterhand, 1960. xvii, 313 p. **4875**

Stelling-Michaud in his review *infra:* " ... dans un chapitre très remarquable sur l'éthique de Rousseau, M. Fetscher a montré comment la théorie rousseauiste de ' l'amour de soi ' et de ' l'amour propre ' dérive de Fénelon, de Malebranche, de la *Logique de Port Royal*, de Pascal et de Vauvenargues, qui a établi clairement la distinction des deux amours, dont Rousseau attribuera la transforma-

tion à la société et non pas au péché, comme l'avaient fait les théologiens."

Distinguished study, both analytical and historical, of the moral foundations of R.'s political philosophy; the sources and consequences of his thought are placed in an illuminating perspective.

Review : S. Stelling-Michaud in AJJR 35:327–39, 1959–62.

Gossman, Lionel. Rousseau's idealism. RR 52:173–82, 1961. **4876**

Emphasizes the austerity of R.'s moral idealism.

" In the society of the *Contrat social* order and justice are bought at the same cost as in *La nouvelle Héloïse*. It is a society without joy " (p. 180).

— Time and history in Rousseau. SVEC 30: 311–49, 1964. **4877**

Gossman emphasizes the historicity of R.'s conception of individuality, which he finds at the root of R.'s vision of the appropriate relations between individuals and their society. To be compared with Grimsley (4799), Plamenatz (4930), Poulet (4852), and Starobinski (4809).

Groethuysen, Bernhard. J.-J. Rousseau. Gallimard, 1949. 338 p. **4878**

One of the most penetrating of all studies of R.'s thought, of particular value for its analysis of his psychological and moral theories and their interrelationships.

Reviews : O. Haac in MLQ 12:377–80, 1951; J. Starobinski in AJJR 32:211–13, 1950–52.

Hall, H. Gaston. The concept of virtue in La nouvelle Héloïse. YFS 28:20–33, 1961–62. **4879**

Sympathetic and illuminating analysis of the moral import of *La nouvelle Héloïse*.

Hyppolite, Jean. Genèse et structure de la Phénoménologie de l'esprit de Hegel. Aubier, 1956 [c. 1946]. 2 v. **4880**

" L'individualisme de Rousseau, puis l'individualisme romantique sont une protestation du cœur contre cette violence faite à l'individualité humaine. Il faut libérer l'homme, ce qui ne signifie pas opposer les hommes les uns aux autres, mais au contraire les réconcilier les uns avec les autres puisque mon bien est le bien de l'humanité ..." (1:276).

R.'s psychological and moral ideas are clarified by comparisons with those of Hegel. *See* particularly 1:42–48, 274–79; 2:364–412, 439–49.

Jost, François. La nouvelle Héloïse, roman suisse. RLC 35:538–65, 1961. **4881**

" Egalité sur toute la ligne, égalité surtout entre l'homme de la ville et l'homme de la campagne : idée foncièrement suisse " (p. 562).
Jost seeks to establish the Swiss origins and qualities of R.'s morality.

Lovejoy, Arthur O. Reflections on human nature. Baltimore, Johns Hopkins press, 1961. p. 217–45. **4882**

Lovejoy discounts the significance of the doctrine of natural goodness in R.'s thought. The implications of his interpretation would appear to have been worked out in the analyses of Lester G. Crocker (4869–70).

Mazauric, Claude. Le rousseauisme de Babeuf. AHRF 34:439–64, 1962. **4883**

" Lorsque dans ses méthodes et ses objectifs concrets, le babouvisme s'éloigne de l'idéal institutionnel de Rousseau, il demeure conforme à son idéal moral et social qui fut celui d'une Société égalitaire, vertueuse, austère ..." (p. 464).
A comparative and historical study which throws light on R.'s political ethics.

Palmer, R. R. The age of the democratic revolution; a political history of Europe and America, 1760–1800. Princeton, Princeton univ. press, 1959–64. 1:111–39. **4884**

" He was the revolutionary *par excellence* because it was a moral revolution that he called for, a revolution in the personality and in the inclination of the will " (p. 114).
Brilliant appraisal of the moral and historical significance of R.'s thought.

Plamenatz, John. " Ce qui signifie autre chose sinon qu'on le forcera d'être libre " : a commentary. APP 5:137–52, 1965. **4885**

Definitive explanation of the meaning of the most controversial and misleading of all R.'s cryptic assertions, achieved through the analysis of this notorious statement in the light of the totality of R.'s theories and thought.

Polin, Raymond. Le sens de l'égalité et de l'inégalité chez J.-J. Rousseau. *In:* Etudes sur le Contrat social de Jean-Jacques Rousseau. *See* 4791. p. 143–64. **4886**

" ... Rousseau n'a jamais défendu d'autre égalité qu'une forme proportionnelle et modérée de l'égalité, qui reconnaît la légitimité des distinctions et des différences morales et politiques, pourvu qu'elles soient accordées aux inégalités établies par la nature " (p. 163).
Brilliant analysis of R.'s conceptions of justice and equality in which their Aristotelian sources are demonstrated. With reference to Starobinski (4889), Polin emphasizes the importance of the meaning of equality.

Raymond, Marcel. Rousseau et la rêverie. *In:* Jean-Jacques Rousseau. *See* 4787. p. 153–70. **4887**

Both nature and society are for R. manifestations of the divine, access to the unity of which may be had through contemplation.

Shklar, Judith N. Rousseau's images of authority. APSR 58:919–31, 1964. **4888**

" If Rousseau's images of authority show any one thing it is the intensity and consistency of his hatred for all forms of personal dependence and social inequality, and for their psychological roots, weakness and *amour-propre* " (p. 931).
Remarkably perceptive analysis of R.'s conception of authority in its relations to his psychological and moral theories.

Starobinski, Jean. La pensée politique de Jean-Jacques Rousseau. *In:* Jean-Jacques Rousseau. *See* 4787. p. 81–99. **4889**

Psychological analysis and exposition of R.'s political theory, the key to understanding which is held to be his need for spiritual union, a need which has its roots in his childhood experience.

Stelling-Michaud, Sven. Rousseau et l'injustice sociale. *In:* Jean-Jacques Rousseau. *See* 4787. p. 171–86. **4890**

" Le sentiment de l'injustice sociale et la prise de position de Rousseau, loin d'avoir sa source avant tout dans des réactions d'amour-propre blessé, étaient fondées sur une analyse et une critique approfondies de la société de son temps " (p. 179).
R.'s vision of a free society of equals is based on his diagnosis of contemporary society and continues to inspire social reform.

Temmer, Mark J. Time in Rousseau and Kant; an essay on French pre-romanticism. Geneva, Droz, 1958. 79 p. **4891**

" ... Rousseau and Kant sought to halt the ever-present threat to the oneness of the Western mind through a radical transformation of their contemporary values—Rousseau achieving his *Umwertung der Werte* by expiating and illustrating the cleavage of eighteenth-century life, Kant by undertaking a vast critique of its intellectual and metaphysical assumptions " (p. 75).

Illuminating comparative analysis of the historical and moral significance of R.'s thought.

Reviews : P. Burgelin in RLC 33:432–34, 1959; P. Chaix in AJJR 34:240, 1956–58; L. Gossman in MLN 75:74–77, 1960; J. Spink in MLR 55:284–85, 1960.

Watkins, Frederick. Introduction. *In:* Rousseau, Jean-Jacques. Political writings. *See* 4780. p. i–xliii.   **4892**

" As a liberal, Rousseau was unwilling to admit any element of coercion that would in the slightest detract from the moral responsibility of the individual. . . . As a totalitarian pessimist, on the other hand, he was unable to believe in the creative potentialities of ordinary individuals " (p. xxxii).

Striking analysis and presentation of R.'s political theory and ethics, especially noteworthy for its sensitivity to their ambiguities, held to be the source of his ultimate failure as a political thinker.

Literary and Artistic

Bellenot, Jean-Louis. Les formes de l'amour dans La nouvelle Héloïse et la signification symbolique des personnages de Julie et de Saint-Preux.   AJJR 33:149–207, 1953–55.   **4893**

Perceptive analysis of R.'s conceptions of love.

Bloom, Allan. Introduction. *In:* Rousseau, Jean-Jacques. Politics and the arts, letter to M. d'Alembert on the theatre.   Ed. and trans. by Allan Bloom.   Glencoe, Ill., Free Press, 1960. p. i–xxxviii.   **4894**

Brilliant introduction explaining R.'s insight into the morally enervating consequences of popularized art and comparing his views with those of the classics.

Broome, Jack Howard. Rousseau, a study of his thought.   New York, Barnes and Noble, 1963. 231 p.   **4895**

R. " was trying courageously to do what somebody has to do in every age : namely, to work out for his own times a practical and acceptable synthesis of old traditions and new philosophies, in the belief that there is value in all of them " (p. 210).

Sympathetic, lucid introductory exposition of R.'s works, giving particular attention to the more literary.

Reviews : R. Ellrich in RR 55:295–96, 1964; P. Jimack in FS 18:273–74, 1964; T. Morris in MLR 60:118–19, 1965.

Dédéyan, Charles.   J.-J. Rousseau : La nouvelle Héloïse. Centre de documentation universitaire, 1958.   192 p. (Les cours de Sorbonne)   **4896**

Comprehensive exposition of R.'s thought centering upon La nouvelle Héloïse.

Review : M. Raymond in AJJR 35:318, 1959–62.

Fabre, Jean. Deux frères ennemis : Diderot et Jean-Jacques. DS 3:155–213, 1961.   **4897**

" Pour Diderot la nature est principe d'exaltation; pour Rousseau d'apaisement et même quand il souhaite de se fondre en elle, c'est pour se réfugier en son sein " (p. 170).

Sensitive and illuminating comparative analysis of the thought of R. and Diderot.

— Jean-Jacques Rousseau. *In:* Histoire des littératures. *See* 3384. 3:746–72.   **4898**

Interpretation which emphasizes the tension in R.'s thought between the natural and the social.

Review : B. Gagnebin in AJJR 35:319–20, 1959–62.

Gagnebin, Bernard, and Marcel Raymond. Les confessions. *In:* Rousseau, Jean-Jacques. Œuvres complètes. *See* 4774. 1:xvi–xliv.   **4899**

" Histoire et mythe consubstantiels à la vérité d'une âme, à la vérité la plus claire comme à la plus obscure, à la mieux masquée à la conscience, Les confessions sont une peinture complète, qui appelle seulement un lecteur sachant lire dans tous les sens " (p. xliv).

An appreciation to the Confessions in all that work's complexities, diversities, and ambiguities of meaning.

Gay, Peter. Three stages on love's way : Rousseau, Laclos, Diderot. *In his:* The party of humanity; essays in the French Enlightenment.   New York, Knopf, 1964. p. 133–61.   **4900**

Critical and novel appraisal of the moral attitudes portrayed in La nouvelle Héloïse.

Grosclaude, Pierre. Rôle et caractères de l'analyse intérieure chez Rousseau. *In:* Jean-Jacques Rousseau et son œuvre : problèmes et recherches. *See* 4790. p. 317–26.   **4901**

" Rien n'est plus éloigné de la grandiloquence et même du lyrisme que le style de Rousseau dans les pages d'analyse intérieure " (p. 325).

An appreciation of R.'s style, particularly notable for its precision and simplicity, which creates nevertheless a poetical quality.

Guyon, Bernard. La nouvelle Héloïse. *In:* Rousseau, Jean-Jacques. Œuvres complètes. *See* 4774. 2:xviii–lxx. **4902**

La nouvelle Héloïse " dépasse de très haut la simple ' littérature .' Un homme qui parle à d'autres hommes leur livre les secrets de son cœur, leur propose un message de bonheur " (p. lxix).

Masterly biographical and contextual study of the novel, presented as an enduring work of art, liberating and ennobling in nature.

Havens, George R. Diderot, Rousseau and the Discours sur l'inégalité. DS 3:219–62, 1961. **4903**

" ... paradoxically, it seems that Diderot's advice tended in two directions at once, toward boldness in content and prudence in form " (p. 262).

Biographical study showing Diderot's influence on the composition and content of the *Discours.*

Launay, Michel. L'art et l'écrivain dans le Contrat social. *In:* Etudes sur le Contrat social de Jean-Jacques Rousseau. *See* 4791. p. 351–78. **4904**

" La recherche de la concision trouve son achèvement dans la création des formules : ' L'homme est né libre, et partout il est dans les fers '; le Manuscrit de Genève porte, plus faiblement : ' L'homme est né libre, et cependant partout il est dans les fers ' " (p. 366).

Perceptive analysis of R.'s style and its dramatic uses and cryptic impact, including an examination of typical images and symbols.

Mauzi, Robert. La conversion de Julie dans La nouvelle Héloïse. AJJR 35:29–47, 1959–62. **4905**

" La conversion de Julie pourrait se définir comme un cas d'absorption spontanée de l'impératif moral par la personnalité tout entière, et non pas du tout comme une pure victoire de la volonté forçant le cœur à se sacrifier à la vertu " (p. 34).

Study which attempts to establish the fundamentally moral nature of the action.

Morphos, Panos Paul. Renaissance tradition in Rousseau's Second discours. MLQ 13:81–89, 1952. **4906**

" ... Rousseau illustrates the point that the eighteenth-century French thinkers, while familiar with classical and Christian thought, were not unaware of Renaissance thought, which they sometimes found closer to their way of thinking " (p. 88).

Historical study which further illuminates the sources of R.'s thought.

Osmont, Robert. Rousseau juge de Jean Jaques : dialogues. *In:* Rousseau, Jean-Jacques. Œuvres complètes. *See* 4774. 1: xlv–lxxii. **4907**

" L'œuvre des *Dialogues* représente le plus patient effort que puisse accomplir un homme pour combattre l'absurdité, recenser ses richesses intérieures, épurer son espérance " (p. lxxi–lxxii).

Biographical and analytical study which seeks to establish as the central purposes of the *Dialogues* communication and purification.

— Les théories de Rousseau sur l'harmonie musicale et leurs relations avec son art d'écrivain. *In:* Jean-Jacques Rousseau et son œuvre : problèmes et recherches. *See* 4790. p. 329–45. **4908**

Original, sensitive, and illuminating comparison of R.'s musical and literary works. Desirability of further research suggested.

Raymond, Marcel. Les confessions. *In:* Jean-Jacques Rousseau. *See* 4787. p. 33–50. **4909**

" Depuis Rousseau, à travers le romantisme, à travers le symbolisme, à travers l'existentialisme ... la connaissance de soi, la conscience de soi sont devenues une hantise et une passion " (p. 41).

Analysis of R.'s motives in writing his autobiography, which reveals him as both a man and a poet, with reflection upon the significance of his effort at self-understanding and self-revelation.

— Jean-Jacques Rousseau et le problème de la connaissance de soi. SF 6:457–72, 1962. **4910**

" ... il a glissé d'une attitude qu'on appellerait sommairement scientifique ... à une attitude qu'on nommerait, tout aussi sommairement, existentielle " (p. 462).

To be compared with Isaiah Berlin (4966).

— Les rêveries du promeneur solitaire. *In:*
Rousseau, Jean-Jacques. Œuvres complètes. *See* 4774. 1:lxiii–xcv.   **4911**

" ... les mystiques n'ont de paix qu'ils
ne soient délivrés d'eux-mêmes, tandis
que Jean-Jacques croit trouver la paix
dans le sentiment de sa propre existence "
(p. xcv).
Analytical and sensitive account of the
moral attitudes conveyed in this work,
with emphasis upon R.'s quest for self-
understanding and possession.

Roddier, Henri. Introduction. *In:* Rousseau,
Jean-Jacques. Les rêveries du promeneur
solitaire. Ed. by Henri Roddier. *See* 4781.
p. i–xcvii.   **4912**

" Le dernier ouvrage de Jean-Jacques,
point final d'une évolution psychologique,
ne fut pas composé d'autre façon que les
précédents " (p. lxxxiii).
An attempt to place this work in the
perspective of R.'s psychological and
moral development.

Rousset, Jean. Rousseau romancier : La
nouvelle Héloïse. *In:* Jean-Jacques Rousseau. *See* 4787. p. 67–80.   **4913**
Analysis of the techniques and symbolism employed by R. in this novel.

Temmer, Mark J. Art and love in the Confessions of Jean-Jacques Rousseau. PMLA
73:215–20, 1958.   **4914**
The analysis is " presented with the
intention of showing how a seemingly
sincere style and a moving appeal to the
reader's sympathy made possible a self-
recreation which reconciles art to life "
(p. 215).
The *Confessions* is a work to be valued
more for its artistic achievement than
for its truthfulness and literal accuracy.

Wolpe, Hans. Psychological ambiguity in
La nouvelle Héloïse. UTQ 28:279–90,
1958–59.   **4915**
" The whole force of illusion of the
characters in *La nouvelle Héloïse* is
founded on this subtle psychology which
appears so straightforward, on this ambiguity which assumes the semblance of
clarity " (p. 289).
Suggestive and provocative examination
of some neglected features of the novel.

Political

Burgelin, Pierre. Hors des ténèbres de la
nature. APP 5:21–34, 1965.   **4916**
Rationality, both personal and political,
is to be achieved only through respect for

the dynamics of human nature and development, for this is, as R. conceives it, an
emergent characteristic of humanity.

Candaux, Jean-Daniel. Lettres écrites de la
montagne. *In:* Rousseau, Jean-Jacques.
Œuvres complètes. *See* 4774. 3:clix–cxcviii.
          4917
" La vision du petit Etat aux mœurs
simples et démocratiques, où l'égalité des
conditions fût gage de justice, de bien-être
et de liberté, s'était restreinte à la seule
bourgeoisie de Genève, mais elle ne
l'avait pas quitté " (p. cxcviii).
The work is placed in the context of
Genevan society and history and is compared with R.'s other political writings.

Chevallier, Jean-Jacques. Le mot et la
notion de gouvernement chez Rousseau.
In: Etudes sur le Contrat social de Jean-
Jacques Rousseau. *See* 4791. p. 291–313.
          4918
R.'s supreme political originality is
revealed in his distinction between sovereignty and government, the point of
which is that government must be conceived as the agent of the people.

Davy, Georges. Thomas Hobbes et J.-J.
Rousseau. Oxford, Clarendon press, 1953.
29 p. *See* 5701.   **4919**
Comparative and analytical study emphasizing similarities and hence inclined
to underestimate R.'s originality.
Reviews : R. Derathé in AJJR 33:340–
41, 1953–55.

Derathé, Robert. Du contrat social. *In:*
Rousseau, Jean-Jacques. Œuvres complètes.
See 4774. 3:xci–cxv.   **4920**
" L'Emile s'adresse aux hommes des
sociétés corrompues pour qu'ils se pré-
servent eux-mêmes de la corruption,
tandis que le *Contrat social* est destiné
aux peuples qui ont su conserver leur
liberté " (p. xcviii).
Analytical study setting forth the principles upon which the work is based and
showing its inspiration and purpose in
R.'s conception of freedom.

— Jean-Jacques Rousseau et la science politique de son temps. Presses univ. de France,
1950. xiv, 463 p.   **4921**
B. Gagnebin in his review *infra:* " Par
des citations empruntées à la correspondance, aux *Lettres de la montagne,* à l'*Emile*
et même à *La nouvelle Héloïse,* M. Derathé
montre que loin de rejeter l'idée d'une
loi supérieure à celle de l'Etat, Rousseau
admet qu'il existe une loi sacrée, que

l'homme ne saurait enfreindre, mais qui n'apparaît qu'avec la vie sociale et le développement de la raison."

In a work of scholarship of the highest order, Derathé corrects many misconceptions of R.'s politics, illuminates every aspect of his political thinking, lays bare its sources, and shows it to be fundamentally rationalist in nature. Indispensable.

Reviews : C. Frankel in RR 43:134–39, 1952; B. Gagnebin in AJJR 32:220–23, 1950–52; G. Lefebvre in Rhist 207:310–14, 1952.

— Les rapports de l'exécutif et du législatif chez J.-J. Rousseau. APP 5:153–69, 1965. **4922**

" De toute façon, les libertés publiques risquent d'être plus menacées et moins bien défendues dans les grands Etats modernes que dans les petites Républiques antiques. Telle est, en somme, la conclusion pessimiste à laquelle nous conduit la lecture du *Contrat social* " (p. 169).

An examination of R.'s reflections on the institutional requisites of freedom.

Fabre, Jean. Considérations sur le gouvernement de Pologne. *In:* Rousseau, Jean-Jacques. Œuvres complètes. *See* 4774. 3:ccxvi–ccxlv. **4923**

" Moderne Lycurgue ou Numa, il a substitué à la Pologne moderne une Pologne spartiate ou romaine et proposé aux Polonais cette image idéale non comme le reflet de la réalité, mais comme l'exigence de la vérité " (p. ccxlii).

Biographical and historical study combined with recognition of R.'s adherence to principle and practicality.

— Jean-Jacques Rousseau et le destin polonais. Eur 391–92:206–27, Nov.–Dec. 1961. **4924**

An appreciation of R.'s work on Poland, calling attention to the ways in which he seeks to institutionalize his ideals in their full integrity.

Fetscher, Iring. Rousseau, auteur d'intention conservatrice et d'action révolutionnaire. APP 5:51–75, 1965. **4925**

" Il y a surtout sa conception de la nécessaire dégénérescence du genre humain au cours du progrès de la société moderne, conception qui exclut toute interprétation franchement révolutionnaire de ses idées politiques " (p. 52).

Survey of R.'s political writings reveals him to be an essentially conservative

thinker, dubious as to the prospects for human progress.

Friedrich, Carl J. Law and dictatorship in the Contrat social. APP 5:77–97, 1965. **4926**

" Beginning with the Jacobins, followed by the restauration conservatives, by the Marxists and other socialists in turn, and finally topped by the critics of totalitarianism, Rousseau has been misquoted and distorted instead of being seen as the thinker he was : one of the genuine believers in and defenders of constitutionalism " (p. 96).

Examination of R.'s writings reveals that they incorporate and embody the basic principles of constitutionalism.

Healey, F. G. Rousseau, Voltaire and Corsica; some notes on an interesting enigma. SVEC 10:413–19, 1959. **4927**

" ... given the idealized picture of Corsica which had emerged from stories of the struggle against Genoa, both Voltaire and Rousseau, to say nothing of the enlightened European public in general, probably had no idea of the true complexity of the Corsican scene, nor of the genius of that nation for political intrigue " (p. 419).

Leigh, R. A. Liberté et autorité dans le Contrat social. *In:* Jean-Jacques Rousseau et son œuvre : problèmes et recherches. *See* 4790. p. 249–62. **4928**

" Dans un sens, pour Rousseau, la liberté, *c'est* l'autorité ... de même que, pour certains théologiens, le libre-arbitre n'est autre chose que la grâce même qui agit en nous " (p. 267).

A defence of R. against the charge that his political theory is illiberal. Authority has its source in freedom and as its purpose the expansion of freedom.

Lévy, Yves. Machiavel et Rousseau. CSoc 6:169–74, 1962. **4929**

" Pour Rousseau, la présence d'un maître suffit à détruire le corps social. Pour Machiavel, il y a toujours un chemin qui mène à la liberté, et il peut se faire que l'instauration d'un prince soit la première étape d'un avenir démocratique " (p. 174).

Illuminating comparative and analytical study which shows R.'s profound distrust of any form of personal authority.

Plamenatz, John. Rousseau. *In his:* Man and society; political and social theory, Machiavelli through Rousseau. New York, McGraw-Hill, 1963. 1:364–442. **4930**

Note especially Plamenatz's comparison of Plato and R. and his analysis of R.'s view of the relations between justice and moral freedom. Indispensable.

Polin, Raymond. La fonction du législateur chez J.-J. Rousseau. *In:* Jean-Jacques Rousseau et son œuvre : problèmes et recherches. *See* 4790. p. 231–47.   **4931**

Excellent analysis of the place of the legislator in R.'s political theory. He is the constitution-maker, designs the institutions which form the character of citizens, but he does not have political authority, which is reserved to the general will.

Starobinski, Jean. Du Discours de l'inégalité au Contrat social. *In:* Etudes sur le Contrat social de Jean-Jacques Rousseau. *See* 4791. p. 97–109.   **4932**

" ... le contrat n'est pas seulement un repère ou un système idéal de mensuration, il est un modèle, il désigne ce que doit accomplir l'homme s'il remplit sa vocation sociale " (p. 108).

Argues that R.'s philosophy of history and his political philosophy are mutually consistent.

Stelling-Michaud, Sven. Ce que Jean-Jacques Rousseau doit à l'abbé de Saint-Pierre. *In:* Etudes sur le Contrat social de Jean-Jacques Rousseau. *See* 4791. p. 35–45.   **4933**

" C'est incontestablement à l'abbé de Saint-Pierre que Rousseau doit d'avoir saisi l'importance du principe fédératif pour éliminer les causes de conflit en Europe " (p. 42).

Excellent study of the influence exerted on R. by the work of Saint-Pierre.

— Ecrits sur l'abbé de Saint-Pierre. *In:* Rousseau, Jean-Jacques. Œuvres complètes. *See* 4774. 3:cxx–clviii.   **4934**

" Les sociétés civiles, régies par le contrat ou pacte d'union et soumises au droit naturel, ne connaissent pas la guerre qui est le résultat de l'anarchie internationale inhérente au système politique des grandes puissances " (p. cxlix).

See also the studies of Stanley Hoffmann (4973) and Kenneth Waltz (4983).

— Projet de constitution pour la Corse. *In:* Rousseau, Jean-Jacques. Œuvres complètes. *See* 4774. 3:cxcix–ccxv.   **4935**

" En réduisant la propriété privée à ce minimum exigé par les besoins de la cellule familiale, Rousseau veut asseoir l'égalité sociale et la liberté politique sur une base solide, assurer par là le bonheur de l'individu et supprimer la tyrannie du pouvoir " (p. ccxii).

Biographical and historical study which also relates the *Projet* to the fundamentals of R.'s political theory.

Touchard, Jean. Révoltes et utopies. *In:* Touchard, Jean, *et al.* Histoire des idées politiques. 3ᵉ édition revue. Presses univ. de France, 1965. 2:420–31, 447–48.   **4936**

" Les conditions historiques de la démocratie n'étant pas réunies, Rousseau se trouvait contraint soit d'accepter l'idéologie du libéralisme bourgeois qui était alors dominante (liberté, inégalité, propriété), soit de construire une cité d'utopie. Utopie, mais utopie rationnelle " (p. 422).

Study which seeks to place R.'s political ideas in their institutional and historical contexts. Accompanied by bibliography.

Watkins, Frederick. The problem of the general will. *In his:* The political tradition of the West : a study in the development of modern liberalism. Cambridge, Harvard univ. press, 1948. p. 90–118.   **4937**

Authoritative interpretation of the historical and institutional significance of R.'s contributions to the development of liberalism, tempered by an appreciation of his ambiguities.

Historical and Political Influence

Cobban, Alfred. In search of humanity : the role of the Enlightenment in modern history. *See* 4121.   **4938**

" The modern mind is essentially the romantic mind, and it begins with the first man in whom the romantic spirit shines through clearly, Jean-Jacques Rousseau. In Rousseau, although the infectious optimism of his age was continually asserting itself, there was a more personal strain of pessimism, which provided the model for romantic gloom and foreshadowed the deeper and more tragic outlook of the greatest minds of the nineteenth century " (p. 215).

R.'s historical significance lies in the romantic rather than the rationalist side of his personality and thought. *See* especially *Rousseau*, p. 147–60, and *The politics of the Enlightenment*, p. 161–79.

Cole, G. D. H. Rousseau's political theory. *In his:* Essays in social theory. London, Macmillan, 1950. p. 113–31.   **4939**

" Rousseau was not a nationalist; but his ideas went to the making of the new belief in national sovereignty, vested in the entire people, but exercised by a sovereign representative assembly, which the French Revolution proclaimed " (p. 130).

An appraisal of the ways in which R.'s ideas were transformed in their institutional applications.

Dahrendorf, Ralf. On the origin of social inequality. *In:* Philosophy, politics and society (second series). Ed. by Peter Laslett and W. G. Runciman. New York, Barnes and Noble, 1962. p. 88–109. **4940**

" ... the new meaning given by Rousseau and his contemporaries to the question of the origins of inequality involved a revolution in terms of politics as well as intellectual history " (p. 92).

An appraisal of the historical significance of R.'s views on inequality presented in the context of the author's own theory.

Friedrich, Carl J. Man and his government : an empirical theory of politics. New York, McGraw–Hill, 1963. 737 p., *passim.* **4941**

" ... Rousseau stressed the close link between state and nation, between the political community and its order in the specific modern form which was to generate nationalism as a pseudo-religious alternative to Christianity's universal brotherhood of man " (p. 555).

R. is presented as encouraging the formation of nationalist sentiment, despite his not being an explicit exponent thereof.

Godechot, Jacques. Le Contrat social et la révolution occidentale de 1762 à 1789. *In:* Etudes sur le Contrat social de Jean-Jacques Rousseau. *See* 4791. p. 393–403. **4942**

" Le mot ' citoyen ' employé en anglais dans la constitution du Massachusetts a le sens que lui donne Rousseau, et non son acception habituelle dans la langue anglaise " (p. 400).

An examination of R.'s influence on political thought prior to the French Revolution. Of special interest is the acquaintance of John Adams with his work. The constitution of Pennsylvania also shows his influence.

Hartz, Louis. United States history in a new perspective. *In:* Hartz, Louis, *et al.* The founding of new societies : studies in the history of the United States, Latin America, South Africa, Canada, and Austra-

lia. New York, Harcourt, Brace & World, 1964. p. 69–122. **4943**

" The Americans when they turned to Locke were extending, rather than contradicting, their intellectual heritage, which precisely is why they turned to Locke rather than to Rousseau after the fashion of the Spanish creole. Rousseau and the French thinkers symbolize precisely the break with tradition which, because of a liberal inheritance, the Americans were able to avoid " (p. 74).

Highly illuminating comparative study of the historical and intellectual significance of Locke, as contrasted with R. for the American political tradition.

Healey, F. G. Rousseau et Napoléon. Geneva, Droz, 1957. 107 p. **4944**

Illuminating study of Napoleon's debts to and differences from R.

Reviews : F. Bouchardy in AJJR 35: 325–26, 1959–62; H. Hunt in MLR 53: 121–22, 1958; N. Tomiche in RHL 59: 231–32, 1959.

Huang, Chia-cheng. Le néo-hégélianisme en Angleterre : la philosophie de Bernard Bosanquet, 1848–1923, par François Houang. Vrin, 1954. 232 p. **4945**

Study of Bosanquet's political philosophy revealing some of the ways in which it was influenced by R.'s political conceptions, in particular that of the general will, which Bosanquet sought to adapt to the national and constitutional state. *See* particularly p. 157–63.

Hyppolite, Jean. Introduction à la Philosophie de l'histoire de Hegel. Rivière, 1948. 98 p. **4946**

" Il y a une certaine transcendance de la volonté générale sur les volontés individuelles, et le fait de considérer l'Etat comme volonté est pour Hegel la grande découverte de Rousseau " (p. 22).

Illuminating study of Hegel's philosophy of history and what it owed to the inspiration of R. *See* particularly p. 15–24.

Jost, François. La fortune de Rousseau aux Etats-Unis : esquisse d'une étude. SVEC 25:899–959, 1963. **4947**

" La présence de Rousseau dans la culture nord-américaine est aussi évidente que difficile à isoler. Et surtout, les voies par lesquelles Jean-Jacques a pénétré dans la vie intellectuelle du nouveau continent demeurent, partiellement du moins, mystérieuses " (p. 956).

Exploratory investigation of R.'s influence in America.

Leśnodorski, B. La pensée politique de Rousseau en Pologne. AHRF 34:497–514, 1962. **4948**

" C'est dans les ' Considérations ' que les plus sensibles et les plus intelligents patriotes polonais trouvèrent une raison d'espérer, malgré les sombres perspectives d'un avenir immédiat, en répétant, avec leur auteur, que la nation continue à vivre, même après la perte de l'indépendance " (p. 505).

An investigation and appraisal of R.'s actual influence on Polish thought and aspiration.

McDonald, Joan. Rousseau and the French Revolution, 1762–1791. London, Univ. of London, Athlone press, 1965. 190 p. **4949**

" The pre-revolutionary and the revolutionary cult had a common rationale in the basic and fundamental idea of the moral regeneration of mankind " (p. 164).

Careful, comprehensive, and persuasive analysis of the uses made of R. before and during the Revolution. Invocation of his name and authority was for different purposes, and yet was not an irrational process. He symbolized the human aspiration for justice.

McNeil, Gordon H. The anti-revolutionary Rousseau. AHR 58:808–23, 1953. **4950**

The " stereotype of Rousseau's close causal connection with the French Revolution is particularly open to question in the light of the essentially conservative, anti-revolutionary tone of much of his political thought..." (p. 808).

A more intellectual than contextual assessement of R.'s connections with the Revolution.

Mondolfo, Rodolfo. Rousseau e la coscienza moderna. Florence, Nuova Italia, 1954. 114 p. **4951**

An appreciation of R.'s impact upon the modern moral consciousness, based upon a thorough and sympathetic examination of his moral and political novelty. Reviews : M. Campagnalo-Bouvier in AJJR 33:356–57, 1953–55.

Mornet, Daniel. The development of literature and culture in the eighteenth century. See 3385. **4952**

" What Rousseau did try to teach was that actually we can all seek and find happiness in the simple life and the simple pleasures which Providence never denies us.... in France and Switzerland, and to some extent in Germany, the ideal of

Rousseau had a prestige and influence of the first order " (p. 323).

Illuminating observations on the meaning which R.'s writings had for the cultured.

Palmer, R. R. Jean-Jacques Rousseau et les Etats-Unis. AHRF 34:529–40, 1962. **4953**

" L'influence de Rousseau ne disparut pas, mais elle s'infiltra dans des chenaux différents et plus profonds, dans les problèmes de religion, de psychologie, d'éducation, répandant des idées de liberté personnelle, et d'une dignité commune à tous les hommes. Elles ont ainsi continué d'agir sur les conceptions américaines de la justice politique " (p. 539–40).

Comprehensive and penetrating appraisal of R.'s influence in both its diffuseness and particularity.

Passerin d'Entrèves, Alessandro. Natural law; an introduction to legal philosophy. London, Hutchinson's university library, 1951. 126 p. **4954**

" Rousseau's theory of the ' general will ' is the real source of the theory of the ethical state " (p. 75).

An evaluation of the historical importance of the theory of the general will presented in the context of the author's study of the doctrine of natural law. See particularly p. 74–76.

Roddier, Henri. J.-J. Rousseau en Angleterre au XVIIIᵉ siècle; l'œuvre et l'homme. Boivin, 1950. 435 p. See 5710. **4955**

C.-E. Engel in her review infra: " L'étude de M. Roddier est d'une richesse de documentation, d'une précision dans l'observation, d'une netteté dans l'expression qui ne faiblissent jamais."

Remarkable study of the influence of R.'s works, comprehensive, detailed, and persuasive.

Reviews : J.-M. Carré in RLC 24:464–67, 1950; C.-E. Engel in AJJR 32:227–31, 1950–52; R. Leigh in MLR 46:272–76, 1951; E. Mossner in RR 42:65–67, 1951.

Shklar, Judith N. Rousseau's two models : Sparta and the age of gold. PSQ 81:25–51, 1966. **4956**

" The just civic order is not based on extremes of inequality, but it cannot expect to be either fully egalitarian or democratic " (p. 37).

An analysis of R.'s ideas on justice and equality in the light of his historical models; this article is consistent with the work of Polin (4886).

Soboul, Albert. Audience des lumières; classes populaires et rousseauisme sous la Révolution. AHRF 34:421–38, 1962. **4957**

"Dans l'œuvre de Rousseau, le monde de l'artisanat contemple avec complaisance sa propre image. De l'un à l'autre, plus peut-être que filiation, il y a résonance" (p. 438).

Meticulous and subtle appreciation of R.'s meaning for this social segment during the Revolution.

— Jean-Jacques Rousseau et le jacobinisme. *In:* Etudes sur le Contrat social de Jean-Jacques Rousseau. *See* 4791. p. 405–24. **4958**

"Entre rousseauisme et jacobinisme, il y a à la fois identité et dépassement, parfois contradiction" (p. 424).

The Jacobins were inspired by R. and driven to violate his political principles; both lacked realistic appreciation of the social requisites of policy.

Strange, M. Jean-Jacques Rousseau et ses contemporains russes. AHRF 34:515–28, 1962. **4959**

"Les sujets qu'elles traitaient présentaient une acuité particulière pour les contemporains russes, dans le domaine des conceptions sociales, philosophiques et politiques; ils invitaient à réviser fondamentalement les anciennes opinions et les vieilles notions" (p. 528).

Unusual study of R.'s influence.

Talmon, Jacob Leib. Totalitarian democracy (Rousseau). *In his:* The rise of totalitarian democracy. Boston, Beacon press, 1952. p. 38–49. **4960**

"Rousseau's sovereign is the externalized general will, and ... stands for essentially the same as the natural harmonious order. In marrying this concept with the principle of popular sovereignty and popular self-expression, Rousseau gave rise to totalitarian democracy" (p. 43).

R.'s rationalism is presented as the intellectual antecedent of modern political authoritarianism.

Taylor, Samuel S. B. Rousseau's contemporary reputation in France. SVEC 27: 1545–74, 1963. **4961**

"In Rousseau's day ... the *Héloïse* and *Emile* formed the bed-rock on which his reputation was based" (p. 1554).

Illuminating study of R.'s contemporary significance, which suggests that this was less political than moral.

Trénard, Louis. La diffusion du Contrat social, 1762–1832. *In:* Etudes sur le Contrat social de Jean-Jacques Rousseau. *See* 4791. p. 425–58. **4962**

Prior to the Revolution the *Contrat social* was not well known. During the Revolution it achieved a vulgarized popularity and afterwards became the subject of scholarly study.

Voisine, Jacques. J.-J. Rousseau en Angleterre à l'époque romantique; les écrits autobiographiques et la légende. Didier, 1956. x, 482 p. **4963**

"Depuis la Révolution française l'influence de l'homme n'avait cessé de grandir par rapport à celle de ses écrits —exception pour la seule *Nouvelle Héloïse* " (p. 433).

Comprehensive and penetrating study of R.'s influence, moral, political, and literary.

Reviews : D. Bernet in Tro 106:121–23, Oct. 1956; G.-A. Bonnard in EA 11:59–63, 1958; A. Engstrom in CL 13:91–94, 1961; M. Gerhardt in Est 39:216–19, 1958; F. Green in FS 11:64–66, 1957; R. Leigh in RLC 31:285–91, 1957; R. Osmont in RHL 58:384–86, 1958; C. Pichois in Lmod 50:243–44, 1956; R. Pouilliart in LR 13:340–43, 1959; H. Roddier in AJJR 34:202–07, 1956–58; L. Trénard in Ihist 19:162–63, 1957.

Volpe, Galvano della. Du discours sur l'inégalité à l'Etat et la révolution. Eur 391–92:181–88, Nov.–Dec. 1961. **4964**

"Comment nier que l'attention extrême du marxisme-léninisme au problème de la reconnaissance économico-proportionnelle, par la société, des *différences* entre les individus et de leurs *capacités* et *nécessités*, exprime la continuité et le développement, sur un nouveau plan historique, du plus original esprit égalitaire de Rousseau ? " (p. 188).

An appraisal of R.'s significance in a Marxist perspective.

Contemporary Relevance and
Research Perspectives

Barbu, Zevedei. Problems of historical psychology. London, Routledge and Kegan Paul, 1960. x, 222 p. **4965**

" ... historical psychology opens a new perspective to the study of the human mind. As a branch of psychology its task is to study the human mind as an historical phenomenon " (p. 4).

Barbu's work in historical psychology

would appear to be an extension of R.'s theory of mind.

Berlin, Isaiah. Does political theory still exist? *In:* Philosophy, politics and society (second series). Ed. by Peter Laslett and W. G. Runciman. New York, Barnes and Noble, 1962. p. 1–33.   **4966**

"... attempts by the *philosophes* of the eighteenth century to turn philosophy, and particularly moral and political philosophy, into empirical science, into individual and social psychology, did not succeed. They failed over politics because our political notions are part of our conception of what it is to be human, and this is not solely a question of fact, as facts are conceived by the natural sciences ..." (p. 22).

R.'s resolutely normative approach to politics deserves, in this light, comparative re-examination.

Bluhm, William T. Theories of the political system : classics of political thought and modern political analysis. Englewood Cliffs, Prentice-Hall, 1965. p. 36–88.   **4967**

" In refashioning the traditional view of the common man, Professor Friedrich in effect returns to the image created by Rousseau, the first great theorist of democracy " (p. 380).
See Carl J. Friedrich, *The new image of the common man* (Boston, Beacon press, 1950). An example of the continuing influence exerted by R. on liberal democratic theory.

Burns, J. H. Du côté de chez Vaughan : Rousseau revisited. PolS 12:229–34, 1964.   **4968**

This article illustrates the way in which R.'s thought is being reevaluated in the light of the work of Derathé, Plamenatz, and others.

Chapman, John W. Political theory : logical structure and enduring types. APP 5:57–96, 1965.   **4969**

" Rousseau held that justice is intrinsic to human nature in the sense that men whose moral potentialities have been fully developed come to feel that a life of justice is the only life worth living " (p. 90).

Fabre, Jean. Réalité et utopie dans la pensée politique de Rousseau. AJJR 35:181–216, 1959–62.   **4970**

A review of interpretations of R.'s thought and an appreciation of his realism and concern for authenticity.

Fetscher, Iring. Rousseau's concepts of freedom in the light of his philosophy of history. *In:* Nomos IV : Liberty. Ed. by Carl J. Friedrich. New York, Atherton press, 1962. p. 29–56.   **4971**

" His rejection of inalienable rights of freedom for individuals and of party divisions in society is the direct result of his aversion to the social and economic dynamics of the modern world, of his insight into the spiritual burdens and moral dangers which threaten mankind in the era of liberalism and free competition " (p. 56).

R. is presented as fearful of the moral consequences of economic progress achieved under liberal auspices.

Frankel, Charles. Bureaucracy and democracy in the new Europe. *In:* A new Europe? Ed. by Stephen R. Graubard. Boston, Houghton Mifflin, 1964. p. 538–59.   **4972**

Suggests need for reformulation of democratic theory in ways less dependent upon Rousseauistic models.

Hoffman, Stanley. Rousseau on war and peace. APSR 57:317–33, 1963.   **4973**

" ... Rousseau's remarks point to the same conclusions as the exhaustive and systematic study of peace and war recently completed by the most profound contemporary writer on the subject, Raymond Aron " (p. 317).

R.'s theory of war is found to be supported by historical analysis and evidence.

Jouvenel, Bertrand de. Rousseau, the pessimistic evolutionist. YFS 28:83–96, 1961–62.   **4974**

R. seen as cautionary with respect to the psychological and moral tensions associated with economic and political change.

Kateb, George. Aspects of Rousseau's political thought. PSQ 76:519–43, 1961.   **4975**

" ... the principles of distributive justice, autonomy, and fair play are principles the absence of which reduce men in society to the status of slavery. They are principles, which, taken together, constitute the necessary conditions for the creation of a society of *persons*, in the strictest meaning of that word " (p. 542).

Kateb's article combines an appreciation of Derathé's work with the contention that R.'s central concerns were for justice, fairness, and moral autonomy. *See also* John Rawls, *Justice as fairness* in PhR 67: 164–94, 1958, and John W. Chapman, *Justice and fairness* in *Nomos VI: Justice*, ed. by Carl J. Friedrich and John W. Chapman (New York, Atherton press, 1963), p. 147–69.

Lakoff, Sanford A. Equality in political philosophy. Cambridge, Harvard univ. press, 1964. p. 105–12. **4976**

" Like Calvin and Hobbes, but very much unlike Liberals and Socialists, the Rousseau of the second *Discourse* could not conceive of the possibility of an equality in society other than an equality of depravity " (p. 111).

Provocative and somewhat overly sharply focused examination of R.'s views on equality presented in a historical perspective.

Lindblom, Charles E. The intelligence of democracy; decision making through mutual adjustment. New York, Free Press, 1965. viii, 352 p. **4977**

" A simple idea is elaborated in this book : that people can coordinate with each other without anyone's coordinating them, without a dominant common purpose, and without rules that fully prescribe their relations to each other " (p. 3).

Lindblom's explication of the rationality evident in democratic political processes constitutes a modernized version of the theory of the general will, not only as presented by R. but also in the work of Bernard Bosanquet and Mary Parker Follett.

Löwith, Karl. The problem of bourgeois society. *In his:* From Hegel to Nietzsche; the revolution in nineteenth-century thought. Trans. by David E. Green. New York, Holt, Rinehart and Winston, 1964. p. 235–62. **4978**

" Rousseau's writings contain the first and clearest statement of the human problem of bourgeois society. It consists in the fact that man, in bourgeois society, is not a unified whole. On the one hand, he is a private individual, and on the other, a citizen of the state ... " (p. 235).

Suggestive appraisal of R.'s historical significance.

Plamenatz, John. The belief in progress. *In his:* Man and society. New York, McGraw-Hill, 1963. 2:409–57. **4979**

" Neither Condorcet nor Comte saw

the real point of Rousseau's indictment of modern society : that the increase of knowledge has social consequences which strengthen the harmful passions " (p. 456).

Plamenatz throws new light upon the meaning and the significance of R.'s first *Discourse*.

Ricoeur, Paul. Finitude et culpabilité. Aubier, 1960. 1:132–62; 2:285–321. **4980**

" ... un mythe de chute n'est possible que dans le contexte d'un mythe de création et d'innocence. Si l'on avait compris cela ... on n'aurait pas plus accusé Rousseau d'inconsistance quand il professait, avec opiniâtreté, la bonté naturelle de l'homme *et* sa perversité historique et culturelle " (1:161).

Brilliant although highly specific insights into R.'s thought in the light of the phenomenology of myth.

Runciman, W. G., and **A. K. Sen.** Games, justice and the general will. Mind 74:554–62, 1965. **4981**

" The conflict between the will of all and the general will arises not because the individual must be required to change his preference orderings, but because of the difference between the outcomes of individual strategy and of enforced collusion which arises under the conditions of the non-cooperative, non-zero-sum game " (p. 557).

An interpretation of the general will in terms of game theory and the contractual conception of justice presented by John Rawls. The general will is an enforceable alternative to mutually destructive atomistic strategies. As such the general will wills justice, but not everything that may be considered just, for justice is the broader concept.

Strauss, Leo. The city and man. Chicago, Rand McNally, 1964. 245 p. **4982**

" The moral law demands from each virtuous activity, *i.e.* the full and uniform development of all his faculties and their exercise jointly with others. Such a development is not possible as long as every one is crippled as a consequence of the division of labor or of social inequality. It is therefore a moral duty to contribute to the establishment of a society which is radically egalitarian and at the same time on the highest level of the development of man " (p. 40).

Provocatively comparative observations on R.'s theory of equality and that of classical thinkers. *See* especially p. 38–42.

Waltz, Kenneth N. The third image : international conflict and international anarchy. *In his:* Man, the state and war. New York, Columbia univ. press, 1959. p. 159–86.   **4983**

" Rousseau's explanation of the origins of war among states is, in broad outline, the final one so long as we operate within a nation-state system. It is a final explanation because it does not hinge on accidental causes—irrationalities in men, defects in states—but upon his theory of the framework within which *any* accident can bring about a war " (p. 231).

R.'s theory of war is presented and appraised in the light of alternatives.

Weil, Eric. Philosophical and political thought in Europe today. *In:* A new Europe ? Ed. by Stephen R. Graubard. Boston, Houghton, Mifflin, 1964. p. 581–601. **4984**

" ... the problems of history, sociology, politics, psychology need not only correction, but radical reformulation " (p. 600).

A thinker, appreciative of R.'s political theory, appears to call for a Rousseauean effort.

Wolin, Sheldon S. Rousseau : the idea of community. *In his:* Politics and vision; continuity and innovation in Western political thought. Boston, Little, Brown, 1960. p. 368–76.   **4985**

" The quest for community undertaken by so many writers, who have reflected so many different political persuasions, suggests that Rousseau's conception of community has turned into a spectre haunting the age of organization, a continuing critic of the sort of life lived within large-scale depersonalized units, a reminder that human needs demanded more than rational relationships and efficient routines " (p. 375).

An adequate political philosophy must take account of the quality of human relationships.

CHAPTER IX. DENIS DIDEROT

(Nos. 4986–5362)

Arthur M. Wilson *and* Mary T. Wilson

Bibliography

See: Bowen (5280), Bowen (5281), Fabre (5146), Lough (5317), Proust (5335), Smiley (5349), Wilson (5103).

Alatri, Paolo. Problemi e figure del Settecento politico francese nella recente storiografia. StS 5:137–68, 333–79, 1964. **4986**
Excellent critical survey of recent writings about the French Enlightenment. Concerns aspects of D. principally. Reprinted and updated *in his: Voltaire, Diderot e il partito filosofico* (Messina and Florence, G. D'Anna, 1965), p. 339–476.

Belaval, Yvon. Nouvelles recherches sur Diderot. Cr 12[11]:793–99, Sept.–Oct. 1955; 14[12]:291–318, Apr. 1956; 14[12]:400–22, May 1956; 14[12]:534–53, June 1956. **4987**
Together with 4988 forms a remarkable series of bibliographical and critical articles, under the form of lengthy reviews of important eds. and monographs being published at that time.

— Le philosophe Diderot. Cr 8:230–53, Mar. 1952. *See* 4987. **4988**

Boutet de Monvel, A. Etat présent des études diderotesques. IL 4:131–36, 1952. **4989**
Excellent critical *aperçu* of eds., monographs, and articles published between 1938 and 1952.

Casini, Paolo. Studi su Diderot. RassF 7:5–26, 150–73, 234–54, 1958. **4990**
Remarkably perceptive and comprehensive criticism of books and monographs concerning D.
Review : E. Benedetti in SF 4:557, 1960.

Centre polonais de recherches scientifiques de Paris. Les traductions polonaises de l'œuvre de Diderot et les études polonaises le concernant. *In their:* Bulletin 8:32–34, Dec. 1950. **4991**

Dieckmann, Herbert. Inventaire du fonds Vandeul et inédits de Diderot. Geneva, Droz, 1951. xlix, 282 p. **4992**
Indispensable tool of criticism and research.
Reviews : R. Niklaus in MLR 47:404–05, 1952; J. Pommier in RHL 51:379–83, 1951; N. Torrey in RR 43:225–27, 1952; I. Wade in Sym 6:204–07, 1952.

Fromm, Hans. Bibliographie deutscher Übersetzungen aus dem Französischen, 1700–1948. *See* 3342. **4993**
V. 2, 266–71 : Diderot.

Proust, Jacques. Diderot et le xviiie siècle français en U.R.S.S. RHL 54:320–28, 1954. *See* 3366. **4994**
Bibliographical survey of Soviet works since 1917 concerning the 18th century in France. For appreciative comment on this article, with amplifications (anonymous), *see: Deni Didro i russkaîa kul'tura XVIII veka* in VFil 234–35, 1955[2].

Svodnyĭ katalog russkoĭ knigi grazhdanskoĭ pechati XVIII veka, 1725–1800 [Union catalog of Russian books printed in non-liturgical type in the xviiith century]. Moscow, 1962–64. 2 v. **4995**
I, 290–91. Items 1860 to 1867 are works of D. translated into Russian before 1800.

Editions

Collected Correspondence

Diderot, Denis. Correspondance. Ed. by Georges Roth. Editions de Minuit, 1955– v. **4996**
Ably edited, complete, and indispensable. Enriched by constant reference to contemporary events or to happenings in D.'s *ambiance.* Previously unpublished D. letters that have appeared since 1950 are not separately listed in this bibliography if they are now incorporated in the Roth ed. For the dating of some of the letters, *see* Philip Koch, *Redating a letter*

to Sophie Volland in Sym 11:296–302, 1957; Jacques Proust, *A propos d'un fragment de lettre de Diderot* in SF 3:88–91, 1959; and Jean Varloot, *La date des lettres 408 et 483 à Sophie Volland* in RHL 61: 419–22, 1961.

Reviews (chronologically listed) : Y. Belaval in NNRF 8:140–42, July 1956; R. Mortier in RBP 34:1093–95, 1956; R. Mortier in RBP 35:823–25, 1957; N. Torrey in RR 48:228–29, 1957; A. Wilson in MLN 72:77–79, 1957; P. Vernière in RHL 59:103–05, 1959; Gita May in RR 51:136–38, 1960; Y. Benot in PRRM n.s. 99:98–105, 1961; A. Delorme in Rsyn n.s. 83:373–75, 1962; R. Mortier in RBP 41:1256–60, 1963; J. Voisine in IL 15:32, 1963; J. Pappas in DS 6:305–11, 1964; A. Freer in SF 9:162–65, 1965; A. Freer in SF 10:160–61, 1966.

Collected Works

Diderot, Denis. Contes. Ed. by Herbert Dieckmann. London, Univ. of London press, 1963. 207 p.			**4997**

Contains : *La marquise de Claye et le comte de Saint-Alban, Cinqmars et Derville, Les deux amis de Bourbonne, Entretien d'un père avec ses enfants, Ceci n'est pas un conte,* and *Madame de la Carlière.* Excellent introduction and notes, as is never failing with this editor.

Reviews : B. Guy in DS 6:369–71, 1964; J. Loy in RR 55:300–01, 1964; J. Proust in RHL 65:317, 1965.

— Diderot, interpreter of nature; selected writings. Trans. by Jean Stewart and Jonathan Kemp. 2nd ed. New York, International Publishers, 1963. viii, 358 p.	**4998**

Unaltered, therefore unimproved, 2nd ed. of 2214.

— Diderot par lui-même; images et textes présentés par Charly Guyot. Editions du Seuil, 1953. 191 p.			**4999**

Profusely illustrated anthology, with a cogent introduction and a bibliography. Useful for both beginners and experts.

Review : J. Loy in RR 45:152–54, 1954.

— Izbrannye ateisticheskie proizvedeniĩa [Selected atheistical writings]. Moscow, Akademiĩa nauk SSSR, 1956. 477 p.	**5000**

Wide selection of D.'s philosophical writings, done by various translators. Introductory essay by Kh. N. Momdzhĩan.

— Le neveu de Rameau. Ed. by Herbert Dieckmann. Club du meilleur livre, 1957. xlviii, 272 p.			**5001**

Reliable ed., with good biographical notes and a chronology. Illustrated. Contains also : *Entretien entre d'Alembert et Diderot, Le rêve de d'Alembert,* and *Suite de l'Entretien.*

Review : E. Benedetti in SF 2:322, 1958.

— Œuvres. Ed. by André Billy. Gallimard, 1951. 1474 p. (Bibliothèque de la Pléiade)			**5002**

Like 2213A, this contains no *Salons* and no *Correspondance.*

— Œuvres choisies. Editions sociales, 1952–64. 7 v.			**5003**

An admirably edited series with meaty introductions, usually with a Marxist orientation. The several editors (Yves Benot, Roland Desné, Jacques Proust, and Jean Varloot), all of them competent scholars, either avail themselves of the best texts already published or establish the text themselves.

Reviews : (I and II) A. Delorme in Rsyn n.s. 33:208–09, 1953; (II) Y. Benot in Eur 102–03:233–36, June–July 1954; (III) R. Desné in PRRM n.s. 108:98–109, 1963; J. Proust in RHL 63:281–87, 1963; (VI) M. Duchet in PRRM n.s. 93:118–20, 1960; A. Freer in SF 5:562–63, 1961.

— Œuvres esthétiques. Ed. by Paul Vernière. Garnier, 1959. xxvii, 843 p.		**5004**

Broad selection. Up-to-date editing of texts, giving variants from the *fonds Vandeul* and the Leningrad mss. Introductions and bibliographies.

Reviews : Gita May (very critical) in MP 58:286–88, 1960–61; R. Niklaus in FS 14:363–65, 1960; C. Rosso in SF 4:157–58, 1960.

— Œuvres philosophiques. Ed. by Paul Vernière. Garnier, 1956. xxvi, 647 p.	**5005**

Wide selection, up to date, and ably edited. Introductions and bibliographies.

Reviews : P. Casini in RassF 6:79, 1957; O. Klapp in Archiv 195:82, 1958–59; R. Mortier in RBP 36: 276–77, 1958; R. Niklaus in FS 11:356–57, 1957; R. Shackleton in MLR 52:283–85, 1957.

— Œuvres politiques. Ed. by Paul Vernière. Garnier, 1963. xliv, 523 p.		**5006**

Excellent ed., containing also 16 photographs and reproductions of some ms pages. Includes introductions, bibliographies, and variants. Contents : some *Encyclopédie* articles ; the *Apologie de l'abbé Galiani* (B.N., *nouv. acq. fr.* 13.765, never before published, Benot [5014] having used *nouv. acq. fr.* 13.755); *Pages contre un tyran; Principes de politique des souverains* (using the Leningrad ms); *Entretiens avec Catherine II* (all of the conversations that were political in nature, reprinted from Tourneux [2223], modified in light of the information given by Kuz'min [5311]; *Observations sur le Nakaz* (B.N., *nouv. acq. fr.* 24.939); and some miscellaneous fragments.

Reviews : Y. Benot in PRRM n.s. 114: 110–19, 1965; G. Cazes in Cr 21:154–64, Feb. 1965; J. Chouillet in RHL 65:318–20, 1965; A. Hytier in DS 6:371–73, 1964; J. Spink in FS 19:189–90, 1965.

— Œuvres romanesques. Ed. by Henri Bénac. Garnier, 1951. 906 p. **5007**

Standard, inexpensive ed., with brief introduction, adequate notes, no information about the various D. mss and texts, nor indeed what texts are followed in this ed. Reprinted in 1959.

Review : A. Freer in SF 5:163, 1961.

— Quatre contes. Ed. by Jacques Proust. Geneva, Droz, 1964. lxxix, 211 p. **5008**

Authoritative texts of *Mystification, Les deux amis de Bourbonne, Ceci n'est pas un conte,* and *Mme de la Carlière.* Contains an excellent introduction, informative notes and appendixes, and a glossary of 18th-century usage.

Reviews : A. Hytier in RR 56:216–17, 1965; J. Proust in PRRM n.s. 122:139–41, 1965; M. Roelens in RScH n.s. 118:290–92, 1965.

— Rameau's nephew and other works. Trans. by Jacques Barzun and Ralph H. Bowen. Garden City, N. Y., Doubleday, 1956. xviii, 333 p. [*Republished:* Indianapolis, Bobbs Merrill, 1964. 317 p.] **5009**

Contains also : *D'Alembert's dream, Supplement to Bougainville's voyage, The two friends from Bourbonne, A conversation between a father and his children, The Encyclopedia* [D.'s article *Encyclopédie*], and *Regrets on parting with my old dressing gown.* Skilfully translated.

— Selected philosophical writings. Ed. by John Lough. Cambridge, Cambridge univ. press, 1953. vii, 222 p. **5010**

Competent annotated ed.

— Le siècle des lumières : Denis Diderot. Mazenod, 1957. 235 p. **5011**

Contains : *Le neveu de Rameau, Entretien entre d'Alembert et Diderot, Le rêve de d'Alembert, Suite de l'Entretien,* and *Supplément au Voyage de Bougainville.*

Illustrated. Useful essay by Pierre Josserand (p. 218–30).

— Textes inédits. *In:* Dieckmann, Herbert. Inventaire du fonds Vandeul et inédits de Diderot. *See* 4992. p. 185–282. **5012**

Comprises many interesting and significant fragments. Also (p. 236–53), the *Lettre apologétique de l'abbé Raynal à M. Grimm.*

Single Works

Defourneaux, Marcelin. La biographie d'Olavide par Diderot. *In his:* Pablo de Olavide ou l'afrancesado (1725–1803). Presses univ. de France, 1959. p. 471–75. **5013**

Published, with brief introduction, from the *fonds Vandeul.* For a very interesting discussion of D.'s relations with Olavide *see* 5113.

Diderot, Denis. Apologie de l'abbé Galiani. PRRM n.s. 55:12–35, 1954. **5014**

A very important text, discovered in the *fonds Vandeul* (B.N., *nouv. acq. fr.* 13.755), preceded by useful introductory remarks (p. 3–11), *Un inédit de Diderot,* by Yves Benot. An earlier text (B.N., *nouv. acq. fr.* 13.765) is made available by Vernière (5006), p. 69–124.

— Diderot et Falconet; correspondance : les six premières lettres, texte en partie inédit. Ed. by Herbert Dieckmann and Jean Seznec. Frankfurt am Main, Klostermann, 1959. 73 p. **5015**

Meticulously edited, and with an excellent introduction. Illustrated.

Reviews : E. Leube in RJa 10:249–53, 1959; A. Wilson in RR 51:229–30, 1960.

— Eléments de physiologie. Ed. by Jean Mayer. Didier, 1964. lxxxi, 387 p. **5016**

Excellent critical ed. based on the ms in the *fonds Vandeul.* The substantial introduction underlines the originality of D.'s observations upon the relation between memory and imagination and emphasizes the largeness of scope of the whole work.

— Est-il bon ? Est-il méchant ? AvS 123:1–29, 1956. *Also in:* L'avant-scène de IT, Supplément au no. 6:1–29, Spring 1956. **5017**

These eds. were occasioned by the production of *Est-il bon ? Est-il méchant ?* at the Comédie Française on Nov. 22, 1955. The latter ed. is followed (p.30–31) by excerpts from 10 leading press reviews of the production.

— Est-il bon? Est-il méchant? Ed. by Jack Undank. Geneva, Institut et musée Voltaire, 1961. 407 p. (SVEC, 16)   **5018**
Authoritative and definitive. Reproduces the *fonds Vandeul* ms, lists all variants from other texts, and confronts page by page *La pièce et le prologue* with *Est-il bon? Est-il méchant?* Excellent critical introduction, including (p. 40–100) *La portée autobiographique de la pièce.*
Reviews : J. D. Candaux in DS 6:363–64, 1964; R. Grimsley in MLR 57:612–13, 1962; J. Loy in RR 53:230–33, 1962; R. Niklaus in FS 16:376–78, 1962; J. Proust in RHL 63:316–19, 1963.

— Jacques le fataliste et son maître. Ed. by Yvon Belaval. Club français du livre, 1953. 379, 58 p.   **5019**
Attractive illustrated ed., with excellent notes and an important critical essay. The text is from Assézat-Tourneux (2209, t. 6, p. 9–287) modified by collation with the ms in the *fonds Vandeul.*
Review : P. Vernière in RHL 55:78, 1955.

— Jacques the fatalist and his master. Trans. and ed. by J. Robert Loy. New York, New York univ. press, 1959. xxii, 289 p.   **5020**
Reviews : R. Arndt in RR 50:220–23, 1959; A. Freer in SF 5:354, 1961; R. Niklaus in FS 14:254–55, 1960.

— Jacques le fataliste. Ed. by J. Robert Loy. New York, Dell, 1962. 302 p.   **5021**
Text follows the Assézat-Tourneux ed. (2209, t. 6, p. 9–287) except where the *fonds Vandeul* and the Leningrad texts agree on a variant. Interesting introduction. Notes especially useful for readers whose mother tongue is not French.

— Jacques le fataliste et son maître. Michel, 1963. 319 p.   **5022**
Préface (p. 7–22) by André Billy, incorporating his *Diderot et le mystère de ses œuvres posthumes* in FL 4, May 11, 1957.

— Lettre sur les aveugles. Ed. by Robert Niklaus. 2nd ed. Geneva, Droz, 1963. lxviii, 123 p.   **5023**
Definitive ed. Excellent introduction, notes, and bibliography.
Reviews : (1st ed., 1951) L. Crocker in RR 43:227–30, 1952; J. Lough in FS 6:255–56, 1952; P. Vernière in RHL 53:375–76, 1953.

— Lettre sur les sourds et muets. Ed. by Paul Hugo Meyer. Geneva, Droz, 1965. xxvi, 232 p. (DS, 7)   **5024**
Definitive ed., with numerous and thorough notes. The scholarly introduction traces the influence of the *Lettre* upon the esthetic ideas of the century. Introductory essay by Georges May.
Review : P. Alatri in SF 10:158, 1966.

— Memoirs of a nun (La religieuse). Trans. with an introduction by Francis Birrell. London, Elek books, 1959. 222 p.   **5025**
Brief but weighty introduction; the whole reprinted from the 1928 London ed.

— Mystification ou histoire des portraits. Ed. by Yves Benot. Preface by Pierre Daix. Illustrated by Picasso. Editeurs français réunis, 1954. 93 p.   **5026**
The text of this *inédit* from the *fonds Vandeul* was first published by Pierre Daix under the same title in LetF, 1, 10, Feb. 4–11, 1954; 12, Feb. 11–18, 1954. *See also* the excellent article by Yves Benot, *A propos de Diderot: Mystification, ironie romantique et recherche de la vérité* in PRRM n.s. 82:65–74, 1958.

— Le neveu de Rameau; texte établi sur le manuscrit autographe avec introduction et notes par Edward J. Geary. Cambridge, Mass., Integral Editions, 1959. xxi, 108 p.   **5027**
Text of the Monval ms in the Pierpont Morgan Library; competent introduction, notes, chronology, and bibliography.

— Le neveu de Rameau ou satire 2de accompagné de la satire première. Edition du deux cent cinquantenaire. Ed. by Roland Desné. Club des amis du livre progressiste, 1963. lxxvii, 186 p.   **5028**
Scholarly and deluxe ed., superbly illustrated. Uses the text as established in the Fabre ed. (2221A) collated with the holograph at the Pierpont Morgan Library. Scholars will want to supplement the introduction by consulting Roland Desné, *Le neveu de Rameu dans l'ombre et la lumière du XVIIIᵉ siècle* in SVEC 25:493–507, 1963.
Reviews : O. Fellows in DS 6:367–69, 1964; A. Hytier in RR 55:297, 1964; M. Launay in RHL 65:706–08, 1965; J. Loy in FR 38:121–22, 1964–65; G. Roger in Eur 421–22:290–96, May–June 1964.

— Le neveu de Rameau. Adapted [for the theater] by Jacques-Henri Duval and Pierre Fresnay. AvS 303:15–27, Jan. 15, 1964.   **5029**

Text of the adaptation presented at the Théâtre de la Michodière, February 4, 1963, preceded (p. 6–12) by brief articles by Ferdinand Alquié, Pierre Fresnay, Jacques-Henri Duval, and Paul-Louis Mignon. Illustrated.

— Paradoxe sur le comédien avec, recueillies et présentées par Marc Blanquet, les opinions de Marcel Achard, *et al.* Nord-Sud, 1949. 189 p.　　　　　　　　　　　　**5030**

Without notes or introduction, but with an interesting collection of opinions by 21 prominent French actors, actresses, and directors concerning the validity of D.'s paradox.

— The paradox of acting by Denis Diderot and Masks or faces? by William Archer. Introduction by Lee Strasberg. New York, Hill and Wang, 1957. xiv, 240 p.　**5031**

Reprints of the Walter Herries Pollock translation of 1883 of the *Paradoxe sur le comédien* (*see* 2216) together with Archer's work of 1888, an excellent discussion at book length of D.'s theory of acting by the eminent translator of Ibsen.

— Pensées philosophiques.　Ed. by Robert Niklaus.　3rd ed.　Geneva, Droz, 1965. xxvii, 75 p.　　　　　　　　　**5032**

Authoritative and definitive critical ed. Revised version of 1st ed., 1950 (Review : A. Vartanian in RR 42:211–12, 1951), and 2nd ed., 1957.

— Le pour et le contre; correspondance polémique sur le respect de la postérité, Pline et les anciens auteurs qui ont parlé de peinture et de sculpture de Diderot et Falconet. Ed. by Yves Benot. Editeurs français réunis, 1958. 384 p.　　　　　　　　**5033**

Contains elaborate notes and lists of variants ed., comparing the Assézat-Tourneux ed. (2209) with B.N. mss *nouv. acq. fr.* 24.936 (used as the basic text of this edition) and 24.983. Illustrated.

Reviews : H. Hinterhäuser in Archiv 197:231–33, 1960–61; E. Leube in RJa 10:249–53, 1959.

— La religieuse. Ed. by Robert Mauzi. Colin, 1961. xliv, 240 p.　　　　　　**5034**

Adequate text, based on a ms in the *fonds Vandeul*, plus a stimulating introduction. Suggests that D. was greatly interested in the phenomenology of alienation.

Reviews : J. Ehrard in DS 6:365–67, 1964; R. Niklaus in FS 17:264–65, 1963; J. Proust in RHL 63:313–15, 1963.

— La religieuse. Ed. by Jean Parrish. Geneva, Institut et musée Voltaire, 1963. 343 p. (SVEC, 22)　　　　　　　　　　**5035**

Text of the *fonds Vandeul* autograph ms, with variants from the 2 other *fonds Vandeul* mss and from the versions in Stockholm and Leningrad, as well as from the 1796 and 1798 printed eds. The introduction consists of a chronological study of the changes in plot and structure made by D. and does not purport to be a full-dress critical study of D.'s thought and style.

Reviews: R. Brooks in MLN 80:406–08, 1965; J. Loy in RR 55:297–300, 1964; Georges May in MLR 59:295–97, 1964; R. Niklaus in FS 18:385–86, 1964; R. Pomeau in RHL 64:306, 1964.

— Le rêve de d'Alembert, Entretien entre d'Alembert et Diderot et Suite de l'Entretien. Ed. by Paul Vernière. Didier, 1951. lxix, 166 p.　　　　　　　　　**5036**

Excellent introduction, though the text itself has been superseded by the Varloot ed. (5003, t. 3).

Review : H. Dieckmann in RR 43:139–43, 1952.

— Salons.　Ed. by Jean Seznec and Jean Adhémar.　Oxford, Clarendon press, 1957– . 4 v.　　　　　　　　　　　　**5037**

Admirable and definitive ed., profusely illustrated and with an abundance of correlative information.　In connection with v. 3, *see also:* Otis E. Fellows and Donal O'Gorman, *Another addition to the Salon de 1767?* in DS 3:215–17, 1961; and Jean Seznec, *L'autographe du Salon de 1767* in CAIEF 13:331–38, 1961.

Reviews : (v. 1, 1759. 1761. 1763). E. Bedford in MLR 53:589–91, 1958; H. Dieckmann in RHL 59:225–30, 1959; M. Gilman in FS 12:164–66, 1958; E. Marcu in MLN 73:629–31, 1958; Gita May in RR 49:132–35, 1958; R. Taylor in FR 32:281–82, 1958–59. (v. 2, 1765). E. Bedford in MLR 57:261–62, 1962; H. Dieckmann in RHL 64:679–82, 1964; S. Dresden in Neo 46:76–77, 1962; Georges May in FS 15:166–69, 1961. (v. 3, 1767). E. Bedford in MLR 60:283–85, 1965; Georges May in FS 18:165–68, 1964; Gita May in RR 55:296–97, 1964; J. Proust in RHL 65:125–26, 1965.

— Supplément au Voyage de Bougainville. Ed. by Herbert Dieckmann. Geneva, Droz, 1955. clv, 86 p.　　　　　　**5038**

The *fonds Vandeul* text, with a remarkable introduction, particularly noteworthy for its relating the *Supplément* to other

writings of D. (especially *Ceci n'est pas un
conte* and *Sur l'inconséquence du jugement
public*) and to D.'s passion for Mme de
Maux.
  Reviews : P. Alatri in Società 12:543–
48, 1956; R. Niklaus in FS 10:267–69,
1956.

— Sur Térence; le texte du manuscrit autographe. Ed. by Herbert Dieckmann. *In:*
Studia philologica et litteraria in honorem
L. Spitzer. Ed. by Anna G. Hatcher and
K. L. Selig. Bern, Francke, 1958. p. 149–
74.   **5039**
  Splendid example of impeccable editing
with notes, variants, and excellent introduction. Photographs.
  Review : A. Pizzorusso in SF 3:323,
1959.

— Three Diderot letters, and Les Eleuthéromanes. Ed. by Herbert Dieckmann.
HLB 6:69–91, 1952.   **5040**
  Letters to Marmontel (Apr. 23, 1757),
Voltaire (June 19, 1776), and Augustin
de Saint-Aubin (Apr. 11, [1781]). *Les
Eleuthéromanes* is edited from a privately
owned holograph ms, with variant readings from the *fonds Vandeul* ms. *See also*
the *same* in *ibid.* 7:231–35, 1953.

— Two unpublished poems by Diderot.
MLN 73:188–91, 1958.   **5041**
  Discovered by Vincent E. Bowen in the
Stockholm ms of Grimm's *Correspondance littéraire: Ils ont passé comme un
moment* (issue of June 1, 1762) and a
*Quatrain de M. Diderot à Sa Majesté
l'Impératrice de Russie* (issue of Jan.,
1774).

— Voce Enciclopedia. *In:* Alembert, Jean d',
and Denis Diderot. L'Enciclopedia;
Discorso preliminare, voce Enciclopedia.
Ed. by Paolo Casini. Bari, Laterza, 1964.
p. 149–228.   **5042**
  Italian translation of the article *Encyclopédie*, with an excellent editorial introduction (p. 5–31).

A Diderot pictorial encyclopedia of trades and
industry, manufacturing and the technical
arts in plates selected from L'Encyclopédie,
ou dictionnaire raisonné des sciences, des
arts et des métiers of Denis Diderot. Ed. by
Charles Coulston Gillispie. New York,
Dover publications, 1959. 2 v.   **5043**
  Admirable introduction, as well as
explanations of the engravings, by one of
the leading authorities in the history of
science.
  Reviews : B. Gille in AIHS 15:157,

1962; F. Kafker in DS 6:275–78, 1964;
A. Wilson in WMQ 3rd s. 17:121–22,
1960.

Hemsterhuis, François. Lettre sur l'homme
et ses rapports, avec le commentaire inédit
de Diderot. Ed. by Georges May. New
Haven, Yale univ. press, 1964. vii, 521 p.
                                            5044
  Recently discovered and extremely
important comments on almost all aspects
of philosophy, written by D. in 1773–74.
This *commentaire* greatly reinforces the
view that D. was indeed a philosopher
and that his philosophy was comprehensive and consistent in content and
rigorous in method.
  Reviews : P. Alatri in StS 6:99–113,
1965; R. Desné in PRRM n.s. 118:93–
110, 1964; J. Doolittle in MP 63:74–75,
1965–66; O. Fellows in FR 39:938–40,
1965–66; A. Freer in Critica Storica
4:800–17, 1965; *same* in SF 10:158–59,
1966; W. Krauss in Archiv 202:76–79,
1965–66; R. Niklaus in MLR 61:131–32,
1966; R. Pouilliart in LR 19:34–35, 1965;
J. Seznec in MLN 80:538–40, 1965;
A. Wilson in RR 56:68–70, 1965.

Loy, John Robert. Diderot's unedited Plan
d'un opéra comique. RR 46:3–24, 1955.
                                            5045
  See also Jacques Proust's discussion
of the *Plan* (5333).

Varloot, Jean. Le poète Diderot : vers incon-
nus ou méconnus. Eur 405–06:203–19,
Jan.–Feb. 1963.   **5046**
  The *Correspondance littéraire* text of
Les Eleuthéromanes (March 1, 1772), taken
from the Gotha ms.

Biography and Biographical Material

Akimova, Alisa Akimovna. Didro. Moscow, Molodaía guardiía, 1963. 479 p.   **5047**
  An accurate biography, but lacking
footnotes, done in something of the
manner of Billy (2255), and based upon
most of the Russian printed sources and
an ample (though spotty) selection of
French ones. Profusely illustrated. Pays
little attention to D. as a philosopher and
slights the last 10 years of his life. A respectable work of vulgarization, but one
which a scholar who does not read
Russian may safely overlook.

Alatri, Paolo. Diderot. *In his:* Voltaire,
Diderot e il partito filosofico. Messina and
Florence, G. D'Anna, 1965. p. 255–338.
                                            5048

Originally delivered as 6 radio lectures on the Terzo Programma in 1964. Excellent and comprehensive, accenting the political aspects of D.'s life and thought.

Basanoff, Anne. La bibliothèque russe de Diderot. BAB 29:71–86, 1959. **5049**
Interesting and informative concerning D.'s journey to Russia and the Russian books he acquired there.

Benot, Yves. La vieillesse de Diderot. Eur 382–83:238–48, Feb.-March 1961. **5050**
Episodes in D.'s later life : D. *sculpteur* (1775); the 1st version of *La pièce et le prologue* (1776); revision of *La religieuse* (1780–81).

Bonfantini, Mario. Introduzione alla lettura di Diderot. Turin, Gheroni, 1963. 119 p. **5051**
Accurate handbook; not intended as a contribution to knowledge but described by the author himself as " una monografia riassuntiva, rapida ma completa e aggiornata."
Review : A. Freer in SF 8:563, 1964.

Booy, Jean Th. de. Diderot et son copiste Roland Girbal. FS 16:324–33, 1962. **5052**
Detailed sifting of evidence concerning D.'s literary activities in the last years of his life (1780–84).

— Diderot, Voltaire et les Souvenirs de Madame de Caylus. *See* 4717. **5053**
Conclusively vindicates D.'s innocence against the allegation that he unscrupulously copied and sold the ms of the *Souvenirs*.

— La fille de Diderot et les premières éditions posthumes du philosophe. RHL 63:237–71, 1963. **5054**
Detailed study of the circumstances surrounding publication of D.'s works between 1784 and 1800. Some incidental information about D. himself.

Bowen, Ralph H. The education of an encyclopedist. *In:* Teachers of history; essays in honor of Laurence Bradford Packard. Ed. by Henry Stuart Hughes. Ithaca, Cornell univ. press, 1954. p. 28–57. **5055**
An account of D.'s life until 1747.

Brugmans, Henri L. Autour de Diderot en Hollande. DS 3:55–71, 1961. **5056**
D.'s relations with Michel van Goens, plus 2 previously unpublished bits of

verse by D. : " *Petit dialogue entre Marmontel et Collé, contre Fréron,*" and "*A Monsieur ou Madame Fréron.*"

— Diderot, le voyage de Hollande. *In:* Connaissance de l'étranger; mélanges offerts à la mémoire de Jean-Marie Carré. Didier, 1964. p. 151–63. **5057**
Focuses on D.'s relations with Hemsterhuis and on the visits of D. to Dutch collections of art.

Les cahiers haut-marnais. 24: 1951. 88 p. **5058**
Devoted exclusively to D. Contains the following documents : (1) *Ecole des cadets de Saint-Pétersbourg: Conventions entre M. Diderot, pour l'Impératrice de Russie, et le Sr Levesque.* 7 May 1773, p. 13–18; (2) *Contrat de mariage de Marie-Angélique Diderot et d'Abel-François-Nicolas Caroillon* (8 *septembre* 1772), p. 19-22; (3) *Notoriété après le décès de Denis Diderot* (17 *janvier* 1785), p. 22. Contents also include following articles : (1) Herbert Dieckmann, *Diderot, membre honoraire de la Société d'antiquaires d'Ecosse*, p. 23–26; (2) Arthur M. Wilson, *Bicentenaire du siècle des lumières; Diderot en prison*, 1749, p. 27–33; (3) Ralph H. Bowen, *La modernité de Diderot*, p. 34–36; (4) A. Bigot, *Diderot et la médecine*, p. 37–47; (5) Dr. Henry Ronot, *La maladie et la mort de Diderot*, p. 47–51. The *Supplément illustré* contains a number of photographs of D.'s letters and other documents, as well as of buildings associated with events in his life.

Casini, Paolo. Rousseau e Diderot. RCSF 19:243–70, 1964. **5059**
A well-rounded, comprehensive, and up-to-date history of the ideological, philosophical, and personal causes of the break between D. and Rousseau. In general, accepts the Jean Fabre theory of the *deux frères ennemis* (5068).

Chevallier, Pierre. Les philosophes et le lieutenant de police (1775–1785). FS 17: 105–20, 1963. **5060**
Valuable recollections of D. by Jean-Pierre-Charles Le Noir, *lieutenant de police* (Bibliothèque municipale d'Orléans, ms 1423).

Cohen, I. Bernard. A note concerning Diderot and Franklin. Isis 46:268–72, 1955. *See* 5808. **5061**
Thorough. The evidence—*hélas*—is negative.

Coiplet, Robert. Images de Diderot à Langres et à Paris. *In:* Demeures inspirées et sites romanesques. Ed. by Raymond Lécuyer. S.N.E.P. – Illustration, 1949–58. 3:87–96. **5062**

Excellent photographs, accompanied by a well-informed but conventional article.

Crocker, Lester G. The embattled philosopher; a biography of Denis Diderot. East Lansing, Michigan State college press, 1954. 442 p. **5063**

Entertaining and well grounded in the sources, but lacks footnotes and bibliography.

Reviews : R. Arndt in RR 46:149–51, 1955; J. Loy in MLQ 16:184–87, 1955; J. Schapiro in SRL 14–15, Jan. 29, 1956; A. Wilson in WMQ 3rd s. 12:501–02, 1955.

Donvez, Jacques. Diderot, Aiguillon et Vergennes. RScH n.s. 87:287–92, 1957. **5064**

Prints some interesting letters from the archives of the Quai d'Orsay regarding D.'s journey to Russia.

Doolittle, James. From hack to editor— Diderot and the booksellers. MLN 75:133–39, 1960. **5065**

Contains previously unknown information that D.'s name was presented (unsuccessfully) as a candidate for *Adjoint Mécanicien* to the Académie des Sciences, Feb. 8, 1749.

Dulac, Georges. La question des blés. Eur 405–06:103–09, Jan.–Feb. 1963. **5066**

Discusses D.'s responses between 1768 and 1770 to the problem of free trade in grain.

Eldridge, Paul. Denis Diderot. *In his:* Seven against the night. New York, Thomas Yoseloff, 1960. p. 245–337. **5067**

Impressionistic and undocumented, not uninformed but quite unsystematic.

Fabre, Jean. Deux frères ennemis : Diderot et Jean-Jacques. *See* 4897. *Reprinted in:* 4127. p. 19–65. **5068**

Meticulous and masterly review of the causes and consequences of the break between D. and Rousseau, extending the analysis to the end of their careers.

— Diderot le langrois. BSHL 193:391–99, 1964. **5069**

Eloquent lecture, tactful but candid,

interpreting D. to an audience of his fellow townsmen.

Fournier, Albert. Ses [Diderot's] logis à Paris. Eur 405–06:48–57, Jan.–Feb. 1963. **5070**

Including also Grandval, Sèvres, Marly, etc. Quite informative.

Havens, George R. Diderot, Rousseau, and the Discours sur l'inégalité. DS 3:219–62, 1961. **5071**

Suggests that D. had great influence on the *Discours*, favoring both boldness in content and prudence in form.

Jean, Raymond. Le sadisme de Diderot. Cr 19:33–50, Jan. 1963. **5072**

" The daily life of Diderot, as well as his intellectual life, swarms with situations in which he puts his reader or interlocutor, a woman, a friend, in the position of being an involuntary witness to some infringement of decency or good taste " (p. 42).

Kesten, Hermann. Denis Diderot : ein Revolutionär in Frankreich. *In his:* Lauter Literaten; Porträts, Erinnerungen. Vienna, Munich, Basel, Kurt Desch, 1963. p. 84–214. **5073**

Accurate and well-informed though rather superficial " portrait " by a prolific contemporaneous German man of letters. No footnotes or bibliography.

Launay, Michel. Madame de Baugrand et Jean Romilly, horloger : intermédiaires entre Rousseau et Diderot. Eur 405–06:247–63, Jan.–Feb. 1963. **5074**

Some interesting information for the years 1763 and 1767, published from the Rousseau mss in the Bibliothèque de la Ville de Neuchâtel.

Leigh, R. A. Les amitiés françaises du Dr Burney; quelques documents inédits. *See* 5572. **5075**

Burney and D., p. 166–71, 175–89.

Lipatti, Valentin. Bătrînețea lui Diderot, în lumina Scrisorii apologetice [Diderot's old age in the light of his Lettre apologétique]. *In:* Omagiu lui Iorgu Iordan cu prilejul împlinirii a 70 de ani. Bucharest, Academia Republicii, Populare Romîne, 1958. p. 513–18. **5076**

Although most of the older biographers have described D.'s powers as flagging in the last 10 years of his life, the *Lettre apologétique de M. l'abbé Raynal à M. Grimm*, discovered in the *fonds Vandeul*, demonstrates how vigorous D. continued to be.

Lîublinskiî, V. S. Sur la trace des livres lus par Diderot. Eur 405–06:276–90, Jan.–Feb. 1963. *See* 5658. **5077**

Interesting and scholarly discussion concerning D.'s library in Russia; first published under the title of : *Po sledam chteniîâ Didro* in FE 512–26, 1959. *See also his: Madrigal'nye pometki Didro* in *Novye metody restavratsii i konservatsii dokumentov i knig* (Moscow and Leningrad, 1960), p. 162–67, concerning D.'s marginalia on a copy of Helvétius' *De l'esprit.*

Lortholary, Albert. Le mirage russe en France au XVIII⁵ siècle. *See* 4742. **5078**

See especially : *Achat de la bibliothèque de Diderot* (p. 95–99, notes p. 318–20) and *Diderot en Russie* (p. 198–242, notes p. 368–81). Searching, caustic.

Lough, John. The Encyclopédie : two unsolved problems. FS 17:121–35, 1963. **5079**

(1) Points out that the *Documents nouveaux sur l'Encyclopédie* published by L.-P. May in Rsyn in 1938 are incomplete : " ... the ' Livre des Délibérations ' breaks off in April 1762, while the expenses stop in 1767 and receipts in 1768" (p. 122). (2) Suggests the possibility that Le Breton's censoring of the *Encyclopédie* was more extensive than Gordon and Torrey (1308) seem to imply.

Luppol, Ivan Kapitonovich. Deni Didro; ocherki zhizni i mirovozzreniya. Moscow, Akademiîâ nauk SSSR, 1960. 294 p. **5080**

New ed. of a work published in Russia in 1934 (French translation : 2276). Brief introduction by M. N. Grigorian, but no other updating.

May, Georges C. L'angoisse de l'échec et la genèse du Neveu de Rameau. DS 3:285–307, 1961. **5081**

Analyzes most convincingly the effect upon D. of the quite qualified success of *Le père de famille* at the Comédie Française.

— Diderot, 1713–1784. *In:* Les écrivains célèbres. Ed. by Raymond Queneau. Mazenod, 1951–53. 2:190–93. **5082**

Comprehensive and accurate, though brief, as to facts; interesting and spirited as to interpretation.

Mesnard, Pierre. Le cas Diderot; étude de caractérologie littéraire. Presses univ. de France, 1952. 245 p. **5083**

Interesting and well-informed case study, fitting D. into the patterns and terminology of the nascent science of characterology : D. was a " choleric ".

Reviews : J.-B. Barrère in RHL 54: 228–30, 1954; A. Devaux in RMéd sér. gén. 59:39–52; 60:182–94, 1954; R. Pouilliart in LR 10:65–67, 1956; L. Tancock in YWML 14:58–59, 1952.

— Sophie Volland et la maturité de Diderot. RScH n.s. 53:12–20, 1949. **5084**

Interesting discussion of " *la liaison éducatrice* " (p. 20).

Nedergaard, Leif. Diderot, filosoffens liv og virke; tillige med en skildring af den store franske Encyklopædis tilblivelseshistorie. Copenhagen, Martin, 1953. 462 p. **5085**

A comprehensive, full-length account, biographical and critical.

Pappas, John N. Diderot, d'Alembert et l'Encyclopédie. *See* 4290. **5086**

Studies in detail the relations between D. and d'Alembert, showing that from the beginning their views differed as to the function the *Encyclopédie* should serve.

—, and **Georges Roth.** Les tablettes de Diderot. DS 3:309–20, 1961. **5087**

Prints from the *fonds Vandeul* a copy, with variants hitherto unpublished, of the *Notte sur la désunion de Diderot et de J.-J. Rousseau.*

Paris. Bibliothèque nationale. Diderot et l'Encyclopédie; exposition commémorative du deuxième centenaire de l'Encyclopédie. 1951. xix, 148 p. *See* 4326. **5088**

Catalog of the B.N. bicentenary exposition, 1951. Contains useful bibliographical notes.

Review : J. Pommier in RHL 51:383–84, 1951.

— Diderot, 1713–1784. 1963. xiv, [1], 136 p. **5089**

A descriptive list of 622 items (mss, books, objects) associated with the career of D. and exhibited at the B.N. Dec., 1963 to Feb., 1964. Illustrated.

Proust, Jacques. La bibliothèque de Diderot. RScH n.s. 90:257–73, 1958; 94:179–83, 1959. *See* 5661. **5090**

Enumeration of the books D. is known to have owned, together with a history of the sale of his library and of what happened to it in Russia, so far as is known. *See also* Wilson (4707).

— La grammaire russe de Diderot. RHL 54: 329–31, 1954.   **5091**
   Studies D.'s personal copy of the *Elémens de la langue russe* (St. Petersburg, 1768) for evidence of his attempting to learn Russian.

— L'initiation artistique de Diderot. GBA 6th per. 55:225–32, Apr. 1960.   **5092**
   Enumerates and analyzes the books on painting in the *Bibliothèque du Roi* borrowed by D. between 1747 and 1751.

Roth, Georges. Notes sur la maladie et la mort de Diderot. CahHM 30:157, 1952.
                                     5093
   Useful excerpts from Grimm's unpublished letters (1783–84) to François Tronchin.

Sauro, Antoine. Diderot. Bari, Adriatica, 1953. 141 p.   **5094**
   In French; a work disfigured by numerous errors. At head of title: Antonio Sauro.

Seznec, Jean. Falconet, Voltaire et Diderot. *See* 4693.   **5095**
   Shows that Falconet was most eager to expose Voltaire's "errors" in his judgment of painters and sculptors of the age of Louis XIV and that D. attempted to restrain the brashness of the ungovernable Falconet.

Tchoutchmariev, V. I. Diderot et l'étude de la langue russe. PRRM n.s. 53:67–74, 1954.
                                     5096
   Speculates on how much Russian D. learned, arguing from marginalia and interlinear translation to be found in some of the books he took back to Paris. The Russian original of this article (*Ob izuchenii Deni Didro russkogo iazyka* in VFil 192–206, 1953[4]) has useful photographs.

— Diderot et les Encyclopédistes devant les progrès de la culture russe. PRRM n.s. 41: 87–96, 1952.   **5097**
   Translated from the author's *Frantsuzckie entsiklopedisty XVIII veka ob uspekhakh razvitiia russkoi kul'tury* in VFil 179–93, 1951[6]; enumerates the books in French or Latin about Russia that D. could have read and lists the Russian books D. collected at St. Petersburg and brought back to France.

Thomas, Jean. Diderot. *In:* Histoire des littératures. *See* 3384. 3:729–45.   **5098**
   Excellent general essay.

— Le rôle de Diderot dans l'Encyclopédie. *See* 4302. p. 7–25.   **5099**
   A judicious and spirited essay, previously published in Dia 3:96–109, April 1952.

Turbet-Delof, Guy. A propos d'Emile et Sophie. RHL 64:44–59, 1964.   **5100**
   Interesting added information regarding the quarrel between D. and Rousseau, 1757–58.

Vernière, Paul. Diderot et Jean Devaines. SRF 2:151–61, 1961.   **5101**
   Important amassing of all information concerning D.'s relations with Devaines (1733–1804).

Walker, T. C. The authorship of Rousseau's Jugement sur Diderot. FS 12:21–29, 1958.
                                     5102
   The item, which is apocryphal, first appeared in Cousin d'Avalon's *Diderotiana* (1810).

Wilson, Arthur M. Diderot: the testing years, 1713–1759. New York, Oxford univ. press, 1957. xii, 417 p. *See* 4346.   **5103**
   Endeavors to round up all the facts about D.'s life and works, as well as give current opinion about them. Emphasizes the history of the *Encyclopédie*.
   Reviews: O. Fellows in FR 31:579–81, 1957–58; A. Goodwin in EHR 74:505–07, 1959; R. Mortier in RBP 36:976–78, 1958; R. Pouilliart in LR 15:378–81, 1961; J. Proust in RHL 58:386–89, 1958; E. Weis in HZ 194:153–54, 1962.

General: Collaborations, Ideas, Influences, Language, Relationships, Reputation, Sources, Style, Techniques

Adam, Antoine. Rousseau et Diderot. RScH n.s. 53:21–34, 1949.   **5104**
   Shows that in their early political writings, D. and Rousseau engaged in a kind of dialogue, writing books at each other.

Alekseev, Mikhail P. D. Didro i russkie pisateli ego vremeni [D. Diderot and the Russian writers of his time]. *In:* XVIII [Vosemnadtsatyi] vek. Sbornik 3. Moscow, Akademiia nauk SSSR, 1958. p. 416–31.
                                     5105
   Starting from the list of Russian books

that D. is known to have owned, discusses what he knew and thought of Lomonosov, Sumarokov, Maïkov, Kheraskov, and others. Summarized by Jacques Proust in RHL 61:589, 1961.

Alexander, Ian W. Philosophy of organism and philosophy of consciousness in Diderot's speculative thought. *In:* Victoria University of Manchester. Studies in Romance philology and French literature presented to John Orr. Manchester, Manchester univ. press, 1953. p. 1–21.   **5106**
A remarkable contribution. " The evolution of Diderot's thought is the passage from the outward to the inward, from the objective to the subjective, from the general to the specific " (p. 2).

Baader, Horst. Diderots Theorie der Schauspielkunst und ihre Parallelen in Deutschland. RLC 33:200–23, 1959. **5107**
Discusses D.'s theories of acting and *sensibilité* and then discusses parallels as seen in the works of Lessing, Goethe, Schiller, Humboldt, and others.

Barzun, Jacques. Why Diderot? *In:* Varieties of literary experience. Ed. by Stanley Burnshaw. New York, New York univ. press, 1962. p. 31–44.   **5108**
Excellent general essay. " Men such as Diderot, then, are *uncompleting* men because they are finders and initiators, not concluders and finishers " (p. 33).

Bassenge, Friedrich. Diderot und die bildende Kunst. WZUB 13:197–205, 1964.
                                                    5109
Emphasizes the moralistic nature of D.'s approach to the arts.

Belaval, Yvon. Note sur Diderot et Leibniz. RScH n.s. 112:435–51, 1963.   **5110**
Profound and erudite. " Is there an influence, direct or indirect, of Leibniz on Diderot? . . . one has the feeling of an influence that is indirect, diffused, and confused " (p. 435, 451).

Bevernis, Christa. Die Weiterentwicklung der ästhetischen Konzeptionen Diderots durch Balzac. WZUB 13:181–87, 1964. **5111**
Studies ways in which the author conceives that Balzac built upon and carried further D.'s esthetic theories.

Bishop, G. Reginald, Jr. The capacity of the senses in Diderot's aesthetic theory. MLF 40:36–40, 1955.   **5112**
Interesting but tantalizingly brief. Thinks D. adequately described the

coordination of the visual, aural, and tactile, but was deficient in respect to describing the olfactory and gustatory. Does not take into account D.'s *Encyclopédie* article *Délicieux.*

Booy, Jean Th. de. A propos de l'Encyclopédie en Espagne : Diderot, Miguel Gijón et Pablo de Olavide. RLC 35:596–616, 1961.
                                                    5113
Ingenious and useful piecing together of information bearing upon D.'s acquaintanceship with Olavide. Compare with 5013.

— Quelques renseignements inédits sur un manuscrit du Rêve de d'Alembert. Neo 40: 81–93, 1956.   **5114**
Starting from letters exchanged between Hemsterhuis and Princess Galitzin, tackles the very difficult and complex problem of the extent of dissemination of D.'s works in ms in Germany.

—, and **Alan J. Freer.** Jacques le fataliste et La religieuse devant la critique révolutionnaire (1796–1800). Geneva, Institut et musée Voltaire, 1965. 344 p. (SVEC, 33)
                                                    5115
A reprinting, admirably edited, of 90 reviews of *La religieuse* or *Jacques le fataliste* (or both) appearing in the Paris press between 1796 and 1804. The useful introduction is an amplification of Booy (5054) and Freer (5302).
Review : A. Hytier in RR 56:303–05, 1965.

Boura, Ferdinand. Diderotovy filosofické a sociálně politické názory [Diderot's philosophical, social, and political ideas]. Prague, Československé Akademie Věd, 1958. 53 p.
                                                    5116
Knowledgeable interpretation from the standard Marxist-Leninist point of view, using a very good spread of quotations from D. Evidently the author did not have access to a number of recent monographs and periodical articles.

Boutet de Monvel, A. Diderot et la notion de style. RHL 51:288–305, 1951.   **5117**
Shows D.'s appreciation of style for itself and his realization of the need for individuation, whether in letters or in the plastic arts.

Bräuning-Oktavio, Hermann. Goethe und Diderot im Jahre 1772; mit ungedruckten Briefen von J. H. Merck und F. M. Leuchsenring. NFJG 24:237–52, 1962. **5118**
Sees the influence of D.'s *Salons* in a

passage written by Goethe for the *Frankfurter gelehrten Anzeigen*, 1772.

Bredvold, Louis I. Diderot : the frustrations of a scientific moralist. *In his:* The natural history of sensibility. Detroit, Wayne State univ. press, 1962. p. 27–49.   **5119**
An unsympathetic essay on D.'s ethics.

Brun, A. Aux origines de la prose dramatique : le style haletant. *In:* MélCB, p. 41–47.   **5120**
Possible effect on Beaumarchais, Le Tourneur, Pixérécourt, etc., of D.'s ideas regarding stage speech, especially as exemplified in *Le père de famille.*

Carson, George Barr, Jr. Natural rights : the Soviet and the bourgeois Diderot. *In:* Ideas in history; essays presented to Louis Gottschalk by his former students. Ed. by Richard Herr and Harold T. Parker. Durham, North Carolina, Duke univ. press, 1965. p. 330–48.   **5121**
Case study in comparative historiography based on the Soviet and the " bourgeois " criticism of D.'s treatment of natural rights. Compares especially Kazarin (5178) and Wilson (5103).

Casini, Paolo. Diderot e Shaftesbury. GCFI 39:253–73, 1960.   **5122**
Definitive.

— Diderot philosophe. Bari, Laterza, 1962. 404 p. *See* 4300.   **5123**
Thoroughgoing and persuasive discussion of D.'s merit as a philosopher, analyzing all aspects of D.'s thought.
Reviews : T. Gregory in Cultura moderna 55:8–11, Feb. 1962; S. Landucci in SF 6:560–61, 1962; *same* in B 18:323–35, 1963; R. Parenti in RCSF 18:111–14, 1963; O. Ragusa in DS 6:313–19, 1964; L. Rebay in RR 55:58–61, 1964; P. Rossi in RIF 54:233–36, 1963; A. Wilson in FR 36:321–22, 1962–63.

Chouillet, Jacques. Le mythe d'Ariste ou Diderot en face de lui-même. RHL 64:565–88, 1964.   **5124**
Analyzes D.'s theory of esthetics, taking off from his self-identification with Aristes in the concluding pages of *De la poésie dramatique* (1758). Though D. never succeeded in becoming the " phantom " Aristes, nevertheless, says the author, this phantom " l'a aidé à devenir lui-même " (p. 588).

Cotta, Sergio. L'illuminisme et la science

politique : Montesquieu, Diderot, et Catherine II. *See* 4423.   **5125**
Contends that Montesquieu was elaborating a sociology *avant la lettre*, while other writers, including D., were constructing ideologies. D.'s ideology was audacious and revolutionary—it was that of democracy.

Creighton, Douglas G. Man and mind in Diderot and Helvétius. *See* 4353.   **5126**
Argues convincingly and concretely that D., unlike Helvétius, had too great a sense of reality ever to fall into the trap of dogmatic environmentalism.

Crocker, Lester G. Diderot and eighteenth century French transformism. *In:* Forerunners of Darwin : 1745–1859. Ed. by Hiram Bentley Glass *et al.* Baltimore, Johns Hopkins press, 1959. p. 114–43.   **5127**
Brilliantly analyzes the birth and growth of D.'s evolutionary thinking.

— Diderot et la loi naturelle. Eur 405–06:57–65, Jan.–Feb. 1963.   **5128**
Capable analysis of D.'s effort in the earlier part of his career to find in natural law a basis for moral evaluation.

— John Toland et le matérialisme de Diderot. RHL 53:289–95, 1953. *See* 5628.   **5129**
Shows how D. was influenced by the fifth of Toland's *Letters to Serena;* but argues that Toland (and, in genetics, Maupertuis) anticipated 20th-century scientific discoveries much more than D., who remained a man of his own century.

— Two Diderot studies : ethics and esthetics. Baltimore, Johns Hopkins press, 1952. viii, 127 p.   **5130**
An important monograph, closely argued. Part I, *A critique of Diderot's ethical philosophy*, has now been incorporated or amplified in the same author's *An age of crisis* (4122). Part II, *Subjectivism and objectivism in Diderot's esthetics*, finds in D. an " irreducible polarity."
Reviews : C. Frankel in RR 44:222–24, 1953; R. Leigh in FS 10:74–78, 1956; J. Loy in MLQ 16:184–87, 1955; Georges May in MLN 68:557–60, 1953; R. Niklaus in MLR 50:343–44, 1955; P. Vernière in RHL 55:75–77, 1955.

Curtius, Ernst Robert. Diderot and Horace. *In his:* European literature and the Latin Middle Ages. Trans. by Willard R. Trask. New York, Pantheon books, 1953. p. 573–83.   **5131**
Translation of 2331.

Dédéyan, Charles. L'Angleterre dans la pensée de Diderot. Centre de documentation universitaire, 1958. 258 p. (Les cours de Sorbonne) *See* 5652.   **5132**

Mimeographed lectures; a comprehensive but not very original monograph, not completely conversant with the relevant secondary authorities.

Desné, Roland. L'apparition du mot philosophe dans l'œuvre de Diderot. AHRF 35:287–94, 1963.   **5133**

Shows that already in his translation (1743) of Stanyan's *Grecian history*, D. was using the word *philosophe* in its Enlightenment meaning.

Diderot studies. Ed. by Otis E. Fellows. (V. 1 and 2) Syracuse, Syracuse univ. press, 1949–52; (Vols. 3–) Geneva, Droz, 1961– .   **5134**

An important series devoted to all aspects of Diderot scholarship. For 1, *see* 2247. Norman L. Torrey was coeditor of 2 and Gita May of 3. Contents will be found listed under individual authors.

Reviews : (v. 2, 1952) F. Green in MLR 51:273–75, 1956; G. Laidlaw in Sym 10:166–73, 1956; A. Vartanian in RR 47:42–48, 1956. (v. 3, 1961) P. Meyer in MP 61:59–62, 1963–64; R. Niklaus in FS 17:66–68, 1963; H. Peyre in RR 52:298–302, 1961; A. Pizzorusso in RLM n.s. 15:67–72, 1962; G. Saba in SF 7:111–19, 1963; J. Smith in MLR 57:613–14, 1962; J. Varloot in RScH n.s. 112:537–50, 1963; P. Vernière in FR 36:650–51, 1962–63. (v. 4, 1963) V. Bowen in MLR 60:285, 1965; R. Desné in Eur 421–22:309–10, May–June 1964; M. Duchet in RHL 65:313–17, 1965; A. Freer in SF 8:357–59, 1964; J. Loy in RR 55:302–05, 1964; J. Perkins in MLN 80:414–17, 1965. (v. 5, 1964) *See* 5268. (v. 6, 1964) P. Alatri in SF 9:112–14, 1965; J. Doolittle in FR 39:169–70, 1965–66; A. Wilson in RR 56:219–24, 1965.

Dieckmann, Herbert. Cinq leçons sur Diderot. Preface by Jean Pommier. Geneva, Droz, 1959. 149 p.   **5135**

Lectures delivered at the Collège de France in 1957 : *Diderot et son lecteur* (also published in MerF 329:620–48, 1957); *Système et interprétation dans la pensée de Diderot, La pensée et ses modes d'expression* (also published in German as *Das Problem der Ausdrucksform des Denkens bei Diderot* in RFor 69:1–27, 1957); *Questions d'esthétique*, and *Les salons*. An important work of criticism.

Reviews : A. Freer in RLM 12:321–24, 1959; R. Mortier in RBP 40:929–32, 1962; R. Niklaus in FS 14:362–63, 1960; R. Pouilliart in LR 16:91–93, 1962; J. Proust in RHL 61:261–64, 1961; J. Spink in MLR 56:114–15, 1961.

— Les contributions de Diderot à la Correspondance littéraire et à l'Histoire des Deux Indes. *See* 5367.   **5136**

The earliest article alerting scholars to the possibility of proving, by utilizing the *fonds Vandeul*, the significance and extent of D.'s contributions to Raynal.

— Diderot und Goldoni. Krefeld, Scherpe, 1961. 47 p. *Also in Italian as:* Diderot e Goldoni. Vel 7⁴:601–26, Aug. 1963. *See* 3639 and 5899–5900.   **5137**

In the *Fils naturel* D. borrowed Goldoni's plot of *Il vero amico* but not his esthetics.

— Observations sur les manuscrits de Diderot conservés en Russie. DS 4:53–71, 1963.   **5138**

Demonstrates the textual superiority, in many instances, of the Leningrad mss.

— The presentation of reality in Diderot's tales. DS 3:101–28, 1961.   **5139**

Masterly analysis of D.'s literary aims and techniques.

— Le thème de l'acteur dans la pensée de Diderot. CAIEF 13:157–72, 1961. *Also in German as:* Das Thema des Schauspielers bei Diderot. SuF 8:438–56, 1961.   **5140**

A subtle study, showing D.'s awareness throughout his life of the relationship of the creative artist to the world of raw facts.

Duchet, Michèle. Bougainville, Raynal, Diderot et les sauvages du Canada : une source ignorée de l'Histoire des Deux Indes. *See* 5382.   **5141**

Portions of Bougainville's *Journal* relating to Canada were published in 1762 in the *Journal étranger*. A comparison of texts shows that D. borrowed some of this material for his contributions to Raynal's 1st ed. (1770).

— Diderot collaborateur de Raynal : à propos des Fragments imprimés du fonds Vandeul. *See* 5383.   **5142**

An epoch-making article, showing the extent of D.'s contributions and their effect upon his thinking.

— Le primitivisme de Diderot. Eur 405–06:126–37, Jan.–Feb. 1963.   **5143**

Proves how complex D.'s ideas were concerning primitivism, as evidenced in all his later works; reminds us, quite rightly, that this is one of the least explored aspects of D.'s thought.

— Le Supplément au Voyage de Bougainville et la collaboration de Diderot à l'Histoire des Deux Indes. *See* 5384.   **5144**

Shows that all the apparently disparate elements of D.'s *Supplément* have an inner cohesion, which later manifested itself unmistakably in D.'s contributions to the *Histoire des Deux Indes*.

Ehrard, Jean. Matérialisme et naturalisme : les sources occultistes de la pensée de Diderot. CAIEF 13:189–201, 1961.   **5145**

Believes that D.'s materialism was intellectually insufficient, thus forcing him to postulate the existence of an " invisible world."

Fabre, Jean. Actualité de Diderot. DS 4:17–39, 1963.   **5146**

Interesting critical and bibliographical comments on 20th-century D. studies.

— Le chemin de Diderot. Eur 405–06:3–16, Jan.–Feb. 1963. *Also in* 4127. p. 85–100.   **5147**

Excellent interpretation of D., serving as introduction to a collection of essays about him.

— Deux définitions du philosophe : Voltaire et Diderot. Tro 122:135–52, 1958. *Also in* 4127. p. 1–18. *See also* 4636.   **5148**

Analyzes the differences in temperament, social origin, and point of view of the two men.

— Diderot et les théosophes. CAIEF 13:203–22, 1961. *Also in* 4127. p. 67–83.   **5149**

Interesting thesis that because D. was really behind his times in chemistry (as in understanding Lavoisier), he owed some of his most prescient and exciting intuitions to ideas inspired by the alchemists.

Folkierski, Władysław. L'anglais de Diderot. RLC 34:226–44, 1960. *See* 5654.   **5150**

Useful study of D.'s faithfulness and skill as a translator, citing especially his translation of Temple Stanyan's *Grecian history*.

Fosca, François [*pseud.* of Georges de Traz]. De Diderot à Valéry : les écrivains et les arts visuels. *See* 5259.   **5151**

Fredman, Alice G. Diderot and Sterne. New York, Columbia univ. press, 1955. 264 p. *See* 3744 and 5655.   **5152**

Shows that D. was no mere plagiarist of Sterne. Compares their literary theories and practices, thus revealing their affinities, but also suggesting the extent of D.'s originality and independence.

Reviews : H. Dieckmann in MLN 71:615–17, 1956; J. Doolittle in RR 47:145–46, 1956; R. Harris in CL 8:268–69, 1956; L. Hartley in SAQ 54:564–65, 1955; A. Hoffman in Sym 10:160–63, 1956; A. McKillop in PQ 35:327–29, 1956; R. Niklaus in MLR 52:115, 1957; J. Seznec in RHL 58:236, 1958; J. Smiley in JEGP 55:330–31, 1956.

Freer, Alan J. Diderot, Angélique et les Confidences de Nicolas. SF 9:283–90, 1965.   **5153**

Probable influence of D. on Gérard de Nerval.

— Diderot et Stendhal. AFLT 11:63–79, 1962.   **5154**

Thorough. D.'s growing reputation in the 19th century owed much to Stendhal, who especially admired *Jacques le fataliste*.

Garcin, Philippe. Diderot et la philosophie du style. Cr 15:195–213, Mar. 1959.   **5155**

Shows that D. is a subtle and conscious artist, aware of ambiguity and of the difficulty of being sincere. A very important article.

Review : R. Niklaus in FS 14:255–56, 1960.

Gendzier, Stephen J. Art criticism and the novel : Diderot and Balzac. FR 35:302–10, 1961–62.   **5156**

Demonstrates that D.'s artistic ideas had a powerful impact on Balzac's conception of the novel.

— Balzac's changing attitudes toward Diderot. FS 19:125–43, 1965.   **5157**

D. had a diminishing influence upon Balzac, who showed, nonetheless, an abiding admiration for *Ceci n'est pas un conte*.

— Diderot's impact on the generation of 1830. SVEC 23:93–103, 1963.   **5158**

Mentions especially Théophile Gautier, Sainte-Beuve, Charles Nodier, and Jules Janin.

— L'interprétation de la figure humaine chez Diderot et chez Balzac. AnB 3:181–93, 1962.   **5159**

Demonstrates and compares D.'s and Balzac's interest in the study of " physiognomy."

Gilman, Margaret. Imagination and creation in Diderot. DS 2:200–20, 1952. **5160**

A thoughtful and compelling essay, consonant with the author's later and larger *The idea of poetry in France* (3551).

— A new vision of poetry : Diderot. *In her:* The idea of poetry in France. *See* 3551. p. 48–85. **5161**

Studies D. as " the greatest champion of the imagination in France." A weighty and meaty discussion of D.'s esthetics.

Giusti, Roberto F. Diderot. Cursos y conferencias (Buenos Aires) 39:223–45, July–Sept. 1951. **5162**

Enthusiastic and well-informed commemorative essay. Interesting comparison of D. and Pirandello (p. 227).

Got, Maurice. Sur le matérialisme de Diderot. Rsyn n.s. 83:135–64, 1962. **5163**

By distinguishing between the materialist, whose thesis is that " mind is only matter," and the vitalist, who holds that " mind and matter are one " (p. 140), argues that what passes for D.'s " materialism " is really " vitalism " or " animism " (p. 163). This is evidenced in D. by his affirming the involution of life and thought in matter (p. 155). A stimulating study, with appendixes of *Leibniz et Diderot* (p. 155–59) and *Diderot et d'Alembert* (159–64), but made unnecessarily difficult by overlong sentences and turgid syntax.

Grava, Arnolds. Diderot and recent philosophical trends. DS 4:73–103, 1963. **5164**

A welcome contribution to the growing body of writing that asserts that D. was a philosopher as well as a *philosophe*. Compares the striking parallels in the philosophy of D. and of Whitehead.

Grimsley, Ronald. L'ambiguité dans l'œuvre romanesque de Diderot. CAIEF 13:223–38, 1961. **5165**

In D.'s literary creation, he " reminds one of some researcher carrying on an experiment the outcome of which he himself does not know " (p. 227–28).

Guy, Basil. The prince de Ligne and Diderot. RR 53:260–68, 1962. **5166**

" ... if only by reaction, he became more deeply indebted to Diderot than we realize " (p. 268).

Guyot, Charly. L'homme du dialogue [Diderot]. Eur 405–06:153–63, Jan.–Feb. 1963. **5167**

Points out the dialectical character—in the pre-Hegelian sense—of D.'s works, including those not overtly cast in dialogue form.

Hall, Max. Benjamin Franklin & Polly Baker; the history of a literary deception. Chapel Hill, Univ. of North Carolina press (For the Institute of early American history and culture at Williamsburg, Va.), 1960. 193 p. **5168**

Traces (p. 66–73) D.'s connection, in Raynal's *Histoire des Deux Indes* and in the *Supplément au Voyage de Bougainville*, with the Polly Baker story.

Havens, George R. Diderot the man; Diderot and the Encyclopédie; Diderot's criticism of drama and art; Diderot, novelist and philosopher. *In his:* The age of ideas. *See* 3383. p. 277–353. **5169**

Very able *mise au point*.

Heitmann, Klaus. Ethos des Künstlers und Ethos der Kunst; eine problemgeschichtliche Skizze anlässlich Diderots. Münster, Aschendorff, 1962. 38 p. **5170**

Traces in Greek and Roman sources, as well as in medieval, Renaissance, and 19th-century ones, the history of a fundamental and recurring problem in ethical and esthetic criticism, namely the relationship of creative genius to morality. Since D. frequently alluded to this problem, most especially in his remarks about Racine in *Le neveu de Rameau*, his point of view is used as the focus of organization of this far-questing essay.

Reviews : E. Leube in RJa 13:237–42, 1962; F. Orlando in SF 6:561, 1962.

Heitner, Robert R. Concerning Lessing's indebtedness to Diderot. MLN 65:82–88, 1950. **5171**

Cautions against exaggerating D.'s influence on Lessing.

— Diderot's own Miss Sara Sampson. *See* 5858. **5172**

Discusses the implications of there being a complete French translation of *Miss Sara Sampson* in the *fonds Vandeul*.

Hinterhäuser, Hans. Utopie und Wirklichkeit bei Diderot; Studien zum Supplément au Voyage de Bougainville. Heidelberg, Carl Winter, 1957. 133 p. **5173**

A general interpretation of D.'s thought using evidence from all of his works and not confining itself simply to the *Supplément*. Shows D.'s tendency to be utopian, but also analyzes (and deplores) his conformism.

Reviews : M. Naumann in RJa 8:266–69, 1957; E. Rzadkowska in KNeo 7:354–58, 1960.

Hofmann, Walter. Diderots Auffassungen vom allgemeinen Empfindungsvermögen, von der Entstehung und Einheit des Bewusstseins. WZUB 13:175–80, 1964. **5174**

Surveys D.'s contributions to the theory of knowledge. Shows that modern neurophysiology is vindicating D.'s intuitions in the *Rêve de d'Alembert* as to the mechanism of the brain in the phenomenology of consciousness.

Hytier, Adrienne D. Le philosophe et le despote : histoire d'une inimitié, Diderot et Frédéric II. DS 6:55–87, 1964. **5175**

Smoothly written and thoroughly researched account.

Jauss, Hans Robert. Nachahmungsprinzip und Wirklichkeitsbegriff in der Theorie des Romans von Diderot bis Stendhal. *In his* (*Ed.*) : Nachahmung und Illusion : Kolloquium Giessen Juni 1963, Vorlagen und Verhandlungen. Munich, Eidos, 1964. p. 157–78. **5176**

Discusses D.'s contribution to the theory of the novel, especially his doctrines in the *Eloge de Richardson*. By speaking of Richardson's novels as *drames* and by analyzing the esthetic effect of Richardson's profuse use of details, D. put the theory of the novel on a new basis. *See also* the ensuing round-table discussion : *ibid.*, p. 237–46.

John, Erhard. Goethes Bemerkungen zu Diderots Versuch über die Malerei. WB 6:1029–39, 1960. **5177**

Analyzes Goethe's theory of art, relating it closely to the " historical position of the German bourgeoisie of that time " (p. 1030). " Goethe expressed and defended, in unison with Diderot, the human and humanistic character of art " (p. 1039).

Kazarin, Aleksandr I. Ekonomicheskie vozzreniíã Deni Didro. [The economic concepts of Denis Diderot]. Moscow, 1960. 206 p. **5178**

Using recently discovered texts, such as the *Apologie de l'abbé Galiani*, shows the evolution of D.'s economic thought from the articles in the *Encyclopédie* to the writings on Russia. Summarized by Jacques Proust in RHL 61:590, 1961.

Kempf, Roger. Deux essais sur Diderot. RScH n.s. 100:415–33, 1960. **5179**

(1) *La présence et le corps chez Diderot.* (p. 415–26). A convincing stylistic examination of D.'s methods of portraying behavior. (2) *Diderot, père et fils* (p. 427–33). D. in relation to his daughter and to his father. Rather sketchy.

— Diderot et le roman; ou le démon de la présence. Editions du Seuil, 1964. 253 p. *See* 5657. **5180**

Based upon an impressive familiarity with D.'s writings (as well as the secondary literature), begins by analyzing D.'s remarkable ability to observe and describe human behavior, individually and in its social and economic context; ultimately transcends simply a study of D.'s theory of the novel by attempting, through observation of his use of masks and mystifications, to seize the biographical essence of the man himself. " On ne saurait parler du romancier sans tout approfondir " (p. 10).

Review : R. Warning in Archiv 202:397–99, 1965–66.

— Zeit und Bewegung bei Diderot. NS n.s. 11:261–67, 1962. **5181**

Demonstrates D.'s aversion to describing duration and his preference for depicting action.

Laidlaw, George Norman. Diderot's teratology. DS 4:105–29, 1963. **5182**

Studies D.'s fondness for perceiving what is normal by observing instances of abnormalities. " Monsters fascinated Diderot " (p. 105).

— Elysian encounter; Diderot and Gide. Syracuse, Syracuse univ. press, 1963. ix, 251 p. **5183**

Study in the parallel of the temperaments, creative gifts, and attitudes toward literary craftsmanship of D. and Gide.

Reviews : A. Freer in RLM 18:149–53, 1965; J. Loy in Sym 18:285–87, 1964; Gita May in DS 6:279–92, 1964; K. O'Neill in MLR 60:456–57, 1965.

Langen, August. Die Technik der Bildbeschreibung in Diderots Salons. RFor 61:324–87, 1948. **5184**

Shows through a wealth of citations how D. solved his two principal problems in describing pictures, that of creating a new style and vocabulary in art criticism and that of enumerating the objects and elements in the composition of a picture. A critical bibliography (p. 384–87).

Langner, Gerhard. Zur Entwicklung des Russlandbildes in Frankreich von Diderot bis Mérimée. WZUR 6:251–94, 1956–57. **5185**

Brings out evidence of D.'s critical opinions of Russia and the czardom.

Lecercle, Jean-Louis. Diderot et le réalisme bourgeois dans la littérature du XVIIIᵉ siècle. PRRM n.s. 38:55–72, 1951. **5186**

A rather ideological piece, by a well-informed Marxist critic.

Lefebvre, Henri. Diderot. Hier et aujourd'hui, 1949. 307 p. **5187**

Influential critical study by a prominent French Marxist scholar and publicist. Review : J.-P. Vernant in PRRM n.s. 29:89–94, 1950.

Lemke, Arno. Diderots Einfluss auf die deutsche Klassik. WZUL 3:221–46, 1953–54. **5188**

Uses the standard eds. of Lessing, Herder, Goethe, Schiller, and Hegel to show the influences of D.'s personality and works. This material covered more comprehensively and thoroughly in Mortier (5207).

Lerel, Abraham C. Diderots Naturphilosophie. Vienna, Brüder Hollinek, 1950. 155 p. **5189**

A vigorous but somewhat repetitious monograph, too much neglected, describing the polarities in D.'s thought and their resolution by dialectical contradictions. Emphasizes the idea of time and becoming (*Das Werden*) in D.'s interest in biology. Stresses also the importance of D.'s *Principes philosophiques sur la matière et le mouvement*.

Livingstone, Leon. The theme of the Paradoxe sur le comédien in the novels of Pérez de Ayala. HR 22:208–23, 1954. **5190**

D.'s influence is especially manifest in Pérez de Ayala's *Belarmino y Apolonio*.

Loy, J. Robert. Diderot aux Etats-Unis. Eur 405–06:263–73, Jan.–Feb. 1963. **5191**

Traces carefully what little evidence there is of D.'s influence on 18th- and 19th-century American thinkers and writers.

— Nature, reason and Enlightenment : Voltaire, Rousseau and Diderot. SVEC 26: 1085–1107, 1963. **5192**

"But as to the central and decisive kernel of the age, Diderot's vision and focus, alone, did not vacillate or dim " (p. 1107).

Mauzi, Robert. Diderot et le bonheur. DS 3:263–84, 1961. **5193**

Especially analyzes the interlacing of D.'s concepts of happiness and of virtue.

— Les rapports du bonheur et de la vertu dans l'œuvre de Diderot. CAIEF 13:255–68, 1961. **5194**

Shows that what was newest and most daring in D.'s later works came from his reconsidering the simplistic equating of happiness and virtue.

May, Georges C. Quatre visages de Denis Diderot. Boivin, 1951. 209 p. **5195**

The *visages* are : *Diderot gastronome, Diderot pessimiste, Diderot et l'été 1769,* and *Diderot entre le réel et le roman.* Excellent essays all, the last three especially useful.

Reviews : J. Pommier in RHL 51:384–87, 1951; R. Pouilliart in LR 10:64–65, 1956; D. Victoroff in Rsyn n.s. 69:147–48, 1951; I. Wade in Sym 6:202–04, 1952.

May, Gita. Chardin vu par Diderot et par Proust. PMLA 72:403–18, 1957. **5196**

Revealing case study of D.'s subtlety as a critic of art.

— Diderot and Burke : a study in aesthetic affinity. PMLA 75:527–39, 1960. *See* 5660. **5197**

Convincing analysis of the nature and extent of D.'s indebtedness to Burke's ideas on esthetics.

— Diderot devant la magie de Rembrandt. PMLA 74:387–97, 1959. **5198**

Although D. persisted in citing Raphael as the great model for painters, he nevertheless felt the constant pull, represented by Rembrandt, toward the appreciation in art of ordinary human beings in everyday situations. Illustrated.

— Diderot et Baudelaire, critiques d'art. Geneva, Droz, 1957. 195 p. **5199**

Important landmark in 20th-century rehabilitation of D. as art critic.

Reviews : L. Austin in RLC 37:634–38, 1963; H. Brugmans in FR 33:302–03, 1959–60; H. Dieckmann in RR 49:215–17, 1958; J. Doolittle in MLN 73:544–47, 1958; C. Engel de Janosi in JAAC

17:531–32, 1958–59; G. Sauerwald in GRM n.s. 12:321–24, 1962; J. Seznec in FS 14:268–70, 1960; H. Żmijewska in KNeo 8:318–23, 1961.

— Diderot et la Présentation au temple de Giotto. MLN 75:229–33, 1960.   **5200**
Study of the probable sources of D.'s acquaintance with the work of Giotto.

Mayer, Jean. Diderot, homme de science. Rennes, Imprimerie bretonne, 1959. 490 p. *See* 4321.   **5201**
Comprehensive analysis of D.'s relationship to the science and the scientists of his day.
Reviews : Anon. in RUB 13:168–70, 1960–61; A. Freer in SF 5:354–55, 1961.

— Der Glücksgedanke bei Diderot. Trans. by I. Schwinzert. WZUB 13:169–73, 1964.   **5202**
D.'s concept of happiness, which is basic to his philosophy, is closely related to his apology for the passions and his belief in the possibility of social progress. Quotes frequently from the unpublished *fonds Vandeul* text of the *Eléments de physiologie.*

Meyer, Martine D. L'art du portrait dans les Lettres à Sophie Volland. FR 32:22–31, 1958–59.   **5203**
Studies D.'s technique of observation and description as exemplified in these letters.

Mølbjerg, Hans. Aspects de l'esthétique de Diderot. Copenhagen, J. H. Schultz, 1964. 272 p.   **5204**
Discusses the totality of D.'s esthetic theory and practice, not just " aspects " of it. Excellent in its understanding of the dynamic development of D.'s ideas, but suffers from a presentation that plunges *in medias res* without adequate introduction or perspectives; therefore baffling even though based on a comprehensive and thorough knowledge of D.'s writings and the literature concerning him.
Reviews : Gita May in RR 56:146–47, 1965; R. Mortier in SF 9:301–03, 1965; P. Nykrog in OrL 19:215–28, 1964; J. Seznec in FS 18:383–84, 1964.

Mortier, Roland. A propos du sentiment de l'existence chez Diderot et Rousseau : notes sur un article de l'Encyclopédie. DS 6:183–95, 1964.   **5205**
Establishes striking parallels (but without attempting to prove influences) of

various of Rousseau's writings with D.'s article *Délicieux.*

— Diderot au carrefour de la poésie et de la philosophie. RScH n.s. 112:485–501, 1963.   **5206**
Shows by exhaustive citation of texts that D. demanded of poetry that it be the product both of inspiration and of study. He " safeguarded the heritage of the past while opening the way to the poetry of the future " (p. 501).

— Diderot en Allemagne, 1750–1850. Presses univ. de France, 1954. 464 p. *See* 4323 and 5868.   **5207**
Comprehensive and definitive. Supplementary to this monumental monograph, *see:* Roland Mortier, *Deux témoignages allemands sur Diderot* in RLC 32: 92–94, 1958; his *Diderot et ses deux petits allemands* in RLC 33:192–99, 1959; and his *La réaction allemande aux premières œuvres philosophiques de Diderot* in DS 4: 131–51, 1963. *See also* 5850.
Reviews : A. Delorme in Rsyn n.s. 77: 101–04, 1956; H. Dieckmann in JEGP 56:95–99, 1957; L. Dieckmann in CL 9:72–74, 1957; J. Fabre in RLC 31:117–22, 1957; S. Gendzier in Sym 10:164–66, 1956; J. Hanse in LR 9:239–42, 1955; Georges May in MLN 71:313–16, 1956; R. Niklaus in MLR 51:116–17, 1956; J. Proust in RHL 57:77–79, 1957; K. Weinberg in RBP 34:465–67, 1956.

— Diderot et la notion de peuple. Eur 405–06: 78–88, Jan.–Feb. 1963.   **5208**
Valuable semantic analysis.

— Diderot et le problème de l'expressivité : de la pensée au dialogue heuristique. CAIEF 13:283–97, 1961.   **5209**
" The apparent oscillation of Diderot is the indication of a line of thought that questions and investigates : it is not synonymous with confusion and disorder " (p. 293). A thoughtful and useful *critique.*

— Diderot sous le prisme de la critique marxiste. NCLS 24:679–91, 1959. *Also in Flemish as:* Diderot in het licht van de marxistische Kritiek. TVUB 3:1–13, 1961.   **5210**
Discusses D. as viewed by Marx, Engels, I. K. Luppol, and Henri Lefebvre.

— L'original selon Diderot. SRF 4:141–57, 1963.   **5211**
Studies D.'s conception of the relationship between originality and genius, both in art and in human character, and

examines the function of the " original " in society.

— Le prince de Ligne, imitateur de Diderot. MR 5:121–29, Aug.-Oct. 1955 **5212**
De Ligne, in his *Le sultan du Congo, ou Mangogul*, wrote a piece for the stage that was based, though without acknowledgment, on D.'s *Les bijoux indiscrets*.

Mourot, Jean. Sur la ponctuation de Diderot. *See* 3509. **5213**
Studies D.'s punctuation in the *Neveu de Rameau* (Fabre ed., 2221A) and in the *Rêve de d'Alembert* (Vernière ed., 5036), showing that punctuation " is one of the means Diderot uses to make the tone, rhythm, and mimesis of the spoken word pass over into a written text " (p. 294).

Naumann, Manfred. Diderot und das Système de la nature. WZUB 13:145–55, 1964. **5214**
Thorough examination of all the evidence and hearsay linking D. with d'Holbach's book. Shows that their ideology was similar but that D. was critical of d'Holbach's one-sidedly mechanistic view of the world.

Niklaus, Robert. Diderot et la peinture : le critique d'art et le philosophe. Eur 405–06: 231–47, Jan.–Feb. 1963. **5215**
Thoroughly documented re-examination of D.'s development as an esthetician.

— Diderot et le conte philosophique. CAIEF 13:299–315, 1961. **5216**
Discusses all of D.'s works, not merely his *contes*, emphasizing that D. is an ambivalent author, so that both author and reader end by saying, " *Que sais-je* ? "

— Diderot et Rousseau : pour et contre le théâtre. DS 4:153–89, 1963. **5217**
Perceptive study of the conflicting philosophies of D. and Rousseau as revealed by their divergent attitudes regarding the social role of the theater.

— Le méchant selon Diderot. SRF 2:139–50, 1961. **5218**
Suggests that *méchant* is a key word in D.'s ethical, social, and political thought and that when he used it he usually had Rousseau in mind.

— La portée des théories dramatiques de Diderot et de ses réalisations théâtrales. RR 54:6–19, 1963. **5219**
" Only ambivalent characters in am-

biguous situations were congenial to him. ... his tales and novels [and not his plays] are his best dramatic writing " (p. 18, 19).

— Présence de Diderot. DS 6:13–28, 1964. **5220**
A valuable *mise au point*. A slightly longer version, but without footnotes, was published under the title of *The mind of Diderot; an enquiry into the nature of Diderot's understanding and thought* in F 14:926–38, 1963.

Perkins, Jean A. Diderot and La Mettrie. *See* 4247. **5221**
Usefully compares and contrasts the philosophy of the two writers. D.'s thought owed more to Leibniz than it did to La Mettrie, and was more dynamic, whereas La Mettrie's philosophy tended to remain mechanistic.

— Diderot's concept of virtue. SVEC 23:77–91, 1963. **5222**
Studies the evolution of D.'s theory of virtue, the final stage being " a new definition in which virtue was accepted as a conflict and a mastery of self " (p. 81). Thoughtful and useful.

Pierre, Jean. Compétence et leçons de Diderot critique d'art. PRRM n.s. 40:81–90; 41:80–86, 1952. **5223**
Combats especially the notion that D.'s ideas of art were inconsistent and contradictory, or that they were over-sentimental or merely literary.

Polt, John H. R. Jovellanos' El delincuente honrado [1773]. RR. 50:170–90, 1959. **5224**
" Jovellanos thus followed the dramatic theories of Diderot and borrowed heavily for his own work from Diderot's most famous *drame* ..." (p. 187).

Pommier, Jean. Comment Balzac relaie Diderot. RScH n.s. 62–63:161–66, 1951. **5225**
Utilizes his masterly knowledge of the works of both authors to show where Balzac may have been influenced by D.

Proust, Jacques. La contribution de Diderot à l'Encyclopédie et les théories du droit naturel. AHRF 173:257–86, 1963. **5226**
Traces the influence of Grotius, Pufendorf, Thomasius, Burlamaqui, Locke, and Hobbes on D.'s early political thought.

— Diderot et la physiognomonie. CAIEF 13: 317–29, 1961. **5227**

Interesting study of the attention that D. ceaselessly paid to the study and description of expressivity and physiognomy.

— Quelques aspects de la création littéraire chez Diderot. *In:* Collège de France. Chaire d'histoire des créations littéraires en France. Ed. by Jean Pommier. Nogent-le-Rotrou, Daupeley-Gouverneur, 1964. p. 42–59. **5228**

Numerous and very interesting examples of how the *Encyclopédie* influenced D.'s strictly literary works, with some instances, inversely, of how his literary works influenced the *Encyclopédie*.

Roddier, Henri. Diderot et la littérature expérimentale. *In:* International congress of modern languages and literatures. Literature and science; proceedings of the sixth triennial congress. Oxford, Blackwell, 1955. p. 192–97. (FILLM, 6) **5229**

Emphasizes D.'s readiness to experiment with literary forms and speaks of the *Rêve de d'Alembert* as " one of the masterpieces of experimental literature of all time " (p. 194).

Roger, Jacques. Diderot et l'Encyclopédie. *In his:* Les sciences de la vie dans la pensée française du XVIIIᵉ siècle. *See* 4146. p. 585–682. **5230**

An exhaustive treatment, both a summary and an analysis, of D.'s philosophy as it was affected by his knowledge of biology. Brings out the affinity between Buffon's doctrines and D.'s ideas, and insists that D. did not believe in transformism, as is so frequently supposed (p. 665–69).

Rosso, Corrado. Aufklaerung e Encyclopédie: Diderot e Lessing. F 6:554–73, 1955. **5231**

A scholarly and heavily documented comparison and contrast, showing that Lessing was more mystical than D., perhaps less influenced by D. than he said he was, and less utilitarian in ethical thought than D., who is represented as being willing to state an untruth if it would serve a good purpose.

Rostand, Jean. La conception de l'homme selon Helvétius et selon Diderot. *See* 4364. **5232**

Interesting confrontation of the views of Helvétius and D., especially as seen in D.'s *Réfutation suivie,* and focused on the old problem of nature versus nurture.

— Diderot et la biologie. RHS 5:5–17, 1952. *Reprinted in* 4308, p. 150–62. **5233**

A very valuable summation.

— La molécule et le philosophe. NL 7, Dec. 19, 1963. **5234**

Most interesting discussion by a great biologist of D.'s biological " philosophy " in the light of recent discoveries in regard to genes, chromosomes, and the origin of life. Compares the 20th-century doctrines of writers such as Le Dantec, J.-E. Charon, and Teilhard de Chardin with D. in respect to the view that matter has sensibility. Amplified under the title of *Diderot, philosophe de la biologie* in his: *Biologie et humanisme* (Gallimard, 1964), p. 211–33. An address given at the Sorbonne (Oct. 25, 1963) in celebration of the 250th anniversary of D.'s birth.

Rzadkowska, Ewa. Encyklopedia i Diderot w polskim oświeceniu [The Encyclopédie and Diderot in the Enlightenment in Poland]. Warsaw, Polska akademia nauk, Instytut Badań Literackich, 1955. 159 p. **5235**

A solid and well-documented monograph, especially emphasizing, in respect to D., his influence in Poland on the theater and on theories of national education.

Review : J. Fabre in RLC 32:133–35, 1958.

Saisselin, Rémy G. Ut pictura poesis : Du Bos to Diderot. JAAC 20:145–46, 1961. **5236**

Discusses the relation of literature to painting in the 18th century; feels that D. does not so much write art criticism as literature inspired by painting.

Schalk, Fritz. Wissenschaft der Sprache und Sprache der Wissenschaft im Ancien Régime. *In:* Joachim Jungius-Gesellschaft der Wissenschaften, Hamburg. Sprache und Wissenschaft : Vorträge gehalten auf der Tagung der Joachim Jungius-Gesellschaft der Wissenschaften. Göttingen, Vandenhoeck & Ruprecht, 1960. p. 101–20. *Reprinted in his:* Studien zur französischen Aufklärung. Munich, Max Hueber, 1964. p. 9–33. **5237**

Mostly devoted to the 17th-century French writers, showing how, in their feeling for rhetoric and semantics, they pursued the ideal of *justesse;* but (p. 114–20) especially studies D.'s theories of vocabulary and of the necessity for new definitions, greater flexibility of language, and more precise and rigorous use of terms. Most of the illustrations are taken from *Le neveu de Rameau*.

Schlegel, Dorothy B. Diderot as the transmitter of Shaftesbury's romanticism. SVEC 27:1457–78, 1963. *See* 5612. **5238**

Searches for evidence of Shaftesbury's influence in D.'s later works as well as in the *Essai sur le mérite et la vertu*.

Schroeder, Eckhart. Diderot und die literarästhetische Tradition : ein Beitrag zu Diderots Antikebild. Marburg, Erich Mauersberger, 1963. 232 p. **5239**

Comprehensive and up-to-date examination of D.'s understanding of the various esthetic traditions of the Ancients and of their influence on him.

Reviews : P. Brockmeier in SF 8:359, 1964; H. Dieckmann in Archiv 202:75–76, 1965–66.

Seznec, Jean. Diderot and Le génie du christianisme. JWCI 15:229–41, 1952. **5240**

Masterly demonstration of D.'s interest in religious painting and his insistence that it be judged by its success in expressing the sacred quality of the subject. Illustrated.

— Diderot et Sarrasine. DS 4:237–45, 1963. **5241**

Shows that Balzac's novella owes part of its inspiration to a passage in D.'s *Salon de 1767*.

— Essais sur Diderot et l'antiquité. Oxford, Clarendon press, 1957. xvi, 149 p. **5242**

Richly documented and abundantly illustrated essays on D.'s relationship with the Greek and Roman world. Indispensable.

Reviews : J.–B. Barrère in RLC 33:287–89, 1959; J. Bayard in AESC 15:1014–15, 1960; L. Dieckmann in CL 11:179–81, 1959; Georges May in MLN 74:91–94, 1959; R. Mortier in AC 27:576–78, 1958; R. Niklaus in MLR 54:281–82, 1959; H. Peyre in FR 32:96, 1958–59; C. Picard in JS 43–45, Jan.–Mar. 1958; R. Pouilliart in LR 15:381–83, 1961; R. Rosenblum in RR 51:138–40, 1960; R. Shackleton in FS 12:270–71, 1958.

— Le musée de Diderot. GBA 6th per. 55:343–56, May–June 1960. **5243**

Excellent article enumerating the old masters that D. was able to see at Paris or on his way to Russia and showing how D. thus broadened his criticism and sharpened his perceptiveness.

Siegel, June S. Grandeur-intimacy : the dramatist's dilemma. DS 4:247–60, 1963. *See* 5663. **5244**

Argues that D.'s failure as a dramatist came from his conviction that a great play must imitate the grandeur of the ancient drama, whereas his forte was in the intimate, richly associational style of the *conte*, the letter, or the novel.

Snyders, Georges. Une révolution dans le goût musical au XVIIIᵉ siècle : l'apport de Diderot et de Jean-Jacques Rousseau. AESC 18:20–43, 1963. **5245**

D. brought about this revolution by insisting that the inherent characteristics of music are energy and passion, insisting also that music communicate, and to very large numbers of persons. Finally, he was aware of the tumultuousness of music and its potentialities of evoking responses in every individual and in each differently.

Spink, John S. L'échelle des êtres et des valeurs dans l'œuvre de Diderot. CAIEF 13:339–51, 1961. **5246**

Vigorous philosophical examination of how much D. subscribed to and deviated from the old concept of the Great Chain of Being.

— La vertu politique selon Diderot ou le paradoxe du bon citoyen. RScH n.s. 112:471–83, 1963. **5247**

A careful analysis of texts suggests that D. believed that the Good Citizen devotes himself to the common weal instead of becoming alienated from it.

Stackelberg, Jürgen von. Rousseau, d'Alembert et Diderot traducteurs de Tacite. *See* 4297. **5248**

Interesting stylistic study : " ... le meilleur interprète de Tacite au XVIIIᵉ siècle en France est Denis Diderot."

Strange, M. Diderot et la société russe de son temps. AHRF 35:295–308, 1963. **5249**

Detailed discussion of 18th-century Russian translations and translators of D.'s *Fils naturel*, *Père de famille*, and collections of articles from the *Encyclopédie*. Does not discuss D.'s personal relationships with Russians. Essentially a translation of the author's " *Enziklopediya* " *Didro i ee russkie perevodchiki* in FE 76–88, 1959 [1961].

Switten, Marlou. Diderot's theory of language as the medium of literature. RR 44:185–96, 1953. *See* 3528. **5250**

Portrays D. as both *grammairien-philosophe*, seeing in language the medium for the communication and preservation of ideas, and as the artist, tormented by the problem of how to express in words ideas and emotions that in their complexity and simultaneity defy expression.

— L'histoire and la poésie in Diderot's writings on the novel. RR 47:259–69, 1956. **5251**

Argues tellingly that D. consciously endeavored to establish the novel as an art form.

Szigeti, József. Denis Diderot : une grande figure du matérialisme militant du XVIIIᵉ siècle. Budapest, Akadémiai Kiadó, 1962. 94 p. *Also in Russian as:* Deni Didro—vydaĭu-shchiĭsĭa predstavitel' voinstvuĭush-chego materializma XVIII veka. Moscow, 1963. 160 p. **5252**

Valuable contribution to an understanding of D. as a philosopher of science, once one has broken through the crust of the author's Marxist-Leninist clichés.
Reviews : J. Egret in Rhist 231:248, 1964; J. Gaucheron in Eur 405–06:274–75, Jan.–Feb. 1963; T. Karpova in VFil 176–78, 1964²; A. Wilson in AHR 68:519, 1962–63.

Thielemann, Leland J. Diderot and Hobbes. DS 2:221–78, 1952. *See* 5664. **5253**

Balanced and well documented. Argues that D. admired Hobbes, though never completely his disciple, and rejected completely the Hobbesian theory of political conduct.

Thomas, Jean. Diderot, les Encyclopédistes et le grand Rameau. Rsyn n.s. 69:46–67, 1951. **5254**

Excellent account of the state of dramatic music in France from 1752 to 1763.

Topazio, Virgil W. Diderot's limitations as an art critic. FR 37:3–11, 1963–64. **5255**

Vigorous asseverations, somewhat *à la* Brunetière. For interesting responses, *see* Gita May in FR 37:11–21, 1963–64, and R. Saisselin in FR 37:457–60, 1963–64.

— Diderot's supposed contribution to d'Holbach's works. *See* 4381. **5256**

Develops the appealing point of view that D. could not have written in that style "... if we can refer to that flat, repetitious, humorless, and monotonous method of writing as style " (p. 188).

— Diderot's supposed contribution to Helvétius' works. *See* 4367. **5257**

Stresses the unlikelihood of D.'s having in any way collaborated with Helvétius.

— Diderot's supposed contributions to Raynal's work. *See* 5385. **5258**

Argues that the contributions were minimal; needs to be compared with the findings of Michèle Duchet (5383).

Traz, Georges de. De Diderot à Valéry : les écrivains et les arts visuels. Michel, 1960. 296 p. **5259**

" Diderot," p. 145–68. Favorable to D., but by mixing early and late quotations, the author confuses any feeling for development in D.'s criticism.

Trousson, Raymond. Diderot et l'antiquité grecque. DS 6:215–45, 1964. **5260**

Searches D.'s work for evidence of his being a Hellenist. Thorough; supplements Seznec's *Diderot et l'antiquité* (5242).

Van Stockum, Th. C. Lessing und Diderot. Neo 39:191–202, 1955. **5261**

Rounds up all the references to D. in Lessing's works.

Van Tieghem, Philippe. Diderot à l'école des peintres. *In:* International congress of modern languages and literatures. Atti del quinto congresso internazionale. Florence, Valmartina, 1955. p. 255–63. (FILLM, 5) **5262**

Many of D.'s ideas regarding the theater and acting were revealed to him by his study of painting.

Vartanian, Aram. Diderot and Descartes; a study of scientific naturalism in the Enlightenment. Princeton, Princeton univ. press, 1953. vi, 336 p. *Also in Italian as:* Diderot e Descartes. Milan, Feltrinelli, 1956. 301 p. **5263**

Argues impressively that Descartes was more skeptical and materialistic, and D. more Cartesian, than has been believed.
Reviews : P. Beik in AHR 59:97–98, 1953–54; Y. Belaval in NNRF 2:901–04, Nov. 1953; P. Casini in RassF 6:72–79, 1957; L. Crocker in MLQ 15:381–86, 1954; H. Dieckmann in MP 53:61–66; 1955–56; Georges May in MLN 69:376–79, 1954; L. Rosenfield in Jph 53:556–64, 1956; P. Rossi in RF 48:444–48, 1957.

— Erotisme et philosophie chez Diderot. CAIEF 13:367–90, 1961. **5264**

Argues tellingly that D.'s eroticism was an " intellectual modality " closely linked with his scientific materialism.

Vernière, Paul. La position de Diderot. *In his:* Spinoza et la pensée française avant la Révolution. *See* 4158. p. 555–611 and *passim.* **5265**

Definitive study.

Vianu, Hélène. Nature et révolte dans la morale de Diderot. Eur 405–06:65–77, Jan.–Feb. 1963. **5266**

In his speculation on ethics D. conceived of nature as essentially dialectical, made up of antitheses that only through revolt could find their potential synthesis.

Volgin, V. P. Politicheskie i sofsial'nye idei Didro. VIst 32–44, March 1955. **5267**

Important Marxist-Leninist evaluation of D.'s social and political philosophy.

Waldauer, Joseph L. Society and the freedom of the creative man in Diderot's thought. DS 5:13–156, 1964. **5268**

By studying D.'s ideas of the connection between the creative person's freedom from social constraint and the internal freedom that the creative act requires, this monograph approaches D.'s esthetics freshly and revealingly. The political and sociological aspects of individual creativity are also recognized but are less amply analyzed. Brief but masterly introduction by Meyer Schapiro.

Reviews : D. Fletcher in FS 19:295–96, 1965; G. Laidlaw in RR 56:217–19, 1965; I. Podolny in FR 39:168–69, 1965–66; V. Topazio in Sym 20:278–80, 1966.

Warning, Rainer. Fiktion und Wirklichkeit in Sternes Tristram Shandy und Diderots Jacques le fataliste. *In:* Nachahmung und Illusion : Kolloquium Giessen Juni 1963, Vorlagen und Verhandlungen. Ed. by Hans Robert Jauss. Munich, Eidos, 1964. p. 96–112. **5269**

Prefers D. to Sterne because the latter's treatment of oddity and eccentricity is morally indifferent, while D.'s treatment of people's behavior is constantly conscious of moral relevancy.

— Illusion und Wirklichkeit in Tristram Shandy und Jacques le fataliste. Munich, Wilhelm Fink, 1965. 123 p. **5270**

Contends that Sterne and D. labored at establishing the theoretical foundations of a new genre in the novel. Their esthetic concerned itself especially with the nature of illusion. Sterne developed his new

technique by exploring " the oddity," D. by exploring " the bizarre."

Review : W. Engler in ZFSL 76:93–94, 1966.

Wartofsky, Marx. Diderot and the development of materialist monism. DS 2:279–329, 1952. **5271**

With professional philosophical technique, relates D.'s materialism to various elements in the thought of Spinoza, Leibniz, Maupertuis, and La Mettrie. Bold and vigorous, somewhat disregardful of earlier contributions in the field.

Weinert, Hermann K. Die Bedeutung des Abnormen in Diderots Wissenschaftslehre. *In:* Festgabe Ernst Gamillscheg zu seinem fünfundsechzigsten Geburtstag am 28. Oktober 1952, von Freunden und Schülern überreicht. Tübingen, Niemeyer, 1952. p. 228–44. **5272**

Interesting discussion of D.'s awareness of the significance of freaks, sports, and other abnormal forms, but based, for sources, too exclusively on D.'s *Prospectus* to the *Encyclopédie*.

Wilson, Arthur M. The development and scope of Diderot's political thought. SVEC 27:1871–1900, 1963. **5273**

Argues that D.'s political thought became less abstract through the years and more aware of history and economics. D.'s political ideas favored civil rights, representative institutions, and a pluralistic society.

Specific Works

Arndt, Richard T. The Vandeul manuscript copy of Jacques le fataliste. DS 3:17–25, 1961. **5274**

Compares the ms in the *fonds Vandeul* with the Leningrad ms.

Barricelli, Jean-Pierre. Music and the structure of Diderot's Le neveu de Rameau. C 5:95–111, 1963. **5275**

Impressive demonstration that the *Neveu*, through the art of subtle association, is organically a musical composition; it " progresses musically by relations, that is, by oblique and affinitive communications " (p. 98).

Belaval, Yvon. Les protagonistes du Rêve de d'Alembert. DS 3:27–53, 1961. *See* 4268. **5276**

Richly documented study of d'Alembert, Julie de Lespinasse, and Dr. Bordeu, showing what D. mirrored and what he invented concerning their relationships.

Benot, Yves. Du nouveau sur Le neveu de Rameau. LetF 1, 5, Sept. 21–27, 1961. **5277**

Documentary evidence that Rameau's nephew was appointed *inspecteur et contrôleur des maîtres à danser* on June 9, 1760; on May 27, 1764, he was paid 2400 *livres* by the community of *maîtres à danser* in compensation for abolition of the office.

Besse, Guy. Observations sur la Réfutation d'Helvétius par Diderot. DS 6:29–45, 1964. *Also in:* WZUB 13:137–43, 1964.   **5278**

Brings to bear most interestingly the results of recent investigations by psychologists on the problems that most concerned D. in his comments on Helvétius, namely, heredity versus environment, and the relationship of the individual to society.

Booy, Jean Th. de. Histoire d'un manuscrit de Diderot : La promenade du sceptique. Frankfurt am Main, Klostermann, 1964. 106 p.   **5279**

Extremely ingenious and meticulous effort to trace the history of D.'s confiscated autograph ms.

Bowen, Vincent E. Diderot's contributions to the Stockholm and Zurich copies of the Correspondance littéraire, 1773–1793. RR 56:30–36, 1965.   **5280**

Useful list, especially for indicating articles not known previously to have been included in Grimm's *Correspondance.*

— Diderot's contributions to the Stockholm copy of the Correspondance littéraire, 1760–1772. RR 55:181–89, 1964. *See* 5512. **5281**

Same comment as for 5280.

Brugmans, Henri L. Les paradoxes du philosophe. Neo 41:173–80, 1957.   **5282**

Interesting discussion of D.'s primitivism and conformism in the *Supplément au Voyage de Bougainville.* " But as is always the case with Diderot, he was the first to refute his own ideas " (p. 176).

Capone Braga, Gaetano. Il significato del Paradoxe sur le comédien di Diderot. AFLC 18:15–56, 1951.   **5283**

Maintains that the *Paradoxe* provides insight into D.'s concept of the nature of all art; shows that D. realized that art is very different from simply imitating nature. Quotes extensively from D. and the older authorities.

Crocker, Lester G. Jacques le fataliste, an expérience morale. DS 3:73–99, 1961. **5284**

Presents *Jacques le fataliste* as standing midway between D.'s " nihilism " and his humanism.

— Le Neveu de Rameau, une expérience morale. CAIEF 13:133–55, 1961.   **5285**

Interprets *Lui* as a nihilist : he achieves greatness, but only in pantomime.

Desné, Roland. Das erste Werk Diderots (Die Übersetzung der Histoire de Grèce von Temple Stanyan). WZUB 13:157–61, 1964. **5286**

Demonstrates that D.'s translation has also the characteristics of an independently creative work. Compare with Desné (5133).

Dieckmann, Herbert. Currents and cross-currents in Le fils naturel. *In:* Linguistic and literary studies in honor of Helmut A. Hatzfeld. Ed. by Alessandro S. Crisafulli. Washington, D.C., Catholic univ. of America press, 1964. p. 107–16.   **5287**

Suggests that many of the effects achieved by D.—both intentional and unintentional, conscious and unconscious—had their origin in the nature of his relationship with Rousseau and in D.'s understanding, as in the portrayal of Dorval, of Rousseau's character and temperament. Discusses the *Entretiens sur Le fils naturel* as well as the play itself.

— Diderot's letters to Falconet; critical observations on the text. FS 5:307–24, 1951.   **5288**

Meticulous comparison of the original letters with the version published in the Assé.zat-Tourneux ed. (2209, t. 18, p. 85–336).

— L'Encyclopédie et le fonds Vandeul. *See* 4305.   **5289**

Fruitful discussion of evidence in the *fonds Vandeul* bearing on the nature and amount of D.'s contributions as an author of articles in the *Encyclopédie.*

— The first edition of Diderot's Pensées sur l'interprétation de la nature. Isis 46:251–67, 1955.   **5290**

Important bibliographical information, as well as excellent comment on the significance of the *Pensées* themselves.

— The Préface-Annexe of La religieuse. DS 2:21–147, 1952.   **5291**

This extremely important article, with

copious illustrations of the original texts, constituted a "break-through" in the appreciation of *La religieuse* and in the understanding of D.'s modes of composition.

— The relationship between Diderot's Satire I and Satire II. RR 43:12–26, 1952. **5292**

Stresses the satirical aspects of *Le neveu de Rameau*, for D. himself entitled it *Satire II*.

—, and **Jean Seznec**. The Horse of Marcus Aurelius; a controversy between Diderot and Falconet. JWCI 15:198–228, 1952. **5293**

Invaluable introduction and elaborate notes concerning D.'s letter to Falconet, May 2, 1773. Illustrated.

Doolittle, James. Hieroglyph and emblem in Diderot's Lettre sur les sourds et muets. DS 2:148–67, 1952. **5294**

Remarkable study of D.'s interest in what would now be called "communication theory."

— Rameau's nephew; a study of Diderot's Second satire. Geneva, Droz, 1960. 136 p. **5295**

An original and controversial interpretation, which searches the text demandingly but perhaps unduly disregards the findings of previous writers on the subject. The author sharply distinguishes the character of *Moi* (whom he despises as self-righteous and endowed with merely a cloistered virtue) from that of D. himself. Reviews : J. Ehrmann in MLN 77:110–12, 1962; V. Hanzeli in MLQ 22:217–18, 1961; R. Niklaus in MLR 56:615–16, 1961.

Ellrich, Robert J. The rhetoric of La religieuse and eighteenth-century forensic rhetoric. DS 3:129–54, 1961. **5296**

Suggests that D. was attempting to present a brief bearing "the eloquence of the great forensic tradition."

— The structure of Diderot's Les bijoux indiscrets. RR 52:279–89, 1961. **5297**

Argues that the *Bijoux* is an early but characteristic example of D.'s making his novels empirical inquiries into morality.

Etiemble, René. Structure et sens des Pensées philosophiques. RFor 74:1–10, 1962. **5298**

Forceful argument that D. revealed himself as an atheist in the *Pensées;* also contains some very thoughtful observations on D.'s rhetoric and style.

Fellows, Otis E. The theme of genius in Diderot's Neveu de Rameau. DS 2:168–99, 1952. **5299**

Ruminates on the distinction made by D. between talent and genius and reveals this as one of the main themes in the confrontation between *Lui* and *Moi*.

Folkierski, Władysław. Comment Lord Shaftesbury a-t-il conquis Diderot? *In:* Studi in onore di Carlo Pellegrini. Turin, Società editrice internazionale, 1963. p. 319–46. **5300**

Elaborate and detailed confrontation of the Shaftesbury original and D.'s *Essai sur le mérite et la vertu*, demonstrating D.'s great skill as a translator and writer, even in so early a work.

François, Y. et T. Quelques remarques sur les Éléments de physiologie de Diderot. RHS 5:77–82, 1952. **5301**

Shows by citation in parallel columns that D. did little more than translate or summarize Haller's *Elementa physiologiae* (8 v., 1757–66) or even the abridged 2-volume ed. of 1769.

Freer, Alan J. Jacques le fataliste e La religieuse nelle testimonianze critiche contemporanee alla loro pubblicazione. SRF 3: 67–103, 1963. **5302**

Numerous reviews in the press from 1796 to 1800 were important in establishing D.'s reputation as a creative artist, where previously he had been thought of as predominantly a *philosophe* and Encyclopedist.

— Une page de La religieuse jugée par la génération romantique : Diderot et l'Amende honorable de Delacroix. RLM 16:180–208, 1963. **5303**

Delacroix' *L'amende honorable* (Philadelphia Museum of Art) was inspired by Maturin's *Melmoth the wanderer*, and thus, indirectly, by D.'s *La religieuse*. Discussed with the author's usual thoroughness.

Gamillscheg, Ernst. Diderots Neveu de Rameau und die Goethesche Übersetzung der Satire. AGSK 1953[1]. 34 p. *Reprinted in his:* Ausgewählte Aufsätze II. Tübingen, Niemeyer, 1962. p. 299–333. **5304**

A closely reasoned but extremely conjectural hypothesis that Goethe's translation was based on the archetypal ms of *Le neveu de Rameau*, a ms coming to Goethe from St. Petersburg and now lost. This denies that the real archetype is the D. holograph now in the Pierpont Morgan Library.

Reviews : J. Fabre in RLC 28:223–27, 1954; R. Mortier in RBP 32:525–32, 1954.

Greshoff, C. Jan. De actualiteit van Le neveu de Rameau. Gids 123⁸:79–94, 1960. *Also in English as:* Diderot's Neveu de Rameau. *In his:* Seven studies in the French novel; from Mme de La Fayette to Robbe-Grillet. Cape Town, A. A. Balkema, 1964. p. 14–25.
                                                5305
Interesting and urbane essay, with the ingenious suggestion that the *Neveu de Rameau* is D.'s *Picture of Dorian Gray* (p. 87). Emphasizes the meaningfulness of the *Neveu* to present-day readers.

Grimsley, Ronald. Morality and imagination in Jacques le fataliste. MLQ 19:283–93, 1958.   **5306**
Illuminating attempt to analyze D.'s psychology while writing *Jacques.*

— Psychological aspects of Le neveu de Rameau. MLQ 16:195–209, 1955.   **5307**
Interesting exploration of " need of the self to resolve an inner conflict which has failed to find adequate solution at the level of lived experience " (p. 196).

Howald, Ernst. Die Exposition von Diderots Père de famille. *In:* Überlieferung und Gestaltung : Festgabe für Theophil Spoerri zum sechzigsten Geburtstag am 10. Juni 1950. Zurich, Speer, 1950. p. 51–76. **5308**
Admires the skill with which D., in his first act, sets the scene for the rest of the play.

Huber, Egon. Bemerkungen zu Diderots Gebrauch von Vergleich und Metapher in Le neveu de Rameau. *In:* Syntactica und Stilistica; Festschrift für Ernst Gamillscheg zum 70. Geburtstag 28. Oktober 1957. Ed. by Günter Reichenkron. Tübingen, Niemeyer, 1957. p. 229–42.   **5309**
Interesting content analysis, with the surprising finding that D. uses rather fewer similes and metaphors than most other authors. In the *Neveu*, D.'s most original metaphors come from social and moral relationships, rather than from physical nature or everyday life.

Jauss, Hans Robert. Diderots Paradox über das Schauspiel (Entretiens sur le Fils naturel). GRM n.s. 11:380–413, 1961. **5310**
Argues that the *Fils naturel* and the accompanying *Entretiens* are a kind of " Paradox on Comedy " corresponding by analogy to the later " Paradox on the Actor." The paradox is the one later developed by Pirandello, of real characters

in search of a creative interpreter. In this light, the *Fils naturel,* even with all its dependence on coincidence, appears as a much more skillful work of art than critics have usually deemed it.

Kuz'min, S. Zabytaĩa rukopis' Didro (Besedy Didro s Ekaterinoĩ II) [A forgotten Diderot manuscript (Conversations of Diderot with Catherine II)]. Literaturnoe nasledstvo 58: 927–58, 1952.   **5311**
History and description of the Noroff ms used extensively by Tourneux in *Diderot et Catherine II* (2223). Elaborate notes and parallel columns demonstrate Tourneux' slips, omissions, and other editorial sins. Illustrated; very important. *See also* Paul Vernière, *Les mémoires à l'Impératrice; autour d'un manuscrit de Diderot perdu et retrouvé* in AUP 36:3–11, 1966.

Laufer, Roger. La structure et la signification de Jacques le fataliste. RScH n.s. 112: 517–35, 1963.   **5312**
Intricate analysis of the subtleties and complexities of *Jacques.*

— Structure et signification du Neveu de Rameau de Diderot. RScH n.s. 100:399–413, 1960. *Reprinted in his:* Style rococo, style des lumières. *See* 4134. p. 113–33. **5313**
Seeks to bring out the " profound unity " of the *Neveu:* " Philosophical reflections and novelistic structure perfectly coincide." Argues that analysis of the work confirms Hegel's " brilliant interpretation " of it (p. 400, 413) and that it " corresponds perfectly to the Kantian and Coleridgian specifications of unity in diversity " (p. 399),

Launay, Michel. Etude du Neveu de Rameau; hypothèses pour une recherche collective. PRRM n.s. 118:85–92, 1964.   **5314**
Preliminary report of results being achieved by a team of researchers at the Sorbonne and at the Ecole Normale Supérieure. By analyzing the composition, structure, and linguistics of the *Neveu de Rameau,* evidently using quantitative techniques to some degree, the study re-investigates the nature, role, significance, and mutual relations of the two protagonists. The nephew, after taking the initiative and seeming to triumph, breaks down physically and intellectually.

Leov, Nola M. Literary techniques in Les bijoux indiscrets. AUMLA 19:93–106, 1963.   **5315**

Interesting comparison and contrast of D.'s techniques with those of his predecessors and contemporaries. Shows how *Les bijoux* " contains the seeds of most of Diderot's qualities as a fiction writer " and " how, on occasion, he coped with his deficiencies, and even turned them to good advantage " (p. 105).

Ley, Hermann. Diderots Réfutation des Helvétius. WZUB 13:119–35, 1964. **5316**

Meaty comparison and contrast of Helvétius and D., introducing also the ideas of La Mettrie and of 19th-century materialists. Deals with such problems as the relationship between nature and nurture in human personality, and the role of perception and of reflection in cognition. Emphasizes the materialism of both writers.

Lough, John. The problem of the unsigned articles in the Encyclopédie. *See* 4319. **5317**

Adds to the number of articles attributed to D. by Proust (5335), enumerates the many erroneously attributed to D. in the Assézat-Tourneux ed. of his works, and lists the numerous ones that " may fairly be attributed " to D. on various grounds, including stylistic analysis. An indispensable treatment of a difficult and elusive subject.

Loy, J. Robert. L'Essai sur les règnes de Claude et de Néron. CAIEF 13:239–54, 1961. **5318**

Draws attention to the importance of this work in D.'s system of ethics, at the cost of slighting its comparable importance in D.'s political thought.

Maurer, Karl. Die Satire in der Weise des Horaz als Kunstform von Diderots Neveu de Rameau. RFor 64:365–404, 1952. **5319**

Thoroughgoing discussion of the Horatian models of satire forms. " Diderot seems to me to be a pupil of Horace to an astounding degree " (p. 388).

Mauzi, Robert. La parodie romanesque dans Jacques le fataliste. DS 6:89–132, 1964. **5320**

Masterly analysis, studying the complexities of the novel's structure, the significance of D.'s insistence that it is not a novel, the interlocking of the several planes of narrative, and the intentional intrusions of the author. Concludes that D. wrote " a marvelous novel, and, indeed, perhaps several at once " (p. 132).

May, Georges C. Diderot et La religieuse;

étude historique et littéraire. New Haven, Yale univ. press, 1954. viii, 245 p. **5321**

Extremely informative; with chapters about the composition, publication, reputation, and significance of *La religieuse*, as well as about D. " *sexologue*," the monastery of Saint-Eutrope, and the royal abbey of Notre-Dame de Chelles.

Reviews : J. Boorsch in FR 28:458–60, 1954–55; L. Crocker in MLQ 16:283–84, 1955; A. Delorme in Rsyn n.s. 77:99–101, 1956; H. Dieckmann in MLN 70:228–34, 1955; R. Mortier in RBP 33:646–51, 1955; R. Niklaus in FS 9:77–79, 1955; J. Proust in RHL 55:235–38, 1955; J. Quignard in LR 10:73–78, 1956; N. Torrey in RR 45:211–13, 1954.

— Le maître, la chaîne et le chien dans Jacques le fataliste. CAIEF 13:269–82, 1961. **5322**

The central idea of *Jacques le fataliste* is liberty; *maître* is one of the key words of the novel, which presents the leading personages of *Don Quixote*, but with the roles reversed. A fruitful contribution to recent criticism concerning *Jacques le fataliste*.

Mayer, Hans. Diderot und sein Roman Jacques le fataliste. *In:* Grundpositionen der französischen Aufklärung. Ed. by Werner Krauss and Hans Mayer. Berlin, Rütten und Loening, 1955. p. 55–82. *Reprinted in his:* Deutsche Literatur und Weltliteratur. Berlin, Rütten und Loening, 1957. p. 317–49. **5323**

A solid article, showing familiarity with much of D.'s work while concentrating especially on the artistic characteristics, as well as the social philosophy, of *Jacques*.

Mayer, Jean. Diderot et la quadrature du cercle. RGS 62:132–38, 1955. **5324**

D.'s *Première proposition de cyclométrie*, hitherto unpublished, and Naigeon's devastating remarks concerning it. *See* the expert and useful critique of D.'s effort by R. J. Gillings, *The mathematics of Denis Diderot* in AMT 11:2–4, 1955.

Meyer, Paul H. The Lettre sur les sourds et muets and Diderot's emerging concept of the critic. DS 6:133–55, 1964. **5325**

Thorough and stimulating analysis, confirming how perceptive Sainte-Beuve was when he declared D. to be the originator of the genre of literary criticism that seeks to honor excellence rather than to identify defects. This attitude also explains D.'s constant attempt to discover a sympathetic and responsive reader and establish communication with him.

— The unity and structure of Diderot's Neveu de Rameau. C 2:362–86, 1959–60. **5326**
Convincing and important analysis of how the *Neveu* " is probably the most lively and engrossing specimen of a conversation with an unforgettable character ever put on paper " (p. 386).

Mylne, Vivienne. Truth and illusion in the Préface-Annexe to Diderot's La religieuse. MLR 57:350–56, 1962. **5327**
Analyzes the logical and esthetic complexities of the implications of the *Préface-Annexe*. " Diderot, one feels, would have relished our confusion " (p. 356).

Nykrog, Per. Les étapes des amours de Jacques. Etudes romanes dédiées à Andreas Blinkenberg à l'occasion de son 70ᵉ anniversaire. Copenhagen, Munksgaard, 1963. p. 113–26. (OrL, Supplement 3) **5328**
Excellent dissection of the complex anatomy of *Jacques le fataliste*. " ... the underlying subject of the novel is the rôle played by human personality—be it impassioned or clear-headed—in the play of events that constitutes a destiny " (p. 126). Useful and revelatory.

Parrish, Jean. Conception, évolution, et forme finale de La religieuse. RFor 74: 361–84, 1962. **5329**
Traces the chronology of the 3 revisions of *La religieuse* and the transformation subtly entailed in each as a result of D.'s changing the audience he had in mind. Should be read in connection with the author's ed. of *La religieuse* (5035).

Pommier, Jean. Autour de la Lettre sur les sourds et muets. RHL 51:261–72, 1951. **5330**
Traces the circumstances of the publication of the *Lettre*, and of the allusions therein to Batteux, Bernis, and Berthier, with reflections on what these allusions reveal of D.'s character.

— La copie Naigeon du Rêve de d'Alembert est retrouvée. RHL 52:25–47, 1952. **5331**
Textual and stylistic study of the *Rêve*, based on a ms (privately owned and unpublished) permitting comparison with the Leningrad and *fonds Vandeul* mss.

— Lueurs nouvelles sur les manuscrits de Diderot. BBB 201–17, 1954. **5332**

Discusses the history of the several mss of D.'s *Eléments de physiologie*.

Proust, Jacques. A propos d'un Plan d'opéra-comique de Diderot. RHT 7:173–88, 1955. **5333**
Using a wealth of knowledge about the 18th-century theater, shows that D. employed a number of old and reliable theatrical devices in his *Plan* and was evidently cognizant of all forms of dramatic art, especially that of the *théâtre populaire*.

— A propos du Shérif. CahHM 75:162–70, 1963. **5334**
Revealing comparison, using unpublished notes by D., of the literary treatment by D., John Pomfret, Addison, Christian Fürchtegott Gellert, and Dorat of an incident in Rapin de Thoyras' *Histoire d'Angleterre*.

— Diderot et l'Encyclopédie. See 4327. **5335**
Brilliant and fruitful analysis of D.'s middle years, by which is revealed how much the *Encyclopédie* affected D.'s development as an ethical and political thinker and contributed to his mastery of technological, scientific, and philosophical characteristics of his time. The work is also a history of the *Encyclopédie* itself and is a momentous contribution to biography and intellectual history. Useful appendixes and bibliography. For complementary research on the attribution of articles to D., *see* Lough (5317).

— La documentation technique de Diderot dans l'Encyclopédie. RHL 57:335–52, 1957. **5336**
Highly informative; includes a classified list of sources and throws light on the history of the *planches*.

— Pour servir à une édition critique de la Lettre sur le commerce de la librairie. DS 3:321–45, 1961. **5337**
Dates the *Lettre* between Sept., 1763, and Feb., 1764, and usefully compares the ms of it in the B.N. with the version published in the name of the booksellers (1764).

— Recherches nouvelles sur La religieuse. DS 6:197–214, 1964. **5338**
Contemporary evidence from the Jansenist *Nouvelles ecclésiastiques* that proves that D., in his description of conventual life, knew what he was talking about.

Variations sur un thème de l'Entretien avec d'Alembert. RScH n.s. 112:453–70, 1963. **5339**

Taking D.'s analogy of " resonant strings that feel " with " the fibres of our organs," shows parallels in the writings of Cartaud de la Villate, Castel, La Mettrie, Bonnet, Simmias, Marcel Proust, and Claudel.

Riffaterre, Michael. Diderot et le philosophe esclave : de Diogène Laërce à Victor Hugo. DS 3:347–67, 1961. **5340**

Shows how wide an array of classic sources D. used in his *Réflexions sur Térence;* also studies the stylistics of the piece and points out its influence on Victor Hugo.

Roelens, Maurice. L'art de la digression dans l'Entretien d'un père avec ses enfants. Eur 405–06:172–82, Jan.–Feb. 1963. **5341**

Through tracing the various stages of the text, demonstrates D.'s elaboration of the difficulty of moral choice. Useful.

Roger, Jacques. Diderot et Buffon en 1749. DS 4:221–36, 1963. **5342**

Searches the probable influences of the first 3 v. of Buffon's *Histoire naturelle* on the *Lettre sur les aveugles.*

Sandomirsky, L. Natalie. The ethical standard of the genius in Diderot's Neveu de Rameau. Sym 18:46–55, 1964. **5343**

" Rameau is not a genius, not in any field, and yet, believing in his excellence, he has allowed himself moral freedom. Diderot shows that the results have been disastrous ..." (p. 52).

Schalk, Fritz. Diderots Artikel Mélancolie in der Enzyklopädie. ZFSL 66:175–85, 1956. *Reprinted in his:* Studien zur französischen Aufklärung. Munich, Max Hueber, 1964. p. 127–38. **5344**

Studies D.'s sources, and also the development and change in meaning of the word *mélancolie* in 18th-century French literature.

— Diderots Essai über Claudius und Nero. Cologne, Westdeutscher Verlag, 1956. 30 p. *Reprinted in his:* Studien zur französischen Aufklärung. Munich, Max Hueber, 1964. p. 148–70. **5345**

An important essay, the first to point out the significance in D.'s political thought of his defense of Seneca.

Reviews : R. Mortier in RLC 31:284–85, 1957; O. Seel in HZ 186:96–97, 1958.

Seznec, Jean. Les derniers Salons de Diderot. FS 19:111–24, 1965. **5346**

" It must be admitted that the author of the last *Salons* is no longer Diderot at his best; and sometimes he is not even Diderot " (p. 124).

— Diderot and historical painting. *In:* Aspects of the eighteenth century. Ed. by Earl R. Wasserman. Baltimore, Johns Hopkins press, 1965. p. 129–42. **5347**

Explores the implications of the fact that D. " has the highest regard for hitorical paintings, for what he calls ' les grandes machines ' ..." (p. 130). Illustrated. Quotations translated; no footnotes or page citations.

— Les Salons de Diderot. HLB 5:267–89, 1951. **5348**

Spirited and urbane description of D.'s critical methods and of his qualifications for criticizing art. Illustrated.

Smiley, Joseph R. A list of Diderot's articles for Grimm's Correspondance littéraire. See 5515. **5349**

Useful as far as it goes; does not include 19 items appearing in the Stockholm ms between 1760 and 1772 and listed by Vincent E. Bowen (5281) nor 37 additional items appearing in either the Stockholm or the Zurich ms between 1773 and 1793 and listed by *same* (5280).

Smith, Ian H. Diderot's Jacques le fataliste; art and necessity. AUMLA 8:17–23, 1958. **5350**

Argues that D. derived a feeling of liberating himself from the logic of inexorable determinism through a self-awareness of being creative.

— The Mme de la Pommeraye tale and its commentaries. AUMLA 17:18–30, 1962. **5351**

Analyzes the technical devices by which D. makes this tale in *Jacques le fataliste* believable, and shows how D. tends intentionally to dissolve and confuse the concepts of " goodness " and " badness." Believes that D. remains deeply puzzled and was not, " by some vaguely Hegelian dialectic process, working towards a solution in favour of libertarianism " (p. 24).

Thielemann, Leland J. Diderot's Encyclopedic article on justice : its sources and significance. DS 4:261–83, 1963. **5352**

Argues that D.'s ultimate source for *Juste* was the Grotian school of natural law.

Tilquin, Charles. Diderot et la théorie de la nature de la morale d'après le Supplément au Voyage de Bougainville. CahHM 75:178–94, 1963.   **5353**

Thoughtful exploration of D.'s efforts to understand morality in historical and sociological terms. Argues that D. wished to replace traditional ethics by a new technique, clinical in type.

Undank, Jack. A new date for Jacques le fataliste. MLN 74:433-37, 1959.   **5354**

Suggests convincingly that *Jacques* was begun in 1771.

Varloot, Jean. Les copies du Rêve de d'Alembert. CAIEF 13:353–66, 1961. **5355**

Meticulous examination and comparison of the various mss. Indispensable for the textual study of the *Rêve*.

— Jacques le fataliste et la Correspondance littéraire. RHL 65:629–36, 1965.   **5356**

The Gotha ms of the *Correspondance littéraire* lends proof that *Jacques le fataliste* was composed in 3 stages : not later than 1771, 1778–80, and 1780–82. The nature of the additions suggests to the author that D. was more of a story-teller than a novelist (p. 636).

— Le projet antique du Rêve de d'Alembert de Diderot. BRP 2:49–61, 1963.   **5357**

Detailed study of ancient sources, as well as minor early-Enlightenment ones, that might have served as *ambiance* to D.'s *Rêve de d'Alembert*.

Vernière, Paul. Diderot et C. L. de Hagedorn : une étude d'influence. RLC 30: 239–54, 1956. See 5871.   **5358**

Abundant evidence that D., in his *Pensées détachées sur la peinture*, was more extensively influenced by Hagedorn's *Betrachtungen über die Malerei* (1762; French translation, 1775) than he saw fit to acknowledge.

— Diderot et l'invention littéraire: à propos de Jacques le fataliste. RHL 59:153–67, 1959.   **5359**

Gives us insight into D.'s creative methods by showing convincingly how he transfused real-life episodes into *Jacques le fataliste*. Also, like Undank (5354), dates the composition of *Jacques* from 1771.

Wilson, Arthur M. The biographical implications of Diderot's Paradoxe sur le comédien. DS 3:369–83, 1961.   **5360**

H. Peyre (in RR 52:300, 1961) : "... poses the disturbing question of Diderot's sincerity, or of his masks and his ambivalence. ..."

Wolpe, Hans. Diderot et l'Histoire des Deux Indes. *In* 5386. p. 186–252.   **5361**

Elaborate comparison and tabulation of the D. contributions to the 1770, 1774, and 1781 eds.

Yamamoto, Yuko. Diderot et Kaempfer; note sur l'article Japonais de l'Encyclopédie. Hikaku Bungaku 2:60–79, 1959.   **5362**

A study, using parallel columns, of how D. used and adapted Kaempfer's history of Japan. D. added to the bland and neutral Kaempfer some very sharp comments on religious faith and religious intolerance.

CHAPTER X. MISCELLANEOUS PROSE

(Nos. 5363–5540)

OTIS E. FELLOWS, JEANNE R. MONTY, MADELEINE FIELDS MORRIS, MERLE L. PERKINS, EDWARD D. SEEBER, ARAM VARTANIAN, *and* FERNAND VIAL

Friedrich Melchior, *baron* de Grimm
(Nos. 5363–5372)

JEANNE R. MONTY

See Bowen (5280–81).

Grimm, Friedrich Melchior, *baron* **de.** Une lettre inédite de Grimm. Ed. by A. Seznec. FS 13:113–24, 1959. **5363**

Letter to Ernest II, duke of Saxe-Gotha, shows G. in his role as factotum for the ducal family. Extensive notes on the text.

— Lettres inédites de Grimm à la reine-mère de Suède. Ed. by Vincent Bowen. RLC 32:565–72, 1958 **5364**

Nine letters which do not deal with any literary topic but reveal G.'s usual mixture of familiarity and obsequiousness in his relations with the queen of Sweden.

Booy, J. Th. de. Henri Meister et la première édition de la Correspondance littéraire (1812–1813). SVEC 23:215–69, 1963. **5365**

Important clarification of Meister's role in the 1813 publication of the *Correspondance littéraire, 1782–1790*. Based on series of 24 letters to and from Meister, some of which were previously unpublished.

Diderot, Denis. Lettre apologétique de l'abbé Raynal à M. Grimm. *In:* Inventaire du fonds Vandeul et inédits de Diderot. *See* 4992. p. 236–53. **5366**

Violent letter of reproach to G., suspected of having been corrupted by court life, in defense of Raynal's *Histoire des Deux Indes.* Reaffirms D.'s liberal political opinion and throws light on his relations with Grimm in his later years. Unknown to Smiley (2413A). Letter permits no doubt that G. was the real author of the dedication to the comtesse de La Marck and the princesse de Robecq.

Dieckmann, Herbert. Les contributions de Diderot à la Correspondance littéraire et à l'Histoire des Deux Indes. RHL 51:417–40, 1951. *See* 5136 and 5381. **5367**

Comparison between certain passages of the *Histoire,* the *Correspondance littéraire,* and the mss of the *fonds Vandeul* shows that some articles of Diderot were used both by G. and by Raynal in their works. A list of corrections made by G. on Diderot's mss proves that " Grimm n'a point trahi la pensée de son ami, et qu'il était un éditeur habile et consciencieux qui n'a pas abusé du droit que Diderot lui concédait de le corriger " (p. 440).

Monty, Jeanne R. The criticism of Rousseau in the Correspondance littéraire. *See* 5513. **5368**

Brief comparison between the criticism of G. and that of Meister, contrasting the latter's generally fair and sound judgment of Rousseau with G.'s consistently hostile attitude after 1757. Sainte-Beuve's admiration for G. and his impartiality toward Rousseau based on an article by Meister.

— La critique littéraire de Melchior Grimm. Geneva, Droz, 1961. 137 p. *See* 5514. **5369**

Systematic study of G.'s criticism of the main authors of the second half of the 18th century. Rousseau, Diderot, Voltaire treated in individual chapters. Concludes G. does not deserve the high praise given him by most historians of literature because of his rigidity, partiality, and sometimes narrowness of vision.

Reviews : C. Aldrich in MLJ 46:323–24 1962; L. Gossman in FS 17:65–66, 1963; R. Grimsley in MLR 58:475, 1963; W. Krauss in Archiv 199:64, 1962–63; M. Launay in RHL 64:110–11, 1964.

— Grimm et les Nouvelles littéraires de Raynal. *See* 5538. **5370**

Contests Meister's claim that the

Correspondance littéraire is a continuation of Raynal's work. It was rather a completely independent enterprise.

Smiley, Joseph R. A list of Diderot's articles for Grimm's Correspondance littéraire. *See* 5515. **5371**
Important list of 89 articles written by Diderot for G., of which only 49 appear with the proper acknowledgment in both the Assézat-Tourneux ed. of the *Œuvres complètes* and the Tourneux ed. of the *Correspondance littéraire*. Must now be revised in light of mss from the *fonds Vandeul*. *See also* Bowen (5280–81).

Wilson, Arthut M. The unpublished portion of Grimm's critique of La nouvelle Héloïse. MLR 59:27–29, 1964. **5372**
From the Stockholm ms of the *Correspondance littéraire*, Jan. 15, 1761.

Jean François de La Harpe
(Nos. 5373–5374)

JEANNE R. MONTY

Jovicevich, Alexander. An unpublished letter of La Harpe. MLN 78:304–07, 1963. **5373**
Letter to a M. Dupoirier, dated Aug. 1767, gives picture of L.'s literary activities during his stay at Ferney in 1766–67.

Meyer, Paul H. The French Revolution and the legacy of the philosophes. FR 30:429–34, 1956–57. **5374**
Main part of the article devoted to L., whose indictment of the *philosophes* on religious grounds provided ammunition to writers hostile to the Enlightenment. L. greatly responsible for neglect of Diderot and attacks on Rousseau for many years. It was also due to him that a greater emphasis was placed on Voltaire as *littérateur* than as thinker and philosopher.

Jean Le Clerc
(No. 5375)

JEANNE R. MONTY

Le Clerc, Jean. Lettres inédites de Le Clerc à Locke. Ed. by Gabriel Bonno. Berkeley, Univ. of California press, 1959. 135 p. *See* 5601. **5375**
Excellent edition of 65 letters of L. to Locke, with copious notes on the text.

Does not alter greatly the image of L. given by Mrs. Barnes (2426), but contains useful information concerning L.'s unsuccessful attempts to leave Holland for England between 1691 and 1697, his intellectual interests and friendship with Locke, and the part he played in the publication and first dissemination of the *Essay concerning human understanding.*
Reviews : W. Krauss in Archiv 198: 282–83, 1961–62; J. Tucker in MLJ 46: 185–86, 1962; A. Vartanian in MP 60: 221–23, 1962–63.

Guillaume Thomas Raynal
(Nos. 5376–5386)

JEANNE R. MONTY

Raynal, Guillaume Thomas François. L'anticolonialisme au XVIIIᵉ siècle : histoire philosophique et politique des établissements et du commerce des Européens dans les Deux Indes. Introduction, choix de texte et notes par Gabriel Esquer. Presses univ. de France, 1951. 318 p. **5376**
Excerpts from R.'s work, arranged by topics, give general view of the *Histoire* as an arsenal of anticolonialism. 45-page introduction includes a brief biography of R. based on Feugère and a discussion of the main themes of the *Histoire*, but fails to distinguish between R.'s and Diderot's contributions. Useful only as a general, popular introduction to the *Histoire* and its main themes.

Courtney, C. P. Antoine-Laurent de Jussieu, collaborateur de l'abbé Raynal; documents inédits. RHL 63:217–27, 1963. **5377**
Identifies almost 50 passages in the 1780 ed. of the *Histoire des Deux Indes* written or revised by Jussieu. Based on Jussieu and Raynal mss in the library of the Muséum d'Histoire Naturelle.

— Burke, Franklin et Raynal; à propos de deux lettres inédites. RHL 62:78–86, 1962. *See* 5811. **5378**
Letters asking for specific data about the American colonies for the 1780 ed. of the *Histoire*. Shows R.'s inquisitiveness and concern for accurate information.

— David Hume et l'abbé Raynal; une source de l'Histoire philosophique des Deux Indes. RLC 36:565–71, 1962. *See* 5585. **5379**
Source is Hume's *History of England*, which furnished R. with copious details on the history of religion in England. R. did not always follow this source

literally, but omitted passages which he considered to be too favorable to the Church and strengthened others which underlined his antireligious views.

Diderot, Denis. Lettre apologétique de l'abbé Raynal à M. Grimm. *See* 4992. p. 236–53. **5380**

Violent letter of reproach to Grimm, in defense of R.'s liberal philosophy. Reaffirms Diderot's liberal political opinions and confirms the nature of his contributions to the *Histoire des Deux Indes*, although no precise passages are identified.

Dieckmann, Herbert. Les contributions de Diderot à la Correspondance littéraire et à l'Histoire des Deux Indes. *See* 5367. **5381**

Based on mss of the *fonds Vandeul*. Reaffirms and amplifies Feugère's conclusions (2443, 2445) concerning nature and extent of Diderot's contributions to the *Histoire*. Many articles utilized by both Grimm and R. in their works.

Duchet, Michèle. Bougainville, Raynal, Diderot et les sauvages du Canada; une source ignorée de l'Histoire des Deux Indes. RHL 63:228–36, 1963. *See* 5141. **5382**

Excerpts from Bougainville's *Journal* (1756–60), published in the *Journal étranger* of 1762, utilized by R. for data concerning American Indians. Passages of the *Histoire* written by Diderot also reflect the influence of Bougainville's views on the " noble savage."

— Diderot collaborateur de Raynal : à propos des Fragments imprimés du fonds Vandeul. RHL 60:531–56, 1960. *See* 5142. **5383**

Most detailed study and comparison between the mss of the *fonds Vandeul* and the *Histoire des Deux Indes*, concluding that the *Fragments imprimés*, the *Mélanges XXXVIII*, and the *Pensées détachées* ... represent part of Diderot's contributions to the *Histoire*. Believes that Diderot gave many articles to the 1774 ed., and that, in the 1780 ed., " c'est Diderot qui a pris la plume et l'ouvrage en main " (p. 542). The *Histoire* thus became the vehicle for Diderot's political and historical ideas.

— Le Supplément au Voyage de Bougainville et la collaboration de Diderot à l'Histoire des Deux Indes. CAIEF 13:173–87, 1961. *See* 5144. **5384**

Important study of the analogies between the *Supplément* and the *Histoire*, with a comparison between passages written by Diderot in both works, shows evolution of Diderot's thought. Nuances introduced in the *Histoire* clarify certain of Diderot's ideas in the *Supplément*, particularly regarding the state of nature and the ethics of sexuality.

Topazio, Virgil W. Diderot's supposed contributions to Raynal's work. Sym 12: 103–16, 1958. *See* 5258. **5385**

Basing arguments mainly on Diderot's correspondence, rejects view of Diderot as a major contributor to the *Histoire des Deux Indes*. Diderot, a reluctant contributor to the 1774 ed., did not do much more for the 1780 ed. Rejects Wolpe's evidence of Diderot's style and content in the *Histoire, infra*. But *see* articles of Dieckmann and Duchet, *supra*.

Wolpe, Hans. Raynal et sa machine de guerre; l'Histoire des Deux Indes et ses perfectionnements. Stanford, Stanford univ. press, 1957. 252 p. **5386**

Useful, systematic, comparative study of the variants in the 1770, 1774, and 1780 eds. of the *Histoire*, divided by subject matter. *Histoire* is not a mere compilation but has its own elastic, internal structure which allowed later additions. Sees duality between theoretical radicalism and practical moderation with general progression towards radical polemicism. Conclusions on Diderot's contributions, similar to Feugère's (2443, 2445), discussed and amplified by Topazio and Duchet, *supra*.

Reviews : L. Crocker in MLN 73:309–10, 1958; A. Pizzorusso in SF 2:323–24, 1958; V. Topazio in RR 48:308–09, 1957.

Charles Irénée Castel,
abbé de Saint-Pierre
(Nos. 5387–5417)

Merle L. Perkins

A number of significant items published before 1950 and not included in CBFL, v. 4, are listed below.

Bahner, W. Der Friedensgedanke in der Literatur der französischen Aufklärung. *In:* Grundpositionen der französischen Aufklärung. Berlin, Rütten & Loening, 1955. p. 141–207. (Neue Beiträge zur Literaturwissenschaft. Ed. by Werner Krauss and Hans Meyer. V. 1) **5387**

Monograph on peace and war in the literature of the French Enlightenment. Deals with S.-P. on p. 151–70 and in footnotes on p. 305ff.

Barni, Jules. Histoire des idées morales et politiques en France au xviiie siècle. Baillière, 1865–73. 1:49–104.   **5388**

Material on S.-P. is in 3 parts. The first treats briefly his life and character, the second examines his moral and political ideas, the third studies the *Projet de paix perpétuelle.* The *Polysynodie,* in spite of its defects, revealed the vices of the existing system. The *Paix perpétuelle* served humanity by attacking militarism. A rather general treatment of the abbé's thought.

Blanchet, Jules Adrien. Un pacifiste sous Louis XV : la Société des Nations de l'abbé de Saint-Pierre. Mâcon, 1917. 20 p.   **5389**

Analysis of the abbé's ideas on European and world government at a time when efforts were underway to promote the establishment of a League of Nations. Inclination to interpret project out of 18th-century context.

Borner, Wilhelm. Das Weltstaatsprojekt des Abbé de Saint-Pierre. Berlin and Leipzig, 1913. vii, 80 p.   **5390**

S.-P. does not deserve mockery. Many of his ideas which are today active in international unions or in the field of arbitration prove him to be no mere dreamer.

Bury, John Bagnell. The idea of progress : an inquiry into its origin and growth. *See* 1031. p. 127–43.   **5391**

Emphasizes S.-P.'s optimism, which " touched *naïveté,*" but concedes that he had an important role in the development of revolutionary ideas and a significance in fact which " has hardly been appreciated yet." Many penetrating insights.

Constantinescu-Bagdat, Elise. Etudes d'histoire pacifiste. Presses univ. de France, 1924–25. 2:105–70.   **5392**

Aware of the immediate impossibility of the *Projet de paix perpétuelle,* S.-P. nevertheless propagated his ideas to call attention to the errors and misdeeds of princes of his time. Similarly, he had little hope of accomplishing the reforms of the *Polysynodie.* That work was primarily an attack on the government and reign of Louis XIV. Constantinescu-Bagdat is inclined to exaggerate the abbé's influence: " Il a élaboré le programme de la philosophie de Montesquieu, de Rousseau, de Voltaire et a engagé tous les philosophes à lutter contre la guerre …. ces philosophes ont-ils tous immortalisé avec leur nom, les idées de leur vénérable Maître, l'abbé de Saint-Pierre."

Droysen, J. G. Über die Schrift Anti St. Pierre und deren Verfasser. Preuss. Akademie der Wissenschaften (Berlin). Monatsberichte 711–46, 1878.   **5393**

After Frederick II conquered Silesia, the abbé severely criticized this action in a pamphlet, *Enigme politique.* The King had its argument refuted by an anonymous article, *Anti-Saint-Pierre, ou, réfutation de l'énigme de l'abbé de Saint-Pierre.*

Dupuis, Charles. Le projet précis et complet de l'abbé de Saint-Pierre pour rendre la paix perpétuelle en Europe. ADI 60:28–46, 1937.   **5394**

Sympathetic treatment of the abbé's aims and specific proposals by an authority in the field of international law.

François, Alexis. L'abbé de Saint-Pierre et les travaux de l'Académie française. RHL 36:242–45, 1929.   **5395**

Concise discussion of original ed. of S.-P.'s *Discours* on the *Travaux.*

Friedrich, Carl Joachim. Inevitable peace. Cambridge, Harvard univ. press, 1948. xii, 294 p.   **5396**

S.-P.'s thought is treated *passim* as indicated in the index. Friedrich accepts J.-J. Rousseau's judgment that the *Paix perpétuelle* too optimistically assumed that " men, and more especially princes and their ministers, are rational and follow their true, long-range interest." The abbé, unlike Rousseau, is supposed to appeal to " the higher reason in princes." Friedrich uses the short, one-volume 1712 ed. of the *Projet,* which does not include the lengthy philosophic discussions found in the three-volume 1713–17 ed. As a result, the Hobbesian intellectual framework of the project is omitted by Friedrich.

Gilson, Etienne. Les métamorphoses de la cité de Dieu. Louvain, Publications univ. de Louvain, 1952. p. 207–27.   **5397**

The significance to the United Europe concept of S.-P.'s general idea that peace must be made perpetual among all Christian states.

Hemleben, Sylvester John. Plans for world peace through six centuries. Chicago, Univ. of Chicago press, 1943. p. 56–74.   **5398**

Deals almost exclusively with the *Paix perpétuelle* and treats in some detail the machinery of the plan as presented in the 1713 French and 1714 English eds. of the *Projet*.

Hendel, Charles William. Jean–Jacques Rousseau, moralist. *See* 2080. **5399**

S.-P. treated *passim*. The abbé's doctrine of utility, his ideas on federation and pact, his views about governmental reform and his concept of natural right. Treatment is usually thorough and carefully documented. Hendel may weigh too heavily, without sufficient evidence, supposed innovations Rousseau made in his own versions of the abbé's *Paix perpétuelle* and *Polysynodie*.

Houwens-Post, H. La Société des Nations de l'abbé de Saint-Pierre. Amsterdam, Uitgevershbedrijf de Spieghel, 1932. 200 p. **5400**

Competent thesis. The idea of establishing a European union was not new, but the abbé's project was original in certain of its principal ideas. Houwens-Post compares the abbé's project to Sully's plan (the Grand Design of Henry IV), to the Germanic Confederation, and to the Pact of the League of Nations.

Lavergne, Léonce de. L'abbé de Saint-Pierre. RDM 2ᵉ pér. 79:557–89, 1869. **5401**

Offers survey of abbé's many activities, his relations with figures of his day, some details about the Club de l'Entresol.

Martin, Kingsley. The rise of French liberal thought; a study of political ideas from Bayle to Condorcet. Ed. by J.P. Mayer. 2nd rev. ed. New York, New York univ. press, 1954. 316 p. **5402**

S.-P. is discussed *passim*. Emphasizes the abbé's state socialism. Martin thinks S.-P. " stood alone in his generation " by his confidence that men are perfectible and that laws derived from natural principles can eliminate social evil.

Meulen, Jacob ter. Der Gedanke der internationalen Organisation in seiner Entwicklung. The Hague, Nijhoff, 1917–40. 3 v. **5403**

Many references to S.-P. in all 3 volumes of this work, but *see* especially 1:180–221. Relates main events of abbé's life, analyzes in some detail his machinery for European organization, and presents comments about the project in the *Journal littéraire* and the *Journal des savants* and criticisms by figures like Dubois, Voltaire, Leibniz, Huldenberg, d'Argenson, Fleury, Rousset, Frederick II, d'Alembert, and others.

Perkins, Merle L. The abbé de Saint-Pierre and the seventeenth-century intellectual background. APSP 97:69–76, 1953. **5404**

Article examines the abbé's efforts at documentation. He read pre-1717 texts on politics, economics, and international law. Apparently only after a long apprenticeship did he write and publish his peace project.

— Civil theology in the writings of the abbé de Saint-Pierre. JHI 18:242–53, 1957. **5405**

In the tradition of the civil theologian, the abbé concerns himself with the articles of faith which a nation's people is to use. In doing so, he avoids on the one hand the truth-seeking of the natural theologian and deist which to him seems infertile and on the other the propensity to local absolutes which in his opinion characterizes and often debases many of the teachings of the religions of history.

— Descartes and the abbé de Saint-Pierre. MLQ 19:294–302, 1958. **5406**

The Cartesian resolutive-compositive devices which S.-P. applies and considers the instruments of discovery are in no way inconsistent with the false Cartesianism of the abbé's assumption that fear is " le plus puissant ressort qui fasse agir les hommes."

— Documentation of Saint-Pierre's Projet de paix perpétuelle. MLQ 16:210–17, 1955. **5407**

In his economic thinking S.-P. never broke away from beliefs common to his age. He was original in the sense that he sought to apply well-known economic premises to the solution of problems admitting no solution in the minds of his contemporaries.

— Late seventeenth-century scientific circles and the abbé de Saint-Pierre. APSP 102:404–12, 1958. **5408**

Discusses the influence on the abbé of the men of science he met between 1680 and 1700 : Varignon, Fontenelle, Bourdelot, Régis, Du Vernay, Tauvry, Méry, Lémery, Cassini, Huygens, Picard, etc. Examines his research during these years when he became convinced that experimentation, observation, and reasoning must go hand in hand, and describes his search for universally applicable mechanistic laws in politics.

— The Leviathan and Saint-Pierre's Projet de paix perpétuelle. APSP 99:259–67, 1955. *See* 5712. **5409**

The *Paix perpétuelle* is supported by a definite body of theory which consistently follows to the national level ideas about man, social contract, and sovereignty expressed in the *Leviathan*. The new European republic itself is an extension of the Hobbesian civil commonwealth.

— The moral and political philosophy of the abbé de Saint-Pierre. Geneva, Droz, 1959. 157 p. *See* 5713.   **5410**

Uses ms sources at Neuchâtel not cited by earlier scholars and collections in Paris, Rouen, London and in libraries of the United States. Gives more complete picture of S.-P.'s intellectual background and development.

Reviews : W. Barber in MLR 56:612–13, 1961; R. Mortier in RHL 63:308–10, 1963; A. Novelli in SF 5:555, 1961; J. Spink in FS 15:165–66, 1961; J. Stevens in AHR 65:963, 1960.

— An unpublished letter from Saint-Pierre to Daguesseau. MLN 70:110–13, 1955.   **5411**

The abbé complains about legal procedures which allow convictions on insufficient evidence.

— Unpublished maxims of the abbé de Saint-Pierre. FR 31:498–502, 1957–58.   **5412**

Maxims show that S.-P. gives the passions a strong role in human motivation. He finds that instinctive love of self guides the majority of men, but emphasizes the constructive side of this constant.

— Voltaire and the abbé de Saint-Pierre. FR 34:152–63, 1960–61. *See* 4669.   **5413**

Attacking abuses in the abbé's name, Voltaire took liberties which in his own name would have been dangerous. Disturbed by the shallowness of S.-P.'s views on the arts and sciences, he senses also in his utopianism a threat to the human spirit, for in the abbé's utopia progress was equated to the perfecting of social machinery.

— Voltaire and the abbé de Saint-Pierre on world peace. SVEC 18:9–34, 1961. *See* 4670   **5414**

Shows Voltaire's position with respect to key issues raised by S.-P., especially in the *Paix perpétuelle*, the major object of Voltaire's attack.

Pomeau, René. De la paix perpétuelle à la nation armée. Tro 147:73–85, March 1960.   **5415**

The idea of nation conceived in the 18th century is subject to drastic revision now that vast empires have arisen outside of a Europe still " émiettée en nations-états." On the other hand, 18th-century ideas for international organization have a future : " Mais un avenir s'ouvre à une pensée qui se réclamera, si elle n'est ingrate, du bon abbé de Saint-Pierre et du grand Cloots Anacharsis."

Rousseau, Jean-Jacques. The political writings of Jean-Jacques Rousseau. Ed. by Charles Edwyn Vaughan. *See* 1882. 1:359–422.   **5416**

These pages devoted to the relationship of S.-P. and Rousseau and to the texts of Rousseau's versions of the *Paix perpétuelle* and the *Polysynodie*. Vaughan may exaggerate Rousseau's originality in revising these works.

Wade, Ira O. The abbé de Saint-Pierre and Dubois. JMH 2:430–47, 1930.   **5417**

Carefully documented article based on letters of Dubois and the abbé and on the latter's *Réflexions sur la grande alliance*, now to be found in the Archives du Ministère des Affaires Etrangères. S.-P.'s proposals were " neither out of keeping with Dubois' policies nor out of harmony with the spirit of his time."

Quesnay and the Physiocrats
(Nos. 5418–5434)

EDWARD D. SEEBER

Many additional titles bearing on the economic doctrines of the physiocrats can be found in the several volumes of the *Index of Economic Journals* (Homewood, Ill., Richard D. Irwin), the UNESCO *International Bibliography of Economics*, and in the bibliography of *François Quesnay et la physiocratie, infra*. A number of significant items published before 1950 and not included in CBFL, v. 4, are listed below.

Quesnay, François. Les manuscrits économiques de François Quesnay et du marquis de Mirabeau aux Archives nationales. Ed. by Georges Weulersse. P. Geuthner, 1910. vii, 150 p.   **5418**

Extracts and critical notes on several mss from 1756 to 1776. *See* 2505.

Association française de science économique. Bi-centenaire du Tableau économique de François Quesnay, 1758–1958. Sirey, 1958. 48 p.   **5419**

Papers and discourses on the occasion of the bicentenary held at the Sorbonne. Reproduces pages from original ms.

Reviews : Anon. in REP 69:246–47, 1959; Anon. in REc 10:472, 1959.

Baudeau, Nicolas. Explication du Tableau économique à Madame de ***. Extrait des Ephémérides de 1767 et 1768. Delalain, 1776. 172 p. **5420**

A lucid explanation of the terms and theories advanced in Q.'s work.

Bourthoumieux, Charles. Essai sur le fondement philosophique des doctrines économiques, Rousseau contre Quesnay. M. Rivière, 1936. viii, 140 p. **5421**

Opposes physiocrats' concept of economics based on les lois naturelles de la société and l'ordre naturel, and Rousseau's view of society as un acte de volonté.

Chavegrin, Ernest. Les doctrines politiques des physiocrates. In: Mélanges R. Carré de Malberg. Recueil Sirey, 1933. p. 59–70. **5422**

Traces physiocrats' belief in the efficacy of reforms controlled by a despote légal as they swung towards acceptance of a more democratic rule.

Cheinisse, Léon. Les idées politiques des physiocrates. A. Rousseau, 1914. 192 p. **5423**

Points out the physiocrats' weakness in viewing society as a part of l'ordre naturel; in their antidemocratic bent; in their preoccupation with the abstract at the expense of reality.

Coleman, Earle E. Ephémérides du citoyen, 1767–1772. See 5516. **5424**

Presents bibliographical data on editors, contributors, eds., and various issues, including variants. Gives locations of the journal in various libraries.

Dupont de Nemours, Pierre-Samuel. L'enfance et la jeunesse de Du Pont de Nemours, racontées par lui-même. Plon-Nourrit, 1906. viii, 294 p. **5425**

His relations with Q.; publication of Q.'s Tableau économique; analysis of Q.'s doctrines.

Einaudi, Mario. The physiocratic doctrine of judicial control. Cambridge, Harvard univ. press, 1938. x, 96 p. **5426**

The physiocrats were criticized for attempting to set up a legal despotism; but, though they looked to the king to introduce their reforms, they held that the royal power should be subject to the control of judges.

Reviews : W. Carpenter in APSR 33: 146–47, 1939; C. Mulett in AHR 44:979, 1938–39.

François Quesnay et la physiocratie. Institut national d'études démographiques, 1958. 2 v. **5427**

V. 1 (p. xx–392) contains a prefatory essay on the physiocrats by Luigi Einaudi; 10 essays on Q.'s thought and works; an excellent life of Q. by Jacqueline Hecht (p. 211–93); a Tableau chronologique des œuvres de Quesnay; and a Liste bibliographique commentée by Jacqueline Hecht, containing over 300 works and articles relating to Q. V. 2 (p. 393–1005) contains 32 letters and annotated texts, and an index of Q.'s Vocabulaire économique.

Garnier, Joseph. Quesnay (François). In: Dictionnaire de l'économie politique, publié sous la direction de MM. Ch. Coquelin et Guillaumin. Guillaumin and Hachette, 1854. 2: 485–90. **5428**

The best early account of Q.'s life and works and of the physiocratic movement.

Lorion, André. Les théories politiques des premiers physiocrates. Jouve, 1918. 192 p. **5429**

Their views on society from legislative point of view; their insight, shortcomings, and influence on the French Revolution and the Declaration of the Rights of Man.

Meek, Ronald L. The economics of physiocracy; essays and translations. Cambridge, Harvard univ. press, 1963. 432 p. **5430**

Contains a nonspecialist introduction to physiocracy; 17 translations (some hitherto unavailable) from Q., Mirabeau, the Encyclopédie, and Journal de l'agriculture, du commerce et des finances; and 5 original and revealing essays (4 previously published) including The interpretation of physiocracy. Good index; no bibliography. Reviews : J. Conan in RHES 42:134–36, 1964; E. Roll in EJ 74:207–09, 1964.

Neill, Thomas P. Quesnay and physiocracy. See 4141. **5431**

Shows important differences between Q. and the younger physiocrats who were supposedly his disciples.

Oncken, August. Zur Biographie des Stifters der Physiokratie, François Quesnay. ZLGS 2:389–415, 1894; 3:180–85, 245–64, 1894; 4:35–57, 152–72, 1895. **5432**

Q.'s background, ancestors, medical career, as they prepared him for the field of economics and blended with his ideas

of a natural order embracing the moral and social world.
Review : S. Bauer in EJ 5:660–61, 1895.

Weulersse, Georges. La physiocratie à la fin du règne de Louis XV, 1770–1774. Presses univ. de France, 1959. xi, 238 p. *See* 5518. **5433**
The movement from 1770 to 1774 : its programs and critics.

— La physiocratie sous les ministères de Turgot et de Necker, 1774–1781. Presses univ. de France, 1950. xvi, 374 p. *See* 5519. **5434**
A definitive work on the program of the physiocrats (especially during the movement's last years), its supporters and critics.
Reviews : C. Fohlen in REc 5:474–76, 1954; L. Gershoy in AHR 56:874–75, 1950–51; R. Howey in JPE 59:365–66, 1951.

Pierre Louis Moreau de Maupertuis
(Nos. 5435–5447)

ARAM VARTANIAN

Maupertuis, Pierre Louis Moreau de. Œuvres. Éd. by G. Tonelli. Hildesheim, Georg Olms, 1965. 4 v. **5435**
Basic texts of M. made available once again in this reprint ed.

— Maupertuis, le savant et le philosophe. Ed. by Emile Callot. Rivière, 1964. 178 p. **5436**
Useful publication, which is the 1st anthology of selected texts by M., with aim of making him better known to modern reader. The *extraits* are rather fragmentary, but have merit of discriminating choice, and succeed in covering wide range of M.'s philosophical and scientific interests. They are preceded by a summary and appreciation by Callot of M.'s thought.

Bachelard, Suzanne. Les polémiques concernant le principe de moindre action au XVIIIe siècle. 1961. 24 p. **5437**
The latest, apparently, in a series of studies on the same general subject (cf. Guéroult, 2589; Brunet, 2581; Abelé, 2577; etc.). By means of a careful analysis of Leibniz' views concerning the notion of least action, Bachelard brings out the originality of M.'s principle.

Brown, Harcourt. Maupertuis philosophe : Enlightenment and the Berlin Academy. SVEC 24:255–69, 1963. **5438**
Valuable article. Shows how M.'s writings after 1746 were inspired by his duties as president of Berlin Academy and competently appraises their importance in advancement of both science and enlightenment in terms of special problems and opportunities pertaining to M.'s official position as promoter of research.

Callot, Emile. Maupertuis. *In his:* La philosophie de la vie au XVIIIe siècle. Rivière, 1965. p. 149–93. **5439**
Penetrating analysis. Its special focus, accounting for its originality, is to study M.'s biological ideas and theories in the context of his speculative philosophy, thereby clarifying many subtle links between his thought as a " metaphysician " and his suggestive opinions in the field of biology, where he remained an *amateur de génie*.

— L'universalité de Maupertius. *In his:* Six philosophes français du XVIIIe siècle. Annecy, Gardet, 1963. p. 77–95. **5440**
Author seeks to further rehabilitate M.'s neglected " genius " by pointing out, for the benefit of nonspecialists, the breadth and variety of his intellectual activities and his originality in more than one field. M. tends to emerge as ideal type of 18th-century scientist.

Crombie, Alistair Cameron. P. L. Moreau de Maupertius, F.R.S. (1698–1759), précurseur du transformisme. Rsyn sér. gén. 78: 35–56, 1957. **5441**
Lucid *mise au point* of the question of M.'s role in the origins of the transformistic hypothesis. While saying little that is startlingly new, author rightly places emphasis on geneticist basis of M.'s most important contributions to biology.

Dufrenoy, Marie Louise. Maupertius et le progrès scientifique. SVEC 25:519–87, 1963. **5442**
Competent review of M.'s scientific achievements in the many fields in which he was active. In most matters, Dufrenoy follows earlier authorities, specially Brunet (2579). She makes contributions of her own, however, in use of Besterman ed. of Voltaire's correspondence to document more thoroughly complex relations between M., Mme du Châtelet, and Voltaire; in discussion of M.'s linguistic philosophy; and generally, in attempts to make

clearer how M.'s investigations—notably regarding principle of least action and genetic phenomena—were related to subsequent scientific progress.

Gooch, George Peabody. Madame du Châtelet and her lovers : I. Maupertuis. Crev 200:648–53, 1961. **5443**

Traces relations between Mme du Châtelet and M., mainly during 1730's, on basis of her correspondence recently published by Besterman. Chatty rather than scholarly tone prevails. General impression is that Mme du Châtelet attached more importance to their liaison than did her mathematician-lover, about whom she complained perceptively : " Unfortunately it is easier to make calculations than to be in love."

Gossman, Lionel. Berkeley, Hume and Maupertuis. FS 14:304–24, 1960. *See* 5684. **5444**

Penetrating analysis, establishing considerable extent of Berkeley's influence (and discounting presumed influence of Hume) on M. in problems of epistemology. M. emerges as only *philosophe* to have taken seriously Berkeleyan subjectivism, so cavalierly dismissed as futile paradox in 18th-century France. Author contends plausibly enough that M.'s affinity with British metaphysician was rooted in his desire to counteract mechanistic and materialist philosophy by undercutting it on epistemological grounds.

Maillet, Pierre L. Pierre-Louis Moreau de Maupertuis, (1698–1759), pour le bicentenaire de sa mort. Edition du Palais de la découverte. 1960. 32 p. **5445**

Seeks to rehabilitate M.'s still undeservedly limited reputation by offering a glowing sketch of his career and ideas as a scientist. Mediocre and secondhand presentation typical of a commemorative *conférence*.

Ostoya, Paul. Maupertuis et la biologie. RHS 7:60–78, 1954. **5446**

Surveys M.'s experiments and theories as a biologist, commenting on their value in relation to more modern developments. Stresses particularly importance of his ideas on genetics and the transformation of species. Despite author's competence in biology, article is of limited originality from a historical standpoint (cf. Brunet, 2579; Bentley, 2587).

Politzer, Robert L. On the linguistic

philosophy of Maupertuis and its relation to the history of linguistic relativism. Sym 17:5–16, 1963. **5447**

Well-informed article, crediting M. with early insights concerning relationship between structure of knowledge and that of a particular language. Evaluates M.'s originality as exponent of linguistic relativism by means of judicious comparisons with philosophy of language of Condillac, Berkeley's subjectivism, and later developments in thought of Kant and von Humboldt.

Georges Louis Leclerc, *comte* de Buffon (Nos. 5448–5476)

OTIS FELLOWS

Buffon, Georges Louis Leclerc, *comte* de. Œuvres philosophiques. Ed. by Jean Piveteau, Maurice Fréchet and Charles Bruneau. Presses univ. de France, 1954. xxxvii, 616 p. **5448**

Annotated text of passages philosophical in nature, taken from the Imprimerie Royale ed. of B.'s complete works. For individual contributions to volume by Jean Piveteau, Maurice Fréchet, Charles Bruneau, E. Genet-Varcin, and Jacques Roger, see *infra*.

Review : O. Fellows in RR 47:130–33, 1956.

— Les époques de la nature. Edition critique avec le manuscrit, une introduction et des notes par Jacques Roger. Editions du Muséum, 1962. clii, 343 p. (Mémoires du Muséum national d'histoire naturelle, n.s., série C., sciences de la terre, 10) **5449**

Rather than a study limited in scope, as the title might suggest, Roger has written the best over-all book to date on B. Insistence as never before upon the need to study B.'s thought in terms of the progressive developments of a number of key concepts.

Reviews : M. Duchet in RHL 64:111–13, 1964; Y. Laissus in RHS 17:191–92, 1964; S. Milliken in DS 6:292–303, 1964; R. Rappaport in Isis 55:392–94, 1964.

— Lettres inédites de Buffon. Ed. by Franck Bourdier and Yves François. *In:* Buffon. *See* 5451. p. 181–224. **5450**

Some 30 unpublished letters representing an important addition to the 2 eds. of B.'s general correspondence. Also an inventory of still unpublished letters to Thouin with names of persons mentioned and a catalog of topics discussed.

Bertin, Léon, Franck Bourdier, *et al.*
Buffon. Muséum national d'histoire naturelle et Publications françaises, 1952. 244 p.
5451

A collection of articles on various aspects of B. published in the series *Les grands naturalistes français* under the direction of Roger Heim. Contributors include Roger Heim, Franck Bourdier, Léon Bertin, Yves François, Jean Piveteau, Jean Pelseneer, E. Genet-Varcin, Ed. Dechambre, and Georges Heilbrun.

Bourdier, Franck. Principaux aspects de la vie et de l'œuvre de Buffon. *In:* Buffon. *See* 5451. p. 15–86.   **5452**

Written with great clarity; perhaps best brief over-all picture of B.'s life and works yet published. Emphasis given certain important details hitherto neglected or unstressed.

Bruneau, Charles. Buffon et le problème de la forme. *In:* Buffon. Œuvres philosophiques. *See* 5448. p. 491–99.   **5453**

Carefully documented article in which writer accredits B. with a distinguished place in the history of the French language. Gives a clear account of what is now the commonly accepted interpretation of the celebrated but often misunderstood formula : *le style est l'homme même.*

Dechambre, Ed. L'article des chiens dans l'Histoire naturelle. *In:* Buffon. *See* 5451. p. 157–66.   **5454**

Work of B. and Daubenton on the family Canidae; first comprehensive study of the subject, with special stress on the domestic dog. Interesting and informative.

Fellows, Otis. Buffon and Rousseau : aspects of a relationship. PMLA 75:184–96, 1960.   **5455**

The intellectual debt of Rousseau to B.'s *Histoire naturelle*, occasionally acknowledged by former, is considerable. Unflagging esteem for B. offset by B.'s diminishing regard for Jean-Jacques.

— Buffon's place in the Enlightenment. SVEC 25:603–29, 1963.   **5456**

Revaluation and rehabilitation of a disconcerting figure in the history of scientific ideas in 18th-century France.

— Voltaire and Buffon : clash and conciliation. Sym 9:222–35, 1955.   **5457**

Intellectual differences between two figures, each profoundly distrustful of the scientific pretentions of the other but careful to preserve the social amenities.

François, Yves. Buffon au Jardin du Roi (1739–88). *In:* Buffon. *See* 5451. p. 105–24.   **5458**

Supersedes William Falls's still useful *B. et l'agrandissement du Jardin du Roi à Paris* (2605).

Fréchet, Maurice. Buffon comme philosophe des mathématiques. *In:* Buffon. Œuvres philosophiques. *See* 5448. p. 435–46.   **5459**

Reveals B.'s very real mathematical gifts with particular competence in the field of mathematical probability. The author would prefer others to decide how much these talents may have influenced B. in developing or rejecting certain of his biological theories on the one hand and in formulating notions concerning stylistic exactitude on the other.

Genet-Varcin, E. La génération des êtres vivants d'après Buffon. *In:* Buffon. *See* 5451. p. 137–56.   **5460**

Short, clear exposé of B.'s basic ideas, particularly the theory of his famous *molécules organiques*, in relation to living matter.

—, and **Jacques Roger.** Bibliographie de Buffon. *In:* Buffon. Œuvres philosophiques. *See* 5448. p. 513–70.   **5461**

1152 pertinent mss, articles, and books are listed in this indispensable bibliographical tool for the B. specialist.

Haber, Francis C. Time and world process in eighteenth-century outlook : Buffon's Epochs of nature. *In his:* The age of the world : Moses to Darwin. Baltimore, Johns Hopkins press, 1959. p. 115–36.   **5462**

Short, lucid résumé of B.'s evolving theory of the earth, especially as it reaches its final form in his " masterpiece," as Haber rightly calls it, the *Epoques de la nature* (1778).

Hanks, Lesley. Buffon et les fusées volantes. RHS 14:137–54, 1961.   **5463**

B. the scientist in the light of his early experiments with rockets leading to the formulation of his theory on the origin of the planets.

Heim, Roger. Préface à Buffon. *In:* Buffon. *See* 5451. p. 5–13.   **5464**

Eminent scholar and administrator justifies choice of B. to inaugurate series on France's greatest naturalists. Excellent *mise au point*.

Middleton, W. E. Knowles. Archimedes, Kircher, Buffon and the burning-mirrors. Isis 52:533–43, 1961. **5465**

Chiefly concerns B.'s successful experiments in igniting distant objects by means of mirrors, thus suggesting that Archimedes could have, despite Descartes' conclusions to the contrary, carried out his own possibly legendary exploits in the field.

Milliken, Stephen F. Buffon and James Bruce. RMR 1:63–80, 1963–64. **5466**

Through a detailed study of a particular case, article reveals both the tireless enthusiasm with which B. pursued new sources of information and the general fairness of his dealings with his more distinguished collaborators. Impeccable scholarship.

Piveteau, Jean. Introduction à l'œuvre philosophique de Buffon. *In:* Buffon. Œuvres philosophiques. *See* 5448. p. vii–xxxvii. **5467**

Succinct and highly useful essay with chapters on B.'s life and on B. as scientist and thinker. Slightly conservative presentation of B.'s views on geology and paleontology, cosmogony, embryology, anthropology, transformism, etc.

— La pensée religieuse de Buffon. *In:* Buffon. *See* 5451. p. 125–32. **5468**

Good account of attacks on B. by Jansenists and Faculté de Théologie of the Sorbonne, as well as by individual clergymen and laymen. Although suggests that B.'s writings on man and nature show a constant oscillation between spiritualism and materialism, Piveteau prefers to conclude naturalist was a Christian entirely sincere in his religious practices.

Poulet, Georges. La Nausée de Sartre et le cogito cartésien. SF 5:452–62, 1961. **5469**

A study of contrasts in the moment of consciousness especially as revealed in the *cogito cartésien*, the *cogito senti* of Buffon, and the *cogito sartrien*.

Roger, Jacques. Buffon. *In his:* Les sciences de la vie dans la pensée française du XVIIIe siècle. *See* 4146. p. 527–84. **5470**

Brilliantly situates B. in the current of 18th-century scientific thought : " La pensée de B. est une pensée solitaire. Non qu'il ait ignoré son siècle; mais les idées philosophiques ou scientifiques qu'il en a reçues, n'ont jamais été passivement acceptées " (p. 582). Special stress given B.'s theory of generation.

— Diderot et Buffon en 1749. DS 4:221–36, 1963. **5471**

B.'s role in the evolution of Diderot's thought between the *Pensées philosophiques* and the *Lettre sur les aveugles;* partly conjectural, partly demonstrated. Careful scholarship, prudent conclusions.

Starobinski, Jean. Rousseau et Buffon. *In:* Jean-Jacques Rousseau et son œuvre; problèmes et recherches. *See* 4790. p. 135–46. **5472**

Exacting scholarship on the intellectual rapports between Rousseau and B. with the conclusion that Jean-Jacques found in B.'s work an anthropological philosophy for the most part highly acceptable but certain aspects of which he rejected.

Watts, George B. The comte de Buffon and his friend and publisher Charles-Joseph Panckoucke. MLQ 18:313–22, 1957. **5473**

Straightforward, factual account of the relations of these two important figures in the 18th-century world of books.

Weil, Françoise. La correspondance Buffon-Cramer. RHS 14:97–136, 1961. **5474**

Letters between the youthful B. and the famous Swiss mathematician, Gabriel Cramer, fill out the history of the relations of the two correspondents, show the future naturalist's considerable gifts for mathematics and throw added light on the problem of B.'s travels in the years 1731–32.

Wilkie, J. S. The idea of evolution in the writings of Buffon. AnSc 12:48–62, 212–27, 255–66, 1956. **5475**

Most complete statement to date on the problem of B. and transformism. Finds naturalist prevented from producing fully generalized theory of evolution by two factors internal to his system of biology : absence of theory of causal mechanism of sufficient power, and presence of too liberal idea of possibilities of spontaneous generation. Author states B.'s greatest contribution relating to theory of evolution was appreciation of significance of geographical distribution of animals.

Wohl, Robert. Buffon and his project for a new science. Isis 51:186–99, 1960. **5476**

An interesting attempt to reduce B.'s science to a single principle, that of

Newtonian attraction. A well-presented but oversimplified resolution of an intricate problem.

Luc de Clapiers, *marquis* de Vauvenargues
(Nos. 5477–5479)

FERNAND VIAL

Michel, Alain. Vauvenargues et le stoïcisme latin. AGBB 95–102, 1964.   **5477**
V.'s stoicism strongly influenced by Locke and the Christian apologists, but remains essentially Latin and sentimental.

Sacy, Samuel de. Vauvenargues ou qui perd gagne. MerF 326:704–27, 1956.   **5478**
Good psychological biography of V.

Saitschick, Robert. Vauvenargues. *In his:* Denker und Dichter. Zurich, Raschen Verlag, 1948. p. 109–43.   **5479**
Rather subtle study in characterology showing dominance of sentiment in V.

Antoine Rivarol
(Nos. 5480–5489)

FERNAND VIAL

Rivarol, Antoine. Ecrits politiques et littéraires. Ed. by Victor-Henri Debidour. Grasset, 1956. 244 p.   **5480**
Solid preface situating R. accurately between the 17th and the 18th centuries. Good choice of texts divided into topical themes.

— Maximes, pensées et paradoxes, suivis de De l'universalité de la langue française, Lettres à M. Necker, Esprit de Rivarol. Ed. by Pierre-Henri Simon. Livre club du libraire, 1962. 230 p.   **5481**
Excellent definition of R.'s political philosophy described as " un intellectuel de droite." Sober and critical analysis of the *Discours* underlining its deficiencies. Letters to Necker dealing with religion and morality. Good choice of texts to show R.'s witticisms.

— Mémoires de Rivarol. Ed. by M. Berville. GALIC, 1962. xvi, 386 p.   **5482**
Text of *Mémoires* dealing with the French Revolution including some notes mostly by R. himself. Lively and picturesque documents. Interesting *éclaircissements* on particular points taken from contemporary works.

— Les plus belles pages de Rivarol. Ed. by Jean Dutourd. Mercure de France, 1963. 340 p.   **5483**
Presents extracts from *Notes, réflexions et maximes*, complete text of *De l'universalité*, extracts from *Petit almanach de nos grands hommes, Journal politique*, and *Rivaroliana*. Judicious choice of sometimes little-known texts. Interesting documents on R.'s life, marriage, and death. Perceptive and original preface describing R. as a *grammairien engagé* holding keen views on contemporary writers, politics, and the French Revolution.

— Rivarol [Maximen]. Ed. by Ernst Jünger. Frankfurt am Main, Klostermann, 1956. 200 p.   **5484**
Good appreciation of R.'s thought and style. An excellent choice of maxims.
Review : F. Schalk in WWa 11:563–65, 1956.

Castel-Çagarriga, G. Françoise de Rivarol et Dumouriez. RDM 425–38, Nov.–Dec. 1964.   **5485**
Startling revelations on the intrigues and adventures of R.'s sister who became mistress of Dumouriez under the name of Baronne de Beauvert; interesting background information on R.

Garcin, Philippe. Rivarol et la littérature. Cr 14:3–17, Jan. 1958.   **5486**
Keen analysis of the role of imagination and imagery in R.'s style.

Law, Reed G. Rivarol's morale indépendante and Pascal. C 1:249–57, 1959.   **5487**
Although a disciple of Voltaire, R. adapted some of Pascal's thoughts, which became the cornerstone of his ethical system. Recognizes the religious content of his life while rejecting all formal notions of revelation.

Loiseau, Yvan. Rivarol, suivi de Le vrai Laclos. La Palatine, 1961. p. 1–195.   **5488**
R. was above all a political writer related to Machiavelli. Study based mostly on *Mémoires* and shows perspicacity and disenchantment of R. before the French Revolution. Rather disconnected articles and considerations on R. as writer and critic.

Vianu, Hélène. Rivarol ou les incompréhensions de l'exil. SVEC 27:1723–34, 1963.   **5489**
Short but pertinent considerations on

R.'s political ideas during his exile, on his diatribes against philosophy, and on his inner contradictions.

Periodical Literature
(Nos. 5490–5540)

MADELEINE FIELDS MORRIS

General Studies
(Nos. 5490–5493)

The material in this section is, in essence, of such nature that a logical arrangement of it on an alphabetical or chronological basis seems neither desirable nor possible. Items can be located by consulting the Volume's alphabetical index.

Krauss, Werner. La correspondance de Formey. RHL 63:207–16, 1963.   **5490**
Presents a collection of unpublished letters to the secretary of the Berlin Academy by Elie Luzac, publisher of the *Bibliothèque impartiale* (281 letters) and by Pierre Rousseau, director of the *Journal encyclopédique* (55 letters).

Topazio, Virgil W. Art criticism in the Enlightenment. *See* 4155.   **5491**
Author intentionally excludes theoretical works of historians and philosophers to concentrate on reports found in periodicals. Sees in La Font de Saint-Yenne the founder of modern art criticism. Baillet de Saint-Julien, abbé Le Blanc, Mathon de La Cour, and Bachaumont are Diderot's predecessors and teachers. Important for study of *Salons*.

Watts, George B. Voltaire and Charles Joseph Panckoucke. *See* 4500.   **5492**
Panckoucke was editor of *L'avant-coureur, Journal de politique et de littérature, Mercure de France,* and *Journal des savants.* Relationship between Voltaire and Panckoucke. Information not found in Hatin.

Ziotous, G. D. La presse et l'Encyclopédie. Esquisse du développement de la presse française dans la première moitié du XVIIIᵉ siècle. EP n.s. 5:313–25, 1953.   **5493**
Role, legal status, and attitude of the press toward the *savants* and *philosophes.* Treatment of the press in the *Encyclopédie:* typography, journalism, freedom; analysis of articles by Voltaire, Diderot, Marmontel, Jaucourt. Shows *Encyclopédie* to be source of *Article XI* of the *Déclaration des droits de l'homme.*

Desfontaines, Fréron, Prévost
(Nos. 5494–5511)

Desfontaines, Pierre François Guyot
(1685–1745)
See 5502.

Morris, Thelma. Desfontaines journaliste. *In her:* L'abbé Desfontaines et son rôle dans la littérature de son temps. SVEC 19: 95–148, 1961.   **5494**
Writes for *Journal des savants* (1724–27); *Nouvelliste du Parnasse* (1731–32); *Remarques sur différents ouvrages* (1733); *Pour et contre* (1734); *Observations sur les écrits modernes* (1735–43); *Jugements sur quelques ouvrages nouveaux* (1744–46).

Myers, Robert L. A literary controversy in eighteenth-century France : Voltaire vs. Desfontaines. *See* 4589.   **5495**
Evaluation and organization of material brings a somewhat fairer light on Desfontaines. Studies : *Nouvelliste du Parnasse, Observations sur les écrits modernes, Jugements sur quelques ouvrages nouveaux;* retraces phases of deteriorating relationship leading to the *Préservatif* and the *Voltairomanie.*

Fréron, Elie-Catherine (1718–76)
See 5534

Bundy, Jean D. Fréron and the English novel. RLC 36:258–65, 1962. *See* 5675.   **5496**
Waning interest in orientalism replaced after 1740 by Anglomania. In *Lettres sur quelques écrits,* reviews of important novels in translation. *Rasselas* compared to *Candide.* Fréron clearly ahead of contemporaries for interest in Fielding.

Dehergne, Joseph. Une table des matières de L'année littéraire de Fréron. RHL 65:269–73, 1965.   **5497**
Useful guide.

Myers, Robert L. The dramatic theories of Elie-Catherine Fréron. *See* 3581.   **5498**
Copious citations from *Année littéraire* between 1754 and 1775 are basis for evaluation of dramatic theories. Material arranged in 3 categories : tragedy, *drame,* and comedy. Limited to criticism of genres rather than of particular dramatists. Objective study showing Fréron's preference for traditionalism. Bibliography and index.

— Fréron and the drame bourgeois. FR 31: 35–40, 1957–58.   **5499**
Study of *Année littéraire.* At first gave

approbation to *drame bourgeois;* after 1771, use of stage by the *philosophes* as political tribune led Fréron to deny legitimacy of new genre.

— Fréron, critique de Rémond de Saint-Mard. SVEC 37:147–64, 1966.   **5500**

Fréron's reaction to Rémond's esthetics. Fills 90 pages of v. 2 of *Lettres sur quelques écrits de ce temps.* Fréron seen as faithful disciple of Boileau and Desfontaines and as failing to appreciate Rémond's defiance of tradition.

— Fréron's theories on tragedy. FR 31:503–08, 1957–58.   **5501**

Study of *Année littéraire.* Cautions against rash judgment of Fréron who is described here as open-minded, completely in step with contemporaries and willing to experiment with new methods.

Prévost d'Exiles, A. F., *abbé* (1697–1763) *See* 5494.

Deloffre, Frédéric. Un morceau de critique en quête d'auteur : le jugement du Pour et contre sur Manon Lescaut. *See* 3800.   **5502**

Critical review attributed to Desfontaines. Analysis of texts. Notes shifting of interest from des Grieux to Manon.

Engel, Claire-Eliane. L'abbé Prévost collaborateur d'une revue neuchâteloise. *See* 3804.   **5503**

Nineteen short stories by Prévost published first in *Pour et contre,* then in *Mercure suisse* between 1734 and 1750.

Frautschi, R. L. The dating of the Pour et contre. MLR 69:512–15, 1965.   **5504**

Internal evidence establishes that after late Jan. 1734, Desfontaines was no longer affiliated with journal.

Labriolle-Rutherford, Marie-Rose de. Le Pour et contre et les romans de l'abbé Prévost (1733–1740). *See* 3820.   **5505**

— Le Pour et contre et son temps. *See* 3821.   **5506**

Excellent 2-volume survey of Prévost's periodical arranged topically.

— Les procédés d'imitation de l'abbé Prévost dans le Pour et contre (1733–1740). *See* 3822.   **5507**

— La scène tragique dans le Pour et le contre de l'abbé Prévost (1733–1740). *See* 3823.   **5508**

Numerous quotations indicate the

difficult position of tragedy in 1740. Prévost foresaw that Corneille and Racine could not be equalled in this *genre.*

— Les sources du Pour et contre (1733–1734). *See* 3824.   **5509**

Methodical study of a subject merely touched on by G. Havens, P. Hazard, C.-E. Engel, H. Roddier. Limited to first 4 v. List of sources. p. 244–57.

Roddier, Henri. L'abbé Prévost, homme de lettres et journaliste. *See* 3841.   **5510**

In second half of article, study of *Pour et contre.* Commentaries on English press, *Lettres philosophiques* (laudatory), and *Journal étranger.*

Weil, Françoise. L'abbé Prévost et le Gazetin de 1740. *See* 3772.   **5511**

Hand copied sheet (7 or 8 numbers); issues 1 to 4 of incontestable literary value. Goncourt brothers attribute authorship to Bachaumont. Seen here as work of Prévost.

Studies on Periodicals listed in alphabetical order (Nos. 5512–5540)

Correspondance littéraire (1753–1793)

Bowen, Vincent E. Diderot's contributions to the Stockholm copy of the Correspondance littéraire. *See* 5281.   **5512**

Complements Joseph R. Smiley's list of Diderot's articles for Grimm's *Correspondance littéraire.* Aims at rectifying some of the errors of printed ed. by giving list of contributions by Diderot found in Stockholm copy during period 1760–72. *Also see* Smiley (5515).

Monty, Jeanne R. The criticism of Rousseau in the Correspondance littéraire. MLQ 24:99–103, 1963. *See* 5368.   **5513**

Corrects Sainte-Beuve's mistake of attributing to Grimm articles written by the Swiss Meister. Contrasts Grimm's harsh judgment of Rousseau with more detached and comprehensive view of Meister, thus explaining contradictions found in periodical.

— La critique littéraire de Melchior Grimm. *See* 5369.   **5514**

Systematic survey of *Correspondance littéraire.* Reliable and conscientious. History of periodical, list of subscribers, collaboration of Diderot and Meister, and Grimm's judgment of contemporaries. Bibliography, p. 135–37.

Smiley, Joseph R. A list of Diderot's articles for Grimm's Correspondance littéraire. RR 42:189–97, 1951. *See* 5349 and 5371.　**5515**
Comparison based on the printed ed. of the *Correspondance* with the Assézat-Tourneaux ed. of Diderot shows latter to be incorrect with regard to Diderot's participation. *Also see* Bowen (5280–81).

Ephémérides du citoyen (1765–1772)
See 5534

Coleman, Earle E. Ephémérides du citoyen, 1767–1772. PBSA 56:17–45, 1962. *See* 5424.　**5516**
Technical study of periodical; does not touch upon subjects treated except in very general way in introduction; gives precise information on contributors, history of paper, variants, copies, editors, reset tomes, authorship, budget and censors; compares various sets; detailed study of deletions made by censors; examines each tome in the collections of Yale and Kress. Contributors : Baudeau, du Pont de Nemours, Riquetti, Mirabeau, Quesnay, Turgot, Mercier de La Rivière, Saint-Péravy, Vauvilliers.

Spengler, Joseph John. Economie et population : les doctrines françaises avant 1800, de Budé à Condorcet. Institut national d'études démographiques. Travaux et documents. Cahier no. 21, 1954. 389 p.　**5517**
Lists important articles from *Ephémérides du citoyen.*

Weulersse, Georges. La physiocratie à la fin du règne de Louis XV, 1770–1774. *See* 5433.　**5518**
Uses material found in physiocratic press. Bibliography, p. 231–35.

— La physiocratie sous les ministères de Turgot et de Necker (1774–1781). *See* 5434.　**5519**
Uses material found in physiocratic press : *Journal économique* (1751–72); *Ephémérides du citoyen* (1765–72); *Journal de l'agriculture, du commerce, et des arts des finances* (1765–74); *Journal de politique et de littérature* (1774–83). Bibliography, p. 367–71.

Gazetin (1740)
See 5511.

Gazette littéraire de l'Europe (1764–66)
See 5527

Journal de lecture (1775–79)

Mortier, Roland. Le Journal de lecture de F. M. Leuchsenring (1775–1779) et l'esprit philosophique. RLC 29:205–22, 1955. *See* 5850.　**5520**
Minor German writer, friend of Herder, Jacobi, and Diderot. Not mentioned in Hatin or Quérard. Complete collections (36 numbers in 12 volumes) in Arsenal and Sainte-Geneviève libraries; v. 1–7 in B. N. Important for studies in comparative literature. Text of *Taximanes* attributed to Diderot, p. 220–22.

Journal encyclopédique (1756–93)

Birn, Raymond F. Le Journal encyclopédique and the old régime. SVEC 24:219–40, 1963.　**5521**
Study of the difficulties of the press. Consistent doctrinal position of paper but unpredictable behavior of government. Presents the *philosophes* as adversaries of Hobbes and d'Holbach, not as adversaries of Fréron and Palissot.

— Pierre Rousseau and the philosophes of Bouillon. SVEC 29:1–212, 1964.　**5522**
Comprehensive study of role of popularizers and disseminators of Enlightenment, in particular in *Journal encyclopédique.* First chapter presents general view of French journalism in 18th century. Following chapters concern *Journal encyclopédique* and *Encyclopédie* as well. Bibliography, p. 205–12.

Charlier, Gustave, and Roland Mortier. Le Journal encyclopédique, 1756–1793. Nizet, 1952. 134 p. *See* 5844.　**5523**
Introduction retracing history of Pierre Rousseau and his journal. Contains *Prospectus du Journal encyclopédique*, letters from Voltaire to Pierre Rousseau, and extracts from the journal on the *Encyclopédie*, Hume, Rousseau, d'Holbach, and the death of Voltaire.

Froidcourt, Georges de. Pierre Rousseau et le Journal encyclopédique à Liège (1756–1759). VW 27:161–94, 261–301, 1953.　**5524**
Propagator of *Encyclopédie* in a town opposed to the *philosophes;* story of hardship and persecution by Church and *Année littéraire;* important articles taken from *Encyclopédie*, in particular article *Certitude* by abbé de Prades; analysis of *La pucelle.* Important for period from Lisbon earthquake to *Candide.*

Schröder, Winfried. Zur Geschichte des Journal encyclopédique. *In:* Neue Beiträge zur Literatur der Aufklärung. Ed. by Werner Krauss. Berlin, Rütten und Loening, 1964. p. 259–76.   **5525**
    Briefly evaluates studies of Küntziger, Francotte, Hatin, Mornet, Charlier, and Mortier. Emphasizes political role of *Journal* during Revolution. Important for study of ideology in second half of 18th century. Influence of d'Holbach and Sébastien Mercier. Notes and selected bibliography, p. 419–41.

Yons, Maurice. L'imprimerie du Journal encyclopédique de Pierre Rousseau. VW 28:276–78, 1954.   **5526**
    Completes Froidcourt's study (5524); deals less with political problems than with practical difficulties such as moving the printing plant from Liège to Brussels and Bouillon.

Journal étranger (1754–62)
See 5510

Pageard, Robert. L'Espagne dans le Journal étranger (1754–62) et la Gazette littéraire de l'Europe (1764–66). RLC 33:376–400, 1959. *See* 5957.   **5527**
    Appreciation of Spain and Spanish literature in contrast to the general attitude of the Encyclopedists who were mostly pro-British. Offers tables of articles and references pertaining to Spain.

Journal général de l'Europe (1785–89)

Vanderschueren, Bernadette. Les premières années du Journal général de l'Europe. VW 34:245–82, 1960.   **5528**
    Physiocratic tendency, favorable to Joseph II, against Catherine II, Frederick II, and the Pope. After the antiliberal reversal of Joseph, Lebrun leaves the Netherlands and is welcomed by the revolutionary government of Liège in 1789.

Mémoires de Trévoux (1701–67)

Desautels, Alfred R. Les Mémoires de Trévoux et le mouvement des idées au XVIIIᵉ siècle. *See* 4125.   **5529**
    First part of projected study which is to cover the entire period of publication. Careful inquiry into political, esthetic, and ethical attitudes of the Jesuits, in particular in the *Querelle des anciens et des modernes* and on the question of fideism.

Faux, Jean-Marie. La fondation et les premiers rédacteurs des Mémoires de Trévoux (1701–39) d'après quelques documents inédits. AHSJ 23:131–51, 1954. **5530**

— Les journalistes de Trévoux, juges des grands classiques. LR 10:393–407, 1956; 11:3–30, 1957.   **5531**
    Research limited to first 20 years of paper and to *belles-lettres.* Jesuits from Louis-le-Grand judge Malherbe, Quinault, Corneille, Racine, La Fontaine, Boileau, Bourdaloue, Fléchier, La Rochefoucauld, and La Bruyère. Evaluation biased because of reprobation of Jansenism, Cartesianism, or moral laxity of authors, but surprisingly modern at times. Well written.

Pappas, John N. Berthier's Journal de Trévoux and the philosophes. *See* 4142. **5532**
    A scrupulous study of journal's last period, under Berthier's direction (1745–62) : shows a fair, judicious and enlightened Berthier favoring Newtonian physics and championing some causes of the *philosophes;* religious issues only source of opposition to *Encyclopédie.* Perhaps too much importance given to archives discovered by author; bibliography somewhat sketchy.

Mercure de France (1724–91)
See 5492

Deloffre, Frédéric. Aspects inconnus de l'œuvre de Marivaux. RScH n.s. 74:97–115, 1954.   **5533**
    Study of texts omitted by editor La Porte in essays of Marivaux published in the *Mercure de France.* Offers rare example of a *démonstration rigoureusement suivie;* interesting judgment of the *philosophes* and of the importance of understanding the human heart as compared to the understanding of the sciences.

Fields, Madeleine. La dernière escarmouche entre Voltaire et Fréron. FR 36:365–73, 1962–63.   **5534**
    Opposes the abridged text of the *Diatribe à l'auteur des Ephémérides du citoyen* as published in the *Mercure* to the answer of Fréron published in *Année littéraire.* Suggests that in 1775, Voltaire was well aware of the inevitability of a violent revolution.

— La première édition française de la Princesse de Babylone. *See* 4730.   **5535**
    First ed. in France in the *Mercure;*

published without title or author's name in abridged form; does not appear in Bengesco nor in any bibliography to date.

— Voltaire et le Mercure de France. *See* 4637
5536

Comprehensive study of some 800 v. of the *Mercure*, revealing the official image of Voltaire in France from 1717 to 1778 : loyal subject of the King, poet, playwright before Corneille and Racine, pious benefactor of humanity. No mention of exiles, death, or works considered now as his masterpieces.

Mercure suisse (1732–75)
See 5503.

Nouvelles littéraires de Londres (1700–40)

Broome, Jack H. Pierre Desmaizeaux, journaliste; les Nouvelles littéraires de Londres entre 1700 et 1740. RLC 29:184–204, 1955. *See* 5650. 5537

Excellent study of the most important French journalist outside of France. Seen here as the principal agent for diffusion of English thought in early part of 18th century. Contributed articles to *Nouvelles de la république des lettres, Mémoires de Trévoux, Journal des savants, Mercure de France, Nouvelles littéraires, Boerkzael der Geleerde Werelt, Nova literaria in supplementum actorum eruditoram (Journal littéraire de La Haye), Histoire littéraire de l'Europe, Critique désintéressée des journaux littéraires, Bibliothèque raisonnée des ou-*

vrages des savants de l'Europe, Histoire critique de la république des lettres, Bibliothèque britannique.

Nouvelles littéraires de Raynal

Monty, Jeanne R. Grimm et les Nouvelles littéraires de Raynal. MLN 76:536–39, 1961. *See* 5370. 5538

Shows that Grimm's *Correspondance littéraire* is not a sequel to Raynal's paper. Feels that both periodicals are completely independent.

Postillon de Paris (1752)

Shaw, Edward P. The chevalier de Mouhy's newsletter of 20 December 1752. MLN 70: 114–16, 1955. 5539

Deals with issue No. 10 of the *Postillon de Paris*, ms 11,498 of the Bibliothèque de l'Arsenal; comments by Mouhy on contemporary theater, in particular on Jean-Jacques Rousseau's ill-received play, *Narcisse.*

Vendangeur (1749–50)

Holbrook, William C. An unnoticed periodical : Le vendangeur (1749–1750). FR 33: 558–62, 1959–60. 5540

Published in the Hague by Antoine van Dole. Consists of forty 8-page " letters ". Not mentioned in Hatin. Literary criticism weak and sketchy; political letters well informed.

CHAPTER XI. FOREIGN INFLUENCES AND RELATIONS

(Nos. 5541–5962)

ALFRED OWEN ALDRIDGE, OLGA RAGUSA, HENRY H. H. REMAK,
KENNETH SCHOLBERG, *and* MELVIN ZIMMERMAN

English
(Nos. 5541–5812)

ALFRED OWEN ALDRIDGE
and
MELVIN ZIMMERMAN

This section was completed with the very extensive assistance of Rhoda Orme-Johnson and Franco Triolo.

Bibliographies and General Studies

Acomb, Frances Dorothy. Anglophobia in France, 1763–1789; an essay in the history of constitutionalism and nationalism. Durham, Duke univ. press, 1950. xii, 167 p. **5541**

Draws on all contemporaneous sources save purely literary ones (plays, poems, and novels). The decline of Anglophile liberalism and the rise of Anglophobe liberalism studied in the context of the American Revolution and the French Revolution. Nationalism in France, stimulated by the thrill of Franco-American victory, led to a condescending attitude toward the political institutions of the English. There is an ample bibliography, containing Anglophile aspects, followed by an index of names and titles.

Aldridge, Alfred Owen. Le problème de la traduction au XVIIIᵉ siècle et aujourd'hui. RBP 39:747–58, 1961. **5542**

Shows similar theories of translation in Alexander Fraser Tytler's *On the principles of translation* and Valéry Larbaud's *Sous l'invocation de Saint-Jérôme.*

Carr, J. L. A curious eighteenth-century translation. MLR 55:574–77, 1960. **5543**

This rare book, *De la certitude des connoissances humaines, ou examen philosophique des diverses prérogatives de la raison & de la foi, avec un parallèle entre l'un & l'autre* (traduit de l'Anglois par

F.A.D.L.V.) is an anthology of deistic writings. The author probably plagiarized these essays using " traduit de l'Anglois " as a cover, hoping to catch the vogue for English works.

Higgins, D. The terrorists' favorite authors : some statistics from Revolutionary literature. MLR 54:401–04, 1959. **5544**

No English authors in this tabulation of Revolutionary anthologies.

Jacquot, Jean. Sir Hans Sloane and French men of science. NRRSL 10:85–100, 1953. **5545**

Gives evidence of sustained two-way stream of scientific news between Sloane and French Royal academicians, including Tournefort, Antoine and Bernard Jussieu, and the abbé Bignon.

Kadler, Eric H. Eighteenth-century precursors of Romantic poetry in France. LHB 4:1–8, 1962. **5546**

A sketchy review of foreign and native influences.

MacKenzie, Fraser. Some aspects of English philosophical thought in France. AUMLA 3:57–64, 1955. **5547**

Discusses the translation into French of the works of Bacon, Hobbes, Locke, Robert Boyle, Thomas Hyde, John Toland (coined " pantheist "), Ralph Cudworth (coined " theism "), Addison, Anthony Collins, Shaftesbury, and Hume and their contribution to French thought.

May, Georges Claude. Le dilemme du roman au XVIIIᵉ siècle; étude sur les rapports du roman et de la critique, 1715–1761. *See* 3731. **5548**

Some discussion is devoted to the influence of English novels in France, especially *David Simple, Pamela, Tom Jones, Joseph Andrews,* and *Charlotte Summers.* An important book for the history of the novel.

— The influence of English fiction on the French mid-eighteenth-century novel. *In:* Aspects of the eighteenth century. Ed. by Earl Reeves Wasserman. Baltimore, Johns Hopkins press, 1965. p. 265–80.   **5549**

The author attempts to explain which elements the French most enjoyed in English novels which were not present in their own. He concludes that it was neither moralism nor realism separately, but the successful combination of these two seemingly incompatible elements.

Intermediaries

a) Travelers, editors, translators, etc. (*See also* Burney, Chateaubriand, Locke)

Baldensperger, Fernand. Avec les voyageurs anglais du grand tour. EA 6:227–30, 1953.   **5550**

A chatty travelogue of the grand tour taken with the official guidebook.

Bayne-Powell, Rosamond. Travellers in eighteenth-century England.   London, Murray, 1951. 203 p.   **5551**

Anecdotal, picturesque descriptions of sites visited by foreigners. Brief, undocumented quotations from Voltaire, de Saussure, the duc de la Rochefoucauld, *et al.* A brief popular introduction to town and country inn life, road conditions, and *curiosités touristiques.* Illustrated with plates.

French travellers in England, 1600-1900 : selections from their writings. Ed. by Roy Ernest Palmer. London, Hutchinson, 1960. xv, 142 p.   **5552**

Edited selections from writings about England of Voltaire, Montesquieu, Rousseau, and others.

Gooch, G. P. 18th-century Anglo-French contacts. Crev 195:148–51, 226–33, 1959.   **5553**

Discusses the visits of Voltaire, Montesquieu, Rousseau, and Mirabeau to England and the visits of Walpole, Lord Chesterfield, Hume, Gibbon, and Burke to France.

May, Gita. Eighteenth-century England as seen by a disciple of the philosophes. FS 19: 253–65, 1965.   **5554**

Madame Roland was an Anglophile well before setting out in 1784 on a 4-week trip to England. She especially admired the English model parliamentary system. Her travel diary, published in 1800 among her *Œuvres,* touched on concrete, homely aspects of daily life of the kind that Prévost, Montesquieu, and Voltaire had failed to discuss. The brief but engrossing trip permitted her to see in English life " only what confirmed her preconceived notions ..." (p. 262). Unpleasant aspects were perceived, but dimly, e.g., prostitution and larceny.

Roe, Frederick C. La découverte de l'Ecosse entre 1760 et 1830. RLC 27:59–75, 1953.   **5555**

Catalogs the various influences of Scottish economic and philosophic thought upon the Encyclopedists and economists of France as well as the immense influence of Ossian and Sir Walter Scott upon French literature in the late 18th and early 19th centuries.

Rossi, P. Gli Illuministi francesi. Turin, Loescher, 1962. 378 p.   **5556**

A comprehensive work on the French Enlightenment which treats, in part, the influence of Locke and Newton.

Van Tieghem, Philippe. Les influences étrangères sur la littérature française (1550–1880). *See* 5839.   **5557**

A comprehensive study with 3 chapters of interest : Ch. 3, *La découverte de l'Angleterre* (on the influences of 17th-century English authors), Ch. 4, *Les grandes influences anglaises au XVIIIᵉ siècle,* and a section on the influence of Ossian in Ch. 5.

Periodicals
(*See also* D'Argens, Desmaizeaux, Wilkes)

Kitchin, Joanna. Un journal philosophique, La décade (1794–1807). Lettres modernes, 1965. viii, 313 p.   **5558**

This valuable study of a highly important periodical of the Revolution contains a section on the English novel and many references to English and American thinkers.

Labriolle-Rutherford, Marie-Rose de. Les procédés d'imitation de l'abbé Prévost dans le Pour et contre (1733–1740). *See* 3822.   **5559**

Describes Prévost as a journalist with a flair for the romantic. He used English " Newsletters " as sources for the fictional plots in *Pour et contre,* for they were full of accounts of crime, scandal, and bizarre stories. The author presents a comparative table of subjects that *Pour et contre* took from *The gentleman's magazine* as well as textual comparisons with the

Grubstreet journal, Daily post, Defoe, and Pope. The author also proposes sentimental adaptations of crime stories as the probable source of *Manon*. After 1731 the novelist derived most of his subjects from English sources.

Séguin, J. A. R. Voltaire and the Gentleman's magazine, 1731–1868; an index compiled and ed. with an introduction by J.A.R. Séguin. *See* 4495. **5560**

This is an index of the *Gentleman's magazine* compiled for Voltaire scholars.

Tucker, Joseph. The Turkish spy and its French background. RLC 32:74–91, 1958. **5561**

Many versions, both English and French, appeared from 1684 well into the next century. Marana is generally accepted as author of 1st version; then Defoe as author of some 60 letters in *Continuation of letters* ... (1718). Claims that vital questions of form and content of first half of 18th century posed by Hazard in *Crise de la conscience européenne*, by Wade in his 1950 ed. of *Micromégas*, and by Adam's article *Le sentiment de la nature au XVIIᵉ siècle en France* in CAIEF, 1954, can be answered at least in part by examination of *Turkish spy*.

The vogue of English authors in France

Addison

(*See* D'Argens, Desmaizeaux, Du Bos, Marivaux, Shakespeare)

Bacon

(*See also Encyclopédie*)

White, Howard B. The influence of Bacon on the philosophes. SVEC 27:1849–69, 1963. **5562**

Presents textual evidence to demonstrate the influence of Bacon upon Montesquieu and Rousseau.

Beckford

Mahmoud, Fatma Moussa. Beckford, Vathek and the oriental tale. *In:* William Beckford of Fonthill, 1760–1844. Bicentenary essays. Ed. by Fatma Moussa Mahmoud. Cairo, Costa Tsoumas and Co., 1960. p. 63–121. (CSE, Suppl. 1960) **5563**

" Based on Chapters VII and VIII of *The oriental tale in England in the early nineteenth century, 1786–1824*, Ph.D. Thesis, University of London, 1957 " (p. 63). Shows that, partly due to author's discretion, *Vathek* had no impact on the

oriental tale until well into the next century, when Byron gave it great publicity in his Turkish tale, *The Giaour* (1813). Mallarmé himself had never heard of the book until Prosper Mérimée drew his attention to it " (p. 104), as André Parreaux revealed.

Parreaux, André. Beckford's Vathek, Londres 1791. Bcol 7:297–99, 1958. **5564**

An edition of *Vathek* with " Londres, 1791 " on the title page proves to be Hignou's ed. with a new title page.

— Vathek et le conte oriental au XVIIIᵉ siècle. *In his:* William Beckford, auteur de Vathek (1760–1844); étude de la création littéraire. *See* 4063. **5565**

Makes distinction between the phase of the pseudo-oriental tale and the Romantic phase. *Vathek* appeared innopportunely : when decline in the genre, in France as well as England, made it less and less believable and acceptable. The author refuses to compare *Rasselas* to Voltaire's *Zadig, Scarmentado*, and *Babouc*. Copious bibliography and index of proper names. Seven appendixes of Beckfordiana.

— Un Vathek ignoré. BBB 176–79, 1957. **5566**

Demonstrates that a so-called 1791 London ed. was in reality made up from surplus sheets of the 1786 Lausanne ed., with a substituted title page : *Les caprices et les malheurs du calife Vathek* ... .

Berkeley

(*See also* Maupertuis)

Bracken, Harry M. Berkeley and Chambers. JHI 17:120–26, 1956. **5567**

Traces, among other things, the connection between a distorted version of Berkeley's thought and *Encyclopédie*. Such a version of his *Principles* was echoed in the article *Corps*, written by d'Alembert, which possibly influenced Diderot's attitude toward Berkeley.

Boswell

Boswell, James. Boswell on the grand tour : Germany and Switzerland, 1764. Ed. by Frederick A. Pottle. New York, McGraw-Hill, 1953. xxiii, 357 p. **5568**

Gives Boswell's relations with Voltaire and Rousseau including dialogues with both and a letter from Voltaire to Boswell.

Review : J. Vallette in MerF 320:534–36, 1954.

— Boswell on the grand tour : Italy, Corsica, and France, 1765–1766. Ed. by Frank Brady and Frederick A. Pottle. New York, McGraw-Hill, 1955. xxv, 356 p. **5569**
Contains mentions of meetings, anecdotes, etc. of Rousseau and Voltaire.

Burke
(*See also* Diderot, Dupont, Montesquieu, Raynal in American section, Rousseau)

Skalweit, Stephan. Edmund Burke und Frankreich. Cologne, Westdeutscher Verlag, 1956. 75 p. **5570**
Chiefly the French Revolution on Burke.

Weston, John C., Jr. A French pamphlet perhaps by Edmund Burke. NQ 196:366–67, 1951. **5571**
Suggests that Burke may be the author of a pamphlet addressed to the French people written before his *Reflections*.

Burney

Leigh, R. A. Les amitiés françaises du Dr. Burney : quelques documents inédits. RLC 25:161–94, 1951. **5572**
In his trips to Paris, the English musicologist Dr. Burney made friends with Diderot, d'Holbach, Suard, etc., and later corresponded with several of them. Dr. Burney admired the works of Rousseau, Diderot, and Voltaire, and many of his French friends (Rousseau, Diderot, Suard) could have profited either from conversations with Burney or from his *A general history of music*. Diderot acknowledged that he had acquainted him " avec tous les virtuoses, tant compositeurs que chanteurs italiens."

Chesterfield
(*See also* Duclos, Montesquieu)

Barrell, R. A. Chesterfield and France. AUMLA 3:40–47, 1955. **5573**
Discusses Cherterfield's friendship with Crébillon *fils*, Fontenelle, Voltaire, and Montesquieu—especially the last, whom he furnished with much information about the British government.

Dobrée, Bonamy. Chesterfield and France. Emisc 2:107–24, 1951. **5574**
Social and historical rather than literary emphasis.

Clarke
(*See* Prévost)

Collins
(*See* Desmaizeaux)

Defoe
(*See* Rousseau, Prévost)

Dryden

Perkins, Merle L. Dryden's The Indian emperour and Voltaire's Alzire. See 4749. **5575**
Although Voltaire and Dryden's plays differ in philosophic meaning and historical orientation, Dryden showed Voltaire the way to break with French classical tradition and adapt a different structure to his philosophical purposes and fast-moving events.

Fenton
(*See* Voltaire)

Fielding

Jones, B. P. Was there a temporary suppression of Tom Jones in France ? MLN 76:495–98, 1961. **5576**
A scholarly amplification of Shaw's note (5577) on the suppression of *Tom Jones* in France.

Shaw, Edward P. A note on the temporary suppression of Tom Jones in France. MLN 72:41, 1957. **5577**
Tom Jones was suppressed in France in order to punish a bookseller who had sold copies of it before he requested permission to print it.

Foote
(*See* Boissy)

Gibbon

Bonnard, Georges A. Gibbon's Essai sur l'étude de la littérature as judged by contemporary reviewers and by Gibbon himself. Est 32:145–53, 1951. **5578**
A comparative study dealing with Gibbon's *Essai*. Reveals how he himself judged the book soon after writing it, 20 years thereafter, and how French men of letters judged it, especially so on the occasion of a trip to France in 1763, for which Gibbon was prepared with a good number of reference letters.

Goldsmith

Barbier, Carl P. Goldsmith en France au xviiie siècle. RLC 25:385–402, 1951. **5579**
Gives a history of translations of Goldsmith's works in France from 1762 and follows their fortunes, especially of the *Essays* and the *Vicar of Wakefield*.

Hobbes

(*See also* Bayle, d'Holbach, Diderot, *Encyclopédie*, Montesquieu, Rousseau, Saint-Pierre, Voltaire)

Thielemann, L. J. Thomas Hobbes dans l'Encyclopédie. RHL 51:333–46, 1951. **5580**

Although Montesquieu, Voltaire, Rousseau, and numerous authors of the *Encyclopédie* severely criticized Hobbes, Diderot went out of his way to give a fair and careful representation of Hobbes's philosophy. He respected Hobbes's honesty and motives, and considered him an ancestor of 18th-century philosophy.

Hume

(*See also* Crébillon *fils*, Diderot, d'Holbach, Maine de Biran, Maupertius, Rousseau, Voltaire)

Hume, David. New letters of David Hume. Ed. by Raymond Klibansky and Ernest C. Mossner. Oxford, Clarendon press, 1954. xxiv, 253 p. **5581**

Publishes about 100 new letters, including some touching on the Rousseau-Hume quarrel. Letters 69 and 71 concern d'Alembert as well as Mlle de Lespinasse. Particularly important is the full text of the July 15, 1766, letter to d'Alembert. J.-B. Suard's translations of Hume and Robertson's *Charles V* recounted in other letters. Letters to Voltaire on Rousseau, on *Candide*, on the condemnation of the *Histoire générale* by clergy, and to Robertson on Prévost's desire to translate *L'histoire d'Ecosse*. Annotated index of persons, books, and subjects.

Bongie, Laurence L. David Hume and the official censorship of the Ancien Régime. FS 12:234–46, 1958. **5582**

Translations of Hume's works were severely censored by the *ancien régime*, all of which served to increase Hume's popularity and encourage publication of the prohibited books.

— David Hume, prophet of the counter-revolution. Oxford, Clarendon press, 1965. xvli, 182 p. **5583**

The religious traditionalists, the greatest enemies of the *philosophes*, profited greatly from Hume's history of the Stuarts and other historical works in the formulation of their own political principles. The author avers that Burke's influence on French counterrevolutionary thought was, for a time, less important than that of Hume's interpretation of Charles' reign and downfall and the

subsequent republican experiment. He documents enduring fame of this work through the various periods. In a sense, Hume's *History* was almost written for France, as it came to be an integral part of their sense of history. Index of names and titles.

— Hume, philosophe and philosopher in eighteenth-century France. FS 15:213–27, 1961. **5584**

An excellent exposition of Hume's fortunes among the *philosophes*. He was admired for his political, economic, and historical writings but was largely misunderstood as a philosopher. From this arise several interesting distinctions between *philosophe* and philosopher.

Courtney, C. P. David Hume et l'abbé Raynal : une source de l'Histoire philosophique des Deux Indes. *See* 5379. **5585**

Discusses the influence of Hume and his *History of England* upon the abbé Raynal and his *Histoire philosophique*.

Grimsley, Ronald. D'Alembert and Hume. *See* 4278. **5586**

Discusses the relations between the two men, especially during the Hume-Rousseau quarrel, and gives details concerning the publication of the *Exposé*. In spite of their mutual sympathy, the two men "met too late in life for either to have exerted a significant influence on the other's intellectual development."

— A French correspondent of David Hume : Fenouillot de Falbaire. MLR 56:561–63, 1961. **5587**

Falbaire wrote Hume one letter asking him to help him get his plays produced in England.

Manuel, Frank Edward. The eighteenth century confronts the gods. Cambridge, Harvard univ. press, 1959. 336 p. **5588**

Ch. 4, *Président de Brosses: in memory of the little fetish* (p. 184–209), discusses the influence of Hume on de Brosses. The influence of the English deists is dealt with throughout. Index follows.

Meyer, Paul Hugo. The manuscript of Hume's account of his dispute with Rousseau. CL 4:341–50, 1952. **5589**

The ms copy of Hume's *Account* addressed to d'Alembert seems to reveal that the English publisher had followed and translated the French version and did not use the original English ms as Hume later wanted. Thus the English version bears d'Alembert's and d'Holbach's alterations, which serve to moderate Hume's observations on Rousseau's conduct.

— Voltaire and Hume's Descent on the coast of Brittany. MLN 66:429–35, 1951. **5590**

Meyer identifies Voltaire as the author of a satirical passage on the English raid on Lorient and the southern coast of Brittany in 1746 and Hume as the author, or at least originator, of a reply to this account.

Mossner, Ernest Campbell. Hume and the French men of letters. RIP 6:222–35, 1952. **5591**

This article reviews Hume's contact with the French intelligentsia from Montesquieu (1749) on. His disappointment in their misunderstanding of and indifference to his philosophy of mitigated skepticism and his scientific method is related.

— The life of David Hume. Edinburgh, Nelson; Austin, Univ. of Texas press, 1954. xx, 683 p. **5592**

Several sections of the book present detailed information on Hume's influence and fortune in France. *See* especially *Political disourses* (257–71), *The call of France* and *The adulation of France* (423–55), *The " philosophes "* (475–88), and *Jean-Jacques Rousseau* (507–32).

Todd, William B. Hume, Exposé succinct. Bcol 7:191, 1958. **5593**

The order of the two 1776 eds. in The Rothschild Library is confirmed by press figures.

Johnson

Clifford, James L. For Candide and Rasselas all was not for the best. TBR 4, 14, April 19, 1959. *See* 5722. **5594**

Points out differences in tone, style, thinking, and targets between Voltaire and Johnson in their satires on the falsity of unthinking optimism.

—, and **Donald J. Greene.** A bibliography of Johnsonian studies, 1950–1960, with additions and corrections, 1887–1950; a supplement to Johnsonian Studies, 1887–1950. *In:* Johnsonian Studies. Ed. by Magdi Wahba. Cairo, Société orientale de publicité, 1962. p. 263–350. **5595**

Section B, XVII, on *Rasselas* and its influence.

Lillo
(*See also* Dorat, Rousseau)

Price, Lawrence M. George Barnwell abroad. CL 2:126–56, 1950. **5596**

The fortunes of George Lillo's play in Europe, particularly in 18th-century France, through La Harpe's verse drama (p. 126–39). Bibliography follows, giving the names of libraries possessing the books (p. 154–56).

Liston
(*See* Riccoboni)

Locke
(*See also* Bayle, Bouhier, Coste, Crousaz, Cuppé, Diderot, Du Bos, Montesquieu, Rousseau)

Locke, John. Travels in France, 1675–1679, as related in his Journals, Correspondence and other papers. Ed. with an introduction and notes by John Lough. Cambridge, Cambridge univ. press, 1953. lxvi, 308 p. **5597**

The " other papers " of the subtitle are a supplement to the *Journal* for 1679 and a list of philosophical passages in it (1676–79). Main interest is light shed " on the state of France when, both at home and abroad, the prestige of Louis XIV was at its height " (p. xli). During this period, his influence on the French was negligible, but he himself profited thereby in establishing relations with several groups of scholars through his contacts with Justel and Thoynard. One name conspicuous by its absence is Malebranche, the greatest contemporary French philosopher.

Bonno, Gabriel. Les relations intellectuelles de Locke avec la France (d'après des documents inédits). CPMP 38:37–264, 1955. **5598**

This is an extensive scholarly study based on the Locke Papers at the Bodleian Library containing chapters on Locke's stay in France; his correspondence with Justel, Thoynard, and the abbé Du Bos; his French books and the influence of French culture upon his intellectual development. It does not deal with the influence of Locke upon French writers.

Cranston, M. Locke in France. TLS 461, July 17, 1953. **5599**

Only a small portion of the diaries Locke kept in France is in shorthand form.

Hampton, John. Les traductions françaises

de Locke au xviiie siècle. RLC 29:240–51, 1955. *See* 3351.   **5600**

Hampton presents a history of translations and eds. of John Locke's works in French from 1686 to 1732 with an eye to estimating Locke's accessibility and popularity in France during that time.

Le Clerc, Jean. Lettres inédites de Le Clerc à Locke. *See* 5375.   **5601**

These letters reassert the importance of Le Clerc's role in the first diffusion of Locke's works.

Passmore, J. A. The malleability of man in eighteenth-century thought. *In:* Aspects of the eighteenth century. Ed. by Earl Reeves Wasserman. Baltimore, Johns Hopkins press, 1965. p. 21–46.   **5602**

Impact of Locke's *Some thoughts concerning education* on Helvétius, Morelly, and Condillac in France, and on Hartley and Mandeville in England. " In France the doctrine that education is all-powerful led to a demand that it be entrusted to the state; in England it had precisely the contrary effect "(p. 45).

Maréchal

Green, F. C. The letters of Milord Maréchal to Rousseau. FS 9:54–59, 1955.   **5603**

Corrects errors in the printed texts of letters from George Keith, Earl Maréchal, to Rousseau.

Moore
(*See* Rousseau)

Milton

Lutaud, Olivier. D'Aeropagitica à la Lettre à un premier commis et de l'Agreement au Contrat social. SVEC 26:1109–27, 1963.   **5604**

Discusses the influence of Milton (and especially the *Areopagitica*) on Mirabeau, Malesherbes, and Voltaire, as well as that of Lilburne (*Agreement of the people*, 1694) on Rousseau.

Lady Mary Montagu

Halsband, Robert. Lady Mary Wortley Montagu as a friend of Continental writers. JRLB 39:57–74, 1956.   **5605**

Discusses Lady Mary's relations and correspondence with Jean-Baptiste Rousseau, Toussaint, Rémond, Voltaire, and Montesquieu as well as many Italian writers.

Newton
(*See also* Diderot, Fréret, Voltaire)

Guerlac, Henry. Three eighteenth-century social philosophers : scientific influences on their thought. Daed 87:8–24, 1958.   **5606**

Suggests that although Newton may have been the rallying cry of the 18th century, it would seem he had little actual effect or influence in France. Montesquieu and d'Holbach did not understand him. Voltaire seems to have grasped the implications of his thought best.

— Where the statue stood : divergent loyalties to Newton in the eighteenth century. *In:* Aspects of the eighteenth century. Ed. by Earl Reeves Wasserman. Baltimore, Johns Hopkins press, 1965. p. 317–34.   **5607**

Examines the problem of defining Newton's method and the idea of his new science, on the one hand, and that of bridging of the gulf separating Newton from his contemporaries on the Continent, on the other. Avers that this gulf was wide and difficult to traverse, even for a Huygens, and that subsequent interpretations of Newtonian philosophy and science in the 18th century were varied and conflicting. Some of these were by Voltaire, d'Alembert, and Condillac.

Murdoch, Ruth T. Newton and the French muse. JHI 19:323–34, 1958. *See* 3560.   **5608**

Although Newton did have an influence on 18th-century French scientific poetry, his work did not really provide apt inspiration for poets.

Ossian
(*See* Bibliographies and General Studies, Wilkes)

Pope
(*See* Crousaz, Rousseau)

Price
(*See* Condorcet)

Richardson
(*See also* Diderot, Laclos, Malesherbes, Voltaire)

Bonnard, G. A. Samuel Richardson and Guillaume-Antoine de Luc. MLR 46:440–41, 1951.   **5609**

Presents an unpublished note from Richardson to de Luc which accompanied a gift of his works. De Luc thanked him by sending him the Medal of Geneva.

Pons, Christian. Richardson et la Nouvelle Héloise. EA 14:350–51, 1961.   **5610**

Points out several striking parallels between the *Nouvelle Héloïse* and *Pamela* and *Sir Charles Grandison*.

Shaftesbury
(*See also* Bayle, Montesquieu)

Aldridge, Alfred Owen. Shaftesbury and the deist manifesto. APST 41:297–385, 1951. **5611**
Contains a descriptive bibliography of references to Shaftesbury (1700–1800), including the French.

Schlegel, Dorothy B. Diderot as the transmitter of Shaftesbury's romanticism. *See* 5238. **5612**
Discusses the influence of Shaftesbury on Rousseau through the intermediary of Diderot, who, as Shaftesbury's translator, was very much impressed and influenced by his ideas and passed them on verbally to Rousseau. *See also* 5122.

— Shaftesbury and the French deists. Chapel Hill, Univ. of North Carolina press, 1956. 143 p. (NCSL, 15) **5613**
Deals with the fate of Shaftesbury's ideas in France and superficially with his influence on Voltaire, Diderot, d'Holbach, and Rousseau.
Review : K. Whitworth, Jr. in CL 9: 258–61, 1957.

Shakespeare
(*See also* d'Argens)

Bailey, Helen Phelps. Hamlet in France, from Voltaire to Laforgue (with an epilogue). Geneva, Droz, 1964. xv, 180 p. **5614**
Ch. 1, *The dark prince in the Age of Enlightenment* (p. 1–25), deals with the fortunes of *Hamlet*, especially its translations, adaptations, and parodies, before 1800. Succeeding chapters cover the periods from 1800 to 1940.
Review : W. Bowman in FR 39:943–44, 1965–66.

Benchettrit, Paul. Hamlet at the Comédie Française : 1769–1896. ShS 9:59–68, 1956. **5615**
Ducis' classical adaptation for the stage (1769) summarily described, beginning with quotation from his explanatory letter to Garrick setting forth his intentions.

Bonnefoy, Yves. Shakespeare and the French poet. Enc 18:38–43, 1962. **5616**
Mentions the translations of Voltaire and Ducis in dealing with the difficulties of translating Shakespeare into French.

Compares original with Ducis', showing similarities with *Cinna* and *Phèdre*. Summarizes Ducis' 1787 alterations (Comédie Française Library ms).

England, Martha W. Garrick's Stratford Jubilee : reactions in France and Germany. ShS 10:90–100, 1956. **5617**
Gives details of 1769 Jubilee and English satirical reaction to excesses of bardolatry. Discusses French rejoicing at news of the Jubilee, Shakespeare's influence on the French theater, and the Voltaire-Le Tourneur feud about Shakespeare's merits as a dramatist. Notes that the Jubilee marked the end of French cultural domination in Germany. Describes Goethe's Shakespeare festivals.

Jeune, Simon. Hamlet d'Otway, Macbeth de Dryden, ou Shakespeare en France en 1714. RLC 36:560–64, 1962. **5618**
The translator of the *Spectator* rendered some of the included passages and references to Shakespeare into French, but he attributed *Hamlet* to Otway and *Macbeth* to Dryden and did nothing to further Shakespeare's fortunes in France.

Keys, A. C. Shakespeare en France : La mégère apprivoisée en 1767. RLC 31:426–28, 1957. **5619**
Antoine Bret's *Les deux sœurs* (1767) is an adaptation of *The taming of the shrew*, as it was presented in the *Théâtre anglais* of La Place.

— Shakespeare in France, an early stage adaptation. AUMLA 1:15–20, 1953 **5620**
Treats *Les deux amies ...* , a musical adaptation of *Merry wives* and an opéra comique (libretto by Bret, score by Papavoine) performed in 1761, 8 years before Ducis' *Hamlet*. The author shows that in the early sixties there was no more chance of the *Merry wives* being known in France than any other of Shakespeare's comedies.

Lombard, Charles M. Ducis' Hamlet and Musset's Lorenzaccio. NQ 203:72–75, 1958. **5621**
Considers translations of *Hamlet* by La Place, Ducis, and Le Tourneur up to Musset's time.

Mattauch, Hans. A propos du premier jugement sur Shakespeare en France. MLN 78:288–300, 1963. **5622**
Established April 1704 as a date of remark : "... mais ces belles qualités sont obscurcies par les ordures qu'il mêle

dans ses comédies." Demonstrates that P. de Courbeville wrote it in *Journal de Trévoux*, but might well have obtained this judgment from another. This Jesuit priest's role assessed as minor, compared with Voltaire, in introducing Shakespeare to the French.

Pons, Christian. Les traductions de Hamlet par des écrivains français. EA 13:116–29, 1960. **5623**

Briefly discusses the translations of Voltaire, Ducis, and Le Tourneur in this survey of *Hamlet* translators.

Shakespeare in Europe. Ed. by Oswald Le Winter. Cleveland, World publishing, 1963. 382 p. **5624**

An anthology of Continental (non-English) opinions of Shakespeare beginning with Voltaire. The editor briefly discusses Shakespeare's impact on 18th-century France in his introduction.

Review: H. Arnold in CLS 1:76–77, 1964.

Vanderhoof, Mary B. Hamlet : a tragedy adapted from Shakespeare (1770) by Jean François Ducis; a critical edition. APSP 97:88–142, 1953. **5625**

Ducis' adaptation was based on La Place's translation since Ducis knew no English. He freely adapted the play and it was his adaptation, performed in 1769, that was translated into Italian, Spanish, and Dutch and acted in Sweden. The author makes detailed comparison between the eds. and presents the criticism of Collé, Diderot, Fréron, and others. A valuable study.

Review : H. Lancaster in ShQ 4:470–71, 1953.

Sterne
(*See* Chamfort, Crébillon *fils*, Diderot, Rousseau)

Swift
(*See* Coyer, Desmaizeaux, Voltaire)

Thomson
(*See also* Rousseau, Voltaire)

Châlon, Yves. Les Saisons de James Thomson; autour de leur Dédicace française. RLC 32:34–46, 1958. **5626**

Quesnay and Mirabeau were responsible for the *Dédicace* to Mme Bontemps' (1759) popular translation of Thomson's *Seasons*, since these poems of nature with the *Dédicace* advanced their cause against that of the Encyclopedists.

Tillotson
(*See also* Cuppé)

Brown, David D. Voltaire, Archbishop Tillotson and the invention of God. RLC 34:257–61, 1960. **5627**

This suggests a source for Voltaire's aphorism " Si Dieu n'existait pas, il faudrait l'inventer " in the sermons of John Tillotson, whose work was known in France and provided much ammunition for the English deists.

Toland

Crocker, Lester G. John Toland et le matérialisme de Diderot. *See* 5129. **5628**

John Toland's *Letters to Serena* inspired certain of Diderot's ideas in his *Rêve de d'Alembert* and his *Pensées sur la matière et le mouvement*.

Warburton
(*See also* The *Encyclopédie*, Voltaire)

Cherpack, Clifton. Warburton and some aspects of the search for the primitive in eighteenth-century France. PQ 36:221–33, 1957. *See* 4257. **5629**

Traces the influence of Warburton's *Divine legation* upon Court de Gébelin, Goguet, Boulanger, Charles de Brosses, Turgot, and Condillac.

— Warburton and the Encyclopédie. *See* 4301. **5630**

Warburton was utilized without acknowledgment in many articles of the *Encyclopédie*, and numerous ideas in various articles were taken from Warburton's writings (which were translated into French and readily available).

Wilkes
(*See also* Crébillon *fils*, Diderot, d'Holbach)

Wilkes, John. The contributions of John Wilkes to the Gazette littéraire de l'Europe. Ed. by Louis I. Bredvold. Ann Arbor, Univ. of Michigan press, 1950. 36 p. **5631**

Reveals that the Wm. L. Clements Library at Ann Arbor holds 32 letters from Wilkes to Suard, plus drafts of articles for the review which Suard directed. Bredvold shows that 2 articles formerly attributed to Voltaire were the fruit of the Wilkes-Suard " collaboration." Bredvold reproduces the full text of Wilkes's articles written in English and freely adapted into French by Suard. One of these concerns the Welsh bards as published in Rev. Evan Evans' *Speci-*

mens. Suard added to this article a comparison with Ossian's poetry, to the detriment of the Welsh.

Reviews : P. Legouis in RLC 25:279–80, 1951; G. Nobbe in PQ 30:300–01, 1951.

Young
(*See* Rousseau)

English influences on French authors

D'Alembert
(*See* Hume)

D'Argens

Lancaster, H. Carrington. Observations on French, Spanish and English theaters in d'Argens' Lettres juives and Lettres cabalistiques. MLN 69:231–37, 1954.   **5632**

Gives d'Argens' views on the theater, actors, authors of France, Spain, and England. D'Argens used Voltaire's *Lettres philosophiques* to condemn English ignorance of dramatic rules; he put Shakespeare and Addison far below Corneille and Racine. His views on Addison, Wycherley, Vanbrugh, and Congreve accord with Voltaire's, thus helping to confirm his Continental readers in their classical prejudices.

Bayle

Labrousse, Elisabeth R. Bayle et l'établissement de Desmaizeaux en Angleterre. RLC 29:251–57, 1955.   **5633**

Bayle's role in promoting Desmaizeaux among English literati, especially Shaftesbury.

Whitmore, P. J. S. English thought and learning in the works of Pierre Bayle. FS 8:141–48, 1954.   **5634**

Maintains that the use of English sources and interest in England is an essential feature of Bayle's work. He made use of More, Hobbes, Locke, and many others.

Boissy

Berveiller, Michel. Anglais et Français de comédie chez Louis de Boissy et Samuel Foote. CLS 2:259–69, 1965.   **5635**

Recalls that these two now obscure playwrights of the early 18th century, one Marivaudian, the other Hogarthian, were precursors of the theatrical device of *dépaysement.* Notes that their considerable success was due to their *dépaysés* characters. Studies through them malicious

pleasure of mutual mockery of the other nation's real or reputed shortcomings. Attempts to demonstrate interesting thesis that both Frenchmen and Englishmen strove to live up to their ethnic reputations, as perpetuated in comic theater.

Bouhier

Shackleton, Robert. Renseignements inédits sur Locke, Coste et Bouhier. RLC 27:319–22, 1953.   **5636**

Voluminous correspondence of the archeologist-philologist Jean Bouhier, if edited and published, would be a mine of precious information about the literary history of his times.

Brissot
(*See* Bibliographies and General Studies—American)

Castillon

Oake, Roger B. Jean-Louis Castillon and Ambrose Gwinett. RLC 28:318–22, 1954.   **5637**

Oake cites Jean-Louis Castillon as the translator of " Ambrose Gwinett " first in the *Journal encyclopédique* in 1769 and then in a work he entitled *Candide anglois, ou aventures tragi-comiques d'Amb. Gwinett.* This latter is a very free translation and should really be considered as a *Candide* imitation.

Chamfort

Alciatore, J. C. Stendhal, Sterne et Chamfort. MLN 75:582–85, 1960.   **5638**

An epigraph in Stendhal, attributed to Sterne, probably comes from Chamfort.

Chateaubriand

Christophorov, P. Chateaubriand à Londres en 1796. RHL 59:168–79, 1959.   **5639**

Precise documentation on his activities, primarily steps taken to receive aid as an *émigré* from the *Comité français,* so that he might have the means to finish his historical research.

Kahn, Ernest. Chateaubriand in England. Crev 177:157–61, 1950.   **5640**

Studies his exile in Suffolk and London and his contemporary and subsequent writings on England.

Letessier, Fernand. Une source de Chateaubriand : Le voyage du jeune Anacharsis. RHL 59:180–203, 1959. *See* 4062.   **5641**

Compares textually, and at length, *Essai sur les révolutions anciennes et modernes* and Jean-Jacques Barthélemy's *Voyage*. Debt to him is only partial as supplementary readings and research contributed even more to background sources of *Essai*. During his stay as French teacher in Beccles (Suffolk), 1793–96, Chateaubriand studied in libraries containing excellent Hellenistic holdings and frequented Hellenists J. Girdlestone, B. Sparrow, and John Ives. Probably read classics and minor authors. Letessier disagrees with Renan's scoffing denial of Chateaubriand's knowledge of philology.

Voisine, Jacques. Le volcan de René. FS 5:149–53, 1951.   **5642**

René's famous meditation on Mt. Etna may well have been derived from *Letters of an Italian nun and an English gentleman, translated from the French of J. J. Rousseau* (1781). The author gives good reasons for believing that not Rousseau but an unknown Englishman was the author of the famous book. Chateaubriand could well have read *Letters of an Italian nun* during his exile in England for, in 1800, Rousseau's name on the book probably would have attracted his interest.

Condorcet

Lough, John. Condorcet et Richard Price. RLC 24:87–93, 1950.   **5643**

Although Condorcet attributes his ideas on the perfectibility of the human species to Richard Price, it is more likely that Condorcet influenced Price. Price's orientation was too religious to have heavily influenced Condorcet.

Coste
(*See also* Bouhier)

Bonno, Gabriel. Locke et son traducteur français Pierre Coste; avec huit lettres inédites de Coste à Locke. RLC 33:161–79, 1959.   **5644**

Coste's letters throw light on the details concerning his translations of Locke's work, which received the benefit of Locke's judgment, views, and approval.

Coyer

Elsoffer-Kamins, Louise. Un imitateur original de Jonathan Swift : l'abbé Coyer et ses Bagatelles morales (1754). RLC 23:469–81, 1949.   **5645**

L'abbé Coyer drew a great deal of inspiration from Swift's works, especially from *A letter to a young lady on her marriage*. His *Bagatelles* were well received and served to instruct in the Swiftian manner.

Crébillon *fils*

Day, Douglas A. Crébillon *fils*, ses exils et ses rapports avec l'Angleterre; avec deux lettres inédites. *See* 4081.   **5646**

Establishes that Crébillon *fils* met his English friends in France, not England. Sterne, Walpole, Hume, and Wilkes liked his work and visited him when they were in France. The letters are addressed to Wilkes.

Crousaz

La Harpe, Jacqueline Ellen Violette de. Jean-Pierre de Crousaz (1663–1750) et le conflit des idées au siècle des lumières. Preface by Daniel Mornet. Berkeley, Univ. of California press, 1955. 281 p. (CPMP, 47)   **5647**

A comprehensive study of the Swiss philosopher and his importance. Some references to Locke and Pope.

Review : L. Thielemann in CL 9:84–86, 1957.

Cuppé

Briggs, E. R. Pierre Cuppé's debts to England and Holland. SVEC 6:37–66, 1958.   **5648**

See especially " Probable english [sic] sources " (p. 42–50) which discusses the influences of Locke and John Tillotson upon Pierre Cuppé.

Desmaizeaux
(*See also* Bayle)

Broome, J. H. Une collaboration : Anthony Collins et Desmaizeaux. RLC 30:161–79, 1956.   **5649**

Discusses the literary and philosophic relationship between Collins and Desmaizeaux, especially the part Desmaizeaux played in Collins' life and work. Some works attributed to Collins were actually collaborations with Desmaizeaux.

— Pierre Desmaizeaux, journaliste; les Nouvelles littéraires de Londres entre 1700 et 1740. *See* 5537.   **5650**

Desmaizeaux sent to France works or extracts of empiricists, as well as news of latest scientific, religious, and philosophical works, which interested the learned Protestant audience of *Nouvelles littéraires*, but passed by the mainstream of

English literature. Notable, though brief exceptions are his praise of Addison's *Voyages en Italie*, Swift's *Tale of a tub*, and the first mention in a French periodical of Shakespeare (Jan., 1703). By 1715 he was contributing simultaneously to 5 French periodicals, thereby encouraging other journalists to take an interest in England. He supported Collins' deism and subtly influenced French publicists to take sides in current English controversies.

Diderot
(*See also* Burney, Shaftesbury, Toland)

Booy, Jean de. A propos d'un texte de Diderot sur Newton. DS 4:41–51, 1963. **5651**

Relates search for identity of a certain abbé Basset who may have published Diderot's letter on Newton in *Les mémoires de Trévoux* (2e Vol., avril 1761) under title : *Réflexions sur une difficulté proposée contre la manière dont les Newtoniens expliquent la cohésion des corps et les autres phénomènes qui s'y rapportent.*

Dédéyan, Charles. L'Angleterre dans la pensée de Diderot. *See* 5132. **5652**

A distinguished comparatist examines the subject.

Doolittle, James. Robert James, Diderot and the Encyclopédie. MLN 71:431–34, 1956. **5653**

Doolittle points out that Diderot used transcriptions from James' *A medicinal dictionary* in *Encyclopédie* articles ascribed to himself and suggests that a work on Diderot and medecine would be valuable.

Folkierski, Władysław. L'anglais de Diderot. *See* 5150. **5654**

Diderot seriously and conscientiously translated English works into French. A number of the books, Stanyan's *Grecian history* for one, had an influence upon him.

Fredman, Alice Green. Diderot and Sterne. *See* 5152. **5655**

The parallels and divergences between Diderot and Sterne are fully explored through a treatment of their sensibility, humor, literary procedures, and style. A common interest in certain ideas and writers is more important between the two than the influence of each upon the other.

Green, F. C. Autour de quatre lettres iné-

dites de Diderot à John Wilkes. RLC 25: 449–67, 1951. **5656**

These letters testify to Diderot's friendship with Wilkes, which dated from 1765. One letter was previously thought to be addressed to Sir Wm. Jones.

Kempf, Roger. Diderot et le roman; ou le démon de la présence. *See* 5180. **5657**

Discusses briefly (p. 18–26) Richardson's influence on Diderot in Ch. 2, and mentions Richardson in passing throughout the work. No index.

Lublinskiĭ, V. S. Sur la trace des livres lus par Diderot. *See* 5077. **5658**

Contains references to English works, notably the translation of James's *A medicinal dictionary.*

Loy, J. Robert. Diderot's determined fatalist; a critical appreciation of Jacques le fataliste. *See* 2219A. **5659**

Ch. 1, *Jacques le fataliste and the critics* concerns, in part, the history of the critics' belief that *Jacques* was an imitation of *Tristram Shandy*. Ch. 2, *The place of Jacques in the 18th-century novel*, deals with several important influences on Diderot, notably those of Richardson and Sterne. The latter is dealt with thoroughly with a great reliance on the texts. An important book.

May, Gita. Diderot and Burke : a study in aesthetic affinity. *See* 5197. **5660**

Studies Diderot's penchant for borrowing from others' esthetic theory, particularly Edmund Burke's *Philosophical enquiry into the origin of our ideas of the sublime and the beautiful* (1757). Textual collation shows that Diderot rethought and reworked, " manipulated and condensed Burke's most striking passages "; this in turn is revelatory of Diderot's style. Diderot and Burke depart from the position of Locke and Condillac on semantics, imagination, and mental association.

Proust, Jacques. La bibliothèque de Diderot (II). *See* 5090. **5661**

Contains some references to Richardson and Hume.

Schwab, Richard N. The history of medicine in Diderot's Encyclopédie. BuHM 32:216–23, 1958. **5662**

Discusses the importance of the chevalier de Jaucourt to the *Encyclopédie* and the value of his article on medicine. Jaucourt's major source was Diderot's translation of Robert James's *A medicinal dictionary*, which in turn owed much to Le Clerc and Freind. Jaucourt departs from James whenever the latter inserts religious or mystical history to give history in the manner of a true *philosophe*.

Siegel, June S. Grandeur-intimacy : the dramatist's dilemma. *See* 5244. **5663**

Relates the conflict of the visual and the imaginative to Diderot's imperfect translation to the stage of techniques of Richardson's novel.

Thielemann, Leland. Diderot and Hobbes. *See* 5253. **5664**

Deals comprehensively with Hobbes's influence on Diderot and on the 18th century and with Diderot's role in disseminating Hobbes's ideas in France.

Dorat

Hallowell, Robert E. Claude-Joseph Dorat, opponent of the drame bourgeois and critic of the English theatre. FR 25:355–63, 1952. **5665**

Although very critical of contemporary English theater, Dorat was impressed by George Lillo's *The merchant*. This conflict is perhaps due to his emotional Anglophobia.

Du Bos

Bonno, Gabriel. Une amitié franco-anglaise du XVIIe siècle : John Locke et l'abbé Du Bos. RLC 24:481–520, 1950. **5666**

The abbé Du Bos read Locke and became friends with him during his visit to England in the 1690's. Bonno presents 16 letters from Du Bos to Locke which demonstrate their mutual esteem and friendship.

Caramaschi, Enzo. Arte e critica nella concezione dell'arte dell'abate Du Bos. RLM 12:101–18; 13:248–70, 1959. **5667**

This long study, based on Du Bos' *Réflexions critiques sur la poésie et la peinture*, deals with the influence of English empiricism on the esthetic thought of Du Bos. Through Locke and Addison, Du Bos came in contact with English esthetic thought. Du Bos tries to justify " artistic activity " not to explain the beautiful. As a critic Du Bos is interested in the " relative and comparative " evaluation and judgment of art. He aims at classification which ends in a stratification. In this the abbé seems to be looking toward Boileau rather than

toward the other side of the channel. Also included is a critical study and evaluation of the " three faults " (*finalismo, edonismo, associazionismo*) which are usually attributed to empiric writers and thinkers and which a modern critic (M. M. Rossi) also associates with Du Bos.

Gates, Warren. The abbé Du Bos : a harbinger of Locke in France ? FR 33:172–74, 1951–52. **5668**

Jean-Marie Le Clerc, not Du Bos, first introduced Locke to France with his *Extrait* from the *Essay on human understanding* in 1688. Le Clerc also wrote an article on Locke's career and life in 1705 which became " the foundation of later biographies."

Duclos

Duthil, R., and Charles Dédéyan. Duclos et la Société royale de Londres (1763–1764). RLC 24:79–86, 1950. **5669**

Touches slightly upon Duclos' relations with Walpole and Lord Chesterfield and his election to the Royal Society. Letters to Duclos from Chesterfield, Ducarel, William Hanbury, and Matthew Maty are given.

Dupont

Schmitt, Hans A., and John C. Weston, Jr. Ten letters to Edmund Burke from the French translator of the Reflections on the Revolution in France. RLM 12:101–18, 1959; 13:248–70, 1960. **5670**

These letters tell the story of the publication of the French ed. of the *Reflections* and of the French translator Pierre-Gaëtan Dupont (who is not the man to whom the *Reflections* are addressed).

The *Encyclopédie*

(*See also* Berkeley, Diderot, Hobbes, Jefferson in American Section, Thomson, Warburton)

Doolittle, James. Jaucourt's use of source material in the Encyclopédie. MLN 65: 387–92, 1950. **5671**

Discusses Jaucourt's debt to Warburton in his articles for the *Encyclopédie*, especially to the Léonard translation of the *Divine legation*.

Schalk, Fritz. Zur Vorgeschichte der Diderot'schen Enzyklopädie. *See* 4331. **5672**

Discusses Hobbes's views in great detail and posits him as the source for the general idea of the *Encyclopédie*. The author also discusses the fate and fame of Hobbes's ideas in France, England, and Germany.

Wilson, Arthur M. Why did the political theory of the Encyclopedists not prevail? A suggestion. *See* 4347.   **5673**

Discusses Weis's analysis (4345) of all articles in *Encyclopédie* on political theory and related concepts and concludes that Locke, Jefferson, and Paine were the major influences on the writers of these articles (principally Jaucourt and Diderot). Wilson also discusses the fate of these ideas after the Revolution.

Fréret

Simon, Renée. L'affaire Newton. *In her:* Nicolas Fréret, académicien. SVEC 17:32–52, 1961.   **5674**

Discusses Fréret's translation of Newton's *Abrégé chronologique*, his correspondence with Newton, his *Observations sur la chronologie de M. Newton* and Newton's *Réponse aux observations* .... Fréret did not just attempt to refute Newton's scheme of chronology. He tried to ascertain the truth of each point, and was concerned with research, not polemics.

Fréron

Bundy, Jean. Fréron and the English novel. *See* 5496.   **5675**

Discusses the critical response of Fréron to the English novel from 1749 to 1775.

Helvétius

Cumming, Ian. Helvétius in England. *See* 4355.   **5676**

Presents Helvétius' impressions of English legislative and educational life as well as his impressions of the countryside, nobility, etc.

D'Holbach
(*See also* Burney, Hume, Newton, Shaftesbury)

Naumann, Manfred. A propos de deux lettres de d'Holbach à Wilkes. RLC 30:110, 1956.   **5677**

Corrects Paul Vernière's statement (RLC 28:482–84, 1954) that the 2 letters he presented were unpublished by calling attention to the undeservedly neglected volume which contains them, i.e., *Baron d'Holbach: a study of eighteenth-century*

radicalism in France by Max Pearson Cushing (1338).

Topazio, Virgil W. D'Holbach's moral philosophy, its background and development. *See* 4384.   **5678**

Diffuse treatment of the influence of English empiricists (Hobbes to Hume).

Vernière, Paul. Deux lettres inédites de d'Holbach à Wilkes. RLC 28:482–86, 1954.   **5679**

Convinced that d'Holbach's attitude toward England and the English merits a particular study, the author adds 2 more letters (1766 and 67) to the extant canon. But *see* Naumann *supra*.

Laclos

Thelander, Dorothy R. Laclos and the epistolary novel. *See* 3966.   **5680**

Dismisses Richardson as a source or model, for " long before Richardson, the basic premises of the novel by letters had been established."

Maine de Biran

Hallie, Philip P. Hume, Biran and the Méditatifs intérieurs. JHI 18:295–312, 1957.   **5681**

French philosopher, François-Pierre Gontier, or Maine de Biran, criticized Hume's work, thus revealing divergences between French and English schools of philosophy in the 18th century.

Malesherbes
(*See also* Milton)

Shaw, Edward P. Malesherbes, the abbé Prévost and the first French translation of Sir Charles Grandison. *See* 3848.   **5682**

Refutes F. M. Wilcox's charge that the abbé Prévost was refused permission to print his translation of *Sir Charles Grandison.* He gives letters showing Malesherbes' support of the translation and his efforts to prevent a rival translation from being printed in Paris at the same time.

Marivaux

Dédéyan, Charles. Marivaux à l'école d'Addison et de Steele. AUP 25:5–17, 1955.   **5683**

The success of Marivaux' journalistic career stems, in part, from what he learned from Addison and Steele. Although their approach to the classics and their values are different, Marivaux learned much stylistically from the *Spectateur* (translated into French from 1714).

Maupertuis

Gossman, Lionel. Berkeley, Hume and Maupertuis. *See* 5444.   **5684**

Whereas the *philosophes*, though familiar with the philosophical works of Berkeley and Hume, were largely uninterested in them and failed to grasp their significance, Maupertuis was very much attracted to and influenced by the philosophy of Berkeley and Hume, principally the former.

Mirabeau
(*See* Milton, Thomson)

Montesquieu
(*See also* Bacon, Chesterfield, Hume, Montagu, Newton)

Courtney, C. P. Montesquieu and Burke. *See* 4427.   **5685**

While principally on Montesquieu's influence on Edmund Burke, there is material touching on contributions of English life and letters toward the making of Montesquieu's thought; most famous chapter of *Esprit* treats British form of government and was written shortly after Montesquieu's return to France from England in 1731. Briefly discusses the differences in the *Leviathan* and " Troglodyte " approaches to the theory of the state. Emphasizes parallels and affinities between Montesquieu's views on the historical justification for the constitution and English empirical and conservative thought : Coke, Hale, and, later, Burke.

Dimoff, Paul. Cicéron, Hobbes et Montesquieu. *See* 4434.   **5686**

Montesquieu, despite the excellence of his intentions, did not succeed in refuting the key points of Hobbes's theory of the basis and origins of morals and law in *De cive*. He read Hobbes and reacted negatively, as did most thinkers of late 17th and early 18th centuries. He attempted to refute Hobbes in Letter X of the *Lettres persanes* with the episode of the Troglodytes. From 1729 on, his interest in Hobbes declined.

Ludwig, Mario. Montesquieu und die Engländer. *See* 4449.   **5687**

Montesquieu's attitude toward England in general and his attitude toward certain English philosophers and writers in particular, notably Hobbes and Shaftesbury (in *Lettres persanes*), Hobbes (*Analyse du traité des devoirs*), Hobbes and others (*De l'esprit des lois*), and Locke, Black, and Chesterfield. Also discusses Montesquieu's stay in England (Nov., 1729–31).

Weil, Françoise. Les lectures de Montesquieu. *See* 4477.   **5688**

A list of some 400 books Montesquieu probably read, with information as to when they were published, available, and given to or acquired by Montesquieu, with a useful chronological summary.

Prévost
(*See also* Periodicals, Richardson)

Engel, Claire-Eliane. Le véritable abbé Prévost. *See* 3808.   **5689**

Sources such as Penelope Aubin, Steele, Otway, Defoe, and others are studied, but the index is spare and the volume hard to use.

Labriolle-Rutherford, Marie-Rose de. The abbé Prévost and the English theatre, 1730–1740. TN 9:111–18, 1955.   **5690**

Documentation of Prévost's exposure to and opinions of the English theater as expressed in his *Pour et contre* and *Mémoires d'un homme de qualité*.

Malherbe, Henry. La vraie Manon. RevHM 22:193–207, 405–15, 1953.   **5691**

Shows that Prévost was well documented on Louisiana and avers that Des Grieux is virtually autobiographical, but that Manon's model is more elusive. Descriptions of her are generally abstract, probably to prevent identification of a real model. Admits possible influence of Defoe, but refutes the assertion that the abbé had " subi l'ascendant de Richardson " as chronologically inadmissible. Also denies that Prévost-Des Grieux actually left France with Manon—one biographer's hypothesis.

Roddier, Henri. L'abbé Prévost et le problème de la traduction au XVIIIᵉ siècle. *See* 3840.   **5692**

Emphasizes modifications and omissions by Prévost in his translations of Richardson's novels. Shows that the former deemed necessary some small adjustments and corrections so that the latter might be acceptable in Paris. Points out that since novels were then considered " light works," they could be altered with no concern for fidelity of translation; accordingly, the abbé is shown to be rather scrupulously literal in translating works in other genres. Considers Prévost's significant reflections on *prose poétique*, harmony, and rhyme.

— L'abbé Prévost, homme de lettres et journaliste. *See* 3841. **5693**

Expressed admiration for Dr. Samuel Clarke.

— L'abbé Prévost, l'homme et l'œuvre. *See* 3842. **5694**

In his chapter, *Le traducteur de Richardson* (p. 166–76), the author discusses Prévost's translations of Richardson and his role in promoting the Richardsonian influence on French literature, notably on *La nouvelle Héloïse*.

Rodway, A. E. Moll Flanders and Manon Lescaut. ECr 3:303–20, 1953. **5695**

Thematic and philosophic similarities and differences, indicating Prévost's debt to Defoe.

Quesnay
(*See* Thomson)

Ramsay

Henderson, George David. Chevalier Ramsay. London, Nelson, 1952. 246 p. **5696**

Biography of the controversial convert to Romanism, " disciple and biographer of Fénelon; secretary to the Quietist Madame Guyon." Adds much new documentation concerning Ramsay's life and activities as writer, historian, and theologian.
Review : J. Voisine in RLC 28:222–23, 1954.

Raynal
(*See* Hume)

Mme Riccoboni

Green, F. C. Robert Liston et Madame Riccoboni : une liaison franco-écossaise du XVIIIe siècle. RLC 38:550–58, 1964. **5697**

The Liston correspondence contains 83 letters from Mme Riccoboni which reveal an ardent passion for Liston, 29 years her junior.

Rousseau
(*See also* Bacon, Boswell, Burney, Hume, Maréchal, Montagu, Richardson, Shaftesbury, Shakespeare)

Cranston, Maurice. Rousseau in England. *See* 4794. **5698**

Popular, undocumented account of the 1766–67 English sojourn and well-known quarrel.

— Rousseau's visit to England, 1766–67. EDH 31:16–34, 1962. **5699**

Gives an account of Rousseau's visit to England under Hume's protection and of their subsequent quarrel.

Davy, Georges. Le corps politique selon le Contrat social de J.-J. Rousseau et ses antécédents chez Hobbes. *In:* Etudes sur le Contrat social de Jean-Jacques Rousseau. *See* 4791. p. 65–93. **5700**

Compares the thoughts and concepts of the two men and traces the pathways that lead from Hobbes to Rousseau. Rousseau found in Hobbes a storehouse of studies, sketches, and constructions he could make use of.

— Thomas Hobbes et J.-J. Rousseau. *See* 4919. **5701**

Extensively documents evidence of Hobbes's influence on Rousseau in spite of fundamental differences in their philosophies.

Dédéyan, Charles. Rousseau et la sensibilité littéraire à la fin du XVIIIe siècle. Centre de documentation univ., 1961. 233 p. (Les cours de Sorbonne) **5702**

Contains some discussion of the influences of English writers upon Rousseau and the French, notably Richardson, George Lillo, Edward Moore, Young, and Thomson.

Jimack, Peter D. Locke. *In his:* La genèse et la rédaction de l'Emile de J.-J. Rousseau. SVEC 13:288–318, 1960. **5703**

An excellent study of the influence Locke exerted on Rousseau through his *Essai philosophique* and *De l'éducation des enfants.*

Leigh, R. A. Boswell and Rousseau. MLR 47:289–318, 1952. **5704**

Speaks mainly of the influence of Rousseau and his writings upon Boswell, but there is interesting material concerning their meetings, friendship, and correspondence.

— J.-J. Rousseau et ses amis anglais. RLC 30:379–87, 1956. **5705**

Presents 3 new letters from Rousseau to his English friends, exposes some errors in the Rousseau-Duchess of Portland correspondence, and calls for a new ed. of Rousseau's letters.

Nicolas, Jean. Une lettre inédite de Jean-Jacques Rousseau. AHRF 34:385–96, 1962. **5706**

The author describes a sympathy between Rousseau and Pope and suggests the existence of an influence. The letter gives Rousseau's opinions of Pope's works at length.

Osborn, Annie Marion. Rousseau and Burke; a study of the idea of liberty in eighteenth-century political thought. New York, Russell & Russell, 1964. xi, 272 p. **5707**

Discusses the similarity of ideas held by Burke and Rousseau but discounts Rousseau's influence on Burke. The author briefly discusses the influence of Newton, Hobbes, and Locke upon Voltaire and Rousseau.

Pire, G. Jean-Jacques Rousseau et Robinson Crusoé. RLC 30:479–96, 1956. **5708**

Discusses Rousseau's attraction to Defoe's work and its influence on him, especially on the *Profession de foi du vicaire savoyard* and on Rousseau's educational theories.

Redpath, Th. Réflexions sur la nature du concept de contrat social chez Hobbes, Locke, Rousseau et Hume. *In:* Etudes sur le Contrat social de Jean-Jacques Rousseau. *See* 4791. p. 55–63. **5709**

Considers briefly in a work each by Hobbes, Locke, Rousseau, and Hume the questions of the historical existence of a social contract, the purposes and uses of the concept and the validity of Hume's criticism. No question of influence is raised.

Roddier, Henri. J.-J. Rousseau en Angleterre au XVIIIᵉ siècle; l'œuvre et l'homme. *See* 4955. **5710**

Although primarily concerned with the influence of Rousseau in England, the author frequently discusses English influences, such as those of Locke and Richardson upon Rousseau. He also discusses Rousseau's visit to England and his quarrel with Hume. A bibliography and index are appended. An important work.

Wasserman, Earl R. Unedited letters by Sterne, Hume and Rousseau. MLN 66:73–79, 1951. **5711**

Several letters of Hume and Rousseau, not published since 1825 (when they appeared in *European magazine*), are quoted here. They relate to Rousseau's stay in England, Hume's efforts on his behalf, and Mr. Davenport's generosities.

Saint-Pierre

Perkins, Merle L. The Leviathan and Saint-Pierre's Projet de paix perpétuelle. *See* 5409. **5712**

A careful study of Saint-Pierre's large debt to Hobbes's *Leviathan*.

— The moral and political philosophy of the abbé de Saint-Pierre. *See* 5410. **5713**

Shows that Hobbes's thought in the *Leviathan* converges in several important aspects with that of the abbé in the early development of *Projet de paix perpétuelle*. Affirms that the Hobbesian current was strong and lasting, even beyond Saint-Pierre's political and legal readings from 1692–1717, but that there were disagreements too, and other influences.

Voltaire
(*See also* D'Argens, Boswell, Chesterfield, Dryden, Hume, Johnson, Milton, Montagu, Newton, Periodicals, Shaftesbury, Shakespeare, Tillotson)

Voltaire, François-Marie Arouet de. Voltaire's England. Ed. by Desmond Flower. *See* 4533. **5714**

Voltaire's views on English manners, institutions, and eminent personalities presented through quotations from his writings.

Barber, W. H. L'Angleterre dans Candide. *See* 4709. **5715**

Besides discussing the role of England in *Candide*, Barber links Eldorado and its governor to William Penn and his colony in America.

— Voltaire and Quakerism : Enlightenment and the inner light. *See* 4608. **5716**

Traces Voltaire's attitude toward Quakerism through his career and feels that Voltaire's interest was due to a profound sympathy with the Quaker doctrines and ideas.

Beer, Gavin de. Voltaire, F. R. S. NRRSL 8:247–52, 1951. **5717**

Explains that the primary reasons leading Voltaire to an interest in Newton were personal rather than scientific : the Mlle Lecouvreur-Mrs. Oldfield contrast, eloquently put forth in his *Lettres philosophiques*. With Mme du Châtelet, Voltaire conducted experiments on fire and the cause of the increase in weight on calcination. The author includes extracts from correspondence between him and Martin Ffolkes, F.R.S., as well as the certificate of recommendation to membership in 1743.

— Voltaire's British visitors. *See* 4565. **5718**

Documents of British visitors of Voltaire in the period after he had settled in Switzerland. Eighty of the visitors have been identified.

Braybrooke, David. Professor Stevenson, Voltaire and the case of Admiral Byng. Jph 53:787–96, 1956. **5719**

In refuting an argument of Professor Stevenson (*Ethics and language*), the author mentions the Admiral Byng episode and Voltaire's use of it in *Candide*.

Brumfitt, J. H. Voltaire and Warburton. *See* 4569. **5720**

Discusses Warburton's career, Voltaire's reactions to his writings and suggests that Voltaire owed a considerable debt to Warburton. The author cites many borrowings from the *Divine legation* that went into the *Philosophie de l'histoire* and later works.

Citron, P. Voltaire et l'Angleterre. RLC 35:349, 1961. **5721**

Review of the colloquium at the French Institute of London on Voltaire and England.

Clifford, James L. For Candide and Rasselas all was not for the best. *See* 5594. **5722**

Shows that Johnson could not have imitated Voltaire in 1759. Two satires " superficially so much alike " in theme and structure, but dissimilar in tone and style. Also, Imlac frequently speaks for Dr. Johnson, but Voltaire makes Pangloss the butt of the satire. If both attack optimism, their concrete targets differ. Voltaire's thought appears melioristic. Johnson's is pessimistic.

Crowley, Francis J. Voltaire a spy for Walpole ? FS 18:356–59, 1964. **5723**

Avers that Voltaire was the good friend of a notorious English spy, Bacon Morris, said to be Walpole's cousin, and suggests that Voltaire was " guilty " by association rather than an overt spy on his own.

Fenger, Henning. Voltaire et le théâtre anglais. Orl 7:161–287, 1949. **5724**

The author contends that a valid means of penetrating Voltairian dramatic principles is to study the relationship between Voltaire and the English theater. Voltaire's novelties in the tragic genre are attributed to an English origin. Valuable materials include a bibliography of Voltaire's dramatic works; repertories of London's 3 theaters (1726–29); a list of Voltaire's knowledge of English plays that he had not seen performed, and a bibliography of " les ouvrages intéressant directement l'étude du dramaturge " (p. 282).

Review : J. Voisine in RLC 27:227–31, 1953.

Fitch, Robert Eliot. A tale of two pilgrims : a comparison of Bunyan's Pilgrim's progress and Voltaire's Candide. HJ 48:388–93, 1950. **5725**

Compares the 2 works, but does not deal with the question of influence.

Gooch, C. P. Voltaire in England. *See* 4582. **5726**

Discusses the conditions and events of Voltaire's visit to England from 1726 to 1729, the favors he received from Lord Bolingbroke and Everard Falkener, and his relations with Pope, Swift, Congreve, Gay, Young, Thomson. Gooch discusses Voltaire's attempts to publish his *Henriade* in England and his exposure to the sects, especially to the Quakers. The *Lettres philosophiques sur les Anglais* are summarized.

Guicharnaud, Jacques. Voltaire and Shakespeare. *See* 4646. **5727**

A survey of Voltaire's opinions for and against Shakespeare. His reaction was largely critical, any influence minimal.

Hartley, K. H. The sources of Voltaire's Mariamne. *See* 4738. **5728**

Avers that the older Italian and French sources hitherto postulated are conjectural compared with new evidence of Voltaire's contemporary, Elijah Fenton (*Mariamne*, 1723), which connection Voltaire mentions only to disclaim in a 1723 letter. Nevertheless, "... every change [in subsequent reworkings, 1723–25] save one made Voltaire's play more closely akin to its English inspirer " (p. 11).

Jovicevich, Alexandre. A propos d'une Paméla de Voltaire. FR 36:276–83, 1962–63. **5729**

Discusses the correspondence that concerns the *Pamela* Voltaire wanted to write and suggests that he may, in fact, have written it and then suppressed it.

Leigh, R. A. Observations on the Voltaire letters – III (Vols. XVII–XXIV). MLR 53:550–52, 1958.   **5730**

Corrects the dates of some of the letters in the Besterman correspondence included in de Beer's account of Voltaire's British visitors.

Meikle, Henry W. Voltaire and Scotland. *See* 4660.   **5731**

Concerns Voltaire's influence on Scotland and on major Scottish writers. Scotland's influence on Voltaire is but passingly referred to.

Meyer, Paul H. Voltaire and Hume as historians : a comparative study of the *Essai sur les mœurs* and the History of England. *See* 4743.   **5732**

Chooses this more apt comparison than a previous one (with *Siècle de Louis XIV*). Raises question of possible reciprocal sources. Finds no evidence of indebtedness of Hume to either the historian or the historiographer. Judiciously avoids exaggerating significance of findings: Voltaire's debt to Hume " cannot be anything but minute " (p. 52). Final portions of study devoted to evaluation of their contributions to historiography in context of their time. Concludes that both " rescued " history, made it a *science humaine*.

Murdoch, Ruth T. Voltaire, James Thomson, and a poem for the marquise du Châtelet. SVEC 6:147–53, 1958.   **5733**

The poem, *Epître à la marquise du Châtelet*, which prefaced Voltaire's *Eléments de la philosophie de Newton*, was primarily influenced by James Thomson's *To the memory of Newton*, written and published in 1727.

Nivat, Jean. Quelques énigmes de la correspondance de Voltaire. *See* 4590.   **5734**

Letters to his niece Mme Denis (1753–54) contain many intimate indications of his profound feelings and intentions at a turning point of his life. These letters, written shortly after his adaptation of *Pamela*, seem to reveal a thematic unity corresponding to that of *Pamela*, viz., the trials of persecuted virtue.

Pichois, Claude. Préromantiques, rousseauistes et shakespeariens (1770–1778). *See* 4674.   **5735**

Part of Voltaire's reserve toward Shakespeare may be due to the fact that

Rousseau and his friends (Ducis, Le Tourneur) very much admired him.

— Voltaire et Shakespeare : un plaidoyer. *See* 4675.   **5736**

Defends Voltaire's translations of Shakespeare and supports the theory that Voltaire admired and respected Shakespeare all his life.

Price, Lawrence Marsden. Shakespeare as pictured by Voltaire, Goethe, and Oeser. Grev 25:83–84, 1950.   **5737**

A note concerning the influence of Voltaire's criticism of Shakespeare upon Goethe and the German painter Oeser.

Thielemann, Leland. Voltaire and Hobbism. *See* 4699.   **5738**

A careful and scholarly discussion of Voltaire's reaction to Hobbes throughout his career. He returns to Hobbes's ideas again and again in his work.

Wade, Ira O. Voltaire's Micromégas : a study in the fusion of science, myth and art. *See* 1645A.   **5739**

Studies borrowings from and evaluates indebtedness to Swift's *Gulliver* but emphasizes intrinsic merit. Demonstrates that *Micromégas* was written shortly after Voltaire's liberal education (1735–39) and represents successful search for a new form, the *conte philosophique*. Wade shows that *Micromégas* resembles *Gulliver* more than *Gargantua* or Cyrano's *Voyage*, but rejects the generally received view that Voltaire merely adapted *Gulliver*. Concludes that Voltaire's superior exploitation of an astronomical discovery " brings out better than any long disquisition the great difference between their two works ... between satire and ' esprit ' " (p. 87).

Reviews : F. Denoeu in BA 25:282, 1951; M. Nicolson in RR 42:208–11, 1951; M. Prior in PQ 30:305–07, 1951.

American

Bibliographies and general studies

Carrière, Joseph M., John F. McDermott, Howard C. Rice, Jr., and Joseph E. Tucker. Anglo-French and Franco-American studies : a current bibliography. FrAR 3:79–119, 1950.   **5740**

Lists books, articles, and reviews dealing with English-French and Franco-American relations. Continued by the above, in IFWB n.s. 1:5–42, 1951. Continued there for 1952, 1953, and 1954.

Chinard, Gilbert. L'homme contre la nature, essais d'histoire de l'Amérique. Hermann, 1949. 178 p. **5741**

Discusses the role of the *Homo americanus* in the making of America into " a fit place to live." Also presents the subject in the context of the De Pauw polemic and his refuters.

— La littérature comparée et l'histoire des idées dans l'étude des relations franco-américaines. *In:* Proceedings of the second congress of the International comparative literature association, II. Ed. by W. P. Friederich. Chapel Hill, 1959. p. 349–69. **5742**

A brilliant discussion of the " mirages " or " images " which America and France present to each other through their literatures.

— Notes on the American origins of the Déclaration des droits de l'homme et du citoyen. APSP 98:383–96, 1954. **5743**

This study discusses the influence of Washington, Franklin, and the Constitution upon the unknown writer of the *Déclaration*, an important statement of liberal thought in France.

Echeverria, Durand. French publications of the Declaration of Independence and the American Constitutions, 1776–1783. PBSA 47:313–38, 1953. **5744**

Asserts that the U. S. influence on men of 1789 was far deeper than textual imitation, as Americans had established the precedent of the right of constitutional self-determination. The Federal Constitution was published in France too late (1787) to exert much influence, but various state constitutions and other papers combined to become, in Paine's words, " the grammar of French liberty."

— Mirage in the West; a history of the French image of American society to 1815. Foreword by Gilbert Chinard. Princeton, Princeton univ. press, 1957. 300 p. **5745**

Treats the preconceptions of the *philosophes*, the enthusiasm engendered by the American Revolution, and the reaction after the counterrevolution of Thermidor, which led to a strong current of anti-Americanism. An important book.

— Roubaud and the theory of American degeneration. FrAR 3:24–33, 1950. **5746**

V. 5 of Roubaud's *Histoire générale ... de l'Amérique ...* (1st ed.) is shown to contain a refutation of Buffon's and De Pauw's theories on American degeneration, positing that the North American continent is viable human habitat, and defending not only Indians but English colonists, just prior to Revolutionary War.

Fabre, Jean. Un thème préromantique : le nouveau monde des poètes d'André Chenier à Mickiewicz. *See* 3549. **5747**

Covers a wide variety of French references from 1770 to 1827. Reprinted in the author's *Lumières et romantisme* (Klincksieck, 1963).

Gerbi, Antonello. La disputa del Nuevo Mundo, 1750–1900; storia di una polemica, 1750–1900. Milan, Ricciardi, 1955. x, 783 p. **5748**

A continuation of Gerbi's *Viejas polemicas sobre el Nuevo Mundo ...* stressing the 18th century.

— Viejas polemicas sobre el Nuevo Mundo, en el umbral de una conciencia americana. Lima, 1943. 127 p. **5749**

An invaluable work, tracing the beginnings of the doctrine of biological degeneration.

Hoog, Armand. The Romantic spirit and the American elsewhere. YFS 10:14–28, 1953. **5750**

Shows how 18th-century forerunners, and later Romanticists, projected own ethos of " anywhere out of the world " into an imagined, " invented " America-Eldorado. An important study.

Kennedy, John H. Jesuit and savage in New France. New Haven, Yale univ. press, 1950. 206 p. **5751**

Philosophes owe much to America for the idea of the savage which they adapted. The author investigates the growth of this essential idea from the basis of physical reality. Distinguishes between missionaries' and lay critics' approaches : former focused on Indian himself; latter compared civilized Frenchmen unfavorably with Indian. Jean-Jacques drew heavily in *Discourse on inequality* from accounts from New France. So did *Encyclopédistes* (s.v. *Sauvage*). But on the question of savages' reason most *philosophes* disagreed with Rousseau as in *L'ingénu*. Bibliography, maps, and index.

Reviews : J.-C. Bonenfant in CHR 32: 78–79, 1951; G. Chinard in AHR 61:

985–86, 1961, and in FrAR 3:339–40, 1950; R. McNamara in CathHR 36:470–71, 1950; G. Nute in MVHR 38:96–97, 1950; H. Smith in WMQ, 3rd s., 8:130–31, 1951.

Koht, Halvdan. The American spirit in Europe, a survey of transatlantic influences. Philadelphia, Univ. of Pennsylvania press, 1949. ix, 289 p.   **5752**

A general treatment in which France does not hold the center of the stage.

Kraus, Michael. The Atlantic civilization : eighteenth-century origins. Ithaca, Cornell univ. press, 1949. xi, 334 p.   **5753**

Studies " the moral force that America exerted upon Europe in the eighteenth century." The author also notes the influences of Jefferson, Franklin, and Paine upon the French but does not discuss them in any depth.

— The North Atlantic civilization. Princeton, Van Nostrand, 1957. 192 p.   **5754**

Discusses the importance of the U. S. in the Atlantic community. See especially Ch. 4, *America and the Utopian ideal in the 18th century* (p. 30–45), for a discussion of the impact of the American Revolution upon Europe.

O'Gorman, Edmundo. La idea del descubrimiento de América; historia de esa interpretación y critica de sus fundamentos. Mexico City, Centro de estudios filosóficos, 1951. 417 p.   **5755**

The controversy on the *bon sauvage* and meliorism in the American context provided a unique but transitory opportunity to reconstruct the history of the human race. The author studies the thesis of humanity and progress from Bossuet's *Discours sur l'histoire universelle* to Condorcet's *Esquisse d'un tableau historique des progrès de l'esprit humain.* In Condorcet's work, the discovery of America is of special significance.

Pearce, Roy H. The savages of America, a study of the Indians and the idea of civilization. Baltimore, Johns Hopkins press, 1953. xv, 252 p.   **5756**

On Buffon's theory of America, a brief commentary. More on Crèvecœur.

Rice, Howard C., Jr. The Yorktown campaign in verse. IFWB n.s. 3:49–74, 1953.   **5757**

Concerning a narrative by Caron du Chanset.

Skard, Sigmund. The American myth and the European mind; American studies in Europe, 1776–1960. Philadelphia, Univ. of Pennsylvania press, 1961. 112 p.   **5758**

Discusses the impact of the American Revolution in Europe (p. 15–22) and then goes into the American influence in the 19th and 20th centuries.

Viatte, Auguste. Histoire littéraire de l'Amérique française des origines à 1950. Quebec, Presses univ. Laval, 1954. xi, 545 p.   **5759**

An expansion of Viatte's article, *La littérature française au XVIe et au XVIIIe siècle* (RLC 25:5–11, 1951).

— La littérature française d'Amérique au XVIIe et au XVIIIe siècle. RLC 25:5–11, 1951.   **5760**

In 17th and 18th centuries French literature produced in America was in large measure for readers in France. Cites and studies interest of humanistic missionaries who wrote *relations* and travelers who wrote accounts of the wilderness and of the savage. Style of these writers analyzed. *Style sauvage* of Chateaubriand seen as adaptation of the oratorical style of Indians which La Hontan described in his *Voyages ...* (1705).

Villard, Léonie. La France et les Etats-Unis, échanges et rencontres (1524–1800). Lyons, Editions de Lyon, 1952. 407 p.   **5761**

The author intends to shed light upon the purely human, individual, and private aspects of Franco-American relations, heretofore neglected. This aspect is particularly important prior to 1776.

Reviews : C. Arnavon in RLC 28:219–21, 1954; E. de Jaive in BA 27:396, 1953.

Zavala, Silvio Arturo. América en el espíritu francés del siglo XVIII. Mexico City, Colegio nacional, 1949. 314 p.   **5762**

The author analyzes and sums up his conclusions on many original writings in the polemic between Buffon and De Pauw on the one hand and Franklin and Jefferson on the other. Raynal is omitted but those in his wake studied : La Hontan's *Dialogues*, Lafitau's *Mœurs*, Poivre's *Observations curieuses*, and Chastellux, under the theme of the results of the discovery of America for the human race.

Reviews : M. Bataillon in RLC 25:383–84, 1951; G. Chinard in HAHR 31:453–61, 1951; A. Gschaedler in FR 24:265–66, 1950–51; J. Muñoz Pérez in Arbor (Madrid) 21:611–13, 1952; A. Whitaker in AHR 56:528–29, 1951.

Intermediaries

(*See also* Brissot, Chateaubriand, Crèvecœur)

Bayard, Ferdinand Marie. Travels of a Frenchman in Maryland and Virginia, with a description of Philadelphia and Baltimore in 1791; or, travels in the interior of the United States, to Bath, Winchester in the valley of the Shenandoah, etc., etc., during the summer of 1791. Trans. and ed. with introduction, notes, and index by Ben C. McCary. Ann Arbor, Edwards, 1950. xxvii, 182 p.   5763

Excellent translation of the significant *Voyage dans l'intérieur des Etats-Unis ...* (2nd ed.), including Washingtoniana, published in 1798.
Reviews : E. Anderson, Jr. in VMHB 59:124–26, 1951; G. Chinard in FrAR 3:342–43, 1950.

Berthier, Alexandre. Journal de la campagne d'Amérique, 10 mai 1780–26 août 1781. Publié d'après le manuscrit inédit de l'Université de Princeton par Gilbert Chinard. IFWB n.s. 1:43–120, 1951.   5764

Fragment given from the Princeton collection (p. 57–120). Editor presents it as the most detailed account extant of the march of Rochambeau's army in the defense of Newport. Shows that Berthier studied and warmly admired Washington's strategy and became an active disciple of this strategy.

Childs, Frances S. Citizen Hauterive's questions on the United States. IFWB n.s., 5–6:34–44, 1957.   5765

Comte d'Hauterive's full text is reproduced. Compares Volney's investigations in his *Tableau* (1803), but finds " no real parallel in treatment of material or in motivation," despite common concern with physical geography as the key to further American studies. Stresses economic concern in *Questions.* Describes Hauterive's relations with Pierre Samuel Dupont de Nemours, " C[itoy]en Dupont de Nemours, voyageur de l'Institut en Amérique."

Foster, James R. A forgotten noble savage, Tsonnonthouan. MLQ 14:348–59, 1953.
                                                  5766
Shows that unknown author of *Memoirs ... of Tsonnonthouan ...* (1763), translated into French (1778 and 1787), knew the voyage-to-America literature of the period : La Hontan, Lafitau, Le Beau, and Charlevoix.

Miller, William M. Lettres écrites des rives de l'Ohio. MLJ 37:68–71, 1953.   5767

Studies book by marquis de Lezay Marnézia, a Gallipolitan. Three letters reproduced (1790–91).

Monaghan, Frank. French travellers in the United States, 1765–1932. With a supplement by Samuel J. Marino. New York, Antiquarian press, 1961. xxii, 130 p.   5768

An annotated bibliography of French travelers. With a chronological list, index.

Semmes, Raphael. Baltimore as seen by visitors, 1783–1860. Baltimore, Maryland historical society, 1953. xi, 208 p.   5769

The 1790's, a period when many famous Frenchmen came to the U.S., and Baltimore in particular, as seen by Moreau de Saint-Méry, Brissot de Warville, and the duc de la Rochefoucauld-Liancourt.
Reviews : R. Clark, Jr. in PMHB 88: 395–96, 1954; J. Matthews in VMHB 62:376–77, 1954.

Welch, M. L. Some Americans in Napoleon's Paris. LHM 24:25–41, 1953.   5770

Washington Allston, Joel Barlow, Aaron Burr, Robert Fulton, Washington Irving, Thomas Melville, John I. Middleton, Rembrandt Peale, and John Vanderlyn.

Periodicals

Aldridge, Alfred Owen. The debut of American letters in France. FrAR 3:1–23, 1950.   5771

The monthly journal *Ephémérides* (1765–72) is responsible for publishing for the first time a number of Dubourg's translations of Rush, Dickinson, and Franklin, thus introducing American ideas and literature into France and helping to build sympathy toward the American Revolution.

The vogue of American authors in France

Bartram
(*See* Chateaubriand)

Franklin
(*See also* Diderot, Dubourg, Periodicals, Raynal)

Franklin, Benjamin. Franklin's wit & folly : The bagatelles. Ed. by Richard E. Amacher. New Brunswick, N.J., Rutgers univ. press, 1953. xiv, 188 p.   5772

An ed. of Franklin's light essays published at his press in Passy, France.

Review : W. Lingelbach in PMHB 78: 502–04, 1954.

Aldridge, Alfred Owen. Benjamin Franklin and the philosophes. SVEC 24:43–65, 1963. **5773**

Discusses Franklin's relations with Voltaire, Condorcet, the *Encyclopédie*, the physiocrats, and tells several anecdotes related to his stay in France.

— Benjamin Franklin et ses contemporains français. Didier, 1963. 246 p. **5774**

An expanded version of *Franklin and his French contemporaries* (5776).

— Benjamin Franklin, philosopher and man. Philadelphia, Lippincott, 1965. xii, 438 p. **5775**

Naturally contains chapters on his French sojourn. Relates public and private life to his literary career.

— Franklin and his French contemporaries. New York, New York univ. press, 1957. 260 p. **5776**

Discusses Franklin's relations with France and the impact of his writings and personality upon the French.

Bishop, Morris. Franklin in France. Daed 86:214–30, 1957. **5777**

Discusses Franklin's relationships with Mme Helvétius and Mme Brillon, his knowledge of French, his fame in France, and the influence of France on Franklin.

Chinard, Gilbert. Abbé Lefebvre de La Roche's recollections of Benjamin Franklin. APSP 94:214–21, 1950. **5778**

Reproduces texts of 1787 letter to Franklin and a later memoir on him by the abbé.

— The apotheosis of Benjamin Franklin, Paris, 1790–1791. APSP 99:440–73, 1955. **5779**

Analysis of the eulogies delivered in France on the occasion of the death of Franklin and the role they play in history of Franco-American relations.

— Benjamin Franklin et la muse provinciale. APSP 97:493–510, 1953. **5780**

Studies life of Anne-Marie-Henriette de Payan (1746–1802), one of the devoted friends of his Parisian sojourn.

— Franklin en France. FR 29:281–89, 1955–56. **5781**

A review of Franklin's relationship with France, his role in Franco-American

friendship, and his fortunes in France. Aimed at a French audience not very well acquainted with the subject.

— Un message du Congrès des Etats-Unis à l'Assemblée nationale. IFWB n.s. 5–6:48–50, 1957. **5782**

Rectification of error in *L'apothéose de Benjamin Franklin* in IFWB, 1956. Document discovered by E. Wolf II proves Congress warmly responded to message of condolences.

— Random notes on two bagatelles. APSP 103:727–60, 1959. **5783**

A careful, thorough study of documents relating to letters to Madame Helvétius and Madame Brillon, revealing two interesting relationships and certain aspects of Franklin's character.

Cramer, Lucien. Les Cramer, une famille genevoise : leurs relations avec Voltaire, Rousseau et Benjamin Franklin-Bache. *See* 3624. **5784**

Concerns Franklin's relationship with the Cramer family regarding the education of his grandson. *See* Ch. 5, *L'éducation genevoise du petit-fils de Benjamin Franklin.*

Kahn, Robert L. Franklin, Grimm, and J. H. Landolt. APSP 99:401–04, 1955. **5785**

A passing reference to Grimm's mentions of Franklin in his *Correspondance.*

Lopez, Claude-Anne. Mon cher papa, Franklin and the ladies of Paris. New Haven, Yale univ. press, 1966. 400 p. **5786**

Franklin and *les Françaises* seen from a feminine angle.

Nolan, J. Bennett. Monsieur Franklin. Phist 23:347–75, 1956. **5787**

The author describes his own collection of Franklin pamphlets acquired in France. Many are clandestine works containing allusions to Franklin or letters supposedly by him. Interesting for the French reaction to Franklin.

Sachs, Jules R. Benjamin Franklin in Paris. LHM 24:249–59, 323–36, 1953. **5788**

Cursory recollections of some men and women he loved during his years in France.

Jefferson
(*See also* The *Encyclopédie* in English section)

Boehm, Dwight, and **Edward Schwartz.** Jefferson and the theory of degeneracy. AQ 9:448–53, 1957. **5789**

Shows that the theory persisted as late as 1837 despite substantial refutations. Both sides of the controversy were documented, with Italians and Englishmen participating as well as Frenchmen and Americans. Jefferson's refutation of Buffon's climatic theory is described here. Discusses Chief Logan's moving speech which, Jefferson claimed, had put Demosthenes and Cicero in the shade. Extensive coverage of the polemic in contemporary periodicals and books.

Watts, George B. Thomas Jefferson, the Encyclopédie and the Encyclopédie méthodique. FR 38:318–25, 1964–65. **5790**

Discusses Jefferson's interest in the *Encyclopédie* and the *Encyclopédie méthodique* and his role as consultant and contributor to the *Economie politique et diplomatique* of Jean-Nicolas Démeunier. Jefferson contributed heavily to this work and wrote several articles Démeunier made use of.

Paine
(*See also* The *Encyclopédie* in English section)

Aldridge, Alfred Owen. Condorcet et Paine, leurs rapports intellectuels. RLC 32: 47–65, 1958. *See* 4387. **5791**

Condorcet and Paine, as friends and collaborators, influenced each other and benefited mutually from their association.

— The influence of Thomas Paine in the United States, England, France, Germany and South America. *In:* Proceedings of the second congress of the International comparative literature association, II. Ed. by W. P. Friederich. Chapel Hill, 1959. p. 369–89. **5792**

Concerns Paine's *Common sense, Crisis,* and *Decline and fall of the English system of finance.*

— Man of reason, the life of Thomas Paine. Philadelphia, Lippincott, 1959. 348 p. **5793**

Discusses Paine's role in the French Revolution, including a number of newly discovered essays.

— The Rights of man de Thomas Paine, symbole du siècle des lumières et leur influence en France. *In:* Utopie et institutions au XVIIIe siècle. Ed. by Pierre Francastel. Mouton, 1963. p. 277–87. **5794**

As indicated, discusses the influence of *The rights of man* in France.

— La signification historique, diplomatique et littéraire de la Lettre adressée à l'abbé Ray-nal de Thomas Paine. EA 8:223–32, 1955. **5795**

This neglected work, which was translated 4 times after 1782, played a significant role in the diplomatic history of France and had an important impact on French readers. It is suggested that the letter may have been instigated by French diplomats.

Gabrieli, Vittorio. Thomas Paine fra l'America e l'Europa. SA 1:9–53, 1955. **5796**

Translations of Paine's works, their popularity, and possible influence on the French Revolution are briefly mentioned.

Gimbel, Richard. Thomas Paine fights for freedom in three worlds : the new, the old, the next. AASP 70:397–492, 1960. **5797**

This catalog of an exhibition at Yale University Library in October, 1959, is interesting for the French translations and critical commentaries on Paine's writings.

American influences on French authors

Brissot

Brissot de Warville, Jacques Pierre. New travels in the United States of America, 1788. Trans. by Mara Soceanu Vamos and Durand Echeverria. Ed. by Durand Echeverria. Cambridge, Belknap press of Harvard univ. press, 1964. xxviii, 447 p. **5798**

Translation of the *Nouveau voyage dans les Etats-Unis.*

Chateaubriand
(*See also* Beauvois)

Bishop, Morris. Chateaubriand in New York State. PMLA 69:876–86, 1954. **5799**

An exhaustive search reveals that Chateaubriand (in America for 4 1/2 months) perhaps made a journey to Niagara, but not to Pittsburgh, and that most of his travels and encounters were imaginary.

Gautier, Jean-Maurice. L'exotisme américain dans l'œuvre de Chateaubriand : étude de vocabulaire. Manchester, Manchester univ. press, 1951. 65 p. **5800**

In this monograph on stylistics, the author studies common nouns of flora, fauna, and " civilization terms " (in the anthropological sense) of the Indians. Under proper nouns, the author lists and studies names of peoples, names of their heroes and gods, and geographical and topographical features. Contains in ap-

pendix a brief but illuminating study of the pre-Romantic writer who influenced Chateaubriand, the nature-lover, William Bartram (1739–1823). A bibliography is included.
Reviews : G. Chinard in IWFB n.s. 1:127–29, 1951; C. Elkin in WPHM 34: 209–10, 1951; J. Tregle, Jr., in JSH 17: 404–05, 1951.

Guillemin, Henri. Monsieur de Chateaubriand, comme vous mentez bien! FL 4, Feb. 21, 1953.   **5801**
Concerns his *Voyage* in America.

Martino, Pierre. Le voyage de Chateaubriand en Amérique; essai de mise au point, 1952. RHL 52:149–64, 1952.   **5802**
Uses new documents to test Chateaubriand's sincerity and accuracy. The author follows Chateaubriand on his travels, exposing errors, anachronisms, and gaps. Supports the validity of Chinard's suggestion that Chateaubriand had a money-making scheme in mind.

Une sœur aînée d'Atala : Odérahi, histoire américaine. Ed. by Gilbert Chinard. Raymond Clavreuil, 1950. 230 p.   **5803**
In his introduction (p. 7–62), the editor examines attributions to Palisot de Beauvois and to Chateaubriand. Concedes that evidence is not sufficiently conclusive to invalidate Hazard's attributions to Palisot. Hypothesizes that *Natchez* and *Atala* are affiliated with *Odérahi*, the common source being Carver's *Travels*.
Review : F. Roe in MLR 46:113–14, 1951.

Switzer, Richard. A precursor of René : le baron de Saint-Castin. RR 41:179–86, 1950.   **5804**
In 1765 Bricaire de La Dixmérie published *Contes philosophiques*. The author suggests that one of the *contes*, *Azakia*, contained René's precursor.

Condorcet
(*See* Bibliographies and General Studies, Paine)

Crèvecœur

Crèvecœur, Michel Guillaume St. Jean de. Eighteenth-century travels in Pennsylvania & New York. Ed. and trans. by Percy G. Adams. Lexington, Univ. of Kentucky press, 1961. xliv, 172 p.   **5805**
The introduction stresses Crèvecœur's importance. His *Voyages* was the most popular guidebook of America in France.

A summary of the whole *Voyages* is appended, followed by an index.

— Journey into northern Pennsylvania and the State of New York. Trans. by Clarissa S. Bostelmann. Ann Arbor, Univ. of Michigan press, 1964. xviii, 619 p.   **5806**
Asserts that P. G. Adam's translation (5805) included only one-third of Crèvecœur's total *Voyage*. Translator supplies chapter summaries preceding each of the 3 v. bound together in this ed. Biographical sketch briefly records comtesse d'Houdetot's admiration of Crèvecœur, his relations with her coterie (Buffon, Brissot de Warville, others) as well as their editorial advice concerning the notes to *Voyage*. Neither bibliography nor index.

Adams, Percy G. The historical value of Crèvecœur's Voyage dans la haute Pennsylvanie et dans New York. AL 25:152–68, 1953.   **5807**
The *Voyage* is a collection of essays and stories published once in Paris in 1801. It has a number of chapters classifiable as literature, is valuable as history, and deserves a major place among 18th-century travel books.

Diderot

Cohen, I. Bernard. A note concerning Diderot and Franklin. *See* 5061.   **5808**
Diderot was most sensitive to recent discoveries in experimental physics and was influenced by Franklin's work in electricity and the *Aurora borealis*. In his *Interprétation de la nature* he discusses and praises Franklin's work. Cohen searches unsuccessfully to find evidence of a meeting or relationship between the two men.

Dubourg
(*See also* Periodicals)

Aldridge, Alfred Owen. Jacques Barbeu-Dubourg, a French disciple of Benjamin Franklin. APSP 95:331–92, 1951.   **5809**
This work details the biography and intellectual history of the man who was the French translator and editor of Franklin. Dubourg considered Franklin his master and his works after 1768 attest to the profound influence Franklin had upon him.

Grimm
(*See* Franklin)

Palisot de Beauvois
(*See* Chateaubriand)

Perrin du Lac

Grenier, Fernand. Un plagiaire illustre : François Perrin du Lac. RHAF 7:207–23, 1953. **5810**

Demonstrates that numerous plagiarisms are to be found in *Voyages dans les deux Louisianes* (1805) and that the writer freely lifted portions of the journals of J.-B. Trudeau, the French-Canadian *voyageur*.

Raynal
(*See also* Paine)

Courtney, C. P. Burke, Franklin et Raynal : à propos de deux lettres inédites. *See* 5378. **5811**

A letter to Burke and one to Franklin in search of facts for his *Histoire philosophique* (1780) throw light on Raynal's working methods and documentation.

Trudeau
(*See* Perrin du Lac)

Volney

Gaulmier, Jean. Un grand témoin de la Révolution et de l'Empire, Volney. Hachette, 1959. 331 p. **5812**

Ch. on Volney's voyage to the U.S. in which *Tableau du climat et du sol des Etats-Unis* and unpublished family papers are used. Itinerary, complete with maps, meticulously prepared and presented. Pre-positivist in his method of observer-voyager : learned language prior to departure the better to observe firsthand what interested him : sociological, linguistic, geographical, meteorological facts —duly noted and classified.
Review : I.-M. Frandon in RLC 35: 146–47, 1961.

Voltaire
(*See* Franklin)

German
(Nos. 5813–5871)

HENRY H. H. REMAK

Bibliographies and General Studies

Atkins, Stuart. Mirages français—French literature in German eyes. YFS 6:35–44, 1950. **5813**

Retraces literary interrelations from the Middle Ages to the postwar present with special stress on German reaction to French literature at various times.

Baldensperger, Fernand, and Werner P. Friederich. Bibliography of comparative literature. *See* 2885A, 3264A, 3308A. **5814**

Reissued 1960 (New York, Russell & Russell). Annual supplements in YCGL, 1952 to date.

Barber, William Henry. Leibniz in France, from Arnauld to Voltaire; a study in French reactions to Leibnizianism, 1670–1760. Oxford, Clarendon press, 1955. xi, 276 p. *See* 4168 and 4607. **5815**

Excellent, impartial study stressing the not too successful role played by French Protestant writers in Germany and Switzerland in promoting the spread of Leibnizian ideas in France. Includes account of Christian Wolff's reception in France.
Reviews : T. Besterman in SVEC 2: 317–18, 1956; R. Brooks in RR 47:66–68, 1956; R. Fargher in FS 10:70–71, 1956; G. Havens in MP 54:63–64, 1956–57; K. Whitworth, Jr. in CL 9:171–74, 1957.

Bibliographie générale de littérature comparée. Boivin and Didier, 1949–58. 5 v. **5816**

The quarterly bibliographies in the RLC assembled in 1 v. for 2 years each. 5 v., covering the years 1949 to 1958 inclusive.

Dédéyan, Charles. Le thème de Faust dans la littérature européenne. Lettres modernes, 1954–61. 4 v. **5817**

Meager penetration of Faust theme into France via Hamilton, Cazotte, Victor Palma Cayet, and the émigrés.

Downs, John A. The treatment of German literature in the Encyclopédie. SP 54:564–72, 1957. **5818**

Scanty discussions (Jaucourt, Sulzer).

Droz, Jacques. L'Allemagne et la Révolution française. Presses univ. de France, 1949. vi, 500 p. **5819**

Informed study, outlining political, philosophical, religious, humanistic, and literary reactions (Goethe, Schiller, Wieland, Herder) to French Revolution. No bibliography, but copious footnotes and an index.
Reviews : M. Colleville in Lmod 43: 363–64, 1949; J. Dresch in RLC 25:280–81, 1951.

Du Colombier, Pierre. L'architecture française en Allemagne au XVIIIe siècle. Presses univ. de France, 1956. 2 v.   5820

Remarkable, admirably documented study on the penetration of French architecture in 18th-century Germany. Valuable supplement to French literary influences. Excellent reproductions.

Ernst, Fritz. Vom Heimweh. Zurich, Fretz und Wasmuth, 1949. 127 p.   5821

Swiss origin and European propagation of this notion in 18th century. Appears in France from 1719 on (Du Bos), brought to Germany subsequently by Wieland. France acted as intermediary in spreading this concept throughout Continent. Review : W. Friederich in CL 3:190–91, 1951.

Franco-German studies. A current bibliography. *In:* Bbib.   5822

Annual survey of books, dissertations, and articles dealing with Franco-German literary relations. Covers critical literature only. Surveys concentrate on material published in preceding year, but also contain good deal of material published 2 or 3 years previously. Last published in Bbib, May–August, 1955 (for 1954). Since then, Franco-German items incorporated in YCGL.

Die französische Aufklärung im Spiegel der deutschen Literatur des 18. Jahrhunderts. Ed. by Werner Krauss. Berlin, Akademie-Verlag, 1963. clxxxvii, 484 p.   5823

Confrontation of German and French Enlightenment through selection of German 18th-century essays on French Enlightenment. Contains lengthy introduction and an epilogue on the reception of German literature in 18th-century France.

Friederich, Werner P., and **David H. Malone.** Outline of comparative literature from Dante Alighieri to Eugene O'Neill. Chapel Hill, Univ. of North Carolina press, 1954. 451 p.   5824

History of literature along comparative lines with due consideration of French and German influences. Reviews : M. Gaither in YCGL 5:65–66, 1956; S. Palleske in CL 8:355–57, 1956; J. Voisine in RLC 30:585–88, 1956.

Fromm, Hans. Bibliographie deutscher Übersetzungen aus dem Französischen, 1700–1948. *See* 3342.   5825

Alphabetically arranged according to name of author translated. Excellent research tool for studies in reception. V. 6 includes a list of German translations of French works by authors of German nationality (e.g., Frederick the Great, Leibniz), anthologies of French literature in German and an extensive index of translators.

Jost, François. La fortune d'un héros : Guillaume Tell en Europe. *In his:* Essais de littérature comparée. I. Helvetica. Fribourg, Editions universitaires, 1964. p. 223–51.   5826

Knowledge of the Tell tradition or myth among 18th-century French (Voltaire, Mercier, Raynal, Florian) was quite developed.

— Reflets suisses dans les lettres françaises. *In his:* Essais de littérature comparée. I. Helvetica. Fribourg, Editions universitaires, 1964. p. 203–22.   5827

Reputation of Switzerland among French public and writers, especially 18th century (d'Argens, d'Argenson, Mercier).

Krauss, Werner. Studien zur deutschen und französischen Aufklärung. Berlin, Rütten und Loening, 1963. 557 p.   5828

Twelve essays comparing French and German Enlightenment : French sources of German Enlightenment, the reception of literature of French Enlightenment in Germany and of German Enlightenment in 18th-century France. Informed Marxist viewpoint. Extensive notes and index of persons. Review : K. Scholder in Germ 6:54, 1965.

— Über das Schicksal der deutschen Literatur in der französischen Aufklärung. GRM n.s. 11:62–69, 1961.   5829

Succinct exposé of initial French receptivity to German science and scholarship early in 18th century and to literature in the 1760's.

Lévy, Paul. La langue allemande en France; pénétration et diffusion des origines à nos jours. *See* 3502.   5830

Comprehensive, authoritative survey of limited linguistic-cultural penetration of German language in France.

Ludwigsburg, Ger. Deutsch-Französisches Institut. Deutschland-Frankreich; Ludwigsburger Beiträge zum Problem der deutsch-französischen Beziehungen. Stuttgart, Deutsche Verlags-Anstalt, 1954–66. 4 v. **5831**

The 4 v. of this series published so far contain a host of articles on all facets of Franco-German literary, political, cultural, and economic relations. Less emphasis on 18th than on 19th and 20th centuries. Reviews : (v. 1, 1954) K. Bieber in CL 7:275–80, 1955; (v. 2, 1957) K. Bieber in YCGL 8:61–69, 1959; H. Remak in CL 11:171–73, 1959; (v. 3, 1963) W. Friederich in CLS 1:83–85, 1964; U. Goldsmith in YCGL 13:81–84, 1964.

Minder, Robert. Kultur und Literatur in Deutschland und Frankreich. Frankfurt am Main, Insel, 1962. 2nd ed., rev., 1963. 139 p. **5832**

Five essays by the eminent professor of the Collège de France. Three deal with Franco-German literary relations, including an incisive comparison of the social position of German and French writers and a study treating Schiller's attitude toward and his impact in France.

Neubert, Fritz. Das französische Deutschlandbild von 1700 bis zum Weltkrieg. *In his:* Französische Literaturprobleme. Berlin, Duncker und Humblot, 1962. p. 339–64. **5833**

Survey of the French literary image of Germany. Essay somewhat tinged but not vitally affected by the Nazi period.

— Ein Jahrtausend deutsch-französischer geistiger Beziehungen. *In his:* Französische Literaturprobleme. Berlin, Duncker und Humblot, 1962. p. 365–88. **5834**

Survey of broad tendencies in both directions from 9th century on, stressing developments prior to 1800.

— Ein Jahrtausend deutsch-französischer geistiger Beziehungen. Vom Hochmittelalter bis sum Zeitalter der Aufklärung und des Rokoko. *In his:* Studien zur vergleichenden Literaturgeschichte. Berlin, Duncker und Humblot, 1952. p. 147–201. **5835**

Concentrates on 13th to 17th centuries, but gives some attention to 18th century (p. 192–201). Synthesis of trends in either direction.

Oppenheim, F. Horst. Der Einfluss der französischen Literatur auf die deutsche. *In:* Deutsche Philologie im Aufriss. Ed. by Wolfgang Stammler. Berlin, Erich Schmidt, 1962. 3:1–106. **5836**

First German synthesis of the topic,

written with exemplary objectivity. From Middle Ages to end of 19th century; very brief sketch of 20th century. Coverage of large number of names does not obscure *les grandes lignes.* Cumbersome style. References, condensed bibliography.

Revue de littérature comparée. **5837**

Bibliographical section discontinued after January–March, 1960, issue.

Spemann, Adolf. Vergleichende Zeittafel der Weltliteratur, vom Mittelalter bis zur Neuzeit (1150–1939). Stuttgart, Engelhornverlag, 1951. 160 p. **5838**

Differs from van Tieghem (*see* 3210) by including period before 1455 and placing heavy emphasis on 20th century. Arrangement similar to van Tieghem. No descriptive remarks. Very useful index lists works of all authors mentioned in the table by order of their appearance.

Van Tieghem, Philippe. Les influences étrangères sur la littérature française (1550–1880). Presses univ. de France, 1961. 275 p. **5839**

Introductory outline, meant primarily for students. Ch. 5 (*Influences diverses au XVIIIe siècle*) includes section on Gessner (p. 131–36). Ch. 6 (*La découverte de l'Allemagne et de la littérature de langue allemande*) gives rapid sketch of first penetration (p. 140–47). Chronology of translations, index.

Wais, Kurt. An den Grenzen der Nationalliteraturen, vergleichende Aufsätze. Berlin, De Gruyter, 1958. 414 p. **5840**

Collection of comparative studies including Goethe and France, Schiller's influence abroad, 500 years of German evaluation of French literature, etc. *See* 5841.

— Fünfhundert Jahre französischer Literatur im Spiegel der deutschen Meinung. Archiv 192:290–305, 1955–56. *Translated into French as:* La littérature française devant l'opinion allemande. CAIEF 8:89–106, 1956. **5841**

Remarkable survey of the reception of French literature in Germany in the last several centuries.

Intermediaries

Baldensperger, Fernand. C. Denina (1731–1813), précurseur du comparatisme en histoire littéraire. RLC 28:467–73, 1954. **5842**

Introductory sketch of the author of the *Tableau des révolutions de la littérature* (Italian original, 1761; French translation, 1767) and of the *Prusse littéraire sous Frédéric II.* In his *Tableau*, Denina discusses both French and German literature.

Bianquis, Geneviève. Un Allemand dans le midi de la France au xviii⁰ siècle. RLC 25:289–300, 1951. **5843**

Sketch of the contents of Moritz August von Thümmel's *Reise in die mittäglichen Provinzen von Frankreich,* undertaken in the 1770's but not published until 1791 to 1805. In it, Thümmel opposes the rationalism and tolerance of Frederick the Great's monarchy to alleged despotism and clericalism of *ancien régime.*

Charlier, Gustave, and **Roland Mortier.** Le Journal encyclopédique, 1756–1793. *See* 5523. **5844**

Introduction to and excerpts from periodical that was important intermediary between German literature and France (Goethe, Herder, Wieland, etc.).

Grubenmann, Yvonne de Athayde. Un cosmopolite suisse : Jacques-Henri Meister, 1744–1826. Geneva, Droz, 1954. 177 p. **5845**

Sketchy, often very summary, study of the much-neglected editor of the *Correspondance littéraire* from 1773 to 1813. Off balance and much too disparaging toward Grimm. Much vague documentation.

Reviews : F. Jost in RLC 32:604–05, 1958; K. Whitworth, Jr. in CL 8:245–49, 1956.

Jost, François. Muralt, juge des Français : la psychologie des peuples à la fin du xvii⁰ siècle. *In his:* Essais de littérature comparée. I. Helvetica. Fribourg, Editions universitaires, 1964. p. 101–39. **5846**

Analysis of Béat de Muralt's famous characterization of the French (written about 1698 and published in 1725).

— Un pèlerin de la Suisse romande : Jean de Muller. *In his:* Essais de littérature comparée. I. Helvetica. Fribourg, Editions universitaires, 1964. p. 32–59. **5847**

Relations of the famous Swiss historian from Schaffhausen with French-speaking Switzerland in general and with Bonstetten, Tronchin, Trembley, and Bonnet in particular. His attitude toward French as a language.

Karl Friedrich Reinhard, 1761-1837; ein Leben für Frankreich und Deutschland. Ed. by Else R. Gross. Stuttgart, Wittwer, 1961. 152 p. **5848**

Collection of documents on the life of this prominent intermediary. Bibliography, notes. Excellent illustrations. No index.

Kurrelmeyer, William. Wielands Briefwechsel mit Du Vau. MLN 64:361–72, 1949. **5849**

Interesting exchange of letters between Wieland and Auguste du Vau—French émigré in Weimar, friend of Wieland, Böttiger, Knebel, and others—about Du Vau's French translation of Wieland's *Neue Göttergespräche.* All letters except one (about 1803) date from 1795 to 1796.

Mortier, Roland. Le Journal de lecture de F.-M. Leuchsenring (1775–1779) et l'esprit philosophique. *See* 5520. **5850**

Neglected periodical edited by this young German in Paris. Leuchsenring knew Diderot who contributed to his journal. Leuchsenring left France in 1782 and returned in 1792 (pro-Revolution). Journal contains numerous translations extracted from German literature.

— Un précurseur de Madame de Staël : Charles Vanderbourg, 1765–1827. Didier, 1955. 272 p. **5851**

Well-documented investigation. While most of the activities of this significant intermediary occurred after 1800, study also covers his emigration years in Germany (1792–95, 1798–1800), his liaison with the Emkendorf circle (Friedrich Heinrich Jacobi, the Reventlows, etc.) and with Voss, Goethe, and other German writers. Documents, bibliography, index.

Reviews : R. Rosenberg in CL 8:87–89, 1956.

Schaffstein, Friedrich. Wilhelm von Humboldt; ein Lebensbild. Frankfurt am Main, Klostermann, 1952. 358 p. **5852**

Well-documented biography, though not work of original scholarship, of perhaps most admirable representative of Prussian humanism. Basic indications on his fruitful stay in Paris (1797–99, 1800–01), where he wrote his famous reports. Connections with Schlabrendorff, Sieyès, Destutt de Tracy, David, Gérard, Mme Talma, Mme Vandeul (Diderot's daughter), Mme de Condorcet, Mme de Staël. H. published parts of his treatise on Goethe's *Hermann und Dorothea* in Paris newspaper.

Welzig, Werner. W. von Humboldt und Frankreich. RLC 38:497–511, 1964. **5853**

After a briefer soujourn in Paris, in 1789, Humboldt's Parisian stay from 1797 to 1801 led to numerous contacts with the French intelligentsia and observations on the French character. Special attention to Humboldt's comparison of French and German acting. Diderot is, for Humboldt, the " Frenchest " of the 18th-century writers. Observations on Bonaparte whom Humboldt met several times.

Goethe

Colloque international sur Goethe et l'esprit français, Strasbourg, 1957. Goethe et l'esprit français. Actes du Colloque international de Strasbourg, 23–27 avril 1957. Les Belles Lettres, 1958. xvii, 346 p. **5854**

Although limited to the exploration of the contribution of French culture (literature, science, economics, fine arts, etc.) to the development of *one* writer, the status of Goethe and the extraordinary quality of the contributions to this volume make its listing imperative.

Review : H. Remak in JEGP 60:386–89, 1961.

Sauter, Hermann. Goethe in Lob und Tadel seiner französischen Zeitgenossen; Berichte und Urteile. Speyer, Dobbeck, 1952. 154 p. **5855**

Contemporary French reactions to Goethe's personality and work. Utilizes some hitherto inaccessible material. Bibliography and notes.

Review : W. Mönch in Archiv 190: 264–65, 1953–54; F. Oppenheim in RLC 28:230–31, 1954.

Strich, Fritz. Goethe und die Schweiz. CL 1:289–308, 1949. **5856**

Contact and " togetherness " of French and German culture in distinct Swiss environment as Goethe must have experienced them.

Haller

Perrochon, Henri. La poésie de Haller en France. *In:* La France, la Bourgogne et la Suisse au XVIIIᵉ siècle. Actes du troisième congrès national de littérature comparée, Dijon, 1959. Didier, 1960. p. 130–36. **5857**

Haller's work penetrated France in 1750's along with Gessner's. Promoted idealized image of a patriarchal Switzerland foreshadowing a parallel one to be held soon of Germany.

Lessing

Heitner, Robert R. Diderot's own Miss Sara Sampson. CL 5:40–49, 1953. **5858**

French translation of Lessing's play, probably made by Nicolai and de la Fermière for Diderot. Nicolai must be L. Heinrich Nicolai or Nicolay (*see* Heier, 5863), not Friedrich Nicolai, Lessing's friend, who is also mentioned in Heitner's article.

German influences on French authors

Dimoff, Paul. Winckelmann et André Chénier. RLC 21:321–33, 1947. **5859**

Winckelmann as a source of Chénier's *L'invention, L'essai sur les causes et les effets de la perfection et de la décadence des lettres et des arts*, and the fragment of his *Epître sur l'imitation des anciens*.

Ferrazzini, Arthur. Béat de Muralt et Jean-Jacques Rousseau. La Neuveville, Editions du Griffon, 1951. 189 p. **5860**

Judicious analysis of Rousseau's debt to Muralt.

Review : H. Roddier in RLC 30:113–15, 1956.

Grimsley, Ronald. D'Alembert and J. D. Michaelis. *See* 4279. **5861**

D'Alembert's endeavors to aid the German orientalist and Biblical scholar Johann David Michaelis. Based on unpublished correspondence.

— D'Alembert at Potsdam (1763) : an English comment. *See* 4280. **5862**

Unpublished letters about the significance of this visit from Sir Andrew Mitchell, English envoy at Berlin.

Heier, Edmund. The Encyclopedists and L. H. Nicolay (1737–1820). RLC 36:495–509, 1962. **5863**

Personal relations of Heinrich Nicolay (not to be mistaken for Lessing's friend, Friedrich Nicolai) with Diderot, Voltaire, and Rousseau, based on unpublished documents. *See* Heitner (5858).

Jost, François. Histoire d'une amitié et d'une correspondance : Jean-Jacques Rousseau et Nicolas-Antoine Kirchberger. *In his:* Essais de littérature comparée. I. Helvetica. Fribourg, Editions universitaires, 1964. p. 60–98. **5864**

Hitherto unpublished complete texts of 15 letters to Rousseau from a Bernese friend and admirer. Interesting reference to Rousseau's relations with Frederick II, sovereign of the duchy of Neuchâtel (p. 71).

— Jean-Jacques Rousseau Suisse. *See* 4802. **5865**

Exhaustive, beautifully presented study giving full information about Rousseau's many links with the Alemannic heritage of Switzerland. Affinity with Bodmer, Haller, Muralt, Gessner, etc. Extensive bibliography, index.

— La Suisse dans les lettres françaises au cours des âges. Fribourg, Editions universitaires, 1956. 352 p. **5866**

Image of German, French and Italian-speaking Switzerland in French literature, particularly of 18th century (Béat de Muralt, Haller, Gessner, Rousseau, Lavater). But links with various cultures make a " Swiss national character " somewhat problematic. Extensive bibliography, footnotes, index.

Reviews: H. Perrochon in RLC 34:489–92, 1960; A. Viatte in RLC 31:280–81, 1957.

Mönch, Walter. Melchior Grimm und die Correspondance littéraire. *In:* Formen der Selbstdarstellung, Festgabe für Fritz Neubert. Berlin, Duncker und Humblot, 1956. p. 261–78. **5867**

General appreciation of Grimm with due attention to his German origin, interests, and inclinations.

Mortier, Roland. Diderot en Allemagne, 1750–1850. *See* 5207. **5868**

Ch. I (*Diderot et les Allemands*) contains references to Diderot's reactions to Germans and to his trip through Germany on his way to and from Russia. Ch. 8 disposes of the legend of Diderot's " Germanism." Perspicacious work.

Schier, Donald. The abbé de Prades in exile. RR 45:182–90, 1954. **5869**

Diderot's and Voltaire's friend became secretary and reader to Frederick II (1752–57), was imprisoned on suspicion of treason (until 1763), and lived in Glogau (Silesia) until his death (1782).

Stutzer, Walter. Jean-Jacques Rousseau und die Schweiz; zur Geschichte des Helvetismus. Basel, Vineta, 1950. 107 p. **5870**

Rousseau's personal and literary contacts (Haller, Gessner) with German-speaking Switzerland, hampered by his ignorance of German. Author seems to squeeze too much out of Rousseau's Swiss characteristics. Bibliography.

Review : W. Friederich in CL 4:185–86, 1952.

Vernière, Paul. Diderot et C. L. de Hagedorn. *See* 5358. **5871**

Substantial influence on Diderot's *Pensées détachées sur la peinture* by Christian Ludwig Hagedorn's *Betrachtungen über die Malerei* (1762), translated into French by Michael Huber (1775). Wille, Diderot's friend, knew Hagedorn and Huber personally. Diderot may have known Hagedorn in Dresden (1773).

Italian
(Nos. 5872–5947)

OLGA RAGUSA

Bibliographies and General Studies

Appolis, E. Le tiers parti catholique au XVIIIe siècle; entre jansénistes et Zelanti. Picard, 1960. xi, 601 p. **5872**

The *tiers parti* is seen as a typically Italian creation.

Review : S. Landucci in SF 5:360–61, 1961.

Bibliographie générale de littérature comparée. 1949–58. 5 v. *See* 5816. **5873**

Bibliographie italo-française, 1949-1958. Première partie : 1948–1954. Maison du livre italien, 1962. xvi, 292 p. **5874**

Important bibliographical tool. French publications on Italy and Italian publications on France during the period 1948–54.

Review : G. Menichelli in Conv 33:214–18, 1965.

Boudard, René. Gênes et la France dans la deuxième moitié du XVIIIe siècle (1748–97). Paris and The Hague, Mouton, 1962. 539 p. **5875**

P. 101–215, *La représentation diplomatique génoise auprès de la cour de France et pendant la Révolution française;* p. 264–313, *Voyageurs et visiteurs français à Gênes.*

Elwert, W. Theodor. Venedigs literarische Bedeutung. AK 36:261–300, 1954. **5876**

Bibliographical essay.

Horn-Monval, Madeleine. Répertoire bibliographique des traductions et adaptations françaises du théâtre étranger du XVe siècle à nos jours. Centre national de la recherche scientifique, 1958–63. 5 v. **5877**

V. 3 devoted to translations and adaptations of Italian works, including opera libretti. Indexes : works translated, authors, French titles, translators and adapters. Includes collections and anonymous works.

Klapp, Otto. Bibliographie der französischen Literaturwissenschaft. 1960– . *See* 3357. **5878**

Includes section on French-Italian influence.

Pellegrini, Carlo. Relazioni tra la letteratura italiana e la letteratura francese. *In:* Problemi ed orientamenti critici di lingua e di letteratura italiana. Ed. by Attilio Momigliano. Milan, Marzorati, 1948. 4:41–99. **5879**

Oriented toward the importance of French literature for Italian rather than vice versa, but contains useful bibliographical indications (esp., p. 91–93).

Schudt, Ludwig. Italienreisen im 17. und 18. Jahrhundert. Vienna, Schroll, 1959. 448 p. **5880**

Beautifully illustrated. P. 110–24 deal specifically with 18th–century travelers; p. 26–39 with guidebooks. Part II reviews travel impressions in great detail. Indispensable work.

Shackleton, Robert. Comparative literature and the Enlightenment. *In:* Comparative literature; proceedings of the second congress of the International comparative literature association. Ed. by W. P. Friederich. Chapel Hill, Univ. of North Carolina studies in comparative literature, 1959. 1:56–61. **5881**

Mentions among *desiderata* of works in the area a study of Italy in relation to France similar to G. D. Bonno's *La culture et la civilisation britanniques devant l'opinion française* (2889); a re-examination of the roles of Pomponazzi, Bruno, Vanini, Campanella, and Machiavelli in the development of the Enlightenment; a study of Antonio Conti, correspondent of Newton, Malebranche, and Leibniz; and a comparative study of French and Italian Jansenism.

Van Tieghem, Philippe. Les influences étrangères sur la littérature française (1550–1880). *See* 5839. **5882**

Ch. I on Italian influences in 16th and 17th centuries. Nothing on 18th century

as such, but useful chronological listing of principal translations of works which influenced French literature.

Italian Influences on French Authors

Addamiano, Natale. Voltaire e l'Italia. Il Ponte 18:655–76, 1962. **5883**

Cites evidence of Voltaire's interest in Italy, with special emphasis on his evaluation of Italian writers.

Barrière, Pierre. L'expérience italienne de Montesquieu. *See* 4410. **5884**

Different aspects of Italian influence on Montesquieu, with special emphasis on 1728 trip and personal contacts established at that time.

— Montesquieu voyageur. In : Actes du Congrès Montesquieu. *See* 4422. p. 61–67. **5885**

Includes remarks on his trip to Italy.

Bédarida, Paul. Quelques écrivains français à Venise au XVIIIᵉ siècle. *In:* Studi in onore di Vittorio Lugli e Diego Valeri. Venice, Neri Pozza, 1961. 1:53–82. **5886**

De Brosses, Montesquieu, Caylus, Misson, de La Lande, Rousseau, Cochin.

Benot, Yves. Un inédit de Diderot: l'Apologie de l'abbé Galiani. *See* 5014. **5887**

Berselli Ambri, Paola. Influences italiennes sur La nouvelle Héloïse. AJJR 32:155–65, 1950–52. **5888**

Echoes of Petrarch, Tasso, and Metastasio.

— L'opera di Montesquieu nel Settecento italiano. *See* 4413. **5889**

Ch. I, p. 3–22, deals with Montesquieu's trip to Italy and his Italian friends.

Berti Toesca, Elena. Il presidente Dupaty alla scoperta dell'Italia. NA 91:205–18, 1956. **5890**

On Dupaty's 1785 *Lettres sur l'Italie.*

Bertière, A. Montesquieu, lecteur de Machiavel. *In:* Actes du Congrès Montesquieu. *See* 4422. p. 141–58. **5891**

Ambiguity of Montesquieu's reaction to Machiavelli is explained in part by his acquaintance with the ms *Apologie pour Machiavelle* by the *chanoine* Louis Machon. Passages in the *Esprit des lois* cited in support.

Brosses, Charles de. Viaggio in Italia; lettere familiari. Ed. by Carlo Levi and

Glauco Natoli. Rome, Parenti, 1957. 3 v.
5892
Introduction stresses de Brosses' preparations for the voyage, especially his reading of Rogissart's *Les délices de l'Italie*.
Review : H. Roddier in RLC 35:667–70, 1961.

Brun, A. L'abbé Féraud et l'Italie. RLC 25:338–43, 1951.   **5893**
Ms at Marseilles contains correspondence and translations from period of his emigration, 1791–98. Contacts with C. Biondi and S. Bettinelli.

Candaux, Jean-Daniel. Jean-Jacques Rousseau à Gênes et à Venise : quelques documents nouveaux. SF 8:250–54, 1964.   **5894**
The documents, conserved by the Montaigu family, refer to Rousseau's 1743–44 stay in Venice as secretary to the French ambassador.

Castiglione, Tommaso R. Fortunato Bartolomeo de Felice tra Voltaire e Rousseau. *In:* Studi di letteratura storia e filosofia in onore di Bruno Revel. Florence, Olschki, 1965. p. 155–78.   **5895**
Reasons for Voltaire's polemical attacks on de Felice's *Encyclopédie*.

Conlon, P. M. Voltaire's election to the Accademia della Crusca. SVEC 6:133–39, 1958.   **5896**
Unpublished documents from the archives of the Crusca on Voltaire's election in 1746.

Cordié, Carlo. Intorno al Lesage. *See* 3754.
5897
Probable influence of a passage of Folengo's *Baldus* on *Gil Blas*.

Courville, Xavier de. Lélio, premier historien de la comédie italienne et premier animateur du théâtre de Marivaux. *See* 3609.   **5898**
Continues and concludes author's earlier work (528) on Lélio (Luigi Riccoboni). Important contribution to history of the Italian theater in France.

Dieckmann, Herbert. Diderot e Goldoni. *See* 5137   **5899**
Affinities of Diderot and Goldoni, rather than questions of influence and plagiarism. Appendix contains ms version of the unsigned review of Goldoni's *La suivante généreuse* which appeared in *Correspondance littéraire* of 1759 and is attributed to Diderot.

— Diderot und Goldoni. *See* 5137.   **5900**
Relationship between Goldoni's *Vero amico* and *Padre di famiglia* and Diderot's *Le fils naturel* and *Le père de famille*. Revaluation of Diderot's reform of the theater.

—, and **Philip Koch**. The autograph manuscript of Galiani's Dialogues sur le commerce des blés. HLB 9:110–18, 1955.   **5901**
Description of ms with corrections by Mme d'Epinay and Galiani.

Elwert, W. Theodor. La liberté vénitienne vue par les Français. VFH 21:164–72, 1955.
5902
Opinions of Jean Bodin, Nicolas Amelot de la Houssaye, Saint-Didier, Montesquieu, de Brosses, and the author of the article on Venice in the *Encyclopédie*.

Finoli, Anna Maria. Un corrispondente francese del Bettinelli 'italianizant' e filologo. *In:* Studi di letteratura storia e filosofia in onore di Bruno Revel. Florence, Olschki, 1965. p. 235–64.   **5903**
Unpublished letters by the Jesuit, Jean-François Féraud, from Ferrara, 1792–95.

Firpo, Luigi. Rousseau in Italia. Turin, Edizioni di Filosofia, 1963. 32 p.   **5904**
First part deals with Rousseau's sojourn in Turin, 1728–29.
Review : L. Sozzi in SF 9:159–60, 1965.

Folena, Gianfranco. Divagazioni sull'italiano di Voltaire. *See* 4639.   **5905**
Examines Voltaire's view of Italian within the context of 18th-century discussions on language, and his use of the language in his correspondence.

Folkierski, Władysław. Montesquieu et Vico. *In:* Actes du Congrès Montesquieu. *See* 4422. p. 127–40.   **5906**
Vico as a source for Montesquieu's thought.

Friedrich II, *der Grosse, king of Prussia.* L'anti-Machiavel. Ed. by Charles Fleischauer. *See* 4502.   **5907**
E. Marcu in review in RR 51:135–36, 1960 : " En somme, la contribution de Voltaire à *l'Anti-Machiavel* est définitivement établie par cette édition scrupuleuse qui comporte, en plus d'une Introduction, la traduction française du *Prince* que Frédéric avait lue, la Réfutation et une bibliographie des éditions de *l'Anti-Machiavel* parues du vivant de Frédéric."

Gaillard, Emile. Jean-Jacques Rousseau à Turin. AJJR 32:55–120, 1950–52. **5908**

Detailed reconstruction of Rousseau's 1728 stay in Turin and family history of comtesse de Vercellis and comte de la Roque.

Galiani, Ferdinando. Dialogues sur le commerce des bleds; giusta l'editio princeps del 1770 con appendici illustrative di Fausto Nicolini. Milan, Ricciardi, 1959. 603 p. **5909**

First reprint since 1845. Appendixes rich in unpublished material. Also Galiani-Morellet controversy, Galiani and d'Alembert, Suard, and Baudoin.

Review : C. Cases in SF 3:497–98, 1959.

Giudici, Enzo. Jean-Baptiste Rousseau e il Cardinale Passionei. *In:* Studi di letteratura storia e filosofia in onore di Bruno Revel. Florence, Olschki, 1965. p. 281–301. **5910**

Unpublished letters from Rousseau to the Cardinal, 1715–20.

Hartley, K. H. Some Italian sources for La pucelle d'Orléans. MLN 72:512–17, 1957. **5911**

Ariosto, Tasso, and Tassoni.

Jonard, N. Le Journal étranger comme intermédiaire en France de la littérature italienne. RLC 39:575–88, 1965. **5912**

Articles on Italian literature between 1755 and 1762.

Kafker, Frank A. A list of contributors to Diderot's Encyclopedia. *See* 4316. **5913**

Includes some Italian names.

Koch, Philip. The genesis of Galiani's Dialogues sur le commerce des blés. FS 15:314–23, 1961. **5914**

See especially p. 320–21 for Diderot's report to Sophie Volland of Galiani's views on the grain policy.

Matucci, Mario. Marivaux e l'Arlecchino selvaggio del Nouveau Théâtre Italien. *See* 3709. **5915**

Delisle's *Arlequin sauvage* and Marivaux' Arlequins are transformations of the Italian mask.

Neppi Madona, Leo. Per la storia della Encyclopédie in Italia : l'abate Giulio Perini collaboratore della Encyclopédie méthodique. RÉtI 10:81–91, 1964. **5916**

On some Italian contributions to the *Encyclopédie*.

Nicolini, Fausto. Amici e corrispondenti francesi dell'abate Galiani; notizie, lettere, documenti. BABN 7:1–244, 1954. **5917**

Important not only for information on Galiani's contacts with the French milieu but for that of other Italians too.

Review : W. Binni in RLI 58:487–88, 1954.

Niklaus, Robert. Marivaux et la comédie italienne. *See* 3713. **5918**

Italian comedy elements, especially in *Arlequin poli par l'amour.*

Rotta, Salvatore. Giuseppe Maria Galanti e Voltaire. RLI 66:100–19, 1962. **5919**

On Voltaire's acquaintance with the work of Antonio Genovesi.

— Una lettera inedita di Domenico Passionei al Voltaire. RLI 63:264–74, 1959. **5920**

Letter dated Rome, Mar. 9, 1746, completes Besterman 3036. Rotta rearranges correspondence between Voltaire and Passionei.

Shackleton, Robert. Montesquieu and Machiavelli : a reappraisal. *See* 4473. **5921**

Applies the method of chronological study of Montesquieu's mss to a re-examination of his debt to Machiavelli.

— Montesquieu et Doria. RLC 29:173–83, 1955. **5922**

Re-examination of P. M. Doria's *Vita civile* as source for Montesquieu.

Topazio, Virgil W. Voltaire's Pucelle : a study in burlesque. *See* 4760. **5923**

A parallel reading of *Orlando furioso* and *La pucelle.*

Trénard, Louis, Lyon et l'Italie au xviiiᵉ siècle : de Vico à Ballanche. RÉtI 5:192–214, 1958. **5924**

Lyons as an intermediary between Vico and Ballanche; 18th-century opposition to the Enlightenment.

Tuzet, Hélène. La Sicile au xviiiᵉ siècle vue par les voyageurs étrangers. Strasbourg, Heitz, 1955. 529 p. **5925**

Among French travelers discussed are Père Labat, Roland de la Platière, Vivant Desnou, and the abbé Saint-Non.

Review : J. Voisine in RLC 30:267–70, 1956.

Van Bever, Pierre. L'Italie au xviiiᵉ siècle et J.-J. Rousseau. RLC 28:16–23, 1954. **5926**

Parallel tendencies in Italy and France explain Rousseau's fortune in Italy. Humanism seen as a pre-Enlightenment.

— Lettere inedite di italiani a Gian Giacomo Rousseau nella biblioteca di Neuchâtel. GSLI 133:255–61, 1956.   **5927**
Letters from G. Farsetti, F. Mazzucchelli, A. Gulmani, C. Mozzoni.

Vaussard, Maurice. Correspondance Scipione de' Ricci-Henri Grégoire (1796–1807). Florence, Sansoni, and Paris, Didier, 1963. 146 p.   **5928**
Annotated ed.; introduction.
Reviews : W. Binni in RLI 68:524-25, 1964; P. Grunebaum-Ballin in REtI 10: 176–77, 1964; L. Sozzi in SF 8:565, 1964.

Venturi, Franco. Galiani tra enciclopedisti e fisiocrati. RSI 72:45–64, 1960.   **5929**
Controversy over *Dialogues sur le commerce des blés*, with special attention to Diderot's position.

Weil, Françoise. Promenade dans Rome en 1729 avec Montesquieu. TAS 2–12, Oct. 1958.   **5930**
Reconstruction of Montesquieu's 1728–29 trip, with special attention to his sojourns in Florence and Rome.

The Vogue of Italian Authors in France

Attinger, Gustave. L'esprit de la commedia dell'arte dans le théâtre français. Librairie théâtrale, 1950. 489 p. *See* 3570.   **5931**
A history of French dramatic literature as influenced by Italian theatrical traditions. Covers period from the 16th century to the present. For 1750–62, discusses companies of Italian comedians in France.
Reviews : A. Crow in FS 6:68–70, 1952; H. Lancaster in MLN 66:341–43, 1951; J. Lough in MLR 46:509–10, 1951; J. Scherer in RHL 52:514–15, 1952.

Booy, J. Th. de. La traduction française de Di una riforma d'Italia de Pilati di Tassulo. SVEC 12:29–42, 1960.   **5932**
On the abridged translation by Le Brun published in 1769 and a complete translation published the same year in Amsterdam by Marc-Michel Rey.

Brenner, Clarence D. The Théâtre Italien : its repertory, 1716–1793. *See* 3607.   **5933**
Important contribution to the history of the Parisian theater.

Chaubard, A.-H. Livres étrangers dans la bibliothèque du président de Brosses. *In:* Société française de littérature comparée. Actes du troisième congrès national (Dijon, 1959) : La France, la Bourgogne et la Suisse au xviiie siècle. Didier, 1960. p. 27–31. (ELEC, 40)   **5934**
Italian literature predominates, with titles from Dante to Goldoni.

Costa, Gustavo. Un collaboratore italiano del conte di Boulainviller [sic] : Francesco Maria Pompeo Colonna (1644–1726). ATSL 29:207–95, 1964.   **5935**
Completes information in Spink's *French free-thought from Gassendi to Voltaire*, p. 128–32.

Courville, Xavier de. Jeu italien contre jeu français. *See* 3608.   **5936**

Dieckmann, Herbert. Claude Gillot, interprète de la commedia dell'arte. *See* 3610.   **5937**
Claude Gillot's drawings for the *Théâtre italien de Ghérardi* are important documents for studying the transformation in the style of acting which was to lead to Riccoboni's " reform."

Fubini, Mario. Vico e Du Bos. *In:* Studi di letteratura storia e filosofia in onore di Bruno Revel. Florence, Olschki, 1965. p. 275–80.   **5938**
Echoes of Vico in the work of Du Bos.

Fucilla, Joseph G. The European and American vogue of Metastasio's shorter poems. Ital 29:13–33, 1952.   **5939**
Bibliography lists 18th-century French versions classified by genres.

Jonard, Nicolas. La fortune de Goldoni en France au xviiie siècle. *See* 3640.   **5940**
Fréron-Diderot polemic of 1757; Grimm, Voltaire, Rousseau, Mme d'Epinay on *commedia dell'arte* and Goldoni's " reform."

Mamczarz, Irena. Les intermèdes de Carlo Goldoni dans le théâtre français au xviiie siècle. *See* 3641.   **5941**
Study of the reception of Goldoni's comic sketches, and the reasons for their success.

Scanio, Vincent A. Observations on the study of Italian by eighteenth–century French travellers. Ital 31:171–78, 1954.   **5942**
The travelers whose remarks on the advisability of studying Italian are examined are the abbé de Binos, Jean

Dominique Cassini, Jean-Baptiste Labat, and Roland de La Platière.

Siciliano, Italo. Il Tasso e la Francia. LI 7: 14–29, 1955. **5943**

For vogue in 18th century, see p. 21–25. Does not add new material.

Sozzi, Lionello. Un italianisant della fine del settecento : Jean-Baptiste Christophe Grainville. RLC 36:530–47, 1962. **5944**

Translator of Tansillo, Chiari, Metastasio. Ms notes on Dante, Petrarch, Ariosto; ms translation of *L'Italia liberata dai Goti* with historical introduction. May be author of anonymous articles on Parini and Alfieri.

Spaziani, Marcello. Il barone Creuzé de Lesser : interprete del Tassoni e viaggiatore in Italia. *In his:* Francesi in Italia e italiani in Francia. Rome, Edizioni di Storia e letteratura, 1961. p. 81–100. **5945**

Creuzé's translation of *La secchia rapita* was published in 1796.

— Le origini italiane della commedia foraine. SF 6:225–44, 1962. **5946**

Contains unpublished excerpts of a version of *L'enlèvement de Proserpine.*

— L'Orlando innamorato in Francia : traduzioni e riduzioni. *In his:* Francesi in Italia e italiani in Francia. Rome, Edizioni di Storia e letteratura, 1961. p. 13–49. **5947**

See p. 33–47 for translation by Lesage.

Spanish
(Nos. 5948–5962)

Kenneth R. Scholberg

See Defourneaux (3333).

Barrière, Pierre. Montesquieu et l'Espagne. BH 49:299–310, 1947. **5948**

Detailed analysis of Montesquieu's references to Spain, which he knew through literary sources or friends. Asserts Montesquieu too often was not original or profound in his treatment of Spain.

Brooks, Richard A. Voltaire and Garcilaso de la Vega. *See* 4619. **5949**

Detailed discussion of Voltaire's indebtedness to the Inca Garcilaso in chapters 148 and 151 of the *Essai sur les mœurs* and in chapters 16–18 of *Candide.*

Cioranescu, Alejandro. Calderón y el teatro clásico francés. *In his:* Estudios de

literatura española y comparada. Laguna, Univ. de la Laguna, 1954. p. 139–95. **5950**

Deals mainly with French imitations of Calderón in the 17th century, although the author also discusses Voltaire's judgments of Calderón (p. 140–46) and gives interesting details about 18th-century works inspired by the Spaniard's *comedias* (p. 152, 164, 187–88).

Defourneaux, Marcelin. L'Espagne et l'opinion française au xviiie siècle. RLC 34:273–81, 1960. **5951**

Concerns a letter in Spanish sent to Voltaire in 1764, complaining of French attitudes and errors toward Spain. Defourneaux identifies the author as Bernardo de Iriarte.

Derla, Luigi. Voltaire, Calderón e il mito del genio eslege. Aevum (Milan) 36:109–40, 1962. **5952**

A careful study of Voltaire's esthetic ideas and his concept of taste, to explain his attitude toward Calderón and also Lope de Vega and Shakespeare. Derla claims Voltaire could not understand an authentically aristocratic civilization like Spain's.

Fleckniakoska, J.-N. Essai sur les sources du panorama de l'Espagne et de son empire dans l'œuvre de Montesquieu. *See* 4439 **5953**

Useful companion to Barrière (5948). Deals with Montesquieu's comments on Spain's geography, rulers, faults, and cruelty in conquest of America. Considers in detail his sources, oral and written, of information on Spain and shows that his somber picture was based on equally harsh Spanish writings.

Guinard, Paul J. Une fausse lettre espagnole de Voltaire. RLC 35:640–48, 1961. **5954**

Text and study of a false *Carta de Mr. Voltaire a su corresponsal en Madrid,* in reality a political pamphlet against the government of Carlos III.

— Le livre dans la péninsule ibérique au xviiie siècle; témoignage d'un libraire français. BH 59:176–98, 1957. **5955**

Deals with the problems of Antoine Boudet, Parisian printer, in seeking to get the 1753 ed. of Moréri's *Dictionnaire historique* into Spain.

Pageard, Robert. Une curieuse figure d'hispanisant français : Coste d'Arnobat (1731–1808). RLC 32:556–65, 1958. **5956**

Studies the work of Pierre-Nicolas Coste d'Arnobat as a literary intermediary between Spain and France. His collaboration on the *Journal étranger* included translations, résumés, and studies of Spanish authors. A well-documented study.

— L'Espagne dans le Journal étranger (1754–62) et la Gazette littéraire de l'Europe (1764–66). *See* 5527.   **5957**

A detailed study, including a complete list of articles pertaining to Spain that appeared in these 2 journals. The *Gazette* was less interested in and less favorable to things Spanish.

Schier, Donald. Voltaire's criticism of Calderón. CL 11:340–46, 1959.   **5958**

Deals with Voltaire's comments on Calderón's *auto, La devoción de la misa,* and his translation of the Spaniard's play, *En esta vida todo es verdad y todo mentira,* which consistently abridged the original text, completely changing the tone.

Scholberg, Kenneth R. Pierre Bayle and Spain. Chapel Hill, Univ. of North Carolina, Studies in the Romance languages and literatures, 1958. 40 p.   **5959**

Details Bayle's interest in Spanish history and literature and his Spanish sources of information. Points out his reliance especially on Juan de Mariana and Nicolás Antonio. Appendixes give lists of Spanish and Portuguese writers referred to by Bayle and of works in French translation that he mentioned.

Sedwick, B. Frank. Cervantes' El celoso extremeño and Beaumarchais' Le barbier de Séville. *See* 3685.   **5960**

Presents general parallels between the 2 authors and suggests Cervantine influence on Beaumarchais.

Steiger, Arnald. Voltaire und Spanien. *In:* Überlieferung und Gestaltung. Festgabe für Theophil Spoerri. Zurich, Speer, 1950. p. 77–87.   **5961**

General review of Voltaire's negative treatment of events in Spanish history and of Spanish literature.

Van Tieghem, Philippe. Les influences espagnoles (1600–1720). *In his:* Les influences étrangères sur la littérature française (1550–1880). *See* 5839. p. 36–59.   **5962**

Claims that Spanish influence on French literature from *c.* 1720 to 1820 was null, although he mentions a few works that show such influence. A *Tableau chronologique des traductions* at end of book has only 5 entries for French translations of Spanish works in the 18th century.

INDEX

NOTE. — When entries in this Index are followed by more than three serial numbers, these serial numbers are identified according to content, as briefly as possible.

When the subject of the Index entry is the author or editor of or a contributor of prefatory material to the item represented by the serial number, the number is given in italics.

A

Achard, Marcel, *5030*
Acomb, Frances Dorothy, *5541*
Adam, Antoine, Bayle : *4167;* Diderot : *5104;* Fontenelle : *4190–91;* Montesquieu : *4402;* nature : 5561; precursors : *3384;* Rousseau : *5104;* Sade : *3972;* Voltaire : *4538*
Adams, John, 4942
Adams, Percy G., *5805, 5806, 5807*
Addamiano, Natale, *4539, 5883*
Addison, Joseph, d'Argens : 5632; Desmaizeaux : 5650; Du Bos : 5667; Marivaux : 5683; Rapin de Thoyras : 5334; translations : 5547
Adhémar, Jean, *5037*
Aïssé, Charlotte Elisabeth, 3403, 4575
Akimova, Alisa Akimovna, *5047*
Alatri, Paolo, Diderot : *4986, 5048;* Voltaire : *4479–80, 4564,* 4696
Albaum, Martin, *4116*
Alberoni, *Cardinal* Giulio, 3799
Alciatore, Jules C., Chamfort : *5638;* Helvétius : *4350;* Voltaire : *4602–03*
Aldridge, Alfred Owen, Contributor, English influences and relations : 5541–5812; Condorcet : *4387, 5791;* Dubourg : *5771, 5809;* Franklin : *5773–76;* Laclos : *3924;* Paine : *5791–95;* Shaftesbury : *5611;* translation : *5542*
Alekseev, Mikhail P., 4488, *5105*
Alembert, Jean Lerond d', section on : 4266–98; Académie des Sciences : 4286; Bacon : 4164; Berkeley : 4285, 5567; Berlin Academy : 4280; Bordeu : 5276; Bossut : 4275; Cartesianism : 4270, 4273–74; Catherine II : 4742; Condorcet : 4390, 4394; Mme Corneille : 4289; Descartes : 4273; Diderot : 4268, 4286, 4290, 4298, 4325, 5086, 5163, 5276; *Encyclopédie:* 4275, 4281, 4284, 4290, 4299, 4302, 4311, 4325, 4335, 4339, 4341, 4664, 5086; English influences and relations : 5581, 5607; Formey : 4276; German influences and relations : 5861–62; Gustavus III : 4283; d'Holbach : 4380, 4666; Hume : 4273, 4278, 4285, 4291, 5581, 5586, 5589; Italian influences and relations : 3322; Lagrange 4271, 4335; Leibniz : 4273; Leopardi : 4287; Mlle de Lespinasse : 4268–69, 4287, 5276; Linguet : 4289; Michaelis : 4279, 5861; Morellet : 4276; Newton : 4270, 5607; *Querelle des bouffons:* 4288; Rameau : 4276; Rousseau : 4281, 4291; Sainte-Beuve : 4272; Saint-Pierre : 5403; Servan : 4295; Tacitus : 4297, 5248; Turgot : 4311; Voltaire : 4281, 4291–92, 4294, 4380, 4664, 4666, 4676, 4683; Works : *Apologie de l'étude:* 4296; *Correspondance: 4282–83, 4294–95; Discours préliminaire: 4266,* 4274; *Eléments de philosophie:* 4274; *Histoire des membres de l'Académie française:* 4272; *Testament: 4267; Traité de dynamique:* 4275
Alexander, Ian W., *5106*
Alexandre, Dom Nicolas, 3521
Alfieri, Vittorio, *conte,* 5944
Algarotti, Francesco, *conte,* 4468, 4522
Allain, Mathé, *4604*
Allem, Maurice, *3675*
Allers, Ulrich S., *4861*
Allston, Washington, 5770
Alquié, Ferdinand, 5029
Alter, Robert, *3751,* 3770
Althusser, Louis, *4407*
Amann, Peter, *4117*
Ambard, Robert, *3613*
Ambrière, Francis, *3619*
American influences and relations, section on : 5740–5812; Bernardin de Saint-Pierre : 3858; Mme Brillon : 5777, 5783; Brissot de Warville : 5798; Buffon : 5756, 5789; Chateaubriand : 5799–5804; Condorcet : 5755, 5773, 5791; Crèvecœur : 5756, 5805–07; Diderot : 5061, 5191, 5808; Dubourg : 5809; *Encyclopédie:* 4309, 5773, 5790; Mme Helvétius : 5777, 5783; Mme d'Houdetot : 5806; Montesquieu : 4422, 4426, 4457; Mme de Payan : 5780; Perrin du Lac : 5810; Prévost : 3812; Raynal : 5378, 5382, 5795, 5811; Rousseau : 4786, 4942–43, 4953, 5751; Sade : 4012, 4039; Volney : 5812; Voltaire : 4709, 5773
Amilaville, Etienne Noël d', 4310
Amphitromanie, 3587

THE ST-CATHERINE PRESS, LTD. BRUGES, BELGIUM